The R Book

The R Book

Third Edition

Elinor Jones
University College London, UK

Simon Harden
University College London, UK

Michael J. Crawley
Imperial College London, UK

This third edition first published 2023
© 2023 John Wiley & Sons Ltd

Edition History: John Wiley & Sons Ltd (1e, 2007; 2e, 2013)

The right of Elinor Jones, Simon Harden and Michael J. Crawley to be identified as the authors of this work has been asserted in accordance with law.

Registered Offices
John Wiley & Sons, Inc., 111 River Street, Hoboken, NJ 07030, USA
John Wiley & Sons Ltd, The Atrium, Southern Gate, Chichester, West Sussex, PO19 8SQ, UK

Editorial Office
9600 Garsington Road, Oxford, OX4 2DQ, UK

For details of our global editorial offices, customer services, and more information about Wiley products visit us at www.wiley.com.

Wiley also publishes its books in a variety of electronic formats and by print-on-demand. Some content that appears in standard print versions of this book may not be available in other formats.

Library of Congress Cataloging-in-Publication Data

Names: Jones, Elinor (Associate Professor), author. | Harden, Simon,
   author. | Crawley, Michael J., author.
Title: The R book / Elinor Jones, Simon Harden, and Michael J. Crawley.
Description: Third edition. | Hoboken, NJ : Wiley, 2022. | Includes
   bibliographical references and index.
Identifiers: LCCN 2022008352 (print) | LCCN 2022008353 (ebook) | ISBN
   9781119634324 (cloth) | ISBN 9781119634409 (adobe pdf) | ISBN
   9781119634430 (epub)
Subjects: LCSH: R (Computer program language) | Mathematical
   statistics–Data processing.
Classification: LCC QA276.45.R3 J662 2022 (print) | LCC QA276.45.R3
   (ebook) | DDC 005.5/5–dc23/eng20220528
LC record available at https://lccn.loc.gov/2022008352
LC ebook record available at https://lccn.loc.gov/2022008353

Cover design: Wiley
Cover image: Courtesy of Simon Harden; © enjoynz/Getty Images

Set in 10/12pt HelveticaLTStd by Straive, Chennai, India
Printed and bound by CPI Group (UK) Ltd, Croydon, CR0 4YY

C9781119634324_260822

Contents

Detailed Contents

List of Tables

Preface

R is the most powerful tool in the known universe for carrying out statistical analysis, and it's free! This book is aimed at those who wish to carry out such work – exploring, plotting, and modelling data – but who do not have much experience in R and/or statistics. R is described from scratch with instructions for loading and getting going with the software in Chapter 1 and a description of its essential elements in Chapter 3. Later chapters discuss statistical methods and are written so that they can be used either as a beginner's guide or as a reference manual on particular procedures in R. The theory behind the analyses is covered in enough depth, we hope, to make it comprehensible but without overburdening the reader with too much mathematics. The datasets used to illustrate various analyses are available at https://www.wiley.com/go/jones/therbook3e.

Using R has become far simpler with the introduction of RStudio, which is also free (other editors are available). RStudio provides a friendly front end and easy access to tools, all of which seem a long way from R's original rather forbidding command prompt. This book assumes the use of RStudio rather than using R directly, but the code presented will work using the latter setup too.

While there is still the usual hurdle of getting to know powerful software, the benefits, particularly in graphics and modelling, far outweigh the effort. Academic papers in many disciplines routinely use and report results using R. In addition, the open-source nature of the software means that users have added extra functionality by writing packages to broaden R's capabilities. There are currently over 18,000 packages that, together with useful links and information, can be found at the official R distribution site, CRAN: https://cran.r-project.org/.

This book is contingent upon the existence of R. Those involved are too numerous to mention, but we are hugely grateful to all involved in its creation and continuing evolution. When you use R, R packages (e.g. `spatstat`), and RStudio, please cite them. Up-to-date citation details for each of these can be found by typing the following in R, respectively:

```
citation ()
citation ("spatstat")
RStudio.Version ()
```

Elinor Jones
Simon Harden
Michael J. Crawley
August 2022

Acknowledgments

This book would not exist without its previous editions so thanks, firstly, to the originating author, Michael J. Crawley.

It has been a pleasure to revise The R Book to create this third edition. We are very grateful to Professor Crawley for allowing us to use materials from previous versions, including his fantastic array of datasets that make a welcome return in this edition.

Finally, we would like to thank the Department of Statistical Science at University College London for giving us time and space to complete the book during a difficult period for everybody.

Elinor Jones
Simon Harden
August 2022

About the Companion Website

This book is accompanied by a companion website.

www.wiley.com/go/jones/therbook3e

This website include: Datasets

1

Getting Started

1.1   Navigating the book

The material covered in this book has been arranged by topic. The first few chapters cover the essentials, including basic technical knowledge (Chapter 2), the fundamentals of *R* (Chapter 3), and data handling in *R* (Chapter 4). Subsequent chapters deal with statistical procedures, including graphics (Chapters 5 and 6), statistical testing (Chapter 9), and common statistical models (from Chapter 10).

To make navigating the book easier, the following conventions will be used:

- New terms are highlighted in **bold** when first used;

- *R* functions and function arguments written in-line are highlighted in red, for example the `plot ()` function and the `pch` argument (note the use of the round brackets when referring to functions);

- Stand-alone *R* code is written in red, with output in blue, for example:

```
1+3

[1] 4
```

- Datasets, variable names, model names, and so on, are written in `typewriter font`;

- *R* packages (see Section 1.6) are highlighted in blue, for example `MASS`.

1.1.1   How to use this book

This book is intended to serve a wide audience from complete beginners through to those in need of an *R* reference manual. Below, we offer advice on how to use the book depending on level of experience in statistics and computing.

The R Book, Third Edition. Elinor Jones, Simon Harden and Michael J. Crawley.
© 2023 John Wiley & Sons Ltd. Published 2023 by John Wiley & Sons Ltd.
Companion website: www.wiley.com/go/jones/therbook3e

Beginner in both computing and statistics

The book is structured principally with such a reader in mind. There are six key things to learn: how to arrange data, how to read data into *R*, how to check data once within *R*, how to select an appropriate analysis, how to interpret the output, and how to present the analysis for publication. A thorough understanding of the basics is essential before trying to do the more complicated things, so we recommend studying Chapters 3 to 4 carefully to begin with. Do all of the exercises that are illustrated in the text on your own computer.

Now comes the hard part, which is selecting the right statistics to use. Model choice is extremely important and is the thing that will develop most with experience. Don't be afraid to ask for expert help with this. Never do an analysis that is more complicated than it needs to be, so start by reading about graphical representations of data (Chapters 5 and 6). Sometimes this is all that's needed.

Student needing help with project work

A good understanding of variable types is key (broadly, variables are either numeric or categorical, see Section 1.8.1). An analysis of a dataset will depend – at least in part – on the type of variables in the dataset and the research question of interest. Does the research question point to a particular 'response' variable, and if so, what type of variable is this?

From here, the first port of call is to plot or tabulate the data, depending on the nature of the variables (see Chapters 5–7). That might be enough in itself, or further statistical analyses might be needed. For example, if the response variable (if any) is a count, consider using hypothesis tests (Chapter 9), tables (Chapter 7), or possibly a model (Chapter 11). If the response variable is a continuous measure (e.g. a weight), then consider using hypothesis tests (Chapter 9), or a regression model (Chapter 10).

Done some R and some statistics, but keen to learn more of both

The best plan is to skim quickly through the introductory material in case there is anything new to be learned. It is a good idea to read Chapter 3 on the fundamentals of the *R* language and Chapters 5 and 6 on graphics. Much of the rest of the book is organised by analysis type making it easy to jump to the relevant chapter.

Done regression, but want to learn more advanced statistical modelling

For readers who have experience of regression in another language, the best plan is to go directly to Chapters 10 and 11 to see how the output from linear models is handled by *R*. Familiarity with data input and dataframes is essential (Chapter 4), then the chapters on more advanced modelling should be accessible.

Experienced in statistics, but a beginner in R

The first thing is to get a thorough understanding of dataframes and data input to *R*, so start with Chapter 4. Then, chapters on statistical modelling should be accessible. It is a good idea to browse, for example Chapters 9 (Testing) and 10 (Regression) to understand the output from *R*. Working through Chapters 5 and 6 will provide the foundations of graphics in *R*.

Experienced in computing, but a beginner in R

Well-written *R* code is highly intuitive and very readable. The most unfamiliar parts of *R* are likely to be the way it handles functions and the way it deals with environments. It is impossible to anticipate the order in which more advanced users are likely to encounter material and hence want to learn about specific features of the language, but vectorised calculations, subscripts on dataframes, function-writing and suchlike are bound to crop up early (Chapter 3). When faced with an unfamiliar name in some code, just type the name immediately after a question mark; for example to find out more about the `rnbinom ()` function, type:

```
?rnbinom
```

Recognizing mathematical functions is quite straightforward because of their names and the fact that their arguments are enclosed in round brackets ( ). Subscripts on objects have square brackets [ ]. Multi-line blocks of *R* code are enclosed within curly brackets { }. The idea of lists might be new, or applying functions to lists; elements within lists have double square brackets [[ ]].

Look at the sections at the start of Chapter 3 as a starting point. The index is probably the most sensible entry point for queries about specifics.

Familiar with statistics and computing, but need a friendly reference manual

For information about a *topic*, use the chapter list and the Detailed Contents to find the most appropriate section. For aspects of the *R language*, look at the sections mentioned at the start of Chapter 3. Spending time browsing the contents of general material such as Chapters 5 and 6 on graphics is a good idea.

Get used to *R*'s help pages. Each *R* function has a help page which can be accessed by typing a question mark followed directly by the function name. To find out what all the graphics parameters mean, for instance, just type:

```
?par
```

1.2   *R* vs. RStudio

R is a powerful open-source software for statistical computing (R Core Team, 2021). It can be used directly, or for a more pleasing user experience, can be used via the RStudio interface which is freely available (RStudio Team, 2020). We strongly recommend using RStudio rather than *R* directly as it makes managing workspace easy and avoids some of *R*'s rather cumbersome features. The rest of the book will assume the use of RStudio, but all code presented will work – and provide identical results – if used in 'native' *R* instead.

We will generally write '*R*' instead of 'RStudio' throughout this book.

1.3   Installing *R* and RStudio

You will need to install both *R* and RStudio. Both will run under Windows, a number of flavours of Linux (more for *R* than for RStudio so check the links below) and even Apple's Mac OS X.

First download and install *R*. Note that this needs to be done first before attempting to download RStudio.

- Go to the CRAN project webpage https://cran.r-project.org/mirrors.html and choose the closest CRAN site to you (e.g. Imperial College London). It doesn't matter too much which of these is chosen if several are close by;
- Select the link for *Download R for ...* , for your operating system;
- Follow the instructions, noting that the default set-up is perfectly adequate.

Now download RStudio.

- Go to the RStudio webpage https://rstudio.com/products/rstudio/download/#download and select the 'Download' for RStudio Desktop. The free version is generally adequate and is certainly so for this book.
- Follow the instructions. At some point you'll be asked to locate where *R* has been installed. Remember that RStudio is just an *R* interface.

Rather than downloading *R* and RStudio, there is the option of accessing the software online via RStudio Cloud (https://www.rstudio.com/products/cloud/). There are some advantages to using RStudio online, for example when working on a group project. However, for individual use, it is likely that downloading *R* and RStudio is the best way forward.

1.4 Using RStudio

Once installed, open RStudio. The screen is divided into three parts as in Figure 1.1.

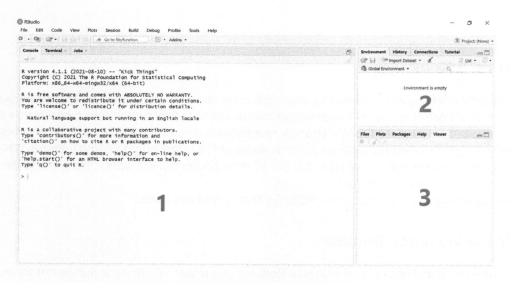

Figure 1.1   RStudio windows. RStudio, PBC

On the left is the **console**, numbered 1 in Figure 1.1. This is *R*. All code will be passed to the console where it will be executed, and numerical output will also be displayed here. The console displays the version number of *R*, its date, and version name (always comedic).

In the top right-hand corner is the **workspace**, numbered 2 in Figure 1.1. This is the control centre and gives an at-a-glance overview of what has been done so far in the session.

The bottom right corner, numbered 3 in Figure 1.1, hosts a number of things. Switch between them by clicking on the relevant tabs:

- **Files**: Shows the accessible file directories (more on this in Section 1.8.4);

- **Plots**: This is where plots and other graphics will be displayed;

- **Packages**: Lists packages that have been installed and provides functionality for installing others (more on this in Section 1.6);

- **Help**: As the name might suggest, help with various functions or procedures can be found here (more on this in Section 1.7);

- **Viewer**: Used for viewing local web content.

1.4.1   Using *R* directly via the console

Before exploring further, we'll return to the console. Below the header – which contains useful information about version number, citation, and a health warning – is a blank line with a > symbol in the left-hand margin. This is called the **prompt** and is *R*'s way of saying 'What now?'. Commands can be typed in directly here, though we suggest a more efficient way of working via **text editors** (see Section 1.4.2).

To begin with, we can use the console as a calculator, for example typing in the following command then pressing enter on the keyboard to execute the command (for neatness, we don't present the > at the start of each line of code in this book):

```
2 + 3
```

```
[1] 5
```

When working, a + is sometimes displayed at the left-hand side of the screen instead of >. This means that the last command typed is incomplete. The most common cause of this is forgetting one or more brackets. If what's missing is clear (e.g. a final right-hand bracket), then just type the missing character and press enter, at which point the command will execute. If a mistake has been made, then press the Esc key and the command line prompt > will reappear. Use the Up arrow key to scroll through previous commands, then use the Left and Right arrow keys to navigate to the mistake and correct it.

1.4.2   Using text editors

Writing commands in the console directly is rarely a good idea. It is good practice to keep a record of the code we use, which makes correcting mistakes, updating analyses, or just running the command(s) again very easy. RStudio has a built-in text editor to store and execute code.

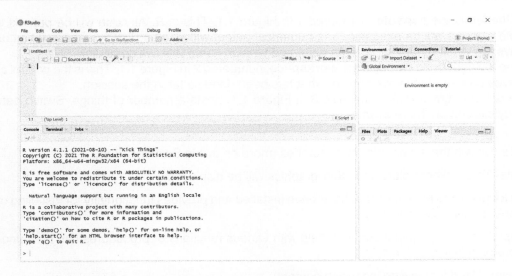

Figure 1.2   RStudio windows with text editor. RStudio, PBC

A failsafe way of opening a blank text editor, which doesn't depend on the operating system of your machine, is to go to *File*, then *New File*, then *R Script*. It will appear in the top left hand corner as in Figure 1.2.

The text editor is where we write commands, using a new line for each one. Click the text editor to activate it, before writing the following:

```
2 + 3
3 * 6
exp (2)
```

To run commands, highlight the relevant lines and click 'Run' (top right corner of the text editor) or press Ctrl and Enter, simultaneously. Output will be displayed in the console (bottom left). For readability, output will be shown directly beneath each of the relevant command throughout this book like this:

```
2 + 3

[1] 5

3 * 6

[1] 18

exp (2)

[1] 7.389056
```

The commands so far request calculations to be performed, but we can also define **objects** (see Chapter 3 for details), for example a is assigned (`<-`) the value 5 while we define b to be ln(10):

```
a <- 5
b <- log (10)
```

When we run this, we notice two things:

- there is no output in the console (because all we've done is define two objects);
- the **Environment** tab in the workspace has been populated with the definitions of a and b.

It is helpful to understand that *R* is an **object-orientated** programming (OOP) language: it is based on applying *actions* (commands) on *objects*. For example, a dataset which we load into *R* (see Chapter 4) will be considered by *R* as an object. Any action applied (e.g. finding the mean for each variable in the dataset) will be an action on a particular object (the dataset in this case). An object doesn't have to be a dataset, however, as we saw above.

   The best way to learn *R* and RStudio is to play with them. The introduction here gives a very brief overview but is in no way complete. A good place to start is with RStudio cheatsheets https://www.rstudio.com/resources/cheatsheets/.

1.5   The Comprehensive *R* Archive Network

CRAN https://cran.r-project.org/ is the first port of call for everything to do with *R*. It is from here that you download and install *R* (see Section 1.3), find contributed packages to solve particular problems (see Section 1.6), find the answers to frequently asked questions, read about the latest developments, get programming tips, and much more besides.

   It is well worth browsing through *The R Journal*, accessible via the CRAN webpage. This is the refereed journal of the *R* project for statistical computing. It features short- to medium-length articles covering topics that might be of interest to users or to developers of *R*, including

- **Add-on packages**: Short introductions to or reviews of *R* extension packages.
- **Changes in *R***: Details of recent changes to *R*.
- **Applications**: Demonstrating how a new or existing technique can be applied in an area of current interest using *R*, providing a fresh view of such analyses in *R* that is of benefit beyond the specific application.

1.5.1   Manuals

There are several manuals available on CRAN, for example (descriptions are taken from the webpage):

- *An Introduction to R* gives an introduction to the language and how to use *R* for doing statistical analysis and graphics.
- A draft of the *R Language Definition*, which documents the language *per se* – that is, the objects that it works on, and the details of the expression evaluation process, which are useful to know when programming *R* functions. This is perhaps the most important of all the manuals.

- *Writing R Extensions* covers how to create your own packages, write *R* help files, and use the foreign language (C, C + +, Fortran, …) interfaces.
- *Data Import/Export* describes the import and export facilities available either in *R* itself or via packages which are available from CRAN.
- *R Installation and Administration*, which is self-explanatory.

These manuals are also available in RStudio by going to the Help tab in the bottom right-hand corner and clicking the 'home' icon.

The most useful part of the site, however, is the Search facility. This is a good starting point for investigating the contents of most of the *R* documents, functions, and searchable mail archives.

1.5.2   Frequently asked questions

R has three collections of answers to FAQs:

- the *R* FAQ, which contains useful information for users on all platforms (Linux, Mac, Unix, Windows);
- the *R* Mac OS X FAQ for all users of Apple operating systems;
- the *R* Windows FAQ for all users of Microsoft operating systems.

Read the first of these, plus the appropriate one for your platform.

1.5.3   Contributed documentation

This contains a wide range of longer (more than 100 pages) and shorter manuals, tutorials, and exercises provided by users of *R*. You should browse these to find the ones most relevant to your needs.

1.6   Packages in *R*

A lot can be done with *R* or RStudio 'straight out of the box', also known as **base-R**. Table 1.1 lists some of the packages that come supplied as part of the base-*R* installation.

Table 1.1   Libraries used in this book that come supplied as part of the base package of *R*.

Package name	Functionality
lattice	graphics for panel plots or trellis graphs
MASS	package associated with Venables and Ripley's book entitled *Modern Applied Statistics using S-PLUS*
mgcv	generalised additive models
nlme	mixed-effects models (both linear and nonlinear)
nnet	feed-forward neural networks and multinomial log-linear models
spatial	functions for kriging and point pattern analysis
survival	survival analysis, including penalised likelihood

However, there is a huge community of *R* users who contribute to its functionality via **packages**. A package contains additional functionality for *R* that can be loaded during a session. Navigating contributed packages can be tricky simply because there are so many of them, and the name of the package is not always as indicative of its function as one might hope.

Viewing existing packages can be done in RStudio by clicking on the Packages tab. Clicking the box next to a package loads it. A far better way of loading a package is to do so via the `library ()` function, which also means we have it as part of our code. For example, to load the `MASS` package (Venables and Ripley, 2002), which has a wide range of useful functions and datasets, type:

```
library (MASS)
```

See Section 1.6.3 for information on installing new packages.

1.6.1   Contents of packages

It is easy to use the `help` function to discover the contents of library packages. Supposing that we wanted to find out about the contents of the `spatial` package, we'd type:

```
library (help = spatial)
```

This brings up general information about the package in a new tab of the text editor in RStudio, including a list of all the functions and data sets.

To find out how to use, say, Ripley's *K* (`kfn ()`) from `spatial`, we load the package and then use `?` to query the function:

```
library (spatial)
?Kfn
```

1.6.2   Finding packages

There is no comprehensive cross-referenced index of packages, but there is a very helpful feature called 'Task Views' on the CRAN website, which explains the packages available under a limited number of usefully descriptive headings. Click on Task Views to see bundles of packages assembled by topic. Currently, there are 40 Task Views on CRAN as listed in Table 1.2.

Click on the Task View to get an annotated list of the packages available under any particular heading. If Base-*R* doesn't cover your needs, it is highly likely that a package exists that does.

1.6.3   Installing packages

The base package does not contain some of the libraries referred to in this book, but installing these is very simple.

It is best to install packages using the `install.packages ()` function, as shown below, rather than doing so via RStudio's Packages tab (therein, click on install, then search for the package needed). The packages used in this book are

```
install.packages ("akima")
install.packages ("boot")
```

Table 1.2   Task Views on CRAN

Bayesian	Bayesian Inference
ChemPhys	Chemometrics and Computational Physics
ClinicalTrials	Clinical Trial Design, Monitoring, and Analysis
Cluster	Cluster Analysis & Finite Mixture Models
Databases	Databases with *R*
DifferentialEquations	Differential Equations
Distributions	Probability Distributions
Econometrics	Computational Econometrics
Environmetrics	Analysis of Ecological and Environmental Data
ExperimentalDesign	Design of Experiments (DoE) & Analysis of Experimental Data
ExtremeValue	Extreme Value Analysis
Finance	Empirical Finance
FunctionalData	Functional Data Analysis
Genetics	Statistical Genetics
Graphics	Graphic Displays & Dynamic Graphics & Graphic Devices & Visualization
HighPerformanceComputing	High-Performance and Parallel Computing with *R*
Hydrology	Hydrological Data and Modeling
MachineLearning	Machine Learning & Statistical Learning
MedicalImaging	Medical Image Analysis
MetaAnalysis	Meta-Analysis
MissingData	Missing Data
ModelDeployment	Model Deployment with *R*
Multivariate	Multivariate Statistics
NaturalLanguageProcessing	Natural Language Processing
NumericalMathematics	Numerical Mathematics
OfficialStatistics	Official Statistics & Survey Methodology
Optimization	Optimization and Mathematical Programming
Pharmacokinetics	Analysis of Pharmacokinetic Data
Phylogenetics	Phylogenetics, Especially Comparative Methods
Psychometrics	Psychometric Models and Methods
ReproducibleResearch	Reproducible Research
Robust	Robust Statistical Methods
SocialSciences	Statistics for the Social Sciences
Spatial	Analysis of Spatial Data
Survival	Survival Analysis
TeachingStatistics	Teaching Statistics
TimeSeries	Time Series Analysis
Tracking	Processing and Analysis of Tracking Data
WebTechnologies	Web Technologies and Services
gR	gRaphical Models in *R*

```
install.packages ("BSDA")
install.packages ("car")
install.packages ("coda")
install.packages ("DescTools")
install.packages ("deSolve")
install.packages ("EMT")
```

```
install.packages ("geoR")
install.packages ("ggplot2")
install.packages ("lme4")
install.packages ("metafor")
install.packages ("nlstools")
install.packages ("PerformanceAnalytics")
install.packages ("plotly")
install.packages ("predictmeans")
install.packages ("psych")
install.packages ("R2jags")
install.packages ("RColorBrewer")
install.packages ("rpart")
install.packages ("SemiPar")
install.packages ("spatstat")
install.packages ("spdep")
install.packages ("stringr")
install.packages ("tree")
```

Installing a package doesn't load it! The `library ()` function needs to be used to load an installed package.

1.7   Getting help in *R*

Help with *R*-related problems is easy to come by. If the name of the function you want help with is known, just type a question mark `?` at the command line prompt followed by the name of the function. For example, to get help on the `read.table ()` function, type:

```
?read.table
```

The help page can then be viewed in the bottom right corner in RStudio.

Sometimes the precise name of the function isn't known, but general subject area is (e.g. data input in this case). Use the `help.search ()` function (without a question mark) with the query in double quotes like this:

```
help.search ("data input")
```

and (with any luck) the names of the *R* functions associated with this query will be displayed. Then use, for example `?read.table` to get detailed help.

Other useful functions are `find ()` and `apropos ()`. The `find ()` function indicates what package something is in

```
find ("lowess")
```

```
[1] "package:stats"
```

while `apropos ()` returns a character vector giving the names of all objects in the search list that match a (potentially partial) enquiry:

```
apropos ("lm")

 [1]  ".colMeans"              ".lm.fit"
 [3]  "anova.lme"              "colMeans"
 [5]  "confint.lm"             "contr.helmert"
 [7]  "contr.Helmert"          "dummy.coef.lm"
 [9]  "extract.lme.cov"        "extract.lme.cov2"
[11]  "getAllMethods"          "glm"
[13]  "glm.control"            "glm.convert"
[15]  "glm.fit"                "glm.nb"
[17]  "glmmPQL"                "KalmanForecast"
[19]  "KalmanLike"             "KalmanRun"
[21]  "KalmanSmooth"           "kappa.lm"
[23]  "lm"                     "lm.fit"
[25]  "lm.gls"                 "lm.influence"
[27]  "lm.ridge"               "lm.wfit"
[29]  "lme"                    "lme.formula"
[31]  "lme.lmList"             "lmeControl"
[33]  "lmeStruct"              "lmList"
[35]  "lmList.formula"         "lmsreg"
[37]  "lmwork"                 "loglm"
[39]  "loglm1"                 "marginalModelPlot"
[41]  "marginalModelPlots"     "model.matrix.lm"
[43]  "nlm"                    "nlme"
[45]  "nlme.formula"           "nlme.nlsList"
[47]  "nlmeControl"            "nlmeStruct"
[49]  "nlminb"                 "panel.lmline"
[51]  "plot.lme"               "predict.glm"
[53]  "predict.lm"             "Predict.matrix.soap.film"
[55]  "prepanel.lmline"        "residuals.glm"
[57]  "residuals.lm"           "rlm"
[59]  "simulate.lme"           "summary.glm"
[61]  "summary.lm"             "USRegionalMortality"
```

There is a huge world-wide *R* user network. An Internet search of a problem is likely to point to a solution if the above approaches don't help.

1.7.1 Worked examples of functions

To see a worked example, just type the function name (e.g. linear models, `lm ()`)

```
example (lm)
```

which provides an example of the printed and graphical output produced by the `lm ()` function.

1.7.2   Demonstrations of *R* functions

These can be useful for seeing the range of things that *R* can do. Try the following to get a flavour of what's on offer:

```
demo (persp)
demo (graphics)
demo (Hershey)
demo (plotmath)
```

1.8   Good housekeeping

1.8.1   Variable types

It is sometimes tempting to dive straight into data analysis without much thought, but before we embark on any data work it is vital to understand the type of variables that we have in our dataset. Choosing suitable statistical methods depends on the type of data you have. Taking time to classify each variable is therefore worthwhile: it isn't always obvious as we'll see.

Broadly, variables are classified as **numeric** (or quantitative) or **categorical** (or qualitative) variables. This two-class system hides some important variable features that we should consider.

- A numeric variable can be **continuous** or **discrete**.

  - A continuous variable can take any value within a given interval, for example height, total precipitation, Olympic 100 m times.
  - A discrete variable can only take particular (numeric) values, for example the number of adults in a household, age in years, and number of daily cases of a virus.

- A categorical variable can be **nominal** or **ordinal**.

  - A nominal variable consists of unordered categories, for example favourite colour, brand of trainers, and gender.
  - An ordinal variable consists of ordered categories, for example letter grade achieved on an exam (e.g. from A to F), a customer's rating of service (e.g. 'poor', 'average', and 'good'), a patient's pain rating from 0 (no pain) to 10 (worst possible pain).

Most of the examples given are straightforward, but a few deserve special attention. Take the number of daily cases of a virus, for example. It is clear that this should be a discrete variable because it can only take whole numbers 0, 1, 2, ... (we can't have, say, 10.462 cases!). Though this is undeniably discrete, we could face difficulty if daily cases varies considerably from no cases to many thousands. With such a vast range of possible values, we might consider treating this variable as continuous instead. This could potentially make an analysis simpler, which is not a bad thing.

It may seem surprising that a patient's pain rating from 0 to 10 is classified as an ordinal (categorical) variable. The possible values are numbers so why isn't this a discrete variable? The numbers here are merely labels for underlying categories, and not meaningful in themselves. Though it would be slightly odd to do so, we could equivalently ask a patient to classify their pain from 100 to 110 instead, or ask them to identify the pain using labels such as 'no pain', 'very mild pain', all the way up to 'worst possible pain'. This would extract the same information from the patients and reveals that there is nothing special about the numeric labels we initially applied to the categories. The moral of the story here is don't jump to the conclusion that any variable with quantitative values is actually numeric.

Once we have a good hold of the variable types in our dataset, we can start thinking about how to approach any analysis.

1.8.2 What's loaded or defined in the current session

To see what variables have been created in the current session, type:

```
objects ()
```

The Environment tab in RStudio also lists everything that has been imported or created. To see which packages and dataframes are currently attached (see Section 1.8.3):

```
search ()
```

1.8.3 Attaching and detaching objects

It is sometimes desirable to **attach** an object, such as a dataset. For example, if we wanted to the mean of a numeric variable, say `myvar`, which sits inside a (loaded) dataset called `mydata`, we would have to instruct R to look inside `mydata` to find `myvar` by using the `$` symbol (read it as 'look inside the object `mydata` and find `myvar`):

```
mean (mydata$myvar)
```

where, of course, the function `mean ()` computes the arithmetic mean. This can get quite cumbersome.

We could `attach ()` `mydata` so that we don't have to do this. By attaching the dataset, its contents become visible to R so that we don't have to specify that `myvar` is located inside `mydata`:

```
attach (mydata)
mean (myvar)
detach (mydata)
```

Attaching objects comes with a serious health warning. It can get very messy and easily lead to mistakes. Once an object is attached, it should be detached as soon as possible using `detach (mydata)` in our example. The `detach ()` command does not make the dataset disappear; it just means that the variables within it are no longer accessible directly by name.

It may also be necessary to remove particular objects created using `rm ()`. That way, the Environment in RStudio doesn't get unnecessarily cluttered:

```
x <- 5
y <- exp(4)
objects ()
rm (x, y)
objects ()
```

To get rid of everything, including all datasets, type:

```
rm (list = ls ())
```

but be absolutely sure that you really want to be as draconian as this before executing the command. There is no going back.

1.8.4 Projects

It is a good idea to keep files relating to a particular piece of work together. An RStudio **project** is a good way of doing this. A project is just a folder containing relevant files which are not necessarily all *R*-related (e.g. code, data, files, notes), together with an `.RProj` file.

Opening the `.RProj` file automatically sets the **working directory** to the project folder, which is more efficient than setting it manually each time RStudio is loaded. The working directory is the folder that *R* searches to find files (see Section 4.1). A list of files in the project can be seen under the Files tab in the bottom right corner in RStudio.

Creating a basic RStudio project is very simple. In RStudio, go to *File*, then *New Project* … then choose *New Directory* followed by *New Project*. Now choose to create a new directory from scratch or use an existing folder. The (new) project folder contains an `.RProj` file. Alternatively, use the Project menu in the top right corner of RStudio to do the same.

The project can be opened by double clicking on the `.RProj` file within the newly created project folder, or by using *File* then *Open Project* in RStudio.

1.9 Linking to other computer languages

Advanced users can employ the functions `.C` and `.Fortran` to provide a standard interface to compiled code that has been linked into *R*, either at build time or via `dyn.load`. They are primarily intended for compiled C and Fortran code, respectively, but the `.C` function can be used with other languages which can generate `C` interfaces, for example C++. The `.Internal` and `.Primitive` interfaces are used to call `C` code compiled into *R* at build time. Functions `.Call` and `.External` provide interfaces which allow compiled code (primarily compiled `C` code) to manipulate *R* objects.

It can be very time-consuming to get these links to work. A particular problem to bear in mind is that if variables are specified as integers in the lower-level language, then they will need to be specified as such in *R* before being passed to the C or Fortran code.

References

R Core Team. (2021). *R: A language and environment for statistical computing*. R Foundation for Statistical Computing. Vienna, Austria. https://www.R-project.org/.

RStudio Team. (2020). *Rstudio: Integrated development environment for R*. RStudio, PBC. Boston, MA. http://www.rstudio.com/.

Venables, W. N., & Ripley, B. D. (2002). *Modern applied statistics with S* (Fourth) [ISBN 0-387-95457-0]. Springer. https://www.stats.ox.ac.uk/pub/MASS4/.

2

Technical Background

2.1 Mathematical functions

There are a number of definitions and rules that we will use frequently in the book. Let's assume that we have a **variable** x, i.e. x could take a range of possible values, and a constant b:

- x^b is x raised to the **power** b. If b is an **integer** or whole number, then x^b is x multiplied by itself b times;

- $e = 2.718\ 28\ \dots$, representing **exponential**, is a number that is probably more important than $\pi = 3.141\ 59\ \dots$ to mathematicians. We will frequently come across expressions such as e^x which is just e raised to the power x, or the **exponential function** of x;

- A **function** is just something that takes a number, or set of numbers, as an input and produces another number as an output. For instance, the function $\ln(x)$ is the inverse of raising x to the power e so that $\ln(e^x) = x$ or $e^{\ln(x)} = x$. This is a form of logarithm (the **natural logarithm**), originally invented to simplify multiplying and dividing large numbers;

- $\ln(x^b) = b\ \ln(x)$;

- $x^{-b} = \frac{1}{x^b}$;

- $x^{\frac{1}{b}}$ is the bth root of x so, for instance, $x^{\frac{1}{2}} = \sqrt{x}$;

- It is often interesting to know what happens when $x \to 0$ or $x \to \infty$, and there are some rules that will help us with that

  - $x^0 = 1$ for any finite value of x;
  - $1^x = 1$;
  - $\infty + x = \infty$ for any x;
  - $\frac{1}{\infty} = 0$;
  - If $x > 1$, then $x^\infty = \infty$ so, in particular, $e^\infty = \infty$;
  - If $0 < x < 1$, then $x^\infty = 0$ so, in particular, $e^{-\infty} = \frac{1}{e^\infty} = \frac{1}{\infty} = 0$.

The R Book, Third Edition. Elinor Jones, Simon Harden and Michael J. Crawley.
© 2023 John Wiley & Sons Ltd. Published 2023 by John Wiley & Sons Ltd.
Companion website: www.wiley.com/go/jones/therbook3e

A common mathematical notation that we will use is, for example [a, b). This represents the interval between a and b, but where a is included in the interval (**closed** at a) but b is not (**open** at b). We will now have a look at some key mathematical functions, and how they are used in R.

2.1.1 Logarithms and exponentials

A typical natural logarithmic equation might be

$$y = a\ln(bx), \qquad\qquad\qquad\qquad (2.1)$$

where a, b are constants. At school, we are often introduced to logarithms to **base** 10, and we use the function log(): here, the base is e, and to be completely clear about that we use ln(). Since e to the power of anything is the inverse of taking natural logarithms, we can re-organise equation (2.1) as follows:

$$\frac{y}{a} = \ln(bx)$$

$$e^{\frac{y}{a}} = e^{\ln(bx)}$$

$$e^{\frac{y}{a}} = bx$$

$$x = \frac{e^{\frac{y}{a}}}{b}.$$

Sometimes we will use exp(), rather than e to refer to the exponential function.

Let's have a look at the simple functions $y = \ln(x)$ and $z = e^x$ for x in the range [0, 10], i.e. the range from 0 to 10, in steps of 0.01, in Figure 2.1:

```
x <- seq (0, 10, 0.01)
plot (x, exp (x), ylab = 'y', type = "l", col = hue_pal ()(2)[1])
plot (x, log (x), ylab = 'z', type = "l", col = hue_pal ()(2)[2])
```

We can see that R uses `exp (x)` to represent e to the power x (so the value for e itself is `exp (1)`) and `log ()` for natural logarithms (i.e. ln()). We can use the latter function for logarithms with any base with, for instance, `log (6, base = 10)`. Now

```
log (0)
```

```
[1] -Inf
```

However, R, sensibly, does not attempt to plot that value. It's also useful to know that

```
log (1)
```

```
[1] 0
```

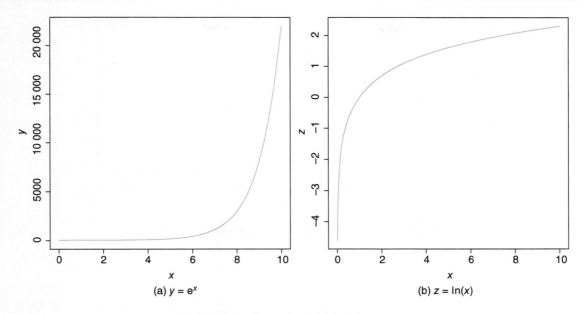

Figure 2.1   Plots of continuous functions

2.1.2   Trigonometric functions

We usually meet trigonometric functions in the context of right-angled triangles with an angle θ, the most common being:

- $\sin(\theta)$: This equals the ratio: (length of side adjacent to θ)/(length of hypotenuse). The **hypotenuse** is the longest side of the triangle;

- $\cos(\theta)$: This is (length of side opposite θ)/(length of hypotneuse);

- $\tan(\theta)$: Or: (length of side adjacent to θ)/(length of side opposite θ).

R does not use degrees for angles but **radians**. It may seem strange to define one radian as 57.295 78 degrees, but all becomes clear if we remember that 360 degrees (one whole revolution of an angle) is equal to 2π radians:

```
360 / (2 * pi)
```

```
[1] 57.29578
```

We can plot the three functions over the range $[0, 2\pi]$ to give Figure 2.2:

```
x <- seq (0, 2 * pi, 0.01)
sinx <- sin (x)
cosx <- cos (x)
```

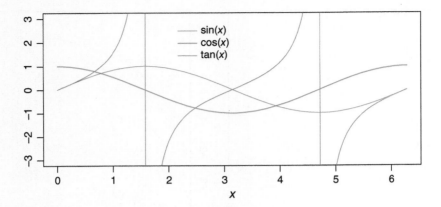

Figure 2.2   Plot of common trigonometric functions

```
tanx <- tan (x)
plot (x, sinx, ylim = c (-3, 3), ylab = "", type = "l", col = hue_pal () (3) [1])
lines (x, cosx, col = hue_pal () (3) [2])
lines (x, tanx, col = hue_pal () (3) [3])
legend (2, 3, legend = c ("sin (x)", "cos (x)", "tan (x)"), lwd = rep (1, 3),
        col = hue_pal () (3), bty = "n")
```

The first two lines are sometimes referred to as a **sine wave** and a **cosine wave**. The tan(x) plot heads off to ∞ as x tends to $\frac{\pi}{2}$ and $\frac{3\pi}{2}$. As x gets little bigger than those two points, tan(x) re-emerges at $-\infty$. The vertical lines 'join' those two points.

We will also on occasion use the inverse of the sin() function, known as the arcsin() or, in *R*, `asin ()`. As usual with inverse functions, this means that

$$\arcsin(\sin(\theta)) = \theta.$$

If we try that in *R* with, say, $\theta = \pi$, we get

```
asin (sin (pi))
```

```
[1] 1.224606e-16
```

This is not zero. It arises as *R* uses approximations for its trigonometric functions. Whenever we see numbers this small in *R*, we should treat them as 0, unless we are specifically looking for extremely small measurements.

2.1.3   Power laws

There is an important family of two-parameter mathematical functions of the form

$$y = ax^b,$$

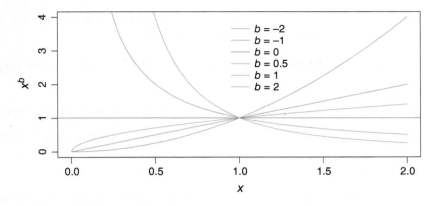

Figure 2.3   Power law plots for various values of b and $a = 1$

known as **power laws**. Depending on the value of the power, b, the relationship can take one of six broad forms as illustrated in Figure 2.3, where we will assume $a = 1$ for simplicity:

```
x <- seq (0, 2, 0.01)
plot (x, 1 / x^2, type = "l", ylab = expression (x^b), col = hue_pal () (6) [1],
      ylim = c (0, 4))
lines (x, 1 / x, col = hue_pal () (6) [2])
abline (h = 1 , col = hue_pal () (6) [3])
lines (x, x^0.5, col = hue_pal () (6) [4])
lines (x, x, col = hue_pal () (6) [5])
lines (x, x^2, col = hue_pal () (6) [6])
legend (0.9, 4, bty = "n",
        legend = c ("b = -2", "b = -1", "b = 0", "b = 0.5", "b = 1", "b = 2"),
              col = hue_pal () (6), lwd = 1)
```

The set of functions where $b < 0$ can be turned into probability distributions (see Chapter 8) over $[1, \infty)$ by a suitable choice for a, so that the function integrates to 1 over the interval: that is why two examples are shown with $b < 0$. However, in order for there to be a finite mean, we require that $b < -2$, and for a finite variance, $b < -3$.

These functions are useful in a wide range of disciplines. The parameters a and b are easy to estimate from data because the function is linearised by a log–log transformation:

$$\log(y) = \log(ax^b) = \log(a) + b\log(x),$$

so that on log–log axes, the intercept is $\log(a)$ and the slope is b. These are often called **allometric** relationships because when $b = 1$ the proportion of x that becomes y varies directly with x.

An important empirical relationship from ecological entomology that has applications in a wide range of statistical analysis is known as **Taylor's power law**. It has to do with the relationship between the variance and the mean of a sample. In elementary statistical models, the variance is assumed not to depend upon the mean. In field data, however, Taylor found that variance increased with the mean according to a power law, such that on log–log axes, the data from most systems fell above a line through the origin with slope = 1 (the pattern shown by data that are Poisson distributed, where the variance is equal to the mean) and below a line through the origin with a slope of 2. Taylor's power law states that for a particular system:

- the log of the variance (log (variance)) is a linear function of the log of the mean (log (mean));
- the scatter about this straight line is small;
- the slope of the regression of log (variance) against log (mean) is greater than 1 and less than 2;
- the parameter values of the log–log regression are fundamental characteristics of the system.

2.1.4 Polynomial functions

Polynomial functions are functions in which x may appear several times, each time raised to a different power, for instance:

$$y = a + bx + cx^2 + \cdots + zx^n.$$

They are useful for describing curves with humps, inflections, or local maxima for a particular range of values of x. So in $[0, 10]$, Figure 2.4 shows the following examples:

- **Decelerating**: The curve increases but increasingly more slowly. The formula is $y = 5x - 0.2x^2$;
- **Humped**: The formula is $y = 5x - 0.4x^2$;

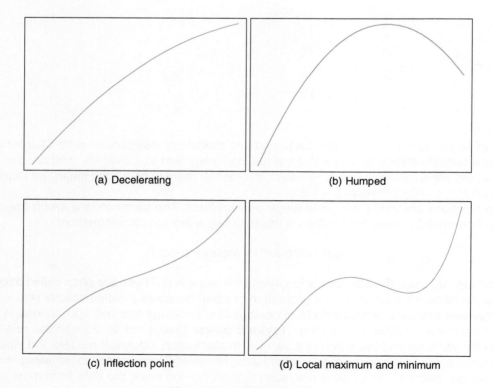

(a) Decelerating   (b) Humped

(c) Inflection point   (d) Local maximum and minimum

Figure 2.4 Polynomial plots

- **Inflection point**: The formula is $y = 2 + 4x - 0.6x^2 + 0.4x^3$;

- **Local maximum and minimum**: The formula is $2 + 4x + 2x^2 - 0.6x^3 + 0.04x^4$.

```
x <- seq (0, 10, 0.01)
y = 5 * x - 0.2 * x^2
plot (x, y, type = "l", col = hue_pal () (4) [1], xaxt = "n", yaxt = "n")
y = 5 * x - 0.4 * x^2
plot (x, y, type = "l", col = hue_pal () (4) [2], xaxt = "n", yaxt = "n")
y = 2 + 4 * x - 0.6 * x^2 + 0.04 * x^3
plot (x, y, type = "l", col = hue_pal () (4) [3], xaxt = "n", yaxt = "n")
y = 2 + 4 * x + 2 * x^2 - 0.6 * x^3 + 0.04 * x^4
plot (x, y, type = "l", col = hue_pal () (4) [4], xaxt = "n", yaxt = "n")
```

Inverse polynomials are an important class of functions which are suitable for setting up generalised linear models with Gamma errors and inverse link functions (see Chapter 11), for instance:

$$\frac{1}{y} = a + bx + cx^2 + \cdots + zx^n.$$

Figure 2.5 shows the following examples:

- **Michaelis–Menten**: The formula is $y = \frac{x}{2+5x}$;

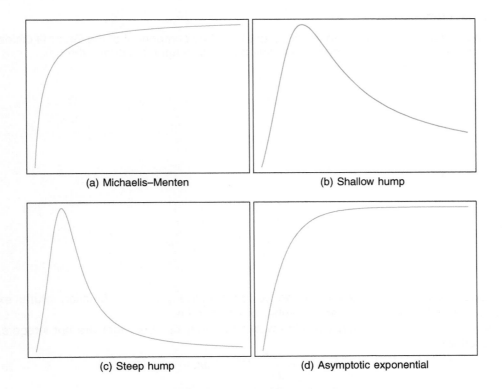

(a) Michaelis–Menten

(b) Shallow hump

(c) Steep hump

(d) Asymptotic exponential

Figure 2.5   Inverse polynomial plots

- **Shallow hump**: The formula is $y = \frac{1}{x-2+4/x}$;
- **Steep hump**: The formula is $y = \frac{1}{x^2-2+4/x}$.

```
x <- seq (0, 10, 0.01)
y = x / (2 + 5 * x)
plot (x, y, type = "l", col = hue_pal () (3) [1], xaxt = "n", yaxt = "n")
y = 1 / (x - 2 + 4 / x)
plot (x, y, type = "l", col = hue_pal () (3) [2], xaxt = "n", yaxt = "n")
y = 1 / (x^2 - 2 + 4 / x)
plot (x, y, type = "l", col = hue_pal () (3) [3], xaxt = "n", yaxt = "n")
```

Note that there are two ways of parameterising the Michaelis–Menten equation:

$$y = \frac{ax}{1 + bx}$$
$$y = \frac{x}{c + dx}.$$

For a practical use of these equations, see Section 14.1.2. In the first case, the asymptotic value of y (as $x \to \infty$) is a/b and in the second it is $1/d$.

2.1.5 Gamma function

The **Gamma** function (sometimes abbreviated to Γ) is a key component of the Gamma distribution (see Section 8.3.6) but is also an important function in its own right. It extends the `factorial ()` function to non-integer values:

```
factorial (6)

[1] 720

gamma (7)

[1] 720

gamma (7.5)

[1] 1871.254
```

So 6 **factorial** $= 6 \times 5 \times 4 \times 3 \times 2 \times 1$ and, as we can see, the `gamma ()` function returns exactly the same value, but we have to insert a number one larger, i.e. `gamma (t + 1) = factorial (t)`. However, the `gamma ()` function also works on other numbers that are not integers. It is defined as follows:

$$\Gamma(t) = \int_0^\infty x^{t-1} e^{-x} \, dx.$$

The function looks like Figure 2.6 in [0.2, 4]:

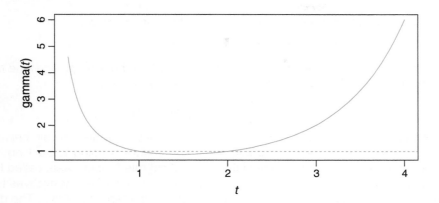

Figure 2.6   Gamma function

```
t <- seq (0.2 ,4, 0.01)
plot (t, gamma (t),type = "l", col = hue_pal ()(2)[1])
abline (h = 1, lty = 2, col = hue_pal ()(2)[2])
```

We can see that $\Gamma(t) = 1$ for $t = 1, 2$. This makes sense as $\Gamma(2) = 1! = 1 = 0! = \Gamma(1)$. Incidentally, in *R* `factorial ()` has been defined to be the same as `gamma ()` and so:

```
factorial (6.5)
```

```
[1] 1871.254
```

2.1.6   Asymptotic functions

An **asymptotic** function of *x* is a function that approaches a fixed value as $x \to \infty$. For instance

$$y = \frac{ax}{1 + bx},$$

which has a different name in almost every scientific discipline. For example, in biochemistry it is called Michaelis–Menten, and shows reaction rate as a function of enzyme concentration; in ecology it is called Holling's disc equation and shows predator feeding rate as a function of prey density. The graph (see Figure 2.5a for an example) passes through the origin and rises with diminishing returns to an asymptotic value at which increasing the value of *x* does not lead to any further increase in *y*.

Another common function is the asymptotic exponential:

$$y = a(1 - e^{-bx}).$$

This, too, is a two-parameter model (*a* and *b*), and in many cases, the two functions would describe data equally well. An example is shown in Figure 2.5d.

Let us work out the behaviour at the limits of our two asymptotic functions, starting with the asymptotic exponential. For $x = 0$ we have:

$$y = a(1 - e^{-b \times 0}) = a(1 - e^0) = a(1 - 1) = a \times 0 = 0,$$

so the graph goes through the origin. At the other extreme, for $x = \infty$, we have

$$y = a(1 - e^{-b \times \infty}) = a(1 - e^{-\infty}) = a(1 - 0) = a \times 1 = a,$$

which demonstrates that the relationship is asymptotic, and that the asymptotic value of y is a.

Turning to the Michaelis–Menten equation, at $x = 0$ the limit is easy:

$$y = \frac{a \times 0}{1 + b \times 0} = \frac{0}{1 + 0} = \frac{0}{1} = 0.$$

However, determining the behaviour at the limit $x = \infty$ is somewhat more difficult, because we end up with $y = \infty/(1 + \infty) = \infty/\infty$, which you might imagine is always going to be 1 no matter what the values of a and b. In fact, there is a special mathematical rule for this case, called **l'Hospital's rule**: when you get a ratio of infinity to infinity, you work out the ratio of the derivatives to obtain the behaviour at the limit. The numerator is ax so its derivative with respect to x is a. The denominator is $1 + bx$ so its derivative with respect to x is $0 + b = b$. The ratio of the derivatives is a/b, and this is the asymptotic value of the Michaelis–Menten function.

We might be in the situation where we have some data which we believe fits either of the two asymptotic functions described above and we want to estimate the values of the parameters, a and b. We can transform the Michaelis–Menten function so that we can fit a linear model or straight line, providing an easy way of estimation. However, that process is not possible for the asymptotic exponential function and an alternative approach must be found (see Section 14.1.1).

For the Michaelis–Menten function, we use the **reciprocal transformation**:

$$\frac{1}{y} = \frac{1 + bx}{ax}.$$

At first glance, this appears to be no great help. But we can separate the terms on the right because they have a common denominator. Then we can cancel the xs, like this:

$$\frac{1}{y} = \frac{1}{ax} + \frac{bx}{ax} = \frac{1}{ax} + \frac{b}{a}.$$

So if we put $Y = 1/y$, $X = 1/x$, $A = 1/a$, and $C = b/a$, we arrive at

$$Y = AX + C,$$

which is linear: C is the intercept and A is the slope. So to estimate the values of a and b from data, we would transform both x and y to reciprocals, plot a graph of $1/y$ against $1/x$, carry out a linear regression to estimate the intercept and slope, then back-transform, to get

$$a = \frac{1}{A}$$

$$b = aC.$$

Suppose that we knew that the graph of the Michaelis–Menten function passed through the two points $(0.2, 44.44)$ and $(0.6, 70.59)$. How do we work out the values of the parameters a and b? First, we calculate the four reciprocals. The slope of the linearised function, A, is the change in $1/y$ divided by the change in $1/x$:

```
A <- (1 / 44.44 - 1 / 70.59) / (1 / 0.2 - 1/0.6)
a <- 1 / A
a
```

```
[1] 399.875
```

Now we rearrange the equation and use one of the points (say $x = 0.2$, $y = 44.44$) to get the value of b:

```
b = 1 / 0.2 * (a * 0.2 / 44.44 - 1)
b
```

```
[1] 3.998088
```

2.1.7 Sigmoid (S-shaped) functions

One of the simplest S-shaped functions is the **two-parameter logistic function** which plays an important role in Generalised Linear Models (see Chapter 11):

$$y = \frac{e^{a+bx}}{1 + e^{a+bx}} = \frac{1}{e^{-(a+bx)} + 1}.$$

We can see that for a value of x, y must lie between zero and one.

The **three-parameter logistic** function allows y to vary on any positive scale:

$$y = \frac{a}{be^{-(cx)} + 1}.$$

The intercept is $a/(1 + b)$, the asymptotic value is a and the initial slope is measured by c. An example with respective parameters 100, 90, and 1 is shown in Figure 2.7a.

The **four-parameter logistic** function has asymptotes at the left (a) and right (b) hand ends of the x axis and scales (c) the response to x about the midpoint (d), where the curve has its inflexion:

$$y = a + \frac{b - a}{e^{c(d-x)} + 1}.$$

An example with parameters 20, 100, 0.8, and 3 is shown in Figure 2.7b. A reversed or **negative sigmoid** function has $c < 0$.

An asymmetric S-shaped curve much used in demography and life insurance work is the **Gompertz growth model**,

$$y = ae^{be^{cx}}.$$

An example with parameters 50, −5, and −0.08 is shown in Figure 2.7c The shape of the function depends on the signs of the parameters b and c. If they are both negative, we have a positive curve, while if b is negative and c positive, then we have a reversed sigmoid. An example of the latter with parameters 100, −1, and 0.2 is given in Figure 2.7d.

The code for all four plots is

```
x <- seq (0, 10, 0.01)
y <- 100 / (1 + 90 * exp(-1 * x))
plot (x, y, type = "l", col = hue_pal ()(4)[1])
y <- 20 +100 / (1 + exp (0.8 * (3 - x)))
plot (x, y, ylim = c (0,140), type = "l", col = hue_pal ()(4)[2])
x <- seq (0, 100, 0.1)
y <- 50 * exp (-5 * exp (-0.08 * x))
plot (x, y, type = "l", col = hue_pal ()(4)[3])
```

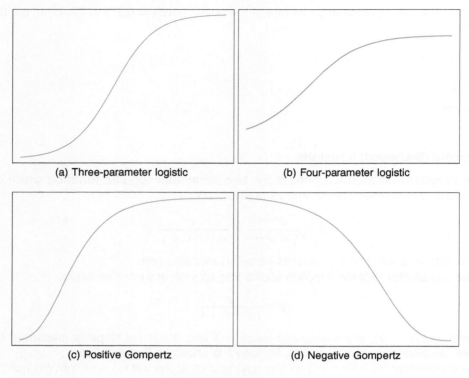

(a) Three-parameter logistic   (b) Four-parameter logistic

(c) Positive Gompertz   (d) Negative Gompertz

Figure 2.7   Sigmoid plots

```
x <- seq (-200, 100, 0.1)
y <- 100 * exp (-exp (0.02 * x))
plot (x, y, type = "l", col = hue_pal ()(4)[4])
```

2.1.8 Biexponential function

The **biexponential** function is a useful four-parameter non-linear function, which is the sum of two exponential functions of *x*:

$$y = ae^{bx} + ce^{dx}.$$

Various shapes depend upon the signs of the parameters *b*, *c*, and *d* (*a* is assumed to be positive): Figure 2.8a shows *c* positive, *b* and *d* negative (it is the sum of two exponential decay curves, so the fast decomposing material disappears first, then the slow, to produce two different phases); Figure 2.8b shows *c* and *d* positive, *b* negative (this produces an asymmetric U-shaped curve); Figure 2.8c shows *c* negative, *b* and *d* positive (this can, but does not always, produce a curve with a hump); and Figure 2.8d shows *b* and *c* positive, *d* negative. When *b*, *c*, and *d* are all negative (not illustrated), the function is known as the **first-order compartment model** in which a drug administered at time 0 passes through the system with its dynamics affected by three physiological processes: elimination, absorption, and clearance. The code for all four plots is

```
x <- seq (0, 10, 0.01)
biexp_plot <- function (a, b, c, d, i) {
```

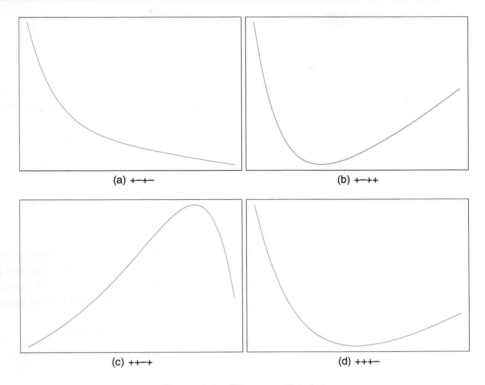

Figure 2.8 Biexponential plots

```
y <- a * exp (b * x) + c *exp (d * x)
plot (x, y, type = "l", col = hue_pal ()(4)[i])
}
biexp_plot (10, -0.8, 10, -0.05, 1)
biexp_plot (10, -0.8, 10, 0.05, 2)
biexp_plot (200, 0.2, -1, 0.7, 3)
biexp_plot (200, 0.05, 300, -0.5, 4)
```

2.1.9 Transformations of model variables

When we build statistical models, we typically denote the variable that we are interested in, the **response** or **outcome** variables by y, and the variables which might affect that outcome, the **covariates**, **explanatory** or **predictors** by x. More details can be found in Chapter 10. If we can create a **linear** (i.e. straight line/plane) relationship between the response and predictors, then building a model is very straightforward. Often, we can transform x and/or y to make the relationship linear (if not then see Chapter 14). We have seen some examples in this chapter and here are some more:

- $\log(y)$ against x for exponential relationships;
- $\log(y)$ against $\log(x)$ for power functions;

- e^y against x for logarithmic relationships;
- $1/y$ against $1/x$ for asymptotic relationships;
- $\log(p/(1-p))$ against x for proportion data.

There are other transformations that are useful for stabilising the variance of y against different values of x:

- $\sqrt{y}$ to stabilize the variance for count data;
- $\arcsin(y)$ to stabilize the variance of percentage data.

2.2 Matrices

Matrices are a useful tool in mathematics and statistics as they allow us to gather together and then manipulate large amounts of data in a relatively straightforward way. In this section, we will go over the basics and show how easy it is to use matrices in R. A **matrix** is just an array of numbers set out in n rows and m columns. We refer to the entry in the rth row and cth column by the coordinates (r, c).

Let's create our first matrix, A. We usually use capital letters for matrices, in R:

```
A <- matrix (c (1, 0, 4, 2, -1, 1), nrow = 3)
A

     [,1] [,2]
[1,]    1    2
[2,]    0   -1
[3,]    4    1
```

There are a few things worth noting:

- the first thing we put into the `matrix ()` function are the data. The default setting is that they will be read into the matrix by going down the columns. This can be changed by the argument `byrow = T`;
- we only have to specify the number of rows (or columns). R knows there are six pieces of data and so $6/3 = 2$ must be the number of columns;
- we can set up an empty matrix which has *NA* everywhere using `matrix (nrow = 3, ncol = 2)`. This can then be filled as the result of some procedure;
- in RStudio, A is shown in the top right-hand corner box and any matrix can be seen in a more pleasing layout by clicking on its entry there or by typing `View (A)`;
- we can create names for the rows or columns of a matrix, or view any already there using `rownames ()` or `colnames ()`, respectively.

More details on matrices in R can be found in Section 3.11.

Our second matrix, *B*, will have the numbers of rows and columns from *A* swapped round:

```
B <- matrix (c (1, -1, 2, 1, 1, 0), ncol = 3)
B


     [,1] [,2] [,3]
[1,]    1    2    1
[2,]   -1    1    0
```

This is a 2 × 3 matrix, i.e. 2 rows and 3 columns.

2.2.1   Matrix multiplication

To multiply one matrix by another matrix, we must have the same number of columns in the first matrix as we do rows in the second. The process is to take each row of the first matrix and multiply it element-wise with every column of the second matrix, summing the result. So to start: put the first row of *A* side by side with the first column of *B*:

```
A[1,]

[1] 1 2

B[,1]

[1]   1 -1
```

and work out the element-wise products:

```
A[1,] * B[,1]

[1]   1 -2
```

then add up those products

```
sum (A[1,] * B[,1])

[1] -1
```

to give the entry in (1, 1) of the product matrix. To find the entry in (1, 2), i.e. row 1, column 2, we do the same but with the second column of *B*:

```
sum (A[1,] * B[,2])

[1] 4
```

To get the entries in the second row of the product matrix, we begin with the second row of *A* and carry out the same calculations with all the columns of *B*, etc. Fortunately, *R* does all the hard work using the matrix multiplication operator `%*%` to create *AB*:

```
A %*% B

      [,1] [,2] [,3]
[1,]   -1    4    1
[2,]    1   -1    0
[3,]    3    9    4
```

This is a 3×3 matrix. More generally, if *A* is a $n_1 \times n_2$ matrix and *B* a $n_2 \times n_3$ matrix, then *AB* will be a $n_1 \times n_3$ matrix: the n_2s, which must be the same, cancel out. In our example, therefore, *BA* will be a 2×2 matrix:

```
B %*% A

      [,1] [,2]
[1,]    5    1
[2,]   -1   -3
```

So, in general, $AB \neq BA$.

2.2.2 Diagonals of matrices

Square matrices, with the same number of rows and columns will have a main diagonal. To create a diagonal matrix of 3 rows and 3 columns, with 1s on the diagonal we use the `diag ()` function like this:

```
C <- diag (1, nrow = 3, ncol = 3)
C

      [,1] [,2] [,3]
[1,]    1    0    0
[2,]    0    1    0
[3,]    0    0    1
```

Matrices with 1s down the diagonal and 0s elsewhere are known as **identity** or **unit** matrices and usually denoted by *I* or, to be specific here, I_3. We can alter the values of the diagonal elements of a matrix like, so

```
diag (C) <- 1:3
C

      [,1] [,2] [,3]
[1,]    1    0    0
[2,]    0    2    0
[3,]    0    0    3
```

We can extract a vector containing the diagonal elements of a matrix:

```
diag (C)
```

```
[1] 1 2 3
```

If we have two variables x and y, each with five elements, then we can create a variance–covariance matrix (an example is given in the multivariate distribution in Section 8.3.12) and extract the diagonal, which contains the variances of x and y:

```
M <- cbind (x = 1:5, y = rnorm(5))
diag (cov (M))
```

```
        x           y
2.5000000 0.3694207
```

2.2.3 Determinants

Determinants are a useful way of summarising a square matrix in just one number. For instance if we have

$$A = \begin{bmatrix} a & b \\ c & d \end{bmatrix},$$

then the **determinant**, sometimes given as $|A|$ is defined as follows:

$$\det(A) = a * d - b * c.$$

Slightly more complicatedly, and using the standard matrix notation, if

$$A = \begin{bmatrix} a_{11} & a_{12} & a_{13} \\ a_{21} & a_{22} & a_{23} \\ a_{31} & a_{32} & a_{23} \end{bmatrix},$$

then the determinant of A is defined to be

$$\det(A) = a_1 \begin{vmatrix} a_{22} & a_{23} \\ a_{32} & a_{33} \end{vmatrix} - a_{12} \begin{vmatrix} a_{21} & a_{23} \\ a_{32} & a_{33} \end{vmatrix} + a_{13} \begin{vmatrix} a_{21} & a_{22} \\ a_{31} & a_{32} \end{vmatrix}.$$

We can then apply the formula for a 2×2 matrix to give

$$\det A = a_{11}a_{22}a_{33} - a_{11}a_{23}a_{32} + a_{12}a_{23}a_{31} - a_{12}a_{21}a_{33} + a_{13}a_{21}a_{32} - a_{13}a_{22}a_{31}.$$

Similar formulae apply for larger matrices.

Let's take a numerical example:

$$A = \begin{bmatrix} 1 & 2 & 3 \\ 2 & 1 & 1 \\ 4 & 1 & 2 \end{bmatrix}.$$

This has determinant

$$\det(A) = (1 \times 1 \times 2) - (1 \times 1 \times 1) + (2 \times 1 \times 4) - (2 \times 2 \times 2) + (3 \times 2 \times 1) - (3 \times 1 \times 4)$$

$$= 2 - 1 + 8 - 8 + 6 - 12 = -5.$$

And in *R*:

```
A <- matrix (c (1, 2, 4, 2, 1, 1, 3, 1, 2), nrow = 3)
A

     [,1] [,2] [,3]
[1,]    1    2    3
[2,]    2    1    1
[3,]    4    1    2

det (A)

[1] -5
```

One neat thing about determinants is that if a row or a column of a matrix is multiplied by a scalar, λ, then the value of the resulting determinant is also multiplied by λ (since a factor λ will appear in each of the products). For instance, here is the bottom row of *A* multiplied by 3:

```
B <- A
B[3,] <- 3 * B[3,]
B

     [,1] [,2] [,3]
[1,]    1    2    3
[2,]    2    1    1
[3,]   12    3    6

det (B)

[1] -15
```

If all the elements of a row or a column are zero, then the determinant is also zero. Again, if all the corresponding elements of any two rows or columns are equal, then $\det(A) = 0$. This final point can be taken one step further: in order for the determinant to be not zero (see Section 2.2.4 for why this is important) no two rows or columns can be a multiple of each other. For example:

```
C <- A
C[,2] <- 4 * C[,1]
C

     [,1] [,2] [,3]
[1,]    1    4    3
```

```
[2,]    2    8    1
[3,]    4   16    2

det (C)


[1] 0
```

2.2.4 Inverse of a matrix

The operation of division is not defined for matrices. However, for a square matrix, A, with a non-zero determinant (**non-singular**), a multiplicative inverse matrix denoted by A^{-1} can be defined. This multiplicative inverse is unique and has the property that

$$A^{-1}A = AA^{-1} = I,$$

where I is the identity matrix. This is analogous to numbers: if $a \neq 0$, then $aa^{-1} = 1$. If A is a square matrix for which $|A| = 0$, the matrix inverse is defined by the relationship:

$$A^{-1} = \frac{\text{adj}(A)}{|A|},$$

where the **adjoint** matrix of A (adj(A)) is the matrix of cofactors of A. The **cofactors** of A are computed as $A_{ij} = (-1)^{i+j}M_{ij}$, where M_{ij} are the **minors** of the elements a_{ij} (these are the determinants of the matrices of A from which row i and column j have been deleted). Probably best to forget all that as R will do the work for us. The properties of the inverse matrix can be laid out for two non-singular square matrices, A and B, of the same size or **order** as follows:

$$(AB)^{-1} = B^{-1}A^{-1}$$
$$(A^{-1})' = (A')^{-1}$$
$$(A^{-1})^{-1} = A$$
$$|A| = \frac{1}{|A^{-1}|},$$

where A' is the **conjugate** or **transpose** of A: $a'_{ij} = a_{ji}$ for all i and j (it is like reflecting A in a mirror down its main diagonal and the function in R is t ( )).

Finding an inverse is straightforward in R using the A defined in Section 2.2.3:

```
solve (A)


       [,1]  [,2]  [,3]
[1,]  -0.2   0.2   0.2
[2,]   0.0   2.0  -1.0
[3,]   0.4  -1.4   0.6


solve (solve (A))
```

```
     [,1] [,2] [,3]
[1,]    1    2    3
[2,]    2    1    1
[3,]    4    1    2
```

We will see why the function is called `solve` in Section 2.2.6. For larger matrices, particularly those with non-integer values and close to non-singular, R may well have rounding issues which can turn into major problems with the solution: in that case it might be worth investigating specialist matrix libraries such as `matlib`.

2.2.5 Eigenvalues and eigenvectors

This section refers to terms that are not used explicitly elsewhere in the book. However, they are carrying out all the work behind the scenes in principal component analysis in Section 19.3. Here we examine a useful example of interest in itself. Consider a square matrix, A, a scalar, λ, and a vector v then λ is an **eigenvalue** and v an **eigenvector** of A if:

$$Av = \lambda v.$$

In fact, in general, an $n \times n$ matrix A will have eigenvalues $\lambda_1, \lambda_2, \dots, \lambda_n$, each with a corresponding eigenvector $v_1, v_2, \dots, v_n$. They are a method of structuring the information held in a matrix.

Here is an example from population ecology. The matrix L shows the demography of different age classes: the top row shows fecundity (the number of females born per female of each age) and the sub-diagonals show survival rates (the fraction of one age class that survives to the next age class). When these numbers are constants, the matrix is known as the **Leslie** matrix. In the absence of density dependence, the constant parameter values in L will lead either to exponential increase in total population size (if $\lambda_1 > 1$) or exponential decline (if $\lambda_1 < 1$) once the initial transients in age structure have damped away. Once exponential growth has been achieved, then the age structure, as reflected by the proportion of individuals in each age class, will be a constant. This is the first eigenvector.

Let's start with the Leslie matrix:

```
L <- matrix (c (0, 0.7, 0, 0, 6, 0, 0.5, 0, 3, 0, 0, 0.3, 1, 0, 0, 0), nrow = 4)
L

     [,1] [,2] [,3] [,4]
[1,]  0.0  6.0  3.0    1
[2,]  0.7  0.0  0.0    0
[3,]  0.0  0.5  0.0    0
[4,]  0.0  0.0  0.3    0
```

The top row contains the age-specific fecundities (e.g. 2-year-olds produce six female offspring per year), and the sub-diagonal contains the survivorships (e.g. 70% of 1-year-olds become 2-year-olds). Now the population sizes at each age go in a column vector, v, which we have defined as a matrix for clarity.

```
v <- matrix (c (45, 20, 17, 3), ncol = 1)
v
```

```
      [,1]
[1,]   45
[2,]   20
[3,]   17
[4,]    3
```

Population sizes next year in each of the four age classes are obtained by matrix multiplication:

```
L %*% v
```

```
        [,1]
[1,]  174.0
[2,]   31.5
[3,]   10.0
[4,]    5.1
```

We can check this the long way. For instance, the number of juveniles next year (the first element of *v*) is the sum of all the babies born last year:

```
45 * 0 + 20 * 6 + 17 * 3 + 3 * 1
```

```
[1] 174
```

Now we can simulate the population dynamics over a period long enough (say, 40 generations) for the age structure to approach stability. If the population growth rate λ is > 1, the population will increase exponentially, once the age structure has stabilised. We will investigate this and produce Figure 2.9:

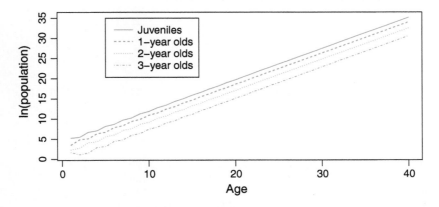

Figure 2.9 Age profile

```
age_profile <- matrix (nrow = 40, ncol = 4)
for (i in 1:40) {
  v <- L %*% v
  age_profile[i,] <- v
}
matplot (1:40, log (age_profile), type = "l", xlab = "age",
         ylab = "ln (population)", col = hue_pal ()(4))
legend (5, 35, legend = c ("juveniles", "1-year olds", "2-year olds",
        "3-year olds"),
        col = hue_pal ()(4),lty = 1:4)
```

We can see that after some initial transient fluctuations, the age structure has more or less stabilised by year 20 (the lines are parallel). By year 40, the population is growing exponentially in size, multiplying by a constant of λ each year (the y-axis is the ln of population sizes).

The population growth rate, λ, is approximated by the ratio of total population sizes in the 40th and 39th years:

```
sum (age_profile[40,]) / sum (age_profile[39,])
```

```
[1] 2.164035
```

and the approximate stable age structure is obtained from the 40th value of v, reweighted so that it sums to one:

```
age_profile[40,] / sum (age_profile[40,])
```

```
[1] 0.709769309 0.230139847 0.052750539 0.007340305
```

The exact values of the population growth rate and the stable age distribution are obtained by matrix algebra: they are the first eigenvalue and its corresponding eigenvector, respectively. We use the function eigen () applied to the Leslie matrix, L, like this:

```
eigen (L)
```

```
eigen() decomposition
$values
[1]  2.1694041+0.0000000i -1.9186627+0.0000000i -0.1253707+0.0975105i
[4] -0.1253707-0.0975105i

$vectors
                  [,1]              [,2]                        [,3]
[1,] 0.949264118+0i -0.93561508+0i -0.01336028-0.03054433i
[2,] 0.306298338+0i  0.34134741+0i -0.03616819+0.14241169i
[3,] 0.070595039+0i -0.08895451+0i  0.36511901-0.28398118i
[4,] 0.009762363+0i  0.01390883+0i -0.87369452+0.00000000i
                       [,4]
```

```
[1,]  -0.01336028+0.03054433i
[2,]  -0.03616819-0.14241169i
[3,]   0.36511901+0.28398118i
[4,]  -0.87369452+0.000000000i
```

The first eigenvalue is 2.1694 (compared with our empirical approximation of 2.1640 after 40 years). The stable age distribution is given by the first eigenvector (column 1, above), which we need to turn into proportions:

```
eigen (L)$vectors[,1] / sum (eigen (L)$vectors[,1])

[1] 0.710569659+0i 0.229278977+0i 0.052843768+0i 0.007307597+0i
```

This compares with our approximation (above) in which the proportion in the first age class was 0.709 77 after 40 years (rather than 0.710 57).

This is a specific example of a more general result linking eigenvalues and eigenvectors to the equilibrium distributions of Markov chains.

2.2.6 Solving systems of linear equations using matrices

Suppose we have two linear equations containing two unknown variables that we can reorganise so that they are laid out in a similar fashion:

$$3x + 4y = 12$$
$$x + 2y = 8. \tag{2.2}$$

Then, we can use the function `solve ()` to find the values of the variables if we provide it with two matrices:

- a square matrix A containing the coefficients of the variables (3, 4, 1, 2), laid out as above;
- a column vector k containing the known values (12 and 8).

We set the two matrices up like this (column-wise, as usual), and solve:

```
A <- matrix (c (3, 1, 4, 2), nrow = 2)
k <- matrix (c (12, 8), nrow = 2)
solve (A, k)

       [,1]
[1,]     -4
[2,]      6
```

It is easy to check that the solution is correct, but why is it? If we think of the variables as a vector, say v, then we can rewrite equation (2.2) as follows:

$$Av = k,$$

and we can then multiply each side of that equation by A^{-1}, on the left, to give

$$v = A^{-1}k.$$

That also explains why the function for the inverse of a matrix, as we discussed in Section 2.2.4 is called `solve ()`. The same technique can be used in much larger sets of simultaneous equations, as long as we use the same number of equations as unknown variables.

2.3 Calculus

R does understand the principles of calculus, differentiation, and integration, and it uses them behind the scenes in a number of areas such as non-linear modelling (see Chapter 14). R can also carry out simple symbolic operations in differentiation and estimate the values of integrals. We will examine these here, as well as looking at how R can estimate the solutions to some differential equations.

2.3.1 Differentiation

If we have a function $f()$ so that

$$y = f(x),$$

then the derivative, $\frac{dy}{dx}$, is just the gradient of our function $f()$, and we can then insert any value of x to find the specific gradient at that point. Here is a simple example where we want to differentiate $2x^3$ and then evaluate the result at $x = 1, 2, 3$:

```
D (expression (2 * x^3), "x")


2 * (3 * x^2)


dxy <- deriv (~ 2 * x^3, "x")
eval (dxy, envir = list (x = 1:3))


[1]   2 16 54
attr(,"gradient")
         x
[1,]   6
[2,]  24
[3,]  54
```

The first line gives the derivative in symbols, i.e. $6x^2$, although it leaves it to us to simplify. The second line then creates an R object containing the derivative. Finally, the third line evaluates both the original expression and the derivative (or gradient) at the points we requested. So, for instance, $2 \times 3^3 = 54$ and, also, $6 \times 3^2 = 54$. Here are some more examples of symbolic derivatives:

```
D (expression (log (x)), "x")


1/x


D (expression (a * exp (-b * x)), "x")
```

```
-(a * (exp(-b * x) * b))

D (expression (a / (1 + b * exp (-c * x))), "x")

a * (b * (exp(-c * x) * c))/(1 + b * exp(-c * x))^2

trig_exp <- expression (sin (x + 2 * y))
D (trig_exp, "x")

cos(x + 2 * y)

D (trig_exp, "y")

cos(x + 2 * y) * 2
```

In `trig_exp`, we have created a function of two variables, x and y, and then (partially) differentiated with respect to each of them. There are more examples in `help (deriv)`.

2.3.2 Integration

The *R* function, `integrate ()` can estimate the area under various curves. For instance, if we want to work out the probability under the standard Normal curve between two points, say $(-1.96, 1.96)$:

```
integrate (dnorm, lower = -1.96, upper = 1.96)

0.9500042 with absolute error < 1e-11

pnorm (1.96) - pnorm (-1.96)

[1] 0.9500042
```

The second line, representing the usual approach, is discussed in Section 8.3.1 along with a more detailed analysis of the distribution.

Or we can define our own function and estimate the area under that

```
our_fn <- function (x) {
  exp (-x)
}
integrate (our_fn, lower = 0, upper = Inf)

1 with absolute error < 5.7e-05
```

Rather neatly, as shown in Figure 2.10, the shaded area under the inverse exponential function, e^{-x}, for positive x, is just 1, plus or minus a little bit as the answer has been estimated rather than derived mathematically.

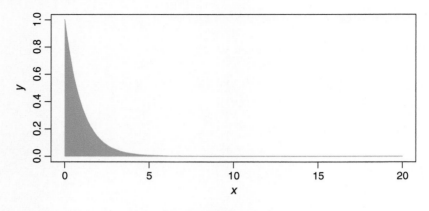

Figure 2.10 e^{-x}

```
x <- seq (0, 20, 0.01)
y <- exp (-x)
plot (x, y, type = "l", col = hue_pal () (2) [1])
polygon (x = c (0, x, 20), y = c (0, y, 0), col = hue_pal () (2) [2], border = NA)
```

2.3.3   Differential equations

There are a number of packages for solving differential equations in *R*. We will look at a relatively simple example using deSolve (Soetaert et al., 2010), without discussing in any technical detail what is going on.

```
library (deSolve, quietly = T)
```

The example involves a simple resource-limited plant herbivore interaction, where *v* is vegetation and *n* is herbivore population. We need to specify two **ordinary differential equations**: one for the change in vegetation over time ($\frac{dv}{dt}$) and one doing the same for the herbivore population ($\frac{dn}{dt}$):

$$\frac{dV}{dt} = rv \left(\frac{K-v}{K} \right) - bvn$$

$$\frac{dN}{dt} = cvn - dn.$$

The steps involved in solving these ODEs in R are as follows:

- define a function (called phmodel () in this case) containing the equations;
  - write the vegetation equation as dv using with;
  - write the herbivore equation as dn using with;
  - combine these vectors into a list called result;

- generate a time series over which to solve the equations in `times`;
- set the parameter values in `parameters`;
- set the starting values for *v* and *n* in `initial`;
- use `ode ()` to create a matrix with the time series of *v* and *n* in output.

None of this is at all complicated, but there are lots of steps, so it looks a bit daunting.

First, we write the function called which tells *R* the structure of the two equations, showing how the change in each population is related to the functional and numerical responses:

```
phmodel <- function (t, state, parameters) {
  with (as.list (c (state, parameters)), {
    dv <- r * v * (K - v) / K - b * v * n
    dn <- c * v * n - d * n
    result <- c (dv, dn)
    list (result)
  }
  )
}
```

The final curly bracket ends the function, the plain right bracket closes the `with ()` function and the penultimate curly bracket ends the definition of the equations.

To run the model, we need to create a vector of times over which to calculate the population dynamics:

```
times <- seq (0, 500)
```

then define the numeric values of the five parameters (these values will determine the behaviour of the two populations):

```
parameters <- c (r = 0.4, K = 1000, b = 0.02, c = 0.01, d = 0.3)
```

and set the initial conditions (plant = 50 and herbivores = 10):

```
initial <- c (v = 50, n = 10)
```

That is the end of the preliminaries.

Solving the equations could not be easier. The important function is `ode ()` (ordinary differential equation solver). The function takes four arguments: the starting values, the vector of times, the function containing the equations, and the list containing the parameter values:

```
phm_output <- ode (y = initial, time = times, func = phmodel, parms = parameters)
```

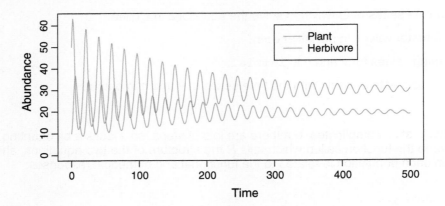

Figure 2.11 Plant herbivore interaction

The output object is a matrix with three columns: time, plant abundance (*v*), and herbivore abundance (*n*):

```
head (phm_output)

     time          v          n
[1,]    0 50.00000 10.00000
[2,]    1 58.29220 12.75106
[3,]    2 62.99695 17.40172
[4,]    3 60.70065 24.09264
[5,]    4 50.79407 31.32860
[6,]    5 37.68312 36.12636
```

We can plot the two time series together to give Figure 2.11:

```
plot (phm_output[,1], phm_output[,2], ylim = c (0, max (phm_output[,2:3])),
      type = "l", ylab = "abundance", xlab = "time", col = hue_pal ()(2)[1])
lines (phm_output[,1], phm_output[,3], col = hue_pal ()(2)[2])
legend (300, 60, legend = c ("plant", "herbivore"), lty = 1,
        col = hue_pal ()(2))
```

The system exhibits damped oscillations to a stable point equilibrium at which $\frac{dv}{dt}$ and $\frac{dn}{dt}$ are both equal to zero, so equilibrium plant abundance $V^* = d/c = 0.3/0.01 = 30$ and equilibrium herbivore abundance $= r(K - V^*)/bK = 19.4$.

An alternative is to plot the output as a phase plane, with herbivore abundance on the *x*-axis and plant abundance on the *y*-axis to give Figure 2.12:

```
plot (phm_output[,2], phm_output[,3], xlim = c (0, max (phm_output[,2:3])),
      ylim = c (0, max (phm_output[,2:3])), type = "l",
      ylab = "plant", xlab = "herbivore", col = hue_pal ()(1))
```

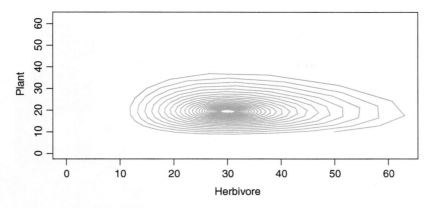

Figure 2.12   Plant herbivore interaction in a phase plane

2.4   Probability

Probability is a branch of mathematics concerned with chance and, sometimes, uncertainty. As with all good mathematical disciplines, there is a set of axioms from which a large number of theorems have been derived, some of which have been found useful in the study of Statistics (see Section 2.5). One slight issue is that there is no consensus on the meaning of the word probability: the problem extends into Statistics. In this section, we will just review some definitions and results that are required elsewhere in the book.

2.4.1   The central limit theorem

The basic idea is that if we take an independent (see Section 8.1.3) sample from a population with finite variance, then the mean of that sample will have a distribution that is close to a Normal distribution. This is known as the **central limit theorem** or **CLT**. We will ignore all the technicalities and look at some simple examples. We can take six uniformly distributed random numbers between 0 and 10 and work out their mean. This will be low when we get, say, 2.7, 3.1, 1.0, 2.8, 1.5, 3.1, and high when we get 9.9, 8.5, 9.2, 6.1, 8.7, 6.9. Typically, of course, the mean will be close to 5. Let us do this 1000 times and look at the distribution of the 6000 *observations* (as a method of simulating the distribution), in Figure 2.13a. The best way to store the data will be in a matrix with 1000 rows and 6 columns:

```
unif_data <- runif (6000, min = 0, max = 10)
unif_samples <- matrix (unif_data, ncol = 6)
hist (unif_data, main = "", xlab = "", col = hue_pal ()(3)[1], breaks = 11)
```

We have set one bar per integer range (`breaks = 11` as we include the start and end as well as the divisions between bars), and it is no surprise to see that each of them has about 600 observations. How about the *means* of each of the 1000 samples? Figure 2.13b shows that histogram:

```
hist (rowMeans (unif_samples), main = "", xlab = "", col = hue_pal ()(3)[2],
      breaks = 21, freq = F)
```

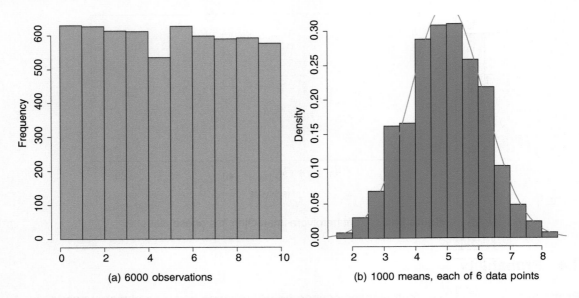

Figure 2.13 Histograms from U(0, 10)

We have requested 21 breaks so that we can see more detail and requested a density rather than a frequency histogram, for reasons that will become clear.

The shape of the second histogram appears roughly similar to that of a Normal distribution. But which Normal distribution, i.e. what are the parameter values for the mean and variance? The CLT says (this is a very informal version of it) that the mean should be what we would expect to see in a sample of 6, namely 5. The variance is a bit more complicated, but it is $\frac{\sigma^2}{n}$, where σ is the variance of the U(0, 10) distribution ($\frac{(10-0)^2}{12}$: see Section 8.3.2) and n the number of independent samples drawn (6), or $\frac{100}{72}$. That gives 1.389 and so the standard deviation we are looking for is the square root of that, or 1.179. We can compare these values to the corresponding values from our sample:

```
mean (rowMeans (unif_samples))

[1] 4.899517

sd (rowMeans (unif_samples))

[1] 1.191412
```

The mean is close and the standard deviation not that far off. We have added the Normal curve with those parameters to Figure 2.13b:

```
x <- seq (0, 10, 0.01)
lines (x, dnorm (x, mean = 5, sd = sqrt (100 / 72)), col = hue_pal () (3) [3],
       lwd = 2)
```

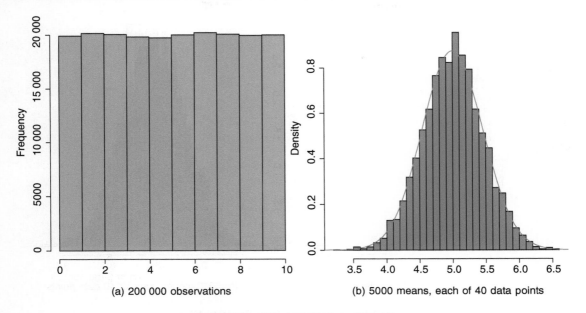

(a) 200 000 observations   (b) 5000 means, each of 40 data points

Figure 2.14   Histograms from U(0, 10)

We can see that the histogram is close to the Normal curve but not that close, particularly in the tails. That is because the CLT says that the distribution will become closer to Normal as the sample size rises. So, let's do the same but with a sample size of 40, and let's take 5000 samples (200 000 observations in total), to give Figures 2.14:

```
unif_data <- runif (200000, min = 0, max = 10)
unif_samples <- matrix (unif_data, ncol = 40)
hist (unif_data, main = "", xlab = "", col = hue_pal ()(3)[1], breaks = 11)
y <- hist (rowMeans (unif_samples), plot = F)
x <- seq (0, 10, 0.01)
hist (rowMeans (unif_samples), main = "", xlab = "", col = hue_pal ()(3)[2],
      breaks = 41, freq = F, ylim = c (0, max (dnorm (x, mean = 5,
      sd = sqrt (100 / (12 * 40))), y$density)))
lines (x, dnorm (x, mean = 5, sd = sqrt (100 / (12 * 40))),
      col = hue_pal ()(3)[3], lwd = 2)
```

That's much better but still not perfect: the CLT is an **asymptotic** result which means that the distribution will never be exactly Normal but will get closer as n gets larger. We can compare the standard deviation of our sample with what we might expect:

```
sd (rowMeans (unif_samples))


[1] 0.4507736


sqrt (100 / (12 * 40))


[1] 0.4564355
```

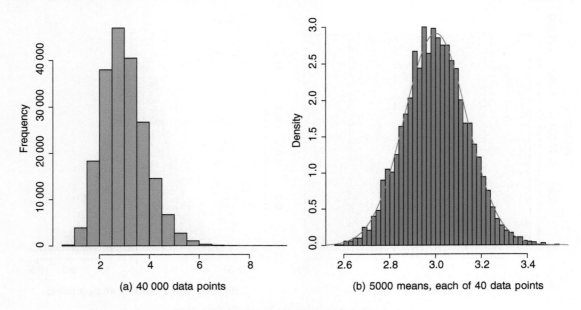

(a) 40 000 data points   (b) 5000 means, each of 40 data points

Figure 2.15   Histograms from Gamma $(12, 4)$

We might think that beginning with the Uniform distribution, which is symmetric and nicely behaved, is cheating: the distribution of the mean of a sample will inevitably itself be symmetric and neat. So, let's repeat the process with a skewed distribution, the Gamma $(12, 4)$ distribution, which has mean $\frac{12}{4} = 3$ and variance $\frac{12}{4*4} = 0.75$, to give Figures 2.15:

```
gamma_data <- rgamma (200000, shape = 12, rate = 4)
gamma_samples <- matrix (gamma_data, ncol = 40)
hist (gamma_data, main = "", xlab = "", col = hue_pal ()(3)[1], breaks = 20)
x <- seq (2.4, 4, 0.01)
y <- hist (rowMeans (gamma_samples), plot = F)
hist (rowMeans (gamma_samples), main = "", xlab = "", col = hue_pal ()(3)[2],
    breaks = 41, freq = F, ylim = c (0, max (dnorm (x, mean = 3,
    sd = sqrt (12 / (4 * 4 * 40))), y$density)))
lines (x, dnorm (x, mean = 3,  sd = sqrt (12 / (4 * 4 * 40))),
    col = hue_pal ()(3)[3], lwd = 2)
```

The starting data are definitely skewed. The right-hand histogram is perhaps not quite as good a fit as for the Uniform distribution, but close. Again, we can compare the means and standard deviations from our sample, and from the Normal distribution:

```
mean (rowMeans (gamma_samples))

[1] 3.001485

sd (rowMeans (gamma_samples))

[1] 0.1347468
```

```
sqrt (12 / (4 * 4 * 40))
```

```
[1] 0.1369306
```

The CLT applies to any distribution with a finite variance, in particular to discrete distributions. In fact, the very first version of the theorem was about the Bernoulli distribution. The upshot was that a sum of Bernoulli distributions, i.e. a Binomial distribution, will get closer to a Normal distribution as the number in the sum increases.

This theorem suggests why approximate Normal distributions appear very often in the natural world: weights or heights of mammals for instance. However, the result is approximate and the natural world a complex place so we should not read too much into the prevalence of roughly bell-shaped curves.

2.4.2 Conditional probability

In probability theory, we discuss the probability of **events**: the probability that our train will arrive in the next five minutes, or that it will rain today or that the sun will rise tomorrow (hopefully close to 1). So if I draw card from a standard pack of playing cards, the probability of the event that it is a heart will be $P(H) = \frac{13}{52}$. Conditional probability is important in many areas of statistics but particularly in Bayesian analysis (see Chapter 22).

Conditional probability is where we examine the probability of an event, given that something else is true. The probability of a heart will be different if I only choose from the red cards in a pack, and we describe this as $P(H|R)$. the definition is

$$P(A|B) = \frac{P(A \cap B)}{P(B)},$$

where $P(A \cap B)$ means the probability of events both A and B occurring. So, for our example:

$$P(H|R) = \frac{P(H \cap R)}{P(R)} = \frac{P(H)}{P(R)} = \frac{\frac{13}{52}}{\frac{26}{52}} = \frac{1}{2},$$

as expected.

There are some simple consequences of the definition:

- $0 \le P(A|B) \le 1$;

- $P(A|A) = 1$;

- $P(A \cap B) = P(A|B) \times P(B) = P(B|A) \times P(A)$;

- $P(A) = P(A|B_1) \times P(B_1) + P(A|B_2) \times P(B_2)$, where B_1 and B_2 are events such that $P(B_1) + P(B_2) = 1$ and $P(B_1 \cap B_2) = 0$.

The final item is the subtle one and is known as the **law of total probability**: it can be extended to as many B_is as we like as long as their probabilities sum to 1 (they are **exhaustive**), and they don't intersect with each other (**exclusive**). Let's look at an example.

Twins can arise from splitting of a single fertilised egg (**monozygotic** twins), or from two separate fertilisations of different eggs (**dizygotic** twins). Not all monozygotic twins look identical, and some dizygotic individuals can look very alike. This means that you cannot reliably tell monozygotic from dizygotic twins just by looking at them. But there is a reliable way of estimating the proportions of monozygotic and dizygotic twins in the population. The key fact is that while dizygotic twins can be born as 2 boys or 2 girls or 1 boy and 1 girl, monozygotic twins are always of the same gender. So if B is the event of a twin being a boy, and G is the event of a twin being a girl, then there are three outcomes for any batch of twins: BB, GG, or GB. Let us define the conception event(s) as either monozygotic (M) or dizygotic (D). We might want to know what is the probability of a pair of twins being monozygotic: $P(M)$. However, all we can do is observe what proportion of twins are, for instance, born as both girls. Assuming that gender at birth is female with a probability of 0.5, the probabilities for the dizygotic twins are easy:

$$P(GG|D) = \frac{1}{4}$$

$$P(BB|D) = \frac{1}{4}$$

$$P(GB|D) = \frac{1}{2},$$

which sum to 1. The probabilities for monozygotic twins are

$$P(GG|M) = \frac{1}{2}$$

$$P(BB|M) = \frac{1}{2}$$

$$P(GB|M) = 0.$$

The law of total probability says that

$$P(GG) = P(GG|M) \times P(M) + P(GG|D) \times P(D),$$

as twins can only be monozygotic or dizygotic (i.e. $P(M) + P(D) = 1$). Applying this and the probabilities from above we find that:

$$P(GG) = \frac{1}{2}P(M) + \frac{1}{4}(1 - P(M))$$

$$P(M) = 4\left(P(GG) - \frac{1}{4}\right),$$

after rearranging. Therefore, in a town where 45% of twins are GG, we can deduce that 80% of twins are monozygotic ($0.8 = 4(0.45 - 0.25)$).

That is a result from probability. In real life, using statistics, we would say that we have only looked at a sample of twins and we would want to add some level of uncertainty or confidence to that result.

2.5 Statistics

Statistics is the art or science of analysing data, looking for explanations and patterns. Sometimes, predictions and decisions are also made. The word 'arose' during the nineteenth century in the first era of **big data** when states (mostly European) began to compile and make available data about births, deaths, crimes, punishments, etc. Some statistical techniques make use of results derived using sometimes quite sophisticated mathematics, and we will mention of few of those in this section. However, statistics is not a branch of mathematics: it just speaks the same language.

At a number of places in this book we build statistical models that attempt, albeit simplistically, to help us analyse aspects of the data we are considering. Many of these models are **parametric** in that they are built around specific named distributions. These distributions all have parameters (e.g. the Exponential distribution has a rate λ), and we introduce the data into the model in order to, among other things, estimate those parameters. Alternatives to parametric models are **non-parametric**, wherein no specific distributions are used, or **semi-parametric**, which are a mixture of the two.

In order to estimate the parameters in a parametric model, a number of different techniques have been developed. These are mentioned and used at various places in the book, and we shall outline them here.

2.5.1 Least squares

In Chapter 10, we see that the parameters in a simple linear regression model, and indeed in a multiple regression model, are estimated using least squares. In this case, the parameters are the coefficients of the line (with one covariate), plane (with two) or hyperplane (more than two) that best fit the data. For one covariate, this is illustrated in Figure 10.3. In mathematical terms, we might have a multiple linear regression model:

$$Y_i = \beta_0 + \beta_1 x_{i1} + \cdots + \beta_p x_{ip} + \epsilon_i, \tag{2.3}$$

for $i = 1, 2, \ldots, n$ where the ϵ_is each come independently from a $N(0, \sigma^2)$ distribution. The idea in estimating the parameters, $\beta_0, \beta_1, \ldots, \beta_p, \sigma^2$, is to minimise the difference between all the actual outcomes, y_is, and the right-hand side of equation (2.3). Obviously, that difference will vary over the different values of i and could be positive or negative: so the **least squares** approach is to minimise the sum of the squared differences.

$$\sum_{i=1}^{n} (Y_i - \beta_0 - \beta_1 x_{i1} - \cdots - \beta_p x_{ip} - \epsilon_i)^2.$$

We treat this as a mathematical expression in $p + 2$ unknowns (the βs plus σ^2). The usual approach to minimising such expressions is to differentiate it in turn with respect to each of the parameters and then set each resulting equation equal to zero: and that is exactly what we do here. We then have $p + 2$ equation in $p + 2$ unknowns which we can solve. For linear regression, there are standard formulae for the solutions. However, if we use least squares in other sorts of models, then we will have to solve those simultaneous equations by hand or, perhaps, estimate the solutions with the help of software (as in generalised linear models: see Chapter 11).

2.5.2 Maximum likelihood

An alternative approach to estimating parameters is to use **maximum likelihood**: this is used, for instance, in spatial point processes (Section 21.1) and factor analysis (Section 19.4). The core concept is to make the assumption that the data we are considering are an independent sample from some specific distribution (e.g. the Exponential), which has parameters (e.g. λ). We then write down the probability or likelihood of getting the data we have, which will be an expression involving the parameters of the distribution, for instance, λ, as well as the data. Finally, we find the value(s) of the parameter(s) which maximise that probability. Simple! In practice, we may not have a single distribution in our model, but a much more complicated expression. However, the same approach can still be used.

If we want any more detail, then it may be simplest to look at an example. We have data, $y_1, y_2, \ldots, y_n$ and make the assumption that they come from a Normal distribution. However, which values of the parameters, μ and σ^2, are the most likely?

The probability density of the Normal is

$$f(y|\mu, \sigma^2) = \frac{1}{\sqrt{\sigma^2 2\pi}} \exp\left[-\frac{(y-\mu)^2}{2\sigma^2}\right],$$

which is read as saying the probability density for a data value y, given (|) a mean of μ and a variance of σ^2, is calculated from this rather complicated-looking two-parameter exponential function on the right-hand side. For any given combination of μ and σ^2, it gives a value between 0 and 1. We have made the expression a function of σ^2 rather than σ as this simplifies the algebra later on.

We then create the **likelihood**, $L()$, which is the product of the probability densities, for each of the values of the response variable, y. So with the data in our experiment, $y_1, y_2, \ldots, y_n$, the likelihood function is

$$L(\mu, \sigma^2) = \prod_{i=1}^{n} \left(\frac{1}{\sqrt{\sigma^2 2\pi}} \exp\left[-\frac{(y_i - \mu)^2}{2\sigma^2}\right] \right)$$

$$= \frac{1}{(\sqrt{\sigma^2 2\pi})^n} \exp\left[-\frac{1}{2\sigma^2} \sum_{i=1}^{n} (y_i - \mu)^2\right].$$

The only change in the first line is that y has been replaced by y_i, and we multiply together the probabilities for each of the n data points. But note that this is now a function of the parameters not the data. The second line does two things:

- it takes any terms not involving i out of the product as they will be the same for every i, and just raises them to the nth power;

- uses the fact that the product of a set of exponentials is just the exponential of the sum of the items. A simple example is that $e^3 \times e^4 = e^{3+4}$.

The two parameters μ and σ^2 are unknown, and the purpose of the exercise is to use statistical modelling to determine their maximum likelihood values from the data (the n different values of y). So how do we find the values of μ and σ^2 that maximize this likelihood? The answer involves calculus: first we find the derivative of the function with respect to the parameters, then set it to zero, and solve.

It turns out that, for various technical reasons, it is easier to work with the ln of the likelihood,

$$l(\mu, \sigma) = \ln(L(\mu, \sigma)) = -\frac{n}{2}\ln(2\pi) - \frac{n}{2}\ln(\sigma^2) - \sum (y_i - \mu)^2 / 2\sigma^2,$$

and maximize this instead. Obviously, the values of the parameters that maximize the **loglikelihood** $l(\mu, \sigma) = \ln(L(\mu, \sigma))$ will be the same as those that maximize the likelihood. From now on, we shall assume that summation is over the index i from 1 to n to simplify the algebraic expressions.

Now for the calculus. We start with the mean, μ. The derivative of the log-likelihood with respect to μ is

$$\frac{dl}{d\mu} = \sum (y_i - \mu)/\sigma^2.$$

We then set the derivative to zero and solve for μ:

$$\sum(y_i - \mu)/\sigma^2 = 0 \quad \text{so} \quad \sum(y_i - \mu) = 0,$$

assuming that $\sigma^2 \neq 0$. Taking the summation through the bracket, and noting that $\sum \mu = n\mu$,

$$\sum y_i - n\mu = 0 \quad \text{so} \quad \sum y_i = n\mu \quad \text{and} \quad \hat{\mu} = \frac{\sum y_i}{n}.$$

The maximum likelihood estimate of μ is just the arithmetic mean: note the hat notation.

Next, we find the derivative of the loglikelihood with respect to σ^2:

$$\frac{dl}{d\sigma^2} = -\frac{n}{2\sigma^2} + \frac{\sum (y_i - \mu)^2}{2\sigma^4},$$

recalling that the derivative of $\ln(x)$ is $1/x$ and the derivative of $-1/x$ is $1/x^2$. Solving, we get

$$-\frac{n}{2\sigma^2} + \frac{\sum (y_i - \mu)^2}{2\sigma^4} = 0 \quad \text{so} \quad \sum (y_i - \mu)^2 = \sigma^4 \left(\frac{n}{\sigma^2} \right) = \sigma^2 n$$

$$\hat{\sigma}^2 = \frac{\sum (y_i - \mu)^2}{n}.$$

The maximum likelihood estimate of the variance σ^2 is the mean squared deviation of the y values from the mean. This is different from the formula we use for the sample variance, where we divide by $(n - 1)$, rather than by n. It is a **biased** estimator which means that its expected value does not equal the variance of the population. However, it does have other advantages.

So we have found estimates of the parameters. However, we will have estimated these from sample data and so we would like to build some uncertainty into the estimates. The maximum likelihood approach allows us to do this by giving these **estimators** a distribution, and so we can work out confidence intervals, etc.

The Normal distribution, although appearing complex, works very neatly with maximum likelihood estimation. In other more complex models, there is no simple algebraic solution and various numerical techniques are used to estimate the parameters.

Reference

Soetaert, K., Petzoldt, T., & Setzer, R. W. (2010). Solving differential equations in R: package deSolve. *Journal of Statistical Software*, *33*(9), 1–25. https://doi.org/10.18637/jss.v033.i09.

3

Essentials of the R Language

There is an enormous range of things that R can do, and one of the hardest parts of learning R is finding our way around. Likewise, there is no obvious order in which different people will want to learn the different components of the R language. It is probably worth quickly scanning down the following bullet points, which represent the order in which the introductory material is presented, and if you are relatively experienced in statistical computing, you might want to skip directly to the relevant section. Beginners are strongly recommended to work through the material in the order presented because successive sections build upon knowledge gained from previous sections. This chapter is divided into the following sections:

- Calculations
- Naming objects
- Factors
- Logical operations
- Sequences
- Class membership
- Missing values and things that are not numbers
- Vectors and subscripts
- Vectorised functions
- Matrices and arrays
- Sampling
- Loops and repeats
- Lists
- Text, character strings, and pattern matching

The R Book, Third Edition. Elinor Jones, Simon Harden and Michael J. Crawley.
© 2023 John Wiley & Sons Ltd. Published 2023 by John Wiley & Sons Ltd.
Companion website: www.wiley.com/go/jones/therbook3e

- Dates and times

- Environments

- Writing *R* functions

- Structure of *R* objects

- Writing to a file from *R*

- Tips for writing *R* code.

Other essential material is elsewhere: beginners will want to master data input and dataframes (Chapter 4), and graphics (Chapters 5 and 6).

3.1 Calculations

The screen prompt > is an invitation to put *R* to work. The convention in this book is that material to be typed into the command line after the screen prompt is shown in red in Courier New font. Just press the Return or Enter key to see the answer. We can use the command line as a calculator, like this:

```
> 7 + 5

[1] 12

> log (42 / 7.3)

[1] 1.749795
```

A further convention is that we use spaces to separate elements of the input. *R* ignores them, but they are helpful for reading code, spotting mistakes, and adding a little elegance to the sometimes mundane world of statistical coding.

Each line can have at most 8192 characters, but if we want to see a lengthy instruction or a complicated expression on the screen, we can continue it on one or more further lines simply by ending the line at a place where the line is obviously incomplete (e.g. with a trailing comma, operator, or with more left parentheses than right parentheses, implying that more right parentheses will follow). When continuation is expected, the prompt changes from > to +, as follows:

```
> 5 + 6 + 3 + 6 + 4 + 2 + 4 + 8 +
+ 3 + 2 + 7
```

Note that the + continuation prompt does not carry out the arithmetic plus operation. If we have made a mistake, and we want to get rid of the + prompt and return to the > prompt, then press the Esc key and use the Up arrow to edit the last (incomplete) line. The latter is incredibly useful, and pressing Up a number of times will retrieve previous commands for editing.

From here onwards and throughout the book, the prompt character > will be omitted. The output from *R* is shown in blue in Courier New font, which uses absolute rather than proportional spacing, so that columns of numbers remain neatly aligned on the page or on the screen.

Two or more expressions can be placed on a single line as long as they are separated by semi-colons:

```
2 + 3; 5 * 7; 3 - 7
```

```
[1]  5
[1]  35
[1]  -4
```

Frankly, this is bad practice and should be avoided wherever possible: it can lead to code that is difficult to follow.

For very big numbers or very small numbers R uses a form of scientific notation called **exponents**:

`1.2e3`	means $1.2 \times 10^3 = 1200$;
`1.2e-2`	means $1.2 \times 10^{-2} = 0.012$;
`3.9 + 4.5i`	is a complex number with real (3.9) and imaginary (4.5) parts, and i is the square root of -1. See Section 3.1.1 for more details.

3.1.1   Complex numbers

If you don't use complex numbers, just skip this section. Complex numbers consist of a real part and an imaginary part, which is identified by a lower-case i like this:

```
z <- 3.5 - 8i
```

Although we might have difficulties in conceiving the square root of -1, it can be very useful mathematically. The elementary trigonometric, logarithmic, exponential, square root, and hyperbolic functions are all implemented for complex values. The following are the special R functions that we can use with complex numbers. Determine the real part:

```
Re (z)
```

```
[1]  3.5
```

Determine the imaginary part:

```
Im (z)
```

```
[1]  -8
```

If we plot the real part (x) of a complex number as being on the x-axis, and the imaginary part (y) on the y-axis, then the **modulus** is the distance from the coordinates (x, y) to the origin: $\sqrt{(x-0)^2 + (y-0)^2}$. Calculate the modulus, in this case $\sqrt{3.5^2 + 8^2}$:

```
Mod (z)
```

```
[1]  8.732125
```

Calculate the argument (don't ask if you don't know: it's to do with representing complex numbers in a different way using **polar coordinates**):

```
Arg (z)

[1] -1.158386
```

Work out the complex conjugate (change the sign of the imaginary part):

```
Conj (z)

[1] 3.5+8i
```

If we want to know whether a number is complex or turn a real number into a complex one:

```
is.complex (z)

[1] TRUE

as.complex (3.8)

[1] 3.8+0i
```

3.1.2 Rounding

We can round to any number of decimal places using round () and to the nearest integer above or below using the companion functions ceiling () and floor (), respectively:

```
round (3.14156, 3)

[1] 3.142

round (16.2, 0)

[1] 16

ceiling (16.2)

[1] 17

floor (16.2)

[1] 16
```

It is a little trickier with negative numbers, but the principles should be clear (remember −5 > −6):

```
round (-3.14156, 3)

[1] -3.142

round (-16.2, 0)

[1] -16

ceiling (-16.2)

[1] -16

floor (-16.2)

[1] -17
```

There are a couple of further functions that can be useful:

```
trunc (5.72, 1)

[1] 5

trunc (-5.72, 1)

[1] -5

signif (2718281, 3)

[1] 2720000

signif (-2718281, 3)

[1] -2720000
```

We can see that `trunc ()` will push the number towards zero with the required number of decimal places, and `signif ()` extracts the first few rounded places, possibly for use in estimation.

3.1.3 Arithmetic

The screen prompt in *R* is a fully functional calculator. We can add and subtract using the obvious + and - symbols, while division is achieved with a forward slash / and multiplication is done by using an asterisk * like this:

```
7 + 3 - 5 * 2

[1] 0
```

Notice from this example that multiplication (5×2) is done *before* the additions and subtractions. Powers (like squared or cube root) use the caret symbol, ˆ, and are done before multiplication or division, as we can see from this example:

```
3^2 / 2

[1] 4.5
```

R follows the usual order or carrying out arithmetic operations which is often abbreviated to **BODMAS** or **PEMDAS**:

1. brackets:

2. powers;

3. multiplication and division (order is irrelevant);

4. addition and subtraction (order is irrelevant).

There are many fundamental arithmetic and mathematical functions available, some key ones are given in Table 3.1. More mathematical details on many of these functions are given in Section 2.1. *R* knows what π is

```
pi

[1] 3.141593
```

Can't we do better?

```
signif_digits <- getOption ("digits")
options (digits = 15)
pi

[1] 3.14159265358979

options (digits = signif_digits)
```

We have created an object (see Section 3.2 for more details), `signif_digits`, containing the default number of digits in *R*: *R* contains a lot of these defaults (see `options ()`), but beware of changing them: there may be unexpected consequences, and it's best to change them back to the default as soon as possible. Too many decimal places may lead to inaccurate answers as the figures are calculated approximately: π is wrong from the 16th decimal place.

All trigonometric functions are calculated in *radians* and not *degrees*: see Section 2.1.2 for more details.

Table 3.1 Mathematical functions.

Function	Meaning
`ln (x)`	log to base e of x
`exp (x)`	inverse of `ln (x)` or e^x
`log (x, n)`	log to base n of x
`log10 (x)`	log to base 10 of x
`sqrt (x)`	square root of x
`factorial (x)`	$x! = x \times (x-1) \times (x-2) \times \cdots \times 3 \times 2 \times 1$
`choose (n, x)`	binomial coefficients or $n!/(x!(n-x)!)$
`gamma (x)`	$\Gamma(x)$: for integer x, equals $(x-1)!$
`lgamma (x)`	$\ln(\Gamma(x))$
`floor (x)`	greatest integer less than x
`ceiling (x)`	smallest integer greater than x
`trunc (x)`	closest integer to 0 between x and 0
`round (x, digits = a)`	round the value of x to a decimal places
`signif (x, digits = b)`	give x to b digits
`runif (n)`	generates n random numbers between 0 and 1 from a uniform distribution
`cos (x)`	cosine of x in radians
`sin (x)`	sine of x in radians
`tan (x)`	tangent of x in radians
`acos (x), asin (x), atan (x)`	inverse trigonometric transformations of real or complex numbers
`acosh (x), asinh (x), atanh (x)`	inverse hyperbolic trigonometric transformations of real or complex numbers
`abs (x)`	the absolute value of x, i.e. ignoring the minus sign if there is one

3.1.4 Modular arithmetic

Suppose we want to know the integer part of a division: say, how many 13s there are in 119:

```
119 %/% 13
```

```
[1] 9
```

Now suppose we wanted to know the remainder (what is left over when 119 is divided by 13): in maths this is known as 119 **modulo** 13, and the value 13 is known as the **modulus**:

```
119 %% 13
```

```
[1] 2
```

Modulo is very useful for testing whether one number is an exact multiple of some other number. For instance, to find out whether 15 421 is a multiple of 7, then ask

```
15421 %% 7
```

```
[1] 0
```

It is as there is no remainder. We can then carry out more complex modular arithmetic:

```
(123 + 456) %% 19
```

```
[1] 9
```

But don't forget to put brackets around the expression for which we want to carry out the modular calculation as follows:

```
123 + 456 %% 19
```

```
[1] 123
```

3.1.5   Operators

We have already seen the standard arithmetic operators in Section 3.1.3. However, there are many more available in *R*, and some are listed in Table 3.2.

We have already seen an example of `<-` in Section 3.1.3 but here is a much simpler one:

```
a <- 16.3
a
```

```
[1] 16.3
```

The model formula will be introduced in anger in Chapter 10.1.2. However, several of these operators have different meaning inside any such expression. Thus, * indicates the main effects plus interaction (rather than multiplication), : indicates the interaction between two variables (rather than generate a sequence) and ^ means all interactions up to the indicated power (rather than raise to the power).

Table 3.2   Common operators

Operator	Meaning
> >= < <= == !=	relational: greater than, greater than or equals, less than, less than or equals, equals, not equals
! & |	logical (not, and, or)
	model formula ('is modelled as a function of')
<-	assignment for giving a value to a variable
$	select elements from a complex data object
:	create an integer sequence

3.1.6 Integers

Historically, memory for computers was very expensive and was at a premium. So integers were stored as whole numbers as distinct from real numbers, which might have many decimal places and would use up more memory. That meant that one had to tell a computer program which numbers were to be treated as integers and which not. This is not such a problem now, but *R* still offers the option of storing a number as an integer. It is only important to do this if we are creating large data objects (such as huge matrices) or using functions in *R* that call programs written in C or Fortran. So don't bother with describing objects as integers unless they are large, as it is a bit of a hassle. The range of integers in *R* is from approximately −2 000 000 000 to approximately +2 000 000 000 (-2×10^9 to $+2 \times 10^9$, which *R* could portray as `-2e+09` to `2e+09`).

Be careful. Do not try to change the class of a vector from numeric by using the `integer ()` function. Here is a numeric vector of whole numbers that we want to convert into a vector of integers:

```
x <- c (5, 3, 7, 8)
is.integer (x)
```

```
[1] FALSE
```

```
is.numeric (x)
```

```
[1] TRUE
```

Applying the `integer ()` function to it doesn't work:

```
x <- integer (x)
```

```
Error in integer(x): invalid 'length' argument
```

Use the `as.integer ()` function in one of two ways like this:

```
x <- c (5, 3, 7, 8)
x <- as.integer (x)
is.integer (x)
```

```
[1] TRUE
```

```
y <- as.integer (c (5, 3, 7, 8))
is.integer (y)
```

```
[1] TRUE
```

The `as.integer ()` function works as `trunc ()` when applied to real numbers and removes the imaginary part when applied to complex numbers:

```
as.integer (5.7)
```

```
[1] 5
```

```
as.integer (-5.7)

[1] -5

as.integer (5.7 - 3i)

Warning: imaginary parts discarded in coercion

[1] 5
```

3.2 Naming objects

We often create named objects in *R*: they might just be a numeric or character variable, a matrix or something more complex such as the results of a linear model. There are three important things to remember when selecting names for our variables:

- Variable names in *R* are case sensitive, so `y` is not the same as `Y`;
- Variable names cannot begin with numbers (e.g. `1y`) or symbols (e.g. `%y`) but can contain such characters (e.g. `y1`);
- Variable names should not contain blank spaces (use `back_pay` not `back pay`).

In terms of work–life balance, it is tempting make variable names as short as possible, so as not to spend too much time typing, and then correcting spelling mistakes in ridiculously long variable names. However, as RStudio completes our variable names once we have typed three letters, it is probably best to make the names meaningful so that we can understand what they are when we come back to look at our code after a period of time.

Objects obtain values in *R* by **assignment**. This is achieved by `<-` which is a composite symbol made up from *less than* and *minus* with no space between them. Thus, to create a scalar constant *x* with value 5 we type:

```
x <- 5
```

and not `x = 5` (which will work some of the time but not all). Notice that there is a potential ambiguity if we get the spacing wrong. Compare our `x <- 5` with `x < - 5` where there is a space between the 'less than' and 'minus' symbols. In *R*, this is actually a question, asking 'is *x* less than minus 5?' and, depending on the current value of *x*, would evaluate to the answer either `TRUE` or `FALSE`.

3.3 Factors

Factors are categorical variables that have a fixed number of levels. A simple example of a factor might be a variable called `gender` with two levels: `female` and `male`. If we had three females and two males, we could create the factor like this:

```
gender <- factor (c ("female", "male", "female", "male", "female"))
class (gender)


[1] "factor"
```

The function `class ()` tells us what sort of data we have: we saw this in Section 3.1.6 when we discussed integers. Incidentally, *R* actually stores factors as numbers:

```
mode (gender)


[1] "numeric"
```

More often, we will create a dataframe by reading our data from a file using `read.table ()`:

```
daphnia <- read.table ("daphnia.txt", header = T)
head (daphnia)


  Growth.rate Water Detergent Daphnia
1   2.919086   Tyne   BrandA   Clone1
2   2.492904   Tyne   BrandA   Clone1
3   3.021804   Tyne   BrandA   Clone1
4   2.350874   Tyne   BrandA   Clone2
5   3.148174   Tyne   BrandA   Clone2
6   4.423853   Tyne   BrandA   Clone2

class (daphnia$Water)


[1] "character"
```

The $ sign enables us to select one of the data columns. Unfortunately, *R* has changed the way it imports data. If we are using a version of *R* less than 4.0 (we really shouldn't: do upgrade), then it would have automatically imported columns of data with a small number of possible non-numeric values as factors. From version 4.0 onwards, it just imports them as **characters** or strings of letters. We can see that we have three columns that we would like to import as factors, and we do this as follows:

```
daphnia <- read.table ("daphnia.txt", header = T,
                    colClasses = c ("numeric", rep ("factor", 3)))
class (daphnia$Water)


[1] "factor"
```

The dataframe contains a continuous response variable (`Growth.rate`: numeric) and three categorical explanatory variables (`Water`, `Detergent` and `Daphnia`), all of which are factors.

There are some important functions for dealing with factors. We will often want to check that a variable is a factor (especially if the factor levels are numbers rather than characters):

```
is.factor (daphnia$Water)
```

```
[1] TRUE
```

To discover the *names* of the factor levels, we use the `levels ()` function:

```
levels (daphnia$Detergent)
```

```
[1] "BrandA" "BrandB" "BrandC" "BrandD"
```

To discover the *number* of levels of a factor, we use the `nlevels ()` function as it is simpler than the alternative:

```
nlevels (daphnia$Detergent)
```

```
[1] 4
```

```
length (levels (daphnia$Detergent))
```

```
[1] 4
```

By default, factor levels are treated in alphabetical order. If we want to change this (as we might, for instance, in ordering the bars of a bar chart), then this is straightforward: we just type the factor levels in the order that we want them to be used and provide this vector as the second argument to the `factor ()` function.

For instance, we might want to reverse the alphabetical ordering of our rivers:

```
levels (daphnia$Water)
```

```
[1] "Tyne" "Wear"
```

```
daphnia$Water <- factor (daphnia$Water, levels = c ("Wear", "Tyne"))
levels (daphnia$Water)
```

```
[1] "Wear" "Tyne"
```

Any results that involve rivers, such as the mean growth rate, would then appear in that order (details of the `tapply ()` function can be found in Section 3.10.1):

```
tapply (daphnia$Growth.rate, daphnia$Water, mean)
```

```
    Wear     Tyne
4.017948 3.685862
```

Only == (not =, see Section 3.4) and != can be used for comparing factors. Note, also, that a factor can only be compared to another factor with an identical set of levels (not necessarily in the same ordering) or to a character vector. For example, we cannot ask quantitative questions about factor levels, like > or <=, even if the levels are numeric.

```
daphnia$Detergent == daphnia$Water

Error in Ops.factor(daphnia$Detergent, daphnia$Water): level sets of factors
                    are different

daphnia$Detergent <= daphnia$Water

 [1] NA NA NA NA NA NA NA NA NA NA NA NA NA NA NA NA NA NA NA NA NA NA NA NA NA
[26] NA NA NA NA NA NA NA NA NA NA NA NA NA NA NA NA NA NA NA NA NA NA NA NA NA
[51] NA NA NA NA NA NA NA NA NA NA NA NA NA NA NA NA NA NA NA NA NA NA
```

We might want to turn factor levels into numbers (integers) in order, say, to colour them in a particular way in a plot, and we use the unclass () function like this:

```
as.vector (unclass (daphnia$Daphnia))

 [1] 1 1 1 2 2 2 3 3 3 1 1 1 2 2 2 3 3 3 1 1 1 2 2 2 3 3 3 1 1 1 2 2 2 3 3 3 1 1
[39] 1 2 2 2 3 3 3 1 1 1 2 2 2 3 3 3 1 1 1 2 2 2 3 3 3 1 1 1 2 2 2 3 3 3
```

3.4 Logical operations

A crucial part of computing involves asking questions about things. Is one thing bigger than other? Are two things the same size? Questions can be joined together using words like and, or and not. Questions in *R* typically evaluate to TRUE or FALSE (which in certain circumstances we can abbreviate to T and F), but there is the option of ignorance (when the answer is not available, NA). Table 3.3 gives some common notation used in logical operations.

Table 3.3 Logical and relational operations

Symbol	Meaning
!	logical NOT
&	logical AND
		logical OR
<	less than
<=	less than or equal to
>	greater than
=	greater than or equal to
==	logical equals (double =)
!=	not equal
&&	AND with IF
||	OR with IF
xor(x,y)	exclusive OR
isTRUE (x)	an abbreviation of identical (TRUE, x)

Here are some simple comparisons with integers. See Section 3.4.2 for a discussion of non-integer values.

```
6 > 5

[1] TRUE

6 == 5

[1] FALSE

6 <= 5

[1] FALSE

6 != 5

[1] TRUE
```

3.4.1 TRUE, T, FALSE, F

We can use T for TRUE and F for FALSE, but we should be aware that T and F might have been allocated as variables. So

```
TRUE == FALSE

[1] FALSE

T == F

[1] FALSE
```

This, however, is not so obvious:

```
T <- 0
T == FALSE

[1] TRUE

F <- 0
TRUE == F

[1] FALSE

T == F

[1] TRUE
```

This arises as *R* also stores T as 1 and FALSE as 0. So never use T or F as variable names, and we can remove them as follows:

```
rm (T, F)
```

3.4.2 Testing for equality of real numbers

There are international standards for carrying out **floating point arithmetic** (i.e. arithmetic using numbers with decimal places), but on our computer these standards are beyond the control of *R*. This is not an issue for integers unless they are enormous (absolute value $> 10^{32}$), but for fractions and other real numbers we lose accuracy because of rounding errors. This is only likely to become a real problem in practice if we have to *subtract* similarly sized but very large numbers. A dramatic loss in accuracy under these circumstances is called **catastrophic cancellation error**. It occurs when an operation on two numbers increases *relative error* substantially more than it increases *absolute error*.

We need to be careful in programming when we want to test whether or not two computed numbers are equal. *R* will assume that we mean *exactly equal*, and what *that* means depends upon machine precision. Typically therefore, two floating point numbers will not reliably be equal unless they were computed by the same algorithm, and not always even then. We can see this by squaring the square root of 2: surely these values are the same?

```
x <- sqrt(2)
x * x == 2
```

```
[1] FALSE
```

The square root of 2 will, inevitably, be approximately calculated and so when it is squared, it will not exactly equal 2. We can see by how much the two values differ by subtraction:

```
x * x - 2
```

```
[1] 4.440892e-16
```

This is not a big number, but it is not zero either. So how do we test for equality of real numbers? The best advice is not to do it. Sometimes, however, we really do want to test for equality. In those circumstances, do not use == to test for equality, but employ the all.equal () function instead. Using an even simpler example:

```
y <- 0.3 - 0.2
z <- 0.1
y == z
```

```
[1] FALSE
```

There is a function for testing for exact equality which applies not just to numbers but to all sorts of objects in *R*:

```
identical (y, z)
```

```
[1] FALSE
```

However, that is no better. But

```
all.equal (y, z)
```

```
[1] TRUE
```

saves the day. If we want to be specifically precise, then we can use the argument `tolerance = ...` to set the level at which we regard two numbers as the same. For instance, if we regard 0.0001 as being small enough not to care about the difference between numbers:

```
all.equal (y, z, tolerance = 0.0001)
```

```
[1] TRUE
```

```
all.equal (pi, 3.141, tolerance = 0.0001)
```

```
[1] "Mean relative difference: 0.0001886475"
```

R then reports on the nature of the difference. We will see in Section 3.18.2 how to use the `if ()` function to determine what to do next on the basis of a comparison. *R* is very strict in `help (all.equal)` and says: 'Do not use `all.equal ()` directly in `if ()` expressions - either use `isTRUE (all.equal ())` or `identical ()` if appropriate'.

3.4.3   Testing for equality of non-numeric objects

The function `all.equal ()` is very useful in for checking that all types of objects, not just numbers, are as we expect them to be. Where differences occur, `all.equal ()` does a useful job in describing all the differences it finds. Here, for instance, it reports on the difference between *a*, which is a vector or list of non-edible pets described using characters and *b*, which is a factor of exactly the same things:

```
a <- c ("cat", "dog", "goldfish")
b <- factor (a)
```

In the `all.equal ()` function, the object on the left, *a*, is called the **target** and the object on the right, *b*, is **current**:

```
all.equal (a, b)
```

```
[1] "Modes: character, numeric"
[2] "Attributes: < target is NULL, current is list >"
[3] "target is character, current is factor"
```

1. The first difference, in [1], is `mode` which tells us how the objects are stored. Recall that factors are stored internally as integers, so they have `mode = numeric`;

2. The reason why `current is list` in item [2] of the output is that factors have two attributes, namely their levels and their class, and these are stored as a list;

3. [3] tells us what class of objects we are dealing with.

We could look at each of these items individually as follows:

```
mode (a)

[1] "character"

mode (b)

[1] "numeric"

attributes (a)

NULL

attributes (b)

$levels
[1] "cat"       "dog"       "goldfish"

$class
[1] "factor"

class (a)

[1] "character"

class (b)

[1] "factor"
```

The `all.equal ()` function is also useful for obtaining feedback on differences in things like the lengths of vectors:

```
n1 <- c (1,2,3)
n2 <- c (1,2,3,4)
all.equal (n1, n2)

[1] "Numeric: lengths (3, 4) differ"
```

It works well, too, for multiple differences:

```
n2 <- as.character (n2)
n2

[1] "1" "2" "3" "4"

all.equal (n1,n2)

[1] "Modes: numeric, character"
[2] "Lengths: 3, 4"
[3] "target is numeric, current is character"
```

Here we have converted the numbers in n2 to characters, so they have quotation marks. If we supply more than two objects to be compared, the third and subsequent objects are simply ignored.

3.4.4   Evaluation of combinations of TRUE and FALSE

It is important to understand how combinations of logical variables evaluate and to appreciate how logical operations (such as those in Table 3.3) work when there are missing values, NA. Here are all the possible outcomes expressed as a logical vector called *x*:

```
x <- c (NA, FALSE, TRUE)
```

To see the logical combinations using & (logical AND), we can use the outer () function with *x* to evaluate all nine combinations like this:

```
outer (x, x, "&")

      [,1]  [,2]  [,3]
[1,]    NA FALSE    NA
[2,] FALSE FALSE FALSE
[3,]    NA FALSE  TRUE
```

Only TRUE & TRUE evaluates to TRUE. FALSE overrides everything else with NA taking priority next. To see the logical combinations | (logical OR) write:

```
outer (x, x, "|")

     [,1]  [,2] [,3]
[1,]   NA    NA TRUE
[2,]   NA FALSE TRUE
[3,] TRUE  TRUE TRUE
```

Here TRUE is dominant followed by NA.

3.4.5   Logical arithmetic

Arithmetic involving logical expressions is very useful in programming and in selection of variables. If logical arithmetic is unfamiliar, then persevere with it, because it will become clear how useful it is, once the penny has dropped. The key thing to understand is that logical expressions evaluate to either true or false (represented in *R* by TRUE or FALSE), and that *R* can **coerce** TRUE or FALSE into numerical values: 1 for TRUE and 0 for FALSE. Suppose that *x* is a sequence of integers from 0 to 6 like this:

```
x <- 0:6
```

Now, we can ask questions about the contents of the vector called *x*. Is each element of *x* less than 4?

```
x < 4
```

```
[1]   TRUE   TRUE   TRUE   TRUE FALSE FALSE FALSE
```

The answer is yes for the first four values (0, 1, 2, and 3) and no for the last three (4, 5, and 6). Two important logical functions are all () and any (). They check an entire vector but return a single logical value: TRUE or FALSE. Are all the *x* values bigger than 0?

```
all (x > 0)
```

```
[1] FALSE
```

No. The first *x* value is a zero. Are any of the *x* values negative?

```
any (x < 0)
```

```
[1] FALSE
```

No. The smallest *x* value is a zero.

We can use the answers of logical functions in arithmetic. We can count the number of values with x < 4, using sum ():

```
sum (x < 4)
```

```
[1]  4
```

We can multiply x < 4 by other vectors, where we only want a non-zero result if the statement is true:

```
(x < 4) * runif (7)
```

```
[1] 0.07904065 0.25855709 0.36850863 0.84638190 0.00000000 0.00000000 0.00000000
```

where runif (7) is a set of seven random numbers between zero and one.

Logical arithmetic is particularly useful in generating simplified factor levels during statistical modelling. Suppose we want to reduce a five-level factor with levels $\{a, b, c, d, e\}$ called `treatment` to a three-level factor called `t2` by lumping together the levels a and e (new factor level 1) and c and d (new factor level 3) while leaving b distinct (with new factor level 2):

```
(treatment <- letters[1:5])

[1] "a" "b" "c" "d" "e"
```

There are a couple of things worth noting here:

- *R* knows the letters of the Roman alphabet, amongst other things: see `help (letters)`;
- if we enclose our statement in brackets, then *R* outputs the value of what we have just created.

```
(t2 <- factor (1 + (treatment == "b") + 2 * (treatment == "c") +
               2 * (treatment == "d")))

[1] 1 2 3 3 1
Levels: 1 2 3
```

Remember that *R* can treat the factors in order as integers. So the new factor `t2` gets a value 1 as default for all the factors levels, and we want to leave this as it is for levels a and e. Thus, we do not add anything to the 1 if the old factor level is a or e. For old factor level b, however, we want the result that `t2` is 2 so we add 1 (`treatment=="b"`) to the original 1 to get the answer we require. This works because the logical expression evaluates to 1 (TRUE) for every case in which the old factor level is b and to 0 (FALSE) in all other cases. For old factor levels c and d, we want the result that `t2` is 3, so we add 2 to the baseline value of 1 if the original factor level is either c or d. Don't forget that *logical equals* is a double equals sign without a space in between (==). It is important to understand the distinction between

```
x <- y   x is assigned the value of y;
x = y    in a function or a list x is set to y unless we specify otherwise;
x == y   produces TRUE if x is exactly equal to y and FALSE, otherwise.
```

3.5 Generating sequences

An important way of creating **vectors** (in this case, just a list of numbers: although they can also be lists of anything, e.g. characters, logical values) is to generate a **sequence** of numbers. The simplest sequences are in steps of 1, and the colon operator is the simplest way of generating such sequences. All we do is specify the first and last values separated by a colon. Here is a sequence from 0 up to 10:

```
0:10

[1]  0  1  2  3  4  5  6  7  8  9 10
```

Here is a sequence from 15 down to 5:

```
15:5
```

```
[1]  15 14 13 12 11 10  9  8  7  6  5
```

To generate a sequence in steps other than 1, we use the `seq ()` function. There are various forms of this, of which the simplest has three arguments: `from = ..., to = ..., by = ...` (the initial value, the final value and the increment). These are the default arguments: what *R* assumes if we just list values. If the initial value is smaller than the final value, the increment should be positive, like this:

```
seq (from = 0, to = 1.5, by = 0.1)
```

```
[1]  0.0 0.1 0.2 0.3 0.4 0.5 0.6 0.7 0.8 0.9 1.0 1.1 1.2 1.3 1.4 1.5
```

```
seq (0, 1.5, 0.1)
```

```
[1]  0.0 0.1 0.2 0.3 0.4 0.5 0.6 0.7 0.8 0.9 1.0 1.1 1.2 1.3 1.4 1.5
```

If the initial value is larger than the final value, the increment should be negative, like this, or we will get an error:

```
seq (6, 4, -0.2)
```

```
[1]  6.0 5.8 5.6 5.4 5.2 5.0 4.8 4.6 4.4 4.2 4.0
```

```
seq (6, 4, 0.2)
```

```
Error in seq.default(6, 4, 0.2): wrong sign in 'by' argument
```

In many cases, we want to generate a sequence to match an existing vector in length. Rather than having to figure out the increment that will get from the initial to the final value and produce a vector of exactly the appropriate length, *R* provides the `along =` and `length =` options. Suppose we have a vector of population sizes which we create using the `c ()` (*combine*) function:

```
N <- c (55, 76, 92, 103, 84, 88, 121, 91, 65, 77, 99)
length (N)
```

```
[1] 11
```

We need to plot this against a sequence that starts at 0.04 in steps of 0.01:

```
seq (from = 0.04, by = 0.01, length = 11)
```

```
[1]  0.04 0.05 0.06 0.07 0.08 0.09 0.10 0.11 0.12 0.13 0.14
```

But this requires us to figure out the length of *N*. A simpler method is to use the `along` argument and specify the vector, *N*, whose length has to be matched:

```
seq (0.04, by = 0.01, along = N)

[1] 0.04 0.05 0.06 0.07 0.08 0.09 0.10 0.11 0.12 0.13 0.14
```

Alternatively, we can get *R* to work out the increment (0.01 in this example), by specifying the start and the end values (`from` and `to`), and the name of the vector (*N*) whose length has to be matched:

```
seq (from = 0.04, to = 0.14, along = N)

[1] 0.04 0.05 0.06 0.07 0.08 0.09 0.10 0.11 0.12 0.13 0.14
```

Notice that when the increment does not match the final value, then the generated sequence stops short of the last value (rather than overstepping it):

```
seq (1.4, 2.1, 0.3)

[1] 1.4 1.7 2.0
```

If we want a vector made up of sequences of unequal lengths, then use the `sequence ()` function. Suppose that the five sequences we want to string together are (1:4, 1:3, 1:4, 1:4, 1:4, 1:5), then:

```
sequence (c (4, 3, 4, 4, 4, 5))

[1] 1 2 3 4 1 2 3 1 2 3 4 1 2 3 4 1 2 3 4 1 2 3 4 5
```

3.5.1 Generating repeats

We will often want to generate repeats of numbers or characters, for which the function is `rep ()`. The object that is named in the first argument is repeated a number of times as specified in the second argument. At its simplest, we would generate five 9s like this:

```
rep (9, 5)

[1] 9 9 9 9 9
```

We can see the issues involved by a comparison of these three increasingly complicated uses of the `rep ()` function:

```
rep (1:4, 2)

[1] 1 2 3 4 1 2 3 4

rep (1:4, each = 2)
```

```
[1] 1 1 2 2 3 3 4 4

rep (1:4, each = 2, times = 3)

[1] 1 1 2 2 3 3 4 4 1 1 2 2 3 3 4 4 1 1 2 2 3 3 4 4
```

In the simplest case, the *entire* first argument is repeated (i.e. the sequence 1–4 appears twice). We often want each *element* of the sequence to be repeated, and this is accomplished with the each argument. Finally, we might want each number repeated and the whole series repeated a certain number of times (here three times).

When each element of the series is to be repeated a different number of times, then the second argument must be a vector of the same length as the vector comprising the first argument (length 4 in this example). So if we want one 1, two 2s, three 3s, and four 4s we would write:

```
rep (1:4, 1:4)

[1] 1 2 2 3 3 3 4 4 4 4
```

In a more complicated case, there is a different but irregular repeat of each of the elements of the first argument. Suppose that we need four 1s, one 2, four 3s, and two 4s. Then we use the combine function c () to create a vector of length 4 which will act as the second argument to the rep () function:

```
rep (1:4, c (4, 1, 4, 2))

[1] 1 1 1 1 2 3 3 3 3 4 4
```

Here is the most complex case with character data rather than numbers: each element of the pet series is repeated an irregular number of times:

```
rep (c ("cat", "dog", "gerbil", "goldfish", "rat"), c (2, 3, 2, 1, 3))

[1] "cat"       "cat"       "dog"   "dog"   "dog"   "gerbil"
[7] "gerbil"    "goldfish"  "rat"   "rat"   "rat"
```

3.5.2 Generating factor levels

The function gl () (*generate levels*) is useful when we want to encode long vectors of factor levels. The syntax for the three arguments is n (number of levels), k (repeated this number of times), length (to total length with default $n * k$). Here is the simplest case where we want 4 factor levels with three repeats (i.e. total length 12):

```
gl (4, 3)

[1] 1 1 1 2 2 2 3 3 3 4 4 4
Levels: 1 2 3 4
```

Here is the function when we want that whole pattern repeated twice:

```
gl (4, 3, 24)

 [1] 1 1 1 2 2 2 3 3 3 4 4 4 1 1 1 2 2 2 3 3 3 4 4 4
Levels: 1 2 3 4
```

If we want text for the factor levels, rather than numbers, we use labels like this:

```
gloss <- gl (2, 2, 24, labels = c ("Low", "High"))
give <- gl (3, 8, 24, labels = c ("Hard", "Medium", "Soft"))
flammable <- gl (2, 4, 24, labels = c ("N", "Y"))
brand <- gl (2, 1, 24, labels = c ("X", "M"))
```

We can then combine these to give all the different combinations (see Section 4.5 for more details on dataframes) for hair gel:

```
data.frame (gloss, give, flammable, brand)

    gloss   give flammable brand
1    Low    Hard        N     X
2    Low    Hard        N     M
3    High   Hard        N     X
4    High   Hard        N     M
5    Low    Hard        Y     X
6    Low    Hard        Y     M
7    High   Hard        Y     X
8    High   Hard        Y     M
9    Low  Medium        N     X
10   Low  Medium        N     M
11   High Medium        N     X
12   High Medium        N     M
13   Low  Medium        Y     X
14   Low  Medium        Y     M
15   High Medium        Y     X
16   High Medium        Y     M
17   Low    Soft        N     X
18   Low    Soft        N     M
19   High   Soft        N     X
20   High   Soft        N     M
21   Low    Soft        Y     X
22   Low    Soft        Y     M
23   High   Soft        Y     X
24   High   Soft        Y     M
```

3.6   Class membership

We have already seen in Section 3.4.3 how data objects can be described by their class, mode, or attributes. We will now examine a fourth classification, **data type**, which is usually how we will refer to a data object. In many cases, the type is the same as class. We can test whether objects are a particular type and also **coerce** them into a different type. For instance, a logical variable has type `logical`. This is how we create the variable:

```
lv <- c (T, F, T)
```

We can assess its membership by asking if it is a logical variable using the `is.logical ()` function:

```
is.logical (lv)
```

```
[1] TRUE
```

It is not a factor, and so it does not have levels:

```
levels (lv)
```

```
NULL
```

But we can coerce it to be a two-level factor like this:

```
(fv <- as.factor (lv))
```

```
[1] TRUE   FALSE  TRUE
Levels: FALSE TRUE
```

```
is.factor (fv)
```

```
[1] TRUE
```

The brackets around an expression will automatically show the outcome, even when we are creating an object from the outcome. We can coerce a logical variable to be numeric: TRUE evaluates to 1 and FALSE evaluates to 0, like this:

```
(nv <- as.numeric (lv))
```

```
[1] 1 0 1
```

This is particularly useful as a short cut when creating new factors with reduced numbers of levels (as we do in model simplification).

Table 3.4 lists functions for testing (`is.`) the type of different objects (arrays, lists, etc.) and for coercing (`as.`) them into a specified form.

Only some types of objects can be coerced into other types. A familiar type of coercion occurs when we interpret the TRUE and FALSE of logical variables as numeric 1 and 0, respectively. Factor levels can be coerced to numbers. Numbers can be coerced into characters, but non-numeric characters cannot be coerced into numbers: we just end up with a load of NAs and a warning.

Table 3.4 Data types.

Type	Testing	Coercing
Array	is.array	as.array
Character	is.character	as.character
Complex	is.complex	as.complex
Dataframe	is.data.frame	as.data.frame
Double	is.double	as.double
Factor	is.factor	as.factor
List	is.list	as.list
Logical	is.logical	as.logical
Matrix	is.matrix	as.matrix
Numeric	is.numeric	as.numeric
Raw	is.raw	as.raw
Time series	is.ts	as.ts
Vector	is.vector	as.vector

```
as.numeric (factor (c ("a", "b", "c")))

[1] 1 2 3

as.numeric (c ("a", "b", "c"))

Warning: NAs introduced by coercion

[1] NA NA NA

as.numeric (c ("1", "4", "3"))

[1] 1 4 3
```

If we try to coerce complex numbers to numeric, the imaginary part will be discarded. Note that `is.complex ()` and `is.numeric ()` are never both TRUE.

We often want to coerce tables (perhaps of counts) into the form of vectors and to turn matrices into dataframes. A lot of testing involves the NOT operator `!` in functions to return an error message if the wrong type is supplied. For instance, if we were writing our own function (see Section 3.18 for more details) to calculate geometric means we might want to test to ensure that the input was numeric using `!is.numeric ()`:

```
geometric <- function (x) {
  if (!is.numeric (x)) stop ("Input must be numeric")
  exp (mean (log (x)))
}
```

Here is what happens when we try to work out the geometric mean of numeric and character data:

```
geometric (c (2, 4, 8))

[1] 4

geometric (c ("a", "b", "c"))

Error in geometric(c("a", "b", "c")): Input must be numeric
```

We might also want to check that there are no zeros or negative numbers in the input, because it would make no sense to try to calculate a geometric mean of such data:

```
geometric <- function (x) {
  if (!is.numeric(x)) stop ("Input must be numeric")
  if (min (x) <= 0) stop ("Input must be greater than zero")
  exp (mean (log (x)))
}
```

Testing this:

```
geometric (c (2, 3, 0, 4))

Error in geometric(c(2, 3, 0, 4)): Input must be greater than zero
```

But when the data are OK there will be no messages, just the numeric answer:

```
geometric (c (10, 1000, 10, 1, 1))

[1] 10
```

When vectors are created by calculation from other vectors, the new vector will be as long as the longest vector used in the calculation and the shorter variable will be recycled as necessary. Here, *A* is of length 10 and *B* is of length 3:

```
A <- 1:10
B <- c (2, 4, 8)
A * B

Warning in A * B: longer object length is not a multiple of shorter object
length

 [1]  2  8 24  8 20 48 14 32 72 20
```

The vector *B* is recycled three times in full and a warning message in printed to indicate that the length of the longer vector *A* is not a multiple of the shorter vector *B*, although the calculation still proceeds.

3.7   Missing values, infinity, and things that are not numbers

Calculations can lead to answers that are plus infinity ($+\infty$), represented in *R* by Inf, or minus infinity ($= \infty$), which is represented as -Inf:

```
3 / 0

[1] Inf

-12 / 0

[1] -Inf
```

Some calculations involving infinity can be evaluated, for instance:

```
exp(-Inf)

[1] 0

0 / Inf

[1] 0

(0:3)^Inf

[1]    0    1 Inf Inf
```

Other calculations, however, lead to quantities that are not numbers. These are represented in *R* by NaN (**not a number**). Here are some of the classic cases:

```
0 / 0

[1] NaN

Inf - Inf

[1] NaN

Inf / Inf

[1] NaN
```

It is important to understand clearly the distinction between NaN and NA (the latter stands for **not available** and is the missing data symbol in *R*; see below). The function is.nan () is provided to check specifically for NaN, and is.na (NaN) also returns TRUE. Coercing NaN to logical or integer type gives an NA of the appropriate type. There are built-in tests to check whether a number is finite or infinite:

```
is.finite (10)

[1] TRUE

is.infinite (10)

[1] FALSE

is.infinite (Inf)

[1] TRUE

is.infinite (-Inf)

[1] TRUE
```

3.7.1   Missing values: NA

Missing values in data are a real source of irritation because, for instance, they affect the way that model-fitting functions operate, and they can greatly reduce the power of the modelling that we would like to do. Unfortunately, they are a feature of real life and we must learn how to deal with them.

We may want to discover which values in a vector are missing. Here is a simple case:

```
y <- c (4, NA, 7)
```

The missing value question should evaluate to FALSE TRUE FALSE. There are two ways of looking for missing values that we might think should work, but do not. These involve treating NA as if it was a piece of text and using double equals (==) to test for it. But this does not work:

```
y == NA

[1] NA NA NA
```

because it records *all* the values as NA (definitely not what was intended). This does not work either:

```
y == "NA"

[1] FALSE    NA FALSE
```

It correctly reports that the numbers are not character strings, but it returns NA for the missing value itself, rather than TRUE as required. This is how to do it properly:

```
is.na (y)
```

```
[1] FALSE  TRUE FALSE
```

There a number of functions to deal with a vector that might contain NAs. Let us add an extra vector with no NAs:

```
x <- c (4, 5, 7)
na.omit (y)
```

```
[1] 4 7
attr(,"na.action")
[1] 2
attr(,"class")
[1] "omit"
```

```
na.fail (x)
```

```
[1] 4 5 7
```

```
na.fail (y)
```

```
Error in na.fail.default(y):  missing values in object
```

The first function gives us not only the data without NAs but also tell us which positions have been omitted, and na.fail () gives an error if there are NAs, but otherwise does nothing.

na.omit () is useful in editing out rows containing missing values from large dataframes (see Section 4.5.5). Here is a very simple example of a dataframe with four rows and four columns:

```
y1 <- c (1, 2, 3, 6)
y2 <- c (5, 6, NA, 8)
y3 <- c (9, 10, 11, 12)
y4 <- c (NA, 14, 15, 16)
(full_frame <- data.frame (y1, y2, y3, y4))
```

```
  y1 y2 y3 y4
1  1  5  9 NA
2  2  6 10 14
3  3 NA 11 15
4  6  8 12 16
```

```
(reduced_frame1 <- na.omit (full_frame))
```

```
  y1 y2 y3 y4
2  2  6 10 14
4  6  8 12 16
```

We might be interested in just deleting those rows which have NA in one particular column, say y1:

```
(reduced_frame1 <- full_frame[!is.na (full_frame$y1),])

   y1 y2 y3 y4
1   1  5  9 NA
2   2  6 10 14
3   3 NA 11 15
4   6  8 12 16
```

This uses both [,] and $ to extract parts of a dataframe. These are discussed in Section 4.5.1.

Some functions do not work with their default settings when there are missing values in the data, and mean () is a classic example of this:

```
x <- c (1:8, NA)
mean (x)
```

```
[1] NA
```

In order to calculate the mean of the non-missing values, we need to specify that the NAs are to be removed, using the na.rm = TRUE argument which is available for many functions by looking in help ():

```
mean (x, na.rm = T)
```

```
[1] 4.5
```

Here is an example where we want to find the locations (7 and 8) of missing values within a vector called vmv:

```
(vmv <- c (1:6, NA, NA, 9:12))
```

```
[1]  1  2  3  4  5  6 NA NA  9 10 11 12
```

Making an index of the missing values in an array could use the seq () function, like this:

```
seq (along = vmv) [is.na (vmv)]
```

```
[1] 7 8
```

However, the result is achieved more simply using the which () function like this:

```
which (is.na (vmv))
```

```
[1] 7 8
```

If the missing values are genuine counts of zero, we might want to edit the NAs to 0s. We can use the `is.na ()` function to generate subscripts for this:

```
vmv[is.na (vmv)] <- 0
vmv
```

```
[1]   1   2   3   4   5   6   0   0   9  10  11  12
```

or, more straightforwardly, use the `ifelse ()` function like this:

```
vmv <- c (1:6, NA, NA, 9:12)
ifelse (is.na (vmv), 0, vmv)
```

```
[1]   1   2   3   4   5   6   0   0   9  10  11  12
```

However, we need to make sure that we know what we are doing, because most missing values are not genuine zeros.

3.8   Vectors and subscripts

A vector is a data object and type with one or more values of the same class (and not, as in maths and physics, an object with magnitude and direction). For instance, the numbers of peas in six pods were 4, 7, 6, 5, 6, and 7. The vector called `peas` is one object of length 6. In this case, the class of the object is `numeric`, but it could equally well be, for instance, `character`, `factor` or `logical`. The easiest way to create a vector in *R* is to combine (link together) the six values using the combine function, `c ()`, like this:

```
peas <- c (4, 7, 6, 5, 6, 7)
```

We can ask all sorts of questions about the vector called `peas`. For instance, what type of vector is it?

```
class (peas)
```

```
[1] "numeric"
```

How big is the vector?

```
length (peas)
```

```
[1] 6
```

The great advantage of a vector-based language is that it is very simple to ask quite complex questions that involve all of the values in the vector. These vector functions are often self-explanatory:

```
mean (peas)
```

```
[1] 5.833333
```

```
max (peas)
```

```
[1] 7
```

```
min (peas)
```

```
[1] 4
```

Others might be more opaque:

```
quantile (peas)
```

```
  0%   25%   50%   75% 100%
4.00 5.25 6.00 6.75 7.00
```

We will examine these type of activities in more detail in Section 3.10.

Another, slightly old-fashioned way to create a vector, is to input data from the keyboard using the function called scan:

```
peas <- scan ()
```

The prompt named 1: appears, which means type in the first number of peas (4) then press the return key; then the prompt 2: appears (type in 7), and so on. When we have typed in all six values, and the prompt 7: has appeared, we just press the return key to tell *R* that the vector is now complete. *R* replies by telling us how many items it has read.

3.8.1 Extracting elements of a vector using subscripts

We will often want to use (read, manipulate, or update) some but not all of the contents of a vector. To do this, we need to master the use of **subscripts** (or **indices** as they are also known). In *R*, subscripts involve the use of square brackets [ ]. It is important to understand that these [ ] refer to the position in a vector not the contents. Our vector called peas shows the numbers of peas in six pods:

```
peas
```

```
[1] 4 7 6 5 6 7
```

The first element of peas is 4, the second 7, and so on. The elements are indexed left to right, 1–6. If we want to extract the fourth element of peas (which we can see is a 5), then this is what we do:

```
peas[4]
```

```
[1] 5
```

If we want to extract several values (say the 2nd, 3rd, and 6th), we use a vector to specify the pods we want as subscripts, either in two stages like this:

```
pods <- c (2, 3, 6)
peas[pods]
```

```
[1] 7 6 7
```

or in a single step, like this:

```
peas[c (2, 3, 6)]
```

```
[1] 7 6 7
```

We can drop values from a vector by using negative subscripts. Here are all but the first values of peas:

```
peas[-1]
```

```
[1] 7 6 5 6 7
```

Here are all but the last (note the use of the `length` () argument to decide what is last):

```
peas[-length (peas)]
```

```
[1] 4 7 6 5 6
```

We can use these ideas to write a function called `trim` () to remove (say) the largest two and the smallest two values from a vector, x (see Section 3.18 for details on writing our own functions). First, we have to `sort` () the vector, then remove the smallest two values (these will have subscripts 1 and 2), then remove the largest two values (which will have subscripts `length` (x) and `length` (x) - 1):

```
trim <- function(x) {
  sorted_x <- sort (x)
  sorted_x[-c (1, 2, length (x) - 1, length (x))]
}
```

We can use `trim` () on the vector called peas, expecting to get 6 and 6 as the result:

```
trim (peas)
```

```
[1] 6 6
```

We can also use sequences of numbers to extract values from a vector. Here are the first three values of `peas`:

```
peas[1:3]

[1]  4  7  6
```

Here are the even-numbered values of `peas`:

```
peas[seq(2, length (peas), 2)]

[1]  7  5  7
```

or alternatively:

```
peas[1:length (peas) %% 2 == 0]

[1]  7  5  7
```

using the modulo function `%%` on the sequence 1–6 to extract the even numbers 2, 4, and 6. Note that vectors in *R* could have length 0, and this can be useful to know:

```
y <- 4.3
z <- y[-1]
length (z)

[1]  0
```

3.8.2 Classes of vector

The vector called `peas` contained numbers: in the jargon, it is of class `numeric`, vector is the data type.

```
class (peas)

[1]  "numeric"
```

R allows vectors of six types, *but* all of the elements in one vector must belong to the same class. The classes that we will meet are `logical`, `integer`, `numeric`, and `character` (or string):

```
trues <- rep (TRUE, 4)
class (trues)
```

```
[1] "logical"

threes <- as.integer (c (3, 3))
class (threes)

[1] "integer"

greetings <- c ("hello", "world")
class (greetings)

[1] "character"
```

3.8.3   Naming elements within vectors

It is often useful to have the values in a vector labelled in some way. For instance, if our data are counts of 0, 1, 2, … occurrences in a vector called `counts`,

```
(counts <- c (25, 12, 7, 4, 6, 2, 1, 0, 2))

[1] 25 12  7  4  6  2  1  0  2
```

so that there were 25 zeros, 12 ones, and so on, it would be useful to name each of the counts with the relevant number 0–8, because if we look at the positions, they will be numbered 1–9:

```
names (counts) <- 0:8
```

Now when we inspect the vector called counts, we see both the names and the frequencies:

```
counts

 0  1  2  3  4  5  6  7  8
25 12  7  4  6  2  1  0  2
```

If we have computed a table of counts, then the object we have created has class `table`. We can remove the names and create a vector like this, where we begin with some random data from a Poisson distribution (frequently used for counts of things):

```
(count_table <- table (rpois (2000, 2.3)))

  0   1   2   3   4   5   6   7   8   9
186 466 537 388 244 112  41  18   6   2

class (count_table)

[1] "table"
```

```
(count_vector <- as.vector (count_table))
```

```
[1]  186 466 537 388 244 112  41  18   6   2
```

```
class (count_vector)
```

```
[1] "integer"
```

3.9 Working with logical subscripts

Take the example of a vector containing the 11 numbers 0–10:

```
x <- 0:10
```

There are two quite different kinds of things we might want to do with this. We might want to *add up* the values of the elements:

```
sum (x)
```

```
[1] 55
```

Alternatively, we might want to *count* the elements that passed some logical criterion. Suppose we wanted to know how many of the values were less than 5:

```
sum (x < 5)
```

```
[1] 5
```

We use the vector function `sum ()` in both cases. However, `sum (x)` adds up the values of the xs and `sum (x < 5)` counts up the number of cases that pass the logical condition $x < 5$. This works because of *coercion* (see Section 3.6): logical `TRUE` has been coerced to numeric 1 and logical `FALSE` has been coerced to numeric 0.

That is all well and good, but how do we list or add up the values of just some of the elements of x? We specify a logical condition, but we do not want to count the number of cases that pass the condition, we want to output or add up all the values of the cases that pass the condition. This involves the use of **logical subscripts**. Note that when we counted the number of cases, the counting was applied to the entire vector, using `sum (x < 5)`. To find the values of x that are less than 5, we write:

```
(x[x < 5])
```

```
[1] 0 1 2 3 4
```

This looks a bit weird as *x* is the vector and is also used in the subscripts, but is a very common tactic in *R*. Let us look at this in more detail. The logical condition `x < 5` is either true or false:

```
x < 5


 [1]   TRUE   TRUE   TRUE   TRUE   TRUE FALSE FALSE FALSE FALSE FALSE FALSE
```

A vector with a load of TRUEs and FALSEs in [ ]s will just output those elements that are TRUE, giving the answer above.

If we want to add up the elements that pass the test above, then:

```
sum (x[x < 5])

[1] 10
```

Suppose we want to work out the sum of the three largest values in a vector, *y*. There are two steps: first `sort ()` the vector into descending order; then add up the values of the first three elements of the reverse-sorted array. Let us do this in stages. First, the values of *y*:

```
y <- c (8, 3, 5, 7, 6, 6, 8, 9, 2, 3, 9, 4, 10, 4, 11)
```

Now if we apply `sort ()` to this, the numbers will be in ascending sequence, and this makes life slightly harder for the present problem:

```
sort (y)

 [1]   2  3  3  4  4  5  6  6  7  8  8  9  9 10 11
```

However, as with most functions, there is a useful argument:

```
sort (y, decreasing = T)

 [1] 11 10  9  9  8  8  7  6  6  5  4  4  3  3  2
```

So the answer to our problem is $11 + 10 + 9 = 30$. But how to compute this? A range of subscripts is simply a series generated using the colon operator. We want the subscripts 1–3, so this is

```
sort (y, decreasing = T)[1:3]

[1] 11 10  9
```

And the answer to the exercise is just:

```
sum (sort (y, decreasing = T)[1:3])

[1] 30
```

Note that we have not changed the vector *y* in any way, nor have we created any new space-consuming vectors during intermediate computational steps.

We will often want to find out which value (i.e. the position) in a vector is the maximum or the minimum (we can find the actual values using `max ()` and `min ()`). This is a question about indices, and the answer we want is an integer indicating which element of the vector contains the maximum (or minimum) out of all the values in that vector. Here is the vector:

```
x <- c (2, 3, 4, 1, 5, 8, 2, 3, 7, 5, 7)
```

So the answers we want are positions 6 (the maximum) and 4 (the minimum). The slow way to do it is like this:

```
which (x == max (x))

[1] 6

which (x == min (x))

[1] 4
```

Better, however, to use the much quicker built-in functions `which.max ()` and `which.min ()` like this:

```
which.max (x)

[1] 6

which.min (x)

[1] 4
```

3.10   Vector functions

One of *R*'s great strengths is its ability to evaluate functions over entire vectors, thereby avoiding the need for loops (which are typically very slow: see Section 3.13) and subscripts. Many of the most important vector functions are listed in Table 3.5.

Here is a numeric vector:

```
y <- c (8, 3, 5, 7, 6, 6, 8, 9, 2, 3, 9, 4, 10, 4, 11)
```

Some vector functions produce a single number:

```
mean (y)

[1] 6.333333
```

Table 3.5 Vector functions

Operation	Meaning
`max (x)`	maximum value in *x*
`min (x)`	minimum value in *x*
`sum (x)`	total of all the values in *x*
`mean (x)`	arithmetic mean of the values in *x*
`median (x)`	median value in *x*
`range (x)`	vector of `min (x)` and `max (x)`
`var (x)`	sample variance of *x*
`cor (x, y)`	correlation between vectors *x* and *y*
`sort (x)`	a sorted version of *x*
`rank (x)`	vector of the ranks of the values in *x*
`order (x)`	integer vector containing the permutation to sort *x* into ascending order
`quantile (x)`	vector containing the minimum, lower quartile, median, upper quartile, and maximum of *x*
`cumsum (x)`	vector containing the sum of all of the elements up to that point
`cumprod (x)`	vector containing the product of all of the elements up to that point
`cummax (x)`	vector of non-decreasing numbers which are the cumulative maxima of the values in *x* up to that point
`cummin (x)`	vector of non-increasing numbers which are the cumulative minima of the values in *x* up to that point
`pmax (x, y, z)`	vector, of length equal to the longest of *x*, *y*, or *z*, containing the maximum of *x*, *y*, or *z* for the *i*th position in each
`pmin (x, y, z)`	vector, of length equal to the longest of *x*, *y*, or *z*, containing the minimum of *x*, *y*, or *z* for the *i*th position in each

Others produce two numbers:

```
range (y)
```

```
[1]   2 11
```

here showing that the minimum was 2 and the maximum was 11 (very useful for setting the axis range in plots). Other functions produce several numbers:

```
fivenum (y)
```

```
[1]   2.0   4.0   6.0   8.5 11.0
```

This is Tukey's famous five-number summary: the minimum, the lower hinge, the median, the upper hinge, and the maximum (the **hinges** are similar to lower and upper quartiles).

A very useful vector function in *R* is `table ()`. Here is a huge vector called `counts` containing 10 000 random integers from a negative binomial distribution (counts of fungal lesions on 10 000 individual leaves, for instance):

```
counts <- rnbinom (10000, mu = 0.92, size = 1.1)
```

Here is a look at the first 30 values:

```
counts[1:30]

 [1] 0 1 1 3 2 4 1 0 1 0 3 1 0 2 0 0 0 0 2 0 0 0 1 1 1 0 0 2 0 2
```

The question is this: how many zeros are there in the whole vector of 10 000 numbers, how many 1s, and so on right up to the largest value within counts? A formidable task, but for *R* it is just:

```
table (counts)

counts
   0    1    2    3    4    5    6    7    8    9   10   11   12   13
5183 2537 1237  548  267  119   59   22   16    7    1    2    1    1
```

There were 5183 zeros, 2537 ones, and so on, up the largest counts. The data have been selected randomly; so each time we run it we will get different outputs. See Chapter 7 for more details on using tables.

3.10.1 Obtaining tables using `tapply ()`

An incredibly useful way of creating tables in *R* is to use the function `tapply ()`. It does not sound like much from the name, but we will use it time and again for calculating means, variances, sample sizes, minima and maxima, etc. With weather data, for instance, we might want the 12 monthly mean temperatures, rather than the whole-year average. We have two variables of interest: a continuous one, `temperature`, and a categorical variable, `month`:

```
temp_data <- read.table ("temp_data.txt", header = T)
head (temp_data)

   yr month temperature
1 1883     1         6.3
2 1883     2         8.0
3 1883     3         4.8
4 1883     4        12.2
5 1883     5        14.7
6 1883     6        17.7
```

We have imported a dataset and then looked at its start. See Section 4.2 for more details. The function that we want to apply is `mean ()`. All we do is invoke the `tapply ()` function with three arguments: the variable for which we want to calculate the mean (`temperatures`), the categorical variable by which we want to break down the answer (`month`), and the name of the function that we want to apply, using the $ sign to select variables:

```
tapply (temp_data$temperature, temp_data$month, mean)

 1  2  3  4  5  6  7  8  9 10 11 12
NA NA NA NA NA NA NA NA NA NA NA NA
```

That doesn't look good, but will teach us to have a look at our data before trying to manipulate them. Clearly, there are some missing data, and we need to deal with them as discussed in Section 3.7.1. If we want to use some of the arguments that go with our function, we can just add them in at the end of the statement as follows:

```
tapply (temp_data$temperature, temp_data$month, mean, na.rm = T)

        1          2          3          4          5          6          7          8
 6.272519   6.619084   8.923664  11.832824  15.408397  18.522901  20.254264  19.863566
        9         10         11         12
17.293798  13.193023   9.151163   6.879845
```

It is easy to apply other functions in the same way: here are the monthly variances:

```
tapply (temp_data$temperature, temp_data$month, var, na.rm = T)

       1        2        3        4        5        6        7        8
3.094931 4.302787 4.116436 2.555607 2.233852 2.167164 3.304532 2.786084
       9       10       11       12
1.953555 1.910185 1.399237 2.452559
```

and the monthly minima

```
tapply (temp_data$temperature, temp_data$month, min, na.rm = T)

   1    2    3    4    5    6    7    8    9   10   11   12
 1.3 -0.6  4.5  8.5 11.9 15.1 16.2 16.0 13.7  9.8  5.9  1.9
```

If *R* does not have a built-in function to do what we want, then we can easily write our own and add them into tapply (). Here, for instance, is a function to calculate the standard error of each mean (these are called **anonymous** functions in *R*, because they are unnamed):

```
tapply (temp_data$temperature, temp_data$month,
        function (x) sqrt (var (x, na.rm = T) / length (x)))

        1          2          3          4          5          6          7          8
0.1531223  0.1805460  0.1765931  0.1391426  0.1300889  0.1281324  0.1582224  0.1452814
        9         10         11         12
0.1216538  0.1202959  0.1029577  0.1363085
```

We use the function function (x) and then just give the formula required by that function (see Section 3.18 for more details of writing our own functions).

The tapply () function is very flexible. It can produce multi-dimensional tables simply by replacing the one categorical variable month by a list () of categorical variables. Here are the monthly means given separately for each year. The variable we name first in the list, yr, will appear as the rows of the results table and the second will appear as the columns:

```
attach (temp_data)
temp_summ <- tapply (temperature, list (yr, month), mean, na.rm = T)
```

```
detach (temp_data)
head (temp_summ)
```

```
        1    2    3     4     5     6     7     8     9    10   11   12
1883  6.3  8.0  4.8  12.2  14.7  17.7  18.8  19.8  16.8  12.7  8.6  7.3
1884  8.4  8.0  9.5  10.6  15.7  18.2  20.8  22.6  18.4  12.3  9.0  6.6
1885  4.7  8.5  7.8  11.6  12.9  18.6  21.0  17.1  16.4  10.5  8.0  7.0
1886  4.5  3.9  6.1  10.9  13.9  17.3  20.8  20.8  17.7  13.8  9.7  4.9
1887  5.1  7.5  7.1  11.0  12.3  21.0  23.7  20.7  15.3  10.6  7.6  6.2
1888  6.4  4.0  5.3   8.9  15.8  16.9  16.2  18.0  16.0  11.8  9.7  7.7
```

We have used the attach () and detach () (which should always go together) to save having to type the dataset name every time we want to select a variable. We have just shown the start of the table, which is a reorganisation of the original data into a more readable form.

We might want to trim some of the extreme values before calculating the mean (the arithmetic mean is famously sensitive to large or small values, unlike the median). The trim argument allows us to specify the fraction of the data (between 0 and 0.5) that we want to be omitted from the left- and right-hand tails of the sorted vector of values before computing the mean of the central values. Let us look at annual values this time, just displaying the first ten:

```
tapply (temp_data$temperature, temp_data$yr, mean, trim = 0.2)[1:10]
```

```
   1883     1884     1885     1886     1887     1888     1889     1890     1891     1892
12.2500  12.7625  11.6000  11.7875  11.5125  11.5625  11.9500  12.7125  11.7375  11.2750
```

3.10.2 Applying functions to vectors using sapply ()

If we want to apply a function to a vector (rather than to the margin of a matrix), then use sapply (). Here is the code to generate a list of sequences from 1:3 up to 1:7:

```
sapply (3:7, seq)

[[1]]
[1] 1 2 3

[[2]]
[1] 1 2 3 4

[[3]]
[1] 1 2 3 4 5

[[4]]
[1] 1 2 3 4 5 6

[[5]]
[1] 1 2 3 4 5 6 7
```

The function sapply () is most useful with complicated iterative calculations. There is a similar function called lapply (), but sapply () is simpler to use. The following data show decay of radioactive emissions (y) over a 50-day (x) period, and we intend to use non-linear least squares (see Section 2.5.1) to estimate the decay rate a in the model $y = e^{-ax}$:

```
sapdecay <- read.table ("sapdecay.txt", header = T)
head (sapdecay)

    x        y
1   0 1.0000000
2   2 0.9602354
3   4 0.8446638
4   6 0.7069363
5   8 0.7086414
6  10 0.6097954
```

We need to write a function to calculate the sum of the squares of the differences between the observed (y) and predicted (yf) values of y, when provided with a specific value of the parameter a:

```
sumsq <- function (a, xv = sapdecay$x, yv = sapdecay$y) {
  yf <- exp (-a * xv)
  sum ((yv - yf)^2)
}
```

We can get a rough idea of the decay constant, a, for these data by linear regression of $\ln(y)$ against x, like this:

```
lm (log (y) ~ x, data = sapdecay)


Call:
lm(formula = log(y) ~ x, data = sapdecay)

Coefficients:
(Intercept)           x
    0.04688     -0.05849
```

So our parameter a is somewhere close to 0.058. We generate a range of values for a spanning an interval on either side of 0.058:

```
a <- seq (0.01, 0.2, 0.005)
```

Now we can use `sapply ()` to apply the sum of squares function for each of these values of a (without writing a loop), and plot the deviance against the parameter value to give Figure 3.1:

```
plot (a, sapply (a, sumsq), type = "l", col = hue_pal ()(1))
```

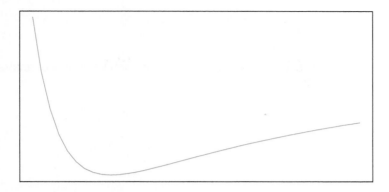

Figure 3.1 Use of `sapply ()` to calculate multiple *y* values.

3.10.3 The `aggregate ()` function for grouped summary statistics

Suppose that we have two variables of interest (*y* and *z*) and two categorical variables (*x* and *w*) that we might want to use to summarise functions like mean or variance of *y* and/or *z*. The `aggregate ()` function (which is a little friendlier than `tapply ()`) has a formula method which allows elegant summaries of four kinds:

one to one	`aggregate (y ~ x, mean)`
one to many	`aggregate (y ~ x + w, mean)`
many to one	`aggregate (cbind (y, z) ~ x, mean)`
many to many	`aggregate (cbind (y, z) ~ x + w, mean)`

These formulae look very much like those we will see in building linear (and other forms of) regression models, see Chapter 10.

This is very useful for removing pseudo-replication from dataframes (see Section 16.2). Here is an example using a dataframe with two continuous variables (`Growth.rate` and `pH`), and three categorical variables (`Water`, `Detergent`, and `Daphnia`):

```
phdaphnia <- read.table ("phdaphnia.txt", header = T)
head (phdaphnia)

  Growth.rate Water Detergent Daphnia       pH
1    2.919086  Tyne    BrandA   Clone1 4.426134
2    2.492904  Tyne    BrandA   Clone1 6.428475
3    3.021804  Tyne    BrandA   Clone1 8.615967
4    2.350874  Tyne    BrandA   Clone2 8.384364
5    3.148174  Tyne    BrandA   Clone2 5.878067
6    4.423853  Tyne    BrandA   Clone2 6.444727
```

Here is one-to-one (i.e. examine `Growth.rate` for each level of one factor) use of `aggregate ()` to find mean growth rate in the two water samples:

```
aggregate (Growth.rate ~ Water, mean, data = phdaphnia)

  Water Growth.rate
```

```
1   Tyne      3.685862
2   Wear      4.017948
```

Here is a one-to-many use (i.e. examine `Growth.rate` for each level of two factors) to look at the interaction between `Water` and `Detergent`:

```
aggregate (Growth.rate ~ Water + Detergent, mean, data = phdaphnia)

    Water Detergent Growth.rate
1   Tyne     BrandA     3.661807
2   Wear     BrandA     4.107857
3   Tyne     BrandB     3.911116
4   Wear     BrandB     4.108972
5   Tyne     BrandC     3.814321
6   Wear     BrandC     4.094704
7   Tyne     BrandD     3.356203
8   Wear     BrandD     3.760259
```

Finally, here is a many-to-many use (i.e. examine `Growth.rate` and `pH` for each level of two factors) to find mean `pH` as well as mean `Growth.rate` for the interaction between `Water` and `Detergent`:

```
aggregate (cbind (Growth.rate, pH) ~ Water + Detergent, mean, data = phdaphnia)

    Water Detergent Growth.rate       pH
1   Tyne     BrandA     3.661807 6.497067
2   Wear     BrandA     4.107857 6.103381
3   Tyne     BrandB     3.911116 5.649101
4   Wear     BrandB     4.108972 6.042897
5   Tyne     BrandC     3.814321 5.817386
6   Wear     BrandC     4.094704 6.432722
7   Tyne     BrandD     3.356203 6.131518
8   Wear     BrandD     3.760259 6.084082
```

3.10.4 Parallel minima and maxima: `pmin` and `pmax`

Here are three vectors, x, y, and z. The parallel minimum function, `pmin ()`, finds the minimum from any one of the three variables for each subscript, and produces a *vector* as its result (of length equal to the longest of x, y, or z):

```
x <- 1:10
y <- 10:1
z <- seq (0, 18, 2)
pmin (x, y, z)

 [1]  0  2  3  4  5  5  4  3  2  1
```

This function just gives the minimum value in each of the 10 positions of each vector. For instance, the smallest value in position one comes from z and is 0. If some of the vectors are shorter than others, then they are just repeated (even partially) up to the length of the longest vector:

```
x <- 1:10
y <- 10:1
z <- seq (0, 8, 2)
pmin (x, y, z)

 [1] 0 2 3 4 5 0 2 3 2 1
```

z has only length five and so is repeated. This mean that the smallest number in position six is, again, 0. pmax () works in a similar way.

3.10.5 Finding closest values

Finding the value in a vector that is closest to a specified value is straightforward using which (). The vector xv contains 1000 random numbers from a Normal distribution with mean 100 and standard deviation 10:

```
xv <- rnorm (1000,100,10)
```

Here, we want to find the value of xv that is closest to 108.0. The logic is to work out the difference between 108 and each of the 1000 random numbers, then find which of these differences is the smallest. This is what the R code looks like, where we use the abs () function to take the absolute value of a number (i.e. any negative sign is ignored):

```
which (abs (xv - 108) == min (abs (xv - 108)))

[1] 311
```

The closest value to 108.0 is in location 311 within xv. But just how close to 108.0 is this value? We use the position as a subscript on xv to find this out:

```
abs (xv[which (abs (xv - 108) == min (abs (xv - 108)))] - 108)

[1] 0.002232716
```

To generalise this, we can write a function (see Section 3.18) to return the closest value to a specified value (sv) in any vector (xv):

```
closest <- function (xv, sv) {
  xv[which (abs (xv - sv) == min (abs (xv - sv)))]
}
```

and run it like this:

```
closest (xv, 108)

[1] 108.0022
```

3.10.6 Sorting, ranking, and ordering

These three related concepts are important, and one of them (ordering) can be difficult to understand on first acquaintance. Let us take a simple example using average house prices in some areas West of London:

```
houses <- read.table ("houses.txt", header = T)
head (houses)

     Location Price
1       Ascot   325
2 Sunninghill   201
3   Bracknell   157
4   Camberley   162
5     Bagshot   164
6     Staines   101
```

We apply the three different functions to the vector called `Price`:

```
ranked <- rank (houses$Price)
sorted <- sort (houses$Price)
ordered <- order (houses$Price)
```

Then we make a dataframe (see Section 4.5 for more details) out of the four vectors like this:

```
(view_houses <- data.frame (houses$Price, ranked, sorted, ordered))

   houses. Price ranked sorted ordered
1           325   12.0     95       9
2           201   10.0    101       6
3           157    5.0    117      10
4           162    6.0    121      12
5           164    7.0    157       3
6           101    2.0    162       4
7           211   11.0    164       5
8           188    8.5    188       8
9            95    1.0    188      11
10          117    3.0    201       2
11          188    8.5    211       7
12          121    4.0    325       1
```

The function `rank` ()

The prices themselves are in no particular sequence. The `ranked` column contains the value that is the rank of the particular data point (value of `Price`), where 1 is assigned to the lowest data point and the number of rows in the dataframe – here 12 – is assigned to the highest data point. So the first element, a price of 325, happens to be the highest value. We can see that there are 11 values smaller than 325:

```
houses$Price < 325
```

```
[1] FALSE  TRUE  TRUE  TRUE  TRUE  TRUE  TRUE  TRUE  TRUE  TRUE  TRUE  TRUE
```

Fractional ranks indicate ties. There are two 188s, and their ranks are 8 and 9. Because they are tied, each gets the average of their two ranks $(8 + 9)/2 = 8.5$. The lowest price is 95, indicated by a rank of 1.

The function sort ()

The sorted vector is very straightforward. It contains the values of `Price` sorted into ascending order. If we want to sort into descending order, we can use the argument `decreasing = T` like this:

```
(sorted_rev <- sort (houses$Price, decreasing = T))
```

```
[1] 325 211 201 188 188 164 162 157 121 117 101  95
```

Note that `sort ()` *is potentially very dangerous*, because it uncouples values that might need to be in the same row of the dataframe (e.g. because they are the explanatory variables associated with a particular value of the response variable). It is bad practice, therefore, to sort just one column of a dataframe, not least because there is no unsort () function.

The function order ()

This is the most important of the three functions, and much the hardest to understand on first acquaintance. The numbers in this column are subscripts between 1 and 12. The `order ()` function returns an integer vector *containing the permutation that will sort the input into ascending order*. The lowest value of `Price` is 95. What is the position in the original vector called `Price` where 95 occurred? Scanning down the column, we find it in row number 9. This is the first value in ordered: `ordered[1]`. Where is the next smallest value (101) to be found within `Price`? It is in position 6, so this is `ordered[2]`. The third smallest value of `Price` (117) is in position 10, so this is `ordered[3]`, and so on.

This function is particularly useful in sorting dataframes, as explained in Section 4.5.3. Using `order ()` with subscripts is a much safer option than using `sort ()`, as it enables us to sort whole rows of the dataframe rather than just one column. The beauty of `order ()` is that we can use `order (Price)` as a subscript for `Location` to obtain the price-ranked list of locations:

```
attach (houses)
Location[order (Price)]
```

```
 [1] "Reading"     "Staines"    "Winkfield"   "Newbury"    "Bracknell"
 [6] "Camberley"   "Bagshot"    "Maidenhead"  "Warfield"   "Sunninghill"
[11] "Windsor"     "Ascot"
```

```
Location[order (Price, decreasing = T)]
```

```
 [1]  "Ascot"       "Windsor"      "Sunninghill" "Maidenhead" "Warfield"
 [6]  "Bagshot"     "Camberley"    "Bracknell"   "Newbury"    "Winkfield"
[11]  "Staines"     "Reading"

detach (houses)
```

As we can see, `order ()` also has the `decreasing = T` argument. In a similar fashion, we can see the whole dataframe, ordered:

```
attach (houses)
houses[order (Price),]

        Location Price
9        Reading    95
6        Staines   101
10     Winkfield   117
12       Newbury   121
3      Bracknell   157
4      Camberley   162
5        Bagshot   164
8     Maidenhead   188
11      Warfield   188
2    Sunninghill   201
7        Windsor   211
1          Ascot   325

detach (houses)
```

3.10.7 Understanding the difference between `unique ()` and `duplicated ()`

The difference between these two functions is best seen with a simple example. Here is a vector of common British surnames:

```
names <- c ("Williams", "Patel", "Smith", "Williams", "Patel", "Williams")
```

We can see how many times each name appears:

```
table (names)

names
   Patel    Smith Williams
       2        1        3
```

It is clear that the vector contains just three different names. The function called `unique ()` extracts these three unique names, creating a vector of length 3, unsorted, in the order in which the names are encountered in the vector:

```
unique (names)
```

```
[1] "Williams" "Patel"    "Smith"
```

In contrast, the function called duplicated () produces a vector, of the same length as the vector of names, containing the logical values either FALSE or TRUE, depending upon whether or not that name has appeared already (reading from the left). So

```
duplicated (names)
```

```
[1] FALSE FALSE FALSE  TRUE   TRUE   TRUE
```

The first three names are not duplicated (FALSE), but the last three are (TRUE). We can mimic the unique () function by using this vector as subscripts like this:

```
names[!duplicated (names)]
```

```
[1] "Williams" "Patel"    "Smith"
```

Remember the NOT operator (!) in front of the duplicated () function. There we have it: if we want a shortened vector, containing only the unique values in names, then use unique (), but if we want a vector of the same length as names, then use duplicated (). We might use this to extract values from a different vector. If we wanted the mean salary, ignoring the repeats, because we believe individuals are on the payroll more than once:

```
salary <- c (42, 42, 48, 42, 42, 42)
mean (salary)
```

```
[1] 43
```

```
salary[!duplicated (names)]
```

```
[1] 42 42 48
```

```
mean (salary[!duplicated (names)])
```

```
[1] 44
```

Note that this is not the same answer as would be obtained by omitting the duplicate salaries because two of the people (Patel and Williams) had the same salary (42). Here is the wrong answer:

```
mean (salary[!duplicated (salary)])
```

```
[1] 45
```

3.10.8 Looking for runs of numbers within vectors

The useful function called `rle ()`, which stands for **run length encoding**, is most easily understood with an example. Here is a vector of 150 random numbers from a Poisson distribution with mean 0.7:

```
set.seed (123)
```

```
(poisson <- rpois (150,0.7))

  [1]  0 1 0 2 2 0 1 2 1 0 2 0 1 1 0 2 0 0 0 2 2 1 1 4 1 1 1 1 0 0 2 2 1 1 0 0 1
 [38]  0 0 0 0 0 0 0 0 0 0 0 2 0 0 1 0 1 0 0 1 2 0 1 0 0 0 1 0 1 1 1 0 1 1 1 0
 [75]  0 0 0 1 0 0 0 1 0 1 0 0 3 2 2 0 0 1 0 1 0 0 1 0 0 1 1 0 0 2 0 2 2 1 0 0 2
[112]  0 0 2 1 0 1 2 1 0 1 0 0 0 0 3 0 0 0 1 1 2 1 1 1 1 1 1 3 0 0 0 0 0 1 0 0 0
[149]  0 1
```

The vector runs over several lines, and the number in square brackets at the start of each line tells us the position of the next element (e.g. the 2nd line begins with the 38th element). We can do our own run length encoding on the vector by eye: there is a run of two 1s, then a run of two 0s, then a single 2, then a single 1, then a single 0, and so on. So the run lengths are 2, 2, 1, 1, 1, 1, …. The values associated with these runs were 1, 0, 2, 1, 0, 1, …. Here is the output using `rle ()`:

```
rle (poisson)
```

```
Run Length Encoding
  lengths: int [1:85] 1 1 1 2 1 1 1 1 1 1 ...
  values : int [1:85] 0 1 0 2 0 1 2 1 0 2 ...
```

The object is a list of two vectors, which we can retrieve using double square brackets, [[ ]]: the lengths of the runs ([[1]]) and the values that did the running ([[2]]). To find the longest run, and the value associated with that longest run, we use the indexed lists like this

```
max (rle (poisson) [[1]])
```

```
[1] 12
```

So the longest run in this vector of numbers was 12. But 12 of what? We use `which ()` to find the location of the 12 in lengths, then apply this index to values to find the answer:

```
which (rle (poisson) [[1]] == max (rle(poisson) [[1]]))
```

```
[1] 25
```

```
rle (poisson) [[2]] [which (rle (poisson) [[1]] == max (rle(poisson) [[1]]))]
```

```
[1] 0
```

We should note that what we retrieved in the first line was not the position of the start of the longest run but the index of the run, i.e. run 12 was the longest. If we want to find out where it started, we can just add up the lengths of the previous runs and add 1:

```
sum (rle (poisson) [[1]] [1:(which (rle (poisson) [[1]] ==
                        max (rle(poisson) [[1]])) - 1)]) + 1
```

```
[1] 38
```

The expressions we are using can have quite a few brackets of differing shapes. If a line of code doesn't work, it's often useful to make sure that our start and end brackets are paired up correctly. In RStudio, if we put the cursor to the right of a bracket, then its partner *as R understands it* will be highlighted in grey.

It is sometimes of interest to know the number of runs in a given vector (for instance, the lower the number of runs, the more aggregated the numbers; and the greater the number of runs, the more regularly spaced out). We use the `length ()` function for this:

```
length (rle (poisson) [[1]])
```

```
[1] 85
```

```
length (rle (poisson) [[2]])
```

```
[1] 85
```

indicating that the 150 values were arranged in 85 runs, whether we look at the first or second item in the list.

In a different example, suppose we had n_1 values of 1 representing *present* and n_2 values of 0 representing *absent*, with at least one of each; then the minimum number of runs would be 2 (a solid block of 1s then a sold block of 0s). The maximum number of runs would be $2n + 1$, where $n = \min (n1, n2)$ if they alternated (until the smaller number ran out). Here is a simple **runs test** based on 10 000 randomisations of 25 ones and 30 zeros, so our minimum length would be 2 and our maximum 51:

```
n1 <- 25
n2 <- 30
y <- c (rep (1, n1),rep (0, n2))
len <- numeric (10000)
for (i in 1:10000) {
  len[i] <- length (rle (sample (y)) [[2]])
}
summary (len)
```

```
  Min. 1st Qu.  Median    Mean 3rd Qu.    Max.
 16.00   26.00   28.00   28.27   31.00   41.00
```

Thus, even in 10 000 samples we got nowhere near to achieving the minimum or maximum number of runs.

3.10.9 Sets: `union ()`, `intersect ()`, and `setdiff ()`

There are three essential functions for manipulating sets. The principles are easy to see if we work with an example of two sets:

```
setA <- c ("a", "b", "c", "d", "e")
setB <- c ("d", "e", "f", "g")
```

We can think about what the two sets have in common, and what is unique to each.

The **union** of two sets ($A \cup B$) is everything in the two sets taken together, but counting elements only once that are common to both sets:

```
union (setA, setB)

[1] "a" "b" "c" "d" "e" "f" "g"
```

The **intersection** of two sets ($A \cap B$) is the material that they have in common:

```
intersect (setA, setB)

[1] "d" "e"
```

Note, however, that the **difference** between two sets is order-dependent. It is the material that *is* in the first named set, that *is not* in the second named set. Thus, `setdiff (A, B)` gives a different answer than `setdiff (B, A)`. For our example:

```
setdiff (setA, setB)

[1] "a" "b" "c"

setdiff (setB, setA)

[1] "f" "g"
```

Thus, it should be the case that `setdiff (A, B)` and `intersect (A, B)` and `setdiff (B, A)` is the same as `union (A, B)`. Let us check:

```
union (setdiff (setA, setB), union (intersect (setA, setB),
       setdiff (setB, setA)))

[1] "a" "b" "c" "d" "e" "f" "g"
```

The function `union ()` only works on two sets so we had to use it twice. There is also a built-in function `setequal ()` for testing if two sets are equal:

```
setequal (
  union (setdiff (setA, setB), union (intersect (setA, setB),
```

```
        setdiff (setB, setA))),
union(setA, setB))
```

```
[1]  TRUE
```

We can also use `%in%` for comparing sets. The result is a logical vector whose length matches the vector on the left and which tells us whether members of the first set are in the second one or not:

```
setA %in% setB
```

```
[1] FALSE FALSE FALSE   TRUE   TRUE
```

```
setB %in% setA
```

```
[1]  TRUE   TRUE FALSE FALSE
```

Using these vectors of logical values as subscripts, we can demonstrate, for instance, that those members of the first set that are in the second is the same as $A \cap B$:

```
setA[setA %in% setB]
```

```
[1] "d" "e"
```

```
intersect (setA, setB)
```

```
[1] "d" "e"
```

3.11 Matrices and arrays

An **array** is a multi-dimensional object where all the entries have the same class (e.g. they are all numeric). The dimensions of an array are specified by its `dim` argument, which gives the maximal indices in each dimension. So for a three-dimensional array consisting of 24 numbers in the sequence 1–24, with dimensions $2 \times 4 \times 3$, we write:

```
(y <- array (1:24, dim = c (2, 4, 3)))
```

```
, , 1

     [,1] [,2] [,3] [,4]
[1,]    1    3    5    7
[2,]    2    4    6    8

, , 2

     [,1] [,2] [,3] [,4]
```

```
[1,]     9    11    13    15
[2,]    10    12    14    16


, , 3

       [,1] [,2] [,3] [,4]
[1,]    17   19    21   23
[2,]    18   20    22   24
```

This produces three two-dimensional tables, because the third dimension is 3, and this dimension is given just before each 2×4 table, e.g. , , 1. This is what happens when we change the dimensions:

```
(y <- array (1:24, dim = c (3, 2, 4)))


, , 1

       [,1] [,2]
[1,]     1    4
[2,]     2    5
[3,]     3    6

, , 2

       [,1] [,2]
[1,]     7   10
[2,]     8   11
[3,]     9   12

, , 3

       [,1] [,2]
[1,]    13   16
[2,]    14   17
[3,]    15   18

, , 4

       [,1] [,2]
[1,]    19   22
[2,]    20   23
[3,]    21   24
```

Now we have four two-dimensional tables, each of three rows and two columns.

A **matrix** is just a two-dimensional array. Incidentally, a **dataframe** is a two-dimensional object that looks a bit like a matrix but which can have different content in each column: this is discussed in Section 4.5.

When there are two subscripts [5, 3] to an object like a matrix or a dataframe, the first subscript refers to the row number (5 in this example; the rows are defined as **margin** number 1) and the second subscript refers to the column number (3 in this example; the columns are margin number 2).

There is an important and powerful convention in *R*, such that *when a subscript appears as a blank it is understood to mean 'all of'*. Thus,

- [, 4] means all rows in column 4 of an object;
- [2,] means all columns in row 2 of an object.

When we have an array with more than two dimensions, we use more subscripts, e.g. [2, 4, 5]. So

```
y[2,1,3]
```

```
[1] 14
```

To find this, we need to look in the third table, second row, and first column of the above.

3.11.1 Matrices

There are several ways of making a matrix. We can create one directly like this:

```
(X <- matrix (c (1, 0, 0, 0, 1, 0, 0, 0, 1), nrow = 3))

     [,1] [,2] [,3]
[1,]    1    0    0
[2,]    0    1    0
[3,]    0    0    1
```

where, by default, the numbers are entered column-wise. The class and attributes of *X* indicate that it is a matrix of three rows and three columns:

```
class(X)
```

```
[1] "matrix" "array"
```

```
attributes(X)
```

```
$dim
[1] 3 3
```

In the next example, the data in the vector appear row-wise:

```
y <- c (1, 2, 3, 4, 4, 3, 2, 1)
(Y <- matrix (y, byrow = T, nrow = 2))

     [,1] [,2] [,3] [,4]
[1,]    1    2    3    4
[2,]    4    3    2    1
```

Another way to convert a vector into a matrix is by providing the vector object with two dimensions (rows and columns) using the dim () function like this:

```
dim (y) <- c (4,2)
```

We can check that vector has now become a matrix:

```
is.matrix (y)

[1] TRUE
```

We need to be careful, however, because we have made no allowance at this stage for the fact that the data were entered row-wise into *Y* and so it is different from *y*:

```
y

     [,1] [,2]
[1,]    1    4
[2,]    2    3
[3,]    3    2
[4,]    4    1
```

The matrix we want is the transpose of this matrix:

```
t (y)

     [,1] [,2] [,3] [,4]
[1,]    1    2    3    4
[2,]    4    3    2    1
```

3.11.2 Naming the rows and columns of matrices

By default, matrices have numbers naming their rows and columns (see above). Here is a 4×5 matrix of random integers from a Poisson distribution with mean 1.5:

```
(X <- matrix (rpois (20, 1.5), nrow = 4))

     [,1] [,2] [,3] [,4] [,5]
[1,]    2    1    1    1    3
[2,]    4    1    0    5    2
[3,]    1    1    2    1    1
[4,]    0    2    1    3    1
```

Let us suppose that the rows refer to four different trials, and we want to label the rows Trial.1 etc. We employ the function rownames () to do this. We could use the paste () function (see Section 3.15.1), but here we take advantage of arguments to rownames ():

```
rownames (X) <- rownames (X, do.NULL = FALSE, prefix = "Trial.")
X

        [,1] [,2] [,3] [,4] [,5]
Trial.1    2    1    1    1    3
Trial.2    4    1    0    5    2
Trial.3    1    1    2    1    1
Trial.4    0    2    1    3    1
```

The `do.NULL = FALSE` argument tells *R* not to create row names and then we just add a prefix to the existing ones using the `prefix` argument.

For the columns, we want to supply a vector of different names for the five drugs involved in the trial:

```
drug_names <- c ("aspirin", "paracetamol", "nurofen", "hedex", "placebo")
colnames (X) <- drug_names
X

        aspirin paracetamol nurofen hedex placebo
Trial.1       2           1       1     1       3
Trial.2       4           1       0     5       2
Trial.3       1           1       2     1       1
Trial.4       0           2       1     3       1
```

Alternatively, we can use the `dimnames ()` function to give names to the rows and/or columns of a matrix. This time we want the rows to be unlabelled (`NULL`) and the column names to be of the form `drug.1`, `drug.2`, etc. Each argument to `dimnames ()` has to be a `list ()` (rows first, columns second, as usual) with the elements of the list of exactly the correct lengths (4 and 5 in this particular case):

```
dimnames (X) <- list (NULL, paste ("drug.", 1:5, sep = ""))
X

     drug.1 drug.2 drug.3 drug.4 drug.5
[1,]      2      1      1      1      3
[2,]      4      1      0      5      2
[3,]      1      1      2      1      1
[4,]      0      2      1      3      1
```

3.11.3   Calculations on rows or columns of matrices

Section 2.2 deals with more mathematical aspects of this topic. We can use subscripts to select parts of the matrix, with a blank meaning 'all of the rows' or 'all of the columns'. Here is the mean of the rightmost column (number 5) of *X*, carried over from Section 3.11.2, calculated over all the rows (blank then comma),

```
mean (X[,5])

[1] 1.75
```

or the variance of the bottom row, calculated over all of the columns (comma then blank):

```
var (X[4,])
```

```
[1] 1.3
```

There are some special functions for calculating summary statistics on matrices, with some fairly obvious names:

```
rowSums (X)
```

```
[1]  8 12  6  7
```

```
colSums(X)
```

```
drug.1 drug.2 drug.3 drug.4 drug.5
     7      5      4     10      7
```

```
rowMeans(X)
```

```
[1] 1.6 2.4 1.2 1.4
```

```
colMeans(X)
```

```
drug.1 drug.2 drug.3 drug.4 drug.5
  1.75   1.25   1.00   2.50   1.75
```

These functions are built for speed, and 'blur some of the subtleties of dealing with NA or NaN'. If such subtlety is an issue, then use apply () instead (see Section 3.11.6 for more details). Remember that columns are margin number 2 and rows are margin number 1:

```
apply (X, 2, mean)
```

```
drug.1 drug.2 drug.3 drug.4 drug.5
  1.75   1.25   1.00   2.50   1.75
```

We might want to sum groups of rows within columns, and rowsum () (singular and all lower case, in contrast to rowSums (), above) is a very efficient function for this. In this example, we want to group together row 1 and row 4 (as group *A*) and row 2 and row 3 (group *B*). Note that the grouping vector has to have length equal to the number of rows:

```
group = c ("A", "B", "B", "A")
rowsum (X, group)
```

```
  drug.1 drug.2 drug.3 drug.4 drug.5
A      2      3      2      4      4
B      5      2      2      6      3
```

We could achieve the same ends (but more slowly) with `tapply ()` or `aggregate ():`

```
tapply (X, list (group[row(X)], col(X)), sum)

  1 2 3 4 5
A 2 3 2 4 4
B 5 2 2 6 3
```

This is a little complex, and we have lost the column headings: as usual, there are lots of ways to do things in *R*, but it's worth taking a bit of time to think of the simplest one. A bit better is

```
aggregate (X, list (group), sum)

  Group.1 drug.1 drug.2 drug.3 drug.4 drug.5
1       A      2      3      2      4      4
2       B      5      2      2      6      3
```

Suppose that we want to shuffle the elements of each column of a matrix independently. We apply the randomising function `sample ()` to each column (margin number 2) like this

```
apply (X, 2, sample)

     drug.1 drug.2 drug.3 drug.4 drug.5
[1,]      0      1      1      1      2
[2,]      4      1      0      5      3
[3,]      2      2      1      1      1
[4,]      1      1      2      3      1

apply (X, 2, sample)

     drug.1 drug.2 drug.3 drug.4 drug.5
[1,]      1      1      2      1      1
[2,]      4      1      1      1      2
[3,]      0      1      1      3      3
[4,]      2      2      0      5      1
```

and so on, for as many shuffled samples as we need.

3.11.4 Adding rows and columns to matrices

In this particular case, we have been asked to add a row at the bottom showing the column means, and a column at the right showing the row variances:

```
X <- rbind (X, apply (X, 2, mean))
X <- cbind (X, apply (X, 1, var))
X

     drug.1 drug.2 drug.3 drug.4 drug.5
[1,]   2.00   1.00      1    1.0   3.00 0.80000
```

```
[2,]    4.00    1.00         0     5.0     2.00 4.30000
[3,]    1.00    1.00         2     1.0     1.00 0.20000
[4,]    0.00    2.00         1     3.0     1.00 1.30000
[5,]    1.75    1.25         1     2.5     1.75 0.33125
```

The functions `rbind ()` and `cbind()`, with the `r` and `c` representing row and column, respectively, will bind together whatever is put in their respective brackets. Note that the number of decimal places varies across columns, with one in columns 1 and 2, two in columns 3 and 4, none in column 5 (integers), and five in column 6. The default in *R* is to print the minimum number of decimal places consistent with the contents of the column as a whole.

Next, we need to label the sixth column as `variance` and the fifth row as `mean`:

```
colnames (X) [6] <- "variance"
rownames (X) <- c(1:4, "mean")
X

        drug.1 drug.2 drug.3 drug.4 drug.5 variance
1         2.00   1.00      1    1.0   3.00  0.80000
2         4.00   1.00      0    5.0   2.00  4.30000
3         1.00   1.00      2    1.0   1.00  0.20000
4         0.00   2.00      1    3.0   1.00  1.30000
mean      1.75   1.25      1    2.5   1.75  0.33125
```

When a matrix with a single row or column is created by a subscripting operation, it is by default turned into a vector. In a similar way, if an array with dimension, say, $2 \times 3 \times 3$ is subsetted by just picking the first row it will be coerced into a 3×3 array, losing the unnecessary dimension. After much discussion this has been determined to be a *feature* of *R*. To prevent this happening, add the argument `drop = FALSE` to the subscripting. For example:

```
a <- matrix (1:4, nrow = 2)
(rowmatrix <- a[2, , drop = FALSE])

     [,1] [,2]
[1,]    2    4

(rowvector <- a[2,])

[1] 2 4

(colmatrix <- a[, 1, drop = FALSE])

     [,1]
[1,]    1
[2,]    2

(colvector <- a[, 1])

[1] 1 2
```

```
b <- array (1:18, dim = c (2, 3, 3))
(still_4_dims <- b[1, , , drop = F])


, , 1

     [,1]  [,2]  [,3]
[1,]    1     3     5

, , 2

     [,1]  [,2]  [,3]
[1,]    7     9    11

, , 3

     [,1]  [,2]  [,3]
[1,]   13    15    17
```

The drop = FALSE option should be used **defensively** (i.e. always unless we specifically want to lose a dimension in certain circumstances) when programming.

3.11.5 The sweep () function

The sweep () function is used to **sweep out** array summaries from vectors, matrices, arrays, or dataframes. In this example, we want to express a matrix in terms of the departures of each value from its column mean.

```
sweepdata <- read.table ("sweepdata.txt")
```

First, we need to create a vector containing the parameters that we intend to sweep out of the matrix. In this case, we want to compute the four column means:

```
(colms <- apply (sweepdata, 2, mean))

   V1      V2      V3      V4
4.60   13.30    0.44  151.60
```

Now, it is straightforward to express all of the data in sweepdata as departures from the relevant column means:

```
sweep (sweepdata, 2, colms)

     V1    V2     V3     V4
1  -1.6  -1.3  -0.04  -26.6
2   0.4  -1.3   0.26   14.4
3   2.4   1.7   0.36   22.4
4   2.4   0.7   0.26  -23.6
5   0.4   4.7  -0.14  -15.6
6   4.4  -0.3  -0.24    3.4
```

```
7    2.4  1.7   0.06  -36.6
8   -2.6 -0.3   0.06   17.4
9   -3.6 -3.3  -0.34   30.4
10  -4.6 -2.3  -0.24   14.4
```

Note the use of `margin = 2` as the second argument to indicate that we want the sweep to be carried out on the columns (rather than on the rows). A related function, `scale ()`, is used for centring and scaling data in terms of standard deviations.

We can see what `sweep ()` has done by doing the calculation long-hand. The operation of this particular sweep is simply one of subtraction. The only issue is that the subtracted object has to have the same dimensions as the matrix to be swept (in this example, 10 rows of 4 columns). Thus, to sweep out the column means, the object to be subtracted from `sweepdata` must have the column means repeated in each of the 10 rows of 4 columns:

```
(col.means <- matrix (rep(colms, rep (10, 4)), nrow = 10))

      [,1] [,2] [,3]   [,4]
 [1,]  4.6 13.3 0.44 151.6
 [2,]  4.6 13.3 0.44 151.6
 [3,]  4.6 13.3 0.44 151.6
 [4,]  4.6 13.3 0.44 151.6
 [5,]  4.6 13.3 0.44 151.6
 [6,]  4.6 13.3 0.44 151.6
 [7,]  4.6 13.3 0.44 151.6
 [8,]  4.6 13.3 0.44 151.6
 [9,]  4.6 13.3 0.44 151.6
[10,]  4.6 13.3 0.44 151.6
```

Then the same result as we got from `sweep ()` is obtained simply by

```
sweepdata - col.means
```

There is another helpful use of `sweep ()`. Suppose that we want to obtain the row or column subscripts in a matrix, within the format of a matrix: this might be useful if we want the position of entries that fulfil a particular condition.

```
sweep (sweepdata, 1, 1:10, function (a, b) b)

      [,1] [,2] [,3] [,4]
 [1,]    1    1    1    1
 [2,]    2    2    2    2
 [3,]    3    3    3    3
 [4,]    4    4    4    4
 [5,]    5    5    5    5
 [6,]    6    6    6    6
 [7,]    7    7    7    7
 [8,]    8    8    8    8
 [9,]    9    9    9    9
[10,]   10   10   10   10
```

```
sweep (sweepdata, 2, 1:4, function (a, b) b)

      [,1] [,2] [,3] [,4]
 [1,]    1    2    3    4
 [2,]    1    2    3    4
 [3,]    1    2    3    4
 [4,]    1    2    3    4
 [5,]    1    2    3    4
 [6,]    1    2    3    4
 [7,]    1    2    3    4
 [8,]    1    2    3    4
 [9,]    1    2    3    4
[10,]    1    2    3    4
```

3.11.6 Applying functions to matrices

We have already seen some examples of using the `apply` () function in order to apply other functions to the rows or columns of matrices or dataframes. For example, here is a matrix with four rows and six columns:

```
(X <- matrix (1:24, nrow = 4))

     [,1] [,2] [,3] [,4] [,5] [,6]
[1,]    1    5    9   13   17   21
[2,]    2    6   10   14   18   22
[3,]    3    7   11   15   19   23
[4,]    4    8   12   16   20   24
```

Note that placing the expression to be evaluated in parentheses (as above) causes the value of the result to be printed on the screen. Often, we want to apply a function across one of the **margins** of a matrix. Margin 1 refers to the rows and margin 2 to the columns. Here are the row totals (four of them):

```
apply (X, MARGIN = 1, FUN = sum)


[1] 66 72 78 84
```

The `FUN` = `sum` argument describes the function we want to use across the rows. Here are the column totals (six of them):

```
apply (X, 2, sum)


[1] 10 26 42 58 74 90
```

Note that in both cases, the answer produced by `apply` () is a vector rather than a matrix. We can `apply` () functions to the individual elements of the matrix rather than to the margins. The margin we specify influences only the way the resulting matrix is presented (`sqrt` () is the square root function).

```
apply (X, 1, sqrt)

          [,1]      [,2]      [,3]      [,4]
[1,] 1.000000 1.414214 1.732051 2.000000
[2,] 2.236068 2.449490 2.645751 2.828427
[3,] 3.000000 3.162278 3.316625 3.464102
[4,] 3.605551 3.741657 3.872983 4.000000
[5,] 4.123106 4.242641 4.358899 4.472136
[6,] 4.582576 4.690416 4.795832 4.898979

apply (X, 2, sqrt)

          [,1]      [,2]      [,3]      [,4]      [,5]      [,6]
[1,] 1.000000 2.236068 3.000000 3.605551 4.123106 4.582576
[2,] 1.414214 2.449490 3.162278 3.741657 4.242641 4.690416
[3,] 1.732051 2.645751 3.316625 3.872983 4.358899 4.795832
[4,] 2.000000 2.828427 3.464102 4.000000 4.472136 4.898979
```

Here are the numbers from each of the rows, randomised using `sample ()` without replacement:

```
apply (X, 2, sample)

     [,1] [,2] [,3] [,4] [,5] [,6]
[1,]    3    5   10   16   19   24
[2,]    1    7    9   13   18   21
[3,]    4    6   12   14   20   23
[4,]    2    8   11   15   17   22
```

Note that the resulting matrix has six rows and four columns (i.e. it has been transposed): change the margin to have the output in the original shape.

We can supply our own function definition (here $x^2 + x$) within `apply ()` like this:

```
apply (X, 1, function(x) x^2 + x)

     [,1] [,2] [,3] [,4]
[1,]    2    6   12   20
[2,]   30   42   56   72
[3,]   90  110  132  156
[4,]  182  210  240  272
[5,]  306  342  380  420
[6,]  462  506  552  600
```

This is an **anonymous** function because the function is not named.

3.11.7 Scaling a matrix

For a numeric matrix, we might want to scale the values of the columns so that each has a mean of 0. We might want to go further by scaling the columns so that they have mean 0 *and* a standard deviation of 1. These two actions can be carried out by using `scale ()`. Take the following matrix, for example:

```
mat_a <- matrix (c (1, -2, 5, 4, 15, -8, 1, 10, 19), ncol = 3)
mat_a

       [,1] [,2] [,3]
[1,]    1    4    1
[2,]   -2   15   10
[3,]    5   -8   19
```

If we wanted to linearly scale the matrix `mat_a` so that the columns have mean zero, then we would need:

```
scale (mat_a, scale = FALSE)

           [,1]           [,2] [,3]
[1,] -0.3333333    0.3333333   -9
[2,] -3.3333333   11.3333333    0
[3,]  3.6666667  -11.6666667    9
attr(,"scaled:center")
[1]   1.333333   3.666667 10.000000
```

The output tells us the original mean value for each column. This was then subtracted from the relevant column to produce zero-mean columns.

If we want to scale the matrix so that each column has mean zero and standard deviation of 1, then we need:

```
scale (mat_a)

           [,1]           [,2] [,3]
[1,] -0.0949158    0.02897638   -1
[2,] -0.9491580    0.98519690    0
[3,]  1.0440738   -1.01417328    1
attr(,"scaled:center")
[1]   1.333333   3.666667 10.000000
attr(,"scaled:scale")
[1]   3.511885  11.503623  9.000000
```

This time, the output gives us the mean and standard deviation of each original column, which were then used to scale the matrix as requested.

3.11.8   Using the `max.col ()` function

The task is to work out the number of plots on which a species is dominant in the Park Grass dataframe. This involves scanning each row of a matrix and reporting on the column number that contains the maximum value.

```
pgfull <- read.table ("pgfull.txt", header = T)
names (pgfull)
```

```
 [1] "AC"        "AE"        "AM"        "AO"        "AP"        "AR"
 [7] "AS"        "AU"        "BH"        "BM"        "CC"        "CF"
[13] "CM"        "CN"        "CX"        "CY"        "DC"        "DG"
[19] "ER"        "FM"        "FP"        "FR"        "GV"        "HI"
[25] "HL"        "HP"        "HS"        "HR"        "KA"        "LA"
[31] "LC"        "LH"        "LM"        "LO"        "LP"        "OR"
[37] "PL"        "PP"        "PS"        "PT"        "QR"        "RA"
[43] "RB"        "RC"        "SG"        "SM"        "SO"        "TF"
[49] "TG"        "TO"        "TP"        "TR"        "VC"        "VK"
[55] "plot"      "lime"      "richness"  "hay"       "pH"
```

```
pgfull[1:6, 1:6]
```

```
      AC   AE   AM   AO   AP   AR
1   2.51 1.18 0.45 0.91 0.47 0.00
2   6.85 0.10 0.58 1.02 0.35 0.00
3  10.58 0.11 0.21 1.85 0.00 0.00
4  13.65 0.00 0.00 6.46 0.00 0.00
5   4.84 0.00 1.49 0.36 0.10 0.06
6   4.30 0.32 1.72 1.61 0.09 0.03
```

The species names are represented by 54 two-letter codes (so, for example, 'AC' is *Agrostis capillaris*), and the numerical values, biomass. There are also various other bits of data at the right-hand side. We define the dominant as the species that has the maximum biomass on a given plot. The first task is to reduce the data so that we only have the species abundances (we do not want the plot numbers, or the treatments, or the values of any covariates). For the Park Grass data, the first 54 columns contain species abundance values, so we select all of the rows in the first 54 columns like this:

```
species <- pgfull[,1:54]
```

Now we use the function `max.col` () to go through all of the 89 rows, and for each row return the column number that contains the maximum biomass:

```
max.col (species)
```

```
 [1] 22 22 22  1 32 32 22  1 22 22 22  1 22 22  1  1 22 22 22  4  2  2 51  2  1
[26]  1 22 22  1  1  2  5  1  4  2  2  1  4 22 22 22  4  2  2 25 25  2  2  5 25
[51] 32  1 22 22  2  2  1  1 51  2  2 27  2  2  2  2 35 51 51  1  2  2  1  1 32
[76] 32  1  1  1  1  1  1 14  1  2  1  1  2  2
```

To get the identity of the dominant, we then extract the name of this column, using the index returned by the above as a subscript to the object called `species`:

```
names (species)[max.col (species)]
```

```
 [1] "FR" "FR" "FR" "AC" "LH" "LH" "FR" "AC" "FR" "FR" "FR" "AC" "FR" "FR" "AC"
```

```
[16]  "AC"  "FR"  "FR"  "FR"  "AO"  "AE"  "AE"  "TP"  "AE"  "AC"  "AC"  "FR"  "FR"  "AC"  "AC"
[31]  "AE"  "AP"  "AC"  "AO"  "AE"  "AE"  "AC"  "AO"  "FR"  "FR"  "FR"  "AO"  "AE"  "AE"  "HL"
[46]  "HL"  "AE"  "AE"  "AP"  "HL"  "LH"  "AC"  "FR"  "FR"  "AE"  "AE"  "AC"  "AC"  "TP"  "AE"
[61]  "AE"  "HS"  "AE"  "AE"  "AE"  "AE"  "LP"  "TP"  "TP"  "AC"  "AE"  "AE"  "AC"  "AC"  "LH"
[76]  "LH"  "AC"  "AC"  "AC"  "AC"  "AC"  "AC"  "CN"  "AC"  "AE"  "AC"  "AC"  "AE"  "AE"
```

Finally, we use `table ()` to count up the total number of plots on which each species was dominant. The code looks like this

```
table (names (species) [max.col (species)])

AC AE AO AP CN FR HL HS LH LP TP
26 23  4  2  1 19  3  1  5  1  4
```

So AC was dominant on more plots than any other species, with AE in second place and FR in third. The total number of species that were dominant on one or more plots is given by determining the length of this table:

```
length (table (names (species) [max.col (species)]))


[1] 11
```

So the number of species that were present in the system, but never attained dominance was $54 - 11 = 43$.

There is no such function as min.col (), but we can easily emulate it by using `max.col ()` with the negatives of our data. It makes no sense to do it with this example, because several species are absent from every plot, and the function would just pick one of the absent species at random (i.e. in the event of a tie). But, anyway, just to see how it works:

```
max.col (-species)

 [1]  30 16 23 43 54 36 53 52 45 53 52 49  6 54 28 20 11 16 29 54 20 41 31 43  8
[26]  39 45 45 21 54 20  6 17 39 31 12 23 21 52 19 32 14 20 51 12 17  8 32 16 51
[51]  41  7 48  5 47 43 19 41 19 46 48 29 15 14 16 34 17 45 43 16 15 52 10 23 20
[76]  20 46 49  7 43 19 21 52 29 53 23 31 10  8
```

picks out the identity (the column number) of one of the zeros from each row. In a case where there was a unique minimum in each row, then this would find it.

3.11.9 Restructuring a multi-dimensional array using `aperm` ()

There are circumstances where we may want to reorder the dimensions of an array. Here is an example of an array with three dimensions: two sexes, three ages, and four income groups. For simplicity and ease of illustration, the values in the array are just the numbers 1–24 in order ($2 \times 3 \times 4 = 24$):

```
toy_data <- array (1:24, 2:4)
```

The second argument to the `array ()` function specifies the number of levels in dimensions 1, 2, and 3 using the sequence-generator `2:4` to produce the numbers 2, 3, and 4. This is what the array looks like:

```
toy_data

, , 1

     [,1] [,2] [,3]
[1,]    1    3    5
[2,]    2    4    6

,, 2

     [,1] [,2] [,3]
[1,]    7    9   11
[2,]    8   10   12

, , 3

     [,1] [,2] [,3]
[1,]   13   15   17
[2,]   14   16   18

, , 4

     [,1] [,2] [,3]
[1,]   19   21   23
[2,]   20   22   24
```

There are four sub-tables, each with 2 rows and 3 columns. Now we give names to the factor levels in each of the three dimensions: these are called the `dimnames ()` attributes, and each one is allocated as a `list ()` like this:

```
dimnames (toy_data)[[1]] <- list ("male", "female")
dimnames (toy_data)[[2]] <- list ("young", "mid", "old")
dimnames (toy_data)[[3]] <- list ("A", "B", "C", "D")
dimnames (toy_data)

[[1]]
[1] "male"    "female"

[[2]]
[1] "young" "mid"    "old"

[[3]]
[1] "A" "B" "C" "D"
```

We can see the advantage of naming the dimensions by comparing the output of the array with (below) and without names (above):

```
toy_data

, , A

       young mid old
male       1   3   5
female     2   4   6

, , B

       young mid old
male       7   9  11
female     8  10  12

, , C

       young mid old
male      13  15  17
female    14  16  18

, , D

       young mid old
male      19  21  23
female    20  22  24
```

Suppose, however, that we want the four income groups (A–D) to be the columns in each of the sub-tables, and the separate sub-tables to represent the two genders. This is a job for `aperm ()`. We need to specify the order *age, then income, then gender* in terms of the order of their dimensions (row, column, sub-table, namely 2, then 3, then 1) like this:

```
new_toy_data <- aperm (toy_data, c (2, 3, 1))
new_toy_data

,, male

       A  B  C  D
young  1  7 13 19
mid    3  9 15 21
old    5 11 17 23

,, female

       A  B  C  D
young  2  8 14 20
mid    4 10 16 22
old    6 12 18 24
```

This can be tricky to see at first, but `aperm ()` is a very useful function, so it's worth persevering.

3.12   Random numbers, sampling, and shuffling

When debugging or testing a program, it is often useful to use some randomly generated data. We have already seen a few functions which can do this, `rpois ()` and `sample ()`, for instance. If problems arise, then it can be helpful to get the same string of random numbers as last time. We can use the `set.seed ()` function to control this using our favourite integer as the **seed** to repeat what we get

```
set.seed (375)
runif (3)

[1] 0.9613669 0.6918535 0.7302684

runif (3)

[1] 0.9228566 0.1603804 0.9642799

runif (3)

[1] 0.52880907 0.08660864 0.29075809
```

The `runif ()` function generates randomly from $(0, 1)$, and we get a different set of three each time. If we reset the seed with the same value, we get the same random numbers as last time:

```
set.seed (375)
runif (3)

[1] 0.9613669 0.6918535 0.7302684

runif (3)

[1] 0.9228566 0.1603804 0.9642799

runif (3)

[1] 0.52880907 0.08660864 0.29075809
```

R generates these random data in a sequence, so once we start at the same point, we will continue with the same sequence. The current state of the seed (a vector of numbers) is given by `.Random.seed`, *and it should not be altered*:

```
.Random.seed[1:4]

[1]        10403        9  1743958520 -1985855194

length (.Random.seed)

[1] 626
```

Randomisation is central to a great many scientific and statistical procedures (and is often referred to using the phrase **Monte Carlo**). Generating random numbers from a variety of probability distributions is explained in, for instance, Section 8.3.1. Here we are concerned with randomising (shuffling or sampling from) the elements of a vector, as we might use when planning a designed experiment (e.g. allocating treatments to individuals). There are two ways of sampling:

- sampling **without replacement**, where some or all of the values in the vector appear in the output, but in a randomised sequence; i.e. the values have been shuffled;

- sampling **with replacement**, where some values may be omitted, and other values appear more than once in the output.

3.12.1 The `sample` () function

The default `sample` () function shuffles the contents of a vector into a random sequence while maintaining all the numerical values intact. It is extremely useful for randomisation in experimental design, in simulation, and in computationally intensive hypothesis testing. The vector *y* looks like this:

```
y <- c (8, 3, 5, 7, 6, 6, 8, 9, 2, 3, 9, 4, 10, 4, 11)
```

Here are two different shufflings:

```
sample (y)
```

```
[1]  3 11  9  7  6  8  6  3  9  5  4  2  4  8 10
```

```
sample (y)
```

```
[1]  3  4  3 11  2 10  5  9  4  7  6  8  6  8  9
```

The order of the values is different each time `sample` () is invoked (well, it will repeat but rarely if *y* is not small), but the same numbers are shuffled in every case, and all the numbers in the original vector appear once in the output (so if there are two 9s in the original data, there will be two 9s in the shuffled vector). This is sampling without replacement. We can specify the size of the sample we want as an optional second argument. Suppose we want five random elements from *y*, in any one sample:

```
sample (y, 5)
```

```
[1]  3  2  9 10  6
```

```
sample (y, 5)
```

```
[1]  6  2  6 11  3
```

The argument `replace = T` allows for sampling with replacement, which is the basis of bootstrap-ping (see Section 9.4 for instance). The default vector produced by the `sample ()` function with `replace = T` is the same length as the vector sampled, but some values are left out at random and other values, again at random, appear two or more times:

```
set.seed (888)
sample (y, replace = T)

[1]  9   8 11   9   9   8   5   3   8   3   3   6   8   8   9
```

We have set a seed so that we know that, for instance, 10 does not appear, but 9 appears four times (as opposed to twice in *y*). In this next case, there are three 10s and no 9s:

```
sample (y, replace = T)

[1]  8   8   6   2   5   3 11   7   4   4   3 10 10 10   2
```

More advanced options in `sample ()` include specifying different probabilities with which each element is to be sampled (`prob =`): so far, each number has been chosen with equal probability. For example, if we want to take four numbers at random from the sequence 1:10 without replacement where the probability of selection is 5 times greater for the middle numbers (5 and 6) than for the first or last numbers, and we want to do this five times, we could write:

```
p <- c (1, 2, 3, 4, 5, 5, 4, 3, 2, 1)
x <- 1:10
sapply (1:5, function(i) sample (x, 4, prob = p))

     [,1] [,2] [,3] [,4] [,5]
[1,]    9    5    4    6    7
[2,]    5    1    5    2    5
[3,]    4    7    7    8    3
[4,]    6    4    8    7    4
```

The probabilities are normalised so that they add up to 1. The four random numbers in the first trial are in the first column, etc. To learn more about `sapply ()`, see Section 3.11.6.

3.13   Loops and repeats

The classic, Fortran-like loop is available in *R*. The syntax is a little different, but the idea is identical; we request that an index, *i*, takes on a sequence of values, and that one or more lines of commands are executed as many times as there are different values of *i*. Here is a loop executed five times with the values of *i* from 1 to 5; we print the square of each value:

```
for (i in 1:5) {
  print (i^2)
}
```

```
[1]  1
[1]  4
[1]  9
[1]  16
[1]  25
```

The `for ()` statement introduces the loop with obvious meaning. It is good practice always to use curly brackets { } to enclose material over which the loop is to work (they can be avoided if all the details of the loop are put in the same line as the `for ()` statement, but then it is very difficult to read). It is also good practice to put each element from the loop on a separate line and indent them all, as this helps once we have multiple loops. The final { should also be on a separate line:

```
j <- 0
k <- 0
for (i in 1:5) {
  j <- j + 1
  k <- k + i * j
  print(i + j + k)
}
```

```
[1]  3
[1]  9
[1]  20
[1]  38
[1]  65
```

Here we use a for loop to write a function (see Section 3.18) to calculate factorial x (written $x!$) which is

$$x! = x \times (x - 1) \times (x - 2) \times (x - 3) \times \cdots \times 2 \times 1.$$

So $4! = 4 \times 3 \times 2 = 24$. Here is the function:

```
fac1 <- function (x) {
  f <- 1
  if (x < 2) return (1)
  for (i in 2:x) {
    f <- f * i
  }
  f
}
```

That seems rather complicated for such a simple task, but let us show it works first:

```
fac1 (12)
```

```
[1]  479001600
```

We can also try it out for the numbers 0–5 and compare it with *R*'s alternative:

```
sapply (0:5, fac1)

[1]    1    1    2    6   24 120

factorial (0:5)

[1]    1    1    2    6   24 120
```

There are two other functions which introduce loops in *R*: repeat () and while (). We demonstrate their use for the purpose of illustration, but we can do much better in terms of writing a compact function for finding factorials (see below). First, the while () function:

```
fac2 <- function (x) {
  f <- 1
  t <- x
  while (t > 1) {
    f <- f * t
    t <- t - 1
  }
  f
}
```

The key point is that if we want to use while (), we need to set up an indicator variable (*t* in this case) and change its value *within* each iteration (t <- t-1). We test the function on the numbers 0–5:

```
sapply (0:5, fac2)

[1]    1    1    2    6   24 120
```

Finally, we demonstrate the use of the repeat () function:

```
fac3 <- function (x) {
  f <- 1
  t <- x
  repeat {
    if (t < 2) break
    f <- f*t
    t <- t-1
  }
  f
}
```

Because the repeat () function contains no explicit limit, we need to be careful not to program an infinite loop. We must include a logical escape clause that leads to a break command and, frankly, is not good programming practice: aim to use `for ()` or `while ()`:

```
sapply (0:5, fac3)
```

```
[1]   1   1   2   6   24  120
```

If possible, it is always better (i.e. quicker) to use a built-in function that operates on the entire vector and hence removes the need for loops or repeats of any sort. In this case, we can make use of the cumulative product function, `cumprod ()`. Here it is in action:

```
cumprod (1:5)
```

```
[1]   1   2   6   24  120
```

This is already pretty close to what we need for our factorial function. It does not work for 0! of course, because the whole vector would end up full of zeros if the first element in the vector was zero (try `cumprod (1:5)` and see). The factorial of $x > 0$ is the maximum value from the vector produced by `cumprod`:

```
fac4 <- function(x) {
   max (cumprod (1:x))
}
```

This definition has the desirable side effect that it also gets 0! correct, because when x is 0 the function finds the maximum of 1 and 0 which is 1.

```
max (cumprod (1:0))
```

```
[1] 1
```

```
sapply (0:5, fac4)
```

```
[1]   1   1   2   6   24  120
```

3.13.1   More complicated `while ()` loops

Here is a function (see Section 3.18) that uses the `while ()` function in converting a specified integer to its binary representation (i.e. in base 2, so as a combination of 0s and 1s). As with decimals, the smallest digit (0 for even or 1 for odd numbers) is always at the right-hand side of the answer (in location 32 in this case):

```
binary <- function (x) {
   i <- 0
   string <- numeric (32)
   while (x > 0) {
      string[32-i] <- x %% 2
```

```
      x <- x %/% 2
      i <- i + 1
    }
  first <- match (1, string)
  string[first:32]
}
```

At each step we take the remainder when dividing by 2 to create a digit and then carry on with the preceding value over 2. The value `first` represents the position where we have arrived at the value 1 which must begin our output as leading zeros within the string are not printed. We run the function to find the binary representation of the numbers 15–17:

```
sapply (15:17, binary)

[[1]]
[1] 1 1 1 1

[[2]]
[1] 1 0 0 0 0

[[3]]
[1] 1 0 0 0 1
```

The next function uses `while ()` to generate the Fibonacci series 1, 1, 2, 3, 5, 8, … in which each term is the sum of its two immediate predecessors. The key point about `while ()` loops is that the logical variable controlling their operation is altered inside the loop. In this example, we alter n, the number whose Fibonacci number we want, reducing the value of n by 1 each time around the loop, and ending when it hits 0. Here is the code:

```
fibonacci <- function (n) {
  a <- 1
  b <- 0
  while (n > 0) {
    swap <- a
    a <- a + b
    b <- swap
    n <- n - 1
  }
  b
}
```

An important general point about writing loops involves the use of the `swap` variable above. When we replace a by $a + b$ on line 6, we lose the original value of a. If we had not stored this value in `swap`, we could not set the new value of b to the old value of a. Now we can test the function by generating the Fibonacci numbers 1–10:

```
sapply (1:10, fibonacci)

[1]  1  1  2  3  5  8 13 21 34 55
```

3.13.2 Loop avoidance

It is good *R* programming practice to avoid using loops wherever possible, particularly as in *R* they can be slow. The use of vector functions (Section 3.10) makes this particularly straightforward in many cases. Suppose that we wanted to replace all of the negative values in an array by zeros. We could write a loop:

```
y <- c (1, 3, -2, 0, -6, 17)
for (i in 1:length (y)) {
  if (y[i] < 0) {
    y[i] <- 0
  }
}
y
```

```
[1]  1  3  0  0  0 17
```

Now, however, we can use logical subscripts like this:

```
y <- c (1, 3, -2, 0, -6, 17)
y[y < 0] <- 0
y
```

```
[1]  1  3  0  0  0 17
```

Another useful function in avoiding loops is `ifelse ()`. Sometimes we want to do one thing if a condition is true and a different thing if the condition is false (rather than do nothing, as in the last example). The `ifelse ()` function allows us to do this for entire vectors without using `for ()` or other loops. We might want to replace any negative values of *y* by −1 and any positive values and zero by +1:

```
y <- c (1, 3, -2, 0, -6, 17)
z <- ifelse (y < 0, -1, 1)
z
```

```
[1]  1  1 -1  1 -1  1
```

Next we use `ifelse ()` to convert the continuous variable called `Area` in the dataset `worms` into a new, two-level factor with values `big` and `small` defined by the median `Area` of the fields:

```
worms <- read.table ("worms.txt", header = T)
head (worms)
```

	Field.Name	Area	Slope	Vegetation	Soil.pH	Damp	Worm.density
1	Nashs.Field	3.6	11	Grassland	4.1	FALSE	4
2	Silwood.Bottom	5.1	2	Arable	5.2	FALSE	7
3	Nursery.Field	2.8	3	Grassland	4.3	FALSE	2
4	Rush.Meadow	2.4	5	Meadow	4.9	TRUE	5

```
5 Gunness.Thicket  3.8    0      Scrub    4.2 FALSE              6
6         Oak.Mead  3.1    2  Grassland   3.9 FALSE              2
```

```
ifelse (worms$Area > median (worms$Area), "big", "small")
```

```
 [1] "big"   "big"   "small" "small" "big"   "big"   "big"   "small" "small"
[10] "small" "small" "big"   "big"   "small" "big"   "big"   "small" "big"
[19] "small" "small"
```

We should use the much more powerful function called cut () when we want to convert a continuous variable like Area into many levels (see Section 3.3).

Another use of ifelse () is to override *R*'s natural inclinations. The log of zero in *R*, and mathematics, is -Inf, as we see in these 20 random numbers from a Poisson process with a mean count of 1.5:

```
set.seed (25660)
(y <- log (rpois (20, 1.5)))
```

```
 [1] 0.0000000       -Inf 0.6931472 0.0000000 0.0000000 0.6931472 0.0000000
 [8] 0.0000000 1.0986123 0.0000000      -Inf      -Inf 0.0000000 0.0000000
[15]      -Inf      -Inf 0.6931472      -Inf 0.6931472 0.0000000
```

However, if we want the log of zero to be represented by NA in our particular application, we can write:

```
ifelse (y < 0, NA, y)
```

```
 [1] 0.0000000        NA 0.6931472 0.0000000 0.0000000 0.6931472 0.0000000
 [8] 0.0000000 1.0986123 0.0000000        NA        NA 0.0000000 0.0000000
[15]        NA        NA 0.6931472        NA 0.6931472 0.0000000
```

3.13.3 The slowness of loops

To see how slow loops can be in *R*, we compare two ways of finding the maximum number in a vector of 10 million random numbers from a uniform distribution:

```
x <- runif (10000000)
```

First, using the vector function max ():

```
system.time (max(x))
```

```
user  system elapsed
0.02    0.00    0.01
```

As we see, this operation took just 0.01 seconds to look at the 10 million numbers in *x*. Using a loop, however, took nearly many times longer:

```
pc <- proc.time ()
cmax <- x[1]
for (i in 2:10000000) {
  if (x[i] > cmax) {
    cmax <- x[i]
  }
}
proc.time() - pc

  user   system elapsed
0.29    0.00     0.30
```

The functions `system.time` and `proc.time` produce a vector of three numbers, showing the user, system, and total elapsed times for the currently running *R* process. It is the third number (elapsed time for the calculation) that is typically the most useful.

The take home message from the section so far is

With a large dataset or long program, do everything possible to avoid loops.

Unfortunately, that is not always possible.

3.13.4   Do not 'grow' data sets by concatenation or recursive function calls

Here is an extreme example of what *not* to do. We want to create a vector containing 100 000 numbers in sequence from 1 to 100 000. First, the quickest way using the built-in sequence generator:

```
test1 <- function () {
  y <- 1:100000
}
```

Now we obtain the same result using a loop, where we tell *R* in advance how long the final vector is going to be, using the `numeric ()` function. This is called **pre-allocation** and was (is) a key activity in low-level programming languages.

```
test2 <- function () {
  y <- numeric (100000)
  for (i in 1:100000) {
    y[i] <- i
  }
}
```

Finally, the most inefficient way. Each time we go round the loop, we concatenate the new value onto the right-hand end of the vector that has been created up to this point. We start with a NULL vector, then build it up, one step at a time, which looks like a neat idea, but is extremely inefficient, because changing the size of a vector takes roughly the same size as setting a vector up from scratch, and we change the length of our vector 100 000 times in this example. This ill-advised procedure is called **re-dimensioning**.

```
test3 <- function () {
  y <- NULL
  for (i in 1:100000) {
    y <- c (y, i)
  }
}
```

To compare the efficiency of the three methods, we shall work out how long each takes to complete the task. We shall use the function called `system.time` () as described in Section 3.13.3:

```
system.time (test1 ())

   user  system elapsed
0       0       0

system.time (test2 ())

   user  system elapsed
0       0       0

system.time (test3 ())

   user  system elapsed
7.08    0.06    7.14
```

The first two methods are so lightening fast that they do not even register on the clock. In contrast, the last method, where we grew the vector at each iteration, is comparatively slow. Another moral:*Do not grow vectors by repeated concatenation*.

3.13.5 Loops for producing time series

Wherever we can, we use vectorised functions in *R* because this leads to compact, efficient and easily readable code. Sometimes, however, we need to resort to using loops. Suppose we are interested in the dynamics of a population which is governed by two parameters: the per capita reproductive rate (λ) and the maximum supportable population (N_{max}), which for convenience we shall set to 1.0. Next year's population $N(t + 1)$ is given by this year's population, $N(t)$, multiplied by λ, multiplied again by the fraction of N_{max} that is currently unrealised (i.e. $(N_{max} - N(t))/N_{max} = 1 - N(t)$ in the current case). Thus, we have a difference equation:

$$N(t + 1) = \lambda N(t)[1 - N(t)].$$

To simulate the dynamics of this population in *R*, we start by writing the difference equation as a function:

```
next_year <- function (x) {
  lambda * x * (1 - x)
}
```

So if we begin with a population of $N = 0.6$ and set $\lambda = 3.7$, we can predict next year's population like this

```
lambda <- 3.7
next_year (0.6)
```

```
[1] 0.888
```

The population has increased by 48% (0.888/0.6 = 1.48). What happens in the second year?

```
next_year (0.888)
```

```
[1] 0.3679872
```

The population crashes to less than half its previous value. We could go on repeating these calculations, modelling year after year, but this is an obvious case where using a loop would be the best solution, as we need to know the previous result before we can calculate the next one. Let us assume that we want to model the population over 20 years. It is good practice in cases like this to define a vector to contain the 20 population sizes at the outset as we saw in Section 3.13.2:

```
N <- numeric (20)
```

We set the initial population size (0.6) like this:

```
N[1] <- 0.6
```

Now if we run through a loop to simulate years 2 through 20 using an index called t (for time), we can invoke the function called `next_year` () repeatedly, employing t as a subscript like this:

```
for (t in 2:20) {
  N[t] <- next_year (N[t-1])
}
```

Finally, we might want to plot a time series of the population dynamics over the course of 20 years, to give Figure 3.2.

```
plot (N, type = "l", col = hue_pal ()(1))
```

This famous difference equation is known as the **quadratic map**, and it played a central role in the development of chaos theory. For large values of λ (as we used in the example above), the function is capable of producing series of numbers that are, to all intents and purposes, random. This led to a definition of **chaos** as behaviour that exhibited *extreme sensitivity to initial conditions*: tiny differences in initial population size would lead to radically different time series in population dynamics.

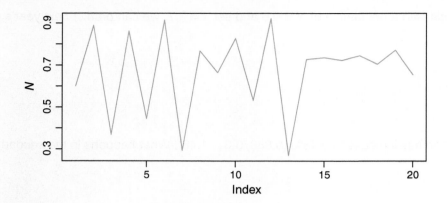

Figure 3.2 The quadratic map.

3.14 Lists

Lists are extremely important objects in *R*. We might come across the problems of 'comparing apples and oranges' or how two things are 'as different as chalk and cheese'. We can think of lists as a way of getting around these problems. Here are four completely different objects: a numeric vector, a logical vector, a vector of character strings, and a vector of complex numbers:

```
apples <- c (4, 4.5, 4.2, 5.1, 3.9)
oranges <- c (TRUE, TRUE, FALSE)
chalk <- c ("limestone", "marl","oolite", "CaC03")
cheese <- c (3.2 - 4.5i, 12.8 + 2.2i)
```

We cannot bundle them together into a matrix or dataframe (see Section 4.5), because the vectors are of different lengths, and this results in an error message:

```
data.frame (apples, oranges, chalk, cheese)

Error in data.frame(apples, oranges, chalk, cheese): arguments imply differ-
ing number of rows: 5, 3, 4, 2
```

Despite their differences, however, we can bundle them together in a single list called `items`:

```
items <- list (apples, oranges, chalk, cheese)
items

[[1]]
[1] 4.0 4.5 4.2 5.1 3.9

[[2]]
[1]  TRUE  TRUE FALSE
```

```
[[3]]
[1] "limestone" "marl"        "oolite"     "CaC03"

[[4]]
[1]   3.2-4.5i 12.8+2.2i
```

Subscripts on vectors, matrices, arrays, and dataframes have one set of square brackets [6], [3, 4], or [2, 3, 2, 1], but subscripts on lists have double square brackets, [[2]] or [[*i*, *j*]]. If we want to extract chalk from the list, we use subscript [[3]]:

```
items[[3]]
```

```
[1] "limestone" "marl"        "oolite"     "CaC03"
```

If we want to extract the third element within chalk (oolite), then we use single subscripts *after* the double subscripts like this:

```
items[[3]][3]
```

```
[1] "oolite"
```

R is forgiving about failure to use double brackets on their own, but not when we try to access a component of an object within a list:

```
items[3]
```

```
[[1]]
[1] "limestone" "marl"        "oolite"     "CaC03"
```

```
items[3][3]
```

```
[[1]]
NULL
```

There is another indexing convention in *R* which is used to extract named components from lists using the element names operator $. This is known as **indexing tagged lists**. For this to work, the elements of the list must have names. At the moment our list called items has no names:

```
names (items)
```

```
NULL
```

We can give names to the elements of a list in the function that creates the list by using the equals sign like this:

```
items <- list (first = apples, second = oranges, third = chalk, fourth = cheese)
```

Now we can extract elements of the list by name:

```
items$fourth

[1]  3.2-4.5i 12.8+2.2i

items$third[2]

[1]  "marl"
```

3.14.1 Summarising lists and `lapply ()`

We can ask a variety of questions about our new list object:

```
class (items)

[1]  "list"

mode (items)

[1]  "list"

is.numeric (items)

[1]  FALSE

is.list (items)

[1]  TRUE

length (items)

[1]  4
```

Note that the length of a list is the number of items in the list, not the lengths of the individual vectors within the list.

We have already seen the use of `tapply ()`, `apply ()` and `sapply ()` to various objects: `lapply ()` does the same thing but for lists: it applies a function to each element in turn, outputting a list. For instance, we might want to know how many elements comprise each component of the list. Technically, we want to know the length of each of the vectors making up the list:

```
lapply (items, length)

$first
[1] 5
```

```
$second
[1] 3

$third
[1] 4

$fourth
[1] 2
```

This shows that `items` consists of four vectors and shows that there were five elements in the first vector, 3 in the second 4 in the third and 2 in the fourth. But 5 of what, and 3 of what? To find out, we apply the function `class` () to the list:

```
lapply (items, class)

$first
[1] "numeric"

$second
[1] "logical"

$third
[1] "character"

$fourth
[1] "complex"
```

So the answer is there were five numbers in the first vector, three logical variables in the second, four character strings in the third vector, and two complex numbers in the fourth.

Applying numeric functions to lists will only work for objects of class `numeric` or `complex`, or objects (like logical values) that can be coerced into numbers. Here is what happens when we try to apply the function `mean` () to `items`:

```
lapply (items, mean)

Warning in mean.default(X[[i]], ...): argument is not numeric or logical:
returning NA

$first
[1] 4.34

$second
[1] 0.6666667

$third
[1] NA

$fourth
[1] 8-1.15i
```

We get a warning message pointing out that the third vector cannot be coerced to a number (it is not numeric, complex or logical), so `NA` appears in the output. The second vector produces the answer 2/3 because logical false (`FALSE`) is coerced to numeric 0 and logical true (`TRUE`) is coerced to numeric 1.

The `summary ()` function works for lists:

```
summary (items)

        Length Class  Mode
first   5      -none- numeric
second  3      -none- logical
third   4      -none- character
fourth  2      -none- complex
```

However, the most useful overview of the contents of a list is obtained with `str ()`, the structure function:

```
str (items)

List of 4
 $ first: num [1:5] 4 4.5 4.2 5.1 3.9
 $ second: logi [1:3] TRUE TRUE FALSE
 $ third: chr [1:4] "limestone" "marl" "oolite" "CaC03"
 $ fourth: cplx [1:2] 3.2-4.5i 12.8+2.2i
```

3.14.2 Manipulating and saving lists

Saving lists to files is tricky because lists typically have different numbers of items in each row so we cannot use, for instance, `write.table ()`. Here is a dataframe on species presence (1) or absence (0) in various locations, with species' Latin binomials in the first column as the row names:

```
pa <- read.csv ("pa.csv", row.names = 1)
pa
```

	Carmel	Derry	Daneswall	Erith	Foggen	Highbury	Slatewell
Bartsia alpina	0	0	1	0	0	0	1
Cleome serrulata	1	1	0	0	0	1	0
Conopodium majus	0	0	0	0	0	0	0
Corydalis sempervirens	1	0	0	1	0	1	0
Nitella flexilis	1	0	0	0	0	0	0
Ranunculus baudotii	1	0	1	1	0	0	0
Rhododendron luteum	1	1	1	1	1	0	1
Rodgersia podophylla	0	1	0	0	0	1	0
Tiarella wherryi	0	0	1	1	1	0	0
Veronica opaca	1	0	0	0	0	1	1

	Uppington	York
Bartsia alpina	0	0
Cleome serrulata	0	0

Conopodium majus	1	1
Corydalis sempervirens	0	0
Nitella flexilis	0	1
Ranunculus baudotii	1	0
Rhododendron luteum	1	1
Rodgersia podophylla	0	0
Tiarella wherryi	0	0
Veronica opaca	1	0

Two kinds of operations, we might want to do with a like this are

- produce lists of the sites at which each species is found;
- produce lists of the species found in any given site.

We shall do each of these tasks in turn.

The problem is that the numbers of place names differ from species to species, and the numbers of species differ from place to place. However, it is easy to create a list (as different elements will have differing lengths) showing the column numbers that contain locations for each species:

```
lapply (1:10, function (i) which (pa[i,] > 0))

[[1]]
[1]  3  7

[[2]]
[1]  1  2  6

[[3]]
[1]  8  9

[[4]]
[1]  1  4  6

[[5]]
[1]  1  9

[[6]]
[1]  1  3  4  8

[[7]]
[1]  1  2  3  4  5  7  8  9

[[8]]
[1]  2  6

[[9]]
[1]  3  4  5

[[10]]
[1]  1  6  7  8
```

This indicates that *Bartsia alpina* (the first species) is found in locations 3 and 7 (Daneswall and Slatewell): for each of the 10 species, we ask which of them is present or TRUE. We can extract the column names at which each species is present, using the elements selected above as subscripts on the `colnames ()` of data, like this:

```
lapply (1:10, function (i) colnames (pa)[pa[i,] > 0])


[[1]]
[1] "Daneswall" "Slatewell"

[[2]]
[1] "Carmel"    "Derry"     "Highbury"

[[3]]
[1] "Uppington" "York"

[[4]]
[1] "Carmel"    "Erith"     "Highbury"

[[5]]
[1] "Carmel" "York"

[[6]]
[1] "Carmel"    "Daneswall" "Erith"     "Uppington"

[[7]]
[1] "Carmel"    "Derry"     "Daneswall" "Erith"     "Foggen"    "Slatewell"
[7] "Uppington" "York"

[[8]]
[1] "Derry"     "Highbury"

[[9]]
[1] "Daneswall" "Erith"     "Foggen"

[[10]]
[1] "Carmel"    "Highbury"  "Slatewell" "Uppington"
```

This completes the first task.

The second task is to get species lists for each location. We apply a similar method to extract the appropriate species (this time using `rownames (pa)`):

```
sapply (1:9, function (j) rownames (pa)[pa[,j] > 0])


[[1]]
[1] "Cleome serrulata"       "Corydalis sempervirens" "Nitella flexilis"
[4] "Ranunculus baudotii"    "Rhododendron luteum"    "Veronica opaca"

[[2]]
[1] "Cleome serrulata"       "Rhododendron luteum"   "Rodgersia podophylla"
```

```
[[3]]
[1] "Bartsia alpina"       "Ranunculus baudotii" "Rhododendron luteum"
[4] "Tiarella wherryi"

[[4]]
[1] "Corydalis sempervirens" "Ranunculus baudotii"    "Rhododendron luteum"
[4] "Tiarella wherryi"

[[5]]
[1] "Rhododendron luteum" "Tiarella wherryi"

[[6]]
[1] "Cleome serrulata"       "Corydalis sempervirens" "Rodgersia podophylla"
[4] "Veronica opaca"

[[7]]
[1] "Bartsia alpina"       "Rhododendron luteum" "Veronica opaca"

[[8]]
[1] "Conopodium majus"     "Ranunculus baudotii" "Rhododendron luteum"
[4] "Veronica opaca"

[[9]]
[1] "Conopodium majus"     "Nitella flexilis"     "Rhododendron luteum"
```

We might want to present this in a more usable way. Because the species lists for different sites are of different lengths, the simplest solution is to create a separate file for each species list. We need to create a set of nine file names incorporating the site name, then use `write.table ()` in a loop:

```
spplists <- sapply (1:9, function (j) rownames (pa)[pa[,j] > 0])
for (i in 1:9) {
  slist <- data.frame (spplists[[i]])
  names (slist) <- names (pa)[i]
  file_name <- paste (names (pa)[i], ".txt", sep = "")
  write.table (slist, file_name)
}
```

We have produced nine separate files. Here, for instance, are the contents of the file `Carmel.txt` as viewed in a text editor like Notepad:

```
"Carmel"
"1" "Cleome serrulata"
"2" "Corydalis sempervirens"
"3" "Nitella flexilis"
"4" "Ranunculus baudotii"
"5" "Rhododendron luteum"
"6" "Veronica opaca"
```

That is all a bit clunky and difficult to analyse. Perhaps the simplest and best solution is to turn the whole presence/absence matrix into a dataframe (see Section 4.5). Then, both tasks become very straightforward. We start by using `stack` `()` to create a dataframe of place names and presence/absence information:

```
newpa <- stack (pa)
head (newpa)

  values    ind
1      0 Carmel
2      1 Carmel
3      0 Carmel
4      1 Carmel
5      1 Carmel
6      1 Carmel
```

We can see in the RStudio Environment window (top right) that whereas `pa` had 10 rows (observations) and 9 columns (variables), `newpa` has 90 (10 × 9) rows, so we have actually *stacked* the data. Now, we extract the species names from the row names, repeat the list of names nine times, and add the resulting vector species names to the dataframe:

```
newpa <- data.frame (newpa, rep (rownames (pa), 9))
```

Finally, give the three columns of the new dataframe sensible names:

```
names (newpa) <- c ("present", "location", "species")
head (newpa)

  present location                 species
1       0   Carmel           Bartsia alpina
2       1   Carmel         Cleome serrulata
3       0   Carmel         Conopodium majus
4       1   Carmel  Corydalis sempervirens
5       1   Carmel          Nitella flexilis
6       1   Carmel       Ranunculus baudotii
```

Unlike the lists, we can easily save this object to a file:

```
write.table (newpa, "spplists.txt")
```

It is also simple to do both our tasks. Here is a location list for `species = Bartsia alpina`:

```
newpa [newpa$species == "Bartsia alpina" & newpa$present == 1, 2]

[1] Daneswall Slatewell
9 Levels: Carmel Derry Daneswall Erith Foggen Highbury Slatewell ... York
```

We have asked for the species and presence we want, but only output column 2, the location. Here is a species list for `location = Carmel`:

```
newpa[newpa$location == "Carmel" & newpa$present == 1, 3]
```

```
[1] "Cleome serrulata"      "Corydalis sempervirens" "Nitella flexilis"
[4] "Ranunculus baudotii"   "Rhododendron luteum"    "Veronica opaca"
```

Again, we are only outputting the species from column 3. Lists are great, but dataframes have many advantages. The cost of using a dataframe is the potentially substantial redundancy in storage requirement. In practice, with relatively small dataframes and modern computers, this seldom matters.

3.15   Text, character strings, and pattern matching

We have seen, albeit in passing, that we can create data objects made up of characters. In *R*, character strings are defined by double quotation marks:

```
a <- "abc"
b <- "123"
class (a)
```

```
[1] "character"
```

```
class (b)
```

```
[1] "character"
```

Numbers can be coerced to characters (as in b above – they just result in NA), but non-numeric characters cannot be coerced to numbers:

```
as.numeric (a)
```

```
[1] NA
```

```
as.numeric (b)
```

```
[1] 123
```

One of the initially confusing things about character strings is the distinction between the length () of a character object (a vector, etc.), and the numbers of characters (nchar ()) in the strings that comprise that object. An example should make the distinction clear:

```
pets <- c ("cat", "dog", "gerbil", "terrapin")
```

Here, pets is a vector comprising four character strings:

```
length (pets)
```

```
[1] 4
```

and the individual character strings have 3, 3, 6, and 7 characters, respectively:

```
nchar (pets)

[1] 3  3  6  8
```

When first defined, character strings are not factors:

```
class (pets)

[1] "character"

is.factor (pets)

[1] FALSE
```

However, if the vector of characters called `pets` was part of a dataframe, then *R* would coerce all the character variables to act as factors:

```
df <- data.frame (pets)
is.factor (df$pets)

[1] FALSE
```

There are built-in vectors in *R* that contain the 26 letters of the alphabet in lower case (letters) and in upper case (LETTERS):

```
letters

 [1] "a" "b" "c" "d" "e" "f" "g" "h" "i" "j" "k" "l" "m" "n" "o" "p" "q" "r" "s"
[20] "t" "u" "v" "w" "x" "y" "z"

LETTERS

 [1] "A" "B" "C" "D" "E" "F" "G" "H" "I" "J" "K" "L" "M" "N" "O" "P" "Q" "R" "S"
[20] "T" "U" "V" "W" "X" "Y" "Z"
```

To discover which number in the alphabet the letter *n* is, we can use the `which ()` function like this:

```
which (letters == "n")

[1] 14
```

For the purposes of printing, we might want to suppress the quotes that appear around character strings by default. The function to do this is called `noquote ()`:

```
noquote (letters)
```

```
[1] a b c d e f g h i j k l m n o p q r s t u v w x y z
```

3.15.1 Pasting character strings together

We can amalgamate individual strings into vectors of character information. First, here is probably the most scintillating command in the book:

```
c (a, b)
```

```
[1] "abc" "123"
```

This shows that the combination using `c ()` produces a vector of two strings. It does *not* convert two 3-character strings into one 6-character string. The *R* function to do that is `paste ()`:

```
paste (a, b, sep = "")
```

```
[1] "abc123"
```

The third argument, `sep = ""`, means that the two character strings are to be pasted together without any separator between them: the default for `paste ()` is to insert a single blank space, like this:

```
paste (a, b)
```

```
[1] "abc 123"
```

Notice that we do *not* lose blanks that are within character strings when we use the `sep = ""` option in `paste ()`.

```
paste(a, b, " a longer phrase containing blanks", sep = "")
```

```
[1] "abc123 a longer phrase containing blanks"
```

If one of the arguments to `paste ()` is a vector, each of the elements of the vector is pasted to the specified character string to produce an object of the same length as the vector:

```
d <- c(a, b, "new")
(e <- paste(d,"a longer phrase containing blanks"))
```

```
[1] "abc a longer phrase containing blanks"
[2] "123 a longer phrase containing blanks"
[3] "new a longer phrase containing blanks"
```

In this next example, we have four fields of information, and we want to paste them together to make a file path for reading data into *R*:

```
drive <- "c:"
folder <- "temp"
file <- "file"
extension <- ".txt"
```

Now, we use the function `paste ()` to put them together:

```
paste (drive, folder, file, extension)
```

```
[1] "c: temp file.txt"
```

This has the essence of what we want, but it is not quite there yet. We need to replace the blank spaces that are the default separator, with no space, and to insert slashes between the drive and the directory, and the directory and file names:

```
paste (drive, "\\", folder, "\\", file, extension, sep = "")
```

```
[1] "c:\\temp\\file.txt"
```

3.15.2 Extracting parts of strings

We being by defining a phrase:

```
phrase <- "the quick brown fox jumps over the lazy dog"
```

The function called `substr ()` is used to extract substrings of a specified number of characters from within a character string. Here is the code to extract the first, the first and second, the first, second, and third, ... , the first 20 characters from our phrase:

```
q <- character (20)
for (i in 1:20) {
  q[i] <- substr (phrase, 1, i)
}
q
```

```
 [1] "t"                    "th"                   "the"
 [4] "the "                 "the q"                "the qu"
 [7] "the qui"              "the quic"             "the quick"
[10] "the quick "           "the quick b"          "the quick br"
[13] "the quick bro"        "the quick brow"       "the quick brown"
[16] "the quick brown "     "the quick brown f"    "the quick brown fo"
[19] "the quick brown fox"  "the quick brown fox "
```

The second argument in `substr ()` is the number of the character at which extraction is to begin (in this case always the first), and the third argument is the number of the character at which extraction is to end (in this case, the `ith`).

3.15.3   Counting things within strings

Counting the total number of characters in a string could not be simpler; just use the `nchar ()` function directly, like this:

```
nchar (phrase)
```

```
[1] 43
```

So there are 43 characters including the blanks between the words. To count the numbers of separate individual characters (including blanks), we need to start by splitting up the character string into individual characters (43 of them), like this:

```
strsplit (phrase, split = character (0))
```

```
[[1]]
 [1] "t" "h" "e" " " "q" "u" "i" "c" "k" " " "b" "r" "o" "w" "n" " " "f" "o" "x"
[20] " " "j" "u" "m" "p" "s" " " "o" "v" "e" "r" " " "t" "h" "e" " " "l" "a" "z"
[39] "y" " " "d" "o" "g"
```

We could use `NULL` in place of `split = character (0)` (see below). We can then resort to our old favourite, `table ()`, to count the number of occurrences of each of the characters:

```
table (strsplit (phrase, split = character (0)))
```

```
  a b c d e f g h i j k l m n o p q r s t u v w x y z
8 1 1 1 3 1 1 2 1 1 1 1 1 1 4 1 1 2 1 2 2 1 1 1 1 1
```

This demonstrates that all of the letters of the alphabet were used at least once within our phrase, and that there were eight blanks within the string called `phrase`, although the heading for the blanks is, not surprisingly but not very helpfully, blank. This suggests a way of counting the number of words in a phrase, given that this will always be one more than the number of blanks (as long as there are no leading or trailing blanks in the string):

```
(words <- 1 + table (strsplit (phrase, split = character (0)))[1])
```

```
9
```

What about the lengths of the words within phrase? Here are the separate words:

```
strsplit (phrase, " ")
```

```
[[1]]
[1] "the"   "quick" "brown" "fox"   "jumps" "over"  "the"   "lazy"  "dog"
```

The second argument says to split wherever a blank is encountered. To work out their lengths, we use four functions starting with `nchar ()`, then applying that using `lapply ()` to each word which are separated using `strsplit ()`, and then summarising everything using `table ()`. This use of multiple functions in one command line is quite common, and in order to understand such instructions, it's often best to start at the innermost set of brackets and work outwards:

```
table (lapply (strsplit (phrase, " "), nchar))

3  4  5
4  2  3
```

showing there were 4 three-letter words, 2 four-letter words, and 3 five-letter words.

This is how to reverse a character string. The logic is that we need to break it up into individual characters, then reverse their order, then paste them all back together again. It seems long-winded until we think about what the alternative might be. Here is the command gradually being put together:

```
strsplit (phrase, NULL)

[[1]]
 [1] "t" "h" "e" " " "q" "u" "i" "c" "k" " " "b" "r" "o" "w" "n" " " "f" "o" "x"
[20] " " "j" "u" "m" "p" "s" " " "o" "v" "e" "r" " " "t" "h" "e" " " "l" "a" "z"
[39] "y" " " "d" "o" "g"

lapply (strsplit (phrase, NULL), rev)

[[1]]
 [1] "g" "o" "d" " " "y" "z" "a" "l" " " "e" "h" "t" " " "r" "e" "v" "o" " " "s"
[20] "p" "m" "u" "j" " " "x" "o" "f" " " "n" "w" "o" "r" "b" " " "k" "c" "i" "u"
[39] "q" " " "e" "h" "t"

sapply (lapply (strsplit (phrase, NULL), rev), paste, collapse = "")

[1] "god yzal eht revo spmuj xof nworb kciuq eht"
```

The `collapse` argument is necessary to reduce the answer back to a single character string. Note that the word lengths are retained, so this would be a poor method of encryption.

When we specify a particular string to form the basis of the split, we end up with a list made up from the components of the string that *do not contain the specified string*. Suppose we split our `phrase` using `the`:

```
strsplit (phrase, "the")

[[1]]
[1] ""                                      " quick brown fox jumps over "
[3] " lazy dog"
```

We end up with a list with only one element. That element has three parts: the first one is the empty string because the first three characters within phrase were exactly `the`; the second contains the part of the phrase between the two occurrences of the string `the`; and the third is the end of the phrase, following the second `the`. Suppose that we want to extract the characters between the first and second occurrences of `the`. This is achieved very simply, using subscripts to extract the second part of the (only) element in the list:

```
strsplit (phrase, "the")[[1]][2]

[1] " quick brown fox jumps over "
```

This emphasises that the output from `strsplit ()` is a list. It is that way as we could put a vector of items into the function to be split (rather than the single item `phrase`) and each would probably have a different structure after the split, requiring a list not a vector as output format. If we want to know how many characters there are between the first and second occurrences of the word `the` within our phrase, we put:

```
nchar (strsplit (phrase, "the")[[1]][2])

[1] 28
```

3.15.4   Upper and lower case text

It is easy to switch between upper and lower cases using the `toupper ()` and `tolower ()` functions:

```
toupper (phrase)

[1] "THE QUICK BROWN FOX JUMPS OVER THE LAZY DOG"

tolower (toupper (phrase))

[1] "the quick brown fox jumps over the lazy dog"
```

3.15.5   The `match ()` function and relational databases

The `match ()` function answers the question: Where (if at all) do the values in the second vector appear in the first vector? It is a really important function, but can be tricky to understand without an example:

```
first <- c (5, 8, 3, 5, 3, 6, 4, 4, 2, 8, 8, 8, 4, 4, 6)
second <- c (8, 6, 4, 2)
match (first, second)

 [1] NA  1 NA NA NA  2  3  3  4  1  1  1  3  3  2
```

The first thing to note is that `match ()` produces a vector as long as the *first* vector (15), of subscripts (index values) and that these are subscripts (or positions) within the *second* vector. If elements of the first vector do not occur anywhere in the second vector, then we get NA. It works like this. Where does 5 (from the first position in the first vector) appear in the second vector?

Answer: it does not (NA). Then, where does 8 (the second element of the first vector) appear in the second vector? Answer: in position number 1, and so on. Why would we ever want to use this? The answer turns out to be very general and extremely useful in data management.

Large and/or complicated databases are always best stored as **relational databases** (e.g. Oracle or Access). In these, data are stored in sets of two-dimensional spreadsheet-like objects called tables. Data are divided into small tables with strict rules as to what data they can contain. You then create relationships between the tables that allow the computer to look from one table to another in order to assemble the data we want for a particular application. The relationship between two tables is based on fields whose values (if not their variable names) are common to both tables. The rules for constructing effective relational databases were first proposed by Dr E.F. Codd of the IBM Research Laboratory at San Jose, California, in an extremely influential paper in 1970 and are, roughly:

- all data are in tables;

- there is a separate table for each set of related variables;

- the order of the records within tables is irrelevant (so we can add records without reordering the existing records);

- the first column of each table is a unique ID number for every row in that table (a simple way to make sure that this works is to have the rows numbered sequentially from 1 at the top so that when we add new rows we are sure that they get unique identifiers);

- there is no unnecessary repetition of data so the storage requirement is minimised, and when we need to edit a record, we only need to edit it once (the last point is very important);

- each piece of data is 'granular' (meaning as small as possible); so we would split a customer's name into title (Dr), first name (Charles), middle name (Urban), surname (Forrester), and preferred form of address (Chuck). If they were promoted, for instance, we would only need to convert Dr to Prof. in the title field.

These are called the **normalisation rules** for creating bullet-proof databases. The use of Structured Query Language (SQL) was designed to work with relational databases. Here, the only point is to see how the match () function relates information in one vector (or table) to information in another.

Take a medical example. We have a vector containing the anonymous identifiers of nine patients (subjects):

```
subjects <- c ("A", "B", "G", "M", "N", "S", "T", "V", "Z")
```

Suppose we wanted to give a new drug to all the patients identified in the second vector called suitable_patients, and the conventional drug to all the others. Here are the suitable patients:

```
suitable_patients <- c ("E", "G", "S", "U", "Z")
```

Notice that there are several suitable patients who are not part of this trial (E and U). This is what the match () function does:

```
match (subjects, suitable_patients)
```

```
[1] NA NA  2 NA NA  3 NA NA  5
```

For each of the individuals in the first vector (subjects), it finds the subscript in the second vector (suitable patients), returning NA if that patient does not appear in the second vector. The key point to understand is that the vector produced is *the same length as the first vector*, and that the numbers in the result are *subscripts within the second vector*.

Let's go through the output term by term and see what each means. Patient A is not in the suitable vector, so *NA* is returned. The same is true for patient B. Patient G is suitable, so we get a number in the third position. That number is a 2 because patient G is the second element of the vector called `suitable_patients`. Neither patient M nor N is in the second vector, so they both appear as NA. Patient S is suitable and so produces a number. The number is 3 because that is the position of S with the second vector.

To complete the job, we want to produce a vector of the drugs to be administered to each of the subjects. We create a vector containing the two treatment names:

```
drug <- c ("new", "conventional")
```

Then we use the result of the match to give the right drug to the right patient:

```
drug [ifelse (is.na (match (subjects, suitable_patients)), 2, 1)]

[1] "conventional" "conventional" "new"          "conventional" "conventional"
[6] "new"          "conventional" "conventional" "new"
```

Note the use of `ifelse ()` with `is.na ()` to produce a subscript 2 (to use with drug) for the unsuitable patients, and a 1 when the result of the match is not NA (i.e. for the suitable patients). It is worth working through this example until it is completely understood.

Alternatively, we might have a table containing personal details about all the possible patients (one row per patient) and want to know which rows to pull out for the suitable patients:

```
which (is.na (match (suitable_patients, subjects)) == F)

[1] 2 3 5
```

It is worth having a look at Section 3.15.9 for an alternative to `match ()` in certain circumstances.

3.15.6 Pattern matching

We need a dataset with a serious amount of text in it to make these exercises relevant:

```
wf <- read.table ("worldfloras.txt", header = T)
head (wf)

      Country Latitude    Area Population Flora Endemism Continent
1 Afghanistan       30   636.0    14.300  3000    0.270      Asia
2     Albania       42    29.0     3.000  3200    0.008    Europe
3     Algeria       35  2382.0    21.300  3139    0.080  N.Africa
4     Andorra       42     0.5     0.034  1000    0.000    Europe
```

```
5        Angola      25   1247.0    8.500  5000   0.250      Africa
6     Antarctica     85  14000.0    0.000     2   0.000  Antarctica

Country <- wf$Country
```

As we can see, there are 161 countries in this dataframe (strictly, 161 places, since some of the entries, such as Sicily and Balearic Islands, are not countries). The idea is that we want to be able to select subsets of countries on the basis of specified patterns within the character strings that make up the country names (factor levels). The function to do this is grep (). This searches for matches to a pattern (specified in its first argument) within the character vector which forms the second argument. It returns a vector of indices (subscripts) within the vector appearing as the second argument, where the pattern was found in whole or in part. The topic of pattern matching is very easy to master once the penny drops, but it can be hard to grasp without simple, concrete examples. Perhaps the simplest task is to select all the countries (extracted into a vector, Country) containing a particular letter – for instance, appropriately, upper-case R:

```
Country[grep ("R", Country)]

[1] "Central African Republic" "Costa Rica"
[3] "Dominican Republic"       "Puerto Rico"
[5] "Reunion"                  "Romania"
[7] "Rwanda"                   "USSR"
```

To restrict the search to countries whose *first* name begins with 'R', we use the ^ character like this:

```
Country[grep("^R", Country)]

[1] "Reunion" "Romania" "Rwanda"
```

To select those countries with multiple names with upper-case R as the first letter of their second or subsequent names, we specify the character string with a blank in like this:

```
Country[grep(" R", Country)]

[1] "Central African Republic" "Costa Rica"
[3] "Dominican Republic"       "Puerto Rico"
```

To find all the countries with two or more names, just search for a blank:

```
Country[grep(" ", Country)]

[1] "Balearic Islands"         "Burkina Faso"
[3] "Central African Republic" "Costa Rica"
[5] "Dominican Republic"       "El Salvador"
[7] "French Guiana"            "Germany East"
[9] "Germany West"             "Hong Kong"
```

```
[11] "Ivory Coast"           "New Caledonia"
[13] "New Zealand"           "Papua New Guinea"
[15] "Puerto Rico"           "Saudi Arabia"
[17] "Sierra Leone"          "Solomon Islands"
[19] "South Africa"          "Sri Lanka"
[21] "Trinidad & Tobago"     "Tristan da Cunha"
[23] "United Kingdom"        "Viet Nam"
[25] "Yemen North"           "Yemen South"
```

To find countries with names ending in y use the $ symbol like this:

```
Country[grep("y$", Country)]


[1] "Hungary"  "Italy"    "Norway"   "Paraguay" "Sicily"   "Turkey"   "Uruguay"
```

For conditions that can be expressed as groups (say, series of numbers or alphabetically grouped lists of letters), use square brackets inside the quotes to indicate the range of values that is to be selected. For instance, to select countries with names containing upper-case letters from C to E inclusive, write:

```
Country[grep("[C-E]", Country)]

 [1] "Cameroon"                 "Canada"
 [3] "Central African Republic" "Chad"
 [5] "Chile"                    "China"
 [7] "Colombia"                 "Congo"
 [9] "Corsica"                  "Costa Rica"
[11] "Crete"                    "Cuba"
[13] "Cyprus"                   "Czechoslovakia"
[15] "Denmark"                  "Dominican Republic"
[17] "Ecuador"                  "Egypt"
[19] "El Salvador"              "Ethiopia"
[21] "Germany East"             "Ivory Coast"
[23] "New Caledonia"            "Tristan da Cunha"
```

Notice that this formulation picks out countries like Ivory Coast and Tristan da Cunha that contain upper-case Cs in places other than as their first letters. To restrict the choice to first letters, use the ˆ operator before the list of capital letters:

```
Country[grep("^[C-E]", Country)]

 [1] "Cameroon"                 "Canada"
 [3] "Central African Republic" "Chad"
 [5] "Chile"                    "China"
 [7] "Colombia"                 "Congo"
 [9] "Corsica"                  "Costa Rica"
[11] "Crete"                    "Cuba"
[13] "Cyprus"                   "Czechoslovakia"
[15] "Denmark"                  "Dominican Republic"
```

```
[17]  "Ecuador"                    "Egypt"
[19]  "El Salvador"                "Ethiopia"
```

How about selecting the counties *not* ending with a specified patterns? The answer is simply to *use negative subscripts* to drop the selected items from the vector. Here are the countries that do not end with a letter between 'a' and 't':

```
Country[-grep("[a-t]$", Country)]

[1]  "Hungary"   "Italy"     "Norway"    "Paraguay" "Peru"      "Sicily"
[7]  "Turkey"    "Uruguay"   "USA"       "USSR"      "Vanuatu"
```

We can see that USA and USSR are included in the list because we specified lower-case letters as the endings to omit. To omit these other countries, put ranges for both upper and lower case letters inside the square brackets, separated by a space:

```
Country[-grep("[A-T a-t]$", Country)]

[1]  "Hungary"   "Italy"     "Norway"     "Paraguay" "Peru"      "Sicily"    "Turkey"
[8]  "Uruguay"   "Vanuatu"
```

Countries with 'y' as their second letter are specified by ˆ.y. The ˆ represents 'starting', then a single dot means one character of any kind, so y is the specified second character:

```
Country[grep("^.y", Country)]

[1]  "Cyprus" "Syria"
```

To search for countries with 'y' as third letter:

```
Country[grep("^..y", Country)]

[1]  "Egypt"        "Guyana"       "Seychelles"
```

If we want countries with 'y' as their sixth letter:

```
Country[grep("^.{5}y", Country)]

[1]  "Norway" "Sicily" "Turkey"
```

Five anything are shown by ., then curly brackets {5}, then y.
   Which are the countries with four or fewer letters in their names?

```
Country[grep("^.{,3}$", Country)]

 [1]  "Chad" "Cuba" "Iran" "Iraq" "Laos" "Mali" "Oman" "Peru" "Togo" "USA"
[11]  "USSR"
```

The '.' means 'anything' while the { , 3 } means 'repeat up to three anythings (dots) before the final string. So to find all the countries with 15 or more characters in their name:

```
Country[grep("^.{15,}$", Country)]

[1] "Balearic Islands"        "Central African Republic"
[3] "Dominican Republic"      "Papua New Guinea"
[5] "Solomon Islands"         "Trinidad & Tobago"
[7] "Tristan da Cunha"
```

3.15.7 Substituting text within character strings

Search-and-replace operations are carried out in *R* using the functions sub () and gsub (). The two substitution functions differ only in that sub () replaces only the first occurrence of a pattern within a character string, whereas gsub () replaces all occurrences. They both come from the same family of functions as grep () and share much of its syntax. Here is a vector comprising seven character strings, called limbs:

```
limbs <- c ("arm", "leg", "head", "foot", "hand", "hindleg", "elbow")
```

We want to replace all lower-case 'h' with upper-case 'H':

```
gsub ("h", "H", limbs)

[1] "arm"       "leg"     "Head"     "foot"     "Hand"     "Hindleg" "elbow"
```

Note that limbs hasn't changed: we are just seeing the effect of the change. Now, suppose we want to convert the first occurrence of a lower-case 'o' into an upper-case 'O'. We use sub () for this:

```
sub ("o", "O", limbs)

[1] "arm"       "leg"     "head"     "fOot"     "hand"     "hindleg" "elbOw"
```

We can see the difference between sub () and gsub () in the following, where both instances of 'o' in foot are converted to upper case by gsub () but not by sub ():

```
gsub ("o", "O", limbs)

[1] "arm"       "leg"     "head"     "fOOt"     "hand"     "hindleg" "elbOw"
```

More general patterns can be specified in the same way as we learned for grep () (Section 3.15.6). For instance, to replace the first character of every string with upper-case 'O', we use the dot notation coupled with ^ (the 'start of string' marker):

```
gsub ("^.", "O", limbs)

[1] "Orm"       "Oeg"     "Oead"     "Ooot"     "Oand"     "Oindleg" "Olbow"
```

There is a very useful string manipulation package, `stringr` (Wickham, 2019), which saves having to use the more esoteric features of `gsub ()`, particularly those coming from the language Perl. Here, we capitalise the first character in each string:

```
library (stringr)


Attaching package: 'stringr'

The following object is masked _by_ '.GlobalEnv':

    words

str_to_title (limbs)

[1] "Arm"     "Leg"     "Head"     "Foot"     "Hand"     "Hindleg" "Elbow"
```

Here we convert all the characters to upper case:

```
str_to_upper (limbs)

[1] "ARM"     "LEG"     "HEAD"     "FOOT"     "HAND"     "HINDLEG" "ELBOW"
```

If we need to do some string manipulation, then it is worth searching through the Index to `stringr`: more details at `help (stringr)`.

3.15.8   Locations of a pattern within a vector

Instead of substituting a pattern as in Section 3.15.7, we might want to know *if* it occurs in a string and, if so, *where* it occurs within each string. The result of `regexpr ()`, therefore, is a numeric vector (as with `grep ()` in Section 3.15.6), but now indicating the position of the first instance of the pattern within the string (rather than just *whether* the pattern was there). If the pattern does not appear within the string, the default value returned is −1. We return to `limbs` from Section 3.15.7:

```
limbs

[1] "arm"     "leg"     "head"     "foot"     "hand"     "hindleg" "elbow"

regexpr ("o", limbs)

[1] -1 -1 -1  2 -1 -1  4
attr(,"match.length")
[1] -1 -1 -1  1 -1 -1  1
attr(,"index.type")
[1] "chars"
attr(,"useBytes")
[1] TRUE
```

This indicates that there were lower-case 'o's in two of the elements of text, and that they occurred in positions 2 and 4, respectively, within those elements. Remember that if we wanted just the subscripts showing which elements of a vector contained an 'o' we would use grep () like this:

```
grep ("o", limbs)

[1] 4 7
```

and we would extract the character strings like this:

```
limbs[grep ("o", limbs)]

[1] "foot"   "elbow"
```

Counting how many 'o's there are in each string is a different problem again, and this involves the use of gregexpr ():

```
freq <- as.vector (unlist (lapply (gregexpr ("o", limbs), length)))
present <- ifelse (regexpr ("o", limbs) < 0, 0, 1)
freq * present

[1] 0 0 0 2 0 0 1
```

indicating that there are no 'o's in the first three character strings, two in the fourth and one in the last string. The best way to understand the first expression is to run subsets of it, starting from the inside, for instance gregexpr ("o", limbs). This will show that gregexpr () contains a lot more output than regexpr (). Using unlist allows us to turn a list into a vector and we then take the elements form that and multiply by whether 'o's were present at all (0 or 1).

The function charmatch () is for matching characters. If there are multiple matches (two or more), then the function returns the value 0 (e.g. when all the elements contain 'm'):

```
charmatch ("m", c ("mean", "median", "mode"))

[1] 0
```

If there is a unique match, the function returns the index of the match within the vector of character strings (here in location number 2):

```
charmatch ("med", c ("mean", "median", "mode"))

[1] 2
```

Pattern matching for use in grep (), grepexpr (), etc., is a huge topic and a rabbit hole from which one might never emerge. There is a long R help page at help (regex), and that then links to even more arcane detail derived from the Perl language, which can be used in *R*. Here are a few more examples. We can look for consecutive characters, in a fairly clear way:

```
grep ("o{1}", limbs, value = T)

[1] "foot"  "elbow"

grep ("o{2}", limbs, value = T)

[1] "foot"

grep ("o{3}", limbs, value = T)

character(0)
```

And here we are counting the number of alphanumeric characters (`alnum`) in each word:

```
grep ("[[:alnum:]]{4, }", limbs, value = T)

[1] "head"    "foot"    "hand"    "hindleg" "elbow"

grep ("[[:alnum:]]{5, }", limbs, value = T)

[1] "hindleg" "elbow"

grep ("[[:alnum:]]{6, }", limbs, value = T)

[1] "hindleg"

grep ("[[:alnum:]]{7, }", limbs, value = T)

[1] "hindleg"
```

3.15.9 Comparing vectors using `%in%` and `which ()`

We might want to know all of the matches between one character vector and another. Here a vehicle hire company has a set of `requests` for items which may or not be in `stock`:

```
stock <- c ("car", "van")
requests <- c ("truck", "suv", "van", "sports", "car", "wagon", "car")
```

We can use `which (... %in% ...)` to find the locations in the first-named vector of any and all of the entries in the second-named vector:

```
which (requests %in% stock)

[1] 3 5 7
```

So we can match the 3rd, 5th, and 7th requests. If we want to know *what* the matches are as well as *where*, they are we use square brackets as an index to `requests`:

```
requests[which (requests %in% stock)]
```

```
[1] "van" "car" "car"
```

We could use the `match ()` function to obtain the same result (see Section 3.15.5):

```
stock[match (requests, stock)][!is.na (match (requests, stock))]
```

```
[1] "van" "car" "car"
```

but that is more clumsy as we need to eliminate the NAs. We could also use `sapply ()`:

```
which (sapply (requests, "%in%", stock))
```

```
van car car
3   5   7
```

but that is unnecessarily long. However, it does bring up an important issue: the use of quotes around the `%in%` function as it does not begin with a letter. This would also be necessary in, for instance, `help ("%in%")`.

3.15.10   Stripping patterned text out of complex strings

Suppose that we want to tease apart the information in these complicated strings:

```
(entries <- c ("Trial 1 58 cervicornis (52 match)",
               "Trial 2 60 terrestris (51 matched)",
               "Trial 8 109 flavicollis (101 matches)"))
```

```
[1] "Trial 1 58 cervicornis (52 match)"
[2] "Trial 2 60 terrestris (51 matched)"
[3] "Trial 8 109 flavicollis (101 matches)"
```

The first task might be to remove the material on numbers of matches including the brackets:

```
gsub (" *$", "", gsub ("\\(.*\\)$", "", entries))
```

```
[1] "Trial 1 58 cervicornis"  "Trial 2 60 terrestris"
[3] "Trial 8 109 flavicollis"
```

The first argument (`*$,  ""`), removes the 'trailing blanks', while the second deletes everything (`".*`) between the left- and the right-hand brackets, substituting this with nothing `""`. The next job is to extract that bracketed material, ignoring the brackets themselves:

```
pos <- regexpr ("\\(", entries)
```

This gives the positions where the material within the brackets begins (the \\ is there as (is not an alphanumeric character).

```
substring (entries, first = pos + 1, last = nchar (entries) - 1)

[1] "52 match"    "51 matched"  "101 matches"
```

We then have the + 1 and - 1 so as not to output the brackets themselves.

3.16   Dates and times in *R*

The measurement of time is highly idiosyncratic. Successive years start on different days of the week. There are months with different numbers of days. Leap years have an extra day in February. Americans and Europeans put the day and the month in different places: 3/4/2006 is March 4 for the former and April 3 for the latter. Occasional years have an additional **leap second** added to them because friction from the tides is slowing down the rotation of the earth from when the standard time was set on the basis of the tropical year in 1900. The cumulative effect of having set the atomic clock too slow accounts for the continual need to insert leap seconds (37 of them by June 2020). There is currently a debate about abandoning leap seconds and introducing a 'leap minute' every century or so instead. Calculations involving times are complicated by the operation of time zones and daylight saving schemes in different countries. All these things mean that working with dates and times is excruciatingly complicated. Fortunately, *R* has a robust system for dealing with this complexity. To see how *R* handles dates and times, let us have a look at Sys.time () with the time taken from the computer on which the command was typed:

```
Sys.time ()

[1] "2021-10-27 10:58:10 BST"
```

This description of date and time is strictly hierarchical from left to right: the longest time scale (years) comes first, then month, then day, separated by hyphens, then there is a blank space, followed by the time, with hours first (using the 24-hour clock), then minutes, then seconds, separated by colons. Finally, there is a character string explaining the time zone (**GMT** stands for Greenwich Mean Time, **BST** for British Summer time, for instance). This representation of the date and time as a character string is user-friendly and familiar, but it is no good for calculations. For that, we need a single numeric representation of the combined date and time. The convention in *R* is to base this on seconds (the smallest time scale that is accommodated in Sys.time ()). It is possible it to aggregate upwards to days or year, but not to do the reverse. The baseline for expressing today's date and time in seconds is 1 January 1970:

```
as.numeric (Sys.time ())

[1] 1635328691
```

This is fine for plotting time series graphs, but it is not much good for computing monthly means (e.g. is the mean for June significantly different from the July mean?) or daily means (e.g. is the Monday mean significantly different from the Friday mean?). To answer questions like these, we have to be able to access a broad set of categorical variables associated with the date: the year, the month, the day of the week, and so forth. To accommodate this, *R* uses the POSIX system for representing times and dates:

```
class (Sys.time ())
```

```
[1] "POSIXct" "POSIXt"
```

We can think of the class POSIXct, with suffix ct, as *continuous time* (i.e. a number of seconds). There is also a more user friendly format, POSIXlt, with suffix lt, as *list time* (i.e. a list of all the various categorical descriptions of the time, including day of the week, and so forth). We shall call these, generically, **date-time** objects. It is hard to remember these acronyms, but it is well worth making the effort. Naturally, we can easily convert to one representation to the other:

```
time.list <- as.POSIXlt (Sys.time ())
unlist (time.list)
```

```
              sec               min              hour              mday
"10.6584351062775"              "58"              "10"              "27"
              mon              year              wday              yday
              "9"             "121"               "3"             "299"
            isdst              zone            gmtoff
              "1"             "BST"            "3600"
```

Here we can see the 11 components of the list, converted into a character vector. The time is represented by the number of seconds (sec to a startling level of accuracy), minutes (min) and hours (on the 24-hour clock). Next comes the day of the month (mday, starting from 1), then the month of the year (mon, starting at January = 0), then the year (starting at 0 = 1900). The day of the week (wday) is coded from Sunday = 0 to Saturday = 6. The day within the year (yday) is coded from 0 = January 1. There is a logical variable (isdst) which asks whether daylight saving time is in operation (0 = FALSE for instance), a description of the time zone and the number of seconds difference from GMT (gmtoff).

3.16.1   Reading time data from files

It is most likely that our data files contain dates in Excel format, for example 03/09/2014 (a character string showing day/month/year separated by slashes).

```
dates <- read.table ("dates.txt", header = T)
head (dates)
```

```
  x        date
1 4  01/01/2021
2 2  02/01/2021
3 0  03/01/2021
4 6  04/01/2021
5 2  05/01/2021
6 8  06/01/2021
```

```
class (dates$date)
```

```
[1] "character"
```

When we read such data into *R* using `read.table ()`, the default option is to turn the data into character variables. For our present purposes, the point is that the data are not recognised by *R* as being dates. To convert a character string or a factor into a date-time object, we employ an important function called `strptime ()`.

To convert a factor or a character string into dates using the `strptime ()` function, we provide a format statement enclosed in double quotes to tell *R* exactly what to expect, in what order, and separated by what kind of symbol. For our present example, we have day (as two digits), then slash, then month (as two digits), then slash, then year (with the century, making four digits).

```
Rdate <- strptime (as.character (dates$date), "%d/%m/%Y")
class (Rdate)
```

```
[1] "POSIXlt" "POSIXt"
```

We don't have any seconds, so there is no `POSIXct`. It is always a good idea at this stage to add the R-formatted date to our dataframe:

```
dates <- data.frame (dates, Rdate)
head (dates)

   x      date       Rdate
1  4  01/01/2021  2021-01-01
2  2  02/01/2021  2021-01-02
3  0  03/01/2021  2021-01-03
4  6  04/01/2021  2021-01-04
5  2  05/01/2021  2021-01-05
6  8  06/01/2021  2021-01-06
```

Now, at last, we can do things with the date information. We might want the mean value of x for each day of the week using `wday` as described in Section 3.16:

```
tapply (dates$x, Rdate$wday, mean)

       0        1        2        3        4        5        6
3.285714 3.000000 4.357143 5.571429 4.357143 4.666667 4.214286
```

The lowest mean is on Tuesdays (`wday = 1`) and the highest on Fridays (`wday = 5`).

It is hard to remember all the format codes for `strptime ()`, but they are sometimes mnemonic, and they are always preceded by a percent symbol. The full list of format components is given in Table 3.6.

Note the difference between the upper case for year `%Y` (this is the unambiguous year including the century, 2014), and the potentially ambiguous lower case `%y` (it is not clear whether 14 means 1914 or 2014).

Table 3.6 Format codes for dates and times

%a	abbreviated weekday name
%A	full weekday name
%b	abbreviated month name
%B	full month name
%c	date and time, locale-specific
%d	day of the month as decimal number (01–31)
%H	hours as decimal number (00–23) on the 24-hour clock
%I	hours as decimal number (01–12) on the 12-hour clock
%j	day of year as decimal number (0–366)
%m	month as decimal number (0–11)
%M	minute as decimal number (00–59)
%p	AM/PM indicator in the locale
%S	second as decimal number (00–61, allowing for two 'leap seconds')
%U	week of the year (00–53) using the first Sunday as day 1 of week 1
%w	weekday as decimal number (0–6, Sunday is 0)
%W	week of the year (00–53) using the first Monday as day 1 of week 1
%x	date, locale-specific
%X	time, locale-specific
%Y	year with century
%y	year without century
%Z	time zone as a character string (output only)

There is a useful function called `weekdays ()` (note the plural) for turning the day number into the appropriate name:

```
y <- strptime ("01/01/2021", format = "%d/%m/%Y")
weekdays (y)
```

```
[1] "Friday"
```

which is converted from

```
y$wday
```

```
[1] 5
```

because the days of the week are numbered from Sunday = 0.

Here is another kind of date, with years in two-digit form, and the months as abbreviated names, with no separators:

```
other_dates <- c ("1jan99", "2jan05", "31mar04", "30jul05")
strptime (other_dates, "%d%b%y")
```

```
[1] "1999-01-01 GMT" "2005-01-02 GMT" "2004-03-31 BST" "2005-07-30 BST"
```

Note that *R* has worked out when British Summer Time starts (in the UK). Here is yet another possibility with year, then month in full, then week of the year, then day of the week abbreviated, all separated by a single blank space:

```
yet_another_date <- c ("2016 January 2 Mon", "2017 February 6 Fri",
  "2018 March 10 Tue")
strptime (yet_another_date, "%Y %B %W %a")


[1] "2016-01-11 GMT" "2017-02-10 GMT" "2018-03-06 GMT"
```

The system is clever in that it knows the date of the Monday in week number 2 of January in 2016, and of the Tuesday in week 10 of 2018, the information on month is redundant in this case:

```
yet_more_dates <- c ("2016 2 Mon", "2017 6 Fri", "2018 10 Tue")
strptime (yet_more_dates, "%Y %W %a")


[1] "2016-01-11 GMT" "2017-02-10 GMT" "2018-03-06 GMT"
```

3.16.2 Calculations with dates and times

We can do the following calculations with dates and times:

- time ± number;
- time1 − time2;
- time1 ==, !=, <, <=, >, >= time2;

The difference between two date-time objects is a **difftime** object. We can add or subtract a number of seconds or a difftime object to/from a date-time object. For obvious reasons, we cannot add two date-time objects. Unless a time zone has been specified two date-time objects are interpreted as being in the current time zone in calculations. It is important to note that the default object being added (or taken away) is seconds, whatever format we begin with

```
(now <- Sys.time ())


[1] "2021-10-27 10:58:10 BST"


now + 1


[1] "2021-10-27 10:58:11 BST"


y


[1] "2021-01-01 GMT"


y + 1


[1] "2021-01-01 00:00:01 GMT"
```

We should convert our dates and times into date-time objects *before* starting to do any calculations. Once we have done that, it is straightforward to calculate means, differences and so on. Here we want to calculate the number of days between two dates, 22 October 2015 and 22 October 2018. Without conversion:

```
y1 <- "2015-10-22"
y2 <- "2018-10-22"
y1 - y2

Error in y1 - y2: non-numeric argument to binary operator
```

But, with conversion:

```
y1 <- as.POSIXlt (y1)
y2 <- as.POSIXlt (y2)
y1 - y2

Time difference of -1096 days
```

Working out the time difference between two dates and/or times involves the `difftime ()` function, which takes two date-time objects as its arguments: the function returns an object of class `difftime` with an attribute indicating the units. The difference we just calculated did just that with the function operating behind the scenes:

```
class (y1 - y2)

[1] "difftime"
```

If we want only the number of days to use in calculation, then write:

```
as.numeric (difftime (y1, y2))

[1] -1096
```

If we have times but no dates, then we can use `difftime ()` to change them into time differences which are appropriate objects for calculations:

```
t1 <- as.difftime ("6:14:21")
t2 <- as.difftime ("5:12:32")
t1 - t2

Time difference of 1.030278 hours
```

We will often want to create date-time objects from components stored in different vectors within a dataframe. For instance, here is a dataframe with the hours, minutes, and seconds from an experiment with two factor levels (A and B) in four separate columns:

```
times <- read.table ("times.txt", header = T)
head (times)

  hrs min sec experiment
1   2  23   6          A
2   3  16  17          A
3   3   2  56          A
4   2  45   0          A
5   3   4  42          A
6   2  56  25          A
```

Because the times are not stored as a date-time object, we need to paste together the hours, minutes, and seconds into a character string, using colons as the separator, and then convert them into time differences:

```
attach (times)
duration <- as.difftime (paste (hrs, min, sec, sep = ":"))
detach (times)
```

Then we can carry out calculations like mean and variance using the `tapply ()` function:

```
tapply (duration, times$experiment, mean)

       A        B
2.829375 2.292882
```

which gives the answer in decimal hours.

3.16.3 Generating sequences of dates

We may want to generate sequences of dates by years, months, weeks, days of the month, or days of the week. Here are four sequences of dates, all starting on 4 November 2015, the first going in increments of one day:

```
seq (as.POSIXlt ("2015-11-04"), as.POSIXlt ("2015-11-15"), "1 day")

 [1] "2015-11-04 GMT" "2015-11-05 GMT" "2015-11-06 GMT" "2015-11-07 GMT"
 [5] "2015-11-08 GMT" "2015-11-09 GMT" "2015-11-10 GMT" "2015-11-11 GMT"
 [9] "2015-11-12 GMT" "2015-11-13 GMT" "2015-11-14 GMT" "2015-11-15 GMT"
```

the second with increments of 2 weeks:

```
seq (as.POSIXlt ("2015-11-04"), as.POSIXlt ("2016-04-05"), "2 weeks")

 [1] "2015-11-04 GMT" "2015-11-18 GMT" "2015-12-02 GMT" "2015-12-16 GMT"
 [5] "2015-12-30 GMT" "2016-01-13 GMT" "2016-01-27 GMT" "2016-02-10 GMT"
 [9] "2016-02-24 GMT" "2016-03-09 GMT" "2016-03-23 GMT"
```

the third with increments of 3 months:

```
seq (as.POSIXlt ("2015-11-04"), as.POSIXlt ("2018-10-04"), "3 months")

 [1] "2015-11-04 GMT" "2016-02-04 GMT" "2016-05-04 BST" "2016-08-04 BST"
 [5] "2016-11-04 GMT" "2017-02-04 GMT" "2017-05-04 BST" "2017-08-04 BST"
 [9] "2017-11-04 GMT" "2018-02-04 GMT" "2018-05-04 BST" "2018-08-04 BST"
```

the fourth with increments of 6 years:

```
seq (as.POSIXlt ("2015-11-04"), as.POSIXlt ("2045-02-04"), by = "6 years")

[1] "2015-11-04 GMT" "2021-11-04 GMT" "2027-11-04 GMT" "2033-11-04 GMT"
[5] "2039-11-04 GMT"
```

If we specify a number, rather than a recognised character string, in the `by` part of the sequence function, then the number is assumed to be a number of seconds, so this generates the time as well as the date:

```
seq (as.POSIXlt ("2015-11-04"), as.POSIXlt ("2015-11-05"), 8955)

 [1] "2015-11-04 00:00:00 GMT" "2015-11-04 02:29:15 GMT"
 [3] "2015-11-04 04:58:30 GMT" "2015-11-04 07:27:45 GMT"
 [5] "2015-11-04 09:57:00 GMT" "2015-11-04 12:26:15 GMT"
 [7] "2015-11-04 14:55:30 GMT" "2015-11-04 17:24:45 GMT"
 [9] "2015-11-04 19:54:00 GMT" "2015-11-04 22:23:15 GMT"
```

As with other forms of `seq ()`, we can specify the length of the vector to be generated, instead of specifying the final date:

```
seq (as.POSIXlt ("2015-11-04"), by = "month", length = 10)

 [1] "2015-11-04 GMT" "2015-12-04 GMT" "2016-01-04 GMT" "2016-02-04 GMT"
 [5] "2016-03-04 GMT" "2016-04-04 BST" "2016-05-04 BST" "2016-06-04 BST"
 [9] "2016-07-04 BST" "2016-08-04 BST"
```

or we can generate a vector of dates to match the length of an existing vector, using `along` instead of `length`:

```
results <- 1:16
seq (as.POSIXlt ("2015-11-04"), by = "month", along = results)

 [1] "2015-11-04 GMT" "2015-12-04 GMT" "2016-01-04 GMT" "2016-02-04 GMT"
 [5] "2016-03-04 GMT" "2016-04-04 BST" "2016-05-04 BST" "2016-06-04 BST"
 [9] "2016-07-04 BST" "2016-08-04 BST" "2016-09-04 BST" "2016-10-04 BST"
[13] "2016-11-04 GMT" "2016-12-04 GMT" "2017-01-04 GMT" "2017-02-04 GMT"
```

We can use the `weekdays ()` function to extract the days of the week from a series of dates:

```
weekdays (seq (as.POSIXlt ("2015-11-04"), by = "month", along = results))

 [1] "Wednesday" "Friday"    "Monday"    "Thursday"  "Friday"    "Monday"
 [7] "Wednesday" "Saturday"  "Monday"    "Thursday"  "Sunday"    "Tuesday"
[13] "Friday"    "Sunday"    "Wednesday" "Saturday"
```

Suppose that we want to find the dates of all the Mondays in a sequence of dates. This involves the use of logical subscripts. The subscripts evaluating to TRUE will be selected, so the logical statement we need to make is `wday == 1` (because Sunday is `wday == 0`). We create an object containing the first 100 days in 2016 (note that *r* starts at day 0), then convert this vector of dates into a date-time object, a list like this:

```
first_100 <- as.Date (0:99, origin = "2016-01-01")
first_100 <- as.POSIXlt (first_100)
```

Now, because `first_100` is a list, we can use the `$` operator to access information on weekday, and we find, of course, that our Mondays are all 7 days apart, starting from the 4 January 2016:

```
first_100[first_100$wday == 1]

 [1] "2016-01-04 UTC" "2016-01-11 UTC" "2016-01-18 UTC" "2016-01-25 UTC"
 [5] "2016-02-01 UTC" "2016-02-08 UTC" "2016-02-15 UTC" "2016-02-22 UTC"
 [9] "2016-02-29 UTC" "2016-03-07 UTC" "2016-03-14 UTC" "2016-03-21 UTC"
[13] "2016-03-28 UTC" "2016-04-04 UTC"
```

Suppose we want to list the dates of the first Monday in each month. This is the first date with `wday == 1` (as above) in each month of the year. This is slightly trickier, because several months will contain five Mondays, so we cannot use `seq ()` with `by = 28 days` to solve the problem (this would generate 13 dates, not the 12 required). Here are the dates of all the Mondays in the year of 2016, together with their months:

```
first_week <- seq (as.POSIXlt ("2016-01-01"), as.POSIXlt ("2016-01-07"), "days")
first_mon <- first_week[weekdays (first_week) == "Monday"]
all_mons <- seq (first_mon, as.POSIXlt ("2016-12-31"), "7 days")
all_mons_months <- data.frame (all_mons, month = months (all_mons))
head (all_mons_months)

    all_mons     month
1 2016-01-04   January
2 2016-01-11   January
3 2016-01-18   January
4 2016-01-25   January
5 2016-02-01  February
6 2016-02-08  February
```

We want a vector to mark the 12 Mondays we require: these are those where `month` is not duplicated (i.e. we want to take the first row from each month). For this example, the first Monday in

January is in row 1 (obviously), the first in February in row 5, the first in March in row 10, and so on. We can use the 'not duplicated' function `!duplicated ()` to tag these rows:

```
wanted <- !duplicated (all_mons_months$month)
```

Finally, select the 12 dates of the first Mondays using `wanted` as a subscript like this:

```
all_mons_months[wanted,]
```

```
              all_mons       month
1   2016-01-04 00:00:00    January
5   2016-02-01 00:00:00   February
10  2016-03-07 00:00:00      March
14  2016-04-04 01:00:00      April
18  2016-05-02 01:00:00        May
23  2016-06-06 01:00:00       June
27  2016-07-04 01:00:00       July
31  2016-08-01 01:00:00     August
36  2016-09-05 01:00:00  September
40  2016-10-03 01:00:00    October
45  2016-11-07 00:00:00   November
49  2016-12-05 00:00:00   December
```

Note that every month is represented, and none of the dates is later than the 7th of the month as required. The time given highlights those Mondays where summer time rules.

3.16.4 Calculating time differences between the rows of a dataframe

A common action with time data is to compute the time difference between successive rows of a dataframe. The vector called `duration` created from the dataset `times` in Section 3.16.2 is of class `difftime` and contains 16 times measured in decimal hours:

```
class (duration)

[1] "difftime"

duration

Time differences in hours
 [1] 2.385000 3.271389 3.048889 2.750000 3.078333 2.940278 3.207778 1.953333
 [9] 2.372778 1.701944 2.521389 3.254444 2.467778 1.926111 2.285278 1.813333
```

We can compute the differences between successive rows using subscripts, like this:

```
(diffs <- duration[1:15] - duration[2:16])

Time differences in hours
 [1] -0.8863889  0.2225000  0.2988889 -0.3283333  0.1380556 -0.2675000
```

```
[7]   1.2544444 -0.4194444   0.6708333 -0.8194444 -0.7330556   0.7866667
[13]   0.5416667 -0.3591667   0.4719444
```

We might want to make the differences between successive rows into part of a dataframe (for instance, to relate change in time to one of the explanatory variables in the dataframe). Before doing this, we need to decide on the row in which we want to put the first of the differences. We should be guided by whether the change in time between rows 1 and 2 is related to the explanatory variables in row 1 or row 2. Suppose it is row 1 that we want to contain the first time difference (−0.8864). Because we are working with differences the vector of differences is shorter by one than the vector from which it was calculated:

```
length (diffs)

[1] 15

length (duration)

[1] 16
```

so we need to add one NA to the bottom of the vector (in row 16):

```
(diffs <- c (diffs, as.difftime ("00:00:00")))

Time differences in secs
 [1] -3191    801   1076  -1182    497   -963   4516  -1510   2415  -2950  -2639   2832
[13]  1950  -1293   1699      0
```

Now we can make this new vector part of the dataframe called times:

```
times$diffs <- diffs
times

    hrs min sec experiment        diffs
1     2  23   6          A -3191 secs
2     3  16  17          A    801 secs
3     3   2  56          A   1076 secs
4     2  45   0          A  -1182 secs
5     3   4  42          A    497 secs
6     2  56  25          A   -963 secs
7     3  12  28          A   4516 secs
8     1  57  12          A  -1510 secs
9     2  22  22          B   2415 secs
10    1  42   7          B  -2950 secs
11    2  31  17          B  -2639 secs
12    3  15  16          B   2832 secs
13    2  28   4          B   1950 secs
14    1  55  34          B  -1293 secs
15    2  17   7          B   1699 secs
16    1  48  48          B      0 secs
```

3.16.5   Regression using dates and times

Here is an example where the number of individual insects was monitored each month over the course of 13 months:

```
timereg <- read.table ("timereg.txt", header = T)
head (timereg)

  survivors        date
1       100 01/01/2011
2        52 01/02/2011
3        28 01/03/2011
4        12 01/04/2011
5         6 01/05/2011
6         5 01/06/2011
```

The first job, as usual, is to use `strptime ()` to convert the date character strings into date-time objects:

```
timereg$date <- strptime (timereg$date,"%d/%m/%Y")
```

We can see that the new object has the following features:

```
class (timereg$date)

[1] "POSIXlt" "POSIXt"

mode (timereg$date)

[1] "list"
```

Then we look at the data to give Figure 3.3a:

```
attach (timereg)
plot (date, survivors, xlab = "month", col = hue_pal ()(3)[1])
plot (date, log (survivors), xlab = "month", col = hue_pal ()(3)[2])
detach (timereg)
```

Inspection of the relationship suggests an exponential decay in numbers surviving, so we shall analyse a model in which `ln (survivors)` is modelled as a function of time (Figure 3.3b): see Chapter 15 for an introduction to these models.

```
timereg_mod1 <- lm (log (survivors) ~ date, data = timereg)

Error in model.frame.default(formula = log(survivors) ~ date, data = timereg, :
invalid type (list) for variable 'date'
```

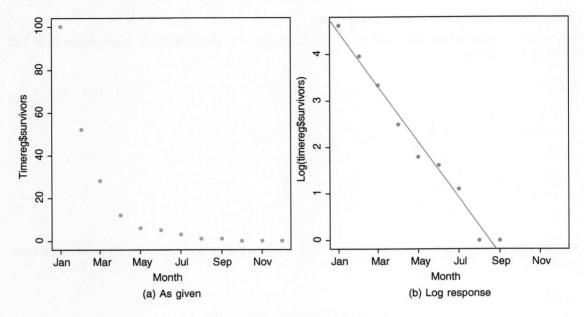

Figure 3.3   Dataset `timereg`.

Well, that didn't work. There are two things we need to correct:

- we need to eliminate the zeros which won't work with a log model;
- the date data need to be converted to something based around seconds, i.e. the `POSIXct` format.

```
timereg_mod2 <- lm (log (survivors) ~ as.POSIXct (date),
                    data = subset (timereg, survivors > 0))
```

We can use the output from this model to add a regression line to the plot in Figure 3.3b using:

```
abline (timereg_mod2, col = hue_pal () (3) [3])
```

We need to take care in reporting the values of slopes in regressions involving date-time objects, because the slopes are rates of change of the response variable *per second*. Here is the summary:

```
summary (timereg_mod2)

Call:
lm(formula = log(survivors) ~ as.POSIXct(date), data = subset(timereg,
    survivors > 0))
```

```
Residuals:
    Min       1Q    Median        3Q       Max
-0.32076 -0.21449  0.09847   0.14596   0.29366

Coefficients:
                    Estimate Std. Error t value Pr(>|t|)
(Intercept)        2.974e+02  1.551e+01   19.18 2.61e-07 ***
as.POSIXct(date)  -2.264e-07  1.189e-08  -19.05 2.74e-07 ***
---
Signif. codes:  0 '***' 0.001 '**' 0.01 '*' 0.05 '.' 0.1 ' ' 1

Residual standard error: 0.2413 on 7 degrees of freedom
Multiple R-squared:  0.9811,    Adjusted R-squared:  0.9784
F-statistic: 362.7 on 1 and 7 DF,  p-value: 2.738e-07
```

The slope is 0; the change in ln (survivors) *per second*. It might be more useful to express this as a monthly rate. So with $60\,\text{sec min}^{-1}$, $60\,\text{min hr}^{-1}$, $24\,\text{hr d}^{-1}$, and (say) $30\,\text{d mo}^{-1}$, the appropriate rate is roughly:

```
(month_rate <- coef (timereg_mod2) [2] * 60 * 60 * 24 * 30)

as.POSIXct(date)
     -0.5868743
```

We can check this out by calculating how many survivors we would expect from 100 starters after two months:

```
100 * exp(month_rate * 2)

as.POSIXct(date)
       30.92057
```

which compares well with our observed count of 28 (see above).

3.17   Environments

R is built around a highly sophisticated system of naming and locating objects. When we start a session in *R*, the variables we create are put in the **global environment**, which is known more familiarly as the user's workspace: details of this can be seen in the default top right-hand window of RStudio (*Environment* tab, *Global Environment* drop down). For instance, if we create the variable a and the matrix b, they should appear in that box:

```
a <- 897932
b <- matrix (c (38, 46, 26, 43), nrow = 2)
```

Any item under the heading `Data`, for instance dataframes, will be given in more detail if clicked upon (using RStudio's `View ()` function). If we create our own function (see Section 3.18), then that will also appear:

```
d <- function (x) {
  f <- log (exp (x))
  f
}
```

The global environment is the first place in which *R* looks for named objects.

An environment consists of a **frame**, which is collection of named objects, and a **pointer** to an enclosing environment. The most common example is the frame of variables that is local to a specific function call (in our example, `f` is a variable only within the environment of the function `d`); its **enclosure** is the environment where the function was defined (in this case the global environment).

There is a strict hierarchy in which *R* looks for things: it starts by looking in the frame, then in the enclosing frame, and so on. Most of the time, we will be operating in the global environment, but, occasionally, we will be working in the environment of a specific function.

3.17.1 Using `attach ()` or not!

When we `attach ()` a dataframe (and some other objects in *R*), we can refer to the variables within that dataframe by name. So, for instance if we consider the built-in dataframe `Orchard-Sprays`:

```
head (OrchardSprays)

  decrease rowpos colpos treatment
1       57      1      1         D
2       95      2      1         E
3        8      3      1         B
4       69      4      1         H
5       92      5      1         G
6       90      6      1         F

OrchardSprays$colpos[1:10]

 [1] 1 1 1 1 1 1 1 1 2 2

attach (OrchardSprays)

The following object is masked _by_ .GlobalEnv:

    treatment

colpos[1:10]

 [1] 1 1 1 1 1 1 1 1 2 2

detach (OrchardSprays)
```

Advanced *R* users do not routinely employ `attach` () in their work, because it can lead to unexpected problems in resolving names (e.g. we can end up with multiple copies of the same variable name, each of a different length and each meaning something completely different: in the example above, we already assigned the object `treatment` in Section 3.4.5 giving rise to the message). When we used `attach` () we can see that an extra environment for the dataset has been created in the drop-down window within Environment in RStudio's top right-hand window.

Most modelling functions like `lm` () or `glm` () have a `data` = argument so `attach` () is unnecessary in those cases. Even when there is a `data` = argument, it is preferable to wrap the call using `with` () like this:

```
with (name_of_dataframe, name_of_function (...))
```

The `with` () function evaluates an *R* expression in an environment constructed from data. We will often use the `with` () function with other functions like `tapply` () or `plot` () which have no built-in data argument. If our dataframe is part of the built-in package called `datasets` (like Orchard Sprays), we can refer to the dataframe directly by name:

```
with (OrchardSprays, boxplot (decrease ~ treatment))
```

Here we calculate the number of n (not infected) cases in the `bacteria` dataframe which is part of the MASS (Venables and Ripley, 2002) library:

```
library (MASS)
with (bacteria, tapply ((y == "n"), trt, sum))

placebo    drug    drug+
     12      18       13
```

Here we plot brain weight against body weight for `mammals` on log–log axes:

```
with (mammals, plot (body, brain, log = "xy"))
```

In neither case did we attach the dataframe. Here we import a dataframe called `regression`:

```
regression <- read.table ("regression.txt", header = T)
```

with which we carry out a linear regression and print a summary:

```
with (regression, {
        model <- lm (growth ~ tannin)
        summary (model)
        }
    )

Call:
lm(formula = growth ~ tannin)
```

```
Residuals:
    Min      1Q   Median       3Q      Max
-2.4556 -0.8889 -0.2389   0.9778   2.8944

Coefficients:
            Estimate Std. Error t value Pr(>|t|)
(Intercept)  11.7556     1.0408  11.295 9.54e-06 ***
tannin       -1.2167     0.2186  -5.565 0.000846 ***
---
Signif. codes:  0 '***' 0.001 '**' 0.01 '*' 0.05 '.' 0.1 ' ' 1

Residual standard error: 1.693 on 7 degrees of freedom
Multiple R-squared:  0.8157,    Adjusted R-squared:  0.7893
F-statistic: 30.97 on 1 and 7 DF,  p-value: 0.0008461
```

The linear model fitting function `lm ()` knows to look in `regression` to find the variables called `growth` and `tannin` because the `with ()` function has used `regression` for constructing the environment from which `lm ()` is called. Groups of statements (different lines of code) to which the `with ()` function applies are contained within curly brackets. An alternative is to define the data environment as an argument in the call to `lm ()` like this:

```
summary (lm (growth ~ tannin, data = regression))
```

Note that whatever form we choose, we still need to get the dataframe into our current environment by using `read.table ()`, etc. (if, as here, it is to be read from an external file), or from a library (like `MASS` to get `bacteria` and `mammals`, as above). To see the names of the dataframes in the built-in package called `datasets`, type:

```
data ()
```

To see all available data sets (including those in the installed packages), type:

```
data (package = .packages (all.available = TRUE))
```

3.17.2 Using `attach ()` in this book

We use `attach ()` in many places throughout this book because experience has shown that it makes the code easier to understand for beginners. In particular, using `attach ()` provides simplicity and brevity so that we can:

- refer to variables by name, so `x` rather than `dataframe$x`;

- write shorter models, so `lm (y ~ x)` rather than `lm (y ~ x,data = dataframe)`;

- go straight to the intended action, so `plot (y ~ x)` not `with (dataframe, plot (y ~ x))`.

Nevertheless, readers are encouraged to use `with ()` or `data =` for their own work, and to avoid using `attach ()` wherever possible. If `attach ()` is used, then it *must* be followed, after the abbreviated names have been used by `detach ()` as we have done at the start of Section 3.17.1:

that will free up the variable names (and the dataset no longer appears as an Environment in RStudio). We have attempted to do this throughout the book: apologies if we have omitted that in one or two examples.

3.18 Writing *R* functions

We typically write our own functions in *R* to carry out operations that require two or more lines of code to execute and that we might want to repeat many times. We have seen a few examples in this chapter so far, but here we will explain in detail how the process works.

Functions in *R* are objects that carry out operations on *arguments* that are supplied to them and return one or more values. The syntax for writing a function is

```
function_name <- function (argument list) {
   body
}
```

The first component of the function declaration is the keyword `function ()`, which indicates to *R* that we want to create a function. An argument list is a comma-separated list of formal arguments. Typically, these will represent data we pass to the function. The `body` can be any valid *R* expression or set of *R* expressions over one or more lines. Generally, the body is a group of expressions contained in curly brackets {, }, with each expression on a separate line. Functions can be written on a single line, with no curly brackets, but we will, in general, avoid that as it can make the code difficult to read. We have usually indented the `body`. We will now have a look at several examples in operation.

3.18.1 Arithmetic mean of a single sample

The mean is the sum of the numbers divided by the number of numbers, typically in a single vector, say *y*, in *R*. The *R* functions involved are `sum (y)` and `length (y)`, so a function to compute arithmetic means is

```
arithmetic_mean <- function (x) {
   sum (x) / length (x)
}
```

If we want the function to output a value, as here, then the last statement in the function must be what we want that output to be. We should test the function with some data where we know the right answer:

```
y <- c (3, 3, 4, 5, 5)
arithmetic_mean (y)
```

```
[1] 4
```

When we used *x* within the function, it only exists in the function environment (see Section 3.17) and when we actually use the function, we can pass it to any data we want (in this case *y* which exists in the global environment). Obviously, we can compare the answer to the built-in function:

```
mean (y)
```

```
[1]  4
```

3.18.2   Median of a single sample

The median (or 50th percentile) is the middle value of the sorted values of a vector of numbers, which we can calculate with this slightly convoluted formula:

```
sort (y)[ceiling (length (y) / 2)]
```

```
[1]  4
```

There is a slight hitch here, of course, because if the vector contains an even number of numbers, then there *is* no middle value. The logic here is that we need to work out the arithmetic average of the two values of *y* on either side of the middle. The question now arises as to how we know, in general, whether the vector *y* contains an odd or an even number of numbers so that we can decide which of the two methods to use. The trick here is to use modulo 2 (see Section 3.1.4). Now we have all the tools we need to write a general function to calculate medians. Let us call the function med () and define it like this:

```
med <- function(x) {
  odd_even <- length (x) %% 2
  if (odd_even == 0) {
    med_x <- (sort (x)[length (x) / 2] + sort (x)[1 + length (x) / 2]) / 2
  } else {
    med_x <- sort(x)[ ceiling (length(x) / 2)]
  }
  med_x
}
```

Notice that when the if () statement is true (i.e. we have an even number of numbers) then the expression immediately following the if () function is evaluated (this is the code for calculating the median with an even number of numbers). When the if () statement is false (i.e. we have an odd number of numbers, and odd_even == 1), then the expression following the else function is evaluated (this is the code for calculating the median with an odd number of numbers). It is good practice in more complex functions to create an object which is the answer (med_x) and leave it as the last line for output.

Let us try it out, first with the odd-numbered vector *y*, then with the even-numbered vector *y*[−1], after the first element of *y* has been dropped (using the negative subscript), and comparing with *R*'s built-in function:

```
med (y)
```

```
[1]  4
```

```
med (y[-1])
```

```
[1] 4.5
```

```
median (y)
```

```
[1] 4
```

```
median (y[-1])
```

```
[1] 4.5
```

We could write the same function in a single (long) line by using `ifelse ()` as follows:

```
med <- function (x) ifelse (length (x) %% 2 == 1,
        sort (x) [ceiling (length (x) / 2)],
      (sort (x) [length (x) / 2] + sort (x) [1 + length (x) / 2]) / 2)
```

However, that is pretty incomprehensible compared with the layout above, and we suggest that lots of lines, space, and indents are used to produce readable code (particularly if we come back to a function after a break).

3.18.3   Geometric mean

For processes that change multiplicatively rather than additively, neither the arithmetic mean nor the median is an ideal measure of central tendency. Under these conditions, the appropriate measure is the **geometric mean**. The formal definition of this is somewhat abstract: the geometric mean is the nth root of the product of the data. If we have data $y_1, y_2, \ldots, y_n$, then the geometric mean, y_{gm} is

$$y_{gm} = \sqrt[n]{y_1 \times y_2 \times \cdots \times y_n}.$$

Let us take a simple example we can work out by hand: the numbers of insects on five plants were as follows: 10, 1, 1000, 1, 10. Multiplying the numbers together gives 100 000. There are five numbers, so we want the fifth root of this. Roots are hard to do in our head, so we will use R as a calculator. Remember that roots are fractional powers, so the fifth root is a number raised to the power $1/5 = 0.2$. In R, powers are denoted by the ^ symbol:

```
100000^0.2
```

```
[1] 10
```

So the geometric mean of these insect numbers is 10 insects per stem. Note that two of the data were exactly like this, so it seems a reasonable estimate of central tendency. The arithmetic mean, on the other hand, is a hopeless measure of central tendency in this case, because the large value (1000) is so influential. This may be interesting but doesn't match the way that insects are represented on plants.

```
insects <- c (1, 10, 1000, 10, 1)
mean (insects)
```

```
[1] 204.4
```

Another way to calculate geometric mean involves the use of logarithms. Recall that to multiply numbers together we add up their logarithms. And to take roots, we divide the logarithm by the root. So we should be able to calculate a geometric mean by finding the antilog (`exp ()`) of the average of the logarithms (`log ()`) of the data:

```
exp (mean (log (insects)))
```

```
[1] 10
```

So here is a function to calculate geometric mean of a vector of numbers *x*:

```
g_mean <- function (x) {
  exp (mean (log (x)))
}
```

When we create a function, it is always worth checking that *R* does not already have a function with that name, which would cause confusion: it's best to choose a name that is clearly distinct from that of existing functions. We can test it with the insect data:

```
g_mean (insects)
```

```
[1] 10
```

The use of geometric means draws attention to a general scientific issue. Look at the Figure 3.4, which shows numbers varying through time in two populations. We could ask which population is the more variable. Chances are, we will pick the upper line:

But now look at the scale on the *y* axis. The upper population is fluctuating 100, 200, 100, 200, and so on. In other words, it is doubling and halving, doubling and halving. The lower curve is fluctuating 10, 20, 10, 20, 10, 20, and so on. It, too, is doubling and halving, doubling and halving. So the answer to the question is that they are equally variable, relative to their mean value. It is just that one population has a higher mean value than the other (150 vs. 15 in this case). In order not to fall into the trap of saying that the upper curve is more variable than the lower curve, it is good practice to graph the logarithms rather than the raw values of things like population sizes that change multiplicatively, as in Figure 3.5.

Now it is clear that both populations are equally variable. Note the change of scale, to logarithms.

3.18.4 Harmonic mean

Consider the following problem. An elephant has a territory which is a square of side 2 km. Each morning, the elephant walks the boundary of this territory. He begins the day at a sedate pace, walking the first side of the territory at a speed of 1 km hr^{-1}. On the second side, he has sped up to

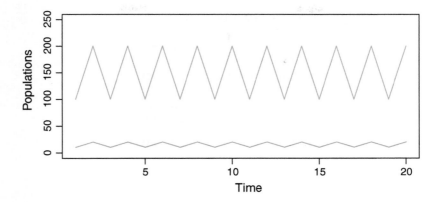

Figure 3.4 Numbers of species varying in two populations.

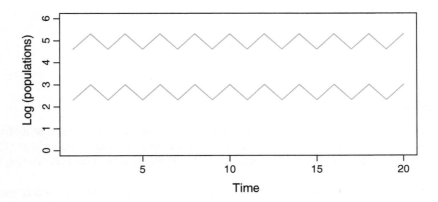

Figure 3.5 Log (numbers) of species varying in two populations.

$2 \, km \, hr^{-1}$. By the third side, he has accelerated to an impressive $4 \, km \, hr^{-1}$, but this so wears him out, that he has to return on the final side at a sluggish $1 \, km \, hr^{-1}$. So what is his average speed over the ground? You might say he travelled at 1, 2, 4, and $1 \, km \, hr^{-1}$ so the average speed is $(1 + 2 + 4 + 1)/4 = 8/4 = 2 \, km \, hr^{-1}$. But that is wrong. Recall that velocity is defined as distance travelled divided by time taken. The distance travelled is easy: it is just $4 \times 2 = 8$ km. The time taken is a bit harder. The first edge was 2 km long, and travelling at $1 \, km \, hr^{-1}$ this must have taken 2 hours. The second edge was 2 km long, and travelling at $2 \, km \, hr^{-1}$ this must have taken 1 hours. The third edge was 2 km long and travelling at $4 \, km \, hr^{-1}$ this must have taken 0.5 hours. The final edge was 2 km long and travelling at $1 \, km \, hr^{-1}$ this must have taken 2 hours. So the total time taken was $2 + 1 + 0.5 + 2 = 5.5$ hours. So the average speed is not $2 \, km \, hr^{-1}$ but $8/5.5 = 1.4545 \, km \, hr^{-1}$. The way to solve this problem is to use the **harmonic mean**.

The harmonic mean is the reciprocal of the average of the reciprocals. The average of our reciprocals is

$$\frac{\frac{1}{1} + \frac{1}{2} + \frac{1}{4} + \frac{1}{1}}{4} = \frac{2.75}{4} = 0.6875.$$

The reciprocal of this average is the harmonic mean

$$\frac{4}{2.75} = \frac{1}{0.6875} = 1.4545.$$

In symbols, therefore, the harmonic mean, $\tilde{y}$, for data y is given by

$$\tilde{y} = \frac{1}{\left(\sum(1/y)\right)/n} = \frac{n}{\sum(1/y)}.$$

An R function for calculating harmonic means, therefore, could be

```
harmonic <- function (x) {
  1 / mean (1 / x)
}
```

and testing it on our elephant data gives

```
harmonic (c (1, 2, 4, 1))
```

```
[1] 1.454545
```

3.18.5   Variance

A measure of variability or uncertainty is perhaps the most important quantity in statistical analysis. The greater the variability in the data, the greater will be our uncertainty in the values of parameters estimated from the data, and the less will be our ability to distinguish between competing hypotheses about the data.

The variance of a sample is measured as a function of *the sum of the squares of the difference between the data and the arithmetic mean*. This important quantity is called the 'sum of squares', *SS*:

$$SS = \sum (y - \bar{y})^2.$$

Naturally, this quantity gets bigger with every new data point we add to the sample (unless that point happens to be the arithmetic mean). An obvious way to compensate for this is to measure variability as the average of the squared departures from the mean (the 'mean square deviation'.). There is a slight problem, however. Look at the formula for the sum of squares, *SS*, above and ask what we need to know before we can calculate it. We have the data, y, but the only way we can know the sample mean, $\bar{y}$, is to calculate it from the data (we will never know $\bar{y}$ in advance).

To allow for this and to complete our calculation of the variance, we need the **degrees of freedom** (d.f.). This important concept in statistics is defined, for our purposes, as follows:

$$\text{d.f.} = n - k,$$

which is the sample size, n, minus the number of parameters, k, estimated from the data. For the variance, we have estimated one parameter from the data, $\bar{y}$, and so there are $n - 1$ degrees of freedom. In a simple linear regression (see Section 10.1), we estimate two parameters from the data, the slope, and the intercept, and so there are $n - 2$ degrees of freedom in a regression analysis.

Variance is denoted by the lower-case Latin letter s squared: s^2. The square root of variance, s, is called the **standard deviation**. We always calculate the variance of a sample as

$$\text{variance} = s^2 = \frac{\text{sum of squares}}{\text{degrees of freedom}}.$$

Consider the following data:

```
y <- c (13, 7, 5, 12, 9, 15, 6, 11, 9, 7, 12)
```

We need to write a function to calculate the sample variance: we call it `samp_var` variance and define it like this:

```
samp_var <- function (x) {
  sum ((x - mean (x))^2) / (length (x) - 1)
}
```

and use it like this:

```
samp_var (y)
```

```
[1] 10.25455
```

Our measure of variability in these data, the variance, is thus 10.254 545 5. It is said to be an unbiased estimator of the variance of the population because we divide the sum of squares by the degrees of freedom $(n - 1)$ rather than by the sample size, n, to compensate for the fact that we have estimated one parameter from the data. So the variance is *close* to the average squared difference between the data and the mean, especially for large samples, but it is not exactly equal to the mean squared deviation. We can compare this answer to the built in function:

```
var (y)
```

```
[1] 10.25455
```

3.18.6 Variance ratio test

How do we know if two variances are significantly different from one another? One of several sensible ways to do this is to carry out Fisher's F-test, which simply examines the ratio of the two variances (see Section 9.2.6). Here is a function to print the p-value (see Section 9.1.3) associated with a comparison of the larger and smaller variances:

```
vrt <- function (x,y) {
    v1 <- var (x)
    v2 <- var (y)
  if (var (x) > var (y)) {
      vr <- var (x) / var (y)
      df1 <- length (x)-1
```

```
      df2 <- length (y)-1
   } else {
      vr <- var (y) / var (x)
      df1 <- length (y) - 1
      df2 <- length (x) - 1
   }
   p_val <- 2 * (1 - pf (vr, df1, df2))
   p_val
}
```

This is the longest function we have written, so it's worth mentioning:

- the liberal use of space and indents. In particular, we need to be very clear about where the }s appear so we understand where loops, etc., end;

- we have a `if () else ()` statement. It is probably clearer to use this than the `ifelse` function;

- the `} else {` layout is recommended by *R*;

- rather than leave the final calculation as the last line, we have given it a name and then put that last. This is a good habit to get into so it is clear what the program is outputting;

- *R* already has a function called `pvalue ()` so we should avoid using that name.

The technical details aren't important, but they follow anyway. The last line of our function works out the probability of getting an *F* ratio as big as `vr` or bigger by chance alone *if the two variances were really the same*, using the cumulative probability of the *F* distribution, which is an *R* function called `pf ()`. We need to supply `pf ()` with three *arguments*: the size of the variance ratio (`vr`), the number of degrees of freedom in the numerator (`df1`), and the number of degrees of freedom in the denominator (`df2`).

Here are some data to test our function. They are normally distributed random numbers, but the first set has a variance of 4 and the second a variance of 16 (i.e. standard deviations of 2 and 4, respectively):

```
a <- rnorm (20, 15, 2)
b <- rnorm (10, 15, 4)
```

Here is our function in action:

```
vrt (a, b)
```

```
[1] 0.565174
```

We can compare our *p*-value with the *p*-value given by *R*'s built-in function:

```
var.test (a,b)

     F-test to compare two variances
```

```
data:   a and b
F = 0.74775, num df = 19, denom df = 9, p-value = 0.5652
alternative hypothesis: true ratio of variances is not equal to 1
95 percent confidence interval:
 0.2030086 2.1535570
sample estimates:
ratio of variances
        0.7477493
```

3.18.7   Using the variance

The variance is used in many ways. Here we will concentrate on establishing a measure of unreliability, a confidence interval (CI) for the mean of the population. This, along with hypothesis testing, is examined in more detail in Chapter 9.

Consider the properties that we would like a measure of unreliability to possess. As the variance of the data increases, what would happen to the unreliability of estimated parameters? Would it go up or down? Unreliability would go up as variance increased, so:

$$\text{unreliability} \propto s^2.$$

What about sample size? Would we want our estimate of unreliability to go up or down as sample size, n, increased? We would want unreliability to go down as sample size went up, so:

$$\text{unreliability} \propto \frac{s^2}{n}.$$

Finally, consider the units in which unreliability is measured. What are the units in which our current measure is expressed? Sample size is dimensionless, but variance is based on the sum of squared differences, so it has dimensions of mean squared. So if the mean was a length in cm, the variance would be an area in cm^2. This is an unfortunate state of affairs. It would make good sense to have the dimensions of the unreliability measure and of the parameter whose unreliability it is measuring the same. That is why all unreliability measures are enclosed inside a big square root term. Unreliability measures are called *standard errors*. What we have just worked out is the *standard error of the mean* (of the population), estimated from a sample:

$$se_{\bar{y}} = \sqrt{\frac{s^2}{n}},$$

where s^2 is the variance and n is the sample size. We can write a function to calculate the standard error of a mean:

```
se <- function (x) {
  sqrt (var (x) / length (x))
}
```

We can refer to functions we have written from within other functions. Recall (see Section 9.1.3), although the details are not important here, that a CI is based around a value from the t-distribution:

$$\text{CI} = \text{sample mean} \pm t_{1-\alpha/2,\text{d.f.}} \times se.$$

The *R* function `qt` () gives the value of the t-distribution, with $1 - \alpha/2 = 0.975$ and degrees of freedom d.f. = `length (x) - 1`. Here is a function called `ci95` () which uses our function `se` () to compute a 95% CI for a mean:

```
ci95 <- function (x) {
  t_value <- qt (0.975, length(x) - 1)
  ci <- t_value * se (x)
  return (list (lower_CI = mean (x) - ci,
                upper_CI = mean (x) + ci))
}
```

Here we want the function to output two things: the lower and upper limits of the CI. The final line shows us how to do that and gives names to the two outputs. We can test the function with 150 normally distributed random numbers with mean 25 and standard deviation 3:

```
x <- rnorm (150, 25, 3)
ci95 (x)

$lower_CI
[1] 24.18495

$upper_CI
[1] 25.11273
```

If we were to repeat the experiment many times, then the mean of the population would lie in approximately 95% of the intervals we create.

We can also use the `se` () function to investigate how the standard error of the mean changes with the sample size. We will take progressively larger samples from the standard Normal distribution (mean 0, variance 1) and plot their standard errors to give Figure 3.6:

We can see clearly that as the sample size falls below about $n = 15$, so the standard error of the mean increases rapidly. The lack of smoothness is caused by randomness in the data being

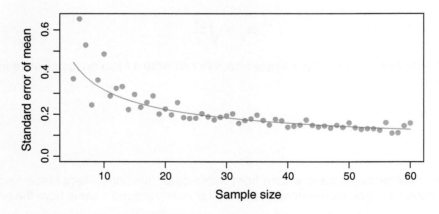

Figure 3.6 Effect of sample size on standard error of the mean.

selected and decreases with sample size. The smooth curve we have added is easy to compute: since the values in our data came from a standard Normal distribution with mean 0 and standard deviation 1, the expected curve would be $1/\sqrt{n}$.

3.18.8 Plots and deparsing in functions

There is no function in the base package of *R* for drawing error bars on bar charts, although several contributed packages use the `arrows ()` function for this purpose as described in Section 5.4.3. Here is a simple, stripped-down function that is supplied with three arguments: the positions of the bars (yv), the lengths (up and down) of the error bars (z), and the labels for the bars on the *x* axis (nn).

In addition, sometimes we write functions which produce output that we want to label with the names of the variables that were passed to the function. The process of **deparsing** does this and turns an unevaluated expression into a character string. For instance, if the function is written in terms of a continuous response variable *y* and a categorical explanatory variable *x*, we might want to label the axes of a plot produced by the function with, say, `biomass` in place of *y*, where that label is the name of the data. We will use the `deparse ()` function to do that.

```
error.bars <- function (yv, z, nn){
    xv <- barplot(yv, ylim = c (0, max(yv) + max(z)), col = hue_pal ()(2)[1],
             names = nn, ylab = deparse (substitute (yv)))
    g = (max (xv) - min (xv)) / 50 # 2g is width of error bar
    for (i in 1:length (xv)) {
        lines (c (xv[i], xv[i]), c (yv[i] + z[i], yv[i] - z[i]),
            col = hue_pal ()(2)[2], lwd = 2)
        lines (c (xv[i] - g, xv[i] + g), c (yv[i]+z[i], yv[i] + z[i]),
            col = hue_pal ()(2)[2], lwd = 2)
        lines (c (xv[i] - g, xv[i] + g), c (yv[i]-z[i], yv[i] - z[i]),
            col = hue_pal ()(2)[2], lwd = 2)
    }
}
```

The first `lines ()` function adds the vertical line, and the subsequent two lines the crossbars. Our function will output just a plot. We have also added a comment after the # symbol. Anything after such a symbol will be ignored by *R* when running the code. A good program or function will have many whole or part lines explaining what is going on.

Here is the `error.bars ()` function in action with the plant competition data (see Section 16.3.2):

```
comp <- read.table ("competition.txt", header = T,
                 colClasses = list (clipping = "factor"))
head (comp)

   biomass clipping
1      551      n25
2      457      n25
3      450      n25
4      731      n25
```

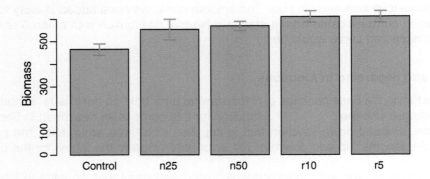

Figure 3.7 Function to generate a plot with error bars.

```
5       499       n25
6       632       n25
```

```
se <- tapply (comp$biomass, comp$clipping, function (x) sd (x) /
              sqrt (length (x)))
labels <- as.character (levels (comp$clipping))
biomass <- tapply (comp$biomass, comp$clipping, mean)
```

Notice that within the line for se, we have created a little function (known as an **anonymous** argument as it is not named) to calculate the standard error of each type of clipping. More details about tapply () can be found in Section 3.10.1. Now, we invoke the function with the means, standard errors, and bar labels to give Figure 3.7:

```
error.bars (biomass, se, labels)
```

3.18.9 The switch () function

When we want a function to do different things in different circumstances, particularly in functions we write, then the switch () function can be useful. Here we write a function that can calculate any one of four different measures of central tendency: arithmetic mean, median, geometric mean, or harmonic mean, using functions we have created in Sections 3.18.1–3.18.4. The argument measure should take one value of Mean, Geometric, Harmonic, or Median; any other text will lead to the error message Measure not included. Alternatively, we can specify the number of the switch (e.g. 1 for Mean, 2 for Median).

```
central_tend <- function (y, measure) {
  switch (measure,
          Mean = arithmetic_mean (y),
          Median = med (y),
          Geometric = g_mean (y),
          Harmonic = harmonic (y),
          stop ("Measure not included"))
}
```

Note that we have to include the character strings in quotes as arguments to the function when we call it, but they must not be in quotes within the `switch ()` function itself. We must also get the name exactly right.

```
our_data <- rnorm (100, 10, 2)
central_tend (our_data, "Median")
[1]  9.97455

central_tend (our_data, 2)

[1]  9.97455

central_tend (our_data, "median")

Error in central_tend(our_data, "median"): Measure not included
```

3.18.10 Arguments in our function

When we create a function, we normally specify some **arguments**. For instance in the function `central_tend ()` at the end of Section 3.18.9 we specify that the user *must* supply values for the arguments y and `measure`. The names of these arguments are only valid within the environment (see Section 3.17 for more details) of the function `central_tend ()`. They have no meaning outside the function and, in fact it is possible to have the same names used globally. So

```
y <- 1:6
central_tend (y = y, 2)


[1]  3.5
```

In the global environment, y is the vector of integers from 1 to 6. The first argument to the function, $y = y$ says that we should give to the argument y in the function the values of the global y. *R* will then evaluate `central_tend (y = y, 2)` with y having the values 1:6 (which could be changed within the function). Once it has finished evaluating the function, it will revert to the global y.

What we have just described are known as **supplied** arguments (i.e. the user *must* supply a value for the argument). We can also set **default** arguments in our functions. These are where we set up a function so that the value of an argument will default to a particular value unless the user suggests otherwise. We have seen this already in *R*'s built-in functions. For instance, we saw in Section 3.7.1 that by default the function `mean ()` will just return NA if any of the data supplied are themselves NA. That is because (as we can see by looking at `help (mean)`) there is an argument to the function, `na.rm = FALSE`. That is a default argument specifying that NAs should not be removed unless otherwise specified.

It is very straightforward to add default arguments to our own functions. Sticking with `central_tend ()`, let's change the `measure` argument so that it defaults to Median:

```
central_tend <- function (y, measure = "Median") {
  switch (measure,
          Mean = arithmetic_mean (y),
          Median = med (y),
```

```
        Geometric = g_mean (y),
        Harmonic = harmonic (y),
        stop ("Measure not included"))
}
central_tend (y)

[1] 3.5

central_tend (y, measure = "Geometric")

[1] 2.993795
```

We can still use the function for other measures of central tendency, but we need to specify them.
   Some applications are much more straightforward if the number of arguments does not need to be specified in advance. There is a special formal name ... (**triple dot**) which is used in the argument list to specify that an arbitrary number of arguments are to be passed to the function. Here is a function that takes any number of vectors and calculates their means and variances:

```
many_means_vars <- function (...) {
  data <- list (...)
  n <- length (data)
  means <- numeric (n)
  vars <- numeric (n)
  for (i in 1:n) {
    means[i] <- mean (data[[i]])
    vars[i] <- var (data[[i]])
  }
  print (means)
  print (vars)
}
```

The main features to note are these:

- the function definition has ... as its only argument. This allows the function to accept additional arguments of unspecified name and number and introduces tremendous flexibility into the structure and behaviour of functions;

- the first thing done inside the function is to create an object (in fact a list) called data out of the list of vectors that are actually supplied in any particular case. The length of this list is the number of vectors, not the lengths of the vectors themselves (these could differ from one vector to another, as in the example below);

- the two output variables (means and vars) are defined to have as many elements as there are vectors in the parameter list. The loop goes from 1 to the number of vectors, and for each vector uses the built-in functions mean () and var () to compute the answers we require;

- because data is a list, we use double [[ ]] subscripts in addressing its elements;

- the outputs have been printed directly to the screen, rather than saved. We will discuss this in more detail below in Section 3.18.12.

Now let's try it out. To make things difficult, we shall create three vectors of different lengths. All come from the standard Normal distribution (with default arguments of mean 0 and variance 1), but the three vectors will have different lengths:

```
x <- rnorm (100)
y <- rnorm (200)
z <- rnorm (300)
```

Now we invoke the function for different numbers of inputs:

```
many_means_vars (x, y, z)

[1]  0.23911128 0.01472836 0.03127244
[1]  1.0012944 0.8792163 1.0185302


many_means_vars (x, z)

[1]  0.23911128 0.03127244
[1]  1.001294 1.018530


many_means_vars (z)

[1]  0.03127244
[1]  1.01853
```

The first line in each output contains the means, the second the variances. Unsurprisingly, all the means are close to 0, and all three variances are close to 1.

We can use ... to absorb some arguments into an intermediate function which can then be extracted by functions called subsequently. *R* has a form of **lazy evaluation** of function arguments in which arguments are not evaluated until they are needed (in some cases the argument will never be evaluated).

3.18.11 Errors in our functions

Sometimes our functions might give rise to errors. In that case, we might want the function to continue and just report the error. One way to **trap** these errors (i.e. identify and then deal with them) is to use the `try ()` function. The following function can be used to attempt to load a dataset using `read.table ()`. Here are the standard error and warning messages:

```
read.table ("compitition.txt", header = T)

Warning in file(file, "rt"): cannot open file 'compitition.txt': No such file or
directory

Error in file(file, "rt"): cannot open the connection
```

As we can see, they are not very helpful if the file can't be found, as is the case here (due to a misspelling). So our function turns them off at the start, produces a bespoke message, and then turns them on again at the end. The key middle part of the function tries to read the file, and the output from that is saved in `try_read`. If that is an error (`class (try_read) == "try-error"`), then the bespoke error is generated. Otherwise, the start of the file is printed to the screen.

```
try.dataset <- function (x) {
  options (show.error.messages = FALSE)
  options (warn = -1)
  try_read <- try (read.table (x, header = T))
  if (class (try_read) == "try-error") {
    cat ("The file named", x, "does not appear to exist in the working direc-
tory\n")
  } else {
    data_in <- read.table (x, header = T)
    cat ("The first records in", x, "are\n")
    print (head (data_in))
  }
  options (show.error.messages = TRUE)
  options (warn = 0)
}
```

We can now run it with a misspelled one, and then a correct dataset, `competition.txt`, from Section 3.18.8, which is then saved as `our_data`:

```
our_data <- try.dataset ("compitition.txt")

The file named compitition.txt does not appear to exist in the working
directory.

our_data <- try.dataset ("competition.txt")

The first records in competition.txt are
  biomass clipping
1     551      n25
2     457      n25
3     450      n25
4     731      n25
5     499      n25
6     632      n25
```

The object `our_data` can be seen in the `Environment` tab in the top right-hand window of RStudio. There are many other functions for dealing with errors and a good starting point can be found at

```
help (tryCatch)
```

3.18.12 Outputs from our function

So far we have seen three ways of outputting information from functions: standard output using the final line, plots and the `print ()` function. We will look at each of these in turn.

The standard option is to put the value to be output in the last line of the function or by using the `return (list ())` line for multiple outputs as in Section 3.18.7. If we do that, we can create an object from the output and use $ or [] for picking out elements. Let us create a simple function with multiple outputs for producing squares of two numbers:

```
simple.function <- function (a, b) {
  a2 <- a^2
  b2 <- b^2
  return (list (asquared = a2, bsquared = b2))
}
```

And now we can run it:

```
run1 <- simple.function (6, 13)
run1

$asquared
[1]  36

$bsquared
[1]  169

run1[1]

$asquared
[1]  36

run1$bsquared

[1]  169
```

and when we enter `run1$`, we are presented with the various names we have set up.

Producing plots is very straightforward as we saw in Section 3.18.7. If we just want a plot, then there is no need for the final line of the function to represent the output.

In other circumstances, we might want to see some output to the screen (perhaps, if we have a loop, a counter showing which loop is being run). We have seen a very poor example of this in Section 3.18.10 using the `print ()` function: we don't know what the output actually represents! Let us add some screen output to `simple.function ()`:

```
simple.function <- function (a, b) {
  a2 <- a^2
  b2 <- b^2
  cat ("The value of", a, "squared is", a2,
       "\nand the value of", b, "squared is", b2)
  return (list (asquared = a2, bsquared = b2))
}
```

The key function for screen output is `cat` (). It works in a similar way to `paste` () by con*cat*enating elements; text or variables. Using \n in quotation marks creates a new line, but it is often simplest just to use multiple `cat` () functions. So

```
simple.function (71, 245)

The value of 71 squared is 5041
and the value of 245 squared is 60025
$asquared
[1] 5041

$bsquared
[1] 60025
```

That looks a mess. We forgot to put in a line break at the end of the screen output and now we have both that, and the values returned by the function. It's best practice to do one or the other, although in some cases, we might want to see output while the function is running (a counter) and then have the function output saved for further use as described above. Here is a final version of our function with an example:

```
simple.function <- function (a, b) {
  a2 <- a^2
  b2 <- b^2
  cat ("The value of", a, "squared is", a2,
      "\nand the value of", b, "squared is", b2, "\n\n")
  return (list (asquared = a2, bsquared = b2))
}
run2 <- simple.function (6.3, pi)

The value of 6.3 squared is 39.69
and the value of 3.141593 squared is 9.869604.

run2$bsquared

[1] 9.869604
```

When we run a function, it's best to save the output as we have done here to `run2`. The screen output will still appear, and we can use the output in other functions or calculations later. When outputting results to screen, it can be good to think about rounding. Although we should store the data to as many decimal places as we need, it can be simpler to output using the `round` () function.

We saw above the use of \n. There are other **escape sequences** (harking back to the days of manual typewriters) we can use and they are given in Table 3.7.

Here is an example of using some of these sequences, where we create a simple model but would like the ANOVA output to appear differently to usual. The details of the numbers are not important.

```
tannin <- read.table ("tannin.txt", header = T)
head (tannin)
```

Table 3.7 Escape sequences for use with `cat ()`

Escape sequence	Effect
\n	newline
\r	carriage return
\t	tab character
\b	backspace
\a	bell (particularly useful)
\f	form feed
\v	vertical tab

```
   growth tannin
1      12      0
2      10      1
3       8      2
4      11      3
5       6      4
6       7      5


tannin_model <- lm (growth ~ tannin, data = tannin)
summary.aov (tannin_model)


            Df Sum Sq Mean Sq F value    Pr(>F)
tannin       1  88.82   88.82   30.97 0.000846 ***
Residuals    7  20.07    2.87
---
Signif. codes:  0 '***' 0.001 '**' 0.01 '*' 0.05 '.' 0.1 ' ' 1
```

Suppose that we wanted to produce a slightly different layout

```
ANOVA table
Source          SS        d.f.     MS               F
Treatment       99.2      2        49.6             4.244691
Error           315.5     27       11.68519
Total           414.7     29
```

First, we extract the necessary numbers from the `summary.aov ()` object:

```
df1 <-unlist (summary.aov (tannin_model)[[1]] [1])[1]
df2 <-unlist (summary.aov (tannin_model)[[1]] [1])[2]
ss1 <-unlist (summary.aov (tannin_model)[[1]] [2])[1]
ss2 <-unlist (summary.aov (tannin_model)[[1]] [2])[2]
```

Here is the *R* code to produce the ANOVA table, using `cat()` with multiple tabs (`"\t\t"`) and single new-line markers (`"\n"`) at the end of each line:

```
{cat ("ANOVA table", "\n")
cat ("Source", "\t\t", "SS", "\t", "\t", "d.f.", "\t", "MS", "\t",
    "\t\t", "F", "\n")
```

```
cat ("Treatment","\t", ss1, "\t", df1, "\t", ss1/df1, "\t\t",
                                (ss1 / df1) / (ss2 / df2), "\n")
cat ("Error", "\t\t", ss2, "\t", df2, "\t", ss2 / df2, "\n")
cat ("Total", "\t\t", ss1 + ss2, "\t", df1 + df2, "\n")}
```

Note the use of curly brackets to group the five `cat` () functions into a single print object rather than alternating the commands with the output.

As we saw in Section 3.18.10, it is also possible to output to screen using the `print` () function. This should only be used when what we want to output has an intrinsic structure, as in

```
print (summary (1:20))

   Min. 1st Qu.  Median    Mean 3rd Qu.    Max.
  1.00    5.75   10.50   10.50   15.25   20.00

cat (summary (1:20))

1 5.75 10.5 10.5 15.25 20
```

The `print` () function preserves the structure while `cat` () does not. However, we would need to use `cat` () as well, in order to add some sort of description of what the output represents.

3.19   Structure of *R* objects

We have discussed (or will discuss throughout the book) a range of types of objects in *R* from simple numbers to the outputs of complex models. There is a simple way to examine what these objects contain. For instance, here is one of the simplest objects in *R* – a vector of length 7 containing real numbers:

```
(y <- seq (0.9 ,0.3, -0.1))

[1] 0.9 0.8 0.7 0.6 0.5 0.4 0.3
```

We can ask *R* about the structure of the object called y using `str` ():

```
str (y)



num [1:7] 0.9 0.8 0.7 0.6 0.5 0.4 0.3
```

We discover that it is `numeric` (well, actually, its *mode*, which describes how it is stored, is), a vector of length 7 [1:7], and (because the vector is short) we see all of the values listed. For longer vectors, we would see the first few values, depending on what would fit on a single printed line (as affected by the number of decimal places displayed). For such a simple object, this information is available in RStudio in the top right-hand window of the screen.

What about a slightly more complicated object? Here is a dataframe with two columns:

```
spino <- read.table ("spino.txt", header = T, colClasses = rep ("factor", 2))
str (spino)


'data.frame':   109 obs. of  2 variables:
 $ condition: Factor w/ 5 levels "better","much.better",..:
   4 2 4 4 4 5 2 4 3 1 ...
 $ treatment: Factor w/ 3 levels "drug.A","drug.B",..: 3 2 2 1 2 1 2 1 2 3 ...
```

We learn that spino is a dataframe with 109 rows and 2 columns, then we get detailed information on each of the columns in turn. The first is a variable called condition which is a factor with five levels (the first two levels of which (in alphabetical order) are better and much.better). The second variable is called treatment and is a factor with three levels. The numbers are the integer representations of the factor levels in the first 10 rows of the dataframe (the numbers represent the levels of the factors in alphabetical order). Because we can see only factor levels 1 and 2, we would need to do more work to discover what factor level 4 of condition, or level 3 of treatment, actually represented:

```
levels (spino$condition)

[1] "better"      "much.better" "much.worse"  "no.change"   "worse"

levels (spino$treatment)

[1] "drug.A"  "drug.B"  "placebo"
```

We can also click on spino to view all the data in a more comfortable format.

Frequently, in this book, we will be dealing with objects that are statistical models. Here is the simplest case, a linear regression model (see Section 10.1 for details):

```
tannin <- read.table ("tannin.txt", header = T)
tannin_model <- lm (growth ~ tannin, data = tannin)
str (tannin_model)


List of 12
 $ coefficients: Named num [1:2] 11.76 -1.22
  ..- attr(*, "names")= chr [1:2] "(Intercept)" "tannin"
 $ residuals    : Named num [1:9] 0.244 -0.539 -1.322 2.894 -0.889 ...
  ..- attr(*, "names")= chr [1:9] "1" "2" "3" "4" ...
 $ effects      : Named num [1:9] -20.67 -9.42 -1.32 2.83 -1.01 ...
  ..- attr(*, "names")= chr [1:9] "(Intercept)" "tannin" "" "" ...
 $ rank         : int 2
 $ fitted.values: Named num [1:9] 11.76 10.54 9.32 8.11 6.89 ...
  ..- attr(*, "names")= chr [1:9] "1" "2" "3" "4" ...
 $ assign       : int [1:2] 0 1
 $ qr           :List of 5
  ..$ qr: num [1:9, 1:2] -3 0.333 0.333 0.333 0.333 ...
```

```
 .. ..- attr(*, "dimnames")=List of 2
 .. .. ..$ : chr [1:9] "1" "2" "3" "4" ...
 .. .. ..$ : chr [1:2] "(Intercept)" "tannin"
 .. ..- attr(*, "assign")= int [1:2] 0 1
 ..$ qraux: num [1:2] 1.33 1.26
 ..$ pivot: int [1:2] 1 2
 ..$ tol  : num 1e-07
 ..$ rank : int 2
 ..- attr(*, "class")= chr "qr"
$ df.residual: int 7
$ xlevels    : Named list()
$ call       : language lm(formula = growth ~ tannin, data = tannin)
$ terms    :Classes 'terms', 'formula'  language growth ~ tannin
 .. ..- attr(*, "variables")= language list(growth, tannin)
 .. ..- attr(*, "factors")= int [1:2, 1] 0 1
 .. .. ..- attr(*, "dimnames")=List of 2
 .. .. .. ..$ : chr [1:2] "growth" "tannin"
 .. .. .. ..$ : chr "tannin"
 .. ..- attr(*, "term.labels")= chr "tannin"
 .. ..- attr(*, "order")= int 1
 .. ..- attr(*, "intercept")= int 1
 .. ..- attr(*, "response")= int 1
 .. ..- attr(*, ".Environment")=<environment: R_GlobalEnv>
 .. ..- attr(*, "predvars")= language list(growth, tannin)
 .. ..- attr(*, "dataClasses")= Named chr [1:2] "numeric" "numeric"
 .. .. ..- attr(*, "names")= chr [1:2] "growth" "tannin"
$ model       :'data.frame':  9 obs. of  2 variables:
 ..$ growth: int [1:9] 12 10 8 11 6 7 2 3 3
 ..$ tannin: int [1:9] 0 1 2 3 4 5 6 7 8
 ..- attr(*, "terms")=Classes 'terms', 'formula'  language growth ~ tannin
 .. .. ..- attr(*, "variables")= language list(growth, tannin)
 .. .. ..- attr(*, "factors")= int [1:2, 1] 0 1
 .. .. .. ..- attr(*, "dimnames")=List of 2
 .. .. .. .. ..$ : chr [1:2] "growth" "tannin"
 .. .. .. .. ..$ : chr "tannin"
 .. .. ..- attr(*, "term.labels")= chr "tannin"
 .. .. ..- attr(*, "order")= int 1
 .. .. ..- attr(*, "intercept")= int 1
 .. .. ..- attr(*, "response")= int 1
 .. .. ..- attr(*, ".Environment")=<environment: R_GlobalEnv>
 .. .. ..- attr(*, "predvars")= language list(growth, tannin)
 .. .. ..- attr(*, "dataClasses")= Named chr [1:2] "numeric" "numeric"
 .. .. .. ..- attr(*, "names")= chr [1:2] "growth" "tannin"
- attr(*, "class")= chr "lm"
```

There are 12 elements in the list (which is much longer than the data!) representing the structure of this linear model object: coefficients, residuals, effects, rank, fitted values, assign, qr, residual degrees of freedom, xlevels, call, terms, and model. Each of these, in turn, is broken down into components; for instance, the two coefficients are numbers (11.76 and −1.22), and their names are (Intercept) and tannin. It is worth coming back to this after understanding linear models (Chapter 10).

The summary () function will typically pull out just some of the elements from a **model object**, so it is worth spending a bit of time becoming familiar with all the available information.

```
summary (tannin_model)

Call:
lm(formula = growth ~ tannin, data = tannin)

Residuals:
    Min      1Q  Median      3Q     Max
-2.4556 -0.8889 -0.2389  0.9778  2.8944

Coefficients:
            Estimate Std. Error t value Pr(>|t|)
(Intercept)  11.7556     1.0408  11.295 9.54e-06 ***
tannin       -1.2167     0.2186  -5.565 0.000846 ***
---
Signif. codes:  0 '***' 0.001 '**' 0.01 '*' 0.05 '.' 0.1 ' ' 1

Residual standard error: 1.693 on 7 degrees of freedom
Multiple R-squared:  0.8157,    Adjusted R-squared:  0.7893
F-statistic: 30.97 on 1 and 7 DF,  p-value: 0.0008461
```

More complex models, such as GLMs (Chapter 11) give rise to even more complex objects. All these objects are just lists, and we can create such things by building our own functions (see Section 3.18).

3.20   Writing from *R* to a file

There are many ways to save a variety of objects in *R*: data, plots, commands, current session, etc. We will examine those in this section.

3.20.1   Saving data objects

Sometimes we might be interrupted halfway through a session and need to close down *R*, but wish to keep all the data objects and functions we have created (in RStudio, the list in the top right-hand corner: Environment/Global Environment). To do that we can type:

```
save (list = ls (all = TRUE), file = "session15092021.RData")
```

The file will be saved to our current working directory (other locations can just be typed into the start of file = ()). To restore the session later, we can just launch the file (which RStudio should recognise) or type:

```
load ("session15092021.RData")
```

Alternatively, we can just use RStudio mean options: Session/Save Workspace as ... , and then type in the filename as above. There is a Load Workspace ... menu option for restoring data objects, etc. We can just save specific data objects by using the save () command described above and just listing the objects we want to save. Unless some data objects take a long time to generate (and are thus worth saving and retrieving), we suggest that it is *not* worth saving all data objects every time we exit *R*. If we do that, we end up with hundreds of objects that we might not need and which might have names that could clash with new work we are carrying out.

The *best way to save what we have done* is to do all our work in an RStudio script (or program) session in a window in the top left-hand corner of RStudio (see Section 1.4 for more details). This is just a text file that can be reopened on next entering *R*, and the relevant commands run again to generate any key data objects.

3.20.2   Saving command history

Alternatively, or additionally, we might wish to save all the commands that we have entered during a session. Again, the best way to do this is with an *R* program or script. However, there is an alternative:

```
savehistory (file = "commandhistory15092021.txt")
```

This can then be loaded using:

```
loadhistory (file = "commandhistory15092021.txt")
```

3.20.3   Saving graphics or plots

This is dealt with thoroughly in Section 5.1.3.

3.20.4   Saving data for a spreadsheet

We might wish to export some spreadsheet style data (typically a dataframe, table, or matrix) to an actual spreadsheet (we hope we persuade you in this book that there will usually be very little call for that). Anyway, the simplest approach is to save the data object to a .csv file. Here are some simple examples:

```
# matrices
amatrix <- matrix (1:24, nrow = 6)
write.csv (amatrix, file = "amatrix.csv", row.names = F)

# dataframes
adataframe <- as.data.frame (amatrix)
row.names (adataframe) <- paste ("row", 1:6, sep = "")
colnames (adataframe) <- paste ("col", 1:4, sep = "")
write.csv (adataframe, file = "adataframe.csv")

# tables
atable <- table (rpois (100, 6))
write.csv (atable, "atable.csv", row.names = F)
```

Although most of the datasets for this book have been saved to .txt files with spaces separating the pieces of data, .csv are more widely used and use commas to separate the data. Obviously, we can then retrieve the data into *R* using read.csv (). Note that this function, unlike read.table () assumes that there is a single row of header information. That option can be changed.

3.20.5 Saving output from functions to a file

Sometimes when we run a program, we would like to put the results directly into a file: perhaps we have written a program that we wish to run against a number of different datasets, with each dataset producing its own output document. This requires us to do two things:

- run a whole program;
- direct the output from that program to a file.

Let's create a simple program which takes as input a vector of numbers, in a csv file whose name we are required to input, and then outputs some basic summary statistics:

```
# import data
filename <- readline ("Enter csv file name without the extension,
                      and press Enter: ")
input <- read.csv (paste (filename, ".csv", sep = ""), header = F)
input <- unlist (input) # create a vector from the imported dataframe

# produce summary statistics
inp_sum <- summary (input)
inp_var <- var (input)

# create output
cat ("Summary statistics for data in ", filename, ".csv\n", sep = "")
cat (rep ("=", 35 + nchar (filename)), sep = "")
cat ("\nThe usual summary statistics are:\n")
print (inp_sum)
cat ("\nThe variance of the data is", round (inp_var, 2), "\n\n")
print (Sys.Date ())
```

When we run the first line, it asks us to enter a name in the *R* console (use the data file trial.csv which has random data in the first column, or create our own). Running each line after that will create the summary statistics and then print them to screen. However, that looks a bit of a mess. So there is a copy of the program saved as Test_program.R. We can now run that program using the source () function:

```
source ("Test_program.R")
```

We then just get the output from the analysis printed to screen. The program should work with any set of data in the first column of a csv file, which we can generate in a spreadsheet. That has completed the first task.

Pointing the output to a file rather than the screen is very straightforward:

```
sink ("Test_output.txt")
source ("Test_program.R")
sink ()
```

Nothing will be output to the screen but, if all has gone well, a file will have been created from the `sink ()` function with our output. It is very important that the second `sink ()` command is run: only then will the file be complete.

3.21 Tips for writing *R* code

Here are some suggestions for good programming, particularly in *R*:

- create a script or program to store *R* commands;
- use RStudio;
- lay out the program with lots of spaces, indents and comments (using #);
- be clear about what is wanted from the code: once that is done, stop;
- test the program, line by line, as it is written;
- use object names that mean something;
- try not to use `attach ()`: if it is absolutely necessary, then use `detach ()` immediately after finishing use of the dataframe;
- always look for an alternative to loops, although there may not be one.

References

Venables, W. N., & Ripley, B. D. (2002). *Modern applied statistics with S* (Fourth) [ISBN 0-387-95457-0]. Springer. https://www.stats.ox.ac.uk/pub/MASS4/.

Wickham, H. (2019). *Stringr: simple, consistent wrappers for common string operations* [R package version 1.4.0]. https://CRAN.R-project.org/package=stringr.

4

Data Input and Dataframes

In this chapter, we will explore how to import data into *R* and then, when it has arrived, how to manipulate its default structure, known as a **dataframe**. Obviously, data can be typed directly into *R* using `c ()` and other functions, but we will assume from now on that the data is held in a file, usually a spreadsheet.

4.1 Working directory

R always has a **working directory** which is where it will attempt to read and write files. It's easy to find the current working directory:

```
getwd ()
```

The simplest way to organise things is to set the working directory to wherever (directory or folder) the project we are working on is based, as soon as *R* is started. Presumably, any data files we import will already be located there and then when we save a program, plot, data file, etc., it will automatically be saved to the same place. There are a number of ways to do this. Let us assume that the directory is `C:/project`. Then we could type:

```
setwd ("C:/project")
```

Alternatively, in RStudio, we can click on the `Files` tab in the bottom right-hand window, move to the directory we want and then, from the menu in that window, select `More` and then `Set As Working Directory`. Another good option is to open the program or script we are working on (see Section 1.4.2), perhaps by double clicking on it in its folder or directory, which will open *R* and RStudio, and then from the main menu selecting `Session`, `Set Working Directory`, and then `To Source File Location`.

Whichever method we use, it's best to have the working directory set before we attempt any work. See also Section 1.8.4 for a discussion of projects.

The R Book, Third Edition. Elinor Jones, Simon Harden and Michael J. Crawley.
© 2023 John Wiley & Sons Ltd. Published 2023 by John Wiley & Sons Ltd.
Companion website: www.wiley.com/go/jones/therbook3e

4.2 Data input from files

The easiest way to get data into *R* is to make the data into the shape of a dataframe in a spreadsheet before trying to read it into *R*. As explained in detail in Section 4.5, we should put all of the values of each variable into a single column, and put the name of the variable in row 1 (called the **header** row). Sometimes the rows and the columns of the dataframe are referred to as **cases** and **fields**, respectively. In our terminology, the fields are the *variables* and the cases are *rows*. Once we have the spreadsheet laid out correctly we can save it as file types `text` (Tab delimited) or CSV (Comma delimited).

   When data is read into *R* from a file, that file will need to have a **separator** between elements of the dataset. Most of the datasets we import in this book will have a space or a tab as a separator as they have been saved as file type `text` (Tab delimited). We can then use `read.table ()` to read in the file as that is the default separator. Where there are text strings (either in the column names or in the data themselves) containing blanks (e.g. place names like 'New Brighton') then `read.table ()` is no good because it will think that 'New' is the value of one variable and 'Brighton' is another, causing the input to fail because the number of data items does not match the number of columns. In such cases, we save them as CSV (Comma delimited) and read the data from a **.csv** file using the function `read.csv ()` (the suffix `.csv` stands for 'comma separated values'). The function `read.csv2 ()` is the variant for countries where a comma is used as the decimal point: in this case, a semicolon is the field separator.

4.2.1 Data input using `read.table ()` and `read.csv ()`

Here is an example of the standard means of data entry used in this book, creating a dataframe within *R* using `read.table ()`, which assumes that the file we are trying to read is in our working directory:

```
yields <- read.table ("yields.txt", header = T)
head (yields)

   sand clay loam
1     6   17   13
2    10   15   16
3     8    3    9
4     6   11   12
5    14   14   15
6    17   12   16
```

The argument `header = T` tells *R* that the first line of the file we are importing contains column names. Alternatively, we can save time by using `read.delim ()`, because then we can omit the argument:

```
yields <- read.delim ("yields.txt")
```

Or we could go the whole way down the labour-saving route and write our own text-minimising function (see Section 3.18), which uses the `paste ()` function like this:

```
rt <- function (x) {
   read.table (paste (x, ".txt", sep = ""), header = TRUE)
}
```

Then we can just type:

```
yields <- rt ("yields")
```

It is possible to import the data from another directory rather than the working directory as in

```
yields <- read.table ("C://temp/yields.txt", header = T)
```

However, it is far simpler to have the data file in the working directory.

At this point, it is worth thinking about what to call the data we input. It's tempting to give the data the name `data`, but that can be confusing and may even overwrite data we have previously imported. It's much better to give the new data object a sensible name, perhaps related to the name of the file we have used.

Importing data often gives rise to errors. The following is a common error message:

```
yield <- read.table ("yield.txt", header = T)

Error in file(file, "rt"): cannot open the connection
```

There are a number of reasons why that could have arisen:

- the file we are trying to import is not in the working directory;
- the file name has been typed incorrectly, which is the case here: it should be `yields` not `yield`. Similar errors would be using capital or lower case letters, or inserting spaces when they are not used that way in the file name;
- quotation marks for the whole file name (including other directory if that is used) have been omitted;
- the file extension, `.txt`, has been omitted.

Another common cause of failure is that the number of variable names (characters strings in row 1) does not match the number of columns of information. This is usually because there are blank spaces in the variable names; so for instance, if we have five column names:

1. `state name`;
2. `population`;

3. home ownership;

4. cars;

5. insurance,

R will expect seven columns of numbers (because of the spaces in the first and third names). The following will work:

1. state_name;

2. population;

3. home_ownership;

4. cars;

5. insurance.

There are two possible reasons why spaces in the data area of the file we are importing might cause problems. The first is when there is no data for a particular row and column. This might arise if we are collecting the data in a spreadsheet and one cell is empty, perhaps because of some missing data. The safest thing is to put NA in that cell. Alternatively, the character data in a cell ("dark chocolate") might contain a blank. In both cases, the best solution is to save the file in the spreadsheet as a .csv file (often Save as type, then select CSV (Comma delimited)) and then read the file into *R* using read.csv ():

```
map <- read.csv ("bowens.csv")
head (map)

              place east north
1           Abingdon    50    97
2       Admoor Copse    60    70
3       AERE Harwell    48    87
4      Agates Meadow    70    73
5        Aldermaston    59    65
6 Aldermaston Court    60    65
```

As a bonus, this function assumes that the data have a header and so we don't need to tell *R* that.

4.2.2 Input from files using scan ()

For dataframes with data in a fixed number of rows and columns, read.table () and read.csv () are superb. But we can now see what happens when we try to use those functions with a more complicated file structure:

```
read.table ("rt.txt")

Error in scan(file = file, what = what, sep = sep, quote = quote, dec = dec,
: line 1 did not have 4 elements
```

It simply cannot cope with lines having different numbers of fields (check out the file using a word or text processor) which is what we have here: 5 lines of data with 1, 2, 4, 2, 1 numbers in each. However, scan () and readLines () (see Section 4.2.3) come into their own with these complicated, non-standard files.

The scan () function reads data into a list when it is used to read from a file. It is much less friendly for reading dataframes than read.table () or read.csv (), but it is substantially more flexible for tricky or non-standard files.

By default, scan () assumes that we are inputting double precision numbers. If not, then we need to use the what argument to explain what exactly we are inputting (character, logical, integer, complex or list). By default, scan () expects to read space-delimited or tab-delimited input fields. If our file has separators other than blank spaces or tab markers, \t, then we can specify the separator option (e.g. sep = ",") to specify the character which delimits fields.

With scan (), we may want to skip the header row (because this contains variable names rather than data). The argument for this is skip = 1, or however many lines we want to skip (this option is also available for read.table () and read.csv ()). If a single record occupies more than one line of the input file, then we can use the argument multi.line = TRUE.

Anyway, back to the datafile rt.txt that we failed to read earlier. It is an image of a file containing information on the identities of the neighbours of five individuals from a population: the first individual has one neighbour (number 138), the second individual has two neighbours (27 and 44), the third individual has four neighbours, and so on.

```
138
27       44
19       20       345      48
115      2366
59
```

Let's attempt three different readings of the same file with different separators: the first has 10 items, the second 5 items, and the third 20 items:

```
scan ("rt.txt")

 [1]   138    27    44    19    20   345    48   115  2366    59

scan ("rt.txt", sep = "\n")

 [1]        138      2744 192034548     1152366        59

scan ("rt.txt", sep = "\t")

 [1] 138    NA    NA    NA    27    44    NA    NA    19    20   345    48   115  2366    NA
[16]  NA    59    NA    NA    NA
```

- the first line uses the default separator which is blanks: the 10 items are the 10 numbers that we are interested in, but information about their grouping has been lost;

- the second line uses the sep = "\n" end of line control character as the separator: the contents of each of the five lines have been stripped out and trimmed to create meaningless numbers, except for 138 and 59 which were the only numbers on their respective lines;

- the third uses tabs `sep = "\t"` as separators (we have no information on lines, but at least the numbers have retained their integrity), and missing values (`NA`) have been used to pad out each line to the same length, 4.

To get the result we want, we need to use the information on the number of lines from method 2 and the information on the contents of each line from method 3. The first step is easy:

```
no_lines <- length (scan ("rt.txt", sep = "\n"))
```

So we have five lines of information in this file. To find the maximum number of items per line, we divide the total number of items by the number of lines:

```
len <- length (scan ("rt.txt", sep = "\t")) / no_lines
```

To extract the information on each line, we want to take a line at a time, and extract the missing values (i.e. remove the `NA`s). So, for line 1 we start with:

```
scan ("rt.txt", sep = "\t") [1:len]

[1] 138  NA  NA  NA
```

then, to remove the `NA` we use `na.omit ()`, to remove the `Read 20 items` we use `quiet = T` and to leave only the numerical value we use `as.numeric ()`:

```
as.numeric (na.omit (scan ("rt.txt", sep = "\t", quiet = T) [1:len]))

[1] 138
```

To complete the job, we need to apply this logic to each of the five lines in turn, creating a function to produce a list of vectors of variable lengths (1, 2, 4, 2, and 1):

```
sapply (1:no_lines, function (i)
         as.numeric (na.omit (scan ("rt.txt", sep = "\t", quiet = T)[(4*i-3):(4*i)])))

[[1]]
[1] 138

[[2]]
[1] 27 44

[[3]]
[1]  19  20 345  48

[[4]]
[1]  115 2366

[[5]]
[1] 59
```

We have created a list of five items, each of the appropriate length. That was about as complicated a procedure as we are likely to encounter in reading information from a file (apart from having to specify the data type). In hindsight, we might have created the data as a dataframe with missing values explicitly added to the rows that had less than four numbers. Then a single `read.table` () statement would have been enough.

4.2.3 Reading data from a file using `readLines` ()

Now let's have a look at the example of the neighbours file that we analysed in Section 4.2.2 using `readLines` ():

```
readLines ("rt.txt")

[1] "138\t\t\t"    "27\t44\t\t"    "19\t20\t345\t48" "115\t2366\t\t"    "59\t\t\t"
```

We can see that the function has produced a vector of length 5 (one element for each row in the file), with the contents of each row reduced to a single character string (including the literal tab markers "\t"). We need to split this up within the lines using `strsplit` (), as discussed in Section 3.15.3. We split first on the tabs, then on the new lines in order to see the distinction:

```
strsplit (readLines ("rt.txt"), "\t")

[[1]]
[1] "138" ""      ""

[[2]]
[1] "27" "44" ""

[[3]]
[1] "19"  "20"  "345" "48"

[[4]]
[1] "115"  "2366" ""

[[5]]
[1] "59" ""      ""

strsplit (readLines ("rt.txt"), "\n")

[[1]]
[1] "138\t\t\t"

[[2]]
[1] "27\t44\t\t"

[[3]]
[1] "19\t20\t345\t48"

[[4]]
[1] "115\t2366\t\t"

[[5]]
[1] "59\t\t\t"
```

The split by tab markers is closest to what we want to achieve, so we shall work on that. First, turn the character strings into numbers:

```
(neighbour_rows <- lapply (strsplit (readLines ("rt.txt"), "\t"), as.numeric))

[[1]]
[1] 138  NA  NA

[[2]]
[1] 27 44 NA

[[3]]
[1]  19  20 345  48

[[4]]
[1]  115 2366   NA

[[5]]
[1] 59 NA NA
```

Now all that we need to do is to remove the NAs from each of the vectors using a simple function:

```
sapply (1:no_lines, function(i) as.numeric (na.omit (neighbour_rows[[i]])))

[[1]]
[1] 138

[[2]]
[1] 27 44

[[3]]
[1]  19  20 345  48

[[4]]
[1]  115 2366

[[5]]
[1] 59
```

And we have ended up with the same list as with scan (), probably in a more straightforward way. Using both scan () and readLines () was fiddly, but both arrived at what we were looking for in the end. It takes a lot of practice to appreciate which one of the functions to use in any particular circumstance. If possible, it's best to aim for the more straightforward dataframe import.

4.3   Data input directly from the web

We typically use `read.table ()` to read data from a file, but the function also works for complete URLs. In computing, URL stands for **universal resource locator** and is a specific character string that constitutes a reference to an Internet resource, combining domain names with file path syntax, where forward slashes are used to separate folder and file names:

```
canc <- read.table ("http://www.bio.ic.ac.uk/research/mjcraw/therbook/data/
                     cancer.txt", header = T)
head (canc)

  death treatment status
1     4    DrugA       1
2    26    DrugA       1
3     2    DrugA       1
4    25    DrugA       1
5     7    DrugA       1
6     6    DrugA       0
```

4.4   Built-in data files

There are many built-in data sets within the `datasets` package (or library), which is automatically enabled when *R* is launched. We can see their names by typing:

```
data ()
```

We can see the data sets in all or individual installed packages, whether we have started them by using `library ()` or not, by typing:

```
data (package = .packages (all.available = TRUE))
data (package = "MASS")
```

We can read the documentation for a particular data set with the usual query:

```
?lynx
```

Some very large packages, such as `spatstat`, are actually multiple packages and all are launched when we type:

```
library (spatstat)
```

We can see all installed packages in RStudio in the `Packages` tab in the bottom right-hand window. Those with a tick in the box have been launched or enabled. So if we have `spatstat` installed, then we can see that we will need to type the following to see the datasets:

```
data (package = "spatstat.data")
```

4.5   Dataframes

Learning how to handle our data, how to enter them into the computer, and how to read them into *R* are among the most important topics we will need to master. *R* handles data in objects known as dataframes. A **dataframe** is an object with rows and columns (a bit like a matrix). The rows, typically, contain different observations from our study, or measurements from our experiment (these are sometimes called *cases*). The columns contain the values of different variables (these are often called *fields*). The values in the body of a matrix must all be of the same type (numbers, etc.,), but the values in the body of a dataframe can vary by column: numbers, text (e.g. the names of factor levels for categorical variables, like male or female in a variable called gender), calendar dates (e.g. 23/5/04), or logical variables (TRUE or FALSE). Table 4.1 is a spreadsheet in the form of a dataframe with seven variables, the leftmost of which comprises the row names, and other variables are numeric (`Area`, `Slope`, `Soil pH`, and `Worm Density`), categorical (`Field Name` and `Vegetation`) or logical (`Damp` is either true = `T` or false = `F`).

Perhaps the most important thing about analysing data properly is getting the data absolutely right to be imported into a dataframe. The expectation is that we will have used a spreadsheet to

Table 4.1   Correctly set out dataset for importing into a dataframe

Field name	Area	Slope	Vegetation	Soil pH	Damp	Worm density
Nash's Field	3.6	11	grassland	4.1	F	4
Silwood Bottom	5.1	2	arable	5.2	F	7
Nursery Field	2.8	3	grassland	4.3	F	2
Rush Meadow	2.4	5	meadow	4.9	T	5
Gunness' Thicket	3.8	0	scrub	4.2	F	6
Oak Mead	3.1	2	grassland	3.9	F	2
Church Field	3.5	3	grassland	4.2	F	3
Ashurst	2.1	0	arable	4.8	F	4
The Orchard	1.9	0	orchard	5.7	F	9
Rookery Slope	1.5	4	grassland	5	T	7
Garden Wood	2.9	10	scrub	5.2	F	8
North Gravel	3.3	1	grassland	4.1	F	1
South Gravel	3.7	2	grassland	4	F	2
Observatory Ridge	1.8	6	grassland	3.8	F	0
Pond Field	4.1	0	meadow	5	T	6
Water Meadow	3.9	0	meadow	4.9	T	8
Cheapside	2.2	8	scrub	4.7	T	4
Pound Hill	4.4	2	arable	4.5	F	5
Gravel Pit	2.9	1	grassland	3.5	F	1
Farm Wood	0.8	10	scrub	5.1	T	3

Table 4.2 Dataset that will not form a dataframe correctly

Control	Preheated	Prechilled
6.1	6.3	7.1
5.9	6.2	8.2
5.8	5.8	7.3
5.4	6.3	6.9

enter and edit the data, and that we will have used plots to check for errors. The thing that takes some practice is learning exactly how to put the data into the spreadsheet. There are countless ways of doing it wrong, but only one way of doing it right. And this way is *not* the way that most people find intuitively to be the most obvious.

The key thing is this: all the values of the same variable must go in the same column. It does not sound like much, but this is what people tend to get wrong. If we had an experiment with three treatments (`control`, `preheated`, and `prechilled`), and four measurements per treatment, it might seem like a good idea to create the spreadsheet as in Table 4.2:

However, this is not correct to be imported into a dataframe, because values of the response variable appear in three different columns, rather than all in the same column. The correct way to enter these data is to have two columns: one for the response variable and one for the levels of the experimental factor called `Treatment` (`control`, `preheated`, and `prechilled`). Table 4.3 has the same data, entered correctly:

A good way to practice this layout is, for instance, to use the Excel function called `PivotTable` (found under `Insert` on the main menu bar): it requires the spreadsheet to be in the form of a dataframe, with each of the variables in its own column.

Once we have made our dataframe in a spreadsheet in the correct format, and corrected all the inevitable data entry and spelling errors, then we need to save it in a file format that can be read by *R*. One way is to save each tab from the spreadsheet as a tab-delimited text file. In Excel, for instance, click on `File Save As ...` then from the `Save as type` options choose `Text (Tab delimited)`. There is no need to add a suffix, because Excel will automatically add `.txt` to the file name. This file can then be read into *R* directly as a dataframe, using the `read.table ()`

Table 4.3 Dataset that will form a dataframe correctly

Response	Treatment
6.1	control
5.9	control
5.8	control
5.4	control
6.3	preheated
6.2	preheated
5.8	preheated
6.3	preheated
7.1	prechilled
8.2	prechilled
7.3	prechilled
6.9	prechilled

function as explained in Section 4.2.1, where an alternative approach using `read.csv ()` is also discussed.

It is important to note that `read.table ()` would fail if there were any spaces in any of the variable names in row 1 of the dataframe (the header row), such as `Field Name`, `Soil pH` or `Worm Density` (above), or between any of the words within the same factor level (as in many of the field names). These should be replaced by dots, '.', or underscores, '_', before the data is saved in the spreadsheet (an alternative is to use `read.csv ()`). Also, it is good idea to remove any apostrophes, as these can sometimes cause problems because there is more than one ASCII code for quotation marks. Now the spreadsheet can be read into *R*. Think of a name for the dataframe (say, `worms` in this case) and then allocate the data from the file to the dataframe like this:

```
worms <- read.table ("worms.txt", header = T,
                     colClasses = list (Vegetation = "factor"))
```

The final argument, `colClasses = list (Vegetation = "factor")`, specifies that entries in the column of data headed `Vegetation` should be treated as coming from a restricted set of options, called **levels**. See Section 3.3 for more details.

Once the file has been imported to *R*, there are a number of things we can do to inspect the data:

- use `names ()` to get a list of the variable names;
- use `head ()` to look at the first few rows of the data;
- use `tail ()` to look at the last few rows of the data.

```
names (worms)

[1] "Field.Name"    "Area"          "Slope"         "Vegetation"   "Soil.pH"
[6] "Damp"          "Worm.density"

head (worms)

        Field.Name Area Slope Vegetation Soil.pH  Damp Worm.density
1      Nashs.Field  3.6    11  Grassland     4.1 FALSE            4
2   Silwood.Bottom  5.1     2     Arable     5.2 FALSE            7
3    Nursery.Field  2.8     3  Grassland     4.3 FALSE            2
4      Rush.Meadow  2.4     5     Meadow     4.9  TRUE            5
5 Gunness.Thicket  3.8     0      Scrub     4.2 FALSE            6
6         Oak.Mead  3.1     2  Grassland     3.9 FALSE            2

tail (worms)

        Field.Name Area Slope Vegetation Soil.pH  Damp Worm.density
15      Pond.Field  4.1     0     Meadow     5.0  TRUE            6
16    Water.Meadow  3.9     0     Meadow     4.9  TRUE            8
17       Cheapside  2.2     8      Scrub     4.7  TRUE            4
18      Pound.Hill  4.4     2     Arable     4.5 FALSE            5
19      Gravel.Pit  2.9     1  Grassland     3.5 FALSE            1
20       Farm.Wood  0.8    10      Scrub     5.1  TRUE            3
```

To see the contents of the whole dataframe, we can just type its name or, for better presentation, click on the name of the dataframe in the `Environment` tab in the top right-hand window of RStudio. This actually runs the command (note the capital `V`):

```
View (worms)
```

Notice that *R* has expanded our abbreviated T and F into `TRUE` and `FALSE`. The object called `worms` is now a dataframe. For example, we can summarise it, using `summary ()`:

```
summary (worms)

   Field.Name          Area            Slope           Vegetation
Length:20         Min.    :0.800    Min.    : 0.00    Arable    :3
Class:character   1st Qu.:2.175    1st Qu.: 0.75    Grassland:9
Mode :character   Median :3.000    Median : 2.00    Meadow    :3
                  Mean    :2.990    Mean    : 3.50    Orchard   :1
                  3rd Qu.:3.725    3rd Qu.: 5.25    Scrub     :4
                  Max.    :5.100    Max.    :11.00

   Soil.pH            Damp          Worm.density
Min.    :3.500    Mode :logical   Min.    :0.00
1st Qu.:4.100    FALSE:14        1st Qu.:2.00
Median :4.600    TRUE :6         Median :4.00
Mean    :4.555                    Mean    :4.35
3rd Qu.:5.000                    3rd Qu.:6.25
Max.    :5.700                    Max.    :9.00
```

Values of continuous variables are summarised under six headings: the arithmetic mean, maximum, minimum, median, 25th percentile or first quartile, and 75th percentile or third quartile. Levels of categorical variables or factors (`Vegetation` in this case) are counted. Note that the field names are not listed in full because they are unique to each row.

The two functions `by ()` and `aggregate ()` (for more details see Section 3.10.3) allow summary of the dataframe on the basis of factor levels. For instance, it might be interesting to know the means of the `Area` for each `Vegetation` type:

```
by (worms$Area, worms$Vegetation, mean)

worms$Vegetation: Arable
[1] 3.866667
-------------------------------------------------------------
worms$Vegetation: Grassland
[1] 2.911111
-------------------------------------------------------------
worms$Vegetation: Meadow
[1] 3.466667
-------------------------------------------------------------
worms$Vegetation: Orchard
[1] 1.9
-------------------------------------------------------------
worms$Vegetation: Scrub
[1] 2.425
```

Or the effect of Vegetation type on Damp:

```
by (worms$Damp, worms$Vegetation, mean)


worms$Vegetation: Arable
[1] 0
-----------------------------------------------------------------
worms$Vegetation: Grassland
[1] 0.1111111
-----------------------------------------------------------------
worms$Vegetation: Meadow
[1] 1
-----------------------------------------------------------------
worms$Vegetation: Orchard
[1] 0
-----------------------------------------------------------------
worms$Vegetation: Scrub
[1] 0.5
```

The logical variable Damp has been coerced to numeric (TRUE = 1, FALSE = 0) and then averaged.

4.5.1 Subscripts and indices

The key thing about working effectively with dataframes is to become completely at ease with using **subscripts** (or **indices**, as some people call them). In *R*, subscripts appear in square brackets, [,]. A dataframe is a two-dimensional object, comprising rows and columns. The rows are referred to by the first (left-hand) subscript, the columns by the second (right-hand) subscript in exactly the same way as with matrices (see Section 3.11). Thus:

```
worms[3, 5]

[1] 4.3
```

is the value in row 3 of Soil.pH (the variable in column 5). To extract a consecutive sequence of values (say the 14th to 19th rows) from worm density (the variable in the seventh column), we use the colon operator : to generate a series of subscripts (14, 15, 16, 17, 18, and 19):

```
worms[14:19, 7]

[1] 0 6 8 4 5 1
```

To extract a group of rows and a group of columns, we need to generate a series of subscripts for both the row and column subscripts. Suppose we want `Area` and `Slope` (columns 2 and 3) from rows 1 to 5:

```
worms[1:5, 2:3]

  Area Slope
1  3.6    11
2  5.1     2
3  2.8     3
4  2.4     5
5  3.8     0
```

This next point is very important and is hard to grasp without practice. To select *all* the entries in a *row*, the syntax is 'number comma blank'. Similarly, to select all the entries in a *column* the syntax is 'blank comma number': the 'blank' tells *R* to select all the entries in that row or column. Thus, to select all the columns in row 3, we type:

```
worms[3,]

     Field.Name Area Slope Vegetation Soil.pH  Damp Worm.density
3 Nursery.Field  2.8     3  Grassland     4.3 FALSE            2
```

whereas to select all the rows in column 3 we need:

```
worms[, 3]

 [1] 11  2  3  5  0  2  3  0  0  4 10  1  2  6  0  0  8  2  1 10
```

This is a key feature of the *R* language. Note that these two apparently similar commands create *objects of different classes* (see Section 3.6):

```
class (worms[3,])

[1] "data.frame"

class (worms[, 3])

[1] "integer"
```

That happens because when we select a single column, all the data must be of the same class, in this case integers. Whereas, when we select a single row we have representatives of all the different data classes present in the dataframe, and so we end up with a dataframe with just one row.

There is an alternative to using column numbers, which is to use their names, and is particularly useful for selecting single columns

```
worms$Slope
```

```
 [1] 11  2  3  5  0  2  3  0  0  4 10  1  2  6  0  0  8  2  1 10
```

In RStudio, this is very straightforward. Once we have typed $, we will be offered a list of column names to choose from.

We can create sets of rows or columns. For instance, to extract all the rows for `Field.Name` and `Soil.pH` (columns 1 and 5), we use the combine function, `c ()`, to make a vector of the required column numbers:

```
worms[, c (1, 5)]

         Field.Name Soil.pH
1        Nashs.Field     4.1
2     Silwood.Bottom     5.2
3      Nursery.Field     4.3
4        Rush.Meadow     4.9
5    Gunness.Thicket     4.2
6           Oak.Mead     3.9
7       Church.Field     4.2
8            Ashurst     4.8
9        The.Orchard     5.7
10      Rookery.Slope    5.0
11       Garden.Wood     5.2
12       North.Gravel    4.1
13       South.Gravel    4.0
14 Observatory.Ridge     3.8
15         Pond.Field     5.0
16       Water.Meadow     4.9
17          Cheapside     4.7
18         Pound.Hill     4.5
19         Gravel.Pit     3.5
20          Farm.Wood     5.1
```

Again, we end up with a smaller dataframe. The commands for selecting rows and columns from the dataframe are summarised in Table 4.4.

4.5.2 Selecting rows from the dataframe at random

In bootstrapping (see Sections 9.4 and 11.6) or cross-validation we might want to select certain rows from the dataframe at random. We use the `sample ()` function to do this: the default `replace = FALSE` performs shuffling (each row is selected once and only once), while the option `replace = TRUE` (sampling with replacement) allows for multiple copies of certain rows and the omission of others. Here we use the default to select a unique 8 of the 20 rows at random:

Table 4.4 Selecting parts of a dataframe called `df_dummy`

Command	Meaning
`df_dummy[n,]`	select all of the columns from row n
`df_dummy[-n,]`	drop the whole of row n
`df_dummy[1:n,]`	select all of the columns from rows 1 to n
`df_dummy[-(1:n),]`	drop all of the columns from rows 1 to n
`df_dummy[c (i,j,k),]`	select all of the columns from rows i, j, and k
`df_dummy[x > y,]`	use a logical test $(x > y)$ to select all columns from certain rows
`df_dummy[, m]`	select all of the rows from column m
`df_dummy[, -m]`	drop the whole of column m
`df_dummy[, 1:m]`	select all of the rows from columns 1 to m
`df_dummy[, -(1:m)]`	drop all of the rows from columns 1 to m
`df_dummy[, c (i, j, k)]`	select all of the rows from columns i, j, and k
`df_dummy[, x > y]`	use a logical test $(x > y)$ to select all rows from certain columns
`df_dummy[, c (1:m, i, j, k)]`	add duplicate copies of columns i, j, and k to columns 1 to m
`df_dummy[x > y, a != b]`	extract certain rows $(x > y)$ and certain columns $(a != b)$
`df_dummy[c (1:n, i, j,k),]`	add duplicate copies of rows i, j, and k to rows 1 to n

```
worms[sample (1:20, 8),]

        Field.Name Area Slope Vegetation Soil.pH  Damp Worm.density
8          Ashurst  2.1     0     Arable     4.8 FALSE            4
15      Pond.Field  4.1     0     Meadow     5.0  TRUE            6
16    Water.Meadow  3.9     0     Meadow     4.9  TRUE            8
7     Church.Field  3.5     3  Grassland     4.2 FALSE            3
2   Silwood.Bottom  5.1     2     Arable     5.2 FALSE            7
19      Gravel.Pit  2.9     1  Grassland     3.5 FALSE            1
18      Pound.Hill  4.4     2     Arable     4.5 FALSE            5
17       Cheapside  2.2     8      Scrub     4.7  TRUE            4
```

Note that the row numbers are in random sequence (not sorted), so that if we want a sorted random sample we will need to order the dataframe after the randomisation (see Section 4.5.3).

4.5.3 Sorting dataframes

It is common to want to sort a dataframe by rows, but rare to want to sort by columns (although the same principles apply). Because we are sorting by rows (the first subscript), we specify the order of the row subscripts *before* the comma. Thus, to sort the dataframe on the basis of values in one of the columns (say, `Slope`), we write:

```
worms[order (worms$Slope),]

         Field.Name Area Slope Vegetation Soil.pH  Damp Worm.density
5   Gunness.Thicket  3.8     0      Scrub     4.2 FALSE            6
8           Ashurst  2.1     0     Arable     4.8 FALSE            4
9        The.Orchard 1.9     0    Orchard     5.7 FALSE            9
15       Pond.Field  4.1     0     Meadow     5.0  TRUE            6
```

16	Water.Meadow	3.9	0	Meadow	4.9	TRUE	8
12	North.Gravel	3.3	1	Grassland	4.1	FALSE	1
19	Gravel.Pit	2.9	1	Grassland	3.5	FALSE	1
2	Silwood.Bottom	5.1	2	Arable	5.2	FALSE	7
6	Oak.Mead	3.1	2	Grassland	3.9	FALSE	2
13	South.Gravel	3.7	2	Grassland	4.0	FALSE	2
18	Pound.Hill	4.4	2	Arable	4.5	FALSE	5
3	Nursery.Field	2.8	3	Grassland	4.3	FALSE	2
7	Church.Field	3.5	3	Grassland	4.2	FALSE	3
10	Rookery.Slope	1.5	4	Grassland	5.0	TRUE	7
4	Rush.Meadow	2.4	5	Meadow	4.9	TRUE	5
14	Observatory.Ridge	1.8	6	Grassland	3.8	FALSE	0
17	Cheapside	2.2	8	Scrub	4.7	TRUE	4
11	Garden.Wood	2.9	10	Scrub	5.2	FALSE	8
20	Farm.Wood	0.8	10	Scrub	5.1	TRUE	3
1	Nashs.Field	3.6	11	Grassland	4.1	FALSE	4

There are some points to notice here:

- because we want the sorting to apply to all the columns, the column subscript (after the comma) is blank;
- the original row numbers are retained in the leftmost column;
- where there are ties for the sorting variable (e.g. there are five ties for `Slope = 0`), then the rows are in their original order.

If we want the dataframe in reverse order:

```
worms[order (worms$Slope, decreasing = TRUE),]
```

	Field.Name	Area	Slope	Vegetation	Soil.pH	Damp	Worm.density
1	Nashs.Field	3.6	11	Grassland	4.1	FALSE	4
11	Garden.Wood	2.9	10	Scrub	5.2	FALSE	8
20	Farm.Wood	0.8	10	Scrub	5.1	TRUE	3
17	Cheapside	2.2	8	Scrub	4.7	TRUE	4
14	Observatory.Ridge	1.8	6	Grassland	3.8	FALSE	0
4	Rush.Meadow	2.4	5	Meadow	4.9	TRUE	5
10	Rookery.Slope	1.5	4	Grassland	5.0	TRUE	7
3	Nursery.Field	2.8	3	Grassland	4.3	FALSE	2
7	Church.Field	3.5	3	Grassland	4.2	FALSE	3
2	Silwood.Bottom	5.1	2	Arable	5.2	FALSE	7
6	Oak.Mead	3.1	2	Grassland	3.9	FALSE	2
13	South.Gravel	3.7	2	Grassland	4.0	FALSE	2
18	Pound.Hill	4.4	2	Arable	4.5	FALSE	5
12	North.Gravel	3.3	1	Grassland	4.1	FALSE	1
19	Gravel.Pit	2.9	1	Grassland	3.5	FALSE	1
5	Gunness.Thicket	3.8	0	Scrub	4.2	FALSE	6
8	Ashurst	2.1	0	Arable	4.8	FALSE	4
9	The.Orchard	1.9	0	Orchard	5.7	FALSE	9
15	Pond.Field	4.1	0	Meadow	5.0	TRUE	6
16	Water.Meadow	3.9	0	Meadow	4.9	TRUE	8

Notice that when there are ties (e.g. `Slope = 0`), the original row order is retained.

More complicated sorting operations might involve two or more variables. This is achieved very simply by separating a series of variable names by commas within the `order ()` function. *R* will sort on the basis of the left-hand variable, with ties being broken by the second variable, and so on. Suppose that we want to order the rows of the database on `Worm.density` within each `Vegetation` type:

```
worms[order (worms$Vegetation, worms$Worm.density),]
```

	Field.Name	Area	Slope	Vegetation	Soil.pH	Damp	Worm.density
8	Ashurst	2.1	0	Arable	4.8	FALSE	4
18	Pound.Hill	4.4	2	Arable	4.5	FALSE	5
2	Silwood.Bottom	5.1	2	Arable	5.2	FALSE	7
14	Observatory.Ridge	1.8	6	Grassland	3.8	FALSE	0
12	North.Gravel	3.3	1	Grassland	4.1	FALSE	1
19	Gravel.Pit	2.9	1	Grassland	3.5	FALSE	1
3	Nursery.Field	2.8	3	Grassland	4.3	FALSE	2
6	Oak.Mead	3.1	2	Grassland	3.9	FALSE	2
13	South.Gravel	3.7	2	Grassland	4.0	FALSE	2
7	Church.Field	3.5	3	Grassland	4.2	FALSE	3
1	Nashs.Field	3.6	11	Grassland	4.1	FALSE	4
10	Rookery.Slope	1.5	4	Grassland	5.0	TRUE	7
4	Rush.Meadow	2.4	5	Meadow	4.9	TRUE	5
15	Pond.Field	4.1	0	Meadow	5.0	TRUE	6
16	Water.Meadow	3.9	0	Meadow	4.9	TRUE	8
9	The.Orchard	1.9	0	Orchard	5.7	FALSE	9
20	Farm.Wood	0.8	10	Scrub	5.1	TRUE	3
17	Cheapside	2.2	8	Scrub	4.7	TRUE	4
5	Gunness.Thicket	3.8	0	Scrub	4.2	FALSE	6
11	Garden.Wood	2.9	10	Scrub	5.2	FALSE	8

Notice that as with single-condition sorts, when there are ties in both sort variables, the rows are in their original sequence (here: 3, 6, 13 for instance). We might want to override this by specifying a third sorting condition (e.g. `Soil.pH`):

```
worms[order (worms$Vegetation, worms$Worm.density, worms$Soil.pH),]
```

	Field.Name	Area	Slope	Vegetation	Soil.pH	Damp	Worm.density
8	Ashurst	2.1	0	Arable	4.8	FALSE	4
18	Pound.Hill	4.4	2	Arable	4.5	FALSE	5
2	Silwood.Bottom	5.1	2	Arable	5.2	FALSE	7
14	Observatory.Ridge	1.8	6	Grassland	3.8	FALSE	0
19	Gravel.Pit	2.9	1	Grassland	3.5	FALSE	1
12	North.Gravel	3.3	1	Grassland	4.1	FALSE	1
6	Oak.Mead	3.1	2	Grassland	3.9	FALSE	2
13	South.Gravel	3.7	2	Grassland	4.0	FALSE	2
3	Nursery.Field	2.8	3	Grassland	4.3	FALSE	2
7	Church.Field	3.5	3	Grassland	4.2	FALSE	3
1	Nashs.Field	3.6	11	Grassland	4.1	FALSE	4
10	Rookery.Slope	1.5	4	Grassland	5.0	TRUE	7

```
4         Rush.Meadow    2.4    5    Meadow     4.9  TRUE       5
15        Pond.Field     4.1    0    Meadow     5.0  TRUE       6
16        Water.Meadow   3.9    0    Meadow     4.9  TRUE       8
9         The.Orchard    1.9    0    Orchard    5.7  FALSE      9
20        Farm.Wood      0.8    10   Scrub      5.1  TRUE       3
17        Cheapside      2.2    8    Scrub      4.7  TRUE       4
5         Gunness.Thicket 3.8   0    Scrub      4.2  FALSE      6
11        Garden.Wood    2.9    10   Scrub      5.2  FALSE      8
```

The rule is this: if in doubt, sort using more variables than we think we need. That way we can be absolutely certain that the rows are in the order we expect them to be in. This is exceptionally important when we begin to make assumptions about the variables associated with a particular value of the response variable on the basis of its row number.

Perhaps we want only certain columns in the sorted dataframe. Suppose we want Vegetation, Worm.density, Soil.pH, and Slope, and we want them in that order from left to right. We specify the column numbers in the sequence we want them to appear as a vector:

```
worms[order (worms$Vegetation, worms$Worm.density, worms$Soil.pH), c (4, 7, 5, 3)]


   Vegetation Worm.density Soil.pH Slope
8      Arable            4     4.8     0
18     Arable            5     4.5     2
2      Arable            7     5.2     2
14  Grassland            0     3.8     6
19  Grassland            1     3.5     1
12  Grassland            1     4.1     1
6   Grassland            2     3.9     2
13  Grassland            2     4.0     2
3   Grassland            2     4.3     3
7   Grassland            3     4.2     3
1   Grassland            4     4.1    11
10  Grassland            7     5.0     4
4      Meadow            5     4.9     5
15     Meadow            6     5.0     0
16     Meadow            8     4.9     0
9     Orchard            9     5.7     0
20      Scrub            3     5.1    10
17      Scrub            4     4.7     8
5       Scrub            6     4.2     0
11      Scrub            8     5.2    10
```

We can select the columns on the basis of their variables names, but this is more fiddly to type, because we need to put the variable names in quotes like this:

```
worms[order (worms$Vegetation, worms$Worm.density, worms$Soil.pH),
            c("Vegetation", "Worm.density", "Soil.pH", "Slope")]


   Vegetation Worm.density Soil.pH Slope
8      Arable            4     4.8     0
18     Arable            5     4.5     2
```

2	Arable	7	5.2	2
14	Grassland	0	3.8	6
19	Grassland	1	3.5	1
12	Grassland	1	4.1	1
6	Grassland	2	3.9	2
13	Grassland	2	4.0	2
3	Grassland	2	4.3	3
7	Grassland	3	4.2	3
1	Grassland	4	4.1	11
10	Grassland	7	5.0	4
4	Meadow	5	4.9	5
15	Meadow	6	5.0	0
16	Meadow	8	4.9	0
9	Orchard	9	5.7	0
20	Scrub	3	5.1	10
17	Scrub	4	4.7	8
5	Scrub	6	4.2	0
11	Scrub	8	5.2	10

Sometimes there are multiple sorting variables, but the variables have to be sorted in opposing directions. In this example, the task is to order the database first by vegetation type in alphabetical order (the default) and then within each vegetation type to sort by worm density in decreasing order (highest densities first). The trick here is to use order () and then put a minus sign in front of Worm.density like this:

```
worms[order (worms$Vegetation, -worms$Worm.density),]
```

	Field.Name	Area	Slope	Vegetation	Soil.pH	Damp	Worm.density
2	Silwood.Bottom	5.1	2	Arable	5.2	FALSE	7
18	Pound.Hill	4.4	2	Arable	4.5	FALSE	5
8	Ashurst	2.1	0	Arable	4.8	FALSE	4
10	Rookery.Slope	1.5	4	Grassland	5.0	TRUE	7
1	Nashs.Field	3.6	11	Grassland	4.1	FALSE	4
7	Church.Field	3.5	3	Grassland	4.2	FALSE	3
3	Nursery.Field	2.8	3	Grassland	4.3	FALSE	2
6	Oak.Mead	3.1	2	Grassland	3.9	FALSE	2
13	South.Gravel	3.7	2	Grassland	4.0	FALSE	2
12	North.Gravel	3.3	1	Grassland	4.1	FALSE	1
19	Gravel.Pit	2.9	1	Grassland	3.5	FALSE	1
14	Observatory.Ridge	1.8	6	Grassland	3.8	FALSE	0
16	Water.Meadow	3.9	0	Meadow	4.9	TRUE	8
15	Pond.Field	4.1	0	Meadow	5.0	TRUE	6
4	Rush.Meadow	2.4	5	Meadow	4.9	TRUE	5
9	The.Orchard	1.9	0	Orchard	5.7	FALSE	9
11	Garden.Wood	2.9	10	Scrub	5.2	FALSE	8
5	Gunness.Thicket	3.8	0	Scrub	4.2	FALSE	6
17	Cheapside	2.2	8	Scrub	4.7	TRUE	4
20	Farm.Wood	0.8	10	Scrub	5.1	TRUE	3

Using the minus sign only works when sorting numerical variables. For factor levels, we can use the `rank ()` function. This treats the levels as numbers in the default order (alphabetical):

```
worms[order (-rank (worms$Vegetation), -worms$Worm.density),]
```

```
                 Field.Name Area Slope Vegetation Soil.pH  Damp Worm.density
11          Garden.Wood  2.9    10      Scrub     5.2 FALSE            8
5        Gunness.Thicket  3.8     0      Scrub     4.2 FALSE            6
17             Cheapside  2.2     8      Scrub     4.7  TRUE            4
20             Farm.Wood  0.8    10      Scrub     5.1  TRUE            3
9            The.Orchard  1.9     0    Orchard     5.7 FALSE            9
16          Water.Meadow  3.9     0     Meadow     4.9  TRUE            8
15            Pond.Field  4.1     0     Meadow     5.0  TRUE            6
4            Rush.Meadow  2.4     5     Meadow     4.9  TRUE            5
10         Rookery.Slope  1.5     4  Grassland     5.0  TRUE            7
1            Nashs.Field  3.6    11  Grassland     4.1 FALSE            4
7           Church.Field  3.5     3  Grassland     4.2 FALSE            3
3          Nursery.Field  2.8     3  Grassland     4.3 FALSE            2
6              Oak.Mead  3.1     2  Grassland     3.9 FALSE            2
13          South.Gravel  3.7     2  Grassland     4.0 FALSE            2
12          North.Gravel  3.3     1  Grassland     4.1 FALSE            1
19             Gravel.Pit  2.9     1  Grassland     3.5 FALSE            1
14     Observatory.Ridge  1.8     6  Grassland     3.8 FALSE            0
2         Silwood.Bottom  5.1     2     Arable     5.2 FALSE            7
18            Pound.Hill  4.4     2     Arable     4.5 FALSE            5
8                Ashurst  2.1     0     Arable     4.8 FALSE            4
```

It is less likely that we will want to select *columns* on the basis of logical operations, but it is perfectly possible. Suppose that for some reason we want to select the columns that contain the character s (upper-case S). In *R*, the function for this is `grep ()` (see Section 3.15.6 for more details), which returns the subscript (a number or set of numbers) indicating which character strings within a vector of character strings contained an upper-case S. The names of the variables within a dataframe are obtained by the `names ()` function:

```
names (worms)
```

```
[1] "Field.Name"    "Area"          "Slope"        "Vegetation"  "Soil.pH"
[6] "Damp"          "Worm.density"
```

So we want our function `grep ()` to pick out variables numbers 3 and 5 because they are the only ones containing upper-case S:

```
grep ("S", names (worms))
```

```
[1] 3 5
```

Finally, we can use these numbers as subscripts to select columns 3 and 5:

```
worms[, grep ("S", names (worms))]

    Slope Soil.pH
1      11     4.1
2       2     5.2
3       3     4.3
4       5     4.9
5       0     4.2
6       2     3.9
7       3     4.2
8       0     4.8
9       0     5.7
10      4     5.0
11     10     5.2
12      1     4.1
13      2     4.0
14      6     3.8
15      0     5.0
16      0     4.9
17      8     4.7
18      2     4.5
19      1     3.5
20     10     5.1
```

4.5.4 Using logical conditions to select rows from the dataframe

A very common operation is selecting certain rows from the dataframe on the basis of values in one or more of the variables (the columns of the dataframe). Suppose that we want to restrict the data to cases from damp fields. We want all the columns, so the syntax for the subscripts is ['which rows', blank]:

```
worms[worms$Damp == T,]

      Field.Name Area Slope Vegetation Soil.pH Damp Worm.density
4     Rush.Meadow  2.4     5     Meadow     4.9 TRUE            5
10  Rookery.Slope  1.5     4  Grassland     5.0 TRUE            7
15     Pond.Field  4.1     0     Meadow     5.0 TRUE            6
16   Water.Meadow  3.9     0     Meadow     4.9 TRUE            8
17      Cheapside  2.2     8      Scrub     4.7 TRUE            4
20      Farm.Wood  0.8    10      Scrub     5.1 TRUE            3
```

Note that because Damp is a logical variable (with just two potential values, TRUE or FALSE) we can refer to true or false in abbreviated form, T or F. Also notice that the T in this case is not enclosed in quotes: the T means true, not the character string T. The other important point is that the symbol for the logical condition is == (two successive equals signs with no gap between them; see Section 3.4).

The logic for the selection of rows can refer to values (and functions of values) in more than one column. Suppose that we wanted the data from the fields where `Worm.density` was higher than the median and `Soil.pH` was less than 5.2. In *R*, the logical operator for AND is the ('ampersand') symbol:

```
worms[worms$Worm.density > median (worms$Worm.density) & worms$Soil.pH < 5.2,]
```

	Field.Name	Area	Slope	Vegetation	Soil.pH	Damp	Worm.density
4	Rush.Meadow	2.4	5	Meadow	4.9	TRUE	5
5	Gunness.Thicket	3.8	0	Scrub	4.2	FALSE	6
10	Rookery.Slope	1.5	4	Grassland	5.0	TRUE	7
15	Pond.Field	4.1	0	Meadow	5.0	TRUE	6
16	Water.Meadow	3.9	0	Meadow	4.9	TRUE	8
18	Pound.Hill	4.4	2	Arable	4.5	FALSE	5

This might seem fiddly to type, but in RStudio, the lists offered after typing three characters of `worms` and after $ make it very simple.

Suppose that we want to extract all the columns that contain numbers (rather than characters or logical variables) from the dataframe. The function `is.numeric ()` can be applied across all the columns of `worms` using `sapply ()` to create the appropriate subscripts like this:

```
worms[, sapply (worms, is.numeric)]
```

	Area	Slope	Soil.pH	Worm.density
1	3.6	11	4.1	4
2	5.1	2	5.2	7
3	2.8	3	4.3	2
4	2.4	5	4.9	5
5	3.8	0	4.2	6
6	3.1	2	3.9	2
7	3.5	3	4.2	3
8	2.1	0	4.8	4
9	1.9	0	5.7	9
10	1.5	4	5.0	7
11	2.9	10	5.2	8
12	3.3	1	4.1	1
13	3.7	2	4.0	2
14	1.8	6	3.8	0
15	4.1	0	5.0	6
16	3.9	0	4.9	8
17	2.2	8	4.7	4
18	4.4	2	4.5	5
19	2.9	1	3.5	1
20	0.8	10	5.1	3

Similarly, we might want to extract the columns that are factors (see Section 3.3):

```
worms[, sapply (worms, is.factor)]


 [1] Grassland Arable    Grassland Meadow    Scrub     Grassland Grassland
 [8] Arable    Orchard   Grassland Scrub     Grassland Grassland Grassland
[15] Meadow    Meadow    Scrub     Arable    Grassland Scrub
Levels: Arable Grassland Meadow Orchard Scrub
```

There is just one.

To drop a row or rows from the dataframe, use *negative subscripts*. Thus, to drop the middle 10 rows (i.e. row numbers 6–15 inclusive) do this:

```
worms[-(6:15),]

       Field.Name Area Slope Vegetation Soil.pH  Damp Worm.density
1      Nashs.Field  3.6    11  Grassland     4.1 FALSE            4
2   Silwood.Bottom  5.1     2     Arable     5.2 FALSE            7
3    Nursery.Field  2.8     3  Grassland     4.3 FALSE            2
4      Rush.Meadow  2.4     5     Meadow     4.9  TRUE            5
5  Gunness.Thicket  3.8     0      Scrub     4.2 FALSE            6
16     Water.Meadow  3.9     0     Meadow     4.9  TRUE            8
17       Cheapside  2.2     8      Scrub     4.7  TRUE            4
18       Pound.Hill  4.4     2     Arable     4.5 FALSE            5
19       Gravel.Pit  2.9     1  Grassland     3.5 FALSE            1
20        Farm.Wood  0.8    10      Scrub     5.1  TRUE            3
```

Here are all the rows that are not grasslands (recall that the logical symbol ! means NOT):

```
worms[!(worms$Vegetation == "Grassland"),]

       Field.Name Area Slope Vegetation Soil.pH  Damp Worm.density
2   Silwood.Bottom  5.1     2     Arable     5.2 FALSE            7
4      Rush.Meadow  2.4     5     Meadow     4.9  TRUE            5
5  Gunness.Thicket  3.8     0      Scrub     4.2 FALSE            6
8          Ashurst  2.1     0     Arable     4.8 FALSE            4
9      The.Orchard  1.9     0    Orchard     5.7 FALSE            9
11     Garden.Wood  2.9    10      Scrub     5.2 FALSE            8
15      Pond.Field  4.1     0     Meadow     5.0  TRUE            6
16     Water.Meadow  3.9     0     Meadow     4.9  TRUE            8
17       Cheapside  2.2     8      Scrub     4.7  TRUE            4
18       Pound.Hill  4.4     2     Arable     4.5 FALSE            5
20        Farm.Wood  0.8    10      Scrub     5.1  TRUE            3
```

If we want to use minus signs rather than logical NOT to drop rows from the dataframe, the expression we use must evaluate to (i.e. produce) numbers. The which () function is useful for this as it just returns the position in the appropriate vector (here, Damp). Let's use this technique to drop the non-damp fields:

```
worms[-which (worms$Damp == F),]
```

```
      Field.Name Area Slope Vegetation Soil.pH Damp Worm.density
4    Rush.Meadow  2.4     5     Meadow     4.9 TRUE            5
10 Rookery.Slope  1.5     4  Grassland     5.0 TRUE            7
15    Pond.Field  4.1     0     Meadow     5.0 TRUE            6
16   Water.Meadow 3.9     0     Meadow     4.9 TRUE            8
17     Cheapside  2.2     8      Scrub     4.7 TRUE            4
20     Farm.Wood  0.8    10      Scrub     5.1 TRUE            3
```

which achieves the same end as the more elegant:

```
worms[!(worms$Damp == F),]
```

or, even simpler:

```
worms[worms$Damp == T,]
```

In this rather more complicated example, we would like to extract a single record for each vegetation type, and that record is to be the case within each vegetation type that has the greatest Worm.density. There are two steps to this: first order all of the rows in a new dataframe in decreasing order of Worm.density, then select the subset of these rows which is not duplicated within each Vegetation type. This will pick out the first of each Vegetation type, which will therefore have the highest Worm.density:

```
worms_new <- worms[order (worms$Worm.density),]
worms_new[!duplicated (worms_new$Vegetation),]
```

```
         Field.Name Area Slope Vegetation Soil.pH  Damp Worm.density
14 Observatory.Ridge  1.8     6  Grassland     3.8 FALSE            0
20         Farm.Wood  0.8    10      Scrub     5.1  TRUE            3
8            Ashurst  2.1     0     Arable     4.8 FALSE            4
4        Rush.Meadow  2.4     5     Meadow     4.9  TRUE            5
9        The.Orchard  1.9     0    Orchard     5.7 FALSE            9
```

4.5.5 Omitting rows containing missing values, NA

In statistical modelling, it is often useful to have a dataframe that contains no missing values (which should be described as NA: see Section 3.7) in the data. We can create a shorter dataframe using the na.omit () function. Here is a sister dataframe of worms in which certain values are NA:

```
(worms_short <- read.table ("worms.missing.txt", header = T))
```

```
      Field.Name Area Slope Vegetation Soil.pH  Damp Worm.density
1     Nashs.Field  3.6    11  Grassland     4.1 FALSE            4
2  Silwood.Bottom  5.1    NA     Arable     5.2 FALSE            7
3   Nursery.Field  2.8     3  Grassland     4.3 FALSE            2
4     Rush.Meadow  2.4     5     Meadow     4.9  TRUE            5
5  Gunness.Thicket 3.8     0      Scrub     4.2 FALSE            6
6        Oak.Mead  3.1     2  Grassland     3.9 FALSE            2
7    Church.Field  3.5     3  Grassland      NA    NA           NA
8         Ashurst  2.1     0     Arable     4.8 FALSE            4
9     The.Orchard  1.9     0     Orchard     5.7 FALSE            9
10   Rookery.Slope  1.5     4  Grassland     5.0  TRUE            7
11    Garden.Wood  2.9    10      Scrub     5.2 FALSE            8
12    North.Gravel  3.3     1  Grassland     4.1 FALSE            1
13    South.Gravel  3.7     2  Grassland     4.0 FALSE            2
14 Observatory.Ridge 1.8    6  Grassland     3.8 FALSE            0
15      Pond.Field  4.1     0     Meadow     5.0  TRUE            6
16    Water.Meadow  3.9     0     Meadow     4.9  TRUE            8
17       Cheapside  2.2     8      Scrub     4.7  TRUE            4
18      Pound.Hill  4.4     2     Arable     4.5 FALSE            5
19      Gravel.Pit   NA     1  Grassland     3.5 FALSE            1
20       Farm.Wood  0.8    10      Scrub     5.1  TRUE            3
```

By inspection we can see that we should like to leave out row 2 (one missing value), row 7 (three missing values), and row 19 (one missing value). This could not be simpler:

```
na.omit (worms_short)
```

```
      Field.Name Area Slope Vegetation Soil.pH  Damp Worm.density
1     Nashs.Field  3.6    11  Grassland     4.1 FALSE            4
3   Nursery.Field  2.8     3  Grassland     4.3 FALSE            2
4     Rush.Meadow  2.4     5     Meadow     4.9  TRUE            5
5  Gunness.Thicket 3.8     0      Scrub     4.2 FALSE            6
6        Oak.Mead  3.1     2  Grassland     3.9 FALSE            2
8         Ashurst  2.1     0     Arable     4.8 FALSE            4
9     The.Orchard  1.9     0     Orchard     5.7 FALSE            9
10   Rookery.Slope  1.5     4  Grassland     5.0  TRUE            7
11    Garden.Wood  2.9    10      Scrub     5.2 FALSE            8
12    North.Gravel  3.3     1  Grassland     4.1 FALSE            1
13    South.Gravel  3.7     2  Grassland     4.0 FALSE            2
14 Observatory.Ridge 1.8    6  Grassland     3.8 FALSE            0
15      Pond.Field  4.1     0     Meadow     5.0  TRUE            6
16    Water.Meadow  3.9     0     Meadow     4.9  TRUE            8
17       Cheapside  2.2     8      Scrub     4.7  TRUE            4
18      Pound.Hill  4.4     2     Arable     4.5 FALSE            5
20       Farm.Wood  0.8    10      Scrub     5.1  TRUE            3
```

and we see that rows 2, 7, and 19 have been omitted in creating the new dataframe.

Alternatively, we can use the `na.exclude ()` function. This differs from `na.omit ()` only when we are considering models (such as linear models in Chapter 10). A model built with `na.omit (worms.missing)` will only produce residuals and predictions of length 17 (20 − 3). However, if we use `na.exclude (worms.missing)`, then the residuals and predictions will be of length 20 with NAs in positions 2, 7, and 19:

```
new_worms_short <- na.exclude (worms_short)
```

The function to test for the presence of missing values across a dataframe is `complete.cases ()`:

```
complete.cases (worms_short)
```

```
 [1]  TRUE FALSE  TRUE  TRUE  TRUE  TRUE FALSE  TRUE  TRUE  TRUE  TRUE  TRUE
[13]  TRUE  TRUE  TRUE  TRUE  TRUE  TRUE FALSE  TRUE
```

We could also use this as a method to pick out the rows with no NAs:

```
worms_short[complete.cases (worms_short),]
```

```
           Field.Name Area Slope Vegetation Soil.pH  Damp Worm.density
1         Nashs.Field  3.6    11  Grassland     4.1 FALSE            4
3       Nursery.Field  2.8     3  Grassland     4.3 FALSE            2
4         Rush.Meadow  2.4     5     Meadow     4.9  TRUE            5
5     Gunness.Thicket  3.8     0      Scrub     4.2 FALSE            6
6            Oak.Mead  3.1     2  Grassland     3.9 FALSE            2
8             Ashurst  2.1     0     Arable     4.8 FALSE            4
9         The.Orchard  1.9     0    Orchard     5.7 FALSE            9
10      Rookery.Slope  1.5     4  Grassland     5.0  TRUE            7
11        Garden.Wood  2.9    10      Scrub     5.2 FALSE            8
12       North.Gravel  3.3     1  Grassland     4.1 FALSE            1
13       South.Gravel  3.7     2  Grassland     4.0 FALSE            2
14  Observatory.Ridge  1.8     6  Grassland     3.8 FALSE            0
15         Pond.Field  4.1     0     Meadow     5.0  TRUE            6
16       Water.Meadow  3.9     0     Meadow     4.9  TRUE            8
17          Cheapside  2.2     8      Scrub     4.7  TRUE            4
18         Pound.Hill  4.4     2     Arable     4.5 FALSE            5
20          Farm.Wood  0.8    10      Scrub     5.1  TRUE            3
```

It is well worth checking the individual variables containing NAs separately, because it is possible that one or more variables contribute most of the missing values, and it may be preferable to remove these variables from the modelling rather than lose the valuable information about the other explanatory variables associated with these cases. We can use `summary ()` to count the missing values for each variable in the dataframe:

```
summary (worms_short)
```

```
  Field.Name            Area            Slope          Vegetation
Length:20         Min.   :0.800    Min.   : 0.000    Length:20
Class :character  1st Qu.:2.150    1st Qu.: 0.500    Class :character
Mode  :character  Median :3.100    Median : 2.000    Mode  :character
```

```
                        Mean    :2.995    Mean     : 3.579
                        3rd Qu.:3.750    3rd Qu.: 5.500
                        Max.    :5.100    Max.     :11.000
                        NA's    :1        NA's     :1
         Soil.pH              Damp             Worm.density
 Min.    :3.500    Mode :logical    Min.     :0.000
 1st Qu.:4.100    FALSE:13         1st Qu.:2.000
 Median :4.700    TRUE :6          Median :4.000
 Mean    :4.574    NA's :1          Mean     :4.421
 3rd Qu.:5.000                      3rd Qu.:6.500
 Max.    :5.700                      Max.     :9.000
 NA's    :1                         NA's     :1
```

We can see that in this case no single variable contributed more missing values than any other.

We would need to think carefully before doing this, but there might be circumstances when we want to replace the missing values, NA, by zero (or by some other missing-value indicator). This is how to replace all the NAs by zeros:

```
worms_short[is.na (worms_short)] <- 0
worms_short
```

	Field.Name	Area	Slope	Vegetation	Soil.pH	Damp	Worm.density
1	Nashs.Field	3.6	11	Grassland	4.1	0	4
2	Silwood.Bottom	5.1	0	Arable	5.2	0	7
3	Nursery.Field	2.8	3	Grassland	4.3	0	2
4	Rush.Meadow	2.4	5	Meadow	4.9	1	5
5	Gunness.Thicket	3.8	0	Scrub	4.2	0	6
6	Oak.Mead	3.1	2	Grassland	3.9	0	2
7	Church.Field	3.5	3	Grassland	0.0	0	0
8	Ashurst	2.1	0	Arable	4.8	0	4
9	The.Orchard	1.9	0	Orchard	5.7	0	9
10	Rookery.Slope	1.5	4	Grassland	5.0	1	7
11	Garden.Wood	2.9	10	Scrub	5.2	0	8
12	North.Gravel	3.3	1	Grassland	4.1	0	1
13	South.Gravel	3.7	2	Grassland	4.0	0	2
14	Observatory.Ridge	1.8	6	Grassland	3.8	0	0
15	Pond.Field	4.1	0	Meadow	5.0	1	6
16	Water.Meadow	3.9	0	Meadow	4.9	1	8
17	Cheapside	2.2	8	Scrub	4.7	1	4
18	Pound.Hill	4.4	2	Arable	4.5	0	5
19	Gravel.Pit	0.0	1	Grassland	3.5	0	1
20	Farm.Wood	0.8	10	Scrub	5.1	1	3

This has had unfortunate side-effects in that the Damp entries have been coerced to 0s and 1s, and, for instance, it is impossible to distinguish between a Slope of 0 (row 5) and one where the datum was missing (row 2).

4.5.6 A dataframe with row names instead of row numbers

We can suppress the creation of row numbers and allocate our own unique names to each row by altering the syntax of the read.table () function. The first column of the worms database contains the names of the fields in which the other variables were measured. Up to now, we have read this column as if it was the first variable.

```
(worms2 <- read.table ("worms.txt", header = T, row.names = 1))
```

	Area	Slope	Vegetation	Soil.pH	Damp	Worm.density
Nashs.Field	3.6	11	Grassland	4.1	FALSE	4
Silwood.Bottom	5.1	2	Arable	5.2	FALSE	7
Nursery.Field	2.8	3	Grassland	4.3	FALSE	2
Rush.Meadow	2.4	5	Meadow	4.9	TRUE	5
Gunness.Thicket	3.8	0	Scrub	4.2	FALSE	6
Oak.Mead	3.1	2	Grassland	3.9	FALSE	2
Church.Field	3.5	3	Grassland	4.2	FALSE	3
Ashurst	2.1	0	Arable	4.8	FALSE	4
The.Orchard	1.9	0	Orchard	5.7	FALSE	9
Rookery.Slope	1.5	4	Grassland	5.0	TRUE	7
Garden.Wood	2.9	10	Scrub	5.2	FALSE	8
North.Gravel	3.3	1	Grassland	4.1	FALSE	1
South.Gravel	3.7	2	Grassland	4.0	FALSE	2
Observatory.Ridge	1.8	6	Grassland	3.8	FALSE	0
Pond.Field	4.1	0	Meadow	5.0	TRUE	6
Water.Meadow	3.9	0	Meadow	4.9	TRUE	8
Cheapside	2.2	8	Scrub	4.7	TRUE	4
Pound.Hill	4.4	2	Arable	4.5	FALSE	5
Gravel.Pit	2.9	1	Grassland	3.5	FALSE	1
Farm.Wood	0.8	10	Scrub	5.1	TRUE	3

We can see that the field names column is not now headed by a variable name, and that the row numbers, as intended, have been suppressed. Now, we can use the row name or the row number as a reference:

```
worms2[1, 1]

[1] 3.6

worms2["Nashs.Field", 1]

[1] 3.6
```

The first column is now `Area`.

4.5.7 Creating a dataframe from another kind of object

We have seen that the simplest way to create a dataframe in *R* is to read a table of data from an external file using the `read.table ()` function. Alternatively, we can create a dataframe by using the `data.frame ()` function to bind together a number of vectors. Here are three vectors of the same length:

```
x <- runif (10)
y <- letters [1:10]
z <- sample (c (rep (T, 5), rep(F, 5)))
```

To make them into a dataframe called `new_df`, we just type:

```
(new_df <- data.frame (y, z, x))

    y     z           x
1   a  FALSE  0.8598338
2   b   TRUE  0.6170012
3   c   TRUE  0.7765110
4   d  FALSE  0.2229500
5   e  FALSE  0.6665438
6   f   TRUE  0.7434039
7   g   TRUE  0.1997147
8   h   TRUE  0.5121942
9   i  FALSE  0.6975335
10  j  FALSE  0.2100809
```

Note that the order of the columns is controlled simply by the sequence of the vector names specified, and the Ts and Fs have been converted into TRUEs and FALSEs.

In this next example, we create a table of counts of 1500 random integers from a Poisson distribution with mean 1.5, and then convert the table into a dataframe. First, we make a table object:

```
x <- rpois (1500, 1.5)
(y <- table (x))

x
  0    1    2    3    4    5    6    7
311  494  395  190   76   23    9    2
```

Now, it is simple to convert this table object into a dataframe with two variables, the value of the variable and the frequency, using the `as.data.frame ()` function (see Section 3.6 for more details). R knows that the count arises in the variable x and, as the source is a table, puts the result of the count in the variable `Freq`:

```
(y_df <- as.data.frame (y))

   x  Freq
1  0   311
2  1   494
3  2   395
4  3   190
5  4    76
6  5    23
7  6     9
8  7     2
```

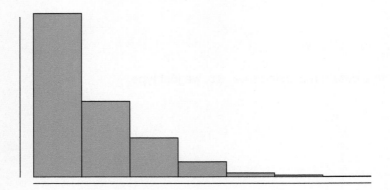

Figure 4.1 Histogram from extended dataframe

In some cases, we might want to expand a dataframe like the one above such that it had a separate row for every distinct count (i.e. 311 rows with $x = 0$, 494 rows with $x = 1$, 395 rows with $x = 2$, etc.). This is very straightforward using subscripts. We need to create a vector of indices containing 311 repeats of 1, 494 repeats of 2 and so on. Note that we need to the row numbers (1, 2, 3, ... ,), not the row values ($x = 0, 1, 2, \dots$,).

```
y_long <- rep (1:nrow (y_df), y_df$Freq)
```

This simple command has produced a vector with the right number of repeats of each of the row numbers, which we can now use to plot the table in Figure 4.1:

```
length (y_long)

[1] 1500

hist (y_long, breaks = 1: (max (x) + 1), main = "",
xlab = "x", col = hue_pal ()(1))
```

To get the long version of the dataframe, `y_df`, we just use our vector, `y_long`, as the row specifier. We can have a look at its bottom:

```
y_long_df <- y_df[y_long,]
tail (y_long_df)

    x Freq
7.5 6    9
7.6 6    9
7.7 6    9
7.8 6    9
8   7    2
8.1 7    2
```

Note the way that *R* has handled the duplicate row numbers, creating a nested series to indicate the repeats of each of the original row numbers.

4.5.8 Eliminating duplicate rows from a dataframe

Sometimes a dataframe will contain duplicate rows where all the variables have exactly the same values in two or more rows, perhaps by mistake. Here is a simple example:

```
(dups <- read.table ("dups.txt", header = T))

  cow dog cat bat
1   1   2   3   1
2   1   2   2   1
3   3   2   1   1
4   4   4   2   1
5   3   2   1   1
6   6   1   2   5
7   1   2   3   2
```

Note that row number 5 is an exact duplicate of row number 3. To create a dataframe with all the duplicate rows stripped out, we can use the `unique ()` function like this:

```
unique (dups)

  cow dog cat bat
1   1   2   3   1
2   1   2   2   1
3   3   2   1   1
4   4   4   2   1
6   6   1   2   5
7   1   2   3   2
```

Notice that the row names in the new dataframe are the same as in the original so that we can spot that row number 5 was removed by. The function will work equally well on vectors, matrices, and arrays.

To view the rows that are duplicates in a dataframe (if any), we can use the `duplicated ()` function to create a vector of TRUEs and FALSEs to act as the filter:

```
dups[duplicated (dups),]

  cow dog cat bat
5   3   2   1   1
```

This will output the second or further instances of any row.

4.5.9 Dates in dataframes

Dates and times, particularly their structure, are dealt with in detail in Section 3.16. Here we illustrate the idea, focused on dataframes, using a simple example of patients' response to a treatment:

```
pat_resp <- read.table ("sortdata.txt", header = T)
head (pat_resp)
```

```
     name         date  response treatment
1  albert 25/08/2003 0.05963704         A
2     ann 21/05/2003 1.46555993         A
3    john 12/10/2003 1.59406539         B
4     ian 02/12/2003 2.09505949         A
5 michael 18/10/2003 2.38330748         B
6     ann 02/07/2003 2.86983693         B
```

We want to order the rows by date. The ordering is to be applied to all four columns of the dataframe. Note that ordering on the basis of our variable called `date` does not work in the way we want it to

```
head (pat_resp[order (pat_resp$date),])
```

```
      name         date  response treatment
53  rachel 01/08/2003 32.987922         B
65  albert 02/06/2003 38.419796         A
6      ann 02/07/2003  2.869837         B
10  cecily 02/11/2003  6.814676         A
4      ian 02/12/2003  2.095059         A
29 michael 03/05/2003 15.598909         B
```

This is because of the format used for depicting the date is a character string in which the first characters are the day, then the month, then the year, so the dataframe has been sorted by day of the month. In order to sort by date, we need first to convert our variable into date-time format using the `strptime ()` function (see Section 3.16.1 for details):

```
(pat_resp_dates <- strptime (pat_resp$date, format = "%d/%m/%Y"))
```

```
 [1] "2003-08-25 BST" "2003-05-21 BST" "2003-10-12 BST" "2003-12-02 GMT"
 [5] "2003-10-18 BST" "2003-07-02 BST" "2003-09-27 BST" "2003-06-05 BST"
 [9] "2003-06-11 BST" "2003-11-02 GMT" "2003-09-24 BST" "2003-11-26 GMT"
[13] "2003-11-08 GMT" "2003-07-11 BST" "2003-09-12 BST" "2003-05-27 BST"
[17] "2003-09-06 BST" "2003-09-30 BST" "2003-05-30 BST" "2003-07-20 BST"
[21] "2003-07-29 BST" "2003-10-15 BST" "2003-09-18 BST" "2003-04-27 BST"
[25] "2003-11-17 GMT" "2003-10-03 BST" "2003-11-23 GMT" "2003-11-11 GMT"
[29] "2003-05-03 BST" "2003-11-20 GMT" "2003-10-30 GMT" "2003-09-15 BST"
[33] "2003-04-30 BST" "2003-06-08 BST" "2003-05-18 BST" "2003-08-04 BST"
[37] "2003-08-13 BST" "2003-08-07 BST" "2003-10-21 BST" "2003-11-29 GMT"
[41] "2003-06-17 BST" "2003-08-19 BST" "2003-10-27 GMT" "2003-10-06 BST"
[45] "2003-11-05 GMT" "2003-07-05 BST" "2003-07-26 BST" "2003-06-20 BST"
[49] "2003-04-21 BST" "2003-05-09 BST" "2003-07-17 BST" "2003-08-31 BST"
[53] "2003-08-01 BST" "2003-10-09 BST" "2003-07-23 BST" "2003-09-21 BST"
[57] "2003-08-28 BST" "2003-06-29 BST" "2003-07-08 BST" "2003-08-22 BST"
```

```
[61]  "2003-06-26 BST" "2003-08-10 BST" "2003-04-24 BST" "2003-10-24 BST"
[65]  "2003-06-02 BST" "2003-09-09 BST" "2003-09-03 BST" "2003-07-14 BST"
[69]  "2003-05-12 BST" "2003-06-14 BST" "2003-05-06 BST" "2003-05-15 BST"
[73]  "2003-05-24 BST" "2003-08-16 BST" "2003-11-14 GMT" "2003-06-23 BST"
```

This has produced a date object (vector) with year first, then a hyphen, then month, then a hyphen, then day, and this will sort into the desired sequence. We bind the new variable to the dataframe like this:

```
pat_resp <- cbind (pat_resp, pat_resp_dates)
```

Now that the new variable is in the correct format, the dates can be sorted correctly:

```
head (pat_resp[order (pat_resp$pat_resp_dates),])

          name       date response treatment pat_resp_dates
49      albert 21/04/2003 30.66633         A     2003-04-21
63       james 24/04/2003 37.04140         A     2003-04-24
24        john 27/04/2003 12.70257         A     2003-04-27
33     william 30/04/2003 18.05707         B     2003-04-30
29     michael 03/05/2003 15.59891         B     2003-05-03
71         ian 06/05/2003 39.97238         A     2003-05-06
```

4.6   Using the `match` () function in dataframes

The `worms` dataframe we have been using contains fields of five different vegetation types:

```
unique (worms$Vegetation)

[1] Grassland Arable    Meadow    Scrub    Orchard
Levels: Arable Grassland Meadow Orchard Scrub
```

and we want to know the appropriate herbicides to use in each of the 20 fields. The herbicides are in a separate dataframe that contains the recommended herbicides for a much larger set of plant community types:

```
(herbicides <- read.table ("herbicides.txt", header = T))

         Type Herbicide
1    Woodland  Fusilade
2     Conifer  Weedwipe
3      Arable  Twinspan
4        Hill  Weedwipe
5     Bracken  Fusilade
```

```
6         Scrub   Weedwipe
7     Grassland   Allclear
8         Chalk   Vanquish
9        Meadow   Propinol
10         Lawn   Vanquish
11      Orchard   Fusilade
12        Verge   Allclear
```

We want to create a vector of length 20 (one for every field in `worms`) containing the name of the appropriate herbicide. The first value needs to be `Allclear` because Nash's Field is `Grassland`, and the second needs to be `Twinspan` because Silwood Bottom is `Arable`, and so on. The first argument in `match ()` is what we want to match, i.e. `worms$Vegetation`, and the second argument selects the appropriate row from `herbicides`. The result is the used as a vector of subscripts to extract the relevant herbicides from `herbicides$Herbicide` like this:

```
(hb <- herbicides$Herbicide[match (worms$Vegetation, herbicides$Type)])

 [1] "Allclear" "Twinspan" "Allclear" "Propinol" "Weedwipe" "Allclear"
 [7] "Allclear" "Twinspan" "Fusilade" "Allclear" "Weedwipe" "Allclear"
[13] "Allclear" "Allclear" "Propinol" "Propinol" "Weedwipe" "Twinspan"
[19] "Allclear" "Weedwipe"
```

We could then add this information as a new column in the `worms` dataframe:

```
worms$hb <- hb
```

That is a very simple way to add a column to a dataframe. An alternative which is a bit clearer about what is happening is

```
data.frame (worms, hb)
```

	Field.Name	Area	Slope	Vegetation	Soil.pH	Damp	Worm.density	hb
1	Nashs.Field	3.6	11	Grassland	4.1	FALSE	4	Allclear
2	Silwood.Bottom	5.1	2	Arable	5.2	FALSE	7	Twinspan
3	Nursery.Field	2.8	3	Grassland	4.3	FALSE	2	Allclear
4	Rush.Meadow	2.4	5	Meadow	4.9	TRUE	5	Propinol
5	Gunness.Thicket	3.8	0	Scrub	4.2	FALSE	6	Weedwipe
6	Oak.Mead	3.1	2	Grassland	3.9	FALSE	2	Allclear
7	Church.Field	3.5	3	Grassland	4.2	FALSE	3	Allclear
8	Ashurst	2.1	0	Arable	4.8	FALSE	4	Twinspan
9	The.Orchard	1.9	0	Orchard	5.7	FALSE	9	Fusilade
10	Rookery.Slope	1.5	4	Grassland	5.0	TRUE	7	Allclear
11	Garden.Wood	2.9	10	Scrub	5.2	FALSE	8	Weedwipe
12	North.Gravel	3.3	1	Grassland	4.1	FALSE	1	Allclear
13	South.Gravel	3.7	2	Grassland	4.0	FALSE	2	Allclear
14	Observatory.Ridge	1.8	6	Grassland	3.8	FALSE	0	Allclear
15	Pond.Field	4.1	0	Meadow	5.0	TRUE	6	Propinol

16	Water.Meadow	3.9	0	Meadow	4.9	TRUE	8	Propinol
17	Cheapside	2.2	8	Scrub	4.7	TRUE	4	Weedwipe
18	Pound.Hill	4.4	2	Arable	4.5	FALSE	5	Twinspan
19	Gravel.Pit	2.9	1	Grassland	3.5	FALSE	1	Allclear
20	Farm.Wood	0.8	10	Scrub	5.1	TRUE	3	Weedwipe

4.6.1 Merging two dataframes

Suppose we have two dataframes, the first containing information on plant life forms and the second containing information on time of flowering. We want to produce a single dataframe showing information on both life form and flowering time. Both dataframes contain variables for genus name and species name:

```
(lifeforms <- read.table ("lifeforms.txt", header = T))


   Genus      species lifeform
1   Acer platanoides     tree
2   Acer    palmatum     tree
3  Ajuga     reptans     herb
4 Conyza sumatrensis   annual
5 Lamium       album     herb


(flowering <- read.table ("fltimes.txt", header = T))


      Genus       species flowering
1      Acer    platanoides      May
2     Ajuga        reptans     June
3  Brassica         napus    April
4 Chamerion angustifolium     July
5    Conyza      bilbaoana   August
6    Lamium         album  January
```

Because at least one of the variable names is identical in the two dataframes (in this case, in fact, two variables are identical, namely `Genus` and `species`) we can use the simplest of all merge commands:

```
merge (flowering, lifeforms)


   Genus     species flowering lifeform
1   Acer platanoides       May     tree
2  Ajuga     reptans      June     herb
3 Lamium       album   January     herb
```

R has looked for rows which had identical entries in both dataframes, where the column names match (i.e. `Genus` and `species`), and then put in the values from the remaining columns from both dataframes. Two rows from the `lifeforms` database were excluded because there were no flowering time data for them (`Acer platanoides` and `Conyza sumatrensis`), and three rows from the `flowering` database were excluded because there were no life-form data for them (`Chamerion angustifolium`, `Conyza bilbaoana`, and `Brassica napus`).

If we want to include all the species, with missing values (`NA`) inserted when flowering times or life forms are not known, then we can use the `all = T` option:

```
(plants_all <- merge (flowering, lifeforms, all = T))

     Genus         species flowering lifeform
1     Acer        palmatum      <NA>     tree
2     Acer      platanoides       May     tree
3    Ajuga         reptans      June     herb
4  Brassica          napus     April     <NA>
5 Chamerion angustifolium      July     <NA>
6    Conyza       bilbaoana    August     <NA>
7    Conyza     sumatrensis      <NA>   annual
8    Lamium           album   January     herb
```

One complexity that often arises is that the same variable has *different names* in the two dataframes that need to be merged. The simplest solution is often to edit the variable names in the spreadsheet before reading them into *R* but, failing this, we need to specify the names in the first dataframe (known conventionally as the *x* dataframe) and the second dataframe (known conventionally as the *y* dataframe) using the `by.x =` and `by.y =` options in `merge ()`. We have a third dataframe containing information on the seed weights of all eight species, but the variable `Genus` is called `name1` and the variable `species` is called `name2`.

```
(seeds <- read.table ("seedwts.txt", header = T))

     name1          name2 seed
1     Acer      platanoides 32.0
2    Lamium           album 12.0
3    Ajuga          reptans  4.0
4 Chamerion angustifolium  1.5
5    Conyza       bilbaoana  0.5
6  Brassica          napus  7.0
7     Acer        palmatum 21.0
8    Conyza     sumatrensis  0.6
```

Just typing `merge (plants_all, seeds)` fails miserably as it is not clear how to merge the dataframes: try it and see. We need to inform the `merge ()` function that `Genus` and `name1` are synonyms (different names for the same variable), as are `species` and `name2`.

```
merge (plants_all, seeds, by.x = c ("Genus", "species"),
       by.y = c ("name1", "name2"))

     Genus       species flowering lifeform seed
1     Acer      palmatum      <NA>     tree 21.0
2     Acer    platanoides      May     tree 32.0
```

```
3      Ajuga        reptans       June      herb   4.0
4    Brassica         napus      April      <NA>   7.0
5  Chamerion  angustifolium       July      <NA>   1.5
6     Conyza      bilbaoana     August      <NA>   0.5
7     Conyza    sumatrensis       <NA>    annual   0.6
8     Lamium          album    January      herb  12.0
```

Note that the variable names used in the merged dataframe are those names that originate in the *x* dataframe.

4.7   Adding margins to a dataframe

Suppose we have a dataframe showing sales by season and by person:

```
(sales <- read.table ("sales.txt", header = T))


             name spring summer autumn winter
1       Jane.Smith     14     18     11     12
2     Robert.Jones     17     18     10     13
3      Dick.Rogers     12     16      9     14
4  William.Edwards     15     14     11     10
5      Janet.Jones     11     17     11     16
```

We want to add margins (i.e. an extra row and column) to this dataframe showing departures of the seasonal means from the overall mean (as an extra row at the bottom) and departures of the people's means from the overall mean (as an extra column on the right). Finally, we want the sales in the body of the dataframe to be represented by departures from the overall mean. Let's start with the extra column:

```
indiv_means <- rowMeans (sales[, 2:5])
overall_mean <- mean (indiv_means)
(people <- indiv_means - overall_mean)


[1]  0.30  1.05 -0.70 -0.95  0.30
```

It is very straightforward to add a new column to the dataframe using cbind ():

```
(new.sales <- cbind (sales, people))


             name spring summer autumn winter people
1       Jane.Smith     14     18     11     12   0.30
2     Robert.Jones     17     18     10     13   1.05
3      Dick.Rogers     12     16      9     14  -0.70
4  William.Edwards     15     14     11     10  -0.95
5      Janet.Jones     11     17     11     16   0.30
```

Robert Jones is the most effective sales person (+1.05) and William Edwards is the least effective (−0.95). The column means are calculated in a similar way:

```
indiv_seasons <- colMeans (sales[,2:5])
overall_seasons <- mean (indiv_seasons)
(seasons <- indiv_seasons - overall_seasons)


spring summer autumn winter
0.35    3.15   -3.05  -0.45
```

Sales are highest in summer (+3.15) and lowest in autumn (−3.05).

Now there is a hitch, however, because there are only four column means, but there are six columns in `new.frame`, so we cannot use `rbind ()` directly. The simplest way to deal with this is to make a copy of one of the rows of the new dataframe and then edit this to include the values we want: a label in the first column to say 'seasonal means' then the four column means, and then a zero for the grand mean of the effects:

```
new.row <- new.sales[1,]
new.row[1] <- "Seasonal effects"
new.row[2:5] <- seasons
new.row[6] <- 0
new.row


              name spring summer autumn winter people
1 Seasonal effects   0.35   3.15  -3.05  -0.45      0
```

Now we can use `rbind ()` to add our new row to the bottom of the extended dataframe:

```
(new.sales <- rbind (new.sales, new.row))

               name spring summer autumn winter people
1       Jane.Smith  14.00  18.00  11.00  12.00   0.30
2      Robert.Jones 17.00  18.00  10.00  13.00   1.05
3      Dick.Rogers  12.00  16.00   9.00  14.00  -0.70
4   William.Edwards 15.00  14.00  11.00  10.00  -0.95
5      Janet.Jones  11.00  17.00  11.00  16.00   0.30
6 Seasonal effects   0.35   3.15  -3.05  -0.45   0.00
```

Our final task is to replace the counts of sales in the dataframe `new.frame[1:5, 2:5]` by departures from the overall mean sale per person per season (the grand mean (gm): overall_mean = overall_seasons = 13.45). We create a vector of length 4 containing repeated values of the grand mean (one for each column of sales). Finally, we use `sweep ()` (see Section 3.11.5) to subtract the grand mean from each value:

```
gm <- rep (overall_mean,4)
new.sales[1:5, 2:5] <- sweep (new.sales[1:5, 2:5], 2, gm)
new.sales
```

```
          name spring summer autumn winter people
1        Jane.Smith    0.55   4.55  -2.45  -1.45   0.30
2      Robert.Jones    3.55   4.55  -3.45  -0.45   1.05
3       Dick.Rogers   -1.45   2.55  -4.45   0.55  -0.70
4  William.Edwards     1.55   0.55  -2.45  -3.45  -0.95
5      Janet.Jones    -2.45   3.55  -2.45   2.55   0.30
6 Seasonal effects     0.35   3.15  -3.05  -0.45   0.00
```

To complete the table we want to put the grand mean in the bottom right-hand corner:

```
new.sales[6,6] <- overall_mean
new.sales

          name spring summer autumn winter people
1        Jane.Smith    0.55   4.55  -2.45  -1.45   0.30
2      Robert.Jones    3.55   4.55  -3.45  -0.45   1.05
3       Dick.Rogers   -1.45   2.55  -4.45   0.55  -0.70
4  William.Edwards     1.55   0.55  -2.45  -3.45  -0.95
5      Janet.Jones    -2.45   3.55  -2.45   2.55   0.30
6 Seasonal effects     0.35   3.15  -3.05  -0.45  13.45
```

The best per-season performance was shared by Jane Smith and Robert Jones who each sold 4.55 units more than the overall average in summer.

4.7.1 Summarising the contents of dataframes

The usual function to obtain cross-classified summary functions like the mean or median for a single vector is `tapply` () (see Section 3.10.1), but there are three useful functions for summarising whole dataframes:

- `summary` () which summarises all the contents of each of the variables;
- `aggregate` () which creates a table after the fashion of `tapply` ();
- `by` () which performs functions for each level of any specified factors.

The use of `summary` () and `by` () with the `worms` database was described in Section 4.5. The `aggregate` () function is used like `tapply` () to apply a function (`mean` () in this case) to the levels of a specified categorical variable (`Vegetation` in this case) for a specified range of variables (`Area`, `Slope`, `Soil.pH`, and `Worm.density`) which are specified using their subscripts as a column index:

```
aggregate (worms[,c (2 ,3, 5, 7)], by = list (veg = worms$Vegetation), mean)

        veg      Area     Slope  Soil.pH Worm.density
1    Arable 3.866667 1.333333 4.833333     5.333333
2 Grassland 2.911111 3.666667 4.100000     2.444444
3    Meadow 3.466667 1.666667 4.933333     6.333333
4   Orchard 1.900000 0.000000 5.700000     9.000000
5     Scrub 2.425000 7.000000 4.800000     5.250000
```

We have created a new heading for the Vegetation column. The by = argument needs to be a list () even if, as here, we have only one classifying factor. Here are the aggregated summaries cross-classified by Vegetation and Damp:

```
aggregate (worms[, c(2, 3, 5, 7)],
          by = list (veg = worms$Vegetation, d = worms$Damp), mean)

        veg     d      Area     Slope   Soil.pH Worm.density
1    Arable FALSE 3.866667 1.333333 4.833333      5.333333
2 Grassland FALSE 3.087500 3.625000 3.987500      1.875000
3   Orchard FALSE 1.900000 0.000000 5.700000      9.000000
4     Scrub FALSE 3.350000 5.000000 4.700000      7.000000
5 Grassland  TRUE 1.500000 4.000000 5.000000      7.000000
6    Meadow  TRUE 3.466667 1.666667 4.933333      6.333333
7     Scrub  TRUE 1.500000 9.000000 4.900000      3.500000
```

Note that this summary is unbalanced (i.e. not all factor combinations are represented) because there were no damp arable or orchard sites and no dry meadows.

5

Graphics

Producing high-quality graphics is one of *R*'s strong points as it offers almost complete control over the look of plots. The particular plot function needed will depend on the number and type of variables you want to plot.

In this introductory chapter on creating graphics, we'll first look at the basics of plotting in *R*. Various plotting functions are then dealt with under four headings:

- plots for single variables;
- plots for two variables;
- plots for three or more variables;
- plotting functions.

5.1 Plotting principles

A plot should be clear, readable, and serve a purpose. It shouldn't be so busy or cluttered that the main message is obscured, nor should its interpretation (or the reason for its inclusion in a report, say) be left to the audience to guess. This depends, at least in part, on having:

- appropriate graphic type;
- appropriate graphic size;
- descriptive title(s) or caption(s);
- informative labels on axes;
- appropriate number of 'tick marks' on axes;
- suitable font and font size for labels and titles;

The R Book, Third Edition. Elinor Jones, Simon Harden and Michael J. Crawley.
© 2023 John Wiley & Sons Ltd. Published 2023 by John Wiley & Sons Ltd.
Companion website: www.wiley.com/go/jones/therbook3e

- strategic use of colour;

- clear legends where necessary.

There are many more aspects we could list here, but this is a good start.

This section is intended to give an overview of the most basic features of plotting – axes, titles, and colour – for which we'll use *R*'s `plot ()` function. This function is the basis for many *R* plots and will be explored in more depth from Section 5.3 onward. The ideas introduced here in terms of changing plot features are similar if not identical to how they are changed for other graphing functions.

For now, though, let us explore its basic use on a simple dataset.

```
scatter1 <- read.table ("scatter1.txt", header = T)
attach (scatter1)
head (scatter1)

        xv        ys
1 90.77212 51.75918
2 16.11536 28.95312
3 31.12350 35.50002
4 39.79581 32.69104
5 48.82297 40.50366
6 78.17519 56.58430
```

You'll see that our dataset has two numeric variables, `xv` and `ys`, and a classic plot to show the relationship (if any) between these would be a **scatterplot**. If you feed *R*'s `plot ()` function two numeric variables, this is exactly what you get, as shown in Figure 5.1. Notice that the variable written as the first argument is plotted on the *x*-axis, and the second argument is plotted on the *y*-axis.

```
plot (xv, ys)
```

The plot is pretty basic: there is no title or caption, the axis labels take the variable name (which may or may not be appropriate), and the observations are plotted as open black circles. It's pretty uninspiring as it is.

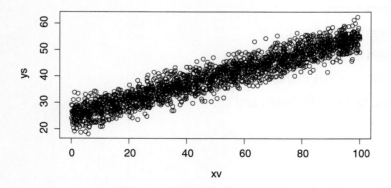

Figure 5.1 A scatterplot of ys against xv

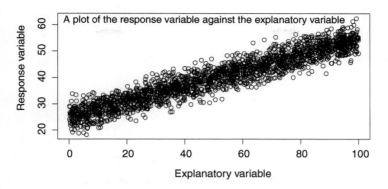

Figure 5.2 Scatterplot with better axes labels

5.1.1 Axes labels and titles

Let us add a title and appropriate axis labels. This can all be done within the `plot ()` function using `main` to specify the title, and `xlab` and `ylab` to specify the *x*- and *y*-axis labels, respectively. If we run the following code, we get Figure 5.2. It certainly looks a lot better already.

```
plot (xv, ys, xlab = "Explanatory variable", ylab = "Response variable",
      main = "A plot of the response variable against the explanatory variable")
```

If the title is a bit long, it might look better spread over a couple of lines. This is easy enough using \n at the point you want to break the line (resulting plot not shown):

```
plot (xv, ys, xlab = "Explanatory variable", ylab = "Response variable",
      main = "A plot of the response variable \n against the explanatory
      variable")
```

5.1.2 Plotting symbols and colours

The default in *R* when producing a scatterplot is to use open circles, but this can be changed very easily in the `plot ()` function using `pch` (which stands or **p**lot **ch**aracter). Figure 5.3 shows the range of plotting symbols that can be used, with the associated numeric code. Symbols 0 through 14 are outline or empty symbols, symbols 15 through 20 are solid filled symbols which have no border to them, and symbols 21 through 25 can be filled (e.g. with colour) but will retain a border (the colour of which can be controlled).

You can change the size of a plotting symbol using `cex`. The default is `cex = 1`, but you can scale the size of the symbol up or down to suit your needs.

Let us try a different plotting symbol (a particular favourite is `pch = 16`), and while we're at it we'll shrink the size of the symbol slightly. We'll drop the title for brevity from now on, given that all figures in the book have a caption instead. Doing all this results in Figure 5.4.

```
plot (xv, ys, xlab = "Explanatory variable", ylab = "Response variable",
      pch = 16, cex = 0.6)
```

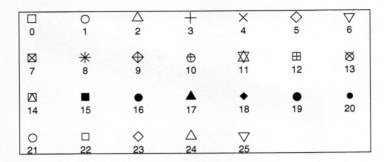

Figure 5.3 pch symbols and their numeric code

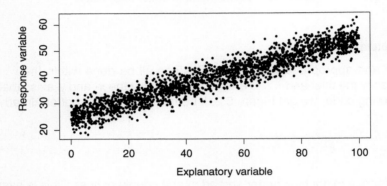

Figure 5.4 Scatterplot with different plotting symbol

A bit of colour can make a graph come alive, but be careful here: it's easy to go overboard with *R*'s possible colours. Make sure that your graphic is still readable. A very easy way to add colour to our plot is using the `col` argument. *R* has built-in colours with a recognisable name, e.g. `col = "red"` or `col = "blue"`, or you can define a very specific colour via a hexadecimal RGB triplet, e.g. `col = "#C69647"`. Let's try a basic named colour, which we see in Figure 5.5.

```
plot (xv, ys, xlab = "Explanatory variable", ylab = "Response variable",
      pch = 16, cex = 0.6, col = "blue")
```

If we had chosen a different plotting symbol, let us say one that had a separate border (plotting symbols number 21–25), then we can specify a colour for the inside of the symbol (via `bg` which stands for 'background') and the border (which we do via the usual `col` argument). For example, in Figure 5.6, we specify blue border filled with `col = "orange"`.

```
plot (xv, ys, xlab = "Explanatory variable", ylab = "Response variable",
      pch = 21, cex = 0.6,
      col = "blue", bg = "orange")
```

The result is OK, but it can be really tricky to define a sequence of colours for a plot when several are needed, for example to highlight different groups. There are ready-made 'palettes' available

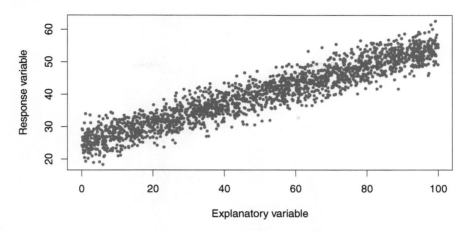

Figure 5.5   Scatterplot with better axes labels

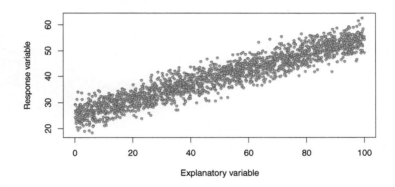

Figure 5.6   Scatterplot with different colour for border and background of plotting symbol

which suggest good colours to combine. More on this later, but you will notice in this book that we use `hue_pal ()` from the `scales` package (Wickham and Seidel, 2020) to generate appropriate colours depending on how many we need in a particular plot. For example, if we need four colours in a plot, we specify `hue_pal()(4)`, which will generate the four nicely contrasting colours in Figure 5.7.

We can then pick out individual colours as needed using square brackets, from `hue_pal()(4)[1]` through to `hue_pal()(4)[4]`. Adding this to our scatterplot, we choose two colours (one for background of the plotting symbol and one for its border), as demonstrated in Figure 5.8. Let's face it, having a circle for each observation, with a different colour for the border and background, doesn't look that great whatever colours are chosen.

```
plot (xv, ys, xlab = "Explanatory variable", ylab = "Response variable",
      pch = 21, cex = 0.6,
      col = hue_pal()(2)[1], bg = hue_pal()(2)[2])

detach (scatter1)
```

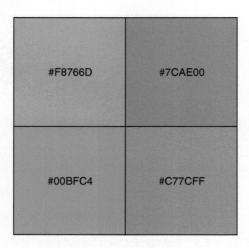

Figure 5.7 Four contrasting colours

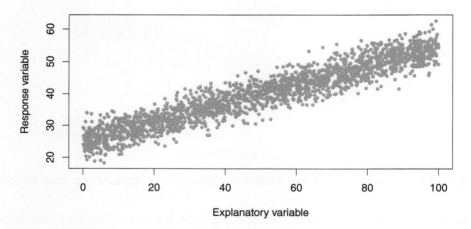

Figure 5.8 Final scatterplot

5.1.3 Saving graphics

For publication-quality graphics, saving each plot as a PDF, PostScript or other type of file will be necessary. By default, plots will generally show up in the **Plots** pane in RStudio in the bottom right-hand corner, which can be saved directly by exporting it to whatever format required. This will give a rough and ready copy of the graph, but it won't be of the highest quality.

If a high-quality PDF, postscript, bmp, png, jpeg, or tiff file is needed, this can be done simply by specifying the 'device' before you start plotting, then turning the device off once finished. Assuming that you've already set your working directory to where the plot should be saved, here is how to save to a pdf file:

```
pdf ("myplot.pdf", width = 7, height = 4)
plot (xv, ys, xlab = "Explanatory variable", ylab = "Response variable",
```

```
    pch = 21, cex = 0.6,
    col = hue_pal()(2)[1],  bg = hue_pal()(2)[2])
dev.off ()
```

Notice that the file is opened using the `pdf ()` function, inside which the intended file name is specified, and the width and height which are in inches (old fashioned, we know). Now close the file using `dev.off ()`. It's possible to change all sorts of other optional arguments too. See `?pdf` for details.

Saving as a postscript file is done in the same way, swapping `pdf ()` for `postscript ()`, with `?postscript` bringing up the relevant help file.

There are further functions with the obvious names if a bmp, png, jpeg, or tiff file is required: `bmp ()`, `png ()`, `jpeg ()`, and `tiff ()`. The height and width for such plots still need to be specified, but this time the measure is pixels by default. This can be changed, if necessary, along with a load of other things. See `?png` for specifics (this also gives information on bmp, jpeg, and tiff file types).

5.2 Plots for single variables

With just one variable to plot, we have a range of options depending on the type of variable. A plot suitable for a numeric variable isn't generally going to be suitable for a categorical variable. Table 5.1 shows some possible options, the type of variable it is suitable for, and the R base function that we can use.

5.2.1 Histograms vs. bar charts

First a word on histograms and bar charts. In Table 5.1, the variable type for histograms and bar charts are starred because there is *some* flexibility in the variable types they are suitable for, but nowhere near as much as some may think. These are *not* the same graphic.

A histogram is for a continuous numeric response, where we have the value of the response on the *x*-axis and the *y*-axis shows the frequency (or, more correctly, the probability density). The *x*-axis is cut into 'bins' which do not need to be of the same length, and the adjacent bars are connected (as long as there are observations in consecutive bins) on account of the *x*-axis representing a *continuous* response. You wouldn't therefore re-order the 'bins' on the *x*-axis as these follow a prescribed order.

A bar chart, on the other hand, is for categorical data where we have the categories on the *x*-axis and frequency on the *y*-axis. These bars are not connected as the categories are distinct and we

Table 5.1 Plotting single variables (starred variable types indicate some flexibility)

Plot name	Variable type	R function
Histogram	Numeric*	hist ()
Density plot	Numeric	density ()
Boxplot	Numeric	box ()
Dotplot	Numeric	stripchart ()
Bar chart	Categorical*	barplot ()
Pie chart	Categorical	pie ()

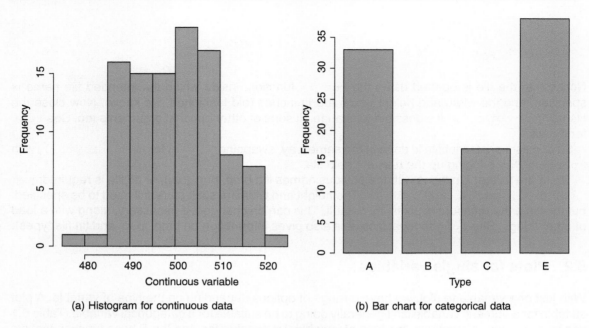

(a) Histogram for continuous data   (b) Bar chart for categorical data

Figure 5.9   A histogram and a bar chart

can in general reorder the bars however we like (compare this with a histogram). Figure 5.9 gives an example of both to highlight the difference.

A grey area is what we do with discrete numeric variables: should these be plotted as a histogram or a bar chart? This depends on the nature of the variable. If you have a variable with lots of (discrete) values, let's say age in years, then we could treat this as continuous and create age-group bins, e.g. 18–24, 25–34, 35–44. A histogram would then be ideal. If we had a variable with only very few discrete values, then we are better off using a bar chart and *not* grouping the values.

5.2.2   Histograms

Let us look at an example where the response variable is the growth rate of daphnia. We can ask *R* for a histogram using the `hist ()` function, colour it using the `col` argument, and specify that no title is produced via `main = ""` (by default, *R* creates a title for the graphic, but we can put whatever we like between the speech marks). The result is shown in Figure 5.10.

```
daph <- read.table ("daphnia.txt", header = T)
attach (daph)
hist (Growth.rate, col = hue_pal ()(4)[1], main = "")
```

The divisions of the *x*-axis into which the values of the response variable are distributed and then counted are called **bins**. Unless you specify your bins, *R* will choose them for you. The convention adopted in *R* for showing bin boundaries is to employ square and round brackets so that `[a,b)` means 'greater than or equal to `a` but less than `b`' [square then round], and `(a,b]` means 'greater than `a` but less than or equal to `b`' (round then square). The point is that it must be unequivocal which bin gets a given number when that number falls exactly on a boundary between two bins.

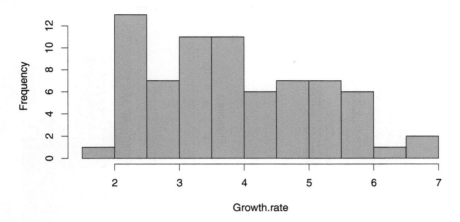

Figure 5.10 Histogram of daphnia growth rate

Histograms are profoundly tricky, because what you see depends on the subjective judgements of where exactly to put the bin margins. Wide bins produce one picture, narrow bins produce a different picture, unequal bins can result in confusion.

Let us produce four different histograms of the same data with varying bin widths which we can do via the argument `breaks`; for example the following specifies that we want breaks every 0.25 units between growth rate of 0 and 8 (which results in Figure 5.11a):

```
hist (Growth.rate, breaks = seq (0, 8, 0.25),
      col = hue_pal () (4) [1], main = "")
```

See `?hist` for more `breaks` options, but the resulting plots are in Figure 5.11.

The narrower the bins, the lower the peak frequencies (note that the *y* scale changes: 7, 12, 40). Small bins produce multimodality (top left), broad bins unimodality (bottom right). When there are different bin widths (bottom right), the default in *R* is for `hist ()` to convert the counts (frequencies) into densities (so that the total area is 1.0).

Histograms are excellent for showing the mode, the spread, and the symmetry (skew) of a set of data, but the *R* function `hist ()` is deceptively simple. Figure 5.12 shows a histogram of 1000 random integers drawn from a Poisson distribution with a mean of 1.7. With the default bins, the histogram produces a graphic that does not clearly distinguish between the zeros and the ones.

The question here is whether we should use a bar chart instead, but if it makes sense to continue with a histogram then it is much better to specify the bins explicitly, using the `breaks` argument. The most sensible breaks for count data are −0.5 to +0.5 to capture the zeros, 0.5–1.5 to capture the 1s, and so on; `breaks = (-0.5: 8.5)` generates such a sequence automatically. Now the histogram in Figure 5.13 makes clear that 1s are almost twice as frequent as 0s. The distribution is said to be 'skewed to the right' (or 'positively skewed') because the long tail is on the right-hand side of the histogram.

```
hist (values, breaks = (-0.5 : 8.5), col = hue_pal () (4) [1], main = "",
      xlab = "random numbers from a Poisson with mean 1.7")
```

So far we've considered only frequency on the *y*-axis of our histograms (admittedly, they're easier to read!), but what we should be doing is producing a histogram with the *density* on the *y*-axis.

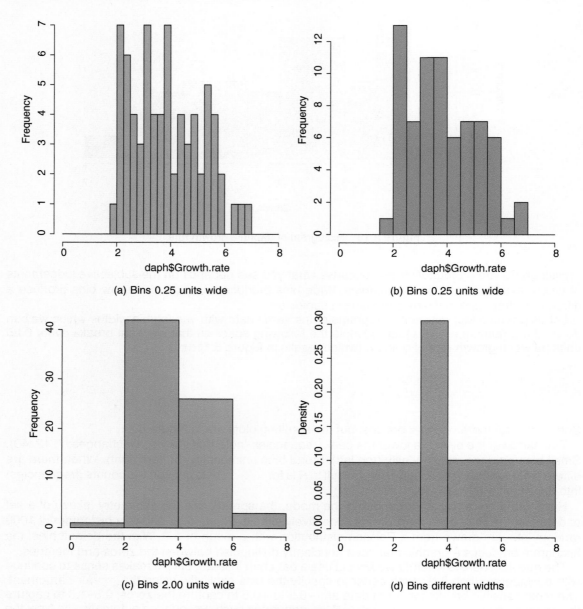

(a) Bins 0.25 units wide   (b) Bins 0.25 units wide

(c) Bins 2.00 units wide   (d) Bins different widths

Figure 5.11 Types of point pattern

This enables different sized bins. We can do this easily with `freq = FALSE` and the plot is in Figure 5.14. Now compare to Figure 5.10: the histogram is identical with only the scale on the *y*-axis having changed.

```
hist (Growth.rate, col = hue_pal ()(4)[1], main = "", freq = FALSE)
```

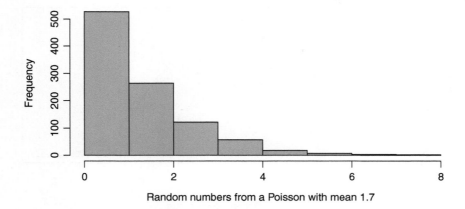

Figure 5.12   Histogram of 1000 Poisson random numbers

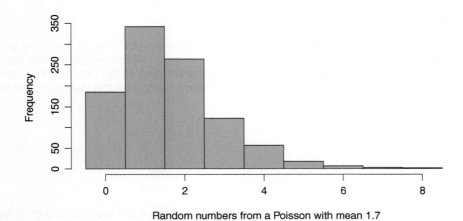

Figure 5.13   Histogram of 1000 Poisson random numbers

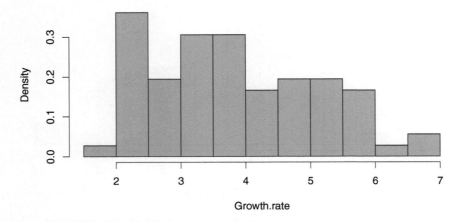

Figure 5.14   Histogram of daphnia with density on *y*-axis and superimposed density

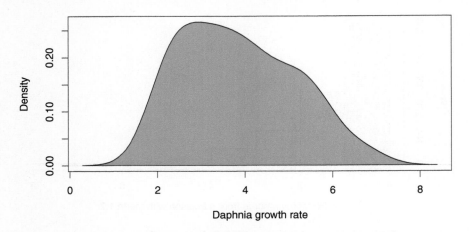

Figure 5.15   Filled density plot of daphnia data

5.2.3   Density plots

A density plot can be a useful alternative to a histogram when you want to see the shape of a distribution of a variable. The relevant function is `density ()` which estimates the density, and from there we can use `plot ()`. If we did this, we'd get an outline of the density. You can colour it in, so to speak, using the `polygon ()` function. We'll demonstrate on the daphnia data here once again, resulting in Figure 5.15.

```
plot (density (Growth.rate), col=hue_pal ()(4)[1],
      xlab="Daphnia growth rate", main="")
polygon (density (Growth.rate), col=hue_pal ()(4)[1],
         xlab="Daphnia growth rate", main="")
```

It's possible to use the `density ()` function to superimpose the estimated density on a histogram, as in Figure 5.16.

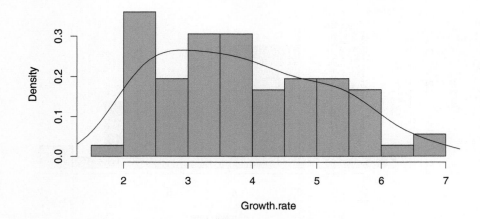

Figure 5.16   Histogram for the daphnia data with density superimposed

```
hist (Growth.rate, col = hue_pal () (4) [1], main = "", freq = FALSE)
lines (density (Growth.rate))
```

Adding a bespoke density function to a plot can be done by specifying it with `lines ()`. See `?lines` for information and examples.

5.2.4 Boxplots

Boxplots are great for showcasing continuous data when it's in abundance. It is a graphical representation of the so-called 'five number summary': it shows the minimum, 25th percentile, median (50th percentile), 75th percentile, and the maximum. This allows us to get a good feel for the 'shape' of the distribution of the underlying variable. Let's draw a boxplot for the growth rate of daphnia, which is displayed in Figure 5.17.

```
boxplot (Growth.rate, col = hue_pal () (4) [1], ylab = "Daphnia growth rate")
```

The box represents the middle 50% of the data (from the 25th percentile at the lower end of the box through to the 75th percentile at the upper end), with the heavy horizontal line in the box representing the median. The end points of the 'whiskers' *usually* show the minimum and maximum values (hence the original name, 'box-and-whisker' plot which has since been shortened to 'boxplot', but see below for an exception). These points correspond to the five number summary of growth rate, *but does not show the mean*:

```
summary (Growth.rate)

 Min. 1st Qu.  Median   Mean 3rd Qu.    Max.
1.762   2.797   3.788  3.852   4.807   6.918
```

We can switch to a horizontal boxplot if we want, by using the extra argument `horizontal = TRUE` in the `boxplot ()` function.

One important point to note is that the minimum and/or maximum may not be captured at the end points of the whiskers. Let's add a couple of spuriously large values to our daphnia growth rate data, say a value of 10.00 and another of 11.00 and re-draw the boxplot. The result is in Figure 5.18.

The added values are showing on the graph but as circles, with the end of the whisker at the previous maximum. This is because *R* uses an automated process to work out if there are any

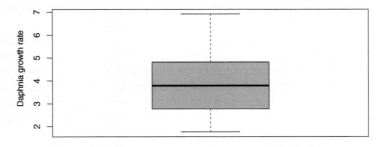

Figure 5.17 Boxplot for the daphnia data

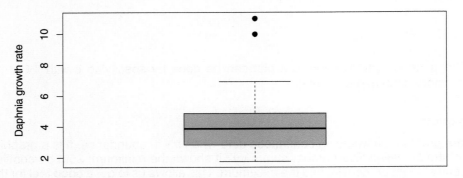

Figure 5.18   Boxplot for the daphnia data with two unusual values added

unusually big or small values, and if there are, it decides to display them as in Figure 5.18 instead of having a very long whisker. This makes sense: an extremely long whisker here would give us a false impression about the skew of the distribution of the data. A word of warning; however, the process that *R* uses to decide on which values to display as circles is arbitrary, and these observations *should not be automatically classified as 'outliers'*. They might well be strange observations worthy of further investigation, or they may be just fine as they are.

5.2.5   Dotplots

For sample sizes that are too small to use box plots, an alternative plotting method is to use **dotplots**. You can do this using the `stripchart ()` function. Let us use this on the caterpillar growth data.

```
caterpillar <- read.table ("caterpillar.txt", header = T)
stripchart (caterpillar$growth, xlab = "Caterpillar growth",
          col = hue_pal ()(2)[1])
stripchart (caterpillar$growth, xlab = "Caterpillar growth",
          col = hue_pal ()(2)[2],
          method = 'jitter', jitter = 1, pch = 16, cex = 2)
```

What we can't see in Figure 5.19a is that there are two identical values (both at 3). To get around this, we vertically jitter the values slightly with `method = 'jitter'` with an amount of jitter set at 1, resulting in Figure 5.19b. Alternatively, we could have used the `method = 'stack'` option, which, as the name suggests, stacks observations. We are now able to see all observations. We've also changed the dot type, and the size of the plotting symbol here to make the plot look a little nicer.

   It is really important to know when dot plots can be used, and when they are unsuitable. For small datasets, by all means use a dotplot. In such cases a boxplot, for example, might well mask the underlying shape of the distribution because it attempts to summarise it in just five numbers. With a small dataset, you have the luxury of being able to plot *all* data points without the graphic becoming cluttered and unreadable, so why not plot everything?

   For large datasets, use a boxplot or other type of display. A dotplot will be too busy and in extreme cases will show just a dense cloud or line of points where the underlying shape will be invisible.

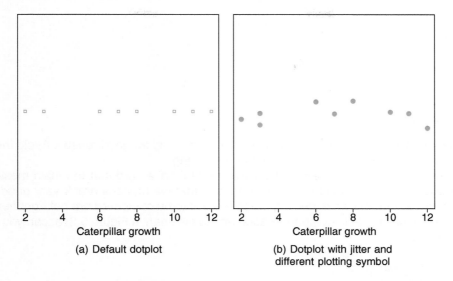

Figure 5.19   Dotplots of the caterpillar data

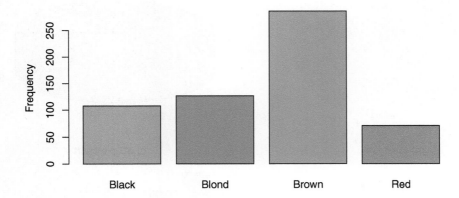

Figure 5.20   Barplot showing frequency of different hair colour types

5.2.6   Bar charts

Bar charts are a great way of displaying categorical data (or perhaps discrete numeric data with limited unique values). Bar plots come in many different flavours, but the simplest is to place the categories of the variable on the *x*-axis with the height of the bars representing the frequency of observations that fall into that category. These are simple enough to create, as we demonstrate with the hair and eye colour dataset from *R*. We'll plot the hair colour of the participants, but first we need to create a table and then pass on this table to the barplot () function. The result is in Figure 5.20.

```
hair_eye <- read.table ("hair_eye.txt", header = T)
table_hair <- table (hair_eye$Hair)
table_hair
```

```
Black Blond Brown   Red
  108   127   286    71


barplot (table_hair, col = hue_pal()(4), ylab = "Frequency")
```

5.2.7 Pie charts

A word of warning here: Statisticians do not like pie charts, and for good reason. Avoid these as far as possible, and let the following example act as a warning.

  When creating graphics to represent data, we want to make sure that the main messages are clear to our audience. The problem with pie charts is that we humans aren't very good at distinguishing, e.g. sizes and angles, especially when the bits to be compared are not right next to each other, or there are lots of bits to compare. Based on the pie chart in Figure 5.21a, can you tell which

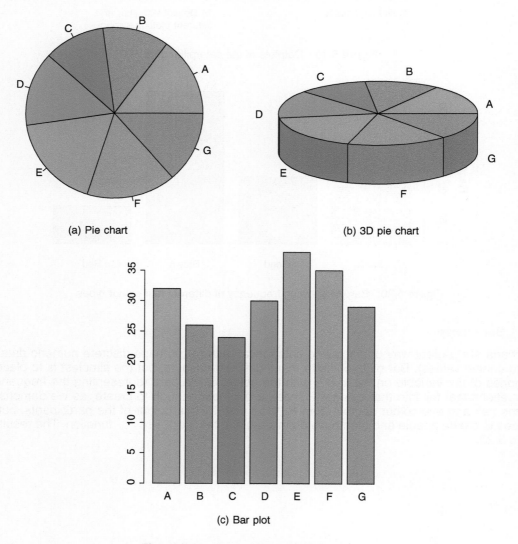

(a) Pie chart   (b) 3D pie chart

(c) Bar plot

Figure 5.21   Three plots of the same data

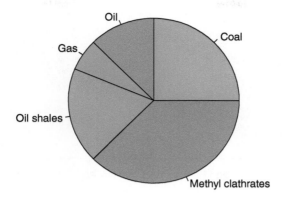

Figure 5.22 Pie chart

category has the most observations? What about in Figure 5.21b? And the truth is patently clear in Figure 5.21c.

If you *absolutely must* use one, then the relevant function is `pie ()`. It takes a vector of numbers, turns them into proportions, and divides up the circle on the basis of those proportions. It is essential to use a label to indicate which pie segment is which. The label is provided as a vector of character strings, here called `data$names`. Because there are blank spaces in some of the names ('oil shales' and 'methyl clathrates') we cannot use `read.table ()` with a tab-delimited text file to enter the data. Instead, we save the file as a comma-delimited file, with a '.csv' extension, and input the data to *R* using `read.csv ()` in place of `read.table ()`. The end result is in Figure 5.22.

```
piedata <- read.csv ("piedata.csv")
piedata

            names amounts
1            coal       4
2             oil       2
3             gas       1
4       oil shales       3
5 methyl clathrates       6

pie (piedata$amounts, labels = as.character (piedata$names), col = hue_pal()(5))
```

Try not to use these sorts of plots, however. It just isn't worth it.

5.3 Plots for showing two numeric variables

5.3.1 Scatterplot

We first met the `plot ()` function in Section 5.1 and now we continue with exploration of it. There are, in fact, two ways of specifying `plot ()` and you should choose whichever you prefer:

- Cartesian `plot (x, y)`
- formula `plot (y ~ x)`

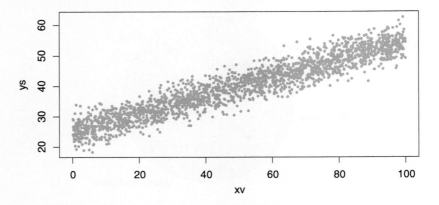

Figure 5.23   Basic scatterplot using plot ()

The advantage of the formula-based plot is that the plot function and the model fit look and feel the same (response variable, tilde, explanatory variable, as will be discussed in Section 10.1.2). If you use Cartesian plots (eastings first, then northings, like the grid reference on a map), then the plot has '*x*, then *y*' while the model has '*y*, then *x*'.

Let us load some data and produce an initial scatterplot as shown in Figure 5.23.

```
scatter1 <- read.table ("scatter1.txt", header = T)
attach (scatter1)
names (scatter1)


[1] "xv" "ys"


plot (xv, ys, col = hue_pal()(3)[1], pch = 16, cex = 0.6)
```

The great thing about graphics in *R* is that it is extremely straightforward to add things to your plots. In the present case, we might want to add a line to the plot, which may represent a particular cut-off to emphasise or perhaps a line of best fit (regression line) through the cloud of points.

The function for this is `abline` () which can take as its arguments either a specified line (as in Figure 5.24a), or a linear model object `lm` (y1 ~ x1) as explained in Section 10.1.2 if you want to superimpose a line of best fit (as in Figure 5.24b). If you want to add the former, then use `abline` (a, b) for a line with intercept a and slope b, or `abline` (v) for a vertical line placed at *v* = *x* or `abline` (h) for a horizontal line placed at *h* = *y*.

You can also change the line thickness (using `lwd`), as we do in Figure 5.24.

```
plot (xv, ys, col = hue_pal()(3)[1], cex = 0.6,
      xlab = "Explanatory variable", ylab = "Response variable")
abline (v = 40, col = hue_pal()(3)[2], lwd = 3)
plot (xv, ys, col = hue_pal()(3)[1], cex = 0.6,
      xlab = "Explanatory variable", ylab = "Response variable")
abline (lm (ys ~ xv), col = hue_pal()(3)[2], lwd = 3)
```

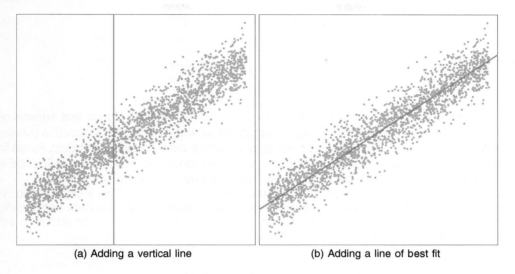

(a) Adding a vertical line   (b) Adding a line of best fit

Figure 5.24   Adding lines to plots

It is just as easy to add more points to the plot. The extra observations are in another file:

```
scatter2 <- read.table ("scatter2.txt", header = T)
attach (scatter2)
names (scatter2)


[1] "xv2" "ys2"
```

The new points (*xv2, ys2*) are added using the points () function, and we can finish by adding a line of best fit through the extra points as in Figure 5.25. Notice that we also change the line type to distinguish between the two regression lines using lty. We'll stick to black lines here to demonstrate (colour is great, but sometimes it all gets a bit too much).

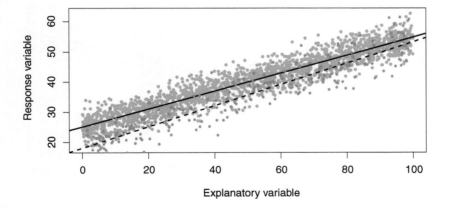

Figure 5.25   Scatterplot with added observations, and a regression line for each dataset

```
plot (xv, ys, col = hue_pal()(3)[1], cex = 0.6,
      xlab = "Explanatory variable", ylab = "Response variable")
abline (lm (ys ~ xv), lty = 1, lwd = 2)
points (xv2, ys2, col = hue_pal()(3)[2], pch = 16, cex = 0.6)
abline (lm (ys2 ~ xv2), lty = 2, lwd = 2)
```

This example shows a very important feature of the `plot ()` function. Notice that several of the lower values from the second data set have *not* appeared on the graph. This is because (unless we say otherwise at the outset) *R* chooses 'pretty' scaling for the axes based on the data range in the *first* set of points to be drawn. If, as here, the range of subsequent data sets lies outside the scale of the *x*- and *y*-axes, then points are simply left off without any warning message.

One way to cure this problem is to plot *all* the data with `type = "n"`. This instructs *R* to create a plot – with axes that area scaled to accommodate all the points from all the data sets (using the concatenation function, `c ()`) – then we can use `points ()` and `lines ()` to add both sets of data to the blank axes, resulting in Figure 5.26.

```
plot (c (xv, xv2), c(ys, ys2),
      xlab = "Explanatory variable",
      ylab = "Response variable",
      type = "n")
points (xv, ys, col = hue_pal()(3)[1], pch = 16, cex = 0.6)
points (xv2, ys2, col = hue_pal()(3)[2], pch = 16, cex = 0.6)
abline (lm (ys ~ xv), lty = 1, lwd = 2)
abline (lm (ys2 ~ xv2), lty = 2, lwd = 2)
```

Now all of the points from both data sets appear on the scatterplot. However, sometimes it is better to take control of the selection of the limits for the *x*- and *y*-axes, rather than accept the 'pretty' default values. In Figure 5.26, for instance, the minimum on the *y*-axis was about 13 (but it is not exactly obvious). Specifying that the minimum on the *y*-axis should be zero, for example is achieved with the `ylim` argument. This is a vector of length 2, specifying the minimum and maximum values for the *y*-axis: `ylim = c (0, 70)`. Similarly, for the *x*-axis using `xlim`. This method is particularly

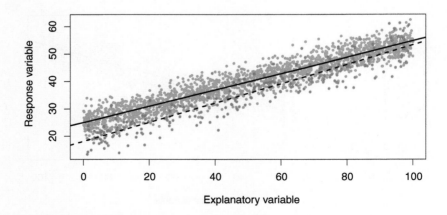

Figure 5.26   Scatterplot with better scaling of axes to accommodate both datasets

convenient when you want two comparable graphs side by side, or when you want to overlay several lines or sets of points on the same axes.

A good way to find out the axis values is to use the `range` () function applied to the data sets in aggregate:

```
range (c (xv, xv2))
```

```
[1]   0.02849861 99.93262000
```

```
range (c (ys, ys2))
```

```
[1] 13.41794 62.59482
```

Here the x-axis needs to go from 0.02 up to 99.93 (0–100 would be pretty), and the y-axis needs to go from 13.4 up to 62.6 (0–70 would be pretty). This is how the axes are drawn; the points and lines are added exactly as before:

```
plot (c (xv, xv2), c (ys, ys2), xlim = c (0, 100), ylim = c (0, 70),
      xlab = "Explanatory variable", ylab = "Response variable",
      type = "n")
points (xv, ys, col = hue_pal () (3) [1], pch = 16, cex = 0.6)
points (xv2, ys2, col = hue_pal () (3) [2], pch = 16, cex = 0.6)
abline (lm (ys ~ xv), lty = 1, lwd = 2)
abline (lm (ys2 ~ xv2), lty = 2, lwd = 2)
```

Adding a legend to the plot to explain the difference between the two colours of points would be useful. The thing to understand about the `legend` () function is that the number of lines of text inside the legend box is determined by the length of the vector containing the labels (two in this case: `c ("Dataset 1", "Dataset 2")`. The other specified vectors must be of the same length as this: in our case, one for the plotting symbols and one for the colours (e.g. `c ("red", "blue")`).

The `legend` () function can also be used with `locator` (1) as one of its arguments to allow you to select exactly where on the plot surface the legend box should be placed like this:

```
legend (locator (1), c ("Dataset 1", "Dataset 2"), pch = c (16, 16),
col = hue_pal () (3) [1:2])
```

Once you run the function, go to your plot viewing pane in *R* and click where you want the *top left* of the box around the legend to be. Otherwise, specify the location of the top left-hand corner of the legend box, like we do to get Figure 5.27. Here we specify the top left of the legend box to be located at the co-ordinate $(0, 70)$.

```
legend (0, 70, c ("Dataset 1", "Dataset 2"), pch = c (16, 16),
        col = hue_pal () (3) [1:2])
detach (scatter1)
detach (scatter2)
```

Figure 5.27 is about as complicated as you would want to make any figure. Adding more information would begin to detract from the message.

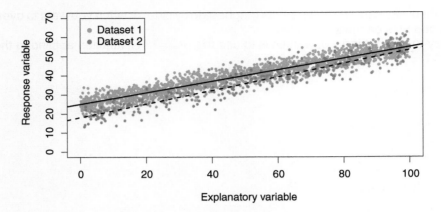

Figure 5.27 Scatterplot with legend, showing a regression line for each of the datasets plotted

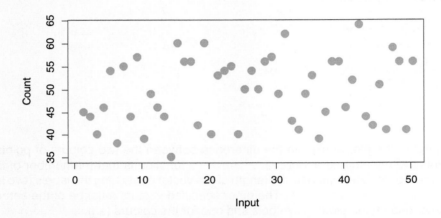

Figure 5.28 Scatterplot with duplicated observations

5.3.2 Plots with many identical values

Sometimes a scatterplot simply won't do. Consider the following example, depicted in Figure 5.28, where we have 1275 observations, but you could be forgiven for thinking that there are far fewer. The problem here is that some of the values are duplicated and so appear as one dot on the plot.

```
longdata <- read.table ("longdata.txt", header = T)
attach (longdata)
names (longdata)

[1] "xlong" "ylong"

plot (xlong, ylong, col = hue_pal()(3)[1], xlab = "Input", ylab = "Count")
```

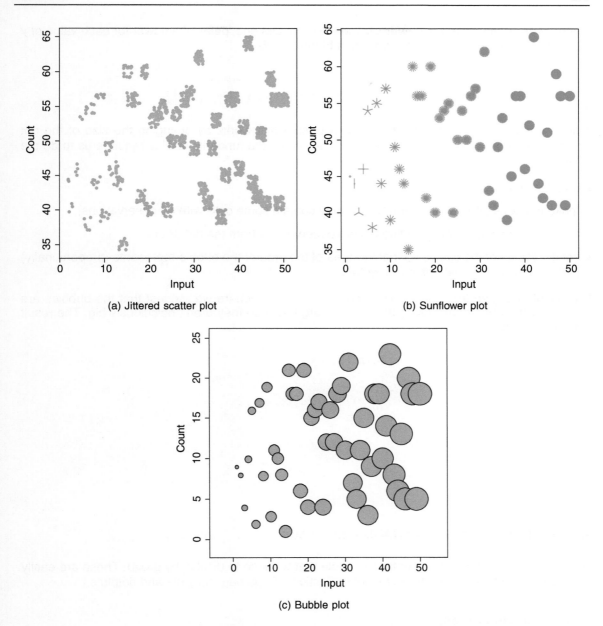

(a) Jittered scatter plot   (b) Sunflower plot

(c) Bubble plot

Figure 5.29   Three plots of the same data

We could 'jitter' the observations (add some random noise to each observation in the *x*- and *y*-direction), but be careful here because too much jitter can obscure the truth and the plot becomes useless. The jittered scatterplot is shown in Figure 5.29a.

```
plot (jitter (xlong, amount = 1), jitter (ylong, amount = 1),
      xlab = "Input", ylab = "Count", col = hue_pal()(4)[1])
```

Another easy option is a **sunflower plot** which produces one 'petal' of a flower for each value of *y* that is located at that point. This is shown in Figure 5.29b.

```
plot (jitter (xlong, amount = 1), jitter (ylong, amount = 1),
     xlab = "Input", ylab = "Count", col = hue_pal()(4)[1])
```

A final attractive option is a **bubble plot**. A bubble plot works by changing the size of the dot (i.e. bubble) depending on the number of observations that underlie it. This requires us to do the following:

- reformat the data into a table;
- make the table into a data frame (which may contain some cells with no observations);
- prune out the rows corresponding to zero observations from the dataframe;
- set the radius of the circles so that the area of the area of the bubble represents (proportionally) the number of observations represented.

The bubble plot can then be drawn using symbols (), where we request that the bubbles are scaled down proportionally using the inches argument so they aren't ridiculously big. The result is shown in Figure 5.29c

```
# Preparing data for the bubble plot
tab_longdata <- table (longdata$ylong, longdata$xlong)
tab_longdata_df <- as.data.frame (tab_longdata)
tab_longdata_df <- tab_longdata_df [!(tab_longdata_df$Freq == 0),]
# Setting the radius of circles so that area of bubble represents frequency
radius_area <- sqrt (tab_longdata_df$Freq / pi)
symbols (tab_longdata_df$Var2, tab_longdata_df$Var1, circles = radius_area,
        xlab = "Input", ylab = "Count",
        inches = 0.3, bg = hue_pal()(4)[1])
```

5.4   Plots for numeric variables by group

Now suppose that we have a numeric variable that we wish to display by group. These are easily conjured using some of the ideas we met in Section 5.2, namely boxplots and dotplots.

5.4.1   Boxplots by group

Our first example uses the factor called month (with levels 1–12) to investigate weather patterns at Silwood Park. There is one bit of housekeeping we need to do before we can plot the data. We need to declare month to be a factor. At the moment, *R* thinks it is just a number:

```
weather <- read.table ("SilwoodWeather.txt", header = T)
weather$month <- as.factor (weather$month)
attach (weather)
names (weather)


[1] "upper" "lower" "rain"  "month" "yr"
```

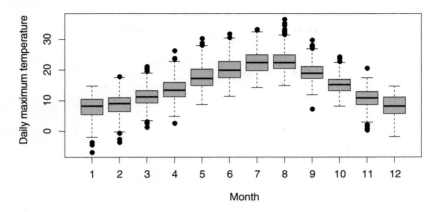

Figure 5.30   Boxplots of daily maximum temperature by month at Silwood Park

Now, we can plot using a categorical explanatory variable (`month`), resulting in Figure 5.30. Incidentally, using `plot ()` instead of `boxplot ()` still yield a set of boxplots because the first variable is a factor.

```
boxplot (upper ~ month, ylab = "daily maximum temperature", xlab = "month",
        col = hue_pal()(1)[1])
```

The boxplot summarises a great deal of information very clearly; see Section 5.2.4 for an explanation of how to interpret each individual boxplot. Boxplots not only show the location and spread of data but also indicate skewness (which shows up as asymmetry in the sizes of the upper and lower parts of the box). For example Figure 5.30 shows that the distribution of daily maximum temperature is fairly symmetric across all 12 month, though there is perhaps a little skewness in, for example, January (skewed to the left, as there is a slightly longer left tail – corresponding to lower temperatures – visible) and in August (skewed to the right, as there is a slightly longer right tail – corresponding to higher temperatures – visible).

Boxplots are also excellent for spotting errors in the data when the errors are represented by extreme points. There don't seem to be any untoward values in Figure 5.30, and you shouldn't assume that R's decision to plot some of the lowest and highest temperatures as dots rather than as part of the whiskers as implying anything is wrong.

Boxplots are very good at showing the distribution of the data points around the median, but they are not so good at indicating whether or not the median values are different from one another. Tukey invented **notches** to get the best of both worlds. The notches are drawn as a 'waist' on either side of the median and are intended to give a rough impression of the extent of the differences between two medians. Boxes in which *the notches do not overlap* are likely to prove to have different medians under an appropriate test. Boxes with overlapping notches probably do not have particularly different medians. The size of the notch increases with the magnitude of the interquartile range and declines with the square root of the replication, like this:

$$\text{notch} = \pm 1.58 \frac{\text{IQR}}{\sqrt{n}}, \tag{5.1}$$

where IQR is the interquartile range and n is the replication per sample. Notches are based on assumptions of asymptotic normality of the median and roughly equal sample sizes for the two

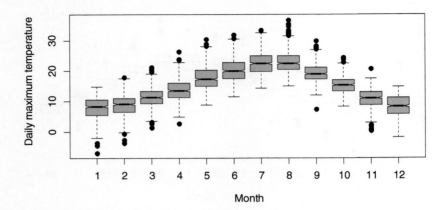

Figure 5.31   Boxplots of daily maximum temperature by month at Silwood Park, with notches

medians being compared and are said to be rather insensitive to the underlying distributions of the samples. The idea is to give roughly a 95% confidence interval for the difference in two medians, but the theory behind this is somewhat vague.

Figure 5.31 are the Silwood Weather data with the option `notch = TRUE` (or `notches = TRUE` if you are using `plot ()`):

```
boxplot(upper ~ month, ylab = "daily maximum temperature", xlab = "month",
        col = hue_pal()(1)[1], notch = TRUE)
```

```
detach (weather)
```

There is not much of a difference in median daily maximum temperature between July and August (the notches for months 7 and 8 overlap completely), but median maxima in September are substantially lower than in August.

When the sample sizes are small and/or the within-sample variance is high, the notches are not drawn as you might expect them (i.e. as a waist within the box). Instead, the notches are extended *above* the 75th percentile and/or *below* the 25th percentile. This looks odd, but it is an intentional feature, supposed to act as a warning of the likely invalidity of using such a method.

5.4.2   Dotplots by group

If you have only a small number of observations by group, you are better off with a dotplot. Data for this example come from an experiment on plant competition, with five factor levels in a single categorical variable called `clipping`: a control (unclipped), two root clipping treatments (`r5` and `r10`) and two shoot clipping treatments (`n25` and `n50`) in which the leaves of neighbouring plants were reduced by 25% and 50%. The response variable is yield at maturity (a dry weight) called `biomass`.

```
compexpt <- read.table ("compexpt.txt", header = T)
attach (compexpt)
names (compexpt)
```

```
[1] "biomass"  "clipping"
```

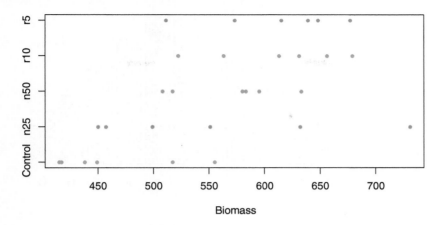

Figure 5.32   Dotplot of biomass, by clipping group

Now we can draw the dotplot by group, as shown in Figure 5.32:

```
stripchart (biomass ~ clipping, col = hue_pal()(5), pch = 16, cex = 0.8)

detach (compexpt)
```

Notice that dotplots would be a silly idea if you have a lot of data. All that would be visible is a mass of points and spotting any shape to the distribution would be near impossible.

5.4.3   An inferior (but popular) option

Rather than using boxplots to display the data, an alternative option (but inferior, as explained below) is to use a `barplot ()` to show the heights of the mean values from the different treatments.

Let's return to the Silwood Park weather data from Section 5.4.1. We need to begin by calculating the heights of the bars, typically by using the function `tapply ()` to work out the mean values for each level of the categorical explanatory variable.

```
weather <- read.table ("SilwoodWeather.txt", header = T)
attach (weather)
means <- tapply (upper, month, mean)
```

Then the barplot is produced very simply, with the result in Figure 5.33:

```
barplot (means, xlab = "Month", ylab = "Mean daily maximum temperature",
         col = hue_pal()(4)[1])
```

Compare Figure 5.33 to the boxplots by group we produced earlier in Figure 5.30. In the former, we are plotting just 12 numbers, one for each group (do you need a plot for just 12 numbers?), while in the latter, we are plotting information about the whole dataset which allows us to see, for

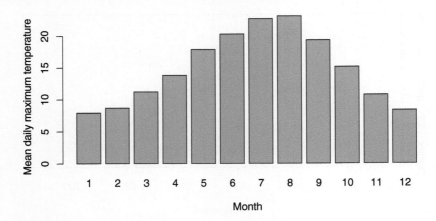

Figure 5.33   Bar plot of mean daily maximum temperature, by month

example the shape of the distribution of maximum daily temperature and the variability by month. Figure 5.30 wins in terms of conveying information by a country mile.

We could add error bars to our barplot, which would go *some* way to indicating the extent of the uncertainty associated with each of the estimated treatment means. There is no built-in function for drawing error bars on barplots, but it easy to write a function to do this. One obvious issue is that the *y*-axis as drawn by the previous call to `barplot ()` may be too short to accommodate the error bar extending from the top of the tallest bar. Another issue is that it is not obvious where to centre each of the error bars (i.e. the *x* coordinates of the middles of the bars).

The next decision to make is what kind of error bar to draw. Many journals prefer plus or minus one standard error of the mean. An old-fashioned approach is to use plus or minus the 95% confidence interval of the mean. On the assumption that you want to publish your work in *Science* or *Nature*, we shall use plus or minus one standard error of the mean, because this is their error bar of choice. First, we need to compute the standard error of the mean (we define a function to do this, as there is no in-built way of doing so in *R*):

```
sem <- tapply (upper, month, function(x) sqrt (var (x) / length (x)))
```

Now we draw the barplot with `arrows ()` creating the error bars, as shown in Figure 5.34.

```
mybarplot <- barplot (means, xlab = "Month",
                ylab = "Mean daily maximum temperature",
                col = hue_pal()(4)[1])
arrows (x0 = mybarplot, y0 = means - sem,
        x1 = mybarplot, y1 = means + sem,
        code = 3, angle = 90, length = 0.1)

detach (weather)
```

The `x0` and `y0` arguments provide the coordinates from which to start the bar, and `x1` and `y1` arguments tells *R* where to stop. The argument `code = 3` instructs that we want a head at both ends of the arrow, while `angle` determines the angle of the arrow head and `length` determines its length.

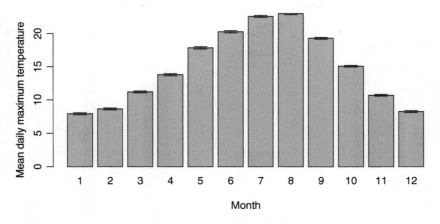

Figure 5.34   Bar plot with error bars

5.5   Plots showing two categorical variables

It is also possible to create plots to display two or more categorical variables, though you may prefer to keep things simple by displaying information in a contingency table instead (see Section 7.1). The following plots are based on the bar chart of Section 5.2.6.

5.5.1   Grouped bar charts

Let us use the hair and eye colour dataset of Section 5.2.6 once again. Suppose we want a barchart of hair colour, but this time by eye colour. Once again, the `barplot ()` function requires a table as its argument (see Section 7.1), which is simple enough, and the result is in Figure 5.35a.

```
hair_eye <- read.table ("hair_eye.txt", header = T)
table_hair_eye <- table (hair_eye$Hair, hair_eye$Eye)
barplot (table_hair_eye, col = c (hue_pal()(4)[1:4]),
        ylab = "Frequency", xlab = "Eye colour",
        legend = rownames (table_hair_eye))
```

You can also add `beside = TRUE` to the `barplot ()` function, which places the bars for each eye colour side by side rather than stacking them. See Figure 5.35b.

	Blue	Brown	Green	Hazel
Black	20	68	5	15
Blond	94	7	16	10
Brown	84	119	29	54
Red	17	26	14	14

5.5.2   Mosaic plots

You can take the idea of the stacked bar chart further by creating a **mosaic plot**. In a bar plot, the height of the bars indicate frequency of observations in a group, but a mosaic plot uses

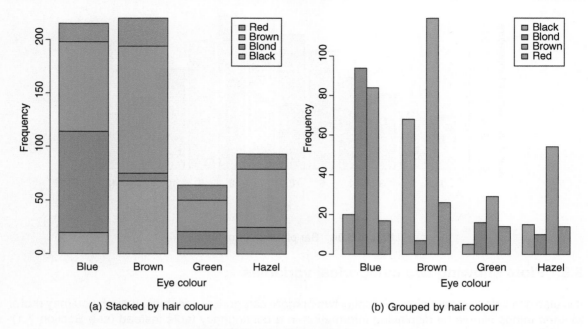

Figure 5.35   Bar chart of eye colour and hair colour

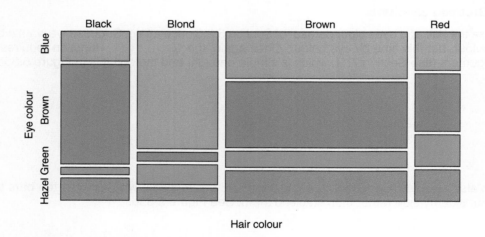

Figure 5.36   Mosaic plot for the hair and eye colour data

the width of the bars to indicate this. Applying this to the eye and hair colour example, we get Figure 5.36.

```
mosaicplot (table_hair_eye, col = c (hue_pal()(4)[1:4]),
            ylab = "Eye colour", xlab = "Hair colour", main = "")
```

Red hair has the narrowest column, while brown hair has the widest. The width of each column is proportional to the number of individuals in each hair colour group. Similarly, the height of each segment is proportional to the number of observations in that group. We can see, for example, that well in excess of half of the blond participants had blue eyes while there were very few green-eyed individuals with black hair.

If you are familiar with contingency tables, you can see that each block of colour represents a cell in the table with its size indicative of the number of observations therein.

5.6 Plots for three (or more) variables

When you want to incorporate information on a third variable (or even more) into the mix, things inevitably get trickier. There are a number of ways we could do this, but we'll stick to looking at simple ways of conveying this information in different situations.

5.6.1 Plots of all pairs of variables

A simple and often effective strategy is to use the `pairs ()` function to create a matrix of scatterplots. This produces a scatterplot (technically two scatterplots) for each pair of variables in the dataset or subset thereof. This couldn't be easier, and we'll demonstrate with the ozone data. This dataset contains information on four continuous variables, and the resulting plot is in Figure 5.37. Notice that we've scaled down the point size using `cex` to make the plots look better:

```
ozone <- read.table ("ozone_pollution.txt", header = TRUE)
head (ozone)

  rad temp wind ozone
1 190   67  7.4    41
2 118   72  8.0    36
3 149   74 12.6    12
```

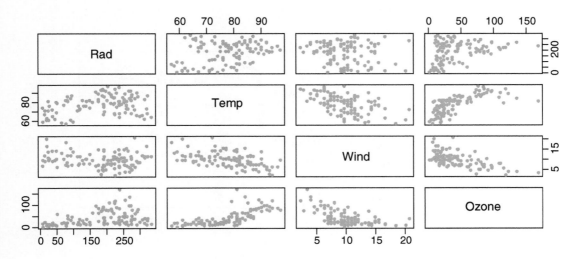

Figure 5.37 Matrix of scatterplots for the ozone data.

```
4 313    62 11.5    18
5 299    65  8.6    23
6  99    59 13.8    19
```

```
pairs (ozone, col = hue_pal()(1), cex = 0.6)
```

If we want to pick out a subset of variables to plot (this can be useful if you have a lot of variables as each scatterplot becomes too small to be useful), you can do this by using, e.g. `pairs (ozone [, c (1:2, 4)])`, which would select the first, second, and fourth variables to plot.

Notice how the scatterplots under the diagonal in Figure 5.37 are mirror images of those above. For example, the first scatterplot of the top row is a scatterplot of `rad` by `temp` with `rad` on the y-axis and `temp` on the x-axis. Meanwhile, the first scatterplot in the first column is of `temp` by `rad` with `temp` on the y-axis and `rad` on the x-axis.

5.6.2 Incorporating a third variable on a scatterplot

The following example concerns the response of a grass species *Festuca rubra* as measured by its biomass in small samples (FR) to two explanatory variables, soil pH, and total hay yield (the mass of all plant species combined). A scatterplot of `pH` against `hay` shows the locations of the various samples. The idea is to use the `text` function to label each of the points on the scatterplot with the dry mass of *F. rubra* in that particular sample, to see whether there is systematic variation in the mass of *Festuca* with changes in hay yield and soil pH, which is in Figure 5.38.

```
pgr <- read.table ("pgr.txt", header = T)
attach (pgr)
names (pgr)

[1] "FR"  "hay" "pH"

plot (hay, pH, col = hue_pal()(2)[1])
text (hay, pH, labels = round (FR, 1), pos = 1, offset = 0.5, cex = 0.7)
```

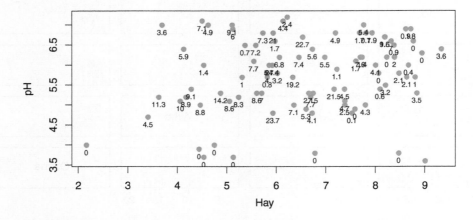

Figure 5.38   pH by hay, labelled using dry mass of *F. rubra* in sample

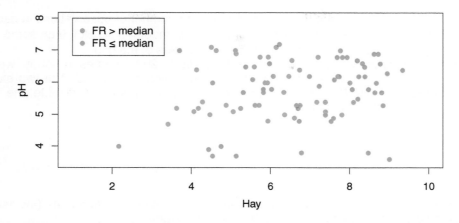

Figure 5.39   pH by hay, coloured by whether dry mass of *F. rubra* in sample was greater than the median

The labels are *centred* on the *x* value of the point (`pos = 1`) and are *offset half a character below* the point (`offset = 0.5`). They show the value of FR rounded to one significant digit (`labels = round (FR, 1)`) at 70% character expansion (`cex = 0.7`). There is an obvious problem with this method when there is lots of overlap between the labels (as in the top right), but the technique works well for more widely spaced points. The plot shows that high values of *Festuca* biomass are concentrated at intermediate values of both soil pH and hay yield.

You can also use a third variable to choose the colour of the points in your scatterplot, as shown in Figure 5.39. We need to specify a legend, which will take up space in the plot, so we extend the range of the *x*- and *y*-axes to accommodate this. Now we'll place the legend so that the top left-hand corner is positioned at (1, 8).

```
plot (hay, pH, pch = 16, xlim = c (1, 10), ylim = c (3.5, 8),
      col = ifelse (FR > median (FR), hue_pal()(2)[1], hue_pal()(2)[2]))
legend (1, 8, c ("FR > median", "FR <= median"),
      pch = 16, col = hue_pal()(2)[1:2])
```

5.6.3   Basic 3D plots

When there are two continuous explanatory variables, it is often useful to plot the response as a contour map. We continue with the example from 5.6.2. This time, we want the biomass of one plant species (the response variable) plotted against soil pH and total community biomass. The species is a grass called *Festuca rubra* once again, that peaks in abundance in communities of intermediate total biomass.

There are many base *R* functions and other packages that build different types of 3D plots in *R*. You could stick to the basic `filled.contour ()` function to create a contour plot. Alternatively, employ a specialist package, for example `rgl` (Murdoch and Adler, 2021) or `plotly` (Sievert, 2020). We'll use `plotly` here, which has a range of excellent plotting options. It's worth exploring their library.

The relevant function in `plotly` is `plot_ly ()` which, roughly speaking, needs us to specify a grid and to say how many observations are in each section of the grid. For example, imagine taking the rectangular area defined by the axes in Figure 5.39, say. Cut this up into a 40 × 40 grid (40 is arbitrary, but will turn out to be the default), and count the number of observations in each square of this grid. Of course, if you want to produce some sort of smoothed 3D plot, then some degree of interpolation is going to be needed between adjacent squares of the grid.

This is where the package `akima` (Akima and Gebhardt, 2021) comes in handy: we can use the `interp ()` function to perform this bivariate interpolation onto a grid. The two explanatory variables are presented first (`hay` and `pH` in this case), with the response variable (the 'height' of the topography), which is `FR` in this case, third:

```
library (plotly)
library (akima)
plot_dat <- interp (hay, pH, FR)
```

Now, we can use `plot_ly ()` to create a contour plot as shown in Figure 5.40. (Incidentally, the interpolation onto a grid is needed for other 3D plotting systems in *R* too.)

```
plot_ly (x = plot_dat$x, y = plot_dat$y,
         z = matrix (plot_dat$z, nrow = length (plot_dat$y), byrow = TRUE),
         type = "contour", colorscale = hue_pal ()(24))
```

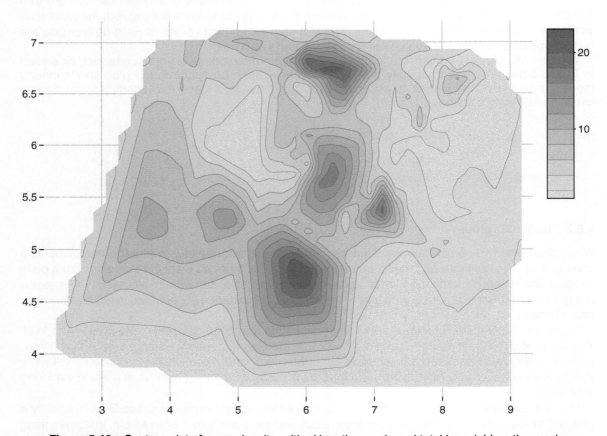

Figure 5.40 Contour plot of grass density, with pH on the *y*-axis and total hay yield on the *x*-axis

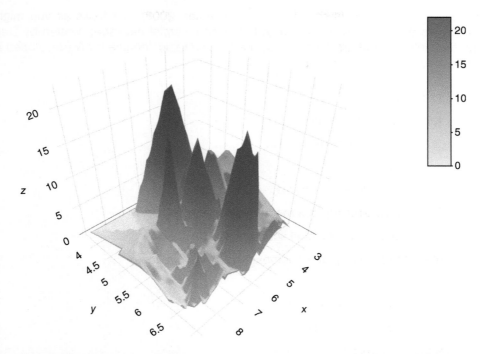

Figure 5.41   3D surface plot of grass density, with pH on the *y*-axis and total hay yield on the *x*-axis

Evidently, the grass peaks in abundance at intermediate biomass, but it also occurs at lower biomasses on soils of intermediate pH (5.0–6.0). It is found in only trace amounts in communities where the biomass is above 7.5 tonnes ha^{-1}, except where soil pH is around 6.6.

Changing to `type = "surface"` in the `plot_ly ()` function gives a nice-looking surface plot of the same data, with the added satisfaction that you can twist the plot around manually in the viewing window to see it from any viewpoint. Figure 5.41 gives the standard view that you get on creating the plot. Notice that the axes have been twisted in comparison to those in Figure 5.40.

```
plot_ly (x = plot_dat$x, y = plot_dat$y,
         z = matrix (plot_dat$z, nrow = length (plot_dat$y), byrow = TRUE),
         type = "surface", colorscale = hue_pal()(24))
```

5.7   Trellis graphics

The main purpose of trellis graphics is to produce multiple plots per page and multi-page plots. The plots are produced in adjacent panels, typically with one plot for each level of a categorical variable (called the **conditioning variable**).

Trellis graphics is a framework for data visualisation developed at Bell Laboratories by Rick Becker, Bill Cleveland, and others, extending the ideas about what makes for an effective graph (layout, colour, style, symbol sizes, and so forth,) presented in Cleveland, 1993. The package for producing trellis graphics in *R* is called `lattice` (Sarkar, 2008) (not trellis as you might have guessed, because that name was pre-empted by a commercial package), written by Deepayan Sarkar, and the plots created are rendered by the Grid Graphics engine for *R* (developed by Paul Murrell). Here are some examples of `lattice` functions:

- `barchart ()` for barplots;
- `bwplot ()` for box-and-whisker plots;
- `densityplot ()` for kernel density plots;
- `dotplot ()` for dot plots;
- `histogram ()` for panels of histograms;
- `qqmath ()` for quantile plots against mathematical distributions;
- `stripplot ()` for a one-dimensional scatterplot;
- `qq ()` for a quantile–quantile plot for comparing two distributions;
- `xyplot ()` for a scatterplot;
- `levelplot ()` for creating level plots;
- `contourplot ()` for contour plots;
- `cloud ()` for 3D scatterplots;
- `wireframe ()` for 3D surfaces;
- `splom ()` for a scatterplot matrix;
- `parallel ()` for creating parallel coordinate plots.

You'll notice that many of the plot types we've already considered are covered by the `lattice` package, but these are generally only used when the base *R* versions we considered earlier are not the best (e.g. when you want to display a variable using a histogram, but you want a separate histogram for each level of some categorical variable).

Let us look at a quick example before we consider some of these functions in more depth. The data used here give the age and weight of seven females and seven males.

```
panels <- read.table ("panels.txt", header = T)
attach (panels)
names (panels)


[1] "age"    "weight" "gender"
```

You might, for instance, plot weight against age for each of two genders (males and females), as displayed in Figure 5.42. The response variable is weight, the continuous explanatory variable is age (also called the **primary covariate** in documentation on trellis graphics) and the categorical explanatory variable is gender (a factor with two levels). In a case like this, the default would produce two panels side by side in one row, with the panel for females on the left (simply because 'f' comes

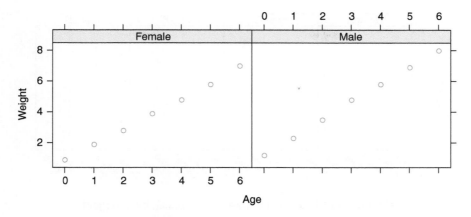

Figure 5.42   Trellis plot of weight by age, separated by gender

before 'm' in the alphabet). In the jargon of trellis graphics, gender is a **grouping factor** that divides the observations into distinct groups.

The panel plots are created by `xyplot ()`, using a formula to indicate the grouping structure: `weight ~ age | gender`. This is read as 'weight is plotted as a function of age, given gender' (the vertical bar is the 'given' symbol).

```
library (lattice)
xyplot (weight ~ age | gender, col = hue_pal()(1)[1])

detach (panels)
```

Lattice plots are highly customisable via user-modifiable settings, but these are completely unrelated to base graphics settings. To read more about the background and capabilities of the lattice package, type `?lattice`.

5.7.1   Panel boxplots

Here is an example trellis plot for the interpretation of a designed experiment where all the explanatory variables are categorical. If we want boxplots, the relevant function is `bwplot ()`, and we request one plot per detergent type.

```
daph <- read.table ("daphnia.txt",header=T)
attach (daph)
names (daph)

[1] "Growth.rate" "Water"        "Detergent"    "Daphnia"

bwplot (Growth.rate ~ Water + Daphnia | Detergent,
        col = hue_pal()(1)[1], scales = list(x = list (rot = 45)))

detach (daph)
```

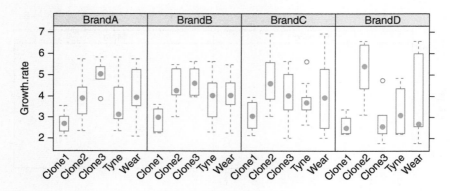

Figure 5.43 Boxplots by water and daphnia, by detergent

Notice that in order to get Figure 5.43, we specify two explanatory variables – `Water` and `Daph-nia` – and get five boxplots for each detergent type in return: one for each of the three levels of `Daphnia` and one for each of the two levels of the variable `Water` (that is, we have two categorical variables on the *x*-axis). The angle of the *x*-axis text has also been rotated for easy reading using the `scales` argument.

5.7.2 Panel scatterplots

The following example is concerned with root growth measured over time, as repeated measures on 12 individual plants:

```
fertilizer_data <- read.table ("fertilizer.txt", header = T)
attach (fertilizer_data)
names (fertilizer_data)

[1] "root"        "week"        "plant"        "fertilizer"
```

A set of 12 scatterplots is given in Figure 5.44, showing `root ~ week` with one panel for each plant. The syntax uses the 'given' bar like this:

```
xyplot (root ~ week | plant, col = hue_pal()(1)[1])
```

Panels are, by default, drawn starting from the bottom left-hand corner, going right and then up, unless `as.table = TRUE` is specified, in which case panels are drawn from the top left-hand corner, going right and then down. Both of these orders can be modified using the `index.cond` and `perm.cond` arguments. In our example, the panels are shown in alphabetical order by plant name from bottom left (ID1) to top right (ID9), which may not be helpful.

  If you want to change things like the plotting symbol, we can do this within the `xyplot ()` function, which gives Figure 5.45 in this case.

```
xyplot (root ~ week | plant, col = hue_pal()(1)[1], pch = 16)
```

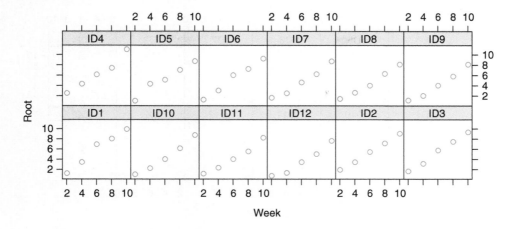

Figure 5.44 Root length by week, displayed by plant

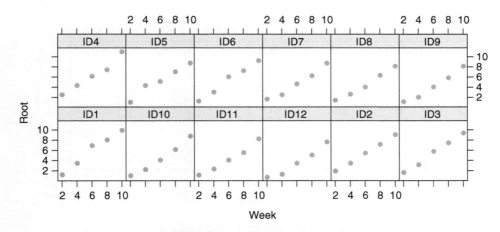

Figure 5.45 A change of plotting symbol

If we want to make more involved changes, we should use a `panel.()` function. There are some grid-compatible replacements for commonly used base *R* graphics functions, for example, `lines` can be replaced by `panel.lines ()`. Note that base *R* graphics functions like `lines ()` simply will not work here.

For example, suppose we want to fit a separate linear regression for each individual plant. This is easy enough, and the output is displayed in Figure 5.46:

```
xyplot (root ~ week | plant,
        panel = function (x, y)
           {panel.xyplot (x, y, pch = 16, col = hue_pal()(2)[1])
            panel.abline (lm (y ~ x), col = hue_pal()(2)[2])
           })
```

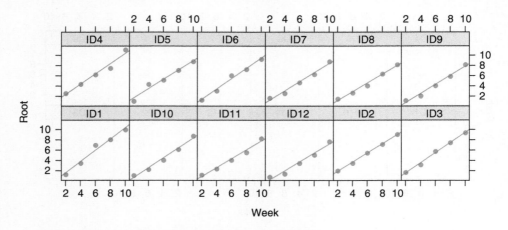

Figure 5.46 Adding a linear regression line for each plant

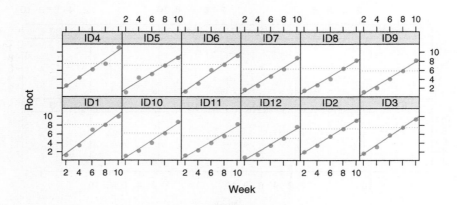

Figure 5.47 Adding a horizontal line

We might want to do different things in different panels. We could draw a horizontal dashed line, as in Figure 5.47 highlighting the location of the fourth data point in each panel using subscripts [4]:

```
xyplot (root ~ week | plant,
        panel = function (x, y)
          {panel.xyplot (x, y, pch = 16, col = hue_pal()(3)[1])
           panel.abline (lm (y ~ x), col = hue_pal()(3)[2])
           panel.abline (h = y [4], col = hue_pal()(3)[3], lty = 3)
           })
```

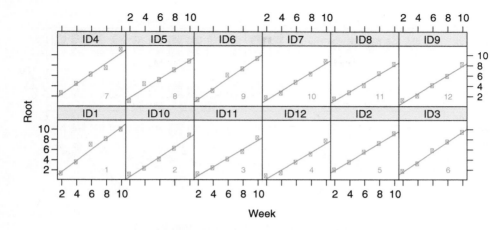

Figure 5.48 Displaying panel number

The panels are numbered by default from lower left to upper right. Here we use `panel.number ()` to illustrate this in Figure 5.48, by adding a text label to each panel showing the panel number:

```
xyplot (root ~ week | plant,
        panel = function (x, y)
           {panel.xyplot (x, y, pch = 16, col = hue_pal()(4)[1])
            panel.abline (lm (y ~ x), col = hue_pal()(4)[2])
            panel.text (8, 2, panel.number (), col = hue_pal()(4)[4], cex = 0.7)
            })
```

```
detach (fertilizer_data)
```

We can add extra points and extra lines to each panel using `panel.lines ()` and `panel.points ()` with `panel.number ()` as a subscript (output not shown):

```
xyplot (root ~ week | plant,
        panel = function (x, y)
           {panel.xyplot (x, y, pch = 16, col = hue_pal()(4)[1])
            panel.abline (lm (y ~ x), col = hue_pal()(4)[2])
            panel.points (xnew [panel.number ()], ynew [panel.number ()])
            })
```

5.7.3 Panel barplots

The following example shows the use of the trellis version of the barchart with the built-in barley data. The data are shown separately for each site in Figure 5.49, and the bars are stacked for each year by specifying `stack = TRUE` in different colours.

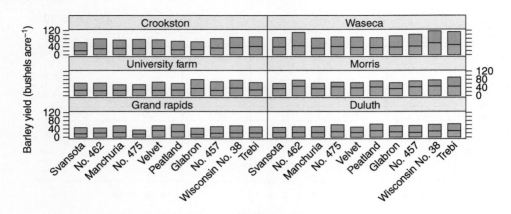

Figure 5.49   Yield by variety and year, by site

The barcharts are produced in three rows of two plots each by specifying `layout = c (2, 3))`. Note the use of `scales` to rotate the long labels on the *x*-axis through 45 degrees:

```
barchart (yield ~ variety | site, data = barley,
          groups = year, layout = c(2,3), stack = TRUE,
          col = c (hue_pal () (2) [1:2]),
          ylab = "Barley Yield (bushels/acre)",
          scales = list(x = list (rot = 45)))
```

5.7.4   Panels for conditioning plots

We'll use the in-built `ethanol` dataset to demonstrate conditioning plots. These are generally plots of two variables, *conditioned* on a third.

We have NOx, the concentration of nitric acid and nitrogen dioxide in engine exhaust; C, the compression ratio of the engine under consideration; and E, the equivalence ratio at which the engine ran.

We want side by side panels of NOx by C, split by E. We need to split E into nine suitable equally sized groups. We'll call the resulting variable EE:

```
EE <- equal.count (ethanol$E, number = 9, overlap = 1/4)
```

Within each panel in Figure 5.50, we create a scatterplot of NOx against C (via `panel.xyplot (x, y)`) and draw an individual linear regression using `panel.abline (lm (y ~ x))`. Notice that we've requested all nine panels to be displayed in one row by specifying `layout = c (9, 1)`:

```
xyplot (NOx ~ C | EE, data = ethanol, layout = c (9, 1),
        panel = function (x, y) {
           panel.xyplot (x, y, col = hue_pal()(2)[1], pch = 16)
           panel.abline (lm (y ~ x), col = hue_pal()(2)[2])
        })
```

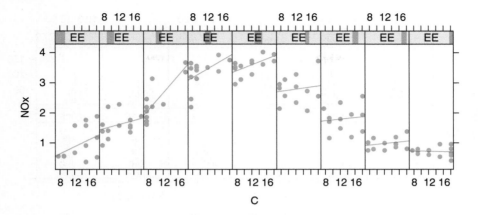

Figure 5.50 NOx by C, by EE, with regression lines added for each panel

This is an excellent way of illustrating that the correlation between NOx and C is positive for all levels of EE except the highest one, and that the relationship is steepest for values of EE just below the median (i.e. in the third panel from the left).

5.7.5 Panel histograms

The task is to use the Silwood weather data to draw a panel of histograms, one for each month of the year, showing the number of days per month during the period 1987–2005 with particular minimum temperatures.

```
weather <- read.table ("SilwoodWeather.txt", header = T)
attach (weather)
head (weather)
```

```
  upper lower rain month    yr
1  10.8   6.5 12.2     1 1987
2  10.5   4.5  1.3     1 1987
3   7.5  -1.0  0.1     1 1987
4   6.5  -3.3  1.1     1 1987
5  10.0   5.0  3.5     1 1987
6   8.0   3.0  0.1     1 1987
```

```
histogram ( ~ lower | month, type = "count",
            xlab = "mimimum temerature", ylab = "frequency",
            breaks = seq (-12, 28, 2), col = hue_pal()(1))
```

```
detach (weather)
```

The panel histogram in Figure 5.51 is drawn using the histogram function which takes a model formula *without a response variable*, ~ lower | month, as its first argument. Though not necessary, we've also specified the bins for the histogram. The month labels, as per the dataset, are displayed above each histogram.

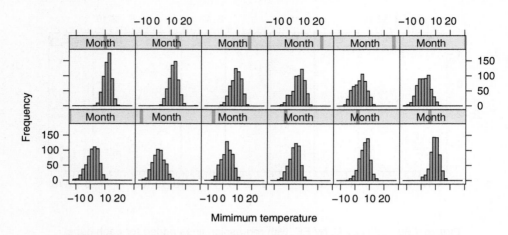

Figure 5.51   Histogram of minimum temperature, by month of year

5.7.6   More panel functions

Rather than having side-by-side panels, plots can be specified by a grouping `groups = rowpos` with one plot produced rather than many. We can indicate that each group should be drawn in a different colour via `panel = "panel.superpose"`, or specify that the dots should be joined by lines for each member of the group `panel.groups = "panel.linejoin"`.

   Here are the built-in orchard spray data with each row shown in a different colour and the treatment means joined together by lines, shown in Figure 5.52. This example also shows how to use `key` to locate a key to the groups on the right of the plot, showing `lines` rather than `points`:

```
xyplot (decrease ~ treatment, OrchardSprays, groups = rowpos,
      type="a", col = c (hue_pal()(8)[1:8]),
      key = list(lines = list (col = c (hue_pal()(8)[1:8])),
                 text = list (as.character (unique (OrchardSprays$rowpos))),
                 space = "right" )
      )
```

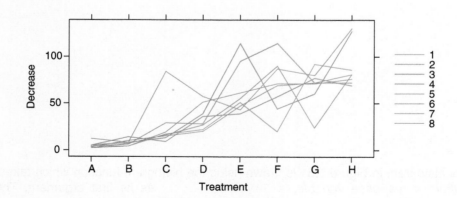

Figure 5.52   Decrease by treatment, plotted by row

5.8 Plotting functions

In this section, we'll turn our attention to plotting deterministic functions, for example mathematical functions or statistical functions such as drawing probability densities. We'll first look at two-dimensional functions before we consider plotting in three-dimensions.

5.8.1 Two-dimensional plots

The `curve ()` function is convenient for this. A plot of $x^3 - 3x$ between $x = -2$ and $x = 2$ is in Figure 5.53:

```
curve (x^3 - 3 * x, -2, 2, col = hue_pal()(1), xlab = "x", ylab = "y")
```

Here is the more cumbersome code to do the same thing using `plot ()`, which results in exactly the same plot:

```
x <- seq (-2, 2, 0.01)
y <- x^3 - 3 * x
plot (x, y, type = "l", col = hue_pal()(1), xlab = "x", ylab = "y")
```

With `plot ()`, you need to decide how many segments you want to generate to create the curve (using `seq ()` with steps of 0.01 in this example), then calculate the matching `y` values, then use `plot ()` with `type = "l"`. This stands for 'type = line' (rather than the default `points ()`) and can cause problems if you misread the symbol as a number 'one' rather than a lower-case letter 'L'.

You can also draw probability distributions in a similar manner, for example a standard Normal distribution (mean = 0 and standard deviation = 1), plotted between $x = -5$ and $x = 5$. To do this we use the built-in `dnorm ()` which gives the density of a Normal distribution with given mean and standard deviation, the result of which is in Figure 5.54:

```
curve (dnorm (x, mean = 0, sd = 1), -5, 5, col = hue_pal()(2)[1],
       xlab = "x", ylab = "Density of standard normal")
```

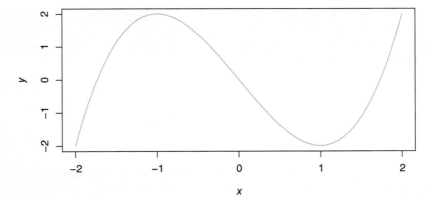

Figure 5.53 Plot of a mathematical function

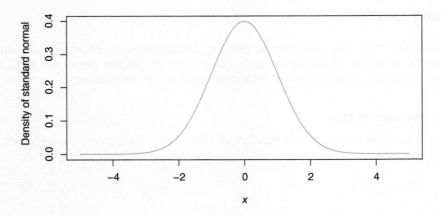

Figure 5.54   Standard Normal distribution function

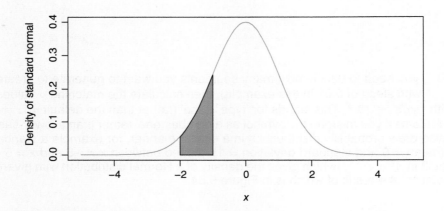

Figure 5.55   Standard Normal distribution function, with section shaded

The `polygon ()` function can be used to draw and fill more complicated shapes, including curved ones. In this example, we are asked to shade the area beneath a standard normal curve between −2 and −1. First draw the probability density as before, then fill the corresponding area. You can see the result in Figure 5.55:

```
curve (dnorm (x, mean = 0, sd = 1), -5, 5, col = hue_pal () (2) [1],
        xlab = "x", ylab = "Density of standard normal")
w <- seq (-2, -1, 0.01)
polygon (c (-2, w, -1), c (0, dnorm (w), 0), col = hue_pal () (2) [2])
```

Note the insertion of the points $(-2, 0)$ and $(-1, 0)$: to create the right-angled corners to the polygon on the *x*-axis and make sure that the bottom line is horizontal. You get a very strange plot if you don't do this!

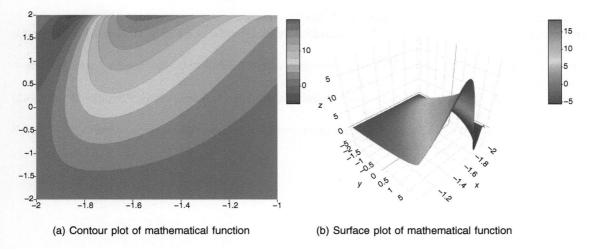

(a) Contour plot of mathematical function   (b) Surface plot of mathematical function

Figure 5.56   Visualising functions with two input variables

5.8.2   Three-dimensional plots

It is straightforward to create 3D images of mathematical functions from regularly spaced grids produced by the `outer ()` function. First, create a series of values for the *x*- and *y*-axis (the base of the plot) and write a function to predict the height of the graph (the response variable, *z*) as a function of the two explanatory variables *x* and *y*. Now use the `outer ()` function to evaluate the function over the complete grid of points defined by *x* and *y*:

```
x <- seq (0, 10, 0.1)
y <- seq (0, 10, 0.1)
func <- function (a, b) 3 * a * exp (0.1 * a) * sin (b * exp (-0.5 * a))
z <- t (outer (x, y, func))
```

Notice that we use `t (outer (y, x,.))` because the `outer ()` function uses the first argument to define the row names first followed by the column names, but `plot_ly ()` from the package `plotly` will need the resulting matrix ordered the other way around. In other words, we need to *transpose* the resulting matrix using `t ()`. Now, we can create a contour or surface plot which results in Figure 5.56:

```
library (plotly)
plot_ly (x = x, y = y, z = z,
        type = "contour", colorscale = hue_pal()(24))
plot_ly (x = x, y = y, z = z,
        type = "surface", colorscale = hue_pal()(24))
```

References

Akima, H., & Gebhardt, A. (2021). *Akima: Interpolation of irregularly and regularly spaced data* [R package version 0.6-2.2]. https://CRAN.R-project.org/package=akima.

Cleveland, W. S. (1993). *Visualizing data*. At & T Bell Laboratories.

Murdoch, D., & Adler, D. (2021). *RGL: 3D visualization using OpenGL* [R package version 0.106.8]. https://CRAN.R-project.org/package=rgl.

Sarkar, D. (2008). *Lattice: multivariate data visualization with R* [ISBN 978-0-387-75968-5]. Springer. http://lmdvr.r-forge.r-project.org.

Sievert, C. (2020). *Interactive web-based data visualization with R, Plotly, and Shiny*. Chapman & Hall/CRC. https://plotly-r.com.

Wickham, H., & Seidel, D. (2020). *Scales: scale functions for visualization* [R package version 1.1.1]. https://CRAN.R-project.org/package=scales.

## 6

Graphics in More Detail

We looked at the basics of plotting in *R* in Chapter 5. Here, we delve into more detail, under the following broad topics:

- Colour in plots;
- Changing the look of graphics;
- Adding items to plots;
- An introduction to an alternative plotting system using `ggplot2`.

We end the chapter with the ultimate graphics cheat-sheet, which goes through a large number of plotting options alphabetically.

6.1 More on colour

Colour can make or break a plot, and it's often tricky to find a set of colours that is easy on the eye and also provides good contrast. In this section, we'll start with colour choice, before looking at how to change the colour of various elements of a plot.

6.1.1 Colour palettes with categorical data

Rather than choose a set of colours explicitly, it's possible to use a colour palette. It is easy to create a vector of colours from a palette, then refer to the colours by their subscripts within the palette. The key is to create the right number of colours for our needs.

Here's a simple example where we use the built-in `heat.colors ()` to shade the temperature bars in our Silwood Weather dataset. We want the colours to grade from cold to hot, then back to cold again from January to December as in Figure 6.1:

```
weather <- read.table ("SilwoodWeather.txt", header = T)
weather$month <- factor (weather$month)
attach (weather)
```

The R Book, Third Edition. Elinor Jones, Simon Harden and Michael J. Crawley.
© 2023 John Wiley & Sons Ltd. Published 2023 by John Wiley & Sons Ltd.
Companion website: www.wiley.com/go/jones/therbook3e

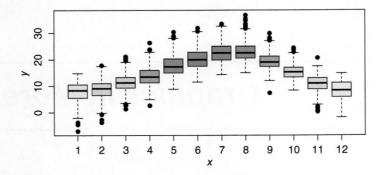

Figure 6.1 Shaded boxplots of temperature by month.

```
season <- heat.colors (12)
temp <- c (11, 10, 8, 5, 3, 1, 2, 3, 5, 8, 10, 11)
plot (month, upper, col = season[temp])
```

```
detach (weather)
```

There are several built-in palettes. For instance, the built-in function called `rainbow ()` takes the seven colours of the rainbow (red, orange, yellow, green, blue, indigo, violet) and splits them into a specified number of colours on the basis of hue, saturation, and value. Here are four examples, with the spectrum split into 7, 14, 28, or 56 segments as displayed in Figure 6.2:

```
pie (rep (1, 7),  col = rainbow (7),  radius = 1)
pie (rep (1, 14), col = rainbow (14), radius = 1)
pie (rep (1, 28), col = rainbow (28), radius = 1)
pie (rep (1, 56), col = rainbow (56), radius = 1)
```

Notice that between them, greens and blues take up more than half of the space, with red, orange, yellow, indigo, and violet making up the remainder. Also, note the use of the margin parameter `radius` to optimise the size of the pie diagrams, while keeping their labels distinct from each other.

There are four other built-in colour functions that can be used to produce graded hues, as displayed in Figure 6.3:

```
pie (rep (1, 14), col = heat.colors (14), radius = 0.9)
pie (rep (1, 14), col = terrain.colors (14), radius = 0.9)
pie (rep (1, 14), col = topo.colors (14), radius = 0.9)
pie (rep (1, 14), col = cm.colors (14), radius = 0.9)
```

It is simple to create customized palettes. Here we use the function `rgb ()` to do it, as displayed in Figure 6.4:

```
custom <- c (rgb (0.6, 0.8,1), rgb (1, 0.8, 0.2), rgb (1, 0.8, 0.4),
             rgb(1, 0.8, 0.6), rgb (1, 0.8, 0.8), rgb (1, 0.8,1),
             rgb(0.8, 0.8,1), rgb (0.7, 0.8,1))
pie (rep (1/8, 8), col = custom)
```

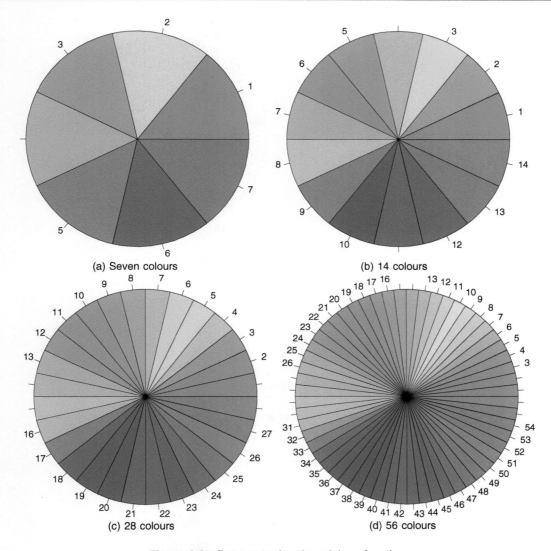

Figure 6.2 Demonstrating the rainbow function.

6.1.2 The RColorBrewer package

RColorBrewer (Neuwirth, 2014) is a very useful package of tried and tested colour schemes, in which carefully selected colours have been grouped together into a set of palettes (more information on ColorBrewer is available at its website, **http://www.colorbrewer.org**). It is necessary to install RColorBrewer in the usual way.

These palettes have a minimum of three colours and a maximum of 8–12 depending on the palette. There are three types of palettes – sequential, diverging, and qualitative:

- Sequential palettes are suited to ordered data that progress from low to high. Lightness steps dominate the look of these schemes, from light colours for low data values to dark colours for high-data values.

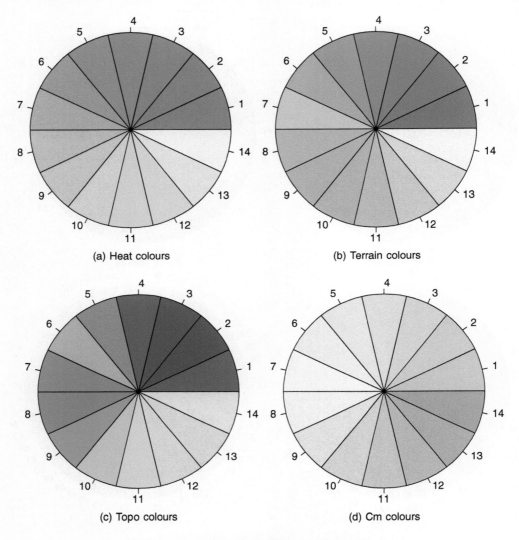

Figure 6.3 Demonstrating other colour functions.

- Diverging palettes put equal emphasis on mid-range critical values and extremes at both ends of the data range. The critical class or break in the middle of the legend is emphasised with light colours, and low and high extremes are emphasised with dark colours that have contrasting hues.

- Qualitative palettes do not imply magnitude differences between legend classes, and hues are used to create the primary visual differences between classes. Qualitative schemes are best suited to representing nominal or categorical data.

Figure 6.5 is a demonstration of three palettes from each of the three palette types. We specify how many colours to use in the palette (eight in these examples). For example, Figure 6.5a was created using:

```
library (RColorBrewer)
mypalette  <- brewer.pal (8, "Reds")
pie (rep (1,8), col = mypalette)
```

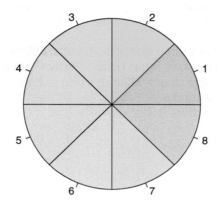

Figure 6.4 Custom colour palatte.

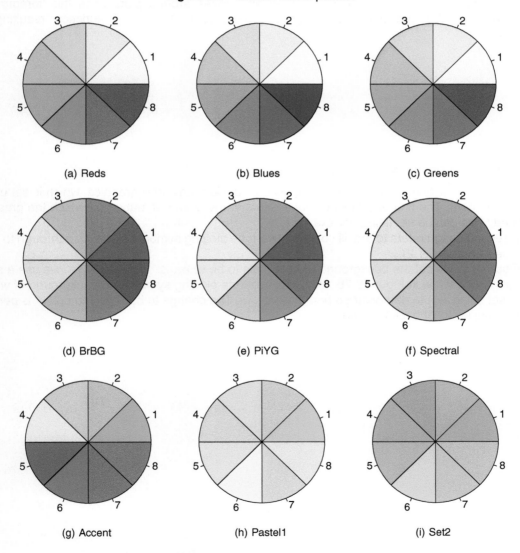

Figure 6.5 Some RColourBrewer palattes with eight colours.

The relevant palatte colour, e.g. Reds in Figure 6.5a, are given as captions under each plot.

The top row in Figure 6.5 contains three classic sequential palettes, the centre row three different diverging palettes, and the bottom row three quite effective qualitative palettes. Once we have defined a palette, we can refer to colours within it using subscripts in any plotting function that accepts a `col` = argument, for example `col = mypalette[3]`.

To reset the palette back to the default use:

```
palette ("default")
```

6.1.3 Foreground colours

Changing the colour of such things as axes and boxes around plots uses the 'foreground' parameter, `fg`. We can add this as an argument to the `plot ()` function resulting in Figure 6.6:

```
plot (1 : 10, 1 : 10, xlab = "x", ylab = "y")
plot (1 : 10, 1 : 10, xlab = "x", ylab = "y", fg = "blue")
plot (1 : 10, 1 : 10, xlab = "x", ylab = "y", fg = hue_pal ()(1))
plot (1 : 10, 1 : 10, xlab = "x", ylab = "y", fg = brewer.pal (3, "Accent")[1])
```

6.1.4 Background colours

It is important to distinguish two contrasting uses of 'background' in *R* graphics, which is set using the `bg` argument. The first and most obvious refers to the colour of 'paper' on which the graph is produced. This can be set using, for example, `par (bg = "wheat2")`.

The second usage refers to the fill colour of two-tone plotting symbols `pch` = 21 through to `pch` = 25 (see Section 5.1.2).

In Figure 6.7, we set the background of both plots to be `wheat2`. In Figure 6.7a, we use a solid plotting symbol, while in Figure 6.7b, we use a two-tone plotting symbol (the background of which can be set using `bg`) to demonstrate both uses of `bg`. The change to background colour is permanent until we switch it back to white.

```
jaws <- read.table ("jaws.txt", header = T)
attach (jaws)
par (bg = "wheat2")
plot (age, bone, pch = 16, cex = 2, col = hue_pal()(1))
plot (age, bone, pch = 21, cex = 2, col = hue_pal()(2)[1], bg = hue_pal()(2)[2])
par (bg = "white")
detach (jaws)
```

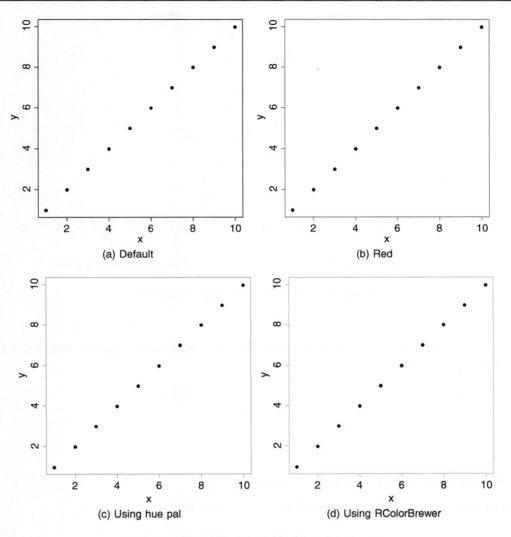

Figure 6.6 Changing the foreground colours.

6.1.5 Background colour for legends

Changing the background colour for a legend box is simple enough, and we can again do it using the `bg` argument, resulting in Figure 6.8a (plot code not shown):

```
legend (0, 50, legend = c ("Control", "Heat", "Dose"), pch = c (16, 16, 16),
        bg = "wheat1", col = hue_pal () (6) [c (2, 4, 6)])
```

As in Section 6.1.4, there is a clash in the use of `bg` in setting a background colour of a legend when we choose to use two-tone plotting symbols (`pch = 21` through to `pch = 25`). We get around this

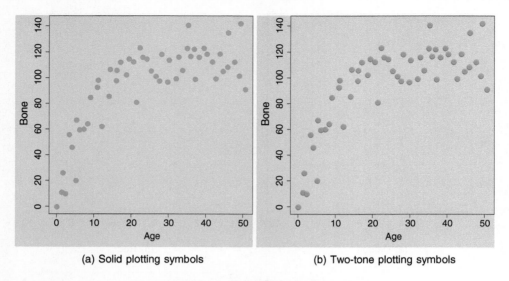

(a) Solid plotting symbols   (b) Two-tone plotting symbols

Figure 6.7   Changing the background colour.

using `pt.bg` to set the background colour of the plotting symbol, when required, resulting in Figure 6.8b (plot code not shown):

```
legend (0, 50, legend = c ("Control", "Heat", "Dose"), pch = c (21, 21, 21),
        bg = "wheat1", col = hue_pal()(6)[c(2, 4, 6)],
        pt.bg = hue_pal()(6)[c (1, 3, 5)])
```

6.1.6   Different colours for different parts of the graph

The colours for different parts of the graph are specified as follows:

`col.axis ()`	is the colour to be used for axis annotation;
`col.lab ()`	is the colour to be used for *x* and *y* labels;
`col.main ()`	is the colour to be used for plot main titles;
`col.sub ()`	is the colour to be used for plot subtitles.

For example, in Figure 6.9, we've changed the colour of the plotting symbols, the labels on the axes, and the tick mark labels on the axes. The result is pretty hideous.

```
plot (1 : 10, 1 : 10, xlab = "x label", ylab = "y label", pch = 16,
      col = hue_pal()(3)[1], col.lab = hue_pal()(3)[2], col.axis = hue_pal()(3)[3])
```

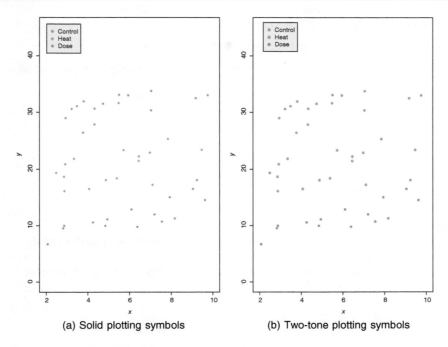

(a) Solid plotting symbols   (b) Two-tone plotting symbols

Figure 6.8   Changing the background colour of legends.

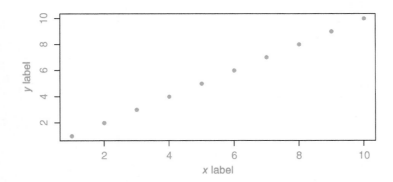

Figure 6.9   Changing colours of various plot elements.

6.1.7   Full control of colours in plots

We could, if we really wanted to, control the colours and line types of all of the components of a plot separately. For example, if we use `plot ()` to create a boxplot (this is the default if we supply one factor variable to the function), we can control the following components:

- the box and its outline `box*`;
- the median, its line type, line width and colour `med*`;

- the whiskers, their line type, width, and colour `whisk*`;
- the staples (this is the jargon for the flat ends of the whiskers) `staple*`;
- the 'outliers' (which may not be actual outliers), their plotting symbol, edge, and fill `out*`.

Here is a full list of arguments that can be controlled in this case:

Box

`boxlty`	line type
`boxlwd`	line width
`boxcol`	line colour
`boxfill`	fill colour

Median

`medlty`	line type (`medlty = "blank"` if we want no line, just a point)
`medlwd`	line width
`medpch`	plotting symbol (added with the line unless specified otherwise)
`medcex`	plotting symbol size
`medcol`	plotting symbol colour
`medbg`	plotting symbol fill for `pch = 21` to `pch = 25`

Whisker

`whisklty`	line type
`whisklwd`	line width
`whiskcol`	colour

Staple

`staplelty`	line type
`staplelwd`	line width
`staplewex`	width expansion
`staplecol`	colour

Outlier

`outlty`	line type
`outlwd`	line width
`outwex`	width expansion
`outpch`	plotting symbol
`outcex`	symbol size
`outcol`	colour of the outline of the plotting symbol
`outbg`	colour of the fill of the plotting symbol

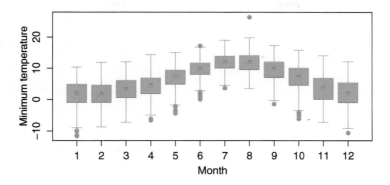

Figure 6.10   Changing colours of various boxplot elements.

Figure 6.10 has many of the options in their non-default settings (but whether we would ever really want to do this is debatable):

```
weather <- read.table ("silwoodweather.txt", header = T)
attach (weather)
plot (factor (month), lower, ylab = "minimum temperature", xlab = "month",
      medlty = "blank", medpch = 21, medbg = hue_pal()(4)[1], medcol = hue_pal()(4)[2],
      boxcol = hue_pal()(4)[1], boxfill = hue_pal()(4)[3], outpch = 21,
      outbg = hue_pal()(4)[2], outcol = hue_pal()(4)[1],
staplecol = hue_pal()(4)[4], whisklty = 1, whiskcol = hue_pal()(4)[4])

detach (weather)
```

6.1.8   Cross-hatching and grey scale

We can control five aspects of shading: the density of the lines, the angle of the shading, the border of the shaded region, the colour of the lines, and the line type. Here are their default values:

```
density = NULL
angle = 45
border = NULL
col = NA
lty = par ("lty"), ...)
```

Other graphical parameters dealing with lines such as xpd, lend, ljoin, and lmitre can be given as arguments. We shall shade each of the bars differently in Figure 6.11:

```
box <- read.table ("box.txt", header = T)
attach (box)
barplot (tapply (response, fact, mean), density = 3 : 10,
        angle = seq (30, 60, length = 8))
```

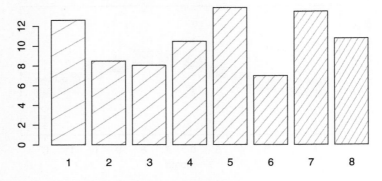

Figure 6.11   Cross-hatching a bar plot.

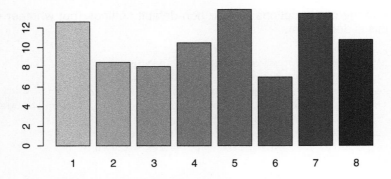

Figure 6.12   Grey scale on a bar plot.

The density and the angle of the shading in Figure 6.11 increase from left to right (the density from 3 lines per inch to 10 lines per inch, and the angle from 30 to 60 degrees).

Figure 6.12 gives the same example with grey scale instead of shading. Remember that the grey scale goes from 0 to 1, which (counter-intuitively) is from dark to light:

```
barplot (tapply (response, fact, mean), col = grey (seq (0.8, 0.2, length = 8)))

detach (box)
```

6.2   Changing the look of graphics

6.2.1   Shape and size of plot

We can resize the `Plots` pane manually in RStudio as we see fit. This alters the size of the graphic, of course. If we choose to save the plot using the `Export` button on the `Plots` pane (remember that this doesn't save a particularly high-quality graphic, see Section 5.1.3), then the height and width of the saved plot depends on how we resized the `Plots` pane. We can check the size of the current graphic by typing:

```
dev.size ()
```

This gives the width then height in inches by default (terribly old fashioned, we know), but we can request the information to be displayed in centimetres (`dev.size ("cm")`) or pixels (`dev.size ("px")`) if preferred.

When we want to save high-quality graphics, it is necessary to specify the size of the saved graphic explicitly. See Section 5.1.3 for more information. A word of warning, however: if we want to preview a plot in the right ratio, this should be done before saving. Otherwise, the final file might look different from what we expect.

6.2.2   Multiple plots on one screen

Often, it is desirable to place more than one graph in a single window. The graphical parameter to do this just happens to be the least intuitive to use. This is the number of graphs per screen, called somewhat unhelpfully, `mfrow ()`. This stands for 'multiple frames by rows'.

The idea is simple, but the syntax is hard to remember. We need to specify the number of rows of plots we want, and number of plots per row, in a vector of two numbers. The first number is the number of rows, and the second number is the number of graphs per row. The vector is made using concatenate `c ()` in the normal way. The default single-plot screen is `par (mfrow = c(1, 1))`. Two plots side by side is `par (mfrow = c (1, 2))` and a panel of four plots in a 2 × 2 square is `par (mfrow = c (2, 2))`.

To move from one plot to the next, we need to execute a new `plot ()` function (it doesn't have to be `plot ()` specifically, though). Control stays within the same plot frame while we execute functions like `points ()`, `lines ()`, or `text ()`. Remember to return to the default single plot when we have finished our multiple plot by executing `par (mfrow = c (1, 1))`. If we have more than two graphs per row or per column, the character expansion `cex` is set to 0.5, and we get half-size characters and labels.

We won't show the plots here, but the following would, for example, generate a single screen with three plots in a row, and once done, we change it back so that we get one plot per screen in future:

```
par (mfrow = c (1, 3))
plot (x1, y1)
plot (x2, y2)
plot (x3, y3)
par (mfrow = c (1, 1))
```

6.2.3   Tickmarks and associated labels

The most likely changes we will be asked to make are to the orientation of the numbers on the tick marks, and to the sizes of the text labels on the axes. There are three functions involved here, which are described in Table 6.1.

Table 6.1   Orientation and sizes of labels.

Argument	Purpose	Values
las	orientation of tick mark labels	0: parallel to each axis 1: horizontal to each axis 2: perpendicular to each axis 3: vertical to each axis
cex.lab	size of axes text labels	> 0, default = 1
cex.axis	size of tick mark labels	> 0, default = 1

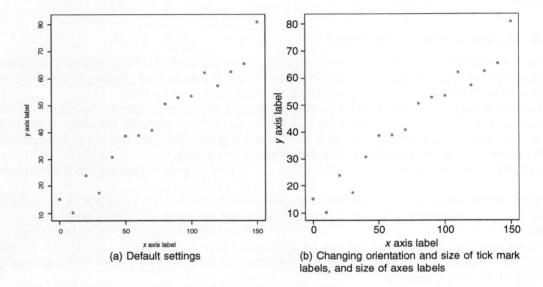

Figure 6.13   Changing tickmarks and associated items.

For example, the scatterplot in Figure 6.13a shows the default settings, while in Figure 6.13b, we have changed the orientation and size of tick mark labels, and size of axes labels. Note the use of `par ()` to generate side-by-side plots.

```
xvals <- seq (0, 150, 10)
yvals <- 16 + xvals * 0.4 + rnorm (length (xvals), 0, 6)
par (mfrow = c (1, 2))
plot (xvals, yvals, pch = 16, col = hue_pal()(1),
     xlab = "x axis label", ylab = "y axis label")
plot (xvals, yvals, pch = 16, col = hue_pal()(1),
     xlab = "x axis label", ylab = "y axis label",
     las = 1, cex.lab = 1.8, cex.axis = 1.5)
par (mfrow = c (1, 1))
```

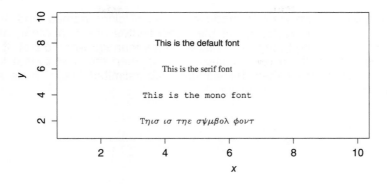

Figure 6.14 Different fonts.

6.2.4 Font of text

To change the typeface used for plotted text, change the name of a font family using `family`. Standard values are `"serif"`, `"sans"` (the default font), `"mono"`, and `"symbol"`, and the Hershey font families are also available. Some devices will ignore this setting completely. Text drawn onto the plotting region is controlled using `par ()` and displayed in Figure 6.14:

```
plot (1 : 10, 1 : 10, type = "n", xlab = "x", ylab = "y")
par (family = "sans")
text (5, 8, "This is the default font")
par (family = "serif")
text (5, 6, "This is the serif font")
par (family = "mono")
text (5, 4, "This is the mono font")
par (family = "HersheySymbol")
text (5, 2, "This is the symbol font")

par (family = "sans")
```

Don't forget to turn the family back to `"sans"`, otherwise we may get some very unexpected symbols in the next text.

The fonts of the various titles are specified in a similar way:

`font.axis`	font to be used for axis annotation;
`font.lab`	font to be used for *x* and *y* labels;
`font.main`	font to be used for plot main titles;
`font.sub`	font to be used for plot subtitles.

6.3 Adding items to plots

6.3.1 Adding text

It is very easy to add text to graphics. Suppose we wanted to add the text '(b)' to a plot at the location *x* = 80 and *y* = 65; just type `text (80, 65, "(b)")`.

In the following example, we want to produce a map of place names, and the place names are in a file called `map.places.csv`, but their coordinates are in another, much longer file called `bowens.csv`, containing many more place names than we want to plot. If we have factor level names with spaces in them (e.g. multiple words), then the best format for reading files is comma-delimited (.csv) rather than the standard tab-delimited (.txt). These are read into a dataframe in *R* using `read.csv ()` in place of `read.table ()`:

```
map_places <- read.csv ("map.places.csv", header = T)
attach (map_places)
head (map_places)


          wanted
1          Ascot
2 AERE Harwell
3        Reading
4         Botley
5   Wytham Wood
6         Cumnor

map_data <- read.csv ("bowens.csv", header = T)
attach (map_data)
head (map_data)


            place east north
1         Abingdon    50    97
2      Admoor Copse    60    70
3      AERE Harwell    48    87
4     Agates Meadow    70    73
5       Aldermaston    59    65
6 Aldermaston Court    60    65
```

There is a slight complication to do with the coordinates. The northernmost places are in a different 100 km square so, for instance, a northing of 3 needs to be altered to 103. It is convenient that all of the values that need to be changed have northings less than 60 in the dataframe:

```
nn <- ifelse (north < 60, north + 100, north)
```

This says: change all of the northings for which `north < 60` is `TRUE` to `nn <- north + 100`, and leave unaltered all the others (`FALSE`) as `nn <- north`.

We begin by plotting a blank space (`type = "n"`) of the right size (eastings from 20 to 100 and northings from 60 to 110) with blank axis labels and no tick marks or numbers:

```
plot (c (20, 100), c (60, 110), type = "n",
xlab = "", ylab = "", xaxt = "n", yaxt = "n")
```

The trick is to select the appropriate places in the vector called `place` and use `text ()` to plot each name in the correct position (`east[ii], nn[ii]`). For each place name in `wanted`, we find the correct subscript for that name within `place` using the `which ()` function to find `ii`:

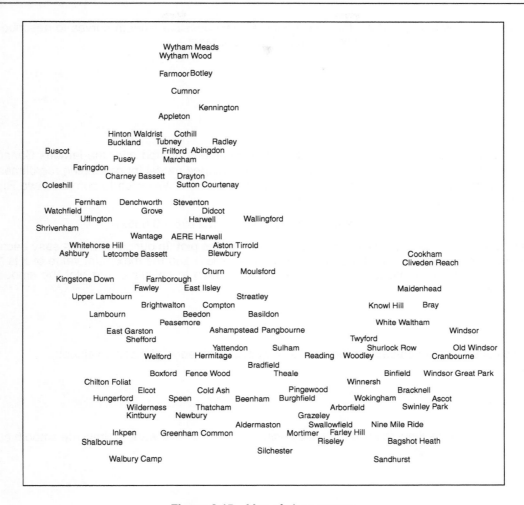

Figure 6.15 Map of place names.

```
for (i in 1:length (wanted)){
  ii <- which (place == as.character (wanted[i]))
  text (east[ii], nn[ii], as.character (place[ii]), cex = 0.6)
}
detach (map_places)
detach (map_data)
```

The result of all this is in Figure 6.15.

6.3.2 Adding smooth parametric curves to a scatterplot

In many cases, we want to add a smooth curve to a scatterplot. The important tip is that to produce reasonably smooth-looking curves in *R*, we should draw about 100 straight-line sections between the minimum and maximum values of the *x*-axis.

Let's start by plotting the data, then we'll consider two possible smooth curves to describe the relationship between the two variables in the following dataset.

```
plotfit <- read.table ("plotfit.txt", header = T)
attach (plotfit)
names (plotfit)
plot (x, y, pch = 16, col = hue_pal()(3)[1])
```

Now let us consider some curve options. The Ricker curve is named after the famous Canadian fish biologist who introduced this two-parameter hump-shaped model for describing recruitment to a fishery y as a function of the density of the parental stock, x. We wish to compare two Ricker curves with the following parameter values:

$$y_A = 482x \exp(-0.045x), \quad y_B = 518x \exp(-0.055x).$$

The first decision to be made is the range of x values for the plot. In our case, this is easy because we know from the literature that the minimum value of x is 0 and the maximum value of x is 100. Next, we need to generate about 100 values of x at which to calculate and plot the smoothed values of y:

```
xv <- 0 : 100
```

Next, calculate vectors containing the values of y_A and y_B at each of these x values:

```
yA <- 482 * xv * exp (-0.045 * xv)
yB <- 518 * xv * exp (-0.055 * xv)
```

We are now ready to draw the two curves by using `lines ()`. We want to draw the smooth curve for y_A as a dashed line:

```
lines (xv, yA, lty = 2, col = hue_pal()(3)[2])
```

and the curve for y_B as a solid line:

```
lines(xv, yA, lty = 1, col = hue_pal()(3)[3])
detach (plotfit)
```

Figure 6.16 implies that the dotted line is a much better description of our data than is the solid line. Estimating the parameters of non-linear functions like the Ricker curve from data is explained in Chapter 14.

6.3.3 Fitting non-parametric curves through a scatterplot

It is common to want to fit a non-parametric smoothed curve through data, especially when there is no obvious candidate for a parametric function. *R* offers a range of options:

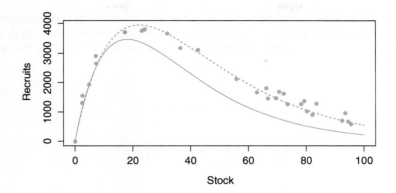

Figure 6.16 Adding smooth curves to a scatterplot.

- `loess ()` (a modelling tool, see Chapter 12);
- `gam ()` (fits generalized additive models, see Chapter 12);
- `lm ()` for linear regression (fit a linear model involving powers of *x*, see Chapter 10).

We will illustrate each of these options using the jaws data. First, we load the data:

```
jaws <- read.table ("jaws.txt", header = T)
attach (jaws)
names (jaws)


[1] "age"   "bone"
```

Let us now plot our four graphs with different smooth functions fitted through the jaws data. First, the simple non-parametric smoother called `lowess ()`. We provide the `lowess ()` function with arguments for the explanatory variable and the response variable, then provide this object as an argument to the `lines ()` function like this:

```
plot (age, bone, pch = 16, col = hue_pal()(2)[1])
lines (lowess (age, bone), col = hue_pal()(2)[2])
```

Figure 6.17a shows that it is a reasonable fit overall, but a poor descriptor of the jaw size for the lowest five ages. Let us try `loess ()`, which is a model-fitting function. We use the fitted model to `predict ()` the jaw sizes:

```
plot (age, bone, pch = 16, col = hue_pal()(2)[1])
model <- loess (bone ~ age)
xv <- 0:50
yv <- predict (model, data.frame (age = xv))
lines (xv, yv, col = hue_pal()(2)[2])
```

The result in Figure 6.17b is much better at describing the jaw size of the youngest animals, but shows a slight decrease for the oldest animals which might not be realistic. Next, we use a generalized additive model (`gam ()`, from the library `mgcv` (Wood, 2011)) to fit bone as `s (age)`, a smooth function of age:

```
library(mgcv)
plot (age, bone, pch = 16, col = hue_pal()(2)[1])
model <- gam (bone ~ s (age))
xv <- 0:50
yv <- predict (model, list (age = xv))
lines (xv, yv, col = hue_pal()(2)[2])
```

The line in Figure 6.17c is almost indistinguishable from the line produced by `loess ()` in Figure 6.17b. Finally, a polynomial:

```
plot (age, bone, pch = 16, col = hue_pal()(2)[1])
model <- lm (bone ~ age + I (age^2) + I (age^3))
xv <- 0:50
yv <- predict (model, list (age = xv))
lines (xv, yv, col = hue_pal()(2)[2])
detach (jaws)
```

As so often is the case with polynomials, the line in Figure 6.17d is more curvaceous than we really want. Note the use of capital `I` (the 'as is' function) in front of the quadratic and cubic terms. The fit is good for young animals, but is rather wavy where we might expect to see an asymptote. It tips up at the end, whereas the last two smoothers tipped down.

6.3.4 Connecting observations

Sometimes we want to join the points on a scatterplot by lines. Let's start with the view of connecting all observations. The trick is to ensure that the points on the *x*-axis are ordered: if they are not ordered, the result is a mess, as we'll see below.

```
smooth <- read.table ("smoothing.txt", header = T)
attach (smooth)
names (smooth)

[1] "x" "y"
```

If we do not order the *x* values, and just use the `lines ()` function, the result is Figure 6.18a: a car crash of a plot.

```
plot (x, y, pch = 16, col = hue_pal()(2)[1])
lines(x, y, col = hue_pal()(2)[2])
```

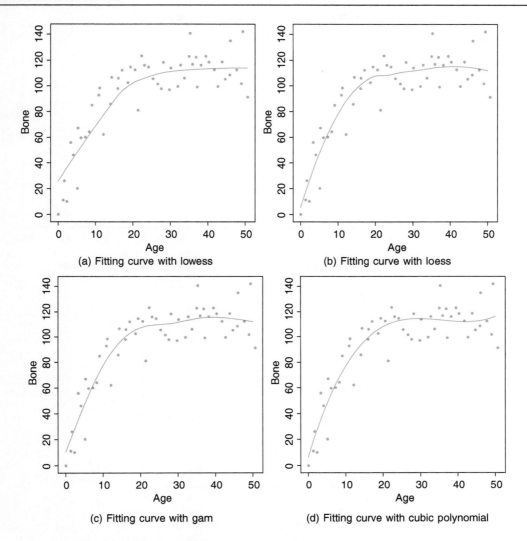

Figure 6.17 Fitting different types of non-parametric curves to data.

We need to order the *x* values. Begin by producing a vector of subscripts representing the ordered values of the explanatory variable. Then draw lines with this vector as subscripts to both the *x* and *y* variables, resulting in Figure 6.18b:

```
plot (x, y, pch = 16, col = hue_pal()(2)[1])
sequence <- order (x)
lines (x[sequence], y[sequence], col = hue_pal()(2)[2])
detach (smooth)
```

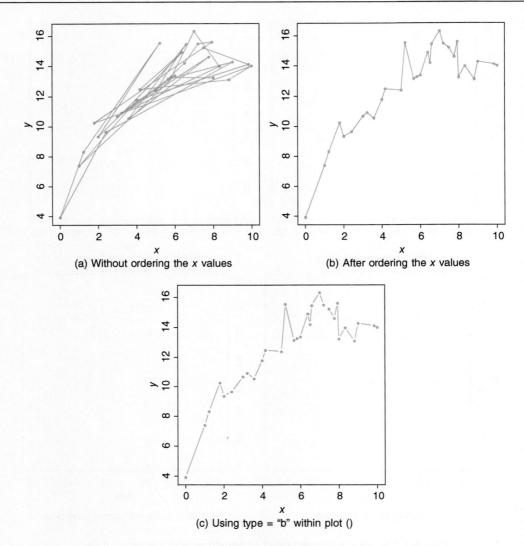

(a) Without ordering the *x* values   (b) After ordering the *x* values

(c) Using type = "b" within plot ()

Figure 6.18   Join the dots.

There is a plot option `type` = `"b"` (this stands for 'both' points and lines) which draws the points and joins them together with lines like in Figure 6.18c. We can choose the plotting symbol (`pch`) and the line type (`lty`) to be used, like this (we still need to order the *x* values!):

```
sequence <- order (x)
plot (x[sequence], y[sequence], pch = 16, col = hue_pal()(2)[1], type = "b", lty = 1)
```

If, instead, we want to plot square edges between two points like in Figure 6.19, we need to decide whether to go across and then up, or up and then across. The issue should become clear with an example. We have two vectors from 0 to 10:

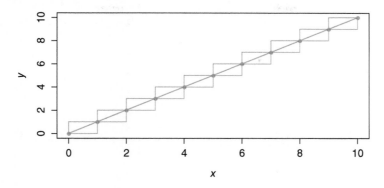

Figure 6.19 Adding stepped lines.

```
x <- 0 : 10
y <- 0 : 10
plot (x, y, pch = 16, col = hue_pal()(4)[1])
```

There are three ways we can join the dots: with a straight line

```
lines (x, y, col = hue_pal()(4)[2])
```

with a stepped line going across first then up, using lower-case 's'

```
lines (x, y, col = hue_pal()(4)[3], type = "s")
```

or with a stepped line going up first, then across using upper-case 'S' ('upper case, up first' is the way to remember it):

```
lines (x, y, col = hue_pal()(4)[4], type = "S")
```

Another common request is to identify multiple individuals in scatterplots using a combination of colours and lines to connect data from an individual. In Figure 6.20, we have an example where reaction time is plotted against duration of sleep deprivation for 18 subjects:

```
sleep <- read.table ("sleep.txt", header = T)
attach (sleep)
plot (Days, Reaction, col = hue_pal()(1))
```

The raw scatterplot in Figure 6.20 is uninformative; the individuals need to stand out more clearly from one another. The main purpose of the graphic is to show the relationship between sleep deprivation (measured in days) and reaction time. Another aim is to draw attention to the differences between the 18 subjects in their mean reaction times and to differences in the rate of increase of reaction time with the duration of sleep deprivation. Because there are so many subjects, the graph is potentially very confusing.

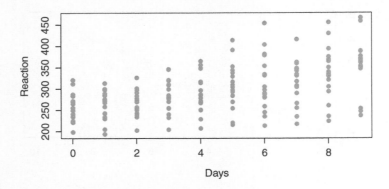

Figure 6.20   Scatterplot of reaction against sleep.

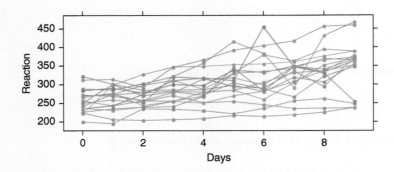

Figure 6.21   Scatterplot of reaction against sleep, by individual.

One improvement is to join together the time series for the individual subjects. We could stick to using `plot ()` to do this, though that would require quite a bit of work. Alternatively, we can use `xyplot ()` from `lattice` (Sarkar, 2008) (see Section 5.7) which does the job with minimal fuss. The function needs to know which observations should be joined (using `groups`), and we specify that we want the observations plotted with points and joined by lines (using `type = c ("p", "l")`). Though not essential, we specify the plotting symbol type and the colours to be used, resulting in Figure 6.21.

```
library (lattice)
xyplot (Reaction ~ Days, groups = Subject, type = c ("p", "l"),
        pch = 16, col = hue_pal ()(18)[c (1 : 18)])

detach (sleep)
```

There's (probably) insufficient room on the plotting surface to insert a legend with 18 labels in it. Perhaps the clearest pattern to emerge from the graphic is that subject 331 (mid-green) clearly had a hangover on day 6, because they were the third fastest reactor after 9 days of deprivation, but their day 6 reaction is rather poor.

6.3.5 Adding shapes

Once we have produced a set of axes using `plot ()`, it is straightforward to locate and insert other kinds of things. To demonstrate, we create two unlabelled axes, without tick marks (`xaxt = "n"`), both scaled from 0 to 10 but without any of the 11 points drawn on the axes (`type = "n"`):

```
plot (0 : 10, 0 : 10, xlab = "", ylab = "", xaxt = "n", yaxt = "n", type = "n")
```

We'll now add items to this blank canvas, such as

- `rect ()` for rectangles;
- `arrows ()` arrows and headed bars;
- `polygon ()` more complicated filled shapes, including objects with curved sides.

For the purposes of demonstration, we shall add a single-headed arrow, a double-headed arrow, a rectangle, and a six-sided polygon to this space.

We want to put a solid square object in the top right-hand corner, and we know the precise coordinates to use. The syntax for the `rect ()` function is to provide four numbers:

```
rect (xleft, ybottom, xright, ytop)
```

We can also specify the colour. Thus, to plot a coloured square from (6, 6) to (9, 9) involves:

```
rect (6, 6, 9, 9, col = hue_pal()(5)[1])
```

Drawing arrows is straightforward. The syntax for the `arrows ()` function is to draw a line from the point (x0, y0) to the point (x1, y1) with the arrowhead, by default, at the 'second' end (x1, y1):

```
arrows (x0, y0, x1, y1, col = hue_pal()(5)[2])
```

Thus, to draw an arrow from (1, 1) to (3, 8) with the head at (3, 8) type:

```
arrows (1, 1, 3, 8, col = hue_pal()(5)[2])
```

A horizontal double-headed arrow from (1, 9) to (5, 9) is produced by adding `code = 3` like this:

```
arrows(1, 9, 5, 9, code = 3, col = hue_pal()(5)[3])
```

A vertical bar with two square ends (e.g. like an error bar) uses `angle = 90` instead of the default `angle = 30`:

```
arrows (4, 1, 4, 6, code = 3, angle = 90, col = hue_pal()(5)[4])
```

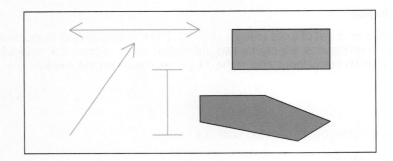

Figure 6.22   Adding shapes to plots.

We now wish to draw a polygon. We can define the corners of a polygon using two vectors; one to define the locations of the x-coordinates and the other to define the locations of the y-coordinates:

```
polygon (c (5, 7, 9, 8, 7, 5), c (4, 4, 2, 0.5, 1, 2), col = hue_pal()(5)[5])
```

Note that the polygon () function has automatically closed the shape, drawing a line from the last point to the first. More complex uses of the polygon () function are discussed in Section 5.8, including defining curved shapes. The result of all this is in Figure 6.22.

A final point on adding items to plots: it's often tricky to know the *exact* co-ordinates of where we want to place a shape or other items. We might want to point with the cursor and get *R* to tell us the coordinates of the locations we pick. First, run the function like this:

```
locator ()
```

This activates the plotting pane. Click however many times we need to in it, then press Escape (or another appropriate method, see ?locator for details). *R* then gives us the *x* and *y* co-ordinates of the locations we chose.

6.3.6   Adding mathematical and other symbols

To write on plots using more intricate symbols such as mathematical symbols or Greek letters, we use expression () or substitute () (see Table 6.2 for a list of the available symbols). Here are some examples of their use. First, we produce a plot of $\sin \phi$ against the phase angle ϕ over the range $-\pi$ to $+\pi$ radians:

```
x <- seq(-4, 4, len = 101)
plot (x, sin (x), type = "l", xaxt = "n", col = hue_pal()(1),
      xlab = expression (paste ("Phase Angle ", phi)),
      ylab = expression ("sin " * phi))
axis (1, at = c (-pi, -pi/2, 0, pi/2, pi),
      lab = expression (-pi, -pi/2, 0, pi/2, pi))
```

Table 6.2 Drawing mathematical expressions in text.

Syntax	Meaning
`x + y`	x plus y
`x - y`	x minus y
`x*y`	juxtapose x and y
`x/y`	x forward slash y
`x %+-% y`	x plus or minus y
`x %/% y`	x divided by y
`x %*% y`	x times y
`x %.% y`	x cdot y
`x[i]`	x subscript i
`x∧2`	x superscript 2
`paste (x, y, z)`	juxtapose x, y, and z
`sqrt (x)`	square root of x
`sqrt (x, y)`	yth root of x
`x == y`	x is equal to y
`x != y`	x is not equal to y
`x < y`	x is less than y
`x <= y`	x is less than or equal to y
`x > y`	x is greater than y
`x >= y`	x is greater than or equal to y
`x %~~% y`	x is approximately equal to y
`x %= ~ % y`	x and y are congruent
`x %==% y`	x is defined as y
`x %prop% y`	x is proportional to y
`plain (x)`	draw x in normal font
`bold (x)`	draw x in bold font
`italic (x)`	draw x in italic font
`bolditalic (x)`	draw x in bold italic font
`symbol (x)`	draw x in symbol font
`list (x, y, z)`	comma-separated list
`...`	ellipsis (height varies)
`cdots`	ellipsis (vertically centred)
`ldots`	ellipsis (at baseline)
`x %subset% y`	x is a proper subset of y
`x %subseteq% y`	x is a subset of y
`x %notsubset% y`	x is not a subset of y
`x %supset% y`	x is a proper superset of y
`x %supseteq% y`	x is a superset of y
`x %in% y`	x is an element of y
`x %notin% y`	x is not an element of y
`hat (x)`	x with a circumflex
`tilde (x)`	x with a tilde
`dot (x)`	x with a dot
`ring (x)`	x with a ring
`bar (x)`	x with bar
`widehat (xy)`	xy with a wide circumflex
`widetilde (xy)`	xy with a wide tilde
`x %<->% y`	x double-arrow y
`x %->% y`	x right-arrow y
`x %<-% y`	x left-arrow y

(continued)

Table 6.2 Continued

Syntax	Meaning
x %up% y	*x* up-arrow *y*
x %down% y	*x* down-arrow *y*
x %<=>% y	*x* is equivalent to *y*
x %=>% y	*x* implies *y*
x %<=% y	*y* implies *x*
x %dblup% y	*x* double-up-arrow *y*
x %dbldown% y	*x* double-down-arrow *y*
alpha	Greek alphabet (lower case)
beta	
...	
omega	
Alpha	Greek alphabet (upper case)
Beta	
...	
Omega	
theta1, phi1, sigma1, omega1	cursive Greek symbols
Upsilon1	capital upsilon with hook
aleph	first letter of Hebrew alphabet
infinity	infinity symbol
partialdiff	partial differential symbol
nabla	nabla, gradient symbol
32*degree	32 degrees
60*minute	60 minutes of angle
30*second	30 seconds of angle
displaystyle (x)	draw *x* in normal size (extra spacing)
textstyle (x)	draw *x* in normal size
scriptstyle (x)	draw *x* in small size
scriptscriptstyle (x)	draw *x* in very small size
underline (x)	draw *x* underlined
x ~~ y	put extra space between *x* and *y*
x + phantom (0) + y	leave gap for "0", but do not draw it
x + over (1, phantom (0))	leave vertical gap for "0" (do not draw)
frac (x, y)	*x* over *y*
over (x, y)	*x* over *y*
atop (x, y)	*x* over *y* (no horizontal bar)
sum (x[i], i==1, n)	sum *x*[*i*] for *i* equals 1 to *n*
prod (plain (P)(X==x), x)	product of P(X = *x*) for all values of *x*
integral (f(x)*dx, a, b)	definite integral of *f*(*x*) with respect to *x*
union (A[i], i==1, n)	union of *A*[*i*] for *i* equals 1 to *n*
intersect (A[i], i==1, n)	intersection of *A*[*i*]
lim (f(x), x %->% 0)	limit of *f*(*x*) as *x* tends to 0
min (g(x), x > 0)	minimum of *g*(*x*) for *x* greater than 0
inf (S)	infimum of *S*
sup (S)	supremum of *S*
x∧y + z	normal operator precedence
x∧(y + z)	visible grouping of operands
x∧y + z	invisible grouping of operands
group ("(",list(a, b),"]")	specify left and right delimiters
bgroup ("(",atop(x,y),")")	use scalable delimiters
group (lceil, x, rceil)	special delimiters

Note the use of `xaxt = "n"` to suppress the default labelling of the *x*-axis, and the use of `expression ()` in the labels for the *x*- and *y*-axes to obtain mathematical symbols such as phi (ϕ) and pi (π). The more intricate values for the tick marks on the *x*-axis are obtained by the `axis ()` function, specifying 1 (the *x*-axis is axis number 1), then using the `at` argument to say where the labels and tick marks are to appear, and `lab` with `expression ()` to say what the labels are to be.

Suppose we wanted to add $\chi^2 = 24.5$ to this graph at location $(-\pi/2, 0.5)$. We use `text ()` with `substitute ()`, like this:

```
text (-pi/2, 0.5, substitute (chi^2 == "24.5"))
```

Note the use of 'double equals' to print a single equals sign, and the use of caret `^` to obtain superscripts. We can write quite complicated formulae on plots using `paste ()` to join together the elements of an equation. Here is the density function of the normal written on the plot at location $(\pi/2, -0.5)$:

```
text (pi/2, -0.5, expression (paste (frac (1, sigma * sqrt(2*pi)), " ",
                              e^{frac (-(x - mu)^2, 2*sigma^2)}))))
```

Note the use of `frac ()` to obtain individual fractions: the first argument is the text for the numerator, the second the text for the denominator. Most of the arithmetic operators have obvious formats (+, -, /, *, `^`," etc.); the only non-intuitive symbol that is commonly used is 'plus or minus' $\pm$; this is written as % + -% like this:

```
text (pi/2, 0, expression (hat (y) %+-% se))
```

To write the results of calculations using text, it is necessary to use `substitute ()`. Here, the coefficient of determination `cd` was calculated earlier, and we want to write its value on the plot, labelled with '$r^2 =$':

```
cd <- 0.63
text(-pi/2, 0, substitute (r^2 == cd, list (cd = cd)))
```

Note the use of 'double equals' and the requirement for a list containing the value calculated earlier. After all that, we end up with Figure 6.23.

There are several other useful plotting symbols (see `?plotmath`) that we refer to in `text ()` functions as symbol (e.g. the 'universal' character is obtained with `expression (symbol ("\042"))`): the full set is:

- universal ∀ : `"\042"`;
- existential ∃ : `"\044"`;
- such that ∋ : `"\047"`;
- therefore ∴ : `"\134"`;
- perpendicular ⊥ : `"\136"`;

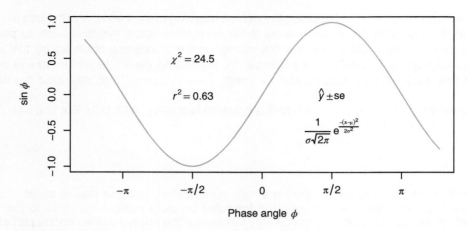

Figure 6.23   Adding mathematical expressions to plots.

- circlemultiply ⊗ : `"\304"`;
- circleplus ⊕ : `"\305"`;
- emptyset ∅ : `"\306"`;
- angle ∠ : `"\320"`;
- leftangle ⟨ : `"\341"`;
- rightangle ⟩ : `"\361"`.

Table 6.2 presents the syntax for including mathematical expressions in plots. If the `text` argument to one of the text-drawing functions (`text ()`, `mtext ()`, `axis ()`, `legend ()`) is an expression, the argument is interpreted as a mathematical expression and the output will be formatted according to TeX-like rules (see Knuth, 2012). Expressions can also be used for titles, subtitles, and x- and y-axis labels (but not for axis labels on `persp ()` plots). It is possible to produce many different mathematical symbols, Greek letters, generate subscripts, or superscripts, produce fractions, etc.

6.4   The grammar of graphics and `ggplot2`

Before finishing off with a broad summary of graphics in Section 6.5, it is worth spending a little time looking at the `ggplot2` package (Wickham, 2016). The package, written by Hadley Wickham, tries to make creating publication-quality graphics as easy as possible. It is based on the philosophy discussed in the book The Grammar of Graphics (Wilkinson, 2012), and the process of creating visualisations with it feels very different to the 'usual' procedures in R for plotting. However, `ggplot2` makes it fairly easy to add layers of complexity to a visualisation (e.g. adding additional data, incorporating legends, creating plots by group).

There is a bewildering amount of information about `ggplot2`, but a good place to start is to explore the `ggplot2` section of the Tidyverse website https://ggplot2.tidyverse.org/.

6.4.1 Basic structure

We can think of `ggplot2` plots as consisting of:

- The dataset to be used;

- An aesthetic mapping `aes ()`, which controls, for example, which variables map to which axes or colours;

- Add any 'layers' to the plot as required.

The general format of the function `ggplot ()` from `ggplot2` is

```
ggplot (dataset, aes ()) + layers
```

A plot will always start with a `ggplot ()` call, and the layers will then specify the type of plot we want (generally of the form `geom_ ()`, referencing 'geometric object') and any other options. Notice the plus sign, `+`, between `ggplot ()` and the layers. Often, as we'll see below, we have a string of various layers which we specify as follows:

```
ggplot (dataset, aes ()) + layer1 + layer2 + layer3 + layer4 + layer5 +
  layer6 + layer7 + layer8
```

We can also save a plot as an object, then add layers to it later, for example:

```
myplot <- ggplot (dataset, aes ()) + layer1 + layer2
myplot + layer3 + layer4
```

Notice the rather subtle differences between adding features using the usual *R* plotting and how we do this with `ggplot2`. In *R*, we could run the `plot ()` function, then add features using, for example `lines ()` or `text ()`. In `ggplot2`, meanwhile, we connect these 'layers' in a plot using `+` (taking care to use `+` before starting a new line if we are still adding layers). In addition, while we can save a `ggplot2` as an object, then continue adding layers to it, this is not how the usual *R* graphics operate.

One of the tricker aspects of `ggplot2` is setting `aes ()` so that we end up with the plot we wanted. It takes a little practice, but is fairly straightforward: just remember that all we're doing here is specifying, for example, how to map variables to axes and colours. Specifying the layers will quickly become natural but may take a little practice initially.

6.4.2 Examples

Learning to use `ggplot2` takes practice, and the best way to do that is to run through some examples. Let us start with the daphnia dataset, and create a range of graphics for the variable `Growth.rate`.

```
daph <- read.table ("daphnia.txt", header = T)
names (daph)
```

```
[1] "Growth.rate" "Water"       "Detergent"   "Daphnia"
```

First, we must load the `ggplot2` package. We'll create several versions of a histogram (`+ geom_histogram ()`) and a boxplot (`+ geom_box ()`) for the data, demonstrating how to add layers to change or update features. These are displayed in Figures 6.24 and 6.25, respectively. Note how easy it is to switch from one graphic type to another.

```
library (ggplot2)
ggplot (daph, aes (x = Growth.rate)) +
  geom_histogram ()
ggplot (daph, aes (x = Growth.rate)) +
  geom_histogram (fill = hue_pal()(1))
ggplot (daph, aes (x = Growth.rate, fill = Water)) +
  geom_histogram ()
ggplot (daph, aes (x = Growth.rate)) +
  geom_histogram (fill = hue_pal()(1)) +
  facet_grid (Water ~ .)
```

The initial `ggplot ()` function supplies the basic information about the dataset and variable(s) of interest. We add to this the type of graphic we want; in this case, a histogram with `geom_histogram ()` and a boxplot with `geom_boxplot ()`. These `geom_ ()` functions can be used as they are (as in Figure 6.24a for example), or we can specify further graphical properties as options in `geom_ ()` (as in Figure 6.24b). Further elements can be added to the graphic, for example in Figure 6.24d, where we also request that the two groups are plotted in separate panels using `facet_grid ()`.

```
ggplot (daph, aes (x = Detergent, y = Growth.rate)) +
  geom_boxplot ()
ggplot (daph, aes (x = Water, y = Growth.rate, fill = Detergent)) +
  geom_boxplot ()
ggplot (daph, aes (x = Water, y = Growth.rate, fill = Water)) +
  geom_boxplot () +
  coord_flip ()
ggplot (daph, aes (x = Water, y = Growth.rate, fill = Water)) +
  geom_boxplot () +
  geom_jitter (shape = 16, position = position_jitter (0.2))
```

Although Figures 6.24 and 6.25 show the basics of what can be done with `ggplot2` with a single variable split into groups, this is by no means exhaustive.

The same procedure applies with other types of graphics. Let us consider our fertiliser data. We are interested in root length by week, by plant.

```
fertilizer_data <- read.table ("fertilizer.txt", header = T)
names (fertilizer_data)

[1] "root"        "week"        "plant"        "fertilizer"
```

We start by plotting root length by week (Figure 6.26a), then identifying plants by colour with larger plotting symbols (Figure 6.26b) and by connected lines (Figure 6.26c), then producing a plot with regression lines added for each plant (Figure 6.26d). For the latter, notice that we didn't need to

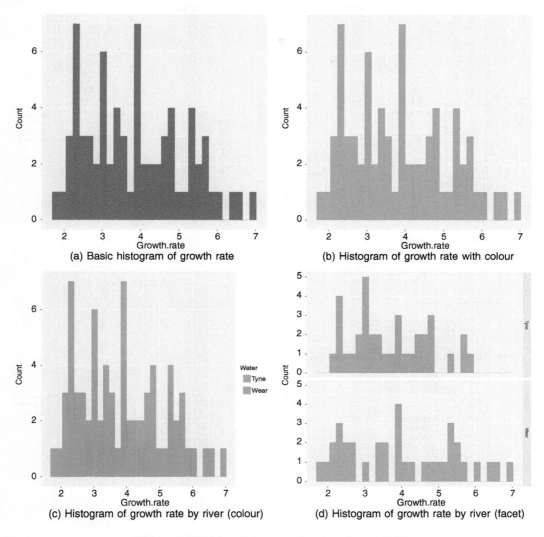

Figure 6.24 Visualising growth rate using ggplot2.

build a regression model first: `ggplot2` takes care of that behind the scenes. All these additional options are mix-and-match and, once again, are intended to give a flavour of what's possible.

```
ggplot (fertilizer_data, aes (x = week, y = root)) +
  geom_point ()
ggplot (fertilizer_data, aes (x = week, y = root, color = plant)) +
  geom_point (size = 4)
ggplot (fertilizer_data, aes (x = week, y = root, group = plant)) +
  geom_point (aes (colour = plant), size = 2) +
  geom_line (aes (colour = plant), size = 1)
ggplot (fertilizer_data, aes (x = week, y = root, color = plant)) +
  geom_point () +
  geom_smooth (method = lm, se = FALSE)
```

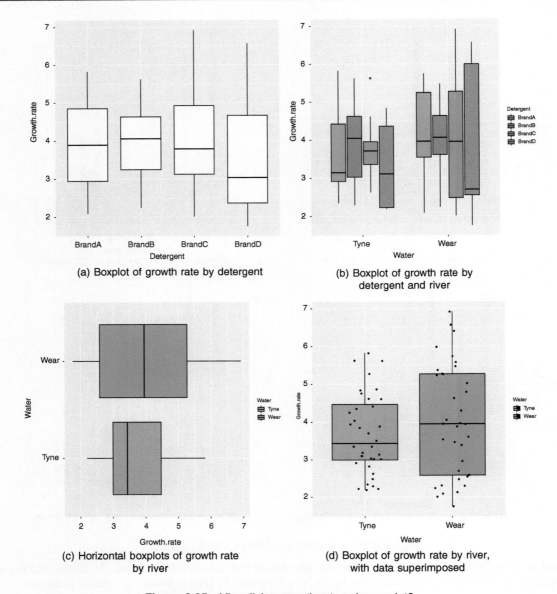

Figure 6.25   Visualising growth rate using ggplot2.

6.5   Graphics cheat sheet

Most of us cannot be expected to remember which graphics attributes are changed with the `par ()` function, which can be changed inside the `plot ()` function, and which stand alone. This section therefore unites all the various kinds of graphics control into a single list (see Table 6.3 at the end of the section): properties that are altered by a call to the `par ()` function are shown as `par (name)`, while properties that can be altered inside a `plot ()` function are shown in that context; other graphics functions that standalone (such as `axis ()`) are not shown in the table.

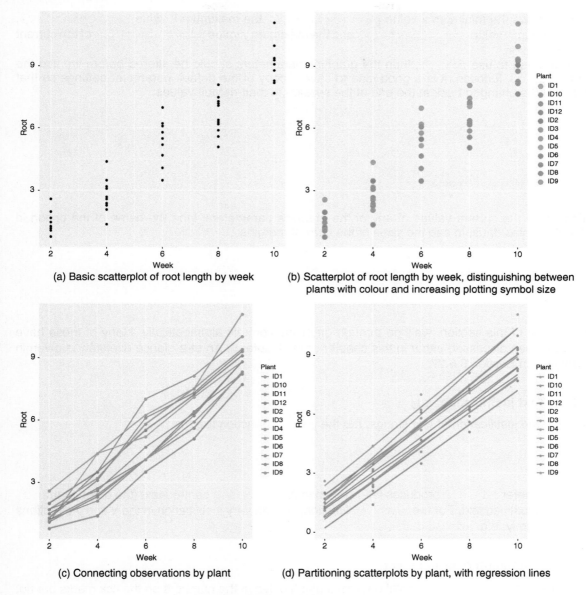

(a) Basic scatterplot of root length by week

(b) Scatterplot of root length by week, distinguishing between plants with colour and increasing plotting symbol size

(c) Connecting observations by plant

(d) Partitioning scatterplots by plant, with regression lines

Figure 6.26   Scatterplots for the fertilizer data.

Before we begin, let us revisit the `par ()` function. When writing functions, we need to know things about the current plotting region. For instance, to find out the limits of the current axes, use

```
par ("usr")

[1] 0 1 0 1
```

which shows the minimum *x* value `par ("usr") [1]`, the maximum *x* value `par ("usr") [2]`, the minimum *y* value `par ("usr") [3]` and the maximum *y* value `par ("usr") [4]` of the current plotting region.

If we need to use `par ()`, then the graphics parameters should be altered *before* we use the first `plot ()` function. It is a good idea to save a copy of the default parameter settings so that they can be changed back at the end of the session to their default values:

```
default.parameters <- par (no.readonly = TRUE)
...
par (...)
...
par (default.parameters)
```

To inspect the current values of any of the graphics parameters, type the name of the option in double quotes: thus, to see the sizes of the current margins:

```
par ("mar")

[1] 5.1 4.1 4.1 2.1
```

In the rest of this section, we'll go through graphical controls alphabetically. Many of these have already been discussed either in this chapter or in Chapter 5. An at-a-glance overview is given in Table 6.3 in Section 6.5.27.

6.5.1 Text justification, `adj`

To alter the justification of text strings, run the `par ()` function like this:

```
par (adj = 0)
```

The parameter `adj = 0` produces left-justified text, `adj = 0.5` centred text (the default) and `adj = 1` right-justified text. For the `text ()` function, we can vary justification in the *x* and *y* directions independently, e.g. `adj = c (1,0)`.

6.5.2 Annotation of graphs, `ann`

If we want to switch off the annotation from a plot (i.e. leave the numbers on the tick marks but not write the *x*- and *y*-axis labels or print any titles on the graph), then set `ann = FALSE`.

6.5.3 Delay moving on to the next in a series of plots, `ask`

Setting `ask = TRUE` means that the user is asked for input before the next figure is drawn.

6.5.4 Control over the axes, `axis`

The attributes of four sides of the graph (1 = bottom (the *x*-axis); 2 = left (the *y*-axis); 3 = above and 4 = right) are controlled by the `axis ()` function.

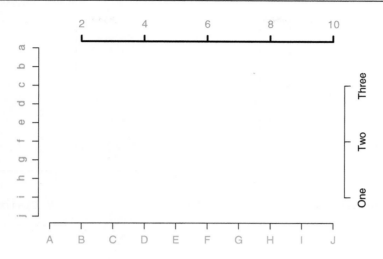

Figure 6.27 Controlling axis style.

When we want to put two graphs with different *y* scales on the same plot, we are likely to want to scale the right axis (`axis = 4`) differently from the usual *y*-axis on the left.

Again, we may want to label the tick marks on the axis with letters (rather than the usual numbers) and this, too, is controlled by the `axis ()` function.

First, draw the graph with no axes at all using plot with the `axes = FALSE` option. For the purposes of illustration only, we use different styles on each of the four axes in Figure 6.27.

```
plot (1 : 10, 10 : 1, type = "n", axes = FALSE, xlab = "", ylab = "")
axis (1, 1 : 10, LETTERS[1:10], col.axis = hue_pal()(3)[1])
axis (2, 1 : 10, letters[10:1], col.axis = hue_pal()(3)[2])
axis (3, lwd = 3, col.axis = hue_pal()(3)[3])
axis (4, at = c (2, 5, 8), labels = c ("one", "two", "three"))
```

On axis 1, there are upper-case letters in place of the default numbers 1 to 10 with red rather than black lettering. On axis 2, there are lower-case letters in reverse sequence in green on each of the 10 tick marks (note the order of the y values `10 : 1` in the original plot function). On axis 3 (the top of the graph), there is blue lettering for the default numbers (2 to 10 in steps of 2) and an extra thick black line for the axis itself (`lwd = 3`). On axis 4, we have overwritten the default number and location of the tick marks using `at`, and provided our own labels for each tick mark (note that the vectors of `at` locations and `labels` must be the same length).

Because we did not use `box ()`, there are gaps between the ends of each of the four axes.

6.5.5 Background colour for plots, bg

The colour to be used for the background of plots is set by `bg` like this:

```
par (bg = "cornsilk")
```

There is an example in Section 6.1.4. The default setting is `par (bg = "transparent")`.

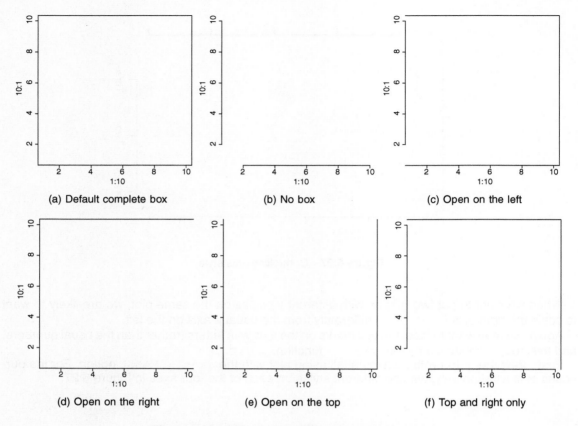

Figure 6.28   Different types of boxes around plots.

6.5.6   Boxes around plots, `bty`

Boxes are altered with the `bty` parameter, and `bty = "n"` suppresses the box. If the character is one of `"o"`, `"l"` (lower-case L, not numeral 1), `"7"`, `"c"`, `"u"`, or `"]"` the resulting box resembles the corresponding *upper*-case letter. There are six options in Figure 6.28:

```
plot (1 : 10, 10 : 1, type = "n")
plot (1 : 10, 10 : 1, type = "n", bty = "n")
plot (1 : 10, 10 : 1, type = "n", bty = "]")
plot (1 : 10, 10 : 1, type = "n", bty = "c")
plot (1 : 10, 10 : 1, type = "n", bty = "u")
plot (1 : 10, 10 : 1, type = "n", bty = "7")
```

6.5.7   Size of plotting symbols using the character expansion function, `cex`

We can use points with `cex` to create 'bubbles' of different sizes. We need to specify the (x, y) coordinates of the centre of the bubble, then use `cex = value` to alter the diameter of the bubble (in multiples of the default character size: `cex` stands for character expansion).

```
plot (0 : 10, 0 : 10, type = "n", xlab = "", ylab = "")
for (i in 1:10) points (2, i, cex = i, col = hue_pal()(10)[i])
for (i in 1:10) points (6, i, cex = (10 + (2 * i)), col = hue_pal()(10)[i])
```

The left column in Figure 6.29 shows points of size 1, 2, 3, 4, etc. (`cex = i`), and the big circles on the right are in sequence `cex = 12, = 14, = 16`, etc. (`cex = (10 + (2 * i))`).

6.5.8 Changing the shape of the plotting region, `plt`

Suppose that we wanted a plot where we specified the shape of the plotting region (e.g. for a map). We can achieve this with the `plt ()` option, which allows us to specify the coordinates of the plot region as fractions of the current figure region. If we imagine the standard plotting region being a unit square, we can specify that we want the x-axis to run from, say, 0.15 to 0.95, while the y-axis runs from 0.3 to 0.7. We can then add the relevant tick marks as appropriate, as in Figure 6.30.

```
par (plt = c (0.15, 0.95, 0.3, 0.7))
plot (c (0, 3000), c (0, 1500), type = "n", ylab = "y", xlab = "x")
```

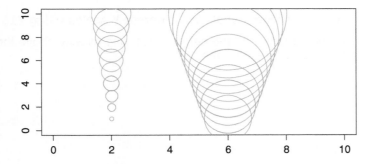

Figure 6.29 Changing size of plotting symbols.

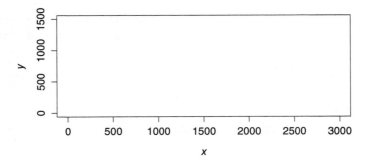

Figure 6.30 A bespoke shape for the plotting region.

6.5.9 Locating multiple graphs in non-standard layouts using `fig`

Generally, we use `mfrow ()` to get multiple plots on the same graphic screen; for instance, `mfrow = c (3, 2)` would give six plots in three rows of two columns each. Sometimes, however, we want a non-standard layout, and `fig` is the function to use in this case.

Suppose we want to have two graphs, one in the bottom left-hand corner of the screen and one in the top right-hand corner. What we need to know is that `fig` considers that the whole plotting region is scaled from (0,0) in the bottom left-hand corner to (1,1) in the top right-hand corner. So we want our bottom left-hand plot to lie within the space $x = c (0, 0.5)$ and $y = c (0, 0.5)$, while our top right-hand plot is to lie within the space $x = c (0.5, 1)$ and $y = c (0.5, 1)$. Here is how to plot the two graphs: `fig` is like a new `plot ()` function and the second use of `fig` would normally wipe the slate clean, so we need to specify that `new = TRUE` in the second `par ()` function to stop this from happening, resulting in Figure 6.31:

```
par (fig = c (0.5, 1, 0.5, 1))
plot (0 : 10, 25 * exp (-0.1 * (0:10)), col = hue_pal()(2)[1],
      type = "l", xlab = "x", ylab = "y")
par (fig = c (0, 0.5, 0, 0.5), new = T)
plot (0 : 100, 0.5 * (0:100)^0.5, col = hue_pal()(2)[2],
      type = "l", xlab = "x", ylab = "y")
```

6.5.10 Two graphs with a common *X* scale but different *Y* scales using `fig`

The idea here is to draw two graphs with the same *x*-axis, one directly above the other, but with different scales on the two y-axes. Here are the data:

```
gales <- read.table ("gales.txt", header = T)
attach (gales)
names (gales)
```

```
[1] "year"      "number"    "February"
```

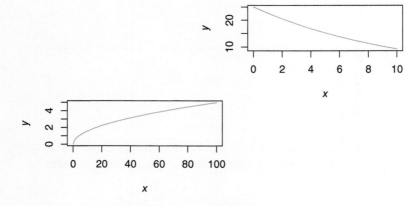

Figure 6.31 Non-standard layout of plots.

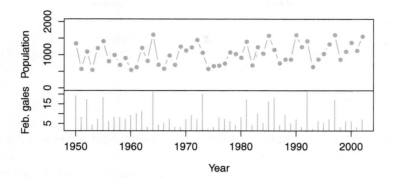

Figure 6.32   Two plots with common *x*-axis.

We use `fig` to split the plotting area into an upper figure (where `number` will be drawn first) and a lower figure (for February gales, to be drawn second but on the same page, so `new = T`). The whole plotting area scales from (0,0) in the bottom left-hand corner to (1,1) in the top right-hand corner, so:

```
par (fig = c (0, 1, 0.5, 1))
```

Now think about the margins for the top graph. We want to label the *y*-axis, and we want a normal border above the graph and to the right, but we want the plot to sit right on top of the lower graph, so we set the bottom margin to zero (the first argument):

```
par (mar = c (0, 5, 2, 2))
```

Now we plot the top graph, leaving off the *x*-axis label and the *x*-axis tick marks:

```
plot (year, number, xlab = "", xaxt = "n", type = "b", pch = 16,
      col = hue_pal()(2)[1], ylim = c (0, 2000), ylab = "Population")
```

Next, we define the lower plotting region and declare that `new = T`:

```
par (fig = c (0, 1, 0, 0.5), new = T)
```

For this graph, we *do* want a bottom margin, because we want to label the common *x*-axes (Year), but we want the top of the second graph to be flush with the bottom of the first graph, so we set the upper margin to zero (argument 3 of `mar`):

```
par (mar = c (5, 5, 0, 2))
plot (year, February, xlab = "Year", type = "h",
      col = hue_pal()(2)[2], ylab = "February gales")
detach (gales)
```

Contrast Figure 6.32 with the overlaid plots in Section 6.5.19.

6.5.11 The `layout` function

If we do not want to use `mfrow ()` or `fig` to configure multiple plots, then `layout ()` might be the function needed. This function allows us to alter both the location and shape of multiple plotting regions independently. The layout function is used like this:

```
layout (matrix, widths = ws, heights = hs, respect = FALSE)
```

where `matrix` is a matrix object specifying the location of the next n figures on the output device (see below), `ws` is a vector of column widths (with `length = ncol (matrix)`) and `hs` is a vector of row heights (with `length = nrow (matrix)`). Each value in the matrix must be 0 or a positive integer. If n is the largest positive integer in the matrix, then the integers {1, ... , $n - 1$} must also appear at least once in the matrix. Use 0 to indicate locations where we do not want to put a graph. The `respect` argument controls whether a unit column width is the same physical measurement on the device as a unit row height and is either a logical value or a matrix object. If it is a matrix, then it must have the same dimensions as `matrix` and each value in the matrix must be either 0 or 1. Each figure is allocated a region composed from a subset of these rows and columns, based on the rows and columns in which the figure number occurs in `matrix`. The function `layout.show (n)` plots the outlines of the next n figures.

Here is an example of the kind of task for which `layout ()` might be used. We want to produce a scatterplot with histograms on the upper and right-hand axes indicating the frequency of points within vertical and horizontal strips of the scatterplot (see the result below). This example was written by Paul R. Murrell and can be found in the `layout ()` help file by typing `?layout`. Here are the data:

```
x <- pmin (3, pmax (-3, rnorm (50)))
y <- pmin (3, pmax (-3, rnorm (50)))
xhist <- hist (x, breaks = seq (-3, 3, 0.5), plot = FALSE)
yhist <- hist (y, breaks = seq (-3, 3, 0.5), plot = FALSE)
```

We need to find the ranges of values within *x* and *y*, where the two histograms will lie:

```
top <- max (c (xhist$counts, yhist$counts))
xrange <- c (-3, 3)
yrange <- c (-3, 3)
```

Now the `layout ()` function defines the location of the three figures: Fig. 1 is the scatterplot which we want to locate in the lower left of four boxes, Fig. 2 is the top histogram which is to be in the upper left box, and Fig. 3 is the side histogram which is to be drawn in the lower right location (the top right location is empty), Thus, the matrix is specified as follows:

```
matrix (c (2, 0, 1, 3), 2, 2, byrow = TRUE)

     [,1] [,2]
[1,]    2    0
[2,]    1    3
```

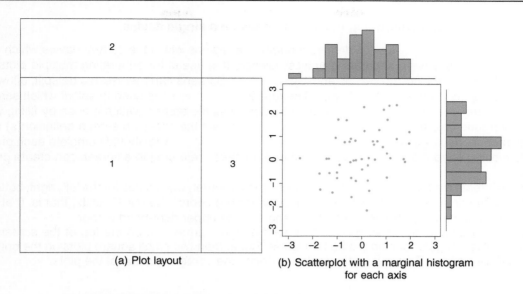

(a) Plot layout

(b) Scatterplot with a marginal histogram for each axis

Figure 6.33   Creating a scatterplot with marginal histograms.

We can view the layout, as in Figure 6.33a:

```
nf <- layout (matrix (c (2, 0, 1, 3), 2, 2, byrow = TRUE),
              c (3, 1), c (1, 3), TRUE)
layout.show (nf)
```

The areas in the first (left) column of the matrix in Figure 6.33a (numbered 1 and 2) are of width 3, while the area in the second column (numbered 3) is of width 1; hence, `c (3, 1)` is the second argument. The heights of the figures in the first column of the matrix (numbered 2 and 1) are 1 and 3, respectively; hence, `c (1, 3)` is the third argument. The 'missing' area is 1 by 1 (top right).

```
par (mar = c (3, 3, 1, 1))
plot (x, y, xlim = xrange, ylim = yrange, pch = 16,
      col = hue_pal()(2)[1], xlab = "", ylab = "")
par (mar = c (0, 3, 1, 1))
barplot (xhist$counts, axes = FALSE, col = hue_pal()(2)[2],
         ylim = c (0, top), space = 0)
par (mar = c (3, 0, 1, 1))
barplot (yhist$counts, axes = FALSE, col = hue_pal()(2)[2],
         xlim = c (0, top), space = 0, horiz = TRUE)
```

Note the way that the margins for the three figures are controlled in Figure 6.33b, and how the `horiz = TRUE` option is specified for the histogram on the right-hand margin of the plot.

6.5.12 Creating and controlling multiple screens on a single device

The function `split.screen ()` defines a number of regions within the current device which can be treated as if they were separate graphics devices. It is useful for generating multiple plots on a single device (see also `mfrow ()` and `layout ()`). Screens can themselves be split, allowing for quite complex arrangements of plots. The function `screen ()` is used to select which screen to draw in, and `erase.screen ()` is used to clear a single screen, which it does by filling with the background colour, while `close.screen ()` removes the specified screen definition(s) and split-screen mode is exited by `close.screen (all = TRUE)`. We should complete each graph before moving on to the graph in the next screen, because returning to a screen can create problems.

We can create a matrix in which each row describes a screen with values for the left, right, bottom, and top of the screen (in that order) in normalized device coordinate (NDC) units, that is, 0 at the lower left-hand corner of the device surface, and 1 at the upper right-hand corner.

We'll use a dataframe called `gales`. We want a long, narrow plot on the top of the screen as Fig. 1, a tall rectangular plot on the bottom left as Fig. 2, then two small square plots on the bottom right as Figs 3 and 4. First, set up the matrix to define the corners of each of the plots.

```
gales <- read.table ("gales.txt", header = T)
attach (gales)
names (gales)


[1] "year"      "number"    "February"

fig.mat <- c (0, 0, .5, .5, 1, .5, 1, 1, .7, 0, .35, 0, 1, .7, .7, .35)
fig.mat <- matrix (fig.mat, nrow = 4)
fig.mat

     [,1] [,2] [,3] [,4]
[1,]  0.0  1.0 0.70 1.00
[2,]  0.0  0.5 0.00 0.70
[3,]  0.5  1.0 0.35 0.70
[4,]  0.5  1.0 0.00 0.35
```

Each row in `fig.mat` corresponds to a screen with values for the left, right, bottom, and top of the screen. Therefore, the first row corresponds to a full width screen, which occupies the upper 30% of the whole window (from 0.7 to 1).

Now we can draw the four graphs as in Figure 6.34.

```
split.screen (fig.mat)


[1] 5 6 7 8

screen (1)
plot (year, number, type = "l", col = hue_pal()(3)[1])
screen (2)
plot (year, February, type = "h", col = hue_pal()(3)[2])
screen (3)
plot (1 : 10, 0.5 * (1 : 10)^0.5, xlab = "concentration",
      ylab = "rate", type = "l", col = hue_pal()(3)[3])
```

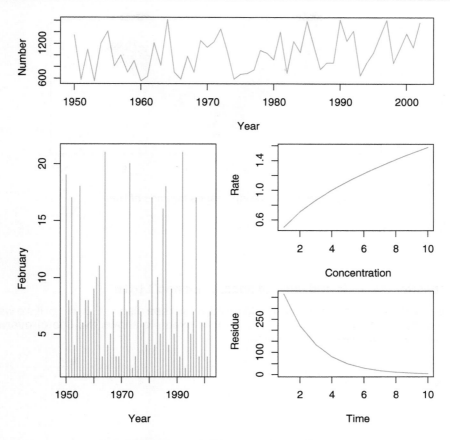

Figure 6.34   Plot layout using split screen.

```
screen (4)
plot (1 : 10, 600 * exp (-0.5 * (1 : 10)), xlab ="time",
      ylab = "residue", type = "l", col = hue_pal()(3)[3])

detach (gales)
```

6.5.13   Orientation of numbers on the tick marks, `las`

Many journals require that the numbers used to label the *y*-axis must be horizontal. To change from the default, use `las`:

`las = 0`	always parallel to the axis (the default);
`las = 1`	always horizontal (preferred by many journals);
`las = 2`	always perpendicular to the axis;
`las = 3`	always vertical.

Note that we cannot use character or string rotation for this.

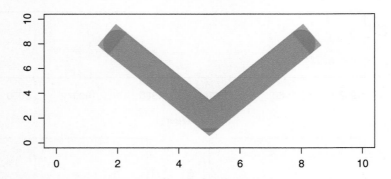

Figure 6.35   Showing shapes for ends of lines.

6.5.14   Shapes for the ends and joins of lines, `lend` and `ljoin`

The default is that the bare ends of lines should be rounded (see also `arrows ()` if we want pointed ends). We can change this to `butt` or `square`. This example shows the use of overwriting with successive colours to achieve special effects:

```
plot (0 : 10, 0 : 10, type = "n", xlab = "", ylab = "")
lines (c (2, 5, 8), c (8, 2, 8), col = hue_pal()(3)[1], lwd = 50,
       lend = "square", ljoin="mitre")
lines(c (2, 5, 8), c (8, 2, 8), col = hue_pal()(3)[2], lwd = 50,
       lend = "round", ljoin = "round")
lines(c (2, 5, 8), c (8, 2, 8), col = hue_pal()(3)[3], lwd = 50,
       lend = "butt", ljoin = "bevel")
```

A V in Figure 6.35 was drawn first with 'square' ends and 'mitre' joins, then the V with 'round' ends and 'round' joins, then finally the V with 'butt' ends and 'bevel' joins.

To get the effect of bordered lines (e.g. to produce roads on a map), first draw wide lines in black (or whatever colour we want the border to be), then draw the colour for the body of the line using a slightly smaller value for the line width. Here is a two-dimensional random walk drawn as a smoothly snaking road in red with black margins:

```
x <- numeric (100)
y <- numeric (100)
x[1] <- 1
y[1] <- 1
for (i in 2:100)  {
  a <- runif (1) * 2 * pi
  d <- runif (1) * 1
  x[i] <- x[i-1] + d * sin (a)
  y[i] <- y[i-1] + d * cos (a)
}
```

Figure 6.36 Bordered lines on a realisation of a smoothed random walk.

We plot blank axes with an intact box around the outside of the map:

```
plot (0 : 10, 0 : 10, type = "n", xaxt = "n", yaxt = "n", xlab = "", ylab = "")
```

The red road with black margins and smooth curves is added like this, resulting in Figure 6.36:

```
lines (x, y, lwd = 13, lend = "round", ljoin = "round")
lines (x, y, lwd = 10, col = hue_pal () (1), lend = "round", ljoin = "round")
```

6.5.15 Line types, `lty`

Line types (like solid, dotted, or dashed) are changed with the line-type parameter `lty`:

```
lty = 1    solid (the default);
lty = 2    dashed;
lty = 3    dotted;
lty = 4    dot-dash;
lty = 5    long-dash;
lty = 6    two-dash.
```

Invisible lines are drawn if `lty = 0` (i.e. the line is not drawn). Alternatively, we can use text to specify the line types with one of the following character strings: `blank`, `solid`, `dashed`, `dotted`, `dotdash`, `longdash`, or `twodash`.

6.5.16 Line widths, `lwd`

To increase the widths of the plotted lines use `lwd = 2` (or greater; the default is `lwd = 1`). The interpretation is device-specific, and some devices do not implement line widths less than 1. The function `abline ()` is so-called because it has two arguments – the first is the intercept (a), and the second is the slope (b) of a linear relationship $y = a + bx$:

```
plot (1 : 10, 1 : 10, xlim = c (0, 10), ylim = c (0, 10),
     xlab = "", ylab = "", type = "n")
for(i in 1 : 7) {
  abline ((-6 + 2 * i), 1, lty = i, col = hue_pal()(7)[i])
}
for (i in 2:7) {
  y <- (-6 + 2 * i) + 2
  x <- 2
  text (x, y, i)
}
abline (-6, 1, lty = 1, lwd = 4)
abline (-8, 1, lty = 1, lwd = 8)
points (5, 1, pch = 16, cex = 3, col = "white")
points (7, 1, pch = 16, cex = 3, col = "white")
points (9, 1, pch = 16, cex = 3, col = "white")
text (5, 1, 1)
text (7, 1, 4)
text (9, 1, 8)
```

The numerals in a vertical line above $x = 2$ in Figure 6.37 indicate the line types 2 to 7 in colours 2 to 7. In the bottom right-hand corner are three solid lines `lty = 1` of widths `lwd = 1,  4` and `8`. Note the use of the large white `pch = 16` across the lines to make a gap in which the red labels indicating the line widths can be printed clearly.

6.5.17 Several graphs on the same page, `mfrow` and `mfcol`

The way to remember the names of these functions is to think of them as standing for 'multiple frames in rows', `mfrow ()`, or 'multiple frames in columns', `mfcol ()`. We can obtain multiple graph panels on the same graphics device by `par (mfrow)`, `par (mfcol)`, `par (fig)`, `split.screen`, and `layout`, but `par (mfrow)` is the most frequently used. We specify the

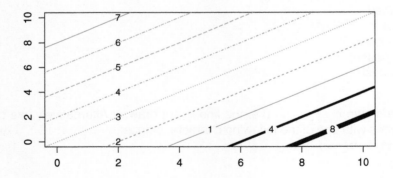

Figure 6.37 Showing line widths and line types.

number of rows of graphs (first argument) and number of columns of graphs per row (second argument) like this:

```
par (mfrow = c (1,1))    the default of one plot per screen;
par (mfrow = c (1,2))    one row of two columns of plots;
par (mfrow = c (2,1))    two rows of one column of plots;
par (mfrow = c (2,2))    four plots in two rows of two columns each;
par (mfrow = c (3,2))    six plots in three rows of two columns each;
par (mfrow = c (3,3))    nine plots in three rows of three columns each.
```

The graphs will be produced row-wise, starting in the top left-hand corner. We need to complete each graph (add all `points`, `lines` and `text`) before going on to the next by issuing a new `plot ()` command or other plotting function.

In a layout with exactly two rows and columns, the base value of `cex` is reduced by a factor of 0.83; if there are three or more of either rows or columns, the reduction factor is 0.66. Remember to set `par ()` back to `par (mfrow = c (1,1))` once finished.

6.5.18 Margins around the plotting area, `mar`

We need to control the size of the margins when we intend to use large symbols or long labels for axes, or when we want to position multiple plots closer together. The four margins of the plot are defined by integers 1 to 4 as follows:

1 = bottom (the *x*-axis);
2 = left (the *y*-axis);
3 = top;
4 = right.

The sizes of the margins of the plot are measured *in lines of text*. The four arguments to `mar` are given in the sequence bottom, left, top, right. The default is

```
par (mar = (c (5, 4, 4, 2) + 0.1))
```

with more spaces on the bottom (5.1) than on the top (4.1) to make room for a subtitle (if needed), and more space on the left (4.1) than on the right (2) on the assumption that we will not want to label the right-hand axis. Suppose that we *do* want to put a label on the right-hand axis, then we would need to increase the size of the fourth number, for instance like this:

```
par (mar = (c (5, 4, 4, 4) + 0.1))
```

To get rid of margins altogether, use

```
par (mar = (c (0, 0, 0, 0)))
```

but bear in mind that there will be no space for any labels under this format.

6.5.19 Plotting more than one graph on the same axes, new

The new parameter is a logical variable, defaulting to new = FALSE. If it is set to new = TRUE, the next high-level plotting command (like plot (y ~ x)) does *not* wipe the slate clean in the default way. This allows one plot to be placed on top of another.

In the next example, we want to plot the number of animals in a wild population as a time series over the years 1950–2000 with the scale of animal numbers on the left-hand axis (numbers fluctuate between about 600 and 1600). Then, on top of this, we want to overlay the number of gales in February each year. This number varies between 1 and 22, and we want to put a scale for this on the right-hand axis, axis = 4.

```
gales <- read.table ("gales.txt", header = T)
attach (gales)
names (gales)
```

```
[1] "year"      "number"    "February"
```

First, we need to make room in the right-hand margin for labelling the axis with the information on February gales:

```
par (mar = c (5, 4, 4, 4) + 0.1)
```

Now draw the time series using a thicker line than usual (lwd=2) for emphasis, specifying the orientation of axis numbers and colour:

```
plot (year, number, type = "l", lwd = 2, las = 1, col = hue_pal()(2)[1])
```

Next, indicate that the next graph will be overlaid on the present one:

```
par (new = T)
```

Now plot the graph of gales against years. This is to be displayed as vertical, type = "h", dashed lines, lty = 2:

```
plot (year, February, type = "h", axes = F, ylab = "",
      lty = 2, col = hue_pal()(2)[2])
```

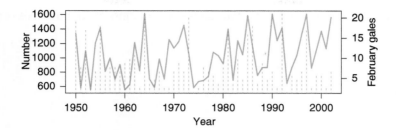

Figure 6.38 Solid line shows time series of number of animals. Dotted lines show number of February gales.

and it is drawn with its own scale (with ticks from 5 to 20, as we shall see). The right-hand axis is ticked and labelled as follows: first use `axis (4)` to create the tick marks and scaling information, then use the `mtext ()` function to produce the axis label (the name stands for 'margin text').

```
axis (4, las = 1)
mtext (side = 4, line = 2.5, "February gales")
detach (gales)
```

From the resulting Figure 6.38, it looks as if unusually severe February gales are associated with the steepest population crashes (contrast this with the separate plots in Section 6.5.10).

6.5.20 Outer margins, oma

There is an area outside the margins of the plotting area called the **outer margin**. Its default size is zero, `oma = c (0, 0, 0, 0)`, but if we want to create an outer margin, we use `oma`.

Here is the function to produce an outer margin big enough to accommodate five lines of text on the bottom and left-hand sides of the plotting region:

```
par (oma = c (5, 5, 0, 0))
```

We want to combine large outer margins with reduced inner margins when producing our own multiple-panel plots.

When using `par (mfrow = c (2,2))` to get a panel of plots, we will probably use `main` to get a unique title for each of the plots, but we may want an overall title (the equivalent of `main` but for the entire set of panel plots). We use `mtext` ('margin text') for this with along with `outer = T`. Here are Anscombe's infamous four plots; he contrived the data so that they all have exactly the same regression models and p-values, but they are obviously very different once we plot them. Moral: always plot the data first, then do the modelling once we know what the data look like. The data are built into *R*:

```
attach (anscombe)
par (mfrow = c (2, 2))
```

We can see the contrasting patterns in the four data sets in Figure 6.39, but there is no room for an overall title:

```
plot (x1, y1, col = hue_pal()(2)[1], pch = 16,
      xlim = c (0,20), ylim = c (0, 16), main = "Set 1")
abline (lm (y1 ~ x1), col = hue_pal()(2)[2])
plot (x2, y2, col = hue_pal()(2)[1], pch = 16,
      xlim = c (0,20), ylim = c (0, 16), main = "Set 2")
abline (lm (y2 ~ x2), col = hue_pal()(2)[2])
plot (x3, y3, col = hue_pal()(2)[1], pch = 16,
      xlim = c (0,20), ylim = c (0, 16), main = "Set 3")
abline (lm (y3 ~ x3), col = hue_pal()(2)[2])
plot (x4, y4, col = hue_pal()(2)[1], pch = 16,
      xlim = c (0,20), ylim = c (0, 16), main = "Set 4")
abline (lm (y4 ~ x4), col = hue_pal()(2)[2])
```

We need to plan ahead and to make space for at least one line of (potentially large) text at the top of the page. This is the *third margin*, and the space we want to create is *outside* the space of the existing plot. Using oma, we specify the width of the margin (in units of text lines) for each of the four margins in a vector (in our case, c (0, 0, 2, 0), to leave two lines at the top (third) margin):

```
par (mfrow = c (2, 2), oma = c (0, 0, 2, 0))
```

Now redraw the four plots (as above), then add the graph title using mtext (), for example like this (result not shown):

```
mtext ("Anscombe's 4 regression data sets", outer = TRUE, cex = 1.5)
detach (anscombe)
```

6.5.21 Packing graphs closer together

In this example, we want to create nine closely spaced plots in a 3 × 3 pattern without any tick marks, and to label only the outer central plot on the x- and y- axes. We need to take care of four things:

- mfrow = c (3, 3) to get the nine plots in a 3 × 3 pattern;
- mar = c (0.2, 0.2, 0.2, 0.2) to leave a narrow strip (0.2 lines looks best for tightly packed plots) between each graph;
- oma = c (5, 5, 0, 0) to create an outer margin on the bottom and left for labels;
- outer = T to write the titles in the outer margin.

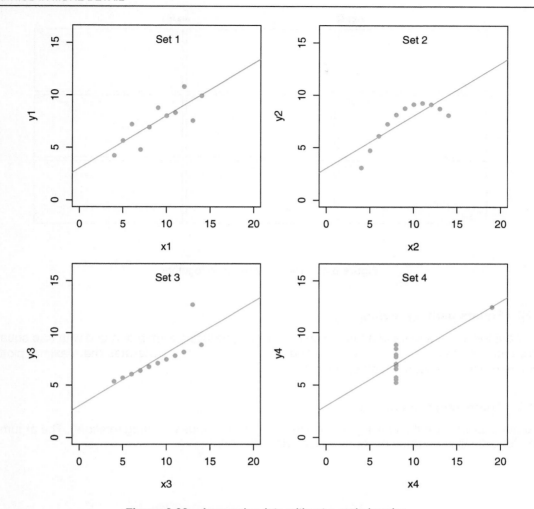

Figure 6.39 Anscombe data without a main header.

The plots consist of 100 pairs of ranked uniform random numbers `sort (runif (100))`, and we shall plot the nine graphs with a `for ()` loop, which results in Figure 6.40:

```
par (mfrow = c (3, 3))
par (mar = c (0.2, 0.2, 0.2, 0.2))
par (oma = c (5, 5, 0, 0))
for (i in 1:9) plot (sort (runif (100)), sort (runif (100)),
                 xaxt = "n", yaxt = "n", pch = 16, col = hue_pal()(1))
title (xlab = "time", ylab = "distance", outer = T, cex.lab = 2)
```

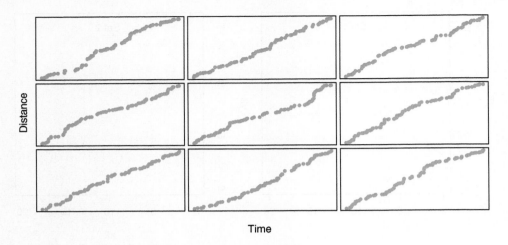

Figure 6.40   Nine graphs close together.

6.5.22   Square plotting region, `pty`

If we want to have a square plotting region (e.g. when producing a map or a grid with true squares on it), then use the `pty = "s"` option. The option `pty = "m"` generates the maximal plotting region which is not square on most devices.

6.5.23   Character rotation, `srt`

To rotate characters in the plotting plane, use `srt` (which stands for 'string rotation'). The argument to the function is in degrees of counter-clockwise rotation:

```
plot (1 : 10, 1 : 10, type = "n", xlab = "", ylab = "")
for (i in 1:10) text (i, i, LETTERS[i], srt = (20 * i), col = hue_pal()(2)[1])
for (i in 1:10) text (10 - i + 1, i, letters[i], srt = (20 * i), col = hue_pal()(2)[2])
```

Observe how the letters i and I have been turned upside down in Figure 6.41 since `srt = 180`.

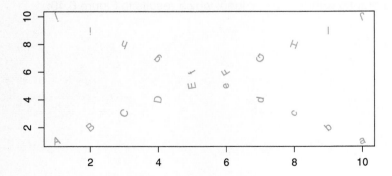

Figure 6.41   A plot with character rotation.

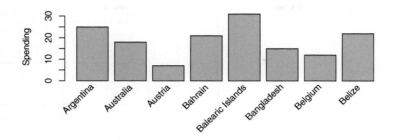

Figure 6.42   A plot with character rotation.

6.5.24   Rotating the axis labels

When we have long text labels (e.g. for bars on a `barplot ()`), it is a good idea to rotate them through 45 degrees so that all the labels are printed, and all are easy to read.

```
spending <- read.csv ("spending.csv", header = TRUE)
attach (spending)
names (spending)
```

```
[1] "spend"   "country"
```

There are three steps involved:

- Make the bottom margin big enough to take the long labels with `mar ()`.
- Find the *x* coordinates of the centres of the bars `xvals` with `usr`.
- Use `text ()` with `srt = 45` to rotate the labels.

```
par (mar = c (7, 4, 4, 2) + 0.1)
xvals <- barplot (spend, ylab = "spending", col = hue_pal()(1))
text (xvals, par ("usr")[3] - 0.25, srt = 45,
      adj = 1, labels = country, xpd = TRUE)
```

```
detach (spending)
```

Note the use of `xpd = TRUE` to allow for text outside the plotting region, and `adj = 1` to place the right-hand end of text at the centre of the bars. The vertical location of the labels is set by `par ("usr")[3] - 0.25` and we can adjust the value of the offset (here 0.25) as required to move the axis labels up or down relative to the *x*-axis.

6.5.25   Tick marks on the axes

The arguments `tck` and `tcl` control the length and location of the tick marks. Negative values put the tick marks *outside* the box (`tcl = -0.5` is the default setting in *R*); `tcl` gives the length of tick marks as a fraction of the height of a line of text.

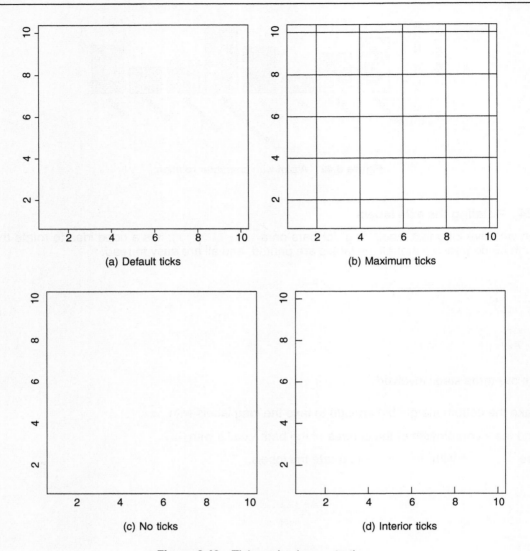

Figure 6.43 Tick marks demonstration.

The default setting for `tck` is `tck = NA`, but we can use this for drawing grid lines: `tck = 0` means no tick marks, while `tck = 1` means fill the whole frame (i.e. the tick marks make a grid). The tick is given as a fraction of the frame width (they are +0.03 in the bottom right-hand graph, so are internal to the plotting region). See Figure 6.43 for examples.

```
plot (1 : 10, 1 : 10, xlab = "", ylab = "", type = "n")
plot (1 : 10, 1 : 10, xlab = "", ylab = "", type = "n", tck = 1)
plot (1 : 10, 1 : 10, xlab = "", ylab = "", type = "n", tck = 0)
plot (1 : 10, 1 : 10, xlab = "", ylab = "", type = "n", tck = 0.03)
```

6.5.26 Axis styles

There are three functions that we need to distinguish:

`axis ()`	select one of the four sides of the plot to work with;
`xaxs, yaxs`	intervals for the tick marks;
`xaxt, yaxt`	suppress production of the axis with `xaxt = "n"`.

The `axis ()` function is described in Section 6.3.6.

The `xaxs` option is used infrequently: style `"r"` (regular) first extends the data range by 4% and then finds an axis with pretty labels that fits within the range; style `"i"` (internal) just finds an axis with pretty labels that fits within the original data range.

Finally, `xaxt` and `yaxt` are often used when we want to specify our own kind of axes with different locations for the tick marks and/or different labelling. If we do not want any tick marks or numbers on the axes, then suppress the tick marks and value labels using `xaxt = "n"` and/or `yaxt = "n"`.

6.5.27 Summary

It is worth restating the really important things about plotting.

- **Plots:** `plot (x, y)` gives a scatterplot if x is continuous, and a boxplot if x is a factor. Some people prefer the alternative syntax `plot (y ~ x)` using 'tilde' as in a model formula; one advantage is that this has a `subset ()` option.

- **Type** of plot: Options include lines `type = "l"` or null (axes only) `type = "n"`.

- **Lines:** `lines (x, y)` plots a smooth function of y against x using the x and y values provided. Some might prefer `lines (y ~ x)`.

- **Line types:** Useful dotted or dashed lines; `lty = 2` (an option in `plot ()` or `lines ()`).

- **Points:** `points(x,y)` adds another set of data points to a plot. Some might prefer `points (y ~ x)`.

- **Plotting characters** for different data sets: `pch = 16` or `pch = "*"` (an option in `points ()` or `plot ()`).

- **Axes:** setting non-default limits to the x- or y-axis scales uses `xlim = c (0, 25)` and/or `ylim = c (0, 1)` as an option in `plot ()`.

- **Labels:** use `xlab` and `ylab` to label the x- and y- axes.

- **Scales:** use `ylim` and `xlim` to control the top and bottom values on axes.

- **Scales:** use `legend ()` to add a legend to a plot.

Table 6.3 gives a more detailed view of the options when plotting. We omit the usual `()` notation from functions for conciseness, unless necessary. Each of the functions is illustrated in more detail in Section 6.5.

Table 6.3 Graphical parameters and their default values.

Parameter	In plot () ?[a]	Default value	Meaning
adj	*	0.5 (centred)	Justification of text
ann	*	TRUE	Annotate plots with axis and overall titles?
ask	*	FALSE	Pause before new graph?
bg	*	"transparent"	Background style or colour
bty		full box	Type of box drawn around the graph
cex	*	1	Character expansion: enlarge if > 1, reduce if < 1
cex.axis	*	1	Magnification for axis notation
cex.lab	*	1	Magnification for label notation
cex.main	*	1.2	Main title character size
cex.sub	*	1	Subtitle character size
cin		0.1354167, 0.1875000	Character size (width, height) in inches
col	*	"black"	colors () to see range of colours
col.axis		"black"	Colour for graph axes
col.lab	*	"black"	Colour for graph labels
col.main	*	"black"	Colour for main heading
col.sub	*	"black"	Colour for subheading
cra		13, 18	Character size (width, height) in rasters (pixels)
crt		0	Rotation of single characters in degrees (see srt)
csi		0.1875	Character height in inches
cxy		0.02255379, 0.03452245	Character size (width, height) in user-defined units
din		7.166666, 7.156249	Size of the graphic device (width, height) in inches (the window is bigger than this)
family	*	"sans"	Font style: from "serif", "sans", "mono" and "symbol" (and see font, below)
fg		"black"	Colour for objects such as axes and boxes in the foreground
fig		0, 1, 0, 1	Coordinates of the figure region within the display region: c (x1, x2, y1, y2)
fin		7.166666, 7.156249	Dimensions of the figure region (width, height) in inches
font	*	1	Font (regular = 1, bold = 2 or italics = 3) in which text is written (and see family, above)
font.axis	*	1	Font in which axis is numbered

font.lab	*	1	Font in which labels are written
font.main	*	1	Font for main heading
font.sub	*	1	Font for subheading
gamma		1	Correction for hsv colours
hsv		1, 1, 1	Values (range [0, 1]) for hue, saturation and value of colour
lab		5, 5, 7	Number of tick marks on the x-axis, y-axis and size of labels
las		0	Orientation of axis numbers: use las = 1 for publication
lend		round	Style for the ends of lines; could be square or butt
lheight		1	Height of a line of text used to vertically space multi-line text
ljoin		round	Style for joining two lines; could be mitre or bevel
lmitre		10	Controls when mitred line joins are automatically converted into bevelled line joins
log	*	Neither	Which axes to log: "log = x", "log = y" or "log = xy"
lty	*	solid	Line type (e.g. dashed: lty = 2)
lwd	*	1	Width of lines on a graph
mai		0.95625, 0.76875, 0.76875, 0.39375	Margin sizes in inches for c (bottom, left, top, right)
mar		5.1, 4.1, 4.1, 2.1	Margin sizes in numbers of lines for c (bottom, left, top, right)
mex		1	Margin expansion specifies the size of font used to convert between mar and mai, and between oma and omi
mfcol		1, 1	Multiple frames per page (same layout as mfrow (see below), but graphs produced columnwise)
mfg		1, 1, 1, 1	Which figure in an array of figures is to be drawn next (if setting) or is being drawn (if enquiring); the array must already have been set by mfcol or mfrow
mfrow		1, 1	Multiple frames per page (first number = rows, second number = columns): mfrow = c (2, 3) gives graphs in two rows each with three columns, drawn row-wise
mgp		3, 1, 0	Margin line (in mex units) for the axis title, axis labels and axis line
new		FALSE	To draw another plot on top of the existing plot, set new = TRUE so that plot does not wipe the slate clean
oma		0, 0, 0, 0	Size of the outer margins in lines of text c (bottom, left, top, right)
omd		0, 1, 0, 1	Size of the outer margins in normalized device coordinate (NDC) units, expressed as a fraction (in [0,1]) of the device region c (bottom, left, top, right)
omi		0, 0, 0, 0	Size of the outer margins in inches c (bottom, left, top, right)
pch	*	1	Plotting symbol; e.g. pch = 16

(continued)

Table 6.3 (Continued)

Parameter	In `plot` () ?[a]	Default value	Meaning
`pin`		6.004166, 5.431249	Current plot dimensions (width, height), in inches
`plt`		0.1072675, 0.9450581, 0.1336245, 0.8925764	Coordinates of the plot region as fractions of the current figure region `c` `(x1, x2, y1, y2)`
`ps`		12	Point size of text and symbols
`pty`		m	Type of plot region to be used: `pty = "s"` generates a square plotting region, `m` stands for maximal
`srt`	*	0	String rotation in degrees
`tck`		−0.5	Big tick marks (grid-lines); to use this set `tcl = NA`
`tcl`		−0.5	Tick marks outside the frame
`tmag`		1.2	Enlargement of text of the main title relative to the other annotating text of the plot
`type`	*	p	Plot type: e.g. `type = "n"` to produce blank axes
`usr`	*	set by the most recent `plot` function	Extremes of the user-defined coordinates of the plotting region `c` `(xmin, xmax, ymin, ymax)`
`xaxp`		0, 1, 5	Tick marks for log axes: `xmin`, `xmax` and number of intervals
`xaxs`		r	Pretty x-axis intervals
`xaxt`		s	x-axis type: use `xaxt = "n"` to set up the axis but not plot it
`xlab`	*	label for the x-axis	`xlab = "label for x axis"`
`xlim`	*	pretty	User control of x-axis scaling: `xlim = c (0, 1)`
`xlog`		FALSE	Is the x-axis on a log scale? If `TRUE`, a logarithmic scale is in use; e.g. following `plot (y ~ x, log = "x")`
`xpd`		FALSE	The way plotting is clipped: if `FALSE`, all plotting is clipped to the plot region; if `TRUE`, all plotting is clipped to the figure region; and if `NA`, all plotting is clipped to the device region
`yaxp`		0, 1, 5	Tick marks for log axes: `ymin`, `ymax` and number of intervals
`yaxs`		r	Pretty y-axis intervals
`yaxt`		s	y-axis type: use `yaxt = "n"` to set up the axis but not plot it
`ylab`	*	label for the y-axis	`ylab = "label for y axis"`
`ylim`	*	pretty	User control of y-axis scaling: `ylim = c (0, 100)`
`ylog`		FALSE	Is the y-axis on a log scale? If `TRUE`, a logarithmic scale is in use; e.g. following `plot (y ~ x, log = "xy")`

[a] The column headed 'In plot?' indicates with an asterisk whether this parameter can be changed as an argument to the `plot`, `points` or `lines` functions.

References

Knuth, D. E. (2012). *The texbook*. Addison-Wesley.

Neuwirth, E. (2014). *Rcolorbrewer: colorbrewer palettes* [R package version 1.1-2]. https://CRAN.R-project.org/package=RColorBrewer.

Sarkar, D. (2008). *Lattice: multivariate data visualization with R* [ISBN 978-0-387-75968-5]. Springer. http://lmdvr.r-forge.r-project.org.

Wickham, H. (2016). *Ggplot2: elegant graphics for data analysis*. Springer-Verlag New York. https://ggplot2.tidyverse.org.

Wilkinson, L. (2012). *Grammar of graphics*. Springer.

Wood, S. N. (2011). Fast stable restricted maximum likelihood and marginal likelihood estimation of semi-parametric generalized linear models.

7

Tables

The alternative to using graphics is to summarise your data in tabular form. Broadly speaking, if you want to convey *detail*, use a table, and if you want to show *effects*, then use graphics. You are more likely to want to use a table to summarise data when your data are categorical (such as people's names, or different commodities) than when they are continuous (in which case a scatterplot is likely to be more informative; see Section 5.1).

7.1 Tabulating categorical or discrete data

We'll first look at tables for categorical data, or discrete (numeric) data with a very limited number of unique values. Our main tools will be the following functions:

- `table ()`: Produces a table of counts;
- `prop.table ()`: Produces a table of proportions.

7.1.1 Tables of counts

The `table ()` function is perhaps the most useful of all the simple vector functions, because it does so much work behind the scenes. We have a vector of objects (they could be numbers or character strings), and we want to know how many of each is present in the vector.

Suppose we generate 1000 integers from a Poisson distribution with mean 0.6. We want to count up all of the zeros, ones, twos, and so on. A big task, but here is the `table ()` function in action:

```
counts <- rpois (1000, 0.6)
table (counts)

counts
  0   1   2   3   4
544 310 115  27   4
```

The R Book, Third Edition. Elinor Jones, Simon Harden and Michael J. Crawley.
© 2023 John Wiley & Sons Ltd. Published 2023 by John Wiley & Sons Ltd.
Companion website: www.wiley.com/go/jones/therbook3e

The function works for characters as well as for numbers and for multiple classifying variables. Let us take the dataset `disease` which contains information on gender and disease status:

```
disease <- read.table ("disease.txt", header = T)
attach (disease)
head (disease)

  gender status
1 females  clear
2 females  clear
3 females  clear
4 females  clear
5 females  clear
6 females  clear
```

This is a large dataset with 1000 rows (observations). You want to know how many males and females were infected and how many were clear of infection:

```
table (status, gender)

          gender
status   females males
  clear      284   515
  infected    53    68
```

If you want the genders as the rows rather than the columns, then put gender first in the argument list to `table ()`:

```
table (gender, status)

        status
gender  clear infected
  females  284       53
  males    515       68
```

You could also go further if you wanted and specify three variables in `table ()`. This would create a stack of two-dimensional tables. The number of tables would depend on the number of levels in the *third* variable specified.

7.1.2 Tables of proportions

Sometimes it is preferable to show tables using *proportions* rather than counts, especially if we are dealing with large tables. Just remember that we also need a decent sample size to do this. If you have a small dataset and try to spread out your data in a large table – making it very sparse – using proportions instead of counts can distort what's really going on.

If you decide that proportions are the way to go, the `prop.table ()` function uses a table's margins (the row totals or the column totals) to calculate cell proportions. We have three options:

- compute the proportion in each cell by considering *row* totals so that proportions in a particular row of the table sum to 1;

- compute the proportion in each cell by considering *column* totals so that proportions in a particular column of the table sum to 1;

- compute the proportion in each cell by considering the *grand* total so that proportions across the whole table sum to 1.

The type of proportion you want is controlled by the second argument of `prop.table ()`, as we'll see.

Let us try this with our `disease` dataset. First, we create an object, `disease_tab`, which is the frequency table we'd like to convert to a table of proportions.

```
disease_tab <- table (gender, status)
disease_tab

         status
gender    clear infected
  females   284       53
  males     515       68
```

Now we can use `prop.table ()` and specify the type of proportions we want computed. If we want *row* proportions, the second argument is `margin = 1` (or just `1` for short). Notice how the rows sum to 1 here.

```
prop.table (disease_tab, 1)

         status
gender         clear  infected
  females  0.8427300 0.1572700
  males    0.8833619 0.1166381
```

If we want *column* proportions, the second argument is `margin = 2` (or just `2` for short). Notice how the columns sum to 1 here.

```
prop.table (disease_tab, 2)

         status
gender         clear  infected
  females  0.3554443 0.4380165
  males    0.6445557 0.5619835
```

Finally, if we want proportions to be computed in relation to the grand total, then we don't need to specify a second argument in `prop.table ()`. Here, the proportions across the table sum to 1.

```
prop.table (disease_tab)

        status
gender          clear    infected
  females 0.30869565 0.05760870
  males   0.55978261 0.07391304


detach (disease)
```

In any particular case, you need to think carefully whether it makes sense to express your counts as proportions of the row totals, the column totals or the grand total.

7.2   Tabulating summaries of numeric data

It is often useful to generate summaries of numeric variables. The most basic function to do this is the summary () function, or we can compute specified summary statistics for particular variables using, for example mean (), median (), sd (), and so on, with the argument of each function being the relevant variable.

We can do more with other functions, however, including generating summaries of variables split by groups. This is what we'll focus on here.

We'll use the Daphnia dataset in this section. The response variable is growth rate of the animals, and there are three categorical explanatory variables: the river from which the water was sampled, the kind of detergent experimentally added, and the clone of daphnia employed in the experiment. Here's a flavour of the content of the dataset:

```
daphnia <- read.table ("Daphnia.txt", header = T)
attach (daphnia)
head (daphnia)

  Growth.rate Water Detergent Daphnia
1    2.919086  Tyne    BrandA  Clone1
2    2.492904  Tyne    BrandA  Clone1
3    3.021804  Tyne    BrandA  Clone1
4    2.350874  Tyne    BrandA  Clone2
5    3.148174  Tyne    BrandA  Clone2
6    4.423853  Tyne    BrandA  Clone2
```

7.2.1   General summaries by group

If you are looking for general summaries by group, the psych package is a good place to start (Revelle, 2021). The package contains a bewildering number of functions which are aimed at those working with psychology-based data as the name would suggest. For generating summaries of numeric data, the describe () and describeBy () functions are very useful. Note the lone capital letter in the latter function.

If you want a numerical summary of a single variable, then use describe (). It gives a lot of output, and most of it is probably unnecessary. You can choose for skew and kurtosis not to be calculated, which streamlines the output.

```
library ('psych')
describe (Growth.rate)

    vars  n mean    sd median trimmed  mad  min   max range skew kurtosis   se
X1     1 72 3.85 1.28   3.79    3.79 1.53 1.76 6.92  5.16 0.37    -0.86 0.15

describe (Growth.rate, skew = FALSE)

    vars  n mean    sd  min  max range   se
X1     1 72 3.85 1.28 1.76 6.92  5.16 0.15
```

For summaries by group, for example numeric summaries of Growth.rate by Detergent, with or without displaying skew and kurtosis, use the describeBy () function:

```
describeBy (Growth.rate, Water)

 Descriptive statistics by group
group: Tyne
    vars  n mean    sd median trimmed  mad min  max range skew kurtosis   se
X1     1 36 3.69 1.05   3.44    3.63 1.21 2.2 5.83  3.63 0.38    -0.97 0.18
------------------------------------------------------------
group: Wear
    vars  n mean    sd median trimmed mad  min   max range skew kurtosis   se
X1     1 36 4.02 1.48   3.96    3.96   2 1.76 6.92  5.16 0.19    -1.22 0.25

describeBy (Growth.rate, Water, skew = FALSE)

Descriptive statistics by group
group: Tyne
    vars  n mean    sd min  max range   se
X1     1 36 3.69 1.05 2.2 5.83  3.63 0.18
------------------------------------------------------------
group: Wear
    vars  n mean    sd  min  max range   se
X1     1 36 4.02 1.48 1.76 6.92  5.16 0.25
```

It is also possible to generate summary tables by two categorical variables, for example

```
describeBy (Growth.rate, list (Water, Daphnia), skew = FALSE)

 Descriptive statistics by group
: Tyne
: Clone1
    vars  n mean    sd min  max range   se
X1     1 12 2.87 0.51 2.2 3.71  1.51 0.15
------------------------------------------------------------
: Wear
: Clone1
```

```
    vars  n mean    sd min  max range   se
X1     1 12 2.81 0.66 2.1 3.95  1.85 0.19
-----------------------------------------------------------
: Tyne
: Clone2
    vars  n mean    sd  min  max range   se
X1     1 12 3.81 0.87 2.35 5.29  2.93 0.25
-----------------------------------------------------------
: Wear
: Clone2
    vars  n mean    sd  min  max range   se
X1     1 12 5.35 1.07 3.89 6.92  3.03 0.31
-----------------------------------------------------------
: Tyne
: Clone3
    vars  n mean   sd  min  max range   se
X1     1 12 4.38 1.1 2.23 5.83   3.6 0.32
-----------------------------------------------------------
: Wear
: Clone3
    vars  n mean    sd  min  max range   se
X1     1 12 3.89 1.36 1.76 5.38  3.62 0.39
```

The `describe ()` and `describeBy ()` functions can be manipulated further. See Revelle, 2021 or search the package help for further details.

7.2.2 Bespoke summaries by group

While all-purpose functions for generating summaries are very useful, you might need more control over exactly what you want to compute. To generate a summary table of a particular statistic of your choosing (by group), a useful function is the somewhat obscurely named `tapply ()`. It is called `tapply ()` because it applies a named function (such as mean or variance) across a grouping variable (categorical variable) to create a table.

Here is `tapply ()` in action using the Daphnia dataset, assuming that we want to tabulate the mean growth rates for the four brands of detergent tested:

```
tapply (Growth.rate, Detergent, mean)


  BrandA    BrandB    BrandC    BrandD
3.884832  4.010044  3.954512  3.558231
```

or for the two rivers:

```
tapply (Growth.rate, Water, mean)


    Tyne      Wear
3.685862  4.017948
```

or for the three daphnia clones:

```
tapply (Growth.rate, Daphnia, mean)


  Clone1    Clone2    Clone3
2.839875  4.577121  4.138719
```

Two-dimensional summary tables are created by replacing the single explanatory variable (the second argument in the function call) by a `list ()` indicating which variable is to be used for the rows of the summary table and which variable is to be used for creating the columns of the summary table. To get the daphnia clones as the rows and detergents as the columns, we write `list (Daphnia, Detergent)` – rows first then columns – and use `tapply ()` to create the summary table as follows:

```
tapply (Growth.rate, list (Daphnia, Detergent), mean)


         BrandA    BrandB    BrandC    BrandD
Clone1 2.732227  2.929140  3.071335  2.626797
Clone2 3.919002  4.402931  4.772805  5.213745
Clone3 5.003268  4.698062  4.019397  2.834151
```

If we wanted the median values (rather than the means), then we would just alter the third argument of the `tapply ()` function like this:

```
tapply (Growth.rate, list (Daphnia, Detergent), median)


         BrandA    BrandB    BrandC    BrandD
Clone1 2.705995  3.012495  3.073964  2.503468
Clone2 3.924411  4.282181  4.612801  5.416785
Clone3 5.057594  4.627812  4.040108  2.573003
```

We're not limited to pre-defined functions like `mean` and `median`. We can also specify our own function. For example, to obtain a table of the standard errors of the means (where each mean is based on six numbers: two replicates and three rivers), the function we want to apply is $\sqrt{s^2/n}$. There is no built-in function for the standard error of a mean in base R, so we create a `function ()` inside `tapply ()` like this:

```
tapply (Growth.rate, list (Daphnia, Detergent),
        function (x)
          sqrt (var (x) / length (x))
        )


         BrandA     BrandB     BrandC     BrandD
Clone1 0.2163448  0.2319320  0.3055929  0.1905771
Clone2 0.4702855  0.3639819  0.5773096  0.5520220
Clone3 0.2688604  0.2683660  0.5395750  0.4260212
```

When `tapply ()` is asked to produce a three-dimensional table, it produces a stack of two-dimensional tables with the number of stacked tables being determined by the number of levels of the categorical variable that comes *third* in the list (`Water` in this case):

```
tapply (Growth.rate, list (Daphnia, Detergent, Water), mean)

,, Tyne

        BrandA    BrandB    BrandC    BrandD
Clone1 2.811265  2.775903  3.287529  2.597192
Clone2 3.307634  4.191188  3.620532  4.105651
Clone3 4.866524  4.766258  4.534902  3.365766

,, Wear

        BrandA    BrandB    BrandC    BrandD
Clone1 2.653189  3.082377  2.855142  2.656403
Clone2 4.530371  4.614673  5.925078  6.321838
Clone3 5.140011  4.629867  3.503892  2.302537
```

In cases like this, the function `ftable ()` (which stands for 'flat table') often produces more pleasing output:

```
ftable (tapply (Growth.rate, list (Daphnia, Detergent, Water), mean))

                 Tyne      Wear

Clone1 BrandA   2.811265  2.653189
       BrandB   2.775903  3.082377
       BrandC   3.287529  2.855142
       BrandD   2.597192  2.656403
Clone2 BrandA   3.307634  4.530371
       BrandB   4.191188  4.614673
       BrandC   3.620532  5.925078
       BrandD   4.105651  6.321838
Clone3 BrandA   4.866524  5.140011
       BrandB   4.766258  4.629867
       BrandC   4.534902  3.503892
       BrandD   3.365766  2.302537
```

Notice that the order of the rows, columns, or tables is determined by the alphabetical sequence of the factor levels (e.g. Tyne comes before Wear in the alphabet). If you want to override this, you must specify that the factor levels are ordered in a non-standard way:

```
water <- factor (Water, levels = c ("Wear", "Tyne"))
ftable (tapply (Growth.rate, list (Daphnia, Detergent, water), mean))

                 Wear      Tyne

Clone1 BrandA   2.653189  2.811265
       BrandB   3.082377  2.775903
```

```
        BrandC   2.855142  3.287529
        BrandD   2.656403  2.597192
Clone2  BrandA   4.530371  3.307634
        BrandB   4.614673  4.191188
        BrandC   5.925078  3.620532
        BrandD   6.321838  4.105651
Clone3  BrandA   5.140011  4.866524
        BrandB   4.629867  4.766258
        BrandC   3.503892  4.534902
        BrandD   2.302537  3.365766
```

The function to be applied in generating the table can be supplied with extra arguments. For example, the `trim` argument is part of the `mean ()` function, specifying the fraction (between 0 and 0.5) of the observations to be trimmed from each end of the sorted vector of values before the mean is computed. Values of `trim` outside that range are taken as the nearest endpoint.

```
tapply (Growth.rate, Detergent, mean, trim = 0.1)


  BrandA    BrandB    BrandC    BrandD
3.874869  4.019206  3.890448  3.482322
```

An extra argument is essential if you want means when there are missing values:

```
tapply (Growth.rate, Detergent, mean, na.rm = T)


  BrandA    BrandB    BrandC    BrandD
3.884832  4.010044  3.954512  3.558231
```

Without the argument specifying that you want to average over the non-missing values (`na.rm = T` means 'it is true that I want to remove the missing values'), the `mean ()` function will simply fail, producing `NA` as the answer.

7.3 Converting between tables and dataframes

7.3.1 From a table to a dataframe

In some situations, you may want to create a dataframe of summary statistics.

For instance, if we wanted a dataframe of mean growth rate classified by detergent and daphnia clone (i.e. averaged over river water and replicates), we can generate the summaries using `tapply ()`, then coerce the result into a dataframe:

```
daph_table <- tapply (Growth.rate, list (Detergent, Daphnia), mean)
daph_table_data <- as.data.frame.table (daph_table)
daph_table_data


    Var1    Var2      Freq
1  BrandA  Clone1  2.732227
```

```
2   BrandB Clone1 2.929140
3   BrandC Clone1 3.071335
4   BrandD Clone1 2.626797
5   BrandA Clone2 3.919002
6   BrandB Clone2 4.402931
7   BrandC Clone2 4.772805
8   BrandD Clone2 5.213745
9   BrandA Clone3 5.003268
10  BrandB Clone3 4.698062
11  BrandC Clone3 4.019397
12  BrandD Clone3 2.834151
```

You need to edit the variable names like this:

```
names (daph_table_data) <- c ("detergents", "daphnia", "mean")
head (daph_table_data)


  detergents daphnia      mean
1     BrandA   Clone1 2.732227
2     BrandB   Clone1 2.929140
3     BrandC   Clone1 3.071335
4     BrandD   Clone1 2.626797
5     BrandA   Clone2 3.919002
6     BrandB   Clone2 4.402931


detach (daphnia)
```

In other situations, you may receive a dataset which is in table format already. For example, for the purpose of model-fitting, we often want to expand a table of explanatory variables to create a dataframe with as many repeated rows as specified by a count. Here is an example of such data:

```
tabledata <- read.table ("tabledata.txt", header = T)
head (tabledata)


  count    sex   age   condition
1    12   male young     healthy
2     7   male   old     healthy
3     9 female young     healthy
4     8 female   old     healthy
5     6   male young parasitized
6     7   male   old parasitized
```

The idea is to create a new dataframe with a separate row for each case. That is to say, we want 12 copies of the first row (for healthy young males), 7 copies of the second row (for healthy old males), and so on.

One way of doing this is to use `lapply ()` to apply the repeat function `rep ()` to each variable in `tabledata` such that each row is repeated by the number of times specified in the vector called count:

```
expanded_table <- lapply (tabledata, function (x) rep (x, tabledata$count))
```

Then we convert this object to a `data.frame` using `as.data.frame` like this:

```
expanded_table <- as.data.frame (expanded_table)
head (expanded_table)


  count  sex   age condition
1    12 male young   healthy
2    12 male young   healthy
3    12 male young   healthy
4    12 male young   healthy
5    12 male young   healthy
6    12 male young   healthy
```

To tidy up, we probably want to remove the redundant vector of counts:

```
expanded_table <- expanded_table [, -1]
head (expanded_table)


   sex   age condition
1 male young   healthy
2 male young   healthy
3 male young   healthy
4 male young   healthy
5 male young   healthy
6 male young   healthy


tail (expanded_table)


     sex   age   condition
57 female young parasitized
58 female   old parasitized
59 female   old parasitized
60 female   old parasitized
61 female   old parasitized
62 female   old parasitized
```

Now we can use the contents of `expanded_table` as explanatory variables in modelling other responses of each of the 62 cases (e.g. the animals' body weights).

This is not the only way of achieving the same result. The alternative is to produce a long vector of row numbers and use this as a subscript on the rows of the short dataframe to turn it into a long dataframe with the same column structure:

```
expanded_table2 <- tabledata [rep (1 : nrow (tabledata),
                                   tabledata [["count"]]),]
head (expanded_table2)

    count  sex   age condition
1      12 male young   healthy
1.1    12 male young   healthy
1.2    12 male young   healthy
```

```
1.3      12 male young    healthy
1.4      12 male young    healthy
1.5      12 male young    healthy
```

Again, the resulting dataset could be tidied up.

7.3.2   From a dataframe to a table

The reverse procedure of creating a table from a dataframe is much more straightforward and involves nothing more than the `table ()` function:

```
table (expanded_table)

,, condition = healthy

         age
sex       old young
  female    8     9
  male      7    12

,, condition = parasitized

         age
sex       old young
  female    5     8
  male      7     6
```

This tabulated object itself could be coerced into another dataframe, in which case use:

```
as.data.frame (table (expanded_table))

      sex    age    condition Freq
1 female    old      healthy    8
2   male    old      healthy    7
3 female  young      healthy    9
4   male  young      healthy   12
5 female    old  parasitized    5
6   male    old  parasitized    7
7 female  young  parasitized    8
8   male  young  parasitized    6
```

R has invented the variable name `Freq` for the counts of the various contingencies. To change this to 'count' use `names ()` with the appropriate subscript for the column number (in this case 4):

```
contract_table <- as.data.frame (table (expanded_table))
names (contract_table) [4] <- "count"
contract_table
```

```
    sex    age   condition count
1 female    old    healthy     8
2   male    old    healthy     7
3 female  young    healthy     9
4   male  young    healthy    12
5 female    old parasitized     5
6   male    old parasitized     7
7 female  young parasitized     8
8   male  young parasitized     6
```

Reference

Revelle, W. (2021). *Psych: Procedures for psychological, psychometric, and personality research* [R package version 2.1.6]. Northwestern University. Evanston, IL. https://CRAN.R-project.org/package=psych.

Probability Distributions in R

Data analysis in essence revolves around attempting to understand as much of the variability in our data as possible. The data used could be *numeric* (e.g. height) or *categorical* (e.g. ethnicity), see Section 1.8.1 for more information, but either way describing the nature of the variability in the data from one observation to the next is done via *probability distributions*.

Before we consider probability distributions, we must think about **random variables**: informally, a random variable is a quantity that varies randomly from unit to unit. For example, height will naturally vary from person to person, while the outcome of a throw of a die will vary from throw to throw. The probability distribution for height or the outcome of a throw of a die then describes the likelihood of an event, occurrence, or outcome of interest. From there we can ask questions such as 'what's the probability (how likely is it) that a person chosen at random from a particular population will be taller than 170 cm?', or 'what are the chances that a six thrown on the next roll of a die?'.

It is useful to have notation so that we can write statements involving random variables succinctly and without ambiguity. It is customary to write random variables using capital letters – this tells us that the value that it can take will vary randomly from unit to unit. Let us say, for example, that X represents the height of an individual from our population of interest, and that Y denotes the outcome of the next roll of the die. Then it makes sense to think about the *distribution* of X and (probably separately!) of Y: what values can they take, and what is the probability of observing a particular event (e.g. that X is larger than 170, or that Y is equal to six)? Our questions above can be written succinctly as $P(X > 170)$ and $P(Y = 6)$, respectively, and as long as we know (or assume) the probability distribution of X and of Y, we can compute these probabilities. More generally, rather than specifying a particular number we can write more generally, for example $P(X > x)$ or $P(Y = y)$ denoting the probability that X is larger than some (yet to be specified) value x or the probability that Y is equal to some (yet to be specified) value y, respectively. Notice that we use lower-case letters, x and y, as these represent particular values, whereas X and Y denote random variables.

There is no end to the probability distributions that we could define, but there are common 'families' of probability distributions that will become very familiar with. You may well have come across some of these already, e.g. the Normal distribution (which is probably the most famous distribution of all). Each of these probability distributions will be characterised by a specific **parameter** or a set of **parameters**. For example, we'll see that a Normal distribution is characterised by its mean and standard deviation (or variance, if preferred) – this is enough to completely specify a particular

The R Book, Third Edition. Elinor Jones, Simon Harden and Michael J. Crawley.
© 2023 John Wiley & Sons Ltd. Published 2023 by John Wiley & Sons Ltd.
Companion website: www.wiley.com/go/jones/therbook3e

Normal distribution – and, of course, there is no end of possible values for these parameters. So in essence there are an infinite number of possible distinct Normal distributions.

When it comes to using probability distributions to answer questions, sometimes there is an 'obvious' probability distribution to use; other times, we *assume* that we can use a specific distribution. Many of the analysis techniques that are discussed later in this book assume specific probability distributions for particular random variables. Methods for checking whether a given set of values does indeed belong to a particular distribution don't exist, but it is possible to look for *evidence* that the set *does not* come from the specified distribution. We won't consider these methods here, but look out for them in Chapter 9.

8.1 Probability distributions: the basics

8.1.1 Discrete and continuous probability distributions

Broadly speaking, probability distributions are categorised as being either **discrete** or **continuous**, though it is possible to have a distribution with both elements (we won't consider them in this book). The distinction sits with the nature of the random variable of interest, see Section 1.8.1 for more information.

If it is possible to list all values that the random variable can take – which may produce an infinite list – the underlying probability distribution is discrete. For example, whether a patient suffered a heart attack (yes or no), the outcome of a roll of a six-sided die (whole numbers from 1 to 6), the number of adults in a household (whole numbers, with no theoretical maximum but with realistic constraints), or the smoking status of an individual (none, light, moderate, and heavy). Some of these random variables are numeric (e.g. the number of adults in a household), while others are categorical (e.g. whether a patient suffered a heart attack). In the latter case, we can map the possible events to numbers. In the heart attack example, we could map 'no heart attack' to 0 and 'heart attack' to 1. This might seem like an unnecessary extra step, but it will be useful in terms of notation: if W is the random variable denoting whether a patient suffered a heart attack, then W can now take on the values 0 or 1, and we no longer need to write out text descriptions of possible options.

A continuous probability distribution is used when the events of interest are not only numeric but also can take on any reasonable value (there may be natural minimum and maximum values). Take for example adult height or the time taken to run 100 m. The values that these variables can take are endless, and indeed, we can't write down all possible eventualities.

8.1.2 Describing probability distributions mathematically

Discrete and continuous distributions are characterised by mathematical functions. For discrete distributions, the **probability mass function** (pmf) gives the probability of a particular event being observed. This is not a suitable description for continuous probability distributions: the probability of observing a particular event is zero (for example the probability that I run 100 m in exactly 13.4607 seconds is zero). Instead, continuous probability distributions are described by a **probability density function** (pdf). This can be used to determine the probability that we observe a random variable falling between two defined values (for example, the probability that I run 100 m in a time between 13.1 and 13.7 seconds).

The idea of a **cumulative distribution function** can also be helpful, but only when the events themselves are ordinal or numeric. These functions describe the probability that a random variable is less than or equal to a particular value. For example, if we had a discrete distribution describing the number of adults in a household, we could look at the probability that a household has three or fewer adults residing: if we let X denote the number of adults in a household, then this would amount to computing $P(X \leq 3)$. For continuous distributions, we could, for example, look at the probability that I run 100 m in less than 11.91 seconds (which is unlikely). If Y denoted the time it takes me to run 100 m (in seconds), I would need $P(Y < 11.91)$.

A note of caution here: $P(X \leq 3)$ is not the same as $P(X < 3)$ when we have a discrete variable. In the former, we want the probability that we have three or fewer adults in the household while the latter asks for the probability we have fewer than three adults (i.e. two or fewer adults) in the household. Meanwhile, for continuous variables such as Y, there is no difference between asking for $P(Y \leq 11.91)$ and $P(Y < 11.91)$ as the probability that I run 100 m in exactly 11.91 seconds (and not a millisecond more or less than this) is zero.

8.1.3 Independence

The concept of **independence** crops up regularly in probability and statistics. It often forms the basis of the assumptions we make during data analysis, and you'll see that it features regularly throughout this book. Let us start with the idea of **independent events**, before considering **independent random variables**.

Suppose we have two events of interest, let us call them A and B. These events are independent if the occurrence of one of these doesn't affect the probability of the other happening. In other words, knowing that A (or B) occurred doesn't affect the chances of B (or A) happening.

For example, if A denoted the event 'roll a six using a six-sided fair die' and B denoted 'two-sided fair coin lands on heads', then intuitively these are independent events: whatever happens when we roll the die isn't going to affect the outcome of the coin flip.

Mathematically speaking, we can formalise this in terms of probability in the following (equivalent) ways:

1. 'Knowledge of B doesn't affect the probability of A occurring': $P(A|B) = P(A)$;

2. 'Knowledge of A doesn't affect the probability of B occurring': $P(B|A) = P(B)$;

3. 'The probability of both A and B occurring is equal to the product of their probabilities: $P(A \cap B) = P(A)P(B)$.

See Section 2.4.2 on conditional probability if the notation $P(A|B)$ is unfamiliar. The first two statements are fairly intuitive, but the third might seem peculiar. This stems from the fact that, for example,

$$P(A \cap B) = P(A|B)P(B) = P(A)P(B),$$

where the second equality uses the first from the list of equivalent statements.

The idea of independence can also be applied to random variables in a similar way. Let us suppose we have two numeric random variables, X and Y. Informally, the two are independent if the value (realisation) of one of these doesn't depend on the value of the other. More formally, X and Y are independent if

$$P(X \leq x, Y \leq y) = P(X \leq x)P(Y \leq y) \tag{8.1}$$

for any values x and y of our choosing. Equation (8.1) uses the cumulative distribution functions of X and Y. Notice that this ties in with the definition of independent events: here our events are $\{X \leq x\}$ and $\{Y \leq y\}$.

The idea of independence will be particularly useful in Chapter 9 on statistical testing, and in later chapters of the book on building models (e.g. regression models in Chapters 10 and 11). Often, in these chapters, we will refer to *observations* in our data being independent of each other. The same broad intuition works here too: if observations are independent of one another, then they don't exert any influence over one another.

For example, if we measured the height of two (unrelated) individuals, then we would (probably) be happy that the measurements are not dependent on each other as knowledge on the height of the first individual wouldn't give us any information on the height of the second. In other words, we could accept that these measurements are *independent* of each other. If, on the other hand, we were to measure the height of two siblings, we would expect that knowing the height of one of the pair gives partial information about the height of the other. In this case, the observations are not independent.

8.2   Probability distributions in *R*

R has a wide range of built-in probability distributions, some of which are listed in Table 8.1. The meanings of the parameters are explained in the remainder of this chapter.

For each of *R*'s supported distributions, four functions are available that complete certain tasks:

- the pdf, which has a d prefix, e.g. for the Beta distribution, dbeta (). This allows us to compute the value of the density at a particular point in the case of a continuous probability distribution, or gives the value of the pmf at a particular point for discrete distributions;

- the cumulative probability, which has a p prefix, e.g. for the Beta distribution, pbeta (). This computes the probability of seeing an observation less than or equal to a particular value;

- the quantiles of the distribution, which has a q prefix, e.g. for the Beta distribution, qbeta (). This asks the reverse question to that asked by pbeta (): what value is required so that the probability of choosing a value less than or equal to this point is a particular probability;

- random numbers generated from the distribution, which has an r prefix, e.g. for the Beta distribution, rbeta ().

Table 8.1   Some commonly used probability distributions supported by *R*

Distribution	Type	Parameters	*R* function	*R* parameter names
Beta	continuous	two shape parameters	beta	shape1, shape2
Binomial	discrete	sample size, probability	binom	size, prob
Exponential	continuous	rate	exp	rate
Chi-squared	continuous	degrees of freedom	chisq	df
F	continuous	degrees of freedom (twice)	f	df1, df2
Gamma	continuous	shape, rate	gamma	shape, rate
Geometric	discrete	probability	geom	prob
Hypergeometric	discrete	two size parameters, number of successes	hyper	m, n, k
Lognormal	continuous	mean, standard deviation	lnorm	meanlog, sdlog
Logistic	continuous	location, scale	logis	location, scale
Negative Binomial	discrete	size, probability	nbinom	size, prob
Normal	continuous	mean, standard deviation	norm	mean, sd
Poisson	discrete	mean	pois	lambda
t	continuous	degrees of freedom	t	df
Uniform	continuous	minimum, maximum	unif	min, max
Uniform	discrete	minimum, maximum	dunif	min, max
Weibull	continuous	shape	weibull	shape

8.3 Continuous probability distributions

The Normal distribution will be used to demonstrate the four functions available in *R* applied to continuous distributions. Other distributions covered in this chapter will receive a much shorter treatment since the same ideas apply.

8.3.1 The Normal (or Gaussian) distribution

Box 8.1: The Normal distribution

Parameters: Mean (μ) and standard deviation (σ).
Mean and variance: μ and σ^2.
Possible values: Any.
Characteristics: Symmetric, bell-shaped pdf.
Notation for a random variable X: $X \sim N(\mu, \sigma^2)$.

The pdf of a Normal distribution is characterised by its 'bell-shaped' curve. The value of the function at any point *x* can be computed in *R* using the function `dnorm ()`, but this isn't really of interest. We can use this function to plot the pdf using the code below which gives Figure 8.1. This Normal distribution has a mean, μ, of 170 and a standard deviation, σ, of 8. It is plotted for values of *x* between 140 and 200 though in reality the minimum and maximum values are infinite. Notice that though the usual notation for a Normal distribution is to give its mean and variance,

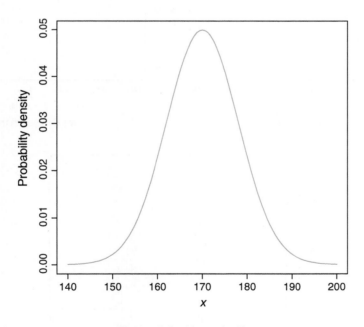

Figure 8.1 Normal pdf.

that is $N(\mu, \sigma^2)$, the suite of `norm` functions require us to specify the mean and standard deviation instead.

```
curve (dnorm (x, 170, 8), 140, 200, xlab = "x",
       ylab = "probability density", col = hue_pal () (1) [1])
```

Computing probabilities based on the Normal distribution is also straightforward. Suppose that we know that height is normally distributed with mean 170 cm and standard deviation 8 cm. What is the probability that a randomly selected individual will be:

- shorter than 160 cm?
- taller than 185 cm?
- between 160 and 185 cm?

The area under the whole curve is exactly 1; this will always be the case for any 'proper' pdf. We won't consider improper probability densities in this book. The area represents *total probability*, for example in our case that the individual is of any height. Then, the required probabilities listed here are defined as the relevant *area under the curve*. Figure 8.2 shows the relevant areas under the curve for each of the questions we posed earlier.

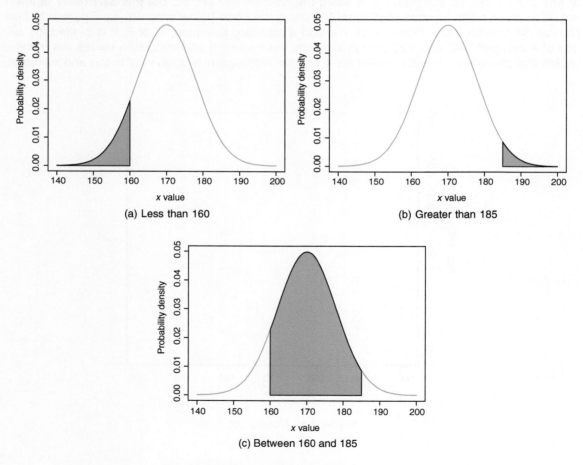

Figure 8.2   Normal probabilities.

For example, the first question can be computed by looking at the area under the curve from minus infinity up to 160 (Figure 8.2a). The function we need for this is pnorm (), which computes the cumulative probability (i.e. the probability of being less than or equal to a specific value); we provide it with the value 160, together with information about the mean and standard deviation of the distribution, to find this probability. The answer to our first question is just over 10% when we feed this request to *R*.

Meanwhile, the answer to our second question requires the complement of what pnorm () gives – remember that pnorm () computes the probability of observing *less than* a particular value. This amounts to subtracting the value pnorm () gives from 1. See Figure 8.2b for a visual representation. A similar argument shows that we must consider the difference between two calls to pnorm () to consider the third question (Figure 8.2c).

```
pnorm (160, mean = 170, sd = 8)

[1] 0.1056498

1 - pnorm (185, mean = 170, sd = 8)

[1] 0.03039636

pnorm (185, mean = 170, sd = 8) - pnorm (160, mean = 170, sd = 8)

[1] 0.8639539
```

We could reverse these probability questions, for example by asking what height are 80% of the population shorter than? What we're asking for here is a particular *quantile* of the Normal distribution, in this case, the 80th quantile of a Normal distribution with mean 170 and standard deviation 8. We can do this using the qnorm () function:

```
qnorm (0.8, mean = 170, sd = 8)

[1] 176.733
```

Therefore, 80% of the population under consideration have a height less than or equal to 176.73. Of course, if we used pnorm () to check the probability of randomly selecting an individual with height less than or equal to 176.73, then we would get an answer of around 0.8 ('around' is due to rounding).

There is one more useful function when it comes to probability distributions: randomly selecting a value from a distribution. If, for example, we wanted to randomly choose a value from a Normal distribution with mean 170 and standard deviation of 8, our tool of choice would be rnorm (). Its first argument is the number of observations that we want to generate from the specified distribution. If we again asked for one observation from the Normal distribution, then we would get a different value as shown in the following code:

```
rnorm (1, mean = 170, sd = 8)

[1] 172.5204

rnorm (1, mean = 170, sd = 8)
```

```
[1] 175.9139

rnorm (5, mean = 170, sd = 8)

[1] 186.6341 162.7192 161.6572 168.6895 177.5674
```

If it is important that we generate the same random numbers every time, we can use the `set.seed` `()` function as follows:

```
set.seed (1604)
rnorm (1, mean = 170, sd = 8)


[1] 178.7003

set.seed (1604)
rnorm (1, mean = 170, sd = 8)


[1] 178.7003

set.seed (3)
rnorm (1, mean = 170, sd = 8)


[1] 162.3045

set.seed (3)
rnorm (1, mean = 170, sd = 8)


[1] 162.3045
```

The seed that we used here – 1604 for the first example and 3 for the second – is arbitrary, but notice as the seed changes so do the randomly generated numbers. This is very useful if we want to, for example, generate simulated data that we can replicate exactly next time.

8.3.2   The Uniform distribution

Box 8.2: The Uniform distribution

Parameters: Minimum and maximum values, a and b.
Mean and variance: $(b - a)/2$ and $(b - a)^2/12$.
Possible values: Any within $[a, b]$.
Characteristics: Symmetric, box-like pdf
Notation for a random variable X: $X \sim U(a, b)$.

The idea is to generate values within an interval (a, b), where the probability of the random value falling in a sub-interval of length l is the same, regardless of where the subinterval lies within (a, b).

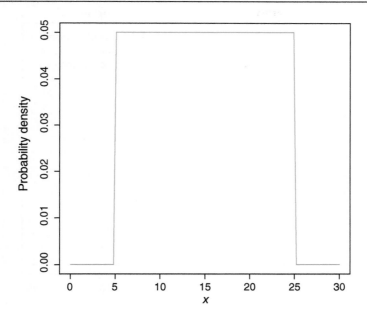

Figure 8.3 Uniform probability density function.

The Uniform distribution is of course symmetric, with a characteristic 'box' shape that is needed to guarantee the above property. See Figure 8.3, which shows the pdf of a Uniform distribution over the range $[5, 25]$. Within this range, the density is $1/(25 - 5)$, while outside this range it is zero. This guarantees that the area under the 'curve' is 1: here the 'curve' is just a rectangle so that we can check this by multiplying the height and width of the box.

Densities, probabilities, quantiles, and random numbers from the Uniform distribution are all possible, with `dunif ()`, `punif ()`, `qunif ()`, and `runif ()` the appropriate functions this time. Supposing we have a random variable such that $X \sim U(5, 25)$, then

- the pdf evaluated at $X = 10$ is `dunif (10, 5, 25)`, which is 0.05;
- the probability that X is less than 14.33 is `punif (14.33, 5, 25)`, which is 0.4665;
- the quantile of the distribution that relates to 0.6 is `qunif (0.6, 5, 25)`, which is 17;
- we can generate 100 random numbers from this Uniform distribution using `runif (100, 5, 25)`.

8.3.3 The Chi-squared distribution

Box 8.3: The Chi-squared distribution

Parameter(s): Degrees of freedom, v.
Mean and variance: v and $2v$.
Possible values: Positive.
Characteristics: Skewed, getting more symmetric as v increases.
Notation for a random variable X: $X \sim \chi_v^2$.

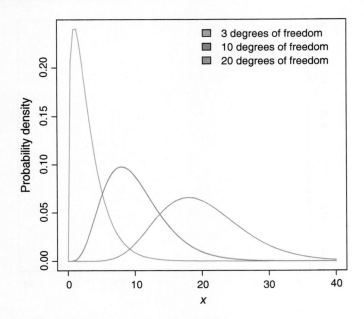

Figure 8.4   Chi-squared probability density function.

The Chi-squared distribution is characterised by a single parameter: the number of degrees of freedom, ν ('nu', pronounced 'new').

 The Chi-squared distribution is always positive (that is, only defined for positive values of the x-axis), and in changing its degrees of freedom, we change its shape. Its shape ranges from being very positively skewed to being (almost) symmetric. See Figure 8.4.

 Densities, probabilities, quantiles, and random numbers using the Chi-squared distribution are all possible, with `dchisq ()`, `pchisq ()`, `qchisq ()`, and `rchisq ()` the appropriate functions this time. For example, if a random variable X had a Chi-squared distribution with 5 degrees of freedom:

- the density function evaluated at $x = 3$ is `dchisq (3, 5)`, which is 0.15;

- the probability that X is less than 4 is `pchisq (4, 5)`, which is 0.45;

- the quantile of the distribution that relates to 0.6 is `qchisq (0.6, 5)`, which is 5.13;

- we can generate 100 random numbers from the Chi-squared distribution by using `rchisq (100, 5)`.

8.3.4   The F distribution

Box 8.4: The F distribution

Parameter(s): Degrees of freedom, ν_1 and ν_2 (it matters in which order these are given).
Mean: $\nu_2/(\nu_2 - 2)$ (for $\nu_2 > 2$).
Variance: $2\nu_2^2(\nu_1 + \nu_2 - 2)/(\nu_1(\nu_2 - 2)^2(\nu_2 - 4))$ for $\nu_2 > 4$.
Possible values: Positive.
Characteristics: Skewed.
Notation for a random variable X: $X \sim F_{\nu_1, \nu_2}$.

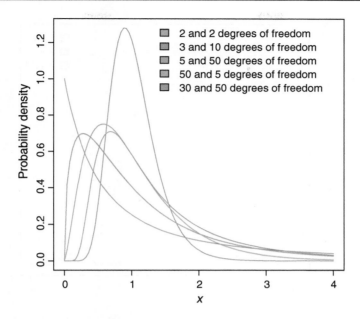

Figure 8.5 F distribution probability density.

Whereas the Chi-squared distribution was characterised by a single parameter – its degrees of freedom – the F distribution is characterised by two parameters, both of which are degrees of freedom. They control the distribution's shape. The density functions for various F distributions are plotted in Figure 8.5. Notice in particular that it matters which way around the degrees of freedom are given: an F distribution with 5 and 50 degrees of freedom is not the same as that with 50 and 5 degrees of freedom.

Densities, probabilities, quantiles, and random numbers using the F distribution are all possible, with `df ()`, `pf ()`, `qf ()`, and `rf ()` the appropriate functions this time. For example, if a random variable X had an F distribution with 5 and 8 degrees of freedom:

- the density function evaluated at $x = 3$ is `df (3, 5, 8)`, which is 0.06;

- the probability that X is less than 4 is `pf (4, 5, 8)`, which is 0.959;

- the quantile of the distribution that relates to 0.6 is `qf (0.6, 5, 8)`, which is 1.17;

- we can generate 100 random numbers from the F distribution by using `rf (100, 5, 8)`.

8.3.5 Student's *t* distribution

Box 8.5: The t-distribution

Parameter(s): Degrees of freedom, r.
Mean: 0.
Variance: $r/(r-2)$ for $r > 2$.
Possible values: Any.
Characteristics: Symmetric, bell-shaped.
Notation for a random variable X: $X \sim t_r$.

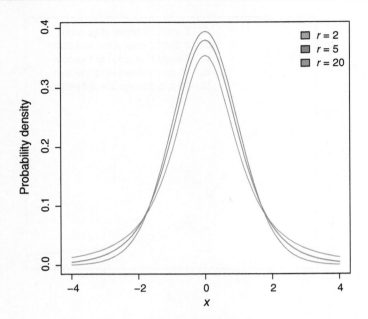

Figure 8.6   t-distribution probability density.

This famous distribution was first published by W.S. Gossett in 1908 under the pseudonym of 'Student' because his then employer, the Guinness Brewing company in Dublin, would not permit employees to publish under their own names. It is a distribution with one parameter – its degrees of freedom, r – and a random variable with a t-distribution can take any value along the real line. The standard version of the t-distribution is to assume its mean is 0. It is possible to define a non-central t-distribution with a non-zero mean, but we won't look at this here (same principles apply, however).

The density for various t-distributions are given in Figure 8.6; all of which are the standard zero-mean versions of the distribution. Notice that the t-distribution is bell-shaped like the Normal distribution, but that it has heavier (or 'fatter') tails. This means that extreme values are more likely with a t-distribution than with a normal. As the degrees of freedom increase however, the t-distribution approaches a Normal distribution with mean 0 and variance 1 (the so-called 'standard Normal distribution'). Technically, the t-distribution with infinite degrees of freedom is equivalent to the standard Normal distribution, while the t-distribution with one degree of freedom is equivalent to the Cauchy distribution.

Densities, probabilities, quantiles, and random numbers using the t-distribution are all possible, with `dt ()`, `pt ()`, `qt ()`, and `rt ()` the appropriate functions this time. For example, if a random variable had a t-distribution with 10 degrees of freedom:

- the density function evaluated at $x = 3$ is `dt (3, 10)`, which is 0.017;

- the probability that X is less than 4 is `pt (4, 10)`, which is almost 1;

- the quantile of the distribution that relates to 0.6 is `qt (0.6, 10)`, which is 0.26;

- we can generate 100 random numbers from the F-distribution by using `rt (100, 10)`.

8.3.6 The Gamma distribution

> **Box 8.6: The Gamma distribution**
>
> **Parameter(s)**: Shape, α, and rate, β.
> **Mean**: α/β.
> **Variance**: α/β^2.
> **Possible values**: Positive.
> **Characteristics**: Skewed.
> **Notation for a random variable** X: $X \sim \text{Gamma}(\alpha, \beta)$.

The Gamma distribution is a two-parameter distribution, where the parameters are traditionally known as *shape*, α, and *rate*, β. *R* also allows the Gamma distribution to be defined using *scale* instead of rate, where scale is the inverse of rate.

The Gamma distribution is defined over only positive values. Examples of gamma probability densities are given in Figure 8.7.

Note how $\alpha \leq 1$ produces strictly declining functions and $\alpha > 1$ produces humped curves, with the degree of skew declining as α increases.

Densities, probabilities, quantiles, and random numbers using the Gamma distribution are all possible, with `dgamma ()`, `pgamma ()`, `qgamma ()`, and `rgamma ()` the appropriate functions this time. For example, if a random variable had a Gamma distribution with parameters 10 and 5:

- the density function evaluated at $x = 1$ is `dgamma (1, 10, 5)`, which is 0.18;

- the probability that X is less than 1.5 is `pgamma (1.5, 10, 5)`, which is 0.22;

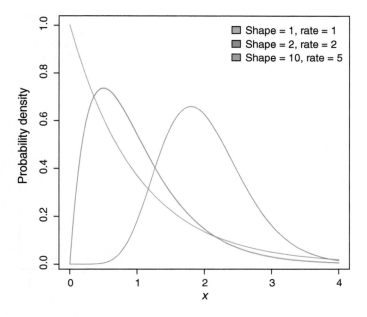

Figure 8.7 Gamma distribution probability density.

- the quantile of the distribution that relates to 0.8 is `qgamma (0.8, 10, 5)`, which is 0.83;

- we can generate 100 random numbers from the Gamma distribution by using `rgamma (100, 10, 5)`.

8.3.7 The Exponential distribution

Box 8.7: The Exponential distribution

Parameter(s): Rate, λ, with $\lambda > 0$.
Mean: $1/\lambda$.
Variance: $1/\lambda^2$.
Possible values: Positive.
Characteristics: Skewed.
Notation for a random variable X: $X \sim \mathrm{Exp}(\lambda)$.

The Exponential distribution is a one parameter distribution; indeed, it is a special case of the Gamma distribution. Its parameter is often known as a *rate* and is useful in modelling the times between events. Values from this distribution are always positive. Examples of the pdf in this case are in Figure 8.8.

Densities, probabilities, quantiles, and random numbers using the Exponential distribution are all possible, with `dexp ()`, `pexp ()`, `qexp ()`, and `rexp ()` the appropriate functions this time. For example if a random variable had an Exponential distribution with rate 1:

- the density function evaluated at $x = 2$ is `dexp (2, 1)`, which is 0.14;

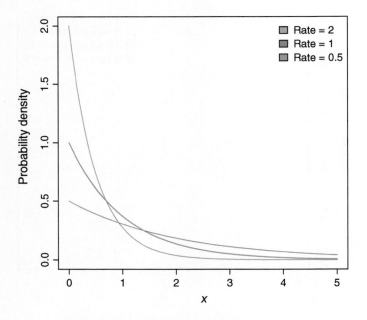

Figure 8.8 Exponential probability density.

- the probability that *X* is less than 4 is `pexp (4, 1)`, which is 0.98;

- the quantile of the distribution that relates to 0.6 is `qexp (0.6, 1)`, which is 0.92;

- we can generate 100 random numbers from the Exponential distribution by using `rexp (100, 1)`.

8.3.8 The Beta distribution

Box 8.8: The Beta distribution

Parameter(s): Two shape parameters, *a* and *b*, both greater than 0.
Mean: $a/(a + b)$.
Variance: $ab/(a + b)^2(a + b + 1)$.
Possible values: Any value in $[0, 1]$.
Characteristics: Bounded between 0 and 1.
Notation for a random variable *X*: $X \sim \text{Beta}(a, b)$.

The only possible values that we can get from a Beta distribution are between 0 and 1. It has two parameters – let us call them *a* and *b* – which are its shape parameters. The order that the shape parameters appear is important: a Beta distribution with shape parameters 1 and 5, say, is not the same as a Beta distribution with shape parameters 5 and 1.

Figure 8.9 shows just how different the Beta distribution's pdf can look as we change *a* and *b*. Notice that when $a = b = 1$, we get the Uniform distribution over $[0, 1]$: this is a special case of the Beta distribution.

Densities, probabilities, quantiles, and random numbers using the Beta distribution are all possible, with `dbeta ()`, `pbeta ()`, `qbeta ()`, and `rbeta ()` the appropriate functions this time.

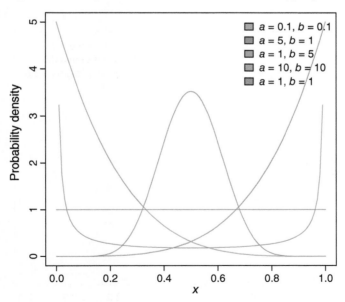

Figure 8.9 Beta probability density.

For example, if a random variable had an Exponential distribution with parameters 1 and 5:

- the density function evaluated at $x = 0.1$ is `dbeta (0.1, 1, 5)`, which is 3.28;

- the probability that X is less than 0.4 is `pbeta (0.4, 1, 5)`, which is 0.92;

- the quantile of the distribution that relates to a probability of 0.5 is `qbeta (0.5, 1, 5)`, which is 0.13;

- we can generate 100 random numbers from the Beta distribution by using `rbeta (100, 1, 5)`.

8.3.9   The Lognormal distribution

Box 8.9: The Lognormal distribution

Parameter(s): μ (any value) and $\sigma > 0$.
Mean: $\exp(\mu + \sigma^2/2)$.
Variance: $(\exp(\sigma^2) - 1)\exp(2\mu + \sigma^2)$.
Possible values: Positive.
Characteristics: Skewed.
Notation for a random variable X: $\ln(X) \sim N(\mu, \sigma^2)$.

Random variables with a Lognormal distribution take only positive values. If the logarithm of a lognormal random variable is taken, the result is a normal random variable, hence the name. Applications for the lognormal include the distribution of particle sizes in aggregates, flood flows, concentrations of air contaminants, and failure times. Examples of lognormal distributions are given in Figure 8.10.

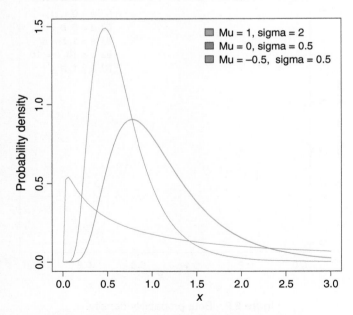

Figure 8.10   Lognormal probability density.

Densities, probabilities, quantiles, and random numbers using the Lognormal distribution are all possible, with `dlnorm ()`, `plnorm ()`, `qlnorm ()`, and `rlnorm ()` the appropriate functions this time. For example, if a random variable had a Lognormal distribution with $\mu = 0$ and $\sigma = 0.3$:

- the density function evaluated at $x = 1$ is `dlnorm (1, 0, 0.3)`, which is 1.33;

- the probability that X is less than 1.1 is `plnorm (1.1, 0, 0.3)`, which is 0.62;

- the quantile of the distribution that relates to a probability of 0.6 is `qlnorm (0.6, 0, 0.3)`, which is 1.08;

- we can generate 100 random numbers from this Lognormal distribution by using `rlnorm (100, 0, 0.3)`.

8.3.10 The Logistic distribution

Box 8.10: The Logistic distribution

Parameter(s): Location, μ (any value), and scale, $\sigma > 0$.
Mean: μ.
Variance: $\sigma^2 \pi^2 / 3$.
Possible values: Positive.
Characteristics: Symmetric, bell-shaped.
Notation for a random variable X: $X \sim \text{Logistic}(\mu, \sigma)$.

The Logistic is a unimodal, symmetric distribution on the real line with tails that are heavier than the Normal distribution. Its most famous role is that in *logistic regression*, which is a very popular model (see Sections 11.4.1, 11.4.2, and 11.4.6). Probability densities of various Logistic distributions are given in Figure 8.11.

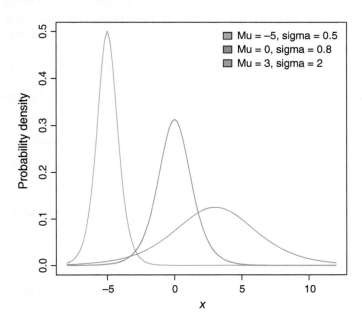

Figure 8.11 Logistic probability density.

When we take the exponential of a Logistic distribution, we get the so-called 'log-Logistic distribution'. It is, of course, positive.

Densities, probabilities, quantiles, and random numbers using the Logistic distribution are all possible, with `dlogis ()`, `plogis ()`, `qlogis ()`, and `rlogis ()` the appropriate functions this time. For example, if a random variable had a Logistic distribution with parameters 1 and 3:

- the density function evaluated at $x = 2$ is `dlogis (2, 1, 3)`, which is 0.08;

- the probability that X is less than 4 is `plogis (4, 1, 3)`, which is 0.73;

- the quantile of the distribution that relates to 0.6 is `qlogis (0.6, 1, 3)`, which is 2.22;

- we can generate 100 random numbers from the Logistic distribution by using `rlogis (100, 1, 3)`.

8.3.11 The Weibull distribution

Box 8.11: The Weibull distribution

Parameter(s): Shape, $\alpha > 0$, and scale, $\beta > 0$.
Mean: A function of α and β.
Variance: A function of α and β.
Possible values: Positive.
Characteristics: Skewed.
Notation for a random variable X: $X \sim \text{Weibull}(\alpha, \beta)$.

The Weibull is a two-parameter distribution, with Weibull random variables always positive. The distribution is characterised by its so-called 'scale and shape'; the larger the shape parameter, the more symmetric the distribution. It is commonly used in reliability and survival analysis and is useful in many other applications involving modelling behaviour. Whenever the shape parameter, α, is equal to 1, the Weibull reduces to the Exponential distribution. Densities of various Weibull distributions are given in Figure 8.12.

Densities, probabilities, quantiles, and random numbers using the Weibull distribution are all possible, with `dweibull ()`, `pweibull ()`, `qweibull ()`, and `rweibull ()` the appropriate functions this time. For example, if a random variable had a Weibull distribution with parameters 1 and 3:

- the density function evaluated at $x = 2$ is `dweibull (2, 1, 3)`, which is 0.17;

- the probability that X is less than 4 is `pweibull (4, 1, 3)`, which is 0.74;

- the quantile of the distribution that relates to 0.6 is `qweibull (0.6, 1, 3)`, which is 2.75;

- we can generate 100 random numbers from the Weibull distribution by using `rweibull (100, 1, 3)`.

8.3.12 Multivariate Normal distribution

Finally, we look at the Normal distribution again, but this time its *multivariate* version. A random quantity generated from this distribution will this time be a vector $(X_1, \ldots, X_k)$, say, where each

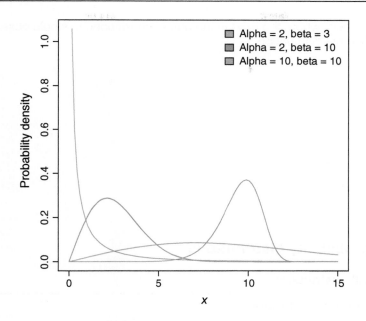

Figure 8.12 Weibull probability density.

element X_i of the vector will have a Normal distribution but the set of variables $\{X_1, \ldots, X_k\}$ are correlated.

The parameters of this distribution are the **mean vector** $\mu = (\mu_1, \ldots, \mu_k)$ and the **covariance matrix**, Σ:

$$\Sigma = \begin{bmatrix} \sigma_1^2 & \sigma_{12} & \cdots & \sigma_{1k} \\ \sigma_{21} & \sigma_2^2 & \cdots & \sigma_{2k} \\ \vdots & \vdots & \ddots & \vdots \\ \sigma_{k1} & \sigma_{k2} & \cdots & \sigma_k^2 \end{bmatrix}.$$

The entries in Σ are as follows: σ_i^2 is the *variance* of the ith element of the vector of random variables $(X_1, \ldots, X_k)$, and σ_{ij} (where $i \neq j$) is the *covariance* between X_i and X_j. Notice that this is the same as the covariance between X_j and X_i, σ_{ji}, hence the covariance matrix is **symmetric**. A matrix is said to be symmetric when it is equal to its transpose (see Section 3.11.6 for details).

With notation now defined, the distribution of a single element of a multivariate normal vector $(X_1, \ldots, X_k)$, let us say X_i, is normally distributed with mean μ_i and variance σ_i^2. The covariances from Σ only come into play when we want to say something about how two elements of the vector, say X_i and X_j where $i \neq j$, behave in relation to each other (i.e. how they co-vary).

In order to generate random numbers from the multivariate Normal distribution (which is the only function we'll consider here), we will need the `mvrnorm ()` function from the package `MASS` (Venables and Ripley, 2002). For example, suppose that we want to simulate five observations from the bivariate Normal distribution – so k is 2 in the above description – under the assumption that the mean vector is $(4, 8)$ and the covariance matrix is

$$\Sigma = \begin{bmatrix} 3 & 1 \\ 1 & 7 \end{bmatrix}.$$

We can do this as follows, where the rows in the output correspond to single observations from the given multivariate Normal distribution.

```
library(MASS)
mvrnorm (5 , mu = c (4, 8), matrix (c (3, 1, 1, 7), 2 ))

          [,1]      [,2]
[1,]  3.681000  7.266784
[2,]  2.353227  9.104023
[3,]  5.260096  4.518117
[4,]  2.070355  8.996658
[5,]  5.223700  7.794384
```

8.4   Discrete probability distributions

8.4.1   The Bernoulli distribution

Box 8.12: The Bernoulli distribution

Parameter(s): Probability of success, p.
Mean: p.
Variance: $p(1 - p)$.
Possible values: $\{0, 1\}$.
Characteristics: Related to the Binomial distribution.
Notation for a random variable X: $X \sim \text{Bern}(p)$.

This is the distribution underlying tests with a binary response variable. The response takes one of only two values: it is 1 with probability p ('a success') and is 0 with probability $1 - p$ (a 'failure'). This in turn defines the distribution's pmf.

It might be instructive to see why the mean of the Bernoulli distribution in R is just the probability p: there are just two possible outcomes which are either a success (a value of 1) with probability p, or a failure (a value of 0) with probability $1 - p$. Thus, the expectation of our random variable X is

$$E(X) = 0 \times (1 - p) + 1 \times p = 0 + p = p.$$

Computations in R involving the Bernoulli distribution are generally done using the binomial, which is discussed next, as the former is a special case of the latter.

8.4.2   The Binomial distribution

Box 8.13: The Binomial distribution

Parameter(s): Probability of success, p, and number of trials, n.
Mean: np.
Variance: $np(1 - p)$.
Possible values: $\{0, 1, 2, \ldots, n\}$.
Characteristics: All trials are independent of one another.
Notation for a random variable X: $X \sim \text{Bin}(n, p)$.

The binomial is an extension of the Bernoulli distribution: instead of just considering what happens in one trial (for which the outcome is either a success or a failure), we now consider what happens in n of these trials. It counts the number of successes in total, out of the n trials, hence a binomial random variable can take on only whole numbers between 0 (indicating that none of the trials was a success) and n (indicating that all trials succeeded).

Suppose that we are interested in the number of successes from four independent trials, where the probability of a success on any given trial is 0.3. Notice that we don't care *which* trials succeeded and which trials didn't; we are just interested in the *count* of the successful trials. Counting how many ways a particular result could have arisen forms a crucial part of the probability calculations for the Binomial distribution.

If, at the end of all four trials, we were told that two of the four were a success, how could this have arisen? We could list all possible ways:

success, success, failure, failure
success, failure, success, failure
success, failure, failure, success
failure, success, success, failure
failure, success, failure, success
failure, failure, success, success

so there are six in total. All six are equally likely, with any of them having probability $(0.3^2 0.7^2)$ which account for two successes and two failures. We can therefore compute the probability of observing two successes out of four trials as

$$6 \times 0.3^2 \times 0.7^2 = 0.2646,$$

where we acknowledge that we see two successes (each with probability 0.3), and therefore, two failures (each with probability 0.7) and that there are six ways of observing this result if we look at the order of the successes and failures.

As the number of trials increases, it becomes rather cumbersome to list all possible ways of finding a particular number of successes among a set number of trials. An easy-to-implement formula to compute the number of ways of getting x items (successes) out of n items (trials) is the combinatorial formula

$$\binom{n}{x} = \frac{n!}{x!(n-x)!} .$$

The 'exclamation mark' means 'factorial'; for instance, $5! = 5 \times 4 \times 3 \times 2 \times 1 = 120$. This formula has immense practical utility. We can certainly use it to help us enumerate binomial probabilities, but it also shows, for example, how unlikely one is to win the National Lottery in which six numbers are selected without replacement between 1 and 59. We can use the built-in choose () function for this, which is roughly a 1 in 45 million chance of winning the jackpot.

```
choose (59, 6)

[1] 45057474
```

The general form of the pmf of the Binomial distribution is given by

$$p(x) = \binom{n}{x} p^x (1-p)^{n-x},$$

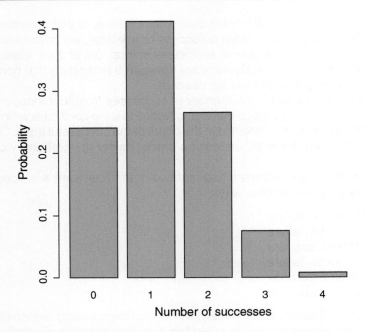

Figure 8.13 Binomial probability mass function for Bin(4, 0.3).

using the combinatorial formula above. Comparing this to the calculation above: this is indeed the form of the probability of two successes in four trials we computed. Again, under the assumption of four trials and probability of success of 0.3 on each one, and now armed with the general formula, we can easily state the pmf (that is, we can quickly compute the probability of 0, 1, 3, and 4 successes out of the four trials). The resulting pmf is given in Figure 8.13.

The mean of the Binomial distribution is np and the variance is $np(1 - p)$. Since $1 - p$ is less than 1, it is obvious that **the variance is less than the mean** for the Binomial distribution (except, of course, in the trivial case when $p = 0$ and the variance is 0).

The mass function, probabilities, quantiles, and random numbers using the Binomial distribution are all possible, with dbinom (), pbinom (), qbinom (), and rbinom () the appropriate functions this time. For example, if a random variable X had a Binomial distribution with $n = 10$ and $p = 0.6$:

- the mass function at $x = 2$ is $P(X = 1)$, which can be evaluated using dbinom (1, 10, 0.6), is 0.01;

- the probability that X is less than or equal to 4 is pbinom (4, 10, 0.6), which is 0.17;

- the smallest value q such that $P(X \le q) \ge 0.5$ is qbinom (0.5, 10, 0.6), which is 6 (note that we will always get a whole number when asking such questions because of the nature of the Binomial distribution);

- we can generate 100 random numbers from this Binomial distribution by using rbinom (100, 10, 0.6).

This is easily adapted to the Bernoulli distribution by specifying the number of trials to be 1. For example, if a random variable X had a Bernoulli distribution with $p = 0.6$, then we can generate 100 random numbers from this Bernoulli distribution by using `rbinom (100, 1, 0.6)`.

8.4.3 The Geometric distribution

Box 8.14: The Geometric distribution

Parameter(s): Probability of success, p.
Mean: $1/p$ or $(1-p)/p$ depending on definition.
Variance: $(1-p)/p^2$.
Possible values: $\{1, 2, 3, \dots\}$ or $\{0, 1, 2, \dots\}$, depending on definition.
Characteristics: All trials are independent of one another.
Notation for a random variable X: $X \sim \text{Geom}(p)$.

There are two 'versions' of the Geometric distribution, with no common consensus as to which one is *the* Geometric distribution.

In one version of the Geometric distribution, suppose that we have a series of independent Bernoulli trials, each with probability p of success. How long do we wait until we see the first success? That is, how many trials do we conduct until we see our first success? Letting W denote the number of trials until the first success occurs, the density function is then

$$f_1(w) = p(1-p)^{w-1}.$$

(That is, we observe $(w-1)$ failures first, each with probability $(1-p)$, and then a success, which happens with probability p). Notice that unlike the Binomial distribution, we do not have to account for how many ways there are of observing this: the whole point is that we stop when we see the first success. This geometric random variable counts *how many trials we undertake until we see a success* and so can take any value in $\{1, 2, 3, \dots\}$. The minimum value is 1 here, which indicates we saw a success on the first trial.

Contrast this to the other version of the Geometric distribution: suppose that we have a series of independent Bernoulli trials, each with probability p of success. Now, let Y be the number of failures until the first success occurs. The density function, therefore, is

$$f_2(y) = p(1-p)^y.$$

(That is, we observe y failures first, each with probability $(1-p)$, and then a success, which happens with probability p). This geometric random variable counts *how many failures we see before observing a success* and so can take any value in $\{0, 1, 2, \dots\}$. The minimum value is 0 here, which indicates we saw a success on the first trial (and therefore there were no failures beforehand). Often, this version of the Geometric distribution is known as the 'shifted Geometric' distribution.

Notice all that has happened in the second version of the Geometric distribution is that the values of the random variable have shifted down by one, but the like-for-like probabilities are the same (e.g. the probability that a geometric random variable using the first formulation is equal to 2 is the same as the probability that a geometric random variable using the second formulation is equal to 1). An example of the pmf of the geometric (with probability of success 0.7 on each trial) is given

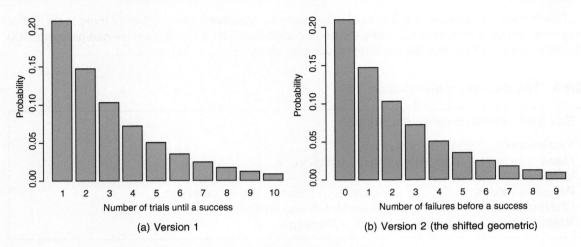

Figure 8.14 Two versions of the Geometric distribution.

in Figure 8.14, for which this relationship should be clear. On the left-hand side is the first formulation, while on the right, we have the second version of the Geometric distribution. The probabilities are the same, but the labels on the x-axis are different: on the right, they are one unit less than those on the left.

Given that the values that the two types of Geometric distribution can take differ, the mean of the two distributions will be different. In the first formulation, the mean is simply $1/p$, while in the second, given that we know it is simply shifted down by a value of one, it is

$$\frac{1}{p} - 1 = \frac{1-p}{p}.$$

The variance is the same for both distributions at $\frac{1-p}{p^2}$: the *spread* of the two distributions doesn't change, only its location.

The mass function, probabilities, quantiles, and random numbers using the Geometric distribution are all possible, with dgeom (), pgeom (), qgeom (), and rgeom () the appropriate functions this time. Note that this is for the first version of the geometric indicated above. For example, if a random variable X had a Geometric distribution with $p = 0.6$ (remember here that the possible values are $\{1, 2, 3, \ldots\}$):

- the mass function at $x = 1$ is $P(X = 1)$, which can be evaluated using dgeom (1, 0.6), gives 0.24;

- the probability that X is less than or equal to 4 is pgeom (4, 0.6), which is 0.99;

- the smallest value q such that $P(X \le q) \ge 0.5$ is qgeom (0.5, 0.6), which is 0;

- we can generate 100 random numbers from this Geometric distribution by using rgeom (100, 0.6).

If we want the shifted Geometric instead, we can still do this using the above functions, but this time adjusting the inputs. For example, if a random variable X had a *shifted* Geometric distribution with $p = 0.6$ (remember here that the possible values are $\{0, 1, 2, \ldots\}$):

- the mass function at $x = 3$ is $P(X = 3)$, which can be evaluated using `dgeom (4, 0.6)`, gives 0.1 (note: we are looking for the probability of 3 failures before then seeing a success, therefore, 4 trials in total in the language of the first type of Geometric distribution);

- the probability that X is less than or equal to 6 is `pgeom (7, 0.6)`, which is 0.99 (see above for reasoning why we use 7 and not 6 in `pgeom ()`);

- the smallest value q such that $P(X \leq q) \geq 0.8$ is `qgeom (0.8, 0.6) - 1`, which is 0 (we need to shift the answer down by one unit – see Figure 8.14 for a graphic representation of why this is the case);

- we can generate 100 random numbers from this Geometric distribution by using `rgeom (100, 0.6)-1` (again we need to shift all random numbers down by one unit so that this is representative of the *shifted* Geometric).

8.4.4 The Hypergeometric distribution

Box 8.15: The Hypergeometric distribution

Parameter(s): Number in population, N, number of specified type, m, number chosen, n.
Mean: nm/N.
Variance: A function of n, m, N.
Possible values: $\{0, \dots, n\}$ (though some of these may have probability zero).
Characteristics: Sampling is with replacement.
Notation for a random variable X: $X \sim$ Hypergeometric(N, m, n).

'Balls in urns' are the classic sort of problem solved by this distribution. Suppose that there are N coloured balls in the statistician's famous urn: b of them are blue and $m = N - b$ of them are red. Now a sample of n balls is removed from the urn; this is sampling *without replacement*. The Hypergeometric distribution counts the number of blue balls that are in our sample. (Note, however, that the Hypergeometric doesn't just apply to balls in urns; this is merely a convenient way of describing it!)

The density function of the hypergeometric is

$$f(x) = \frac{\binom{N-m}{x} \binom{m}{n-x}}{\binom{N}{n}}.$$

This gives the probability that x of these n balls are blue. When we set $N = 20$ (total number of balls in the urn), $m = 16$ (number of blue balls in urn), and $n = 5$ (take a sample of size five), then the pmf is depicted in Figure 8.15. Notice that a value of zero is impossible here: we take five balls without replacement from the urn, and there are only four red balls in there (the rest are blue).

The mass function, probabilities, quantiles, and random numbers using the Hypergeometric distribution are all possible, with `dhyper ()`, `phyper ()`, `qhyper ()`, and `rhyper ()` the appropriate functions this time. For example if a random variable X had a Hypergeometric distribution with $N = 20, m = 16, n = 5$:

- the mass function at $x = 1$ is $P(X = 1)$, which can be evaluated using `dhyper (1, 16, 4, 5)`, gives 0 (note – the parameters required by R are the number of blue balls, and the remaining number of (red) balls, and not the total number of balls);

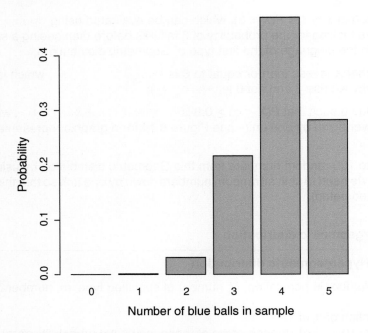

Figure 8.15 Hypergeometric probability mass function.

- the probability that X is less than or equal to 4 is `phyper (4, 16, 4, 5)`, which is 0.72;
- the smallest value q such that $P(X \le q) \ge 0.5$ is `qhyper (0.5, 16, 4, 5)`, which is 4;
- we can generate 100 random numbers from this Geometric distribution by using `rhyper (100, 16, 4, 5)`.

8.4.5 The Multinomial distribution

Box 8.16: The Multinomial distribution

Parameter(s): Number of trials, n, and probability of particular outcomes, $p = (p_1, \ldots, p_t)$.
Mean: Expected number of times we see outcome i, from a set of n trials, $\overline{n}p_i$.
Variance: Variance of the number of times we see outcome i, from a set of n trials, $np_i(1 - p_i)$.
Possible values: Vector of length t, each element between 0 and n.
Characteristics: Outcomes are vectors. Must have that $p_1 + \cdots + p_t = 1$. All trials are independent of one another.
Notation for a random variable N: $N \sim$ Multinomial$(n, \underline{p})$.

The Multinomial distribution is essentially an extension of the Binomial distribution, but this time there are more than two possible outcomes for each trial (hence, *multi-* rather than *bi*-nomial).

Suppose that there are t possible outcomes (let us label these $\{1, 2, \ldots, t\}$) from an experimental trial, and the outcome i has probability p_i. Now allow n independent trials – each of which will result in one of the t outcomes – and ask how many of the trials resulted in each of the t possible outcomes.

What we get, in that case, is a vector $N = (N_1, \ldots, N_t)$, where N_i denotes the number of times we saw outcome i out of the n trials.

The mass function here is an extension of the pmf of the Binomial distribution:

$$P(N = (n_1, \ldots, n_t)) = \frac{n!}{n_1! n_2! n_3! \ldots n_t!} p_1^{n_1} p_2^{n_2} p_3^{n_3} \ldots p_t^{n_t},$$

where $n_1 + \cdots + n_t = n$ (the total number of trials) and $p_1 + \cdots + p_t = 1$ (so that each trial must result in one of the t distinct outcomes). We cannot plot the mass function in this case as it is too cumbersome.

Notice that if we just looked at one of the possible outcomes, let us say the ith outcome, and counted the number of trials which resulted like this, we get the Binomial distribution. That is, if $N = (N_1, \ldots, N_t)$ has a Multinomial distribution with parameters n and $p = (p_1, \ldots, p_t)$, then if we look at the distribution of just N_i, this has a Binomial distribution with n trials and probability of success p_i in each.

R has functions to deal with the Multinomial distribution, which can be found in the `stats` package (R Core Team, 2019). The functions available are the `dmultinom ()` and `rmultinom ()`. (It does not make sense to talk about quantiles or cumulative probabilities here: we are dealing with random vectors instead of random variables.) Take an example with three outcomes (say black, red and blue, so $t = 3$), where the first outcome is twice as likely as the other two ($p_1 = 0.5, p_2 = 0.25, p_3 = 0.25$), noting that the probabilities sum to 1. Let us suppose that we take the number of trials to be 5 (so that each one will result in either black or red or blue):

- the mass function at $(1, 2, 2)$ (so seeing 1 black, 2 red, and 2 blue), or $P(N = (1, 2, 2))$, which can be evaluated using `dmultinom ( c (1, 2, 2), 5, c(0.5, 0.25, 0.25))`, gives 0.06;

- we can generate 100 random numbers from this Multinomial distribution by using `rmultinom (100, 5, c(0.5, 0.25, 0.25))`. Note that this will generate 100 random vectors, each of length 3 (the number of possible outcomes), and will randomly spread five trials among the three possible outcomes according to the given probabilities.

8.4.6 The Poisson distribution

Box 8.17: The Poisson distribution

Parameter(s): λ (often referred to as a rate).
Mean: λ.
Variance: λ.
Possible values: $\{0, 1, 2, \ldots\}$.
Characteristics: All events are independent of one another.
Notation for a random variable X: $X \sim \text{Poisson}(\lambda)$.

This is one of the most useful and important of the discrete probability distributions for describing count data: the random variable describes how many times a particular event was observed (e.g. number of lightning strikes in a particular area over a specified period of time, number of people entering a particular shop each day).

The Poisson is a one-parameter distribution – the rate – which in essence describes the rate or frequency with which the events of interest occur. The mass function of a Poisson distribution with parameter (rate) λ is

$$p(x) = \frac{e^{-\lambda} \lambda^x}{x!}.$$

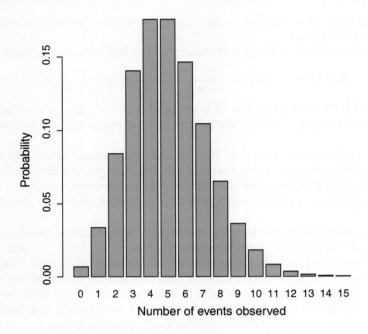

Figure 8.16   Poisson probability mass function.

This gives the probability that we observe *x* events (in a specified time period or space). The mass function when $\lambda = 5$ is shown in Figure 8.16. This distribution has the interesting property that its variance is equal to its mean, both of which are equal to the rate, λ.

The mass function, probabilities, quantiles, and random numbers using the Poisson distribution are all possible, with `dpois ()`, `ppois ()`, `qpois ()`, and `rpois ()` the appropriate functions this time. For example, if a random variable *X* had a Poisson distribution with $\lambda = 5$:

- the mass function at $x = 1$ is $P(X = 1)$, which can be evaluated using `dpois (1, 5)`, gives 0.03;

- the probability that *X* is less than or equal to 4 is `ppois (4, 5)`, which is 0.44;

- the smallest value *q* such that $P(X \leq q) \geq 0.5$ is `qpois (0.5, 5)`, which is 5;

- we can generate 100 random numbers from this Poisson distribution by using `rpois (100, 5)`.

8.4.7   The Negative Binomial distribution

Box 8.18: The Negative Binomial distribution

Parameter(s): Number of failures, *r*, and probability of failure in each trial, *p*.
Mean: $pr/(1 - p)$.
Variance: $pr/(1 - p)^2$.
Possible values: $\{0, 1, 2, \dots\}$.
Characteristics: All trials are independent of each other.
Notation for a random variable *X*: $X \sim \text{NB}(r, p)$.

Suppose that we observe a sequence of trials, each of which can succeed or fail. The negative binomial counts the number of successful trials we observe before we see a particular number of failures. For example, if we are willing to observe up to and including five failures before we stop observing a particular set of trials, how many successes will we have seen up until we stopped? It makes sense that this type of variable can take any (whole) number, starting from 0 (that is, we see five failures in a row, so stop before observing any successes).

The mass function this time, for a specified number of failures r and probability p of any given trial succeeding, is

$$f(x) = \binom{x-1}{r-1} p^r (1-p)^{x-r}.$$

This, of course, gives the probability of observing x successes, when the probability that any given trial succeeds is p and we stop when we see the rth failure. An example of the mass function, when $r = 5$ and $p = 0.4$ is given in Figure 8.17

The mass function, probabilities, quantiles, and random numbers using the Negative Binomial distribution are all possible, with `dnbinom ()`, `pnbinom ()`, `qnbinom ()`, and `rnbinom ()` the appropriate functions this time. For example, if a random variable X had a Negative Binomial distribution with success probability of 0.4 and number of failures equal to 5:

- the mass function at $x = 1$ is $P(X = 1)$, which can be evaluated using `dnbinom (1, 5, 0.4)`, gives 0.03;

- the probability that X is less than or equal to 4 is `pnbinom (4, 5, 0.4)`, which is 0.27;

- the smallest value q such that $P(X \leq q) \geq 0.5$ is `qnbinom (0.5, 5, 0.4)`, which is 7;

- we can generate 100 random numbers from this Negative Binomial distribution by using `rnbinom (100, 5, 0.4)`.

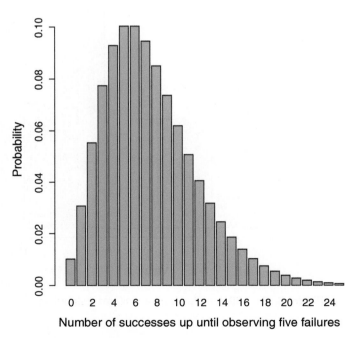

Figure 8.17   Negative binomial probability mass function.

Note that, like the Geometric distribution, there are different formulations of the Negative Binomial distribution. See Ross, 1998 for more information.

8.5   The central limit theorem

Suppose that we have collected data on a particular variable, but we don't know which distribution the data come from. We might want to estimate the population mean, which is straightforward enough: we estimate it using the sample mean. But this gives a single number – how will this vary if we were to repeat the data collection again and again?

The central limit theorem is a very powerful result that enables us to say something useful about the population mean of a random variable, even when we don't know its underlying distribution, as long as we collect enough samples of the random variable.

If we take repeated equally sized samples from a population with finite variance and calculate their averages, then the averages will be normally distributed. This is called the **central limit theorem**.

Let us demonstrate it using *R*'s functions to generate data from a specific distribution. We can take one hundred uniformly distributed random numbers between 0 and 10 and work out the average. Typically, the average will be around 5 – the mean of this Uniform distribution – but, of course, it will vary from sample to sample. Let us look at the histogram of observations for one such sample of 100 observations, given in Figure 8.18. This should look roughly (though not exactly) like the pdf of the uniform, with its characteristic 'flat-top'.

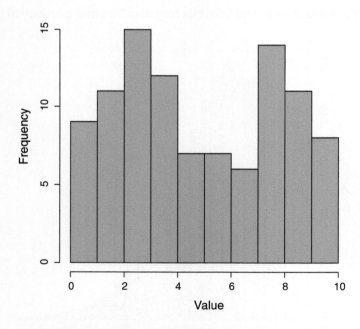

Figure 8.18   100 samples from a Uniform distribution.

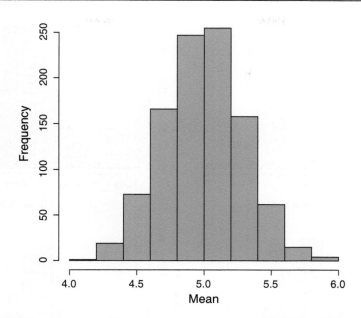

Figure 8.19   1000 sample means from a Uniform distribution. Each sample has 100 observations.

For this particular sample, the mean is 4.8. What if we were to repeat this experiment? The sample mean is likely to change, but by how much? Let us repeat this experiment a further 1000 times. Each time we'll record the sample mean; the histogram of all 1000 sample means is in Figure 8.19.

The histogram indicates a nice bell-shaped curve, and though we won't prove it here, the distribution of the sample mean is approximately normally distributed with mean 4.99 (roughly the mean of the original distribution) and variance 0.08 (roughly the original variance, 100/12, divided by the sample size of 100).

Figure 8.20 shows four more examples of the distribution of sample means when the underlying distribution is non-normal. Each sample has 100 observations, and the sampling is repeated 1000 times.

The central limit theorem really works. Almost any distribution, even a 'badly behaved' one like the Uniform distribution (which for which the distribution looks nothing like the normal), will result in a Normal distribution for the sample means. But we must be careful, however: when we take very small samples from a distribution the central limit theorem might not hold. We can't put a minimum sample size to guarantee the central limit theorem, but a sample size of at least 30 often does the trick.

But aside from novelty, what practical purpose does this result have? It turns out that it helps us in many ways. We won't be using the result directly, and we may not even notice that the mathematics underpinning some of what we discuss in the rest of this book is based on the central limit theorem, but it is there: in creating confidence intervals for population means, in hypothesis testing, and even in inference around building regression models.

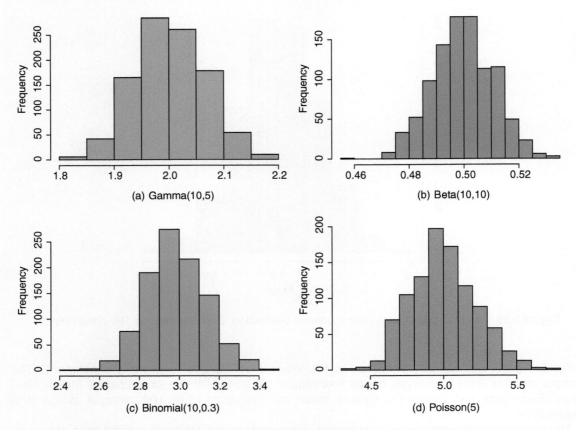

Figure 8.20   Distribution of the sample mean using different sampling distributions.

References

R Core Team. (2019). *R: A language and environment for statistical computing*. R Foundation for Statistical Computing. Vienna, Austria. https://www.R-project.org/.

Ross, S. M. (1998). *A first course in probability* (Fifth). Prentice Hall.

Venables, W. N., & Ripley, B. D. (2002). *Modern applied statistics with S* (Fourth) [ISBN 0-387-95457-0]. Springer. https://www.stats.ox.ac.uk/pub/MASS4/.

9

Testing

Box 9.1:

Population   The group to which we want to apply the conclusion, e.g. Canadian women.

Sample   The subgroup of the population for which we have data.

One of the most popular (as in frequently performed) tasks in statistics is to draw conclusions about a population when we only have data for a subset or a sample of that population. In this chapter, we will consider two such tasks:

- Calculating a confidence interval (**CI**) for a population statistic such as the mean or the variance;

- Comparing population statistics to each other or to specific values or distributions, using statistical **tests**.

The calculations in *R* in both cases are extremely straightforward and, where appropriate, carried out simultaneously. However, selecting and defining an appropriate CI or test, and then interpreting the results are fraught with pitfalls and generally performed badly, frequently in published papers.

The framework for tests (CIs use a subset) is the following:

1. Define the question under consideration in terms of statistical hypotheses. This will determine the general sort of test to be carried out;

2. Check the assumptions that lay behind the tests. This will help pin down the specific test (and possibly the specific hypotheses) that is appropriate;

3. Carry out the test;

4. Interpret the results of the test in terms of the hypotheses;

5. Translate those results into a conclusion for the population being studied.

The R Book, Third Edition. Elinor Jones, Simon Harden and Michael J. Crawley.
© 2023 John Wiley & Sons Ltd. Published 2023 by John Wiley & Sons Ltd.
Companion website: www.wiley.com/go/jones/therbook3e

In this chapter, we will begin by examining the general principles for conducting tests/CIs (items 1, 2, and 4). It is important that these are well understood before moving on to the rest of the chapter where tests/CIs for specific comparisons (item 3) are described. They are organised by data type, initially continuous or discrete. The final issues that we will cover are an alternative approach to testing/CIs known as bootstrapping, how to interpret results when multiple tests are performed, and calculating sample sizes for tests/CIs. There are hundreds of statistical tests: we will touch on a subset of them here.

A final encouragement: before leaping into tests and CIs, have a look at your data by using summary statistics and plots. These may suggest helpful lines of analysis. A summary of all the tests used in this chapter is given in Table 9.1.

9.1 Principles

9.1.1 Defining the question to be tested

We have a question that we want to answer about a population, e.g. are women from Canada taller on average than women from Burundi, or does a hypothetical subatomic particle exist; and some data from a sample of that population. Our first task is to create a statistical **null hypothesis**, H_0, about the population. When we carry out the test (this section does not apply to CIs), we will assume that this null hypothesis, together with the assumptions covered in Section 9.1.2, are true and that will enable us to carry out the mathematics required to draw our conclusion. For the mathematics to work, the null hypothesis needs to be straightforward and it will usually describe the boring or negative outcome. For instance:

- H_0: the average height of women in Canada is the same as the average height of women in Burundi;

- H_0: a new subatomic particle with a specific mass does not exist.

We might then be interested in a specific **alternative hypothesis**, H_1, which may not be the logically exhaustive converse of H_0, for instance: H_1: women in Canada are taller than women in Burundi on average.

The first thing to keep in mind is that we will be testing H_0 and not H_1. It would be much more satisfactory if we could directly test the assumption that Canadian women are taller than Burundian women on average, but the mathematics of the test would not then work. So we can only come to a conclusion about H_0. Second, since we are only examining a sample of the population, we cannot come to a definite conclusion: we have not studied the complete population and so our conclusion will express a level of uncertainty. Finally, as is usual with much scientific testing, we can only express the conclusion in terms of the strength of evidence against H_0.

This all sounds rather depressing and inconclusive. However, there are approaches that will result in more definite conclusions:

- use as large a sample size as possible. This will reduce the level of uncertainty in the conclusion;

- repeat the experiment independently of the original work, and then analyse that. This ought to reduce experimental bias and is essential for the results to have long-term validity.

We will return to interpreting the results of tests in Section 9.1.3.

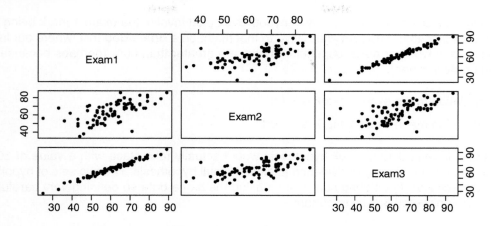

Figure 9.1   Scatter plots comparing the marks from exams.

Let us illustrate these ideas using the exams dataset. This shows the marks out of 100 for 88 students, each taking three exams:

```
exams <- read.csv ("exams.csv")
head (exams)

  Exam1 Exam2 Exam3
1    79    81    80
2    58    72    61
3    44    35    44
4    67    67    69
5    61    61    66
6    53    51    58

plot (exams, pch = 20)
```

We can see from Figure 9.1 that the marks from exams 1 and 3 are highly correlated. In the same way that the plot () function interprets the exams dataframe intelligently, we can examine all correlations in a very straightforward way:

```
cor (exams)

           Exam1      Exam2      Exam3
Exam1 1.0000000 0.6369653 0.9867625
Exam2 0.6369653 1.0000000 0.6127684
Exam3 0.9867625 0.6127684 1.0000000
```

We might be interested in comparing the mean score in exam 1 to a specific mark, say 60%, perhaps because the organisation running the exams has decided that it would like the mean mark to be that. In that case our hypotheses would be

H_0 The population mean exam 1 mark is 60%;

H_1 The population mean exam 1 mark is not 60%.

This is a **two-sided** test as the alternative hypothesis could involve the exam 1 mark being either greater than or less than 60%. An alternative to that might be a **one-sided** test, where our interest might solely lie in whether mean population marks are greater than 60% (perhaps because of an interest in grade inflation):

H_0 The population mean exam 1 mark is $\leq 60\%$;

H_1 The population mean exam 1 mark is $> 60\%$.

The calculations regarding the null hypothesis would actually take place with a value of 60% as they would provide the strongest evidence against the null hypothesis. The two sets of hypotheses above might well lead to differing conclusions using the same data so defining very carefully the question to be answered is very important.

9.1.2   Assumptions

All statistical tests and CIs make assumptions which come in two flavours:

1. That the data in the sample are randomly selected from the population about which we want to draw a conclusion. If this is not the case, then the conclusion may be invalid. For instance, the conclusion of a test to measure the effect that exercise has on cognitive ability where the sample is mostly male university students, should not be extended to the population as a whole. Further discussion is outside the scope of this book and, in practice, the assumption is virtually impossible to achieve. An understanding of the extent to which it has been achieved is important in drawing wider inferences;

2. Some tests (known as **parametric tests**) and CIs make distributional assumptions about the population data. The most common is that population data are normally distributed, and this particular assumption is covered in more detail in Section 9.2.5. Tests that do not make these distributional assumptions are known as **non-parametric**.

For our `exams` dataset, we can assume that the sample was randomly selected from the population (of students). However, we will need to check that the population data come from a Normal distribution and we do this in Section 9.2.5. The outcome is that we are happy with the normality assumption for exams 1 and 3, but not for exam 2.

9.1.3   Interpreting results

The *R* output from a test contains a lot of information, including the CI, that will vary by test. However, the key data to look out for are

- *p*-value This will be present for all tests. It can be defined as the probability that the sample data, or data more extreme, would have arisen *if the assumptions and H_0 are true*.

- **confidence interval** This will be present for all parametric and some non-parametric tests where we are trying to estimate a parameter. It represents a, say, 92% interval for that population parameter, and if we were to sample from the population 100 times, we would expect the actual population parameter to lie in roughly 92 of the resulting confidence intervals. Again, this is based on the assumptions being true.

Interpretations of both of these values are poorly described and frequently, in practice, erroneous.

However, before we consider that, let us go back to our exam data and run a test. We have a sample of 88 students with a mean mark in exam 1 of 60.67, which is close to our target of 60%, but we are interested in the population mean. Fortunately, there are statistical tests that we can use to check that. In this case, as the assumptions are met, we can use a simple t-test and we will request a 92% confidence interval:

```
t.test (x = exams$Exam1, mu = 60, conf.level = 0.92)


One Sample t-test

data:  exams$Exam1
t = 0.51809, df = 87, $p$-value = 0.6057
alternative hypothesis: true mean is not equal to 60
92 percent confidence interval:
 58.37812 62.96279
sample estimates:
mean of x
 60.67045
```

The default setting for H_1 is displayed in the output, as are the p-value and 92% confidence interval. What can we conclude? If our assumptions and H_0 are true, then the probability of ending up with our data or more extreme is 0.606. This does not seem at all unlikely and so *we have no evidence against our null hypothesis that the mean population exam mark is 60%*. This does not imply that H_0 is true nor that H_1 is false. The strongest statement that we can make (in statistical terms) is that the data are not incompatible with H_0. The confidence interval for the population mean is (58.38, 62.96) and a mark of 60 falls comfortably within that.

Box 9.2: Nutritional statistics

The use of p-values is similar to eating fast food: superficially tasty but neither nutritious nor satisfying in the long term. There are healthier statistical techniques: try, for instance, confidence intervals or building (linear) models. These can give you more insight into the data and leave you a happier and healthier statistician.

Before we look at another example, here are some interpretations of p-values (we will use 0.606 from above) that are not valid:

- the probability that the null hypothesis is true is 0.606;

- the null hypothesis should be accepted;

- the alternative hypothesis should be rejected.

And, likewise, incorrect interpretations of confidence intervals (**CI**s) – we will use 92%:

- for a specific CI, the probability that the population value being estimated (e.g. mean) is contained within (or belongs to) that CI is 92%;

- we are 92% certain that the sample mean belongs to the CI (should be population mean).

Assuming that our assumptions are OK, what is the *p*-value where our conclusion might change from no evidence against H_0 (as in our test) to some (or a stronger word) evidence against H_0? There is no right answer and certainly no mathematical justification for a clear cut off point. As the *p*-value becomes smaller, our evidence against H_0 becomes stronger and the results should be interpreted in terms of both the sample size (a larger sample will detect smaller differences) and subject matter relevance (for instance is the confidence interval significant as far as the topic under consideration is concerned?). Large *p*-values tell us nothing about the alternative hypothesis. Experience counts here, so we should involve an experienced statistician in interpreting tests. Above all, *we must not blindly treat 5% as a magical boundary between significant and otherwise*.

We have avoided using the term statistically significant as it has been so badly abused. It might be clearer to say that very small *p*-values indicate **weird shit** in the data, given the null hypothesis and any assumptions.

9.2 Continuous data

We will look at some of the most common topics for testing aspects of a continuous dataset:

- comparing a population average to a specific value (Section 9.2.1);
- comparing the averages of two populations (Section 9.2.2);
- comparing the averages of more than two populations (Section 9.2.3);
- comparing the population distribution to a specific named distribution such as the Gamma (Section 9.2.4).

In many cases, the equivalent CI would give an interval for the average or difference in averages. We might treat a discrete dataset, such as `exams`, as continuous if there is a wide enough range of values: after all, continuous data are usually rounded. The specific test/CI chosen will depend upon assumptions (see Section 9.1.2), the most common being:

- do the population data have a Normal distribution (Section 9.2.5);
- do the two populations have the same variance (Section 9.2.6)?

Checking these assumptions may involve further tests!

9.2.1 Single population average

We have already seen an example of a t-test where we have a single sample of data and wish to know whether the population mean has a specific value (Section 9.1.2).

We can investigate the matter further by examining the data from Michelson's famous experiment in 1879 to measure the speed of light (Michelson, 1880) with a sample of 20 observations. The dataset `light` contains his results in km s^{-1}, but with 299,000 subtracted.

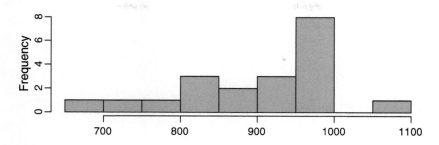

Figure 9.2 Histogram of estimates of the speed of light from `light` (-299,000).

```
light <- read.table ("light.txt", header = T)
head (light)

  speed
1   850
2   740
3   900
4  1070
5   930
6   850

summary (light$speed)

  Min. 1st Qu.  Median   Mean 3rd Qu.   Max.
   650     850     940    909     980   1070
```

Figure 9.2 is a frequency histogram of the data, which is very well spread out and strongly negatively skewed.

```
hist (light$speed,, main = "", xlab = "", col = hue_pal ()(1))
```

We want to test the hypothesis that Michelson's estimate of the speed of light is significantly different from the value of 299,990 thought to prevail at the time. Since the data have all had 299,000 subtracted from them, the test value is 990: this is equivalent to testing whether the data are different from 990. Because of the non-normality (evident in Figure 9.2) and small sample size (20), the use of a t-test in this case is ill advised. However, the non-parametric test we will use (Wilcoxon's signed-rank test) has the following hypotheses, so be careful not to over interpret the results:

H_0: estimates of the speed of light are symmetric about 299,990;

H_1: estimates of the speed of light are not symmetric about 299,990.

```
wilcox.test (light$speed, mu = 990)


Wilcoxon signed rank test with continuity correction

data:  light$speed
V = 22.5, $p$-value = 0.00213
alternative hypothesis: true location is not equal to 990
```

The *p*-value of 0.0021 suggests strong evidence against the null hypothesis: estimates of the speed of light do not appear to be symmetric about 299,990, and the plot indicates that most are lower. Note that this test does not like data points with the same value, as suggested by the warning message that your console may display when running the test.

9.2.2   Two population averages

Comparing averages from two populations is a popular pastime, and the starting point is to decide whether we can pair items. In our `exams` dataset, we can match up results for any pair of exams by picking a student and looking at their marks in those exams. Before we look at those data, we will first examine the `tulips` dataset. This contains measurements of the heights of samples of tulip flowers in two gardens, A and B. The gardeners, Ronald and Karl, are fiercely competitive about their respective approaches to growing tulips. The data come from measurements in two separate gardens and cannot be paired.

```
load ("tulips.RData")
boxplot (list (GardenA, GardenB), ylab = "Height (cm)",
        varwidth = T, names = c ("GardenA", "GardenB"),
        col = hue_pal ()(2), notch = T)
```

Figure 9.3 shows box plots for the samples with slightly differing widths based on the square roots of the sample sizes. It appears that the values in GardenA may be slightly higher than those in GardenB and also more spread out. The `notch = T` argument produces the waist-like effect: their overlap suggests no evidence of difference in medians (see `help (boxplot.stats)` for more details). However, as the datasets appear to be normally distributed (check out the two QQ plots

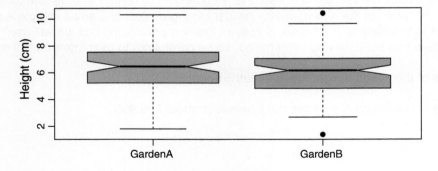

Figure 9.3   Tulip flower heights in 2 gardens.

as described in Section 9.2.5 for an example with another dataset) we will compare means using a t-test. Our hypotheses are

H_0: the populations in GardenA and GardenB have the same mean;

H_1: the populations in GardenA and GardenB do not have the same mean.

This t-test uses the same command as for a single dataset, but we use more of the arguments:

```
t.test (x = GardenA, y = GardenB, conf.level = 0.9,
var.equal = T)


Two Sample t-test

data:  GardenA and GardenB
t = 1.4751, df = 153, $p$-value = 0.1422
alternative hypothesis: true difference in means is not equal to 0
90 percent confidence interval:
 -0.04832176  0.84133842
sample estimates:
mean of x mean of y
6.398133  6.001625
```

We test for equal variances in Section 9.2.6 and accept the default non-paired argument. Combinations of these arguments results in variations of the classic t-test. The p-value of 0.142 suggests no evidence against our null hypothesis, and the 90% CI contains 0.

Reverting to our exams dataset to consider paired data, we might be interested in comparing the results between the first two exams. The assumption we need to check is whether the two sets of population data are normally distributed. As we see in Section 9.2.5, that appears not to be the case for exam 2. This means that we cannot carry out a paired t-test but will need to perform a non-parametric Wilcoxon signed rank test. This has the following hypotheses:

H_0 The differences between marks for pupils in the two exams are symmetric about 0;

H_1 The differences between marks for pupils in the two exams are not symmetric about 0.

Running the test gives:

```
wilcox.test (exams$Exam1, exams$Exam2, paired = TRUE, conf.int = TRUE)


Wilcoxon signed rank test with continuity correction

data:  exams$Exam1 and exams$Exam2
V = 1143, $p$-value = 0.01482
alternative hypothesis: true location shift is not equal to 0
95 percent confidence interval:
 -4.9999700 -0.4999531
sample estimates:
(pseudo)median
-2.500061
```

The confidence interval is the difference in median between the two datasets and defaults to 95%. As we can see, it does not contain zero, and we also have a small p-value, 0.015. This suggests that our assumptions and H_0 would only have a small chance of giving rise to the data, or more extreme: it is very likely that there are problems with either our assumptions or H_0. It does not mean that H_1 is true or that H_0 is false. Formally, we might say that there is evidence against the hypothesis that the two sets of exam marks have the same distributional shape or that there is a problem with one of our assumptions.

Exams 1 and 3 do appear to have normally distributed marks and so we can use a variation on the t-test discussed earlier in this section. First, we need to check for equal variances using `var.test ()` (the values are actually not too far apart: 147.37 and 154.1) and then we put the result of that test into our t-test:

```
if (var.test (x = exams$Exam1, y = exams$Exam3)$p.value < 0.01) {
  exams13_var_equal <- "T"
} else {
  exams13_var_equal <- "F"
}
t.test (x = exams$Exam1, y = exams$Exam3, conf.level = 0.9,
        paired = T, var.equal = exams13_var_equal)


Paired t-test

data:  exams$Exam1 and exams$Exam3
t = -14.541, df = 87, $p$-value < 2.2e-16
alternative hypothesis: true difference in means is not equal to 0
90 percent confidence interval:
 -3.482312 -2.767688
sample estimates:
mean of the differences
                 -3.125
```

There is very strong evidence against our null hypothesis (or any assumptions).

We have seen varieties of the parametric t-test and the non-parametric Wilcoxon test. The non-parametric test is much more appropriate than the t-test when the errors are not Normal, perhaps detected by examining the QQ-plot from the residuals in a t-test. The non-parametric test is about 95% as powerful with Normal errors and can be more powerful than the t-test if the distribution is strongly skewed by the presence of outliers. Typically, the t-test will give the lower p-value, so the Wilcoxon test is said to be conservative: if a difference is very small under a Wilcoxon test it is generally even smaller under a t-test.

9.2.3 Multiple population averages

In Section 9.2.2, we looked at comparing two populations. We might want to compare more than two, for instance if we are looking at the effectiveness of a number of medical interventions. If the populations involved appear to be normally distributed, then this analysis can be carried out using linear regression (Chapter 10). If that is not the case, as in our `exams` dataset, then we have another option, a Kruskal–Wallis test:

```
kruskal.test (exams)


Kruskal--Wallis rank sum test

data:  exams
Kruskal--Wallis chi-squared = 3.589, df = 2, $p$-value = 0.1662
```

This is working with the following hypotheses:

H_0 The medians of the 3 populations of marks are the same.

H_1 The medians of the 3 populations of marks are not the same.

So, in this case, there is no evidence against that null hypothesis. If we did come up with a small p-value, then we would still need to know where the differences occur. A common approach then is to test all pairs of datasets: just be aware that as there are multiple tests, the p-values will need to be adjusted as in Section 9.5.

9.2.4   Population distribution

We might have some data and want to understand their distribution, and could ask one of two different questions:

- Are two sample distributions the same, or are they significantly different from one another in one or more (unspecified) ways?
- Does a particular sample distribution arise from a particular hypothesised distribution?

These apparently simple questions are actually very broad. It is obvious that two distributions could be different because their means were different. But two distributions with exactly the same mean could be significantly different if they differed in variance, or in skew, or in kurtosis. There are some wonderfully named tests that examine these questions.

The tests work on **cumulative distribution functions**. These give the probability that a randomly selected value of X is less than or equal to x:

$$F(x) = P(X <= x).$$

This sounds somewhat abstract. Returning to the size of tulips, we met in Section 9.2.2 and Figure 9.3:

```
load ("tulips.RData")
```

We plot the cumulative frequencies, translated into probabilities (known as **empirical distribution functions**), for the two samples on the same axes in Figure 9.4, bearing in mind that the samples have different lengths. We also show the two boxplots, with very similar profiles.

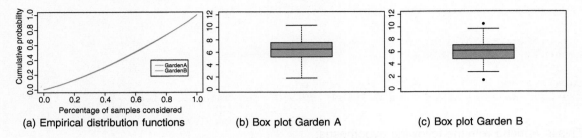

Figure 9.4   Tulip flower heights in 2 gardens.

```
A <- length (GardenA)
B <- length (GardenB)
plot (seq (0, 1, length = A), cumsum (sort(GardenA) / sum(GardenA)), type="l",
     ylab = "cumulative probability", xlab = "percentage of samples consid-
ered",
     col = hue_pal ()(4)[1])
lines (seq (0, 1, length = B), cumsum (sort (GardenB) / sum(GardenB)),
     col = hue_pal ()(4)[2])
legend (x = 0.7, y = 0.4, legend = c ("GardenA", "GardenB"),
     col = hue_pal ()(2), lty = 1)
boxplot (GardenA, col = hue_pal ()(4)[3], ylim =  c (0, 12))
boxplot (GardenB, col = hue_pal ()(4)[4], ylim =  c (0, 12))
```

Although we have seen that the two samples have different means and variability, the plot shows that the two sample distributions are virtually indistinguishable in shape. We can carry out the formal Kolmogorov–Smirnov test:

```
ks.test (GardenA, GardenB)


Two-sample Kolmogorov--Smirnov test

data:  GardenA and GardenB
D = 0.19583, $p$-value = 0.1027
alternative hypothesis: two-sided
```

The *p*-value suggests little evidence against the null hypothesis that the data in the two populations come from the same distribution.

If we wanted to compare the data in GardenA to a specific distribution, say a t-distribution:

```
ks.test(GardenA, "pt", ncp = mean (GardenA), df = length (GardenA) - 1)


One-sample Kolmogorov--Smirnov test

data:  GardenA
D = 0.13273, $p$-value = 0.1423
alternative hypothesis: two-sided
```

then we need to specify the appropriate cumulative distribution function in R (`pt`) together with its parameter values, which we take from the GardenA sample. There is an equally intriguingly named test, the Anderson–Darling test, which one can also use.

Comparisons with the Normal distribution are considered separately in the following section.

9.2.5 Checking and testing for normality

The most common reason for wishing to check that data are normally distributed is because a test that we wish to perform, such as comparing population means, assumes that the population data are normally distributed. That is what we will focus on in this section. For a more general analysis of comparing data to a distribution, see Section 9.2.4.

How might we check whether population data are normally distributed? First, see whether someone else has done it. Reverting to our example from Section 9.1.1, the height of Canadian women will have been thoroughly studied and normality or otherwise should be clear. Usually, however, we will need to perform the review ourselves. In an ideal world, we would have access to the population data and can check those: in practice, we are likely to have only the sample data and, as long as they fulfil the randomness assumption, we can use them.

There are three further conditions that need to be considered before we can actually check for normality:

1. How much data do we have? There is no precise answer to this but, for simplicity's sake, let us say that with fewer than 20 data items, we cannot check for normality (and so cannot make the assumption) but with at least 30 items we definitely can. In between, we should get a bigger sample. If in doubt, let us assume that a check is not possible (i.e. we will either need to perform a non-parametric test or state that we are making the normality assumption without evidence).

2. Are our data genuinely numerical? We may have used numbers as labels and, even if those labels represent some sort of order as in a survey, then normality is not appropriate.

3. What type of data do we have? The Normal distribution is continuous and has a range from minus infinity to plus infinity. So, ideally, our data should be the same. In practice, they may take only integer values and have a much narrower range. Again, it is a judgment call as to whether checking for normality is appropriate. But, for example, 30 data points in $\{11, 12, 13, 14, 15\}$ would not be appropriate for checking but 100 data points in $\{31, 32, \ldots, 70\}$ might be.

Now, let us assume that we have data that meet all the above conditions. How can we actually check for normality? The obvious answer is to carry out a test, and, indeed, there are many such tests. However, they are difficult to interpret and are likely, by default, to suggest normality for small samples and to rule it out for large samples. In addition, trying to capture how well data fit a curve in one number is a little optimistic.

A much better idea is to plot the data. The obvious approach is to plot a histogram (or density plot) of the data and compare it with a Normal curve. But, again, we can do better: there are many histograms for any set of data (depending up on where the breaks between cells occur), so how do we know which one we should use? A Normal **QQ plot** is essentially a mathematical transformation of a Normal curve into a straight diagonal line. We can then carry out the same transformation with the data and see how well the data points match the straight line.

We will illustrate these ideas using the `exams` dataset, introduced in Section 9.1.1. We can build QQ plots with the accompanying Normal straight lines (Figure 9.5) for each of the three exams as follows, with R doing all the heavy lifting:

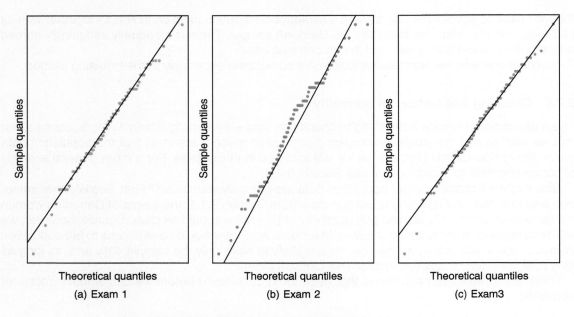

Figure 9.5 QQ plots for the two exams in `exams`.

```
qqnorm (exams$Exam1, main = "", col = hue_pal ()(3)[1], cex.lab = 2, xaxt = "n",
    yaxt = "n")
qqline (exams$Exam1)
qqnorm (exams$Exam2, main = "", col = hue_pal ()(3)[2], cex.lab = 2, xaxt = "n",
    yaxt = "n")
qqline (exams$Exam2)
qqnorm (exams$Exam3, main = "", col = hue_pal ()(3)[3], cex.lab = 2, xaxt = "n",
    yaxt = "n")
qqline (exams$Exam3)
```

In Figures 9.5a and 9.5c the points lie almost exactly on the straight lines, suggesting that the results for Exams 1 and 3 are a good fit to the Normal distribution. However, in Figure 9.5b, things are a little more complicated and this gives us a chance to examine QQ plots in more detail. The heights of the points (on the y-axis) represent the actual values of the data points. So, in the bottom left-hand corner (i.e. for lowest exam marks), they are higher than one might expect from a Normal distribution and in the top right-hand corner, they are lower. This suggests that the data are distributed somewhat like a Normal distribution but where the extreme values have been pushed towards the centre (this is known as **light tailed**). We would usually expect the extreme points on a QQ plot to diverge from the line somewhat, but this plot shows something more serious going on. There is also something a bit weird going on in the middle values, suggesting a bimodal distribution. As you can see, visual comparisons for normality require clear thinking.

To summarise, in order to test for normality: take a decent sized sample of numerical data with a reasonably wide range of values and create a Normal QQ plot. If it is not possible to do that, then we should not assume that our data are normally distributed.

There is one exception to what we have described above. If the summary statistic that is used in the test for which we are checking assumptions is the mean (for instance, in a t-test), then we do not have to test for normality. We can apply the central limit theorem (see Section 2.4.1) and that tells us that we can proceed on the basis that the normality assumption is true, and we can therefore use a z-test, as long as the sample size is large enough. *How much data do we have* earlier on in this section describes how we might interpret large enough.

Slightly surprisingly, there is no function for the z-test in base *R*. There is a function `z.test ()` in the package BSDA (Arnholt and Evans, 2017):

```
library (BSDA)
```

This works in a similar way to `t.test ()` as discussed in Section 9.2.2:

```
z.test (x = exams$Exam1, y = exams$Exam2,
        sigma.x = sd (exams$Exam1),
        sigma.y = sd (exams$Exam2))


Two-sample z-Test

data:  exams$Exam1 and exams$Exam2
z = -1.5965, $p$-value = 0.1104
alternative hypothesis: true difference in means is not equal to 0
95 percent confidence interval:
 -6.3033041 0.6442132
sample estimates:
mean of x mean of y
60.67045  63.50000
```

The *p*-value here is 0.11 compared with 0.015 for the Wilcoxon test for the same data in Section 9.2.2, which may be because the latter is not sensitive to outlying pairs, or because the former does not take pairing into account. The z-test is only an approximate test (i.e. the data will only be approximately Normal), unlike the t-test, so if there is a choice between a z-test and a t-test, use a t-test.

9.2.6 Comparing variances

Before we can carry out a t-test to compare two independent sample means (Section 9.2.2), we need to test whether the sample variances are significantly different. The test could not be simpler. It is called **Fisher's F test** (which uses the F(isher)-distribution) after the famous statistician and eugenicist R.A. Fisher, who worked at Rothamsted in south-east England. To compare two variances, all you do is divide the larger variance by the smaller variance. Obviously, if the variances are the same, the ratio will be 1. In order to be significantly different, the ratio will need to be significantly bigger than 1 (because the larger variance goes on top, in the numerator). We will explore this test using the tulip data introduced in Section 9.2.2 where the means of the populations are compared. We are not sure which population might have the larger variance, so our hypotheses are

H_0 The population variances for the heights of the two tulip populations are the same.

H_1 The population variances for the heights of the two tulip populations are not the same.

In order to test whether the variances of the populations are the same:

```
load ("tulips.RData")
var.test (GardenA, GardenB, conf.level = 0.99)


F-test to compare two variances

data:  GardenA and GardenB
F = 1.2489, num df = 74, denom df = 79, $p$-value = 0.3315
alternative hypothesis: true ratio of variances is not equal to 1
99 percent confidence interval:
 0.6902072 2.2712733
sample estimates:
ratio of variances
        1.248927
```

There is clearly little evidence against H_0.

For multiple samples, you can choose between the Bartlett test and the Fligner–Killeen test. Here are both tests in action using the `refuge` dataset:

```
refs <- read.table ("refuge.txt", header = T)
names(refs)

[1] "B" "T"
```

where T is an ordered factor with nine levels. Each level produces 30 estimates of yields (B) except for level 9 which is a single zero. We begin by looking at the variances:

```
tapply(refs$B, refs$T, var)

      1        2        3        4        5        6        7        8
1354.024 2025.431 3125.292 1077.030 2542.599 2221.982 1445.490 1459.955
      9
     NA
```

When it comes to the variance tests, we shall have to leave out level 9 of T because the tests require at least two replicates at each factor level. We need to know which data point refers to treatment $T = 9$:

```
which (refs$T == 9)

[1] 31
```

We shall omit the 31st data point using negative subscripts. First Bartlett:

```
bartlett.test (refs$B[-31], refs$T[-31])

Bartlett test of homogeneity of variances

data:  refs$B[-31] and refs$T[-31]
Bartlett's K-squared = 13.199, df = 7, $p$-value = 0.06741
```

and then Fligner:

```
fligner.test (refs$B[-31],refs$T[-31])


Fligner--Killeen test of homogeneity of variances

data:  refs$B[-31] and refs$T[-31]
Fligner--Killeen:med chi-squared = 14.386, df = 7, $p$-value = 0.04472
```

The two p-values are either side of 0.05, **WHICH DOES NOT MATTER**, but are not too far apart: both suggest that there is some evidence against H_0, that there is no difference between the group variances.

The Fligner–Killeen test (preferred over Bartlett's test by many statisticians) is a non-parametric test which uses the ranks of the absolute values of the centred samples, and weights. Of the many tests for homogeneity of variances, this is the most robust against departures from normality (Conover et al., 1981), which is assumed for parametric tests such as Bartlett's.

9.3   Discrete and categorical data

We will look at some popular topics for testing a discrete or categorical dataset:

- comparing signs (+/-) of the values in two populations (Section 9.3.1);
- comparing proportions of data with a specific distribution or population. These are known as goodness-of-fit tests (Section 9.3.2);
- testing data in a contingency table (Section 9.3.3).

The latter two sets of tests originally used the χ^2-test for calculations: this was the first test that gave rise to the idea of a p-value, as set out by the famous eugenicist and statistician, K. Pearson. There are better tests now, and there is no need for the χ^2-test to be used any longer. These better tests may be exact (so can be used for small samples) or approximate (for larger samples).

9.3.1   Sign test

This is one of the simplest and most underrated of all statistical tests. Suppose that you cannot *measure* a difference, but you can *see* it as, say, in judging a diving contest. For example, nine springboard divers were scored as better or worse, having trained under a new regime and under the conventional regime (the regimes were allocated in a randomized sequence to each athlete: new then conventional, or conventional then new). Divers were judged twice: one diver was worse on the new regime, and 8 were better. What is the evidence that the new regime produces significantly better scores in competition? The answer comes from a two-tailed binomial test (see Section 9.3.2 for a more general multinomial test). How likely is a response of 1/9 (or 8/9 or more extreme than this, i.e. 0/9 or 9/9) given the null hypothesis where

H_0: there is no difference in performance between the new and conventional training regimes.

H_1: there is a difference in performance between the new and conventional training regimes.

We use a binomial test for this with a probability of success of 0.5, specifying the number of 'failures' (1) and the total sample size (9):

```
binom.test (x = 1, n = 9, p = 0.5)


Exact binomial test

data:   1 and 9
number of successes = 1, number of trials = 9, $p$-value = 0.03906
alternative hypothesis: true probability of success is not equal to 0.5
95 percent confidence interval:
 0.002809137 0.482496515
sample estimates:
probability of success
          0.1111111
```

We would conclude that there is little evidence against the new and conventional training regimes having similar performance.

It is easy to write a function to carry out a sign test to compare two samples, *x* and *y*:

```
sign.test <- function (x, y) {
  if (length(x) != length(y)) stop ("The two variables must be the same length")
  d <- x - y
  binom.test (sum (d > 0), length(d))
}
```

The function starts by checking that the two vectors are the same length, then works out the vector of the differences, *d*. The binomial test is then applied to the number of positive differences and the total number of numbers (i.e. unlike the previous example we create the 1s and 0s from the numeric data). If there was no difference between the samples, then on average, the former would be about half the latter. Here is the sign test used to compare the marks for exams 1 and 2:

```
sign.test (exams$Exam1, exams$Exam2)


Exact binomial test

data:   sum(d > 0) and length(d)
number of successes = 35, number of trials = 88, $p$-value = 0.06935
```

```
alternative hypothesis: true probability of success is not equal to 0.5
95 percent confidence interval:
 0.2948766 0.5076647
sample estimates:
probability of success
              0.3977273
```

Note that the p-value from the sign test (0.069) is larger than that for the equivalent Wilcoxon test that we carried out earlier (0.015)). This will generally be the case: other things being equal, the sign test is cruder, albeit simpler to understand than the Wilcoxon equivalent.

9.3.2 Test to compare proportions

Suppose that a university department wanted to compare how its staff measured up to its country's population in terms of categorisations such as race or gender. We might examine this using a goodness-of-fit test. Let us assume that there are three categories (A, B, and C) with staff numbers and population percentages as follows:

	A	B	C
Staff numbers	4	47	12
Population %	11.1	71.2	17.7

We might want to run our test with the following hypotheses:

H_0: the number of staff in categories A, B, and C are representative of the population as a whole.

H_1: the number of staff in categories A, B, and C are not representative of the population as a whole.

There is an exact test, the **multinomial-test**, for which we need to load a package, EMT (Menzel, 2013):

```
library (EMT)
multinomial.test (observed = c (4, 47, 12),
    prob = c (0.111, 0.712, 0.177))


 Exact Multinomial Test, distance measure: p

    Events    pObs    p.value
      2080   0.0112     0.5154
```

There is no evidence against the null hypothesis that the staff profile for this categorisation represents that of the nation. An alternative approach would be to calculate CIs for the observed proportions and then compare those with the population percentages. For this we need a very useful package, DescTools (Andri et mult. et al., 2021), which has all sorts of statistical goodies and utilities: download it and have a look.

```
library (DescTools)
MultinomCI (x = c (4, 47, 12), conf.level = 0.92)

           est       lwr.ci      upr.ci
[1,]  0.06349206  0.0000000  0.1680624
[2,]  0.74603175  0.6666667  0.8506021
[3,]  0.19047619  0.1111111  0.2950465
```

The output presents our numbers as proportions in the first column and then gives, in this case, 92% CIs for each of the three proportions. We can see that in each case, the population proportion sits well within the CIs. The advantage of this approach, compared to the *p*-value line of attack, is that we can see how each category individually compares with the population.

For large numbers (of, say, staff), the multinomial test can get very slow and an approximate test, the G-test, should be used (and will give very similar answers anyway). What is large? This is one of the most common statistical questions and, as usual, there is no commonly agreed answer. A rule of thumb here is 1000 (although we can see below that that may be far too large). The G-test can also be found in `DescTools`, and we will illustrate it with our data, even if they are small:

```
GTest (x =  c (4, 47, 12), y = c (0.111, 0.712, 0.177))


Log likelihood ratio (G-test) test of independence without correction

data:  c(4, 47, 12) and c(0.111, 0.712, 0.177)
G = 6.5917, X-squared df = 4, $p$-value = 0.1591
```

This gives a similar outcome to the multinomial-test, fortunately!

For a more complex example, we have some data on the numbers of bankruptcies in 80 districts. The question is whether there is any evidence that some districts show greater than expected numbers of cases. What would we expect? Of course, we should expect some variation, but how much, exactly? Well, that depends on our model of the process. Perhaps the simplest model is that absolutely nothing is going on, and that every singly bankruptcy case is absolutely independent of every other. That leads to the prediction that the numbers of cases per district will follow a Poisson distribution in which the variance is equal to the mean. Let us see what the data show.

```
banks <- read.table ("cases.txt", header = T)
names (banks)

[1] "cases"

banks_table <- table (banks$cases)
```

We have used the `table ()` function to summarise the number of districts which have any particular number of cases. There were no cases at all in 34 districts, but one district had 10 cases. A good way to proceed is to compare our distribution with the distribution that would be observed if the data really did come from a Poisson distribution as postulated by our model. We can use the *R* function `dpois` to compute the probability density of each of the 11 frequencies from 0 to 9 and then put the remaining probability (so that the distribution sums to 1) in frequency 10 (we multiply

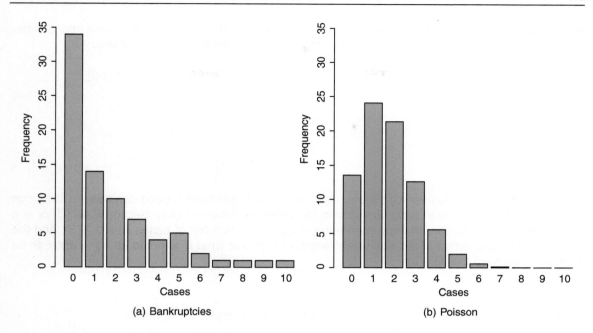

Figure 9.6   Barplots of `banks` data and Poisson distribution.

the probability produced by `dpois` by the total sample of 80 to obtain the predicted frequencies). We need to calculate the mean number of cases per district – this is the Poisson distribution's only parameter:

```
mean (banks$cases)
```

```
[1] 1.775
```

We can compare our data and the Poisson distribution visually in Figure 9.6:

```
barplot (banks_table, ylab = "Frequency", xlab = "Cases", col = hue_pal () (2) [1],
        ylim = c (0, 35), main = "")
barplot (c (dpois (0:9, 1.775), 1 - ppois (9, 1.775)) * 80,
        names = as.character (0:10), ylab = "Frequency", xlab = "Cases",
        col = hue_pal () (2) [2], ylim = c (0, 35), main = "")
```

The distributions are very different: the mode of the observed data is 0, but the mode of the Poisson distribution with the same mean is 1; the observed data contained examples of 8, 9, and 10 cases, but these would be highly unlikely under a Poisson distribution. We would say that the observed data are highly aggregated – they have a variance/mean ratio much greater than 1 (the Poisson distribution, of course, has a variance/mean ratio of 1):

```
var (banks$cases) / mean (banks$cases)
```

```
[1] 2.99483
```

Finally, we can carry out a goodness-of-fit test: the Poisson distribution is definitely not appropriate. We have used the G-test as the data appear to be too much for the multinomial test.

```
GTest (x = banks_table, p = c (dpois (0:9, 1.775), 1 - ppois (9, 1.775)))


Log likelihood ratio (G-test) goodness of fit test

data:  banks_table
G = 69.144, X-squared df = 10, $p$-value = 6.485e-11
```

So, if the data are not Poisson distributed, how are they distributed? A good candidate distribution where the variance - mean ratio can vary is the Negative Binomial (see Section 8.4.7).This is a two-parameter distribution: the first parameter is the mean number of cases ($\mu = 1.775$), and the second can be presented in two equivalent ways. We will use what R refers to as `size` and can be approximated from the data by

$$\frac{\bar{x}^2}{s^2 - \bar{x}}$$

using the usual notation for the mean and variance of the sample. Here, that is

```
mean (banks$cases)^2 / (var (banks$cases) - mean (banks$cases))

[1] 0.8898003
```

We can then compare our data to the Negative Binomial visually in Figure 9.7

```
barplot (banks_table, ylab = "Frequency", xlab = "Cases", col = hue_pal () (2) [1],
         ylim = c (0, 35), main = "")
barplot (c (dnbinom (0:9, size = 0.89, mu = 1.75),
            1 - pnbinom (9, size = 0.89, mu = 1.75)) * 80,
         names = as.character (0:10), ylab = "Frequency", xlab = "Cases",
         col = hue_pal () (2) [2], ylim = c (0, 35), main = "")
```

which appears to be a better fit. A G-test confirms that

```
GTest (x = banks_table,
       p = c (dnbinom (0:9, size = 0.89, mu = 1.75),
              1 - pnbinom (9, size = 0.89, mu = 1.75)))


Log likelihood ratio (G-test) goodness of fit test

data:  banks_table
G = 3.0911, X-squared df = 10, $p$-value = 0.9792
```

Although the tests in Section 9.3.4 appear similar to those we have seen here, they are addressing different questions.

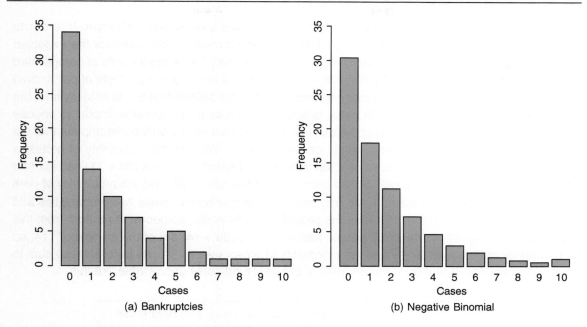

Figure 9.7 Barplots of `banks` data and Negative Binomial distribution.

9.3.3 Contingency tables

A great deal of statistical information comes in the form of **counts** (whole numbers or integers): the number of animals that died, the number of branches on a tree, the number of days of frost, the number of companies that failed, the number of patients who died. With count data, the number 0 is often the value of a response variable (consider, for example, what a 0 would mean in the context of the examples just listed).

The dictionary definition of contingency is 'A possible or uncertain event on which other things depend or are conditional' (OED, 2012). In statistics, however, the contingencies are *all the events that could possibly happen*. A contingency table shows the counts of how many times each of the contingencies actually happened in a particular sample. Consider the following example that has to do with the relationship between hair colour and eye colour in white people. For simplicity, we just chose two contingencies for hair colour: 'fair' and 'dark'. Likewise, we just chose two contingencies for eye colour: 'blue' and 'brown'. Each of these two categorical variables, eye colour and hair colour, has two levels ('blue' and 'brown', and 'fair' and 'dark', respectively). Between them, they define four possible outcomes (the contingencies): fair hair and blue eyes, fair hair and brown eyes, dark hair and blue eyes, and dark hair and brown eyes. We take a random sample of white people and count how many of them fall into each of these four categories. Then we fill in the 2×2 contingency table like this:

	Blue eyes	Brown eyes
Fair hair	38	11
Dark hair	14	51

These are our observed frequencies (or counts). The next step is very important. In order to make any progress in the analysis of these data, we need a **model** which predicts the expected frequencies. What would be a sensible model in a case like this? There are all sorts of complicated models that you might select, but the simplest model (Occam's razor, or the principle of parsimony) is that hair colour and eye colour are *independent*. We may not believe that this is actually true, but the hypothesis has the great virtue of being falsifiable. It is also a very sensible model to choose because it makes it possible to predict the expected frequencies based on the assumption that the model is true. We need to do some simple probability work. What is the probability of getting a random individual from this sample whose hair was fair? A total of 49 people $(38 + 11)$ had fair hair out of a total sample of 114 people. So the probability of fair hair is $\frac{49}{114}$ and the probability of dark hair is $\frac{65}{114}$. Notice that because we have only two levels of hair colour, these two probabilities add up to 1. What about eye colour? What is the probability of selecting someone at random from this sample with blue eyes? A total of 52 people had blue eyes $(38 + 14)$ out of the sample of 114, so the probability of blue eyes is $\frac{52}{114}$ and the probability of brown eyes is $\frac{62}{114}$. As before, these sum to 1. It helps to add the subtotals to the margins of the observed contingency table like this:

	Blue eyes	Brown eyes	Row totals
Fair hair	38	11	49
Dark hair	14	51	65
Column totals	52	62	114

Now comes the important bit. We want to know the *expected* frequency of people with fair hair *and* blue eyes, to compare with our observed frequency of 38. Our model assumption says that the two are independent. This is essential information because it allows us to calculate the expected probability of fair hair and blue eyes. If, and only if, the two traits are independent, then the probability of having fair hair and blue eyes is the product of the two probabilities. So, following our earlier calculations, the probability of fair hair and blue eyes is $\frac{49}{114} \times \frac{52}{114}$. We can do exactly equivalent things for the other three cells of the contingency table:

	Blue eyes	Brown eyes	Total count in each row
Fair hair	$49/114 \times 52/114$	$49/114 \times 62/114$	49
Dark hair	$65/114 \times 52/114$	$65/114 \times 62/114$	65
Total count in each column	52	62	114

Now we need to know how to calculate the expected frequency. It couldn't be simpler. It is just the probability multiplied by the total sample $(n = 114)$. So the expected frequency of blue eyes and fair hair is $\frac{49}{114} \times \frac{52}{114} \times 114 = 22.35$, which is much less than our observed frequency of 38. It is beginning to look as if our hypothesis of independence of hair and eye colour may be false.

You might have noticed something useful in the last calculation: two of the sample sizes cancel out. Therefore, the expected frequency in each cell is just the row total (R) times the column total

(C) divided by the grand total (G) like this:

$$E = \frac{R \times C}{G}.$$

We can now work out the four expected frequencies:

	Blue eyes	Brown eyes	Row totals
Fair hair	22.35	26.65	49
Dark hair	29.65	35.35	65
Column totals	52	62	114

Notice that the row and column totals (the so-called 'marginal totals') are retained under the model. It is clear that the observed frequencies and the expected frequencies are different. But in sampling, everything always varies, so this is no surprise. The important question is to what extent the expected frequencies are different from the observed frequencies. There are a number of ways we could answer that question, which we will address in the next section. Although the tables generated here have only two rows and two columns, contingency tables frequently have more of both.

9.3.4   Testing contingency tables

The first way of looking at the difference between observed and expected contingency tables is to calculate some **Pearson residuals**: these measure the distance between each matching pair of cells and tell us where the larger discrepancies lie. We create a residual table where the entry in location (i,j) is for observed O and expected E:

$$\frac{O_{i,j} - E_{i,j}}{\sqrt{E_{i,j}}}.$$

A useful rule of thumb is that any entries larger than two (or less then minus two) warrant further investigation: particularly if any of the tests we will explore later in this section result in small p-values. For the hair/eye colour table in Section 9.3.3, the residuals table is

	Blue eyes	Brown eyes
Fair hair	3.31	−3.03
Dark hair	−2.87	2.63

All the entries have large absolute values, suggesting that independence is looking unlikely.

It is possible to visualise the relative size of these residuals. We will use a more complicated dataset, also investigating the relationship between hair and eye colour. It is `HairEyeColor` and is built into R. We can tabulate it very easily:

```
ftable (HairEyeColor)

          Sex Male Female
Hair  Eye
Black Brown        32      36
      Blue         11       9
      Hazel        10       5
      Green         3       2
Brown Brown        53      66
      Blue         50      34
      Hazel        25      29
      Green        15      14
Red   Brown        10      16
      Blue         10       7
      Hazel         7       7
      Green         7       7
Blond Brown         3       4
      Blue         30      64
      Hazel         5       5
      Green         8       8
```

The `ftable ()` function produces a **flat** table which attempts to capture the multiple dimensional data in a straightforward way (compare it with the `table ()` function). If we were not concerned about gender, we could produce the association plot in Figure 9.8:

```
assocplot (margin.table (HairEyeColor, c (1, 2)))
```

The `margin.table` argument reduces the three-dimensional contingency table to its first two dimensions. The plot then shows the excess (black bars) of people with black hair who have brown eyes, the excess of people with blond hair who have blue eyes, and the excess of redheads who have green eyes. The red bars show categories where fewer people were observed than expected under the null hypothesis of independence of hair colour and eye colour.

We can now move to formal tests which, as usual, require hypotheses:

H_0: hair colour and eye colour are independent in our population;

H_1: hair colour and eye colour are not independent in our population.

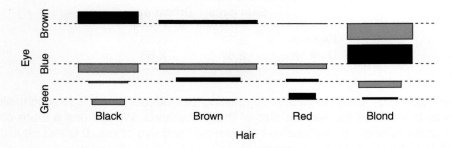

Figure 9.8 Association plot for `HairEyeColor`, ignoring gender.

We can use the approximate G-test (better than the traditional χ^2-test), as described in Section 9.3.2:

```
GTest (x =  matrix (c (38, 14, 11, 51), nrow = 2))


Log likelihood ratio (G-test) test of independence without correction

data:  matrix(c(38, 14, 11, 51), nrow = 2)
G = 37.241, X-squared df = 1, $p$-value = 1.044e-09
```

The observed data have been entered as a matrix which looks like the original contingency table. As we might have expected from the residuals analysis, the very small p-value suggests very strong evidence against independence of hair and eye colour.

In an analogous way to Section 9.3.2, there is an exact test, Fisher's test, which can be used for smaller samples:

```
fisher.test (x =  matrix (c (38, 14, 11, 51), nrow = 2))


Fisher's Exact Test for Count Data

data:  matrix(c(38, 14, 11, 51), nrow = 2)
$p$-value = 2.099e-09
alternative hypothesis: true odds ratio is not equal to 1
95 percent confidence interval:
 4.746351 34.118920
sample estimates:
odds ratio
 12.22697
```

This has a small p-value, similar to that for the G-test but also presents the hypotheses in a different but equivalent way (for 2×2 tables). The **odds ratio** is commonly used in medical statistics. In this case, it compares the odds of having blue eyes as against brown eyes between the two types of hair colour (you can switch hair and eye colour round in the interpretation) and H_0 is that the odds ratio is one.

The tests discussed in this section extend to larger contingency tables, which do not even have to be square. The odds ratio is only used in 2×2 tables.

9.4 Bootstrapping

You have probably heard the old phrase about 'pulling yourself up by your own bootlaces'. That is where the term 'bootstrap' comes from. It is used in the sense of getting 'something for nothing'. The idea is very simple: we replace our population by our sample and produce CIs and p-values by (sub)sampling from that new population. It is most useful when the data are skewed and so parametric methods cannot be used.

So, if we have a single sample of n measurements, we can sample from this in very many ways, as long as we allow some values to appear more than once, and other samples to be left out (i.e.

sampling with replacement). For instance, to calculate a CI, we work out the sample mean of lots of (sub)samples, and then examine the extreme highs and lows of these means using a quantile function to extract the interval we want (e.g. a 93% interval is specified using the $(0.035, 0.965)$, quantile values).

For a very simple example, let us revert to the speed of light data from Section 9.2.1 and sample 10,000 times:

```
boot_means <- numeric (10000)
for (i in 1:10000) {
  boot_means[i] <- mean (sample (light$speed, replace = T))
}
summary (boot_means)

   Min. 1st Qu. Median    Mean 3rd Qu.    Max.
  814.5   894.0  909.5   909.0   925.0   986.0

hist (boot_means, main = "", xlab = "sample means", col = hue_pal ()(1))
```

Figure 9.9 shows a histogram of the (sub)sample means. Unsurprisingly, from the Central Limit Theorem, the distribution is approximately Normal. We might create a 93% CI using the quantile () function:

```
quantile (boot_means, probs = c (0.035, 0.965))

 3.5% 96.5%
865.5 949.0
```

We can also see that there are 0 means at least as large as the postulated speed of light (990 km/s without the 299,000), suggesting that a p-value for the null hypotheses that that is the speed of light (with a one-sided alternative hypothesis) is roughly 0.

Predictably, there is a package, boot (Canty and Ripley, 2021), to do the work for us:

```
library (boot)
```

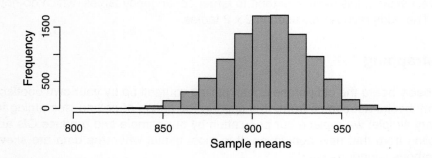

Figure 9.9 Histogram of means of 10,000 samples from Michelsons speed of light data.

We use it as follows:

```
mymean <- function (light, i) {
  mean (light$speed[i])
}
boot_means_package <- boot (light, statistic = mymean, R = 10000)
boot.ci (boot_means_package, conf = 0.93)

BOOTSTRAP CONFIDENCE INTERVAL CALCULATIONS
Based on 10000 bootstrap replicates

CALL:
boot.ci(boot.out = boot_means_package, conf = 0.93)

Intervals:
Level       Normal              Basic
93%    (867.5, 950.8)     (869.5, 952.5)

Level       Percentile            BCa
93%    (865.5, 948.5)     (859.5, 944.5)
Calculations and Intervals on Original Scale
```

Setting up the function for the `statistic` argument is the tricky bit: the *i* is just an index that will be used to run through the 10,000 samples. The default output gives a number of intervals, based on different calculation methods: the BCa interval (using the adjusted bootstrap percentage method) is probably the one to go for (technical details omitted). All the intervals will be different from that calculated by us above, as a different random sample will have been used.

For more depth read the Davison and Hinkley, 1997 book from which the `boot` package was developed.

9.5 Multiple tests

If we carry out a test and get a *p*-value of 0.04, this represents the probability of getting a result at least as extreme as that from our data, by chance, given that our null hypotheses and any assumptions are true. If we carry out two tests with *p*-values of 0.04 and 0.03, what is the probability that we might get a result at least as small in one of them by chance etc (i.e. the rest of the first sentence which I will no longer state for brevity's sake)? It is one minus the probability that neither situation arises or

```
1 - (1 - 0.04) * (1 - 0.03)

[1] 0.0688
```

As the number of tests increases, so does the probability of small *p*-values arising purely by chance. So when we run multiple tests, we need to adjust the resulting *p*-values in order to decide which tests might warrant further investigation. The probability of coming to at least one erroneous conclusion without adjusting the *p*-values is known as the **family-wise error rate**.

 R can carry out the necessary adjustment using the `p.adjust ()` function. However, there are a number of different adjustments that can be carried out and it may be best to take advice from a statistician before deciding which one to use. As an example, if we have carried out 10 tests on a dataset and have p-values of 0.04, 0.03, 0.17, 0.12, 0.01, 0.18, 0.02, 0.04, 0.21, and 0.08, then we might calculate adjusted p-values as follows:

```
p.adjust (p = c (0.04, 0.03, 0.17, 0.12, 0.01, 0.18, 0.02, 0.04, 0.21, 0.08),
method = "holm")

 [1] 0.28 0.24 0.51 0.48 0.10 0.51 0.18 0.28 0.51 0.40
```

None of these appear to be particularly small, despite the fact that in the original tests several of them were.

9.6 Power and sample size calculations

If we carry out a test and would like to come to a conclusion one way or the other (e.g. does a new drug reduce cholesterol more than an old one or does eating chocolate improve blood pressure?), then we could set a threshold, α, for our p-value, p, and go with H_0 if $p < \alpha$ and H_1, otherwise. This could give rise to two sorts of error:

Type I error We reject H_0 when it is, in fact, true. This will have probability α;
Type II error We reject H_1 when it is true. This is defined to have probability β.

Box 9.3: Thresholds

There are two dangers here:

1. The value for the **threshold**. 5% has become the standard **for no good reason** and does not denote a particularly rare event. If we must have a cut-off point, go for something much smaller: 1% or 0.05%.

2. Treating the threshold as absolute: almost identical datasets might give rise to p-values of 0.011 and 0.009. We need to think carefully about whether it is correct that those two values might give rise to completely different decisions.

For our drug example, the hypotheses might be

H_0: the new and old drugs have the same effect on blood pressure;

H_1: the new drug reduces blood pressure more than the old drug.

A lot of money will probably have been invested in the new drug so if it is an improvement on the old drug, we would like to improve our chances of detecting that: i.e. if H_1 is true, then we want to maximise the probability of coming to that decision. This probability is known as **power** and equals $1 - \beta$.

 New drugs usually give rise to drug trials where their efficacy is tested, and this idea has been extended into many other subject areas such as psychology. An important question therefore is how many people should I enrol on my trial? Due to the unknown nature of the new treatment, we would like this number to be as small as possible but large enough to detect the effect we are interested in. This **sample size calculation** requires four inputs when the output we are measuring (e.g. cholesterol) is continuous (other types of output require slightly different information):

1. α, sometimes referred to as the **significance level**;

2. power or, equivalently, β;

3. the mean effect size we wish to detect (often referred to as δ), such as the difference in cholesterol reduction, that, clinically, we might regard as important;

4. the standard deviation of our output (e.g. cholesterol measurements), under the drug regimes (assumed here to be the same for both drugs). This is annoying but is usually found either through a pilot study or from previous research.

Once we have worked through all these, R can carry out a sample size calculation:

```
power.t.test (delta = 2, sd = 3.5, power = 0.8, sig.level = 0.01)


     Two-sample t test power calculation

              n = 73.2095
          delta = 2
             sd = 3.5
      sig.level = 0.01
          power = 0.8
    alternative = two.sided

NOTE: n is number in *each* group
```

As the name of the function suggests, this calculation is based on the t-test and so all the assumptions from that test apply. In the example here, each of our two trial groups would need to have 74 participants. In practice, a larger number would need to be used to allow for people dropping out of the trials.

Changing the values of the four inputs will alter the sample size: reducing α, increasing power, reducing δ, or increasing the standard deviation all lead to larger samples, and vice versa. For instance, we can plot the effect of changing the power on sample size, using the data from the previous example, as follows to give Figure 9.10:

```
powers <- seq (0.5, 0.95, 0.01)
sample_size = numeric (length (powers))
for (i in 1:length (powers)) {
  sample_size[i] <- power.t.test (delta = 2, sd = 3.5, power = powers[i],
                  sig.level = 0.01)$n
}
plot (powers, sample_size, type = "l", xlab = "power", ylab = "sample size",
      col = hue_pal ()(1))
```

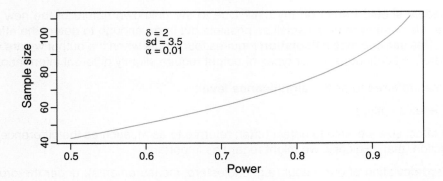

Figure 9.10   Sample sizes for varying power.

```
text (x = 0.6, y = 100, adj = c (0, 0),
     labels = substitute (paste (delta, "= 2")))
text (x = 0.6, y = 95, adj = c (0, 0),
     labels = substitute (paste ("sd = 3.5")))
text (x = 0.6, y = 90, adj = c (0, 0),
labels = substitute (paste (alpha, "= 0.01")))
```

There are other functions in *R* which carry out sample size calculations relating to other tests, for instance `power.prop.test ()` for a proportion test: they all begin `power..`

9.7   A table of tests

We have explored using a number of tests in this chapter, and a summary is given in Table 9.1. There are hundreds of others available, most of them in *R*, but care should be taken to understand exactly what the test does and does not do before use. The table is not intended to be a replacement for working through the appropriate part of this chapter.

Table 9.1   Tests used in Chapter 9.

Name	Function in *R*	Testing what
t-test	`t.test ()`	comparing means in two normally distributed continuous paired data populations
t-test	`t.test (..., paired = F)`	comparing means in two normally distributed continuous unpaired data populations
z-test	`z.test ()` in BSDA	comparing means in two non-normally distributed populations
Wilcoxon signed rank test	`wilcox.test ()`	looking for symmetric data pattern in numeric or ordered populations

Table 9.1   Continued

Name	Function in *R*	Testing what
Kruskal–Wallis rank sum test	`kruskal.test ()`	comparing medians across multiple populations
equality of variances test	`var.test ()`	compare variances in two populations
equality of variances test	`bartlett.test ()`	compare variances in multiple populations
equality of variances test	`fligner.test ()`	compare variances in multiple populations
Kolmogorov–Smirnov test	`ks.test ()`	comparing whether data in two samples come from the same population
Anderson–Darling test	`ad.test ()` in `nortest`	comparing whether data in two samples come from the same population
Binomial test	`binom.test ()`	comparing two proportions from different populations
multinomial test	`multinomial.test ()` in `EMT`	comparing multiple proportions from different populations in small samples
G-test	`GTest.test ()` in `DescTools`	comparing multiple proportions from different populations and independence in contingency tables
Fisher test	`fisher.test ()`	comparing independence in contingency tables (small samples)

References

Andri, S. et al. (2021). *DescTools: Tools for descriptive statistics* [R package version 0.99.42]. https://cran.r-project.org/package=DescTools.

Arnholt, A. T., & Evans, B. (2017). *BSDA: Basic statistics and data analysis* [R package version 1.2.0]. https://CRAN.R-project.org/package=BSDA.

Canty, A., & Ripley, B. D. (2021). *Boot: Bootstrap R (S-plus) functions* [R package version 1.3-28].

Conover, W. J., Johnson, M. E., & Johnson, M. M. (1981). A comparative study of tests for homogeneity of variances, with applications to the outer continental shelf bidding data. *Technometrics, 23,* 351–361.

Davison, A. C., & Hinkley, D. V. (1997). *Bootstrap methods and their application.* CUP.

Menzel, U. (2013). *EMT: Exact multinomial test: goodness-of-fit test for discrete multivariate data* [R package version 1.1]. https://CRAN.R-project.org/package=EMT.

Michelson, A. A. (1880). Experimental determination of the velocity of light made at the U.S. Naval Academy, Annapolis. *Astronomical Papers, 1,* 109–145.

10

Regression

Regression models provide a flexible tool to understand the drivers behind an outcome, response, or phenomenon of interest. These models can be used to complete a variety of tasks, including estimating the collective relationship between variables, hypothesis testing, and prediction of future outcome values.

Perhaps the simplest form of a regression is the **simple linear regression model**, which quantifies the **linear** relationship between a **covariate** (otherwise known as a predictor), X, and an **outcome** (otherwise known as response) of interest, Y. This model assumes a linear – or straight line – relationship between X and Y, of the form

$$Y = \beta_0 + \beta_1 X. \tag{10.1}$$

Box 10.1: Terminology

In other texts, the covariate may be referred to as an 'independent variable' and the outcome as a 'dependent variable', but this is misleading especially in terms of our covariate: the term 'independent' has a special meaning in statistics (see Section 8.1.3), and the covariate here is not necessarily 'independent' of the outcome. Later in this chapter, we'll also consider having multiple covariates, and these do not need to be statistically independent of each other. It's best, therefore, to avoid the term 'independent' variable and use a neutral term like 'covariate' or 'predictor' instead.

Of course, the model in (10.1) is a simplification of the real-world relationship between X and Y, and in particular, we don't expect every observation to lie exactly on this line. Our aim therefore, at least in part, is to find the 'best' estimates of the intercept, β_0, and slope, β_1, of this line, to create what is often referred to as a 'line of best fit'. These models and their extensions are the basis of this chapter.

In this chapter, we consider:

- simple linear regression models;

- multiple linear regression models;

The R Book, Third Edition. Elinor Jones, Simon Harden and Michael J. Crawley.
© 2023 John Wiley & Sons Ltd. Published 2023 by John Wiley & Sons Ltd.
Companion website: www.wiley.com/go/jones/therbook3e

- hypothesis testing in simple and multiple linear regression models;
- checking the assumptions made on simple and multiple linear regression models;
- improving simple and multiple linear regression models (improving model fit).

The models we consider here can be substantially extended, for example in allowing non-linear relationships between covariates and outcome. Later in the book, we cover such extensions (see Table 10.1 in Section 10.7 for a list of *R* functions relating to these types of regression models).

10.1 The simple linear regression model

Let us start with an example which shows the growth of caterpillars fed on experimental diets differing in their tannin content:

```
caterpillardata <- read.table ("caterpillar.txt" , header = T)
attach (caterpillardata)
head (caterpillardata)

  growth tannin
1     12      0
2     10      1
3      8      2
4     11      3
5      6      4
6      7      5

plot (tannin, growth, pch = 19, col = hue_pal ()(3)[1],
      xlab = "% tannin in diet", ylab = "growth rate")

detach (caterpillardata)
```

Though there is no straight line that will pass through all points on the scatterplot in Figure 10.1, (it doesn't need to), there is a general linear trend: a well-chosen straight line through the scatter of points would describe the relationship between tannin and growth well. We would expect this line to have a negative slope, describing the nature of the relationship: the higher the percentage of tannin in the diet, the more slowly the caterpillars grew.

This section looks at the underlying model, the assumptions we make about our data in fitting this model, and how we do so in *R*.

10.1.1 Model format and assumptions

Let us suppose that we have *n* pairs of observations of X and Y, (x_1, y_1), ..., (x_n, y_n). We'll assume that the *i*th observed value of the outcome, y_i, is related to the *i*th observed value of the covariate (or predictor), x_i, by way of a straight line plus an error term.

We can write out the general form as follows:

$$Y_i = \beta_0 + \beta_1 x_i + \epsilon_i .$$ (10.2)

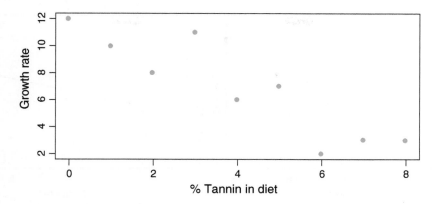

Figure 10.1 Caterpillar growth rate and percentage tannin in diet.

The error term, ϵ_i, is in recognition of the fact that the observations do not need to lie exactly on a straight line. Here, error does not mean 'mistake', but refers to unexplained variation about the line.

Box 10.2: Two important points

First, the distinction between $\{X, Y\}$ and $\{x, y\}$ is important. Lower-case letters are used to denote *observed* data, while capital letters are used to denote random variables (think of this as *before* we observe the data). In (10.2), the covariate is thought of as 'fixed' or observed, but the error term is a random variable. The latter implies that the outcome is also a random variable.

Second, though not explicitly mentioned here, the outcome is a numeric variable and generally a continuous variable. We look at what we can do when this is not the case in later chapters.

There is one obvious assumption that we make about this model: its linear structure. More often than not, however, we also need to make assumptions about the error term. Though the latter is not necessary to find the 'best' estimate of the intercept and slope, it is essential if, for example we want to test hypotheses with our regression model, or provide confidence intervals for predictions. The assumptions we make about the structure of the model, and about the error terms, can be simply stated as follows:

- the relationship between the outcome and covariate is linear;

- the error terms are independent: ϵ_i and ϵ_j are independent, when $i \neq j$;

- the error terms are normally distributed: $\epsilon_i \sim N(0, \sigma^2)$;

- the error terms have the same variance, say σ^2.

The first assumption implies that the relationship between X and Y can be described by a straight line – even if the observations themselves do not lie exactly on any line. For simple linear regression models this can be checked using a scatterplot. Figure 10.2 shows four examples of fitting a simple linear regression model to different data, with commentary below.

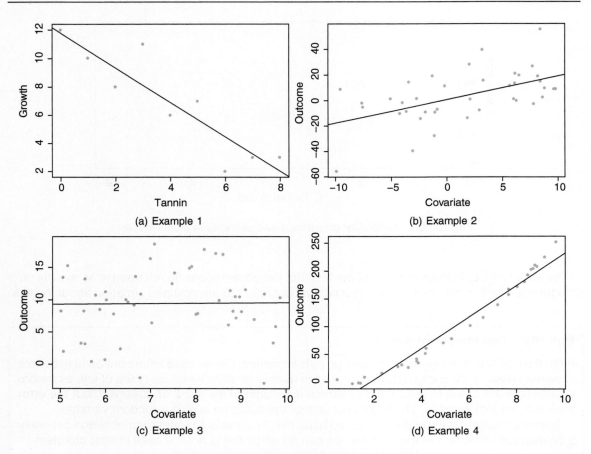

Figure 10.2   Simple linear regression models.

(a) This is the tannin-growth example, where a straight-line model seems to be a good fit for the data.

(b) The relationship here could still be described by a straight line despite there being a lot of variability around the line.

(c) There is little to no relationship between the covariate and outcome here. We can still fit a simple linear regression model, but this time the slope will be close to zero (why does that make sense?).

(d) While a strong relationship between the covariate and outcome is evident here, it isn't linear. Attempting to use simple linear regression here would be foolish. See Section 10.5.8 for suggestions of what could be done in this case.

There are many ways in which we could choose to find the 'best' slope and intercept for any given scatterplot, but they are generally computed using the so-called 'least squares' technique. This procedure minimises ('least') the squared vertical distance ('squares') between each observation and the straight line. These distances (before squaring) are known as **residuals** and are shown by solid blue lines in Figure 10.3. Notice what is happening here: for a specific value *x*, we are comparing the observed outcome *y* to the outcome that is predicted by the model (vertical distance between the green dotted horizontal lines for one observation).

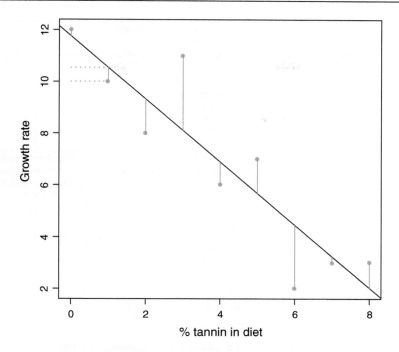

Figure 10.3 Distance between observations and line.

Why do we minimise the *squared* distance and not some other measure of distance between these points? There are convincing mathematical reasons why this is the case which are beyond the scope of this book, but rest assured that this is the method that R uses.

As we will see later in this chapter however, merely estimating the slope and intercept is rarely enough. Usually, we want to do a lot more with our regression model, for which we need to impose assumptions on the error term.

Our error terms, ϵ, are assumed to be independent and follow a Normal distribution with the same variance. Note that it makes sense that the mean of the error terms is zero (this is not really an assumption, per se): suppose that the mean error is, say, 3. Then this implies that we are systematically underestimating our outcome by 3. This can be easily remedied by adding 3 to the intercept, which means that the error term mean is then zero. Incidentally, a common misconception is that the outcome needs to be normally distributed, but this is not the case: we are assuming that the error terms are normally distributed, which happens to have implications for the format of the outcome, but we won't discuss this further here.

Though these assumptions on the error term are often 'hidden', these are exactly what R assumes in order to provide much of the model output. We'll consider this output in detail in Section 10.2, but for now we'll look at how to use R to run a simple linear regression model.

10.1.2 Building a simple linear regression model

The basic steps in building a simple linear regression model are shown in Figure 10.4. The first step is good practice regardless of the analysis that you plan to undertake, and indeed often helps to clarify which analyses might be appropriate. Cleaning will ensure that the data are in an appropriate format and can help in the detection of problems at an early stage.

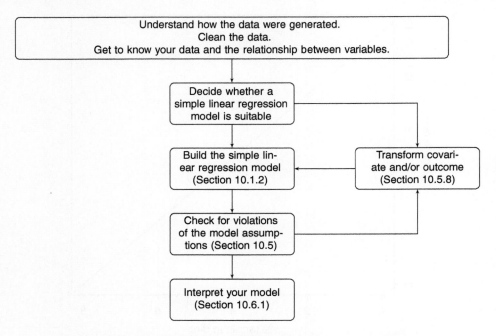

Figure 10.4 Building a simple linear regression model.

The second step – in this case deciding whether the simple linear regression model is an appropriate approach – will generally involve checking that the relationship between the covariate and outcome is linear. This can be simply done using a scatterplot. Steps can be taken at this point to improve any issues around linearity; see Section 10.5.8 on how transformation of variables may help here.

The third step is what we'll consider in this section: building the simple linear regression model in *R*. The remaining suggested steps are discussed in Sections 10.5 and 10.6.1, respectively.

Running a simple linear regression model in *R* is best done using the `lm ()` command (it stands for Linear Model). For the caterpillar growth example, the following code loads the required data and then runs the `lm ()` command on the variables of interest:

```
attach (caterpillardata)
lm (growth ~ tannin)


Call:
lm(formula = growth ~ tannin)

Coefficients:
(Intercept)          tannin
     11.756          -1.217

detach (caterpillardata)
```

Notice the way the variables growth and tannin are fed to the command `lm ()`: we insert the outcome first, followed by a twiddle symbol ~, and then the covariate. We don't have to `attach ()`

our data in order to run `lm ()`: the following code provides identical output where we specify the dataset to be used *within* the `lm ()` command.

```
lm (growth ~ tannin, data = caterpillardata)
```

The output from `lm ()` gives an estimate of the intercept and slope, but we can ask for more information (which will be vital later in the chapter). The most convenient way of doing this is to save the output of the `lm ()` command in an object – called `caterpillar_model` below – then request a summary of this object. This has the advantage that the output is accessible without having to run the model again.

```
caterpillar_model <- lm (growth ~ tannin, data = caterpillardata)
summary (caterpillar_model)


Call:
lm(formula = growth ~ tannin, data = caterpillardata)

Residuals:
    Min      1Q  Median      3Q     Max
-2.4556 -0.8889 -0.2389  0.9778  2.8944

Coefficients:
            Estimate Std. Error t value Pr(>|t|)
(Intercept)  11.7556     1.0408  11.295 9.54e-06 ***
tannin       -1.2167     0.2186  -5.565 0.000846 ***
---
Signif. codes:  0 '***' 0.001 '**' 0.01 '*' 0.05 '.' 0.1 ' ' 1

Residual standard error: 1.693 on 7 degrees of freedom
Multiple R-squared:  0.8157,Adjusted R-squared:  0.7893
F-statistic: 30.97 on 1 and 7 DF,  p-value: 0.0008461
```

An alternative, that will provide identical output but without saving the information in an object, is

```
summary (lm (growth ~ tannin, data = caterpillardata))
```

Box 10.3: Extracting information from the model output

We'll discuss the majority of the output later in the chapter, but for now

- The estimates of the slope and intercept are available in the `Estimate` column.

- The estimated standard deviation of the error term is known as `Residual standard error` in the output. Squaring this number gives an estimate of the variance of the error term.

- Information about the residuals – their five number summary – is given under the heading `Residuals`.

10.2   The multiple linear regression model

While the simple linear regression model provides a convenient way of describing the (linear) relationship between a covariate and an outcome, what should we do if we have more than one possible covariate?

Consider the air pollution dataset for example: our research question of interest may be to investigate how ozone concentration is related to wind speed, air temperature, and the intensity of solar radiation. Specified like this, it is clear that ozone is the outcome of interest, but there are three possible covariates to choose from: wind speed, air temperature, and the intensity of solar radiation. A good place to start might be to view the relationship between each pair of variables, which the `pairs ()` function automates. The resulting scatterplots are in Figure 10.5. Notice that the six plots under the diagonal are mirror images of those above.

```
ozone_pollution <- read.table ("ozone_pollution.txt", header = T)
attach (ozone_pollution)
pairs (ozone_pollution, col = hue_pal ()(3)[1])
```

```
detach (ozone_pollution)
```

The outcome variable, ozone concentration, is shown on the *y*-axis of the bottom row of panels: there is a strong negative relationship with wind speed, a positive correlation with temperature, and a rather unclear, humped relationship with radiation. There are also clear relationships between some of the proposed covariates, for example between wind speed and air temperature.

How do we make the most of all this information about the response? One option is to build a simple linear regression models for each possible covariate. This, however, is an unsatisfactory solution. We wouldn't be making the most of the *combined* information about the outcome contained in our collection of covariates.

A **multiple linear regression model** does just that: it extends the idea of a simple linear regression to allow more than one covariate. This is an exceptionally powerful idea and is a technique that is used extensively in practice.

10.2.1   Model format and assumptions

The multiple linear regression model handles data that come in the form $(y_i, x_{i1}, \ldots, x_{ip})$ for $(i = 1, \ldots, n)$. That is, for the *i*th observation, we have a single observed outcome y_i and in this case, p covariates, $x_{i1}, \ldots, x_{ip}$. The model is written as

$$Y_i = \beta_0 + \beta_1 x_{i1} + \ldots + \beta_p x_{ip} + \epsilon_i . \tag{10.3}$$

Compare this with the general form of the simple linear regression model, and we'll see that this is a 'natural' extension of it. Indeed, the simple linear regression model is just a special case of the multiple linear regression model.

For the simple linear regression model, there was a nice geometric interpretation: we could visualise the model as a straight line passing through a scatterplot, or in other words, a line in two-dimensional space. What does the model in (10.3) 'look' like? This model with p covariates as in (10.3) will produce a **hyperplane**: with p covariates this is a hyperplane in $(p + 1)$-dimensional space. Anything above two covariates therefore means we can't visualise our scatter of points and the resulting hyperplane!

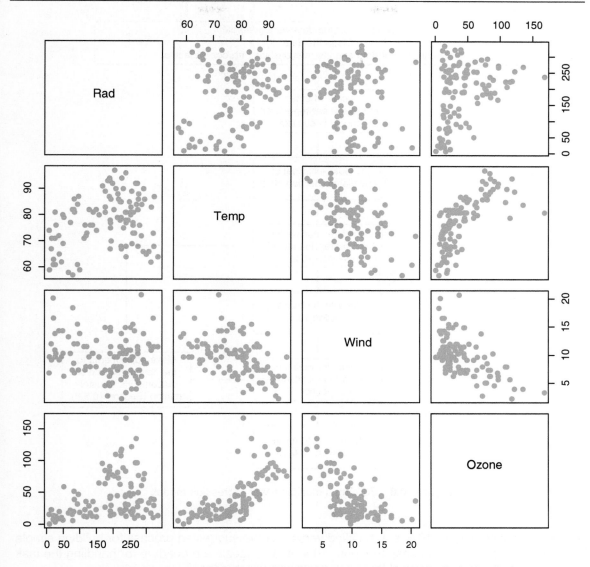

Figure 10.5   Scatterplots of all possible pairs of variables in the ozone dataset.

There are, of course, assumptions to be made in building this model. Once again, we assume linearity, but unlike in the simple linear regression case, we can't easily check this assumption by creating a single scatterplot. We will need alternative methods, which we'll revisit in Section 10.5, to check this assumption. The same assumptions apply to the error terms as did for the simple linear regression model; we'll also discuss how we can check these assumptions in Section 10.5.

10.2.2   Building a multiple linear regression model

Building a simple linear regression model was straightforward as we had only one covariate to consider. With more covariates comes added complexity and the process becomes more of an

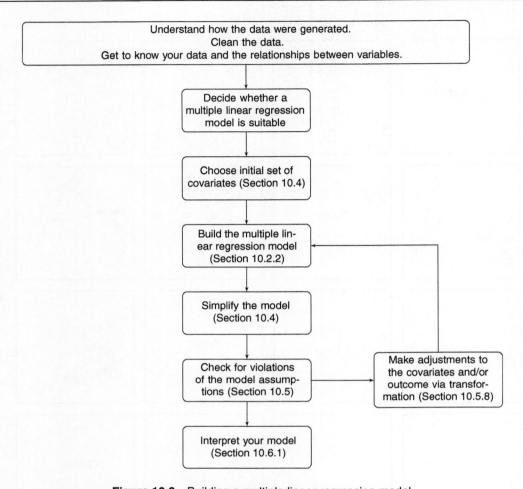

Figure 10.6 Building a multiple linear regression model.

art than a science. Figure 10.6 is a modified version of the suggested process for building simple linear regression models, as seen in Figure 10.4, and suggests a procedure for handling the task of modeling and which sections of this book deals with which parts.

Deciding whether a multiple linear model is suitable in the first place will come from knowledge of the context of the data and how it was generated, for example in ensuring that observations are not obviously dependent on one another which would immediately violate the assumption of independent errors. In particular, no longer can we identify problems with linearity before building the model, as we could for the simple linear regression model, and we have the additional hurdle of deciding how we deal with multiple covariates. These issues are discussed at various points in this chapter.

For now, we'll focus on how to run a multiple linear regression model in R, and do so using the air pollution example. We'll build a multiple linear regression model with ozone concentration as the outcome and wind speed, air temperature, and the intensity of solar radiation as covariates.

Running this model in R follows the same pattern as building a simple linear regression model: we use the `lm ()` command, and feed the covariates to this function, separating them using +.

```
attach (ozone_pollution)
ozone_mod1 <- lm (ozone ~ rad + temp + wind)
summary (ozone_mod1)


Call:
lm(formula = ozone ~ rad + temp + wind)

Residuals:
    Min      1Q  Median      3Q     Max
-40.485 -14.210  -3.556  10.124  95.600

Coefficients:
              Estimate Std. Error t value Pr(>|t|)
(Intercept) -64.23208   23.04204  -2.788  0.00628 **
rad           0.05980    0.02318   2.580  0.01124 *
temp          1.65121    0.25341   6.516 2.43e-09 ***
wind         -3.33760    0.65384  -5.105 1.45e-06 ***
---
Signif. codes:  0 '***' 0.001 '**' 0.01 '*' 0.05 '.' 0.1 ' ' 1

Residual standard error: 21.17 on 107 degrees of freedom
Multiple R-squared:  0.6062, Adjusted R-squared:  0.5952
F-statistic: 54.91 on 3 and 107 DF,  p-value: < 2.2e-16

detach (ozone_pollution)
```

If, for some reason, we do not want an intercept in your model, we can suppress it in one of two ways (the `-1` or `+0` can go anywhere to the right of ~):

```
lm (ozone ~ rad + temp + wind - 1)
lm (ozone ~ rad + temp + wind + 0)
```

This forces the regression line through the origin, (0, 0, 0, 0), implying that if `rad=0`, `temp=0`, and `wind=0`, then we must have `ozone=0`. There is no reason to enforce this here, but this might be a sensible strategy in some cases. Consider, for example predicting the number of calories in 100 g of a product, with fat, carbohydrate, and protein content as covariates. It *might* be desirable to build a model that guarantees a zero calorie prediction if a food product has no fat, carbohydrate or protein; in this case, we could consider a model without intercept. Such cases are rare, and it is advisable to include an intercept unless there are exceptional reasons not to.

10.2.3 Categorical covariates

What if one or more of your covariates is categorical? Can you still use linear regression models? The good news is that yes, you can.

Categorical variables cannot be directly included as covariates in a linear model because their values are names (or labels) and not numbers: we need to convert them into a format that *R* can work with. Essentially, this means turning a categorical variable into a sequence of binary variables, also known as dummy variables. These variables, as the name suggests, can only take one of two values: 0 or 1.

When you pass a categorical variable to *R* as a covariate, or specify that an apparently numeric variable should be treated as categorical (sometimes categorical variables are coded using numbers, but these numbers are just labels), *R* will *automatically create these binary variables so we don't have to*.

Let us take a simple example: we have an experiment in which crop yields per unit area were measured from 10 randomly selected fields on each of three soil types. All fields were sown with the same variety of seed and provided with the same fertilizer and pest control inputs. The question is whether soil type significantly affects crop yield, and if so, to what extent.

```
yields <- read.table ("yields.txt", header = T)
yields

    sand clay loam
1      6   17   13
2     10   15   16
3      8    3    9
4      6   11   12
5     14   14   15
6     17   12   16
7      9   12   17
8     11    8   13
9      7   10   18
10    11   13   14
```

At the moment, these data are not in the correct format to run a linear regression: these data are currently in **wide** format, whereas we want them in **long** format. The long format of these data will involve generating one column with the soil types (this will be our covariate) and another for the yield (our outcome variable). This can easily be achieved by using the `stack ()` function. This would give a long list in the output here, so we limit the displayed results to the first few observations by using the function `head ()`.

```
yields_long <- stack (yields)
head (yields_long)

  values  ind
1      6 sand
2     10 sand
3      8 sand
4      6 sand
5     14 sand
6     17 sand
```

We see that the `stack ()` function has invented names for the outcome variable `values` and the covariate `ind`. We will most likely want to change these:

```
names (yields_long) <- c ("yield", "soil")
head (yields_long)
```

```
   yield soil
1      6 sand
2     10 sand
3      8 sand
4      6 sand
5     14 sand
6     17 sand
```

Now that our data are in the correct format, we need to consider how to convert the categorical variable `soil` into something that R can handle. Notice that there are three categories in total, so we can do this using just two binary variables. Let us call these x_{i1} and x_{i2} for now and define them as follows:

$$x_{i1} = \begin{cases} 1 & \text{if clay} \\ 0 & \text{otherwise} \end{cases} \qquad x_{i2} = \begin{cases} 1 & \text{if loam} \\ 0 & \text{otherwise} \end{cases}$$

Note that x_{i1} and x_{i2} are each dummy variables, and:

- Soil is clay if $x_{i1} = 1$ (in which case $x_{i2} = 0$);
- Soil is loam if $x_{i2} = 1$ (in which case $x_{i1} = 0$);
- Soil is sand if $x_{i1} = 0$ and $x_{i2} = 0$.

The important thing to notice is that *two* dummy variables are enough to code a categorical variable with *three* categories, and in general $(q - 1)$ dummy variables are enough to code a categorical variable with q categories. The subsequent model can be written in the form

$$Y_i = \beta_0 + \beta_1 x_{i1} + \beta_2 x_{i2} + \epsilon_i. \tag{10.4}$$

Notice what happens in (10.4):

- If the soil is clay: $Y_i = \beta_0 + \beta_1 + \epsilon_i$ (because $x_{i1} = 1; x_{i2} = 0$);
- If the soil is loam: $Y_i = \beta_0 + \beta_2 + \epsilon_i$ (because $x_{i1} = 0; x_{i2} = 1$);
- If the soil is sand: $Y_i = \beta_0 + \epsilon_i$ (because $x_{i1} = 0; x_{i2} = 0$).

The mean yield for sand type soil is described by the intercept β_0. If we consider clay or loam, then the additional β_1 or β_2 describes the mean yield difference between sand and each other soil type. Notice, however, that what we have here are three intercept-only models: the intercept is permitted to change by category. More generally, when we have at least one categorical variable as a covariate, the intercept can change for observations from different categories (if there are differences in outcome between the categories).

In our example here, `sand` is considered the **reference category**, but is an arbitrary choice: any of the categories will do. It is best, however, to avoid using a category with very few observations as your reference as this can cause some instability in your model.

When we run a multiple regression model for the yield data, we see that R automatically creates the dummy variables required. It has chosen `sand` as the reference category in this case, but of course the choice is rather arbitrary.

```
yields_model <- lm (yield ~ soil, data = yields_long)
summary (yields_model)


Call:
lm(formula = yield ~ soil, data = yields_long)

Residuals:
   Min    1Q Median    3Q    Max
  -8.5  -1.8    0.3   1.7    7.1

Coefficients:
            Estimate Std. Error t value Pr(>|t|)
(Intercept)    9.900      1.081   9.158 9.04e-10 ***
soilclay       1.600      1.529   1.047  0.30456
soilloam       4.400      1.529   2.878  0.00773 **
---
Signif. codes:  0 '***' 0.001 '**' 0.01 '*' 0.05 '.' 0.1 ' ' 1

Residual standard error: 3.418 on 27 degrees of freedom
Multiple R-squared:  0.2392, Adjusted R-squared:  0.1829
F-statistic: 4.245 on 2 and 27 DF,  p-value: 0.02495
```

We can see that the mean yield for sand soil is 9.9, while the difference between yields for clay and sand soils is 1.6, for example.

In some cases, it doesn't matter which category is chosen as the reference as is probably the case here (unless you specifically want to compare the performance of, say, loam to each of clay and sand). An obvious example of where it *does* matter is in comparing treatments: supposing you want to compare two new treatments against the current gold standard. It would make sense for the current gold standard to be treated as the reference category, so that comparisons can be made between it and each of the new treatments.

Changing the reference category can be done by reordering the categories using factor (). To change the reference category from sand to loam, for example

```
yields_long$soil <- factor (yields_long$soil, levels = c ("loam", "clay", "sand"))
yields_model2 <- lm (yield ~ soil, data = yields_long)
summary (yields_model2)


Call:
lm(formula = yield ~ soil, data = yields_long)

Residuals:
   Min    1Q Median    3Q    Max
  -8.5  -1.8    0.3   1.7    7.1

Coefficients:
            Estimate Std. Error t value Pr(>|t|)
```

```
(Intercept)    14.300         1.081   13.229  2.58e-13 ***
soilclay       -2.800         1.529   -1.832  0.07807.
soilsand       -4.400         1.529   -2.878  0.00773 **
---
Signif. codes:  0 '***' 0.001 '**' 0.01 '*' 0.05 '.' 0.1 ' ' 1

Residual standard error: 3.418 on 27 degrees of freedom
Multiple R-squared:  0.2392,    Adjusted R-squared:  0.1829
F-statistic: 4.245 on 2 and 27 DF,  p-value: 0.02495
```

You can also use other methods to achieve the same, see for example Section 16.3 for an example.

Finally, two questions that you might be asking at this point are 'what would happen if we used *three* dummy variables to describe soil type?', and 'what would happen if we decided not to have an intercept in our model?'.

In answer to the first question, you would run into trouble: you would have four **regression coefficients** to estimate (the intercept and three 'slopes'), but only three pieces of information with which to do this (the yield information from each soil type). This is tantamount to trying to solve a set of three simultaneous equations involving four unknowns, which won't have a unique solution.

The second question is more interesting. If you don't have an intercept, then two dummy variables in this case won't distinguish between the three categories (otherwise, loam in the above example will be assumed to have $y_i = \epsilon_i$, implying a mean yield of zero). In this special case, we therefore need to use three dummy variables to code for our three categories. Remember that going ahead without an intercept is unusual and needs robust justification.

While *R* is perfectly happy to create dummy variables for categorical variables, it is sometimes helpful to create these explicitly. Creating tables of dummy variables for use in statistical modelling is extremely easy with the `model.matrix ()` function. You will see what the function does with a simple example.

In our modelling, we want to create a two-level dummy variable (present or absent) for each soil type (in three extra columns), so that we can ask questions such as whether the mean value of `yield` is significantly different in cases where each soil type was present, and when it was absent. So for the first row of the dataframe, we want `sand = TRUE`, and the rest as `FALSE`.

The long-winded way of doing this is to create a new factor for each soil type separately, but it is easy to do with `model.matrix ()`. The `-1` in the model formula ensures that we create a dummy variable for each of the three soil types (technically, it suppresses the creation of an intercept).

```
dummy_matrix <- model.matrix (~ yields_long$soil - 1)
head (dummy_matrix)

  yields_long$soilloam yields_long$soilclay yields_long$soilsand
1                    0                    0                    1
2                    0                    0                    1
3                    0                    0                    1
4                    0                    0                    1
5                    0                    0                    1
6                    0                    0                    1
```

This matrix has 30 rows, one for each observation in the original dataset. Now, we can join these three columns of dummy variables to the original dataframe, `yields_long`. We just join the new columns to it, after which we can use variable names like `yields_long.soilloam` in the statistical modelling (we might want to update the names to something snappier!):

```
new_frame <- data.frame (yields_long, model.matrix (~ yields_long$soil - 1))
head (new_frame)

  yield soil yields_long.soilloam yields_long.soilclay yields_long.soilsand
1     6 sand                    0                    0                    1
2    10 sand                    0                    0                    1
3     8 sand                    0                    0                    1
4     6 sand                    0                    0                    1
5    14 sand                    0                    0                    1
6    17 sand                    0                    0                    1
```

10.2.4 Interactions between covariates

In many circumstances, we would like to be able to describe the effect of an **interaction** between two (or more) covariates on the response. Interactions are interesting when dependence of the outcome on a specific covariate changes with the value of another covariate. This may sound a little abstract right now, but the next example should put that right.

The following experiment, with weight as the response variable, involved genotype, sex, and age as covariates. There are six levels of genotype and two levels of sex. We initially build a model for weight based on genotype, sex, and age as covariates.

```
gain <- read.table ("Gain.txt", header = T)
attach (gain)
gain_mod1 <- lm (Weight ~ Sex + Age + Genotype)
summary (gain_mod1)


Call:
lm(formula = Weight ~ Sex + Age + Genotype)

Residuals:
     Min       1Q   Median       3Q      Max
-0.40005 -0.15120 -0.01668  0.16953  0.49227

Coefficients:
               Estimate Std. Error t value Pr(>|t|)
(Intercept)     7.93701    0.10066  78.851  < 2e-16 ***
Sexmale        -0.83161    0.05937 -14.008  < 2e-16 ***
Age             0.29958    0.02099  14.273  < 2e-16 ***
GenotypeCloneB  0.96778    0.10282   9.412 8.07e-13 ***
GenotypeCloneC -1.04361    0.10282 -10.149 6.21e-14 ***
GenotypeCloneD  0.82396    0.10282   8.013 1.21e-10 ***
GenotypeCloneE -0.87540    0.10282  -8.514 1.98e-11 ***
```

```
GenotypeCloneF  1.53460     0.10282  14.925  < 2e-16 ***
---
Signif. codes:  0 '***' 0.001 '**' 0.01 '*' 0.05 '.' 0.1 ' ' 1

Residual standard error: 0.2299 on 52 degrees of freedom
Multiple R-squared:  0.9651,Adjusted R-squared:  0.9604
F-statistic: 205.7 on 7 and 52 DF,  p-value: < 2.2e-16
```

We could ask questions such as:

1. Does the effect of Age on Weight depend on Sex?

    - That is, should the coefficient of Age change depending on the given Sex?

2. Does the effect of Age on Weight depend on Genotype?

    - That is, should the coefficient of Age change depending on the given Genotype?

3. Does the effect of Genotype on Weight depend on Sex?

    - That is, should the coefficient of Genotype change depending on the given Sex?

And so on.

These are questions about interactions: how two (or more) covariates interact with each other in their effect on the outcome. Taking into account interactions in a regression model is generally a simple task: just multiply the two (or more) covariates which you think may interact with each other to form a set of new covariates. Of course, we don't need to literally create these covariates: we can simply tell *R* to include an interaction between specified covariates in the lm () function by using * instead of +.

An important point to note is that interactions can be between any type of variable, but the number of interaction terms it produces as extra 'covariates' in our model will depend on the nature of the variables used. Interactions can be between:

- two categorical covariates, which will produce $(p - 1) \times (q - 1)$ additional covariates (where p and q are the number of levels for each covariate);

- one categorical and one numeric covariate, which will produce $(p - 1)$ additional covariates (where p is the number of levels for the categorical covariate);

- two numeric covariates, which will produce one additional covariate.

As adding interactions is straightforward, it might be tempting to include interactions between all variables. This is rarely wise. As a general rule of thumb, if context-specific information leads you to suspect an interaction may be at play, then by all means try adding an interaction to the model.

This being said, it might be helpful to assess potential interactions *before* including them in a model. Interaction plots provide a visual representation of how two covariates interact (if at all). The relevant *R* functions are interaction.plot () for interactions between two categorical covariates, and coplot () which is a more general function that can deal with any type of covariates.

Let us go back to our experimental data, and suppose we have a reason to believe that an interaction between age and sex, and another between genotype and sex, may help us in explaining the outcome. The first is an interaction between a numeric and categorical variable, while the second

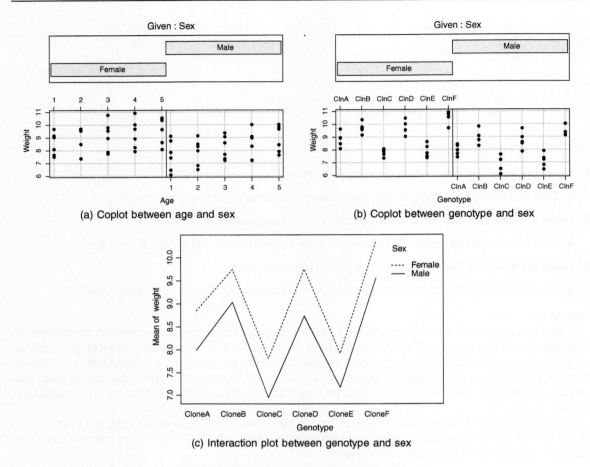

Figure 10.7   Plots to check for interaction.

involves two categorical variables. Figures 10.7a and 10.7b show the `coplot ()` output for both situations, while Figure 10.7c shows the equivalent `interaction.plot ()` function in action for the latter: Figures 10.7b and 10.7c show the same information in slightly different formats.

```
coplot (Weight ~ Age | Sex, data = gain)
coplot (Weight ~ Genotype | Sex, data = gain)
interaction.plot (Genotype, Sex, Weight)
```

What we are looking for here is evidence that males and females differ in terms of gradients/slopes or patterns. There is no obvious difference between males and females by genotype (Figures 10.7b and 10.7c): though females are generally heavier than males, the pattern of change over genotype is very similar. Notice that the difference in weight between females and males will be addressed by the covariate `Sexmale` on its own; this doesn't suggest that we need an interaction.

Meanwhile, a similar story is evident for age and sex: the gradient of a regression line fitted to each window in Figure 10.7a wouldn't differ particularly between men and women so again there is no evidence of an interaction between these two covariates.

No interaction effect could be seen using plots, and therefore unless these effects were of particular scientific interest we wouldn't include them in our model. Supposing, however, the interaction between age and sex *was* of interest, then we can incorporate this using:

```
gain_mod2 <- lm (Weight ~ Sex * Age + Genotype)
summary (gain_mod2)

Call:
lm(formula = Weight ~ Sex * Age + Genotype)

Residuals:
     Min       1Q    Median        3Q       Max
-0.37202  -0.15893  -0.00302   0.15263   0.45188

Coefficients:
               Estimate Std. Error t value Pr(>|t|)
(Intercept)     7.99759    0.11882  67.310  < 2e-16 ***
Sexmale        -0.95277    0.13933  -6.838 9.80e-09 ***
Age             0.27939    0.02970   9.406 9.98e-13 ***
GenotypeCloneB  0.96778    0.10290   9.405 1.00e-12 ***
GenotypeCloneC -1.04361    0.10290 -10.142 7.96e-14 ***
GenotypeCloneD  0.82396    0.10290   8.008 1.41e-10 ***
GenotypeCloneE -0.87540    0.10290  -8.507 2.36e-11 ***
GenotypeCloneF  1.53460    0.10290  14.914  < 2e-16 ***
Sexmale:Age     0.04039    0.04201   0.961    0.341
---
Signif. codes:  0 '***' 0.001 '**' 0.01 '*' 0.05 '.' 0.1 ' ' 1

Residual standard error: 0.2301 on 51 degrees of freedom
Multiple R-squared:  0.9658,    Adjusted R-squared:  0.9604
F-statistic: 179.8 on 8 and 51 DF,  p-value: < 2.2e-16

detach (gain)
```

Box 10.4: Main effects and interaction effects

The term 'interaction effect' is exactly as it sounds: here our only interaction effect was the variable `Sexmale:Age` in the output. The main effects are the covariates listed in our model that are not interaction effects. This includes `Sexmale` and `Age` along with `Genotype`.

Here we have an interaction effect between a categorical and numeric covariate, so given that the categorical variable has two levels we would expect just one additional row to appear in the output relating to the interaction between age and sex. This is indeed the case: the (single) interaction effect is in the last row of the main table in the output. But how does this allocate a different coefficient for `Age` depending on `Sex`?

For a male (so that `Sexmale` is 1), supposing that their genotype is clone D for simplicity (so that `GenotypeCloneD` is 1, but all others are 0), we have

$$\hat{y} = 8 - 0.95 + 0.28 \times \text{age} + 0.82 + 0.04 \times \text{age} = 7.87 + 0.32 \times \text{age}$$

For a female, with the same Genetic type as above, we have:

$$\hat{y} = 8 + 0.28 \times \text{age} + 0.82 = 8.82 + 0.28 \times \text{age}$$

You should see that the regression coefficient for age has changed depending on sex. The different intercept is due to the `Sexmale` **main effect** and *not* due to the interaction.

Interactions of three or more variables are possible by multiplying the relevant covariates. For example, to fit an interaction between all three covariates here:

```
lm (Weight ~ Age * Genotype * Sex, data = gain)
```

The interpretation of a fitted model with such interactions is cumbersome. More on this in Section 10.6.1.

10.3   Understanding the output

We'll use the model that we built in the last section – a model for ozone concentration using wind speed, air temperature, and the intensity of solar radiation as covariates – to understand the output from the function `lm ()`. The output is displayed here again for convenience.

```
summary (ozone_mod1)

Call:
lm(formula = ozone ~ rad + temp + wind)

Residuals:
    Min      1Q  Median      3Q     Max
-40.485 -14.210  -3.556  10.124  95.600

Coefficients:
             Estimate Std. Error t value Pr(>|t|)
(Intercept) -64.23208   23.04204  -2.788  0.00628 **
rad           0.05980    0.02318   2.580  0.01124 *
temp          1.65121    0.25341   6.516 2.43e-09 ***
wind         -3.33760    0.65384  -5.105 1.45e-06 ***
---
Signif. codes:  0 '***' 0.001 '**' 0.01 '*' 0.05 '.' 0.1 ' ' 1

Residual standard error: 21.17 on 107 degrees of freedom
Multiple R-squared:  0.6062,    Adjusted R-squared:  0.5952
F-statistic: 54.91 on 3 and 107 DF,  p-value: < 2.2e-16
```

10.3.1   Residuals

A residual is the difference between an observed outcome for a specific value of the covariate(s), and the outcome predicted by the model using the same value(s) of the covariate(s). The five number summary for the residuals is given. On its own, this is probably not the most helpful of information, but we will be using the residuals later in Section 10.4: these will turn out to be the key to assessing how well a model fits the data.

10.3.2   Estimates of coefficients

The `Estimate` column in the `Coefficients:` table of the output gives us the (least squares) estimates of the regression coefficients. The intercept is listed as `(Intercept)` – in this case it is estimated to be around -64.23. Estimates of the regression coefficients of the covariates are also given. In our case, the predicted model is

$$\hat{y} = -64.23 + 0.06 \times \text{rad} + 1.65 \times \text{temp} + -3.34 \times \text{wind}.$$

10.3.3   Testing individual coefficients

The remaining columns in the `Coefficients:` table of the output are

- `Std. Error`: The standard error of the estimated regression coefficient;
- `t value`: The t-statistic for the null hypothesis that the regression coefficient is zero. This is computed as the ratio of the estimated regression coefficient and its standard error;
- `Pr(>|t|)`: The p-value resulting from the t-test above.

The hypothesis being tested here is particularly interesting. Suppose we look at the case of the j'th regression coefficient, β_j:

$$H_0 : \beta_j = 0 \text{ given the other covariates in the model.}$$

$$H_1 : \beta_j \neq 0 \text{ given the other covariates in the model.}$$

This is an important test: if indeed the null hypothesis is true, then this is equivalent to leaving the jth covariate out of the model. This implies that the covariate doesn't help in explaining the variability in the outcome. The alternative hypothesis, of course, is that it remains in the model: that this particular covariate *does* help in explaining the variability in the outcome. The underlying test is a t-test: the test statistic as given in the `t value` column is compared to a t-distribution with $(n - p)$ degrees of freedom, where n is the number of observations and p is the number of regression coefficients to estimate (including the intercept). See, for example Section 9.1 for an example of a t-test.

Box 10.5: Testing the intercept

Even if we don't reject the hypothesis that the intercept is zero, it is rarely wise to remove it.

These hypothesis tests can be used to check if a *single* regression coefficient is nonzero. We shouldn't be eliminating multiple covariates simultaneously on the basis that their p-values are all 'too large': this is not what's being tested here. It can happen that two or more of the p-values for the regression coefficients are large so may lead us to think that we could remove these covariates simultaneously. However, as we'll see later, an appropriate statistical test to look at whether we can remove two or more covariates simultaneously may find that it is best not to. Remember that the hypothesis is conditional on all other variables being present, so while there may be no evidence to retain covariate A in the model when B is in there, and no evidence to retain covariate B in the model when A is in there, this is not evidence that we can remove *both* A and B.

The stars (if any) next to the p-values give a helpful at-a-glance view of how small the p-value is for each of these t-tests. As noted in the `Signif. codes` legend beneath the table of coefficients, three stars denotes a p-value of less than 0.001, two stars a p-value of between 0.001 and 0.01, and so on. These cut-offs for levels of p-values are arbitrary and should not be taken too seriously.

10.3.4 Residual standard error

The residual standard error is listed beneath the main table in the output. It is the sample estimate of the standard deviation, σ, of the error term, ϵ, in (10.3). For the ozone dataset in hand, the estimate is 21.17, and therefore the estimated variance of the error term is its square, 448.26.

10.3.5 R^2 and its variants

One useful measure we can extract from a model is the coefficient of determination, commonly known as R^2 ('R squared'). This is a sliding scale between 0 and 1 measuring the *proportion of variability in the outcome that is explained by the covariates in the model.* An R^2 of zero indicates that there is no linear relationship between the outcome and covariates (for example in Figure 10.8a), while an R^2 of 1 indicates that (a linear combination of) the covariate(s) can perfectly predict the outcome (for example in Figure 10.8b).

The R^2 can be used as a very rough guide to assessing the strength of the linear relationship between the response variable and the covariates in the model. It should not be used to decide on which model to use, or to compare between models, and should be viewed as just one tool in a modeller's toolkit.

A very important point to note is that a low R^2 isn't necessarily an indication of a poor-fitting model. See, for example Figure 10.8c where a simple linear regression model isn't a bad choice, but due to the amount of variability in the outcome, the R^2 is low. The converse is also true: a high R^2 doesn't necessarily mean you have a 'good' model. In Figure 10.8d, the R^2 is high but a simple linear regression model is clearly the wrong model.

In the R output, there are two versions of R^2: the `Multiple R-squared` and the `Adjusted R-squared`. The R^2 as described here is the `Multiple R-squared`. The `Adjusted R-squared` attempts to get around an undesirable property of R^2: adding covariates into a model will never decrease the R^2, and indeed will very likely increase it. This is undesirable since we could artificially inflate our R^2 by simply increasing the number of covariates we use in the model. Indeed, if we have n observations in our dataset, and we use $(n-1)$ covariates in our model, then we will ensure that $R^2 = 1$: perfect prediction of the outcome from the covariates! To see why this is the case, consider the case that we have two observations and only one covariate. We can guarantee that a simple linear regression model can be found that fits exactly through these two points, yielding an R^2 of 1. This argument extends to however many observations you happen to have. The adjusted R^2 includes a penalty to prevent this happening: the more covariates you add to your model, the bigger the penalty. This penalty is arbitrary, and there's nothing wrong with using `Multiple R-squared` without the penalty, subject to you bearing in mind this property.

10.3.6 The regression F-test

The final line of the `lm ()` output is an F-test, which is sometimes known as an Analysis of Variance for regression (or ANOVA for regression). This is a rather severe statistical test, but serves as a blunt tool to assess your model. Suppose that the model you are building has an intercept, β_0, and

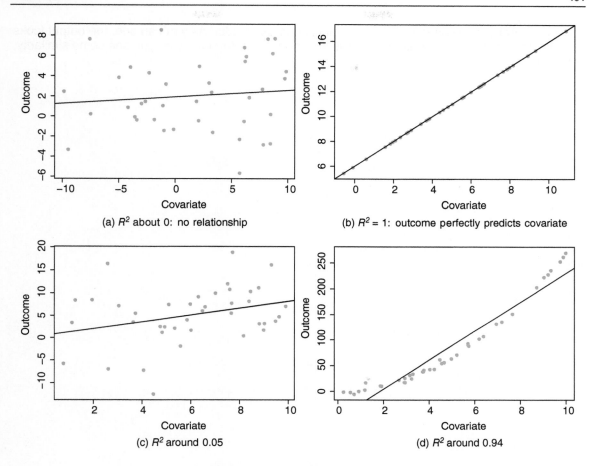

Figure 10.8 R^2 of various relationships.

further regression coefficients $\beta_1, \ldots, \beta_p$ for p covariates. The hypothesis in question here is

$$H_0 : \beta_1 = \ldots = \beta_p = 0 \; ;$$

$$H_1 : \text{At least one of } \beta_1, \ldots, \beta_p \text{ is non-zero.}$$

The null hypothesis can be rephrased as 'remove ALL covariates from the model'. This seems rather extreme, but it tells us something about whether the covariates have any power in describing the outcome. If we fail to reject this hypothesis, then we probably don't have a very powerful model on our hands.

10.3.7 ANOVA: Same model, different output

It is worth spending some time discussing the ANOVA for regression a little more. In Section 10.3.6, we discussed the ANOVA for regression which boils down to an F-test comparing the model in question with the intercept-only model. We'll also be using this function later in the chapter to compare models. There is a lot more going on behind the scenes here, which we'll now consider.

Let us start by applying the `anova ()` function to our model. As you can see, the output looks very different to the `lm ()` output, which is also given for reference. Can you see some similarity, however?

```
summary (ozone_mod1)


Call:
lm(formula = ozone ~ rad + temp + wind)

Residuals:
    Min      1Q   Median      3Q      Max
-40.485 -14.210  -3.556  10.124   95.600

Coefficients:
             Estimate Std. Error t value Pr(>|t|)
(Intercept) -64.23208   23.04204  -2.788  0.00628 **
rad           0.05980    0.02318   2.580  0.01124 *
temp          1.65121    0.25341   6.516 2.43e-09 ***
wind         -3.33760    0.65384  -5.105 1.45e-06 ***
---
Signif. codes:  0 '***' 0.001 '**' 0.01 '*' 0.05 '.' 0.1 ' ' 1

Residual standard error: 21.17 on 107 degrees of freedom
Multiple R-squared:  0.6062,Adjusted R-squared:  0.5952
F-statistic: 54.91 on 3 and 107 DF,  p-value: < 2.2e-16

anova (ozone_mod1)

Analysis of Variance Table

Response: ozone
           Df Sum Sq Mean Sq F value    Pr(>F)
rad         1  14780   14780  32.971 8.853e-08 ***
temp        1  47378   47378 105.692 < 2.2e-16 ***
wind        1  11680   11680  26.057 1.450e-06 ***
Residuals 107  47964     448
---
Signif. codes:  0 '***' 0.001 '**' 0.01 '*' 0.05 '.' 0.1 ' ' 1
```

The `anova ()` output contains the building blocks of the F-test we saw in Section 10.3.6, but we won't worry about that here. What you should look at are the *p*-values. Notice that the last *p*-value – that for `wind` – is the same for both `lm ()` and `anova ()`. Let us do something seemingly innocent and switch around the *order* of the covariates in the model:

```
attach (ozone_pollution)
ozone_mod1a <-lm (ozone ~ wind + rad + temp)
summary (ozone_mod1a)
```

```
Call:
lm(formula = ozone ~ wind + rad + temp)

Residuals:
    Min      1Q  Median      3Q     Max
-40.485 -14.210  -3.556  10.124  95.600

Coefficients:
             Estimate Std. Error t value Pr(>|t|)
(Intercept) -64.23208   23.04204  -2.788  0.00628 **
wind         -3.33760    0.65384  -5.105 1.45e-06 ***
rad           0.05980    0.02318   2.580  0.01124 *
temp          1.65121    0.25341   6.516 2.43e-09 ***
---
Signif. codes:  0 '***' 0.001 '**' 0.01 '*' 0.05 '.' 0.1 ' ' 1

Residual standard error: 21.17 on 107 degrees of freedom
Multiple R-squared:  0.6062,Adjusted R-squared:  0.5952
F-statistic: 54.91 on 3 and 107 DF,  p-value: < 2.2e-16

anova (ozone_mod1a)

Analysis of Variance Table

Response: ozone
          Df Sum Sq Mean Sq F value     Pr(>F)
wind       1  45762   45762 102.088 < 2.2e-16 ***
rad        1   9044    9044  20.176 1.792e-05 ***
temp       1  19032   19032  42.457 2.429e-09 ***
Residuals 107  47964     448
---
Signif. codes:  0 '***' 0.001 '**' 0.01 '*' 0.05 '.' 0.1 ' ' 1

detach (ozone_pollution)
```

Other than switching rows around in the `lm ()` output, it's identical to the previous version. However, the `anova ()` output is different. Notice again that the last *p*-value is the same for both `lm ()` and `anova ()`, but this time this relates to `temp`.

So what is the ANOVA output telling us? Going back to our `ozone_mod1` model, and applying the `anova ()` function:

- the first row of the output compares the model with `rad` to the intercept-only model (no covariates) via an F-test;

- the second row of the output compares the model with `rad, temp` to the model with only `rad` via an F-test;

- the third row of the output compares the model with `rad, temp, wind` to the model with `rad, temp` via an F-test.

By the time we reach the row corresponding to the last-entered covariate in the ANOVA table, we are comparing the 'full' model with removing just one covariate, in this case `wind`. This is identical to the t-test for `wind` that appears in the `lm ()` output, because the F-test in this special case is mathematically identical to a t-test which we saw in Section 10.3.3 (see Section 10.4.3 for full details why the F- and t-test are identical here). The other *p*-values in the ANOVA table are *not* equivalent to the t-tests in the `lm ()` output, so the *p*-values are different in this case.

10.3.8 Extracting model information

We often want to extract material from fitted models (e.g. slopes, residuals, or *p* values), and there are three different ways of doing this:

- extracting from the model object;
- extracting from the summary of the model;
- directly by name, e.g. `coef (model)`.

Let us take a look at what we can extract with each of the methods above from `ozone_mod1`. First, we'll look what was saved inside the model object itself.

```
names (ozone_mod1)

[1] "coefficients"  "residuals"     "effects"       "rank"
[5] "fitted.values" "assign"        "qr"            "df.residual"
[9] "xlevels"       "call"          "terms"         "model"
```

There's a whole host of information here, which we can extract using the name or number attached to each element. For example, if we want to extract just the coefficients, we could do this via one of two ways:

```
ozone_mod1$coefficients

 (Intercept)           rad          temp          wind
-64.23208116    0.05979717    1.65120780   -3.33759763

ozone_mod1[1]

$coefficients
 (Intercept)           rad          temp          wind
-64.23208116    0.05979717    1.65120780   -3.33759763
```

Remembering which numbers go with which bits of the output is probably harder than using the names directly so we'll stick to names.

We may want to extract a *subset* of the coefficients:

```
ozone_mod1$coefficients[[2]]

[1] 0.05979717
```

or save all coefficients as a vector (useful if you're running many analyses and want to keep track of the estimated coefficients, for example):

```
coef_ozone_mod1 <- as.vector (ozone_mod1$coefficients)
coef_ozone_mod1

[1] -64.23208116   0.05979717   1.65120780  -3.33759763
```

A slightly different set of information is contained in the summary of the model:

```
names (summary (ozone_mod1))

[1] "call"          "terms"      "residuals"     "coefficients"
[5] "aliased"       "sigma"      "df"            "r.squared"
[9] "adj.r.squared" "fstatistic" "cov.unscaled"
```

Again, we can access these bits of information by name or by number. For example, if I wanted to extract the residual standard error:

```
summary (ozone_mod1)$sigma

[1] 21.17222
```

or save the residuals as a newly defined object:

```
resid_ozone_mod1 <- summary (ozone_mod1)$residuals
head (resid_ozone_mod1)

        1           2           3           4           5           6
7.9379186   0.9898344 -12.8133444  -0.4769439  -9.2724401  25.9497483
```

Finally, some information can be extracted using a particular function applied to the model object. These include the coefficients, the residual standard error, the residuals, and the fitted values. You get the idea by now, so we won't run these functions:

```
coef (ozone_mod1)
sigma (ozone_mod1)
residuals (ozone_mod1)
fitted (ozone_mod1)
```

10.4 Fitting models

10.4.1 The principle of parsimony

One of the most important themes running through this book concerns model simplification. The principle of parsimony is attributed to the early fourteenth-century English nominalist philosopher,

William of Occam, who insisted that, given a set of equally good explanations for a given phenomenon, *the correct explanation is the simplest explanation*. It is called Occam's razor because he 'shaved' his explanations down to the bare minimum: his point was that in explaining something, assumptions must not be needlessly multiplied. For multiple linear regression models, the principle of parsimony means that:

- models should have as few parameters as possible;
- a model without interactions is preferred to a model containing interactions between factors, all else being equal;
- the levels of a categorical covariate may need to be grouped if they do not differ significantly from each other in terms of the outcome.

In our zeal for model simplification, however, we must be careful not to throw the baby out with the bathwater. Einstein made a characteristically subtle modification to Occam's razor. He said: 'A model should be as simple as possible. But no simpler.' Thus, we should only include an explanatory variable in a model if it significantly improves the fit of the model; the fact that we went to the trouble of measuring something does not mean we have to include it in our model. So, models should have as few covariates as possible, while still explaining as much of the variability in the outcome as is realistically possible.

In practice, the principle of parsimony means that simplifying our models becomes an important task for any modeller. So, given all this, *how* should we go about simplifying a model? There are no fixed rules and no absolutes: how we achieve this is essentially a process of exploration. The thing to remember about multiple regression is that, in principle, there is no end to it. The number of combinations of interaction terms (and curvature terms, which are discussed later in Section 10.5.8) is endless, but a model resulting from any simplifying process:

- must not lead to significant reductions in the model's power to explain the outcome;
- must make good scientific sense;
- should not be more difficult to interpret than is necessary.

The second and third items on this list mainly are mainly concerned with understanding the context of the data and thoughtfully choosing which covariates to retain in the model. For a model to be appropriate in this sense, we may need to incorporate covariates that do not help us particularly in explaining the outcome. This includes, but is by no means limited to, dealing with interactions: if a model includes an interaction term, it is highly recommended that the terms for the individual covariates are kept in the model even if these main effects don't have much of an impact in helping to predict the outcome. Without these however, interpretation gets very tricky indeed (and what use is a model that is either very hard, or not possible, to interpret?). See Section 10.6.1 for further details.

To make matters more complicated, an important point to realise is that it is likely that at least some of the covariates are correlated with each other. Some correlation is expected and won't cause a problem (see Section 10.5.7 for potential problems when correlation is too strong). However, correlation between covariates means that deleting some of these from the model will *change how the remaining covariates influence the outcome*.

For example in our ozone pollution data, the covariates `wind` and `temp` are correlated with one another as we saw in Figure 10.5. If we remove, say, `temp` from the model, the regression coefficient of `wind` changes considerably, as does the intercept and to a lesser extent the regression coefficient of `rad`. The standard errors and *p*-values of the remaining covariates also change, though these are not requested in the output here. This is nothing to worry about per se, but it is something that you should bear in mind when modelling.

```
attach (ozone_pollution)
lm (ozone ~ rad + temp + wind)


Call:
lm(formula = ozone ~ rad + temp + wind)

Coefficients:
(Intercept)            rad           temp           wind
   -64.2321         0.0598         1.6512        -3.3376

lm (ozone ~ rad + wind)


Call:
lm(formula = ozone ~ rad + wind)

Coefficients:
(Intercept)            rad           wind
    77.2687         0.1003        -5.4035

detach (ozone_pollution)
```

10.4.2   First plot the data

A sensible starting point is to visualise the data. Useful ways of doing this include the following:

- Plotting the response against each covariate separately;
  - This will highlight which covariates are highly correlated with the outcome, and therefore, potentially very important in our model.
- Plotting the explanatory variables against one another (e.g. `pairs ()`; see Section 10.2);
  - This will highlight which covariates are highly correlated with each other.
  - Care needs to be taken if they are highly correlated (see Section 10.5.7); one possible option is to remove one or more of these covariates.
  - Don't forget that correlation between covariates means that omitting covariates from the model will change how the remaining covariates influence the outcome.
- Plotting the response against covariates for different combinations of other covariates (checking for interactions) (e.g. conditioning plots via the function `coplot ()` or interaction plots via `interaction.plot ()`, see Section 10.2.4).

- This will highlight interaction terms that may be worth including in the model.

- However, building these plots to look for interactions between covariates generally means that you should have context-specific information to suspect an interaction may be at play.

- When there are lots of covariates, trying to do this for all possible interactions is not a sensible strategy!

Plotting the data will give a good indication of which covariates may play an important role when modelling the outcome. The more of a feel you get for the data the more likely you are to produce a meaningful model at the end of the process. It's also a good opportunity to check for potential problems with your data, for example high correlation between covariates. Only when we start building the model, however, can we assess just how important (or not) covariates really are in explaining the variability in the outcome.

10.4.3 Comparing nested models

There are no specific rules on where to start when building a model, but if you have a reasonably small number of covariates you could do worse than start by building a model with all covariates initially (which may include interaction terms if your initial data exploration suggested that these would be sensible). From this initial model, we must adopt the principle of parsimony and be prepared to simplify the model. This is often done on the basis of **deletion tests**: testing hypotheses about omitting covariates from a model.

You have already met the simplest type of a deletion test in Section 10.3.3: hypotheses relating to omitting a *single* covariate (or equivalently, testing the hypothesis that its regression coefficient is zero), given that the remaining covariates remain in the model. This was conducted using a t-test, and the results of which could be viewed in the output of `lm ()`.

You also saw a more severe form of deletion test in 10.3.6, which tested whether we could omit *all* covariates from the model. This was an F-test, and again, the results of this test could be viewed in the output of `lm ()`.

It would be reasonable to want to test a 'middle ground' hypothesis: whether we can omit a subset of the covariates in the model. For example, supposing that there are several covariates present in the model with associated regression coefficients $\beta_s, \beta_t, \ldots, \beta_u$, interest may be in testing a hypothesis such as

$$H_0 : \beta_s = \beta_t = \ldots = \beta_u = 0 , \tag{10.5}$$

for distinct indices $s, t, \ldots, u \in \{1, \ldots, p\}$. We cannot simply look at the result of the t-test for each of $\beta_s, \beta_t, \ldots, \beta_u$. We need a more sophisticated method that checks whether we can remove all covariates listed *simultaneously* (i.e. $\beta_s = \beta_t = \ldots = \beta_u = 0$). In the context of multiple linear regression, such hypotheses can be tested using F-tests (or possibly likelihood-ratio tests). Notice that the F-test given within the `lm ()` output – which tested whether we could omit *all* covariates – is the same F-test as here but applied to all covariates rather than just a subset.

A very important point to remember when we use these F-tests is that this is a comparison of **nested** models: we compare a model which uses a particular set of covariates with another model in which a *subset* of these covariates have been removed. This test can't be used when we are comparing non-nested models.

Box 10.6: Nested models

A model, let us call it Model A, is nested within another model, let us say Model B, if it contains a subset of the covariates that appear in Model B.

Running these F-tests is simply done in *R*. Let us consider our ozone data once again. At the moment, we have three covariates: `rad`, `temp`, and `wind`. We can test whether we can omit (simultaneously) the variables `rad` and `temp` from the model using:

```
ozone_mod2 <- lm (ozone ~ wind)
anova (ozone_mod2, ozone_mod1)

Analysis of Variance Table

Model 1: ozone ~ wind
Model 2: ozone ~ rad + temp + wind
  Res.Df    RSS Df Sum of Sq      F    Pr(>F)
1    109  76040
2    107  47964  2     28076 31.316 1.965e-11 ***
---
Signif. codes:  0 '***' 0.001 '**' 0.01 '*' 0.05 '.' 0.1 ' ' 1
```

Here, the resulting *p*-value is $1.9647811 \times 10^{-11}$ – which is very small – so we reject the null hypothesis (which said that we could omit these variables from the model with minimal consequences), and we on balance prefer to retain these covariates in the model. This does not mean to say that both are important: only that at least one of them is important enough to prefer to keep both covariates rather than omit both.

Let us check that when we apply this F-test in testing whether we can omit all covariates, we get the same *p*-value as the `lm ()` gave in its output.

```
ozone_mod3 <- lm (ozone ~ 1)
anova (ozone_mod3, ozone_mod1)

Analysis of Variance Table

Model 1: ozone ~ 1
Model 2: ozone ~ rad + temp + wind
  Res.Df    RSS Df Sum of Sq      F    Pr(>F)
1    110 121802
2    107  47964  3     73838 54.907 < 2.2e-16 ***
---
Signif. codes:  0 '***' 0.001 '**' 0.01 '*' 0.05 '.' 0.1 ' ' 1
```

Remember that the nested model this time is the intercept-only model, and in conducting this test, we get the same *p*-value as given by the F-test in the output of `lm ()`, as expected (see Section 10.3.6).

What would happen if we used our F-test to test whether we can omit exactly one covariate? Of course, the `lm ()` output already performs a t-test for this purpose, but if we were to perform the

F-test in this case, then the *p*-value would be identical to the *p*-value from the t-test in the output. In the example below, we conduct an F-test to assess whether we can omit `rad` from the model (i.e. a single covariate). Both give the same *p*-value.

```
ozone_mod4 <- lm (ozone ~ wind + temp)
summary (ozone_mod4)


Call:
lm(formula = ozone ~ wind + temp)

Residuals:
    Min      1Q  Median      3Q     Max
-42.160 -13.209  -3.089  10.588  98.470

Coefficients:
            Estimate Std. Error t value Pr(>|t|)
(Intercept) -67.2008    23.6083  -2.846  0.00529 **
wind         -3.2993     0.6706  -4.920 3.12e-06 ***
temp          1.8265     0.2504   7.293 5.32e-11 ***
---
Signif. codes:  0 '***' 0.001 '**' 0.01 '*' 0.05 '.' 0.1 ' ' 1

Residual standard error: 21.72 on 108 degrees of freedom
Multiple R-squared:  0.5817,Adjusted R-squared:  0.574
F-statistic:  75.1 on 2 and 108 DF, p-value: < 2.2e-16

anova (ozone_mod4, ozone_mod1)

Analysis of Variance Table

Model 1: ozone ~ wind + temp
Model 2: ozone ~ rad + temp + wind
  Res.Df    RSS Df Sum of Sq      F  Pr(>F)
1    108  50948
2    107  47964  1    2983.9 6.6565 0.01124 *
---
Signif. codes:  0 '***' 0.001 '**' 0.01 '*' 0.05 '.' 0.1 ' ' 1
```

So when applied to a single covariate, the F-test gives an identical *p*-value to the t-test. It would be rather inconvenient if this were not the case.

10.4.4 Comparing non-nested models

What if we want to compare two models that are not nested? That is, the outcome is the same in both models, we're using the same data to fit the models, but the covariates in one of the models isn't a subset of the covariates in the other.

If you are looking to perform a statistical test here, you could do worse than consider the `lmtest` package (Zeileis and Hothorn, 2002) which includes tests for comparing non-nested normal linear models. These include the Cox test, `coxtest ()`, the Davidson–MacKinnon J test, `jtest ()`, and the encompassing test, `encomptest ()` (though there are many 'flavours' of encompassing test out there).

Another popular option is to look at Akaike's information criterion (AIC). This is a statistic rather than a test, and comparing (non-nested) models boils down to choosing a model with the smallest AIC. It is known in the statistics trade as a **penalized log-likelihood**. See Section 2.5.2 for details on the likelihood function.

The idea is that the more parameters there are in the model, the better it fits the data, and so the larger the log likelihood. We could obtain a perfect fit if we had a separate parameter for every data point, but this model would have absolutely no explanatory power. The AIC takes the log-likelihood for the model under consideration then penalises it according to how many parameters we need to estimate. Mathematically, we have

$$\text{AIC} = -2 \times \text{log-likelihood} + 2(p + 1),$$

where p is the number of parameters in the model, and 1 is added for the estimated variance of the error terms (you could call this another parameter if you wanted to).

So the smaller the AIC (smaller because we're looking at the negative of the log-likelihood), the better the fit of the model. We could take two (potentially non-nested) models, compute the AIC for each of them, then the better fitting model would be the model with the *smallest* AIC.

There is an *R* function, `AIC ()`, to compute the information criterion directly from the model object. Let us build three models (notice that they aren't nested so the F-test from Section 10.4.3 wouldn't do), and try it out:

```
ozone_mod5 <- lm (ozone ~ temp + wind)
ozone_mod6 <- lm (ozone ~ rad + wind)
ozone_mod7 <- lm (ozone ~ rad + temp)
AIC (ozone_mod5, ozone_mod6)

           df      AIC
ozone_mod5  4 1003.327
ozone_mod6  4 1033.721

AIC (ozone_mod5, ozone_mod6, ozone_mod7)

           df      AIC
ozone_mod5  4 1003.327
ozone_mod6  4 1033.721
ozone_mod7  4 1020.820

detach (ozone_pollution)
```

When comparing `ozone_mod5` and `ozone_mod6`, we would prefer `ozone_mod5` because it has the smallest AIC. This is still the case when we also add `ozone_mod7` into the mix.

10.4.5   Dealing with large numbers of covariates

In Section 10.4, we suggested that a reasonable place to start building a model is to use all covariates in your dataset. With a reasonable sample size and a fairly small number of covariates, this shouldn't pose any problems. Simplifying your model is relatively straightforward too: after all, there are only so many combinations of covariates you could try if we ignore the possibility of transforming the data as we do in Section 10.5.8.

When you have a large number of covariates to deal with however (and hopefully a much larger number of observations), things get more tricky. Now, the process of simplifying your model becomes unwieldly: a natural question to ask is 'where do I start?'. How do I choose subsets of covariates to test whether I can omit them? Lots of covariates in your model may have a large p-value in the individual t-tests of the regression coefficients, but testing whether this subset can be removed entirely may well yield a small p-value: *some* of those covariates were important after all. But which ones? To compound matters, remember that *how* covariates are related to the outcome in a multiple regression model changes depending on which other covariates are present. How do we go about building and simplifying a model in this case?

There are no hard-and-fast rules to apply here: it is a matter of personal choice. There are procedures which automate the selection of covariates for your outcome, but these should be used with extreme care:

1. They are automated routines that cannot take into account the context of the data collection mechanism, and therefore whether certain covariates are 'important' regardless of their impact on the outcome;

2. There is no theoretical justification to these procedures, they simply attempt to make your life easier. These algorithms can fit complicated models to completely random data;

3. The model that results from using these automated procedures should be used as a first model: this is where your model building starts, and it is usually simpler and more manageable to improve this particular model by tinkering with it than try to create one from scratch.

4. This process of tinkering may involve:

   • Adding covariates back into the model (especially if they are known to be important but were omitted by the automated procedure);
   • Simplifying the model further by omitting some of the covariates suggested by the automated procedure;
   • Adding interactions where/if necessary;
   • Transforming variables (see Section 10.5.8 for details).

The main automatic model-building procedures are backward elimination, forward selection, and stepwise regression. Each employs a set of pre-programmed rules to determine which covariates should be kept in the model, and which should not. In summary, these algorithms work as follows:

• forward selection starts with just the intercept and adds covariates to the model one-by-one;

• backward elimination starts by fitting a model with all possible covariates (if possible), and chooses covariates to omit one-by-one;

• stepwise regression is a combination of the above two procedures: this approach allows both entering and removing covariates at each step, allowing to later enter or remove a covariate that has been either removed or entered, respectively, at an earlier step.

Generally, these processes add or remove one covariate at a time, and continue doing so until the programmed 'stop' condition is met. One possible strategy is to run all three types of algorithm and compare their results. If all three methods suggest roughly the same model then this can provide an *initial* direction for the analysis.

Implementation of these will vary from software to software. In *R*, for example, `step ()` provides forward, backward, or stepwise ('both') procedures. The algorithm behind the scenes here – what determines whether a covariate is added or deleted – is based on the current and proposed model's AIC. Implementation is straightforward, for example:

```
model_all <- lm (outcome ~., data = mydata)
model_auto <- step (model_all, direction = "both")
summary (model_auto)
```

The `.` in the `lm ()` function indicates that all variables should be used: we are staring with the model with all possible covariates, and using stepwise regression by choosing `direction = "both"`. Alternatively, `direction = "backward"` or `direction = "forward"` give the obvious other choices.

10.5   Checking model assumptions

In the case of the Normal linear model, as we have been studying here, the assumptions that we have made are

1. *Linearity*: the response is a linear combination of the parameters $\beta_1, \ldots, \beta_p$, and p covariates

$$y_i = \beta_1 x_{i1} + \ldots + \beta_p x_{ip} + \epsilon_i;$$

2. *Homoscedasticity*: the variance of ϵ_i is σ^2 for all $i = 1, \ldots, n$;

3. *Normality*: the error components $\epsilon_1, \ldots, \epsilon_n$ are Normally distributed;

4. *Independence of error components*: the error components are mutually independent (ϵ_i is independent of ϵ_j for $i \neq j$).

If one of the these assumptions fails, then the normal linear model might not be adequate for the data in hand. Nevertheless, given merely the data, it is impossible to *prove* (and hence be certain) that the above assumptions hold. We can merely develop tools that would give *indications against* the above assumptions: the best we can hope for is that we find *no evidence* of departure from these assumptions.

10.5.1   Residuals and standardised residuals

Our main tool in checking for departures from the model assumptions will be the residuals (see Section 10.1.1). We will call these **raw residuals**, and you can think of these as estimators of the error components. However, you should not think that errors and residuals are the same thing. Errors are theoretical constructs, whereas residuals are observed from data using our model.

Our errors are assumed to be independent and identically distributed, and even if this really is the case, the residuals can be dependent and not identically distributed. This poses a problem: even if the underlying assumptions on our error term are correct, our residuals may not behave in the same way. If, in that case, we see that residuals are correlated and/or not identically distributed, then we cannot draw conclusions about the underlying error term. This is a major drawback.

One way of getting around this is to use **standardised residuals** instead of the raw residuals: standardising ensures that *if* the errors are independent and identically normally distributed, then this will approximately be true for the standardised residuals (but not necessarily the raw residuals). There are many ways to standardise residuals – all of which require computing a function of the raw residual – but we'll stick to Pearson residuals here.

Pearson residuals can be computed in *R* painlessly using the `rstandard ()` function. This takes the ratio between the raw residuals and another quantity that is specific to the observation under consideration.

For our ozone data, the residuals and the standardised residuals can be computed as follows. Notice the difference in values between the raw (`ozone_res`) and standardised (`ozone_stres`) residuals.

```
attach (ozone_pollution)
ozone_res <- predict (ozone_mod1) - ozone
ozone_stdres <- rstandard (ozone_mod1)
head (cbind (ozone_res, ozone_stdres))

    ozone_res ozone_stdres
1  -7.9379186    0.38307433
2  -0.9898344    0.04731941
3  12.8133444   -0.60976646
4   0.4769439   -0.02338242
5   9.2724401   -0.45326743
6 -25.9497483    1.25472833
```

Instead of defining the (standardised) residuals ourselves, and creating our own plots for checking assumptions, another alternative is to use the `plot ()` function with our model as the argument like this (output not shown):

```
plot (ozone_mod1)
```

This generates a set of four model checking plots, but we prefer to use our own plots so that we can adjust them as necessary and use standardised residuals in all plots (some of *R*'s model checking plots use raw residuals).

10.5.2 Checking for linearity

The simplest way to check linearity is to plot the values of the response against the values of each covariate, like in Figure 10.5. If these plots indicate roughly linear relationships, then there is no evidence against the linearity assumption.

Another useful way to check linearity is by plotting the standardised residuals against each covariate in turn. If there is no evidence against the linearity assumption, then the plots should show a more or less random scatter around zero. If, on the other hand, you see patterns for a specific covariate, then this provides some evidence that the dependence of the response to that particular covariate isn't linear.

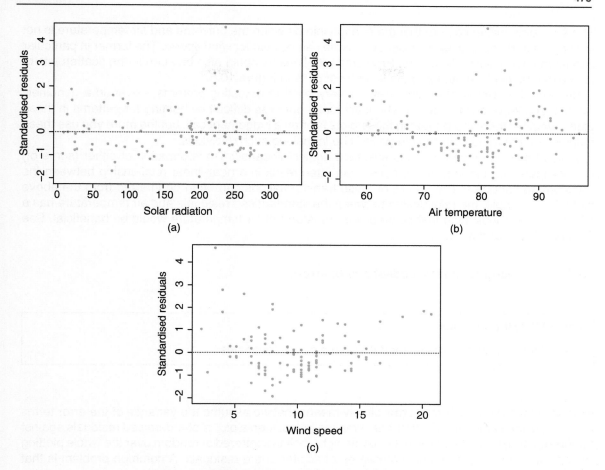

Figure 10.9 Checking for evidence against linearity.

The plots for our ozone data are in Figure 10.9 and are drawn like this (you could use the standard *R* plots by typing `plot (ozone_mod1)`, but this produces generic plots):

```
plot (rad, ozone_stdres, pch = 20, col = hue_pal () (3) [1],
      ylab = "Standardised residuals", xlab = "Solar radiation", ylim = c (-2, 4.5))
abline (a = 0, b = 0, lty = 3)
plot (temp, ozone_stdres, pch = 20,  col = hue_pal () (3) [1],
      ylab = "Standardised residuals", xlab = "Air temperature", ylim = c (-2, 4.5))
abline (a = 0, b = 0, lty = 3)
plot (wind, ozone_stdres, pch=20, col = hue_pal () (3) [1],
      ylab = "Standardised residuals", xlab = "Wind speed", ylim = c (-2, 4.5))
abline (a = 0, b = 0, lty = 3)
```

There is some evidence here that the relationship between the outcome and air temperature is not linear, and perhaps to a lesser extent the same can be said for wind speed. The former in particular seems to have a slight 'U' shape. Problems with linearity could also be seen in the scatterplots of ozone versus each covariate in the last row of plots in Figure 10.5.

Be careful, however: the human eye is very good at detecting patterns – even in a genuinely random scatter of points – so we shouldn't make our lives difficult by hunting for patterns in these plots. Whether there is a pattern in these plots is often a judgement call, but the more you use these techniques, the more comfortable you will be in making such decisions.

What should be done if there is evidence against linearity? Transformation of either (some of) the covariates, or indeed, the outcome, can often result in a near-linear relationship between the transformed variables. The nature of these transformations can often be inferred from the above plots. For example, the relationship between the standardised residuals and air temperature has a slight 'U' shape indicating that some power transform of air temperature would be beneficial. See Section 10.5.8 for details.

10.5.3 Checking for homoscedasticity of errors

Box 10.7: Fitted values

The outcome predicted by the model, given a set of covariates.

Homoscedasticity of the error terms simply means that we assume the variance of the error terms $\epsilon_1, \ldots, \epsilon_n$ is the same for all ϵ_i. If this assumption holds, then a plot of standardised residuals against the **fitted values** should look like the sky at night (points scattered at random over the whole plotting region), with no trend in the size or degree of scatter of the residuals. A common problem is that the variance increases with increasing value of the covariate (or vice versa) so that we obtain an expanding, fan-shaped pattern of residuals.

The plot in Figure 10.10a is what we want to see: no trend in the residuals with the fitted values. The plot in Figure 10.10b is a problem. There is a clear pattern of increasing residuals as the fitted values get larger, indicating that homoscedasticity does not hold in this case. Suggestions of what can be done in this case are given in Section 10.5.8.

10.5.4 Checking for normality of errors

The theory of multiple linear regression is based on the assumption of normal errors. If the errors are *not* normally distributed, then we shall not know how this affects our interpretation of the data or the inferences we make from it. In particular, consequences include but are not limited to inaccurate hypothesis testing and confidence intervals when using the model. This is, of course, a serious problem.

If the assumption of normally distributed errors holds, then the standardised residuals should be, approximately, from a standard Normal distribution. The most convenient way of checking this assumption is to look at normal probability plots. These plot the (ordered) standardised residuals against the quantiles of the standard Normal distribution. If the assumption holds, then we should see that these two quantities, when plotted against each other, roughly lie on the $y = x$ line.

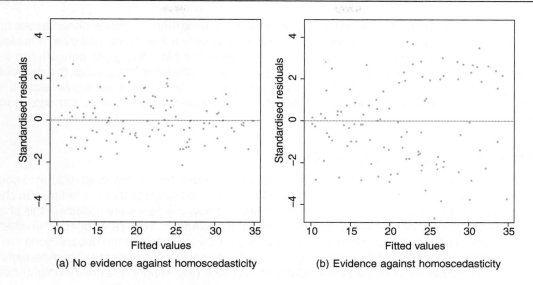

(a) No evidence against homoscedasticity   (b) Evidence against homoscedasticity

Figure 10.10   Checking for evidence against homoscedasticity.

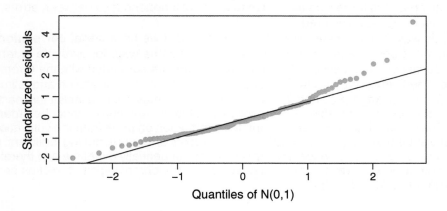

Figure 10.11   Normal probability plot.

Creating these plots is easy: `qqnorm ()` creates the scatterplot of the quantiles and standardised residuals, and `qqline ()` inserts the $y = x$ line for comparison. For the ozone data, the so-called 'QQ-plot' (or quantile-quantile plot) is given in Figure 10.11.

```
qqnorm (ozone_stdres, col = hue_pal ()(3)[1], main = "",
        ylab = "Standardized Residuals", xlab = "Quantiles of N(0,1)")
qqline (ozone_stdres)

detach (ozone_pollution)
```

The QQ-plot alerts us to a problem with the assumption of normality of errors, as the scatter of points form a curve rather than a straight line. It is important to remember, however, that no QQ-plot will ever look perfect, and in particular, the two ends of the plot where there are fewer observations often do no lie exactly on the line even if the assumption of normality holds. Here, however, it is clear it does not: the most worrying features are that the middle of the plot clearly lies beneath the $y = x$ line, and that the tails of the plot lie well above the $y = x$ line. The latter implies that the distribution has a lighter left tail (the smallest standardised residuals are larger than we would expect) and heavier right tail (the largest residuals are larger than we would expect) than a standard Normal distribution.

10.5.5 Checking for independence of errors

The last of our assumptions – that of independence of the error term – is the most difficult to check. Independence can be violated in a number of ways; therefore, no single test or procedure can check this assumption. The best piece of advice is to understand how the data were collected: this should alert you to any obvious problems with this assumption. For example, if data are collected on lifestyle and diet, multiple observations from the same household may indicate that the observations are not truly independent which would likely imply that the errors won't be independent either. Alternatively, data collected repeatedly from the same individual over time (e.g. weight or a child's height) clearly violates this assumption.

Other cursory checks can be made by looking at the residual plots discussed in Sections 10.5.2 and 10.5.3; any patterns therein could be due to a lack of independence between errors, especially if the observations appear clustered.

One specific way that independence can be violated is if we have **serial correlation**. This can only happen if it is possible to order the observations in some way, for example in terms of time or location. Serial correlation occurs if the (ordered) errors are correlated with the errors that come before them. The Durbin–Watson test is used for testing for serial correlation and is implemented as part of the `car` package (Fox and Weisberg, 2019). You may need to install this package first.

Notice that this test isn't suitable for our ozone data: the observations cannot be ordered by time or location. The dataset below, however, contains information on profit from the cultivation of a crop of carrots for a supermarket (`profit`) and associated costs of inputs including fertilizers, pesticides, energy, and labour (`profit`). These data are collected sequentially over time and therefore can be ordered; the order of observations in the dataset is already chronological. It makes sense, in this case, to check for serial correlation.

```
cost_profit <- read.table ("cost_profit.txt", header = T)
attach (cost_profit)
model_cost1 <- lm (profit ~ cost)
library ("car")
durbinWatsonTest (model_cost1)

 lag Autocorrelation D-W Statistic p-value
   1      -0.07946739      2.049899    0.854
Alternative hypothesis: rho != 0

detach (cost_profit)
```

There is no evidence of serial correlation in these residuals – the p-value is large – but note that this is just *one way* that the assumption of independent errors can be violated: a suggested absence of serial correlation in no way guarantees that this assumption holds in general.

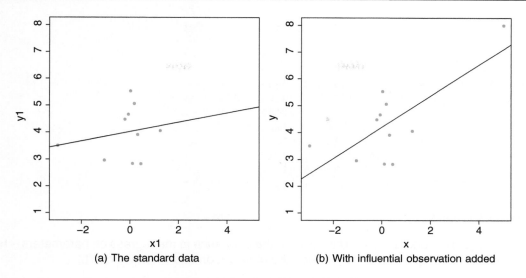

(a) The standard data   (b) With influential observation added

Figure 10.12   The influence of observations.

10.5.6   Checking for influential observations

One of the most common reasons for lack of fit is the existence of influential or unusual observations in the data. It is important to understand, however, that a point may *appear* to be unusual because of misspecification of the model, and not because there is anything wrong with the data. It is also worth noting that the analysis of residuals is a poor way of looking for influence: if a point is highly influential, it forces the regression line close to it, and hence, the influential point may have a very small residual.

Take a look at the data plotted in Figure 10.12a which includes a line of best fit. Now consider what happens when we add a single observation to these data, as in Figure 10.12b. The regression of y on x looks very different. The outlier is said to be highly *influential*. This makes our write-up much more complicated. We need to own up and show that the entire edifice depends upon the single point at (5, 8). This requires an explanation of two models rather than one. We cannot pretend that the point (5, 8) does not exist (that would be a scientific scandal), but we must describe just how influential it is.

Checking for the presence of influential points is an important part of statistical modelling. We cannot rely on analysis of the residuals, because by their very influence, these points force the regression line close to them. If we look at Figure 10.12b, we can see that the line of best fit is close to it, and closer than it is to some of the other observations. Looking at residual plots, therefore, might not be the best way to detect such observations.

One option is to use existing measures of influence. Some of these are usefully reported by the `influence.measures ()` function in *R*. When we run this function on our regression model, it helpfully highlights observations that may be influential using a * in the `inf` column:

```
reg <- lm (y ~ x)
influence.measures (reg)

Influence measures of
 lm(formula = y ~ x):
```

```
    dfb.1_     dfb.x    dffit cov.r  cook.d      hat inf
1  -0.1578   0.03305  -0.1581 1.319 0.01365  0.0951
2   1.3872  -1.49085   1.8979 0.277 0.82823  0.2374    *
3  -0.3649   0.18246  -0.3869 1.100 0.07378  0.1169
4  -0.4103   0.08364  -0.4108 0.969 0.07903  0.0948
5   0.0595   0.02480   0.0687 1.399 0.00264  0.1045
6   0.1635  -0.04472   0.1647 1.320 0.01480  0.0981
7   0.2847  -0.07210   0.2862 1.168 0.04207  0.0971
8  -0.1348   0.02784  -0.1350 1.340 0.01004  0.0949
9  -0.0740   0.02302  -0.0750 1.389 0.00314  0.1004
10 -0.2850   0.00369  -0.2877 1.143 0.04221  0.0909
11  0.8794   4.73210   5.0006 4.511 9.58238  0.8698    *
```

The statistics reported by `influence.measures ()` are

- DFBETAS (`dfb.1` and `dfb.x`): This looks at the difference in the regression parameters – here the intercept and slope – when we include the observation and when we don't.

- DFFITS (`dffit`): This is a function of the difference between the predicted value of an observation versus its predicted value if we dropped the observation from the model.

- Covariance ratio (`cov.r`): This looks at the effect of deleting each observation in turn on the variance–covariance matrix of the estimated regression parameters.

- Cook's distance (`cook.d`): This looks at the effect that omitting an observation has on *all* predicted values. Compare with DFFITS.

- Leverage (`hat`): This reports the *i*th diagonal of the so-called **hat matrix**, which is a measure of influence of the *i*th observation.

The observations with high influence are highlighted by an asterisk. To extract the subscripts of the influential points, use the `is.inf` attribute like this:

```
influence.measures (reg)$is.inf

   dfb.1_  dfb.x dffit cov.r cook.d    hat
1   FALSE  FALSE FALSE FALSE  FALSE  FALSE
2    TRUE   TRUE  TRUE  TRUE   TRUE  FALSE
3   FALSE  FALSE FALSE FALSE  FALSE  FALSE
4   FALSE  FALSE FALSE FALSE  FALSE  FALSE
5   FALSE  FALSE FALSE FALSE  FALSE  FALSE
6   FALSE  FALSE FALSE FALSE  FALSE  FALSE
7   FALSE  FALSE FALSE FALSE  FALSE  FALSE
8   FALSE  FALSE FALSE FALSE  FALSE  FALSE
9   FALSE  FALSE FALSE FALSE  FALSE  FALSE
10  FALSE  FALSE FALSE FALSE  FALSE  FALSE
11  FALSE   TRUE  TRUE  TRUE   TRUE   TRUE
```

So it seems that our additional observation is detected as being unusual in this analysis. There are various rules of thumb for deciding whether an observation is influential according to a particular measure. A nice introduction can be found in the documentation of the `olsrr` package (Hebbali, 2020).

10.5.7 Checking for collinearity

Some dependence between covariates is perfectly normal and to be expected: the covariates are not required to be *independent* of one another. This is a common misconception, probably due to the unfortunate term 'independent variables' used by some when describing covariates.

While dependent covariates are not unusual, too much dependence between them can cause problems when fitting multiple linear regression models. In the worst-case scenario, where a linear combination of at least some of the covariates can be perfectly predicted from a subset of the other covariates, the algorithm that estimates the regression coefficients fails. The result is no output, which may be the first time this problem is encountered if pre-analysis checks, as recommended in Figure 10.6, are not conducted. Common examples where this might occur include accidentally using a two (or more) covariates that contain the same information (e.g. if we had a covariate measuring weight in grams, and another measuring the same weight in pounds, then we can predict precisely one from the other causing collinearity). Removing one of these covariates should resolve the problem. More subtle situations where several covariates act together to perfectly predict another covariate are more difficult to spot.

Box 10.8: Linear combinations

Combination of covariates $x_{ik}, \ldots, x_{ip}$ of the form $a_k x_{ik} + \ldots + a_p x_{ip}$, for constants $a_k, \ldots, a_p$.

Collinearity isn't just a problem when a covariate can be perfectly predicted from a linear combination of other covariates. Far more common, and probably more difficult to spot, is when a covariate is highly correlated with such a combination of other covariates. While in this case it is very probable that the regression coefficients can be estimated, other problems may appear:

- estimated standard errors are unexpectedly large;

- estimated regression coefficients may have signs that don't make sense (e.g. we expect covariate *A* to be negatively correlated with the outcome, but its regression coefficient is large and positive), but this may be the case due to reasons other than collinearity;

- many of the covariates are insignificant, despite strong observed relationships with the outcome observed during preliminary analysis.

Spotting potential collinearity is best done at the preliminary analysis stage thereby avoiding this problem entirely. Good strategies to detect collinearity include the following:

1. Plot covariates against one another, for example using the `pairs ()` function. Are any covariates highly correlated? Of course, this only looks for dependence between *pairs* of variables, but is a good initial strategy.

2. Compute measures such as the **variance inflation factor**, or **VIF** for short, which looks at linear dependence between each covariates and *all the other covariates*. This produces a single number for each covariate: a measure of collinearity.

3. If you have already started building your model, omitting some covariates and looking at the estimates from this simpler model may also be helpful: though they are expected to change as we add or remove covariates, a substantial change may indicate a problem with collinearity.

The first strategy may seem like a poor relation to the second, but this is probably something that you would be doing anyway during your preliminary analysis: you may as well spend a few additional seconds in looking for any signs of collinearity while you're getting to know your data.

Let us return to our ozone pollution data. We have already seen (Figure 10.5) that there is some fairly strong correlation between the covariates that could potentially mean that collinearity could become an issue. But is the correlation sufficiently pronounced to be a cause for concern? At this point, calculating the VIF score for each covariate may be helpful. The function vif () in the car package (Fox and Weisberg, 2019) does just that.

```
attach (ozone_pollution)
library (car)
summary (ozone_mod1)


Call:
lm(formula = ozone ~ rad + temp + wind)

Residuals:
    Min      1Q  Median      3Q     Max
-40.485 -14.210  -3.556  10.124  95.600

Coefficients:
            Estimate Std. Error t value Pr(>|t|)
(Intercept) -64.23208   23.04204  -2.788  0.00628 **
rad           0.05980    0.02318   2.580  0.01124 *
temp          1.65121    0.25341   6.516 2.43e-09 ***
wind         -3.33760    0.65384  -5.105 1.45e-06 ***
---
Signif. codes:  0 '***' 0.001 '**' 0.01 '*' 0.05 '.' 0.1 ' ' 1

Residual standard error: 21.17 on 107 degrees of freedom
Multiple R-squared:  0.6062,Adjusted R-squared:  0.5952
F-statistic: 54.91 on 3 and 107 DF,  p-value: < 2.2e-16

vif (ozone_mod1)

     rad     temp     wind
1.095241 1.431201 1.328979

detach (ozone_pollution)
```

The VIF for each covariate will be at least 1, with a VIF of 1 indicating that the covariate is approximately linearly independent of the other covariates. The higher the VIF, the more problematic the collinearity. As a rule of thumb, a VIF larger than 5 deserves further investigation. Note that the VIF isn't a cure-all: while it may tell you that there is some linear dependence between the covariates it doesn't tell you between exactly which ones, or what you should do next. The latter requires investigation that only you, the researcher, can carry out.

In this case, the VIFs are all fairly close to 1: there is no evidence here that collinearity is an issue.

10.5.8 Improving fit

What should we do if we detect a problem with one of the model assumptions? In this case, the model might not be appropriate as it is (or doesn't *fit* or *describe* the data particularly well). Then what? There are a number of options to try, including (in order or increasing complexity):

- transform the covariate(s) and/or the outcome;
- use weighted least squares;
- abandon the model and try a more sophisticated method such as generalised linear models.

We'll discuss the first of these options, with a brief look at weighted least squares. The models used in the third option are introduced in later chapters of this book. See, for example, Chapters 11, 12 and 14.

Transforming covariates

The idea of transforming covariates and/or the outcome through some function may sound strange: if we, for example, take the square root of (one of) the covariates, is the model still linear? Actually, it is. We assume the outcome is *linear in the parameters (regression coefficients)*. That is, we are free to transform the covariates (and indeed, the outcome). This is easiest to see when we consider simple linear regression models, though the same applies when you have multiple covariates.

In Figure 10.13, we see two examples:

- it is not clear whether the relationship between the untransformed variables in Figure 10.13a is linear. Transforming both the covariate and the outcome produces a clearer pattern which we might be happy to call linear (Figure 10.13b). In this case, both variables are transformed using the (natural) log function;
- the relationship between the untransformed variables in Figure 10.13c is not linear. Transforming just the covariate produces a linear relationship in Figure 10.13d. In this case, the covariate is squared to produce this linear relationship while the outcome remains untouched.

The earlier statement that the outcome is *linear in the parameters (regression coefficients)* might make more sense now. In the first example above, think of $\log(y)$ as the outcome and $\log(x)$ as the covariate, so that simple linear regression is a suitable strategy to model the relationship between $\log(y)$ and $\log(x)$. In the second example, think of the covariate as x^2 – and not x – so that a simple linear regression would be a suitable way of describing the relationship between y and x^2. Note the implication: the idea of building *linear* models isn't as restrictive as it may initially seem.

How should we decide whether to apply a transformation to the covariate(s), outcome, or both? If a transformation is necessary, which transformation should we apply?

This is easiest with the simple linear regression model. A scatterplot will help us in giving an educated guess to which transformation might be suitable. Usually, however, this is a matter of trial-and-error until we find the best transformation(s) to achieve linearity (if indeed this is possible). Common transformations include the following:

- logarithmic functions;
- power functions (including the square root);
- reciprocals.

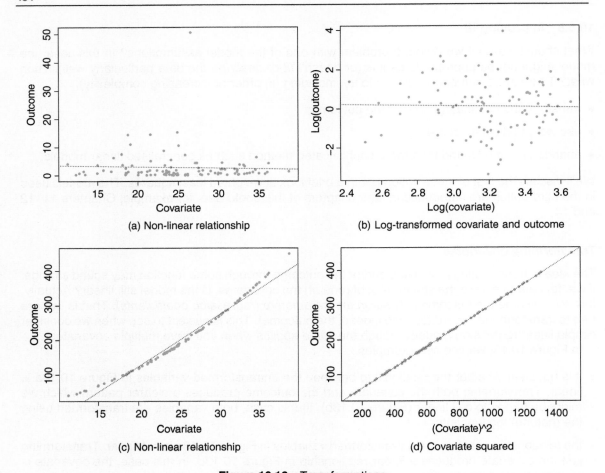

Figure 10.13 Transformations.

It might help to first of all consider common transformation of the covariate, before moving on to transform the outcome if it is necessary (as it was in Figure 10.13a).

For multiple linear regression models where we can't simply draw a scatterplot, we rely on information from the plots used to check linearity in Section 10.5.2: plotting the standardised residuals against each of the covariates. These plots can be used to detect problems in linearity, and therefore, by default we may be able to take an educated guess as to a transformation to 'fix' issues. The plots in Figure 10.14 show various common problems with linearity and suggested fixes.

These plots take experience in deciphering, and there's nothing wrong in trying a variety of transformations to find a combination that improves linearity.

For our ozone pollution data, for example, the plots used to look at linearity are given in Figure 10.9, the plot concerning air temperature (Figure 10.9b) caused the most concern. Here we see a slightly 'U'-shaped pattern to the residuals over the values of air temperature. We could try a square transformation of temperature, or even the reciprocal, but in this case these transformations don't help very much. Figure 10.15 shows the resulting plots when we transform temp by squaring it.

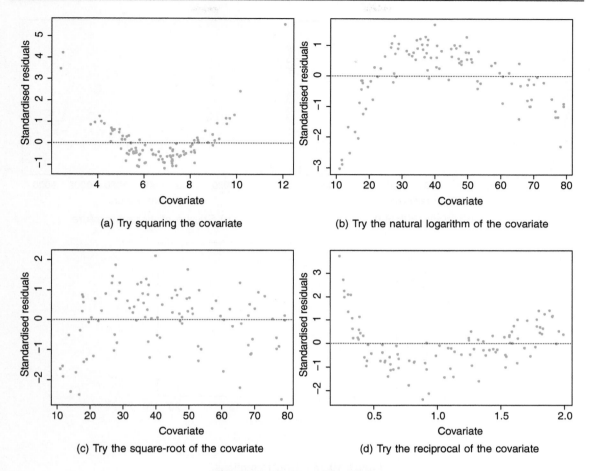

Figure 10.14 Transformations.

```
attach (ozone_pollution)
sq_temp <- temp^2
ozone_mod8 <- lm (ozone ~ wind + rad + sq_temp)
summary (ozone_mod8)

Call:
lm(formula = ozone ~ wind + rad + sq_temp)

Residuals:
    Min      1Q   Median      3Q      Max
-39.831 -13.790   -3.226   10.103   96.975

Coefficients:
            Estimate Std. Error t value Pr(>|t|)
(Intercept) -5.64005   14.17817  -0.398   0.6916
wind        -3.22264    0.64429  -5.002 2.24e-06 ***
```

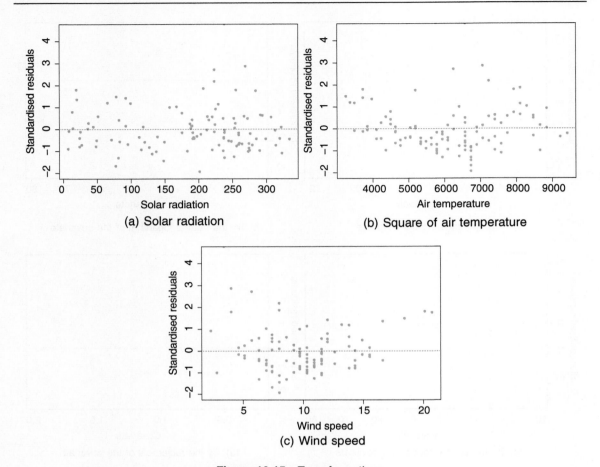

Figure 10.15 Transformations.

```
rad              0.05933    0.02272    2.611   0.0103 *
sq_temp          0.01120    0.00162    6.915 3.54e-10 ***
---
Signif. codes:  0 '***' 0.001 '**' 0.01 '*' 0.05 '.' 0.1 ' ' 1

Residual standard error: 20.8 on 107 degrees of freedom
Multiple R-squared:  0.6199,    Adjusted R-squared:  0.6092
F-statistic: 58.16 on 3 and 107 DF,  p-value: < 2.2e-16

ozone8_stdres <- rstandard (ozone_mod8)
```

Given that a range of transformations (not shown) didn't improve matters here, it's natural to turn our attention to transforming the outcome. From the plots, we have used so far it is hard to know whether we should try this, let alone what the optimal transformation would look like.

In these circumstances, the Box–Cox transformation offers a simple empirical solution. The idea is to find a power, λ (lambda), so that transforming the outcome via y^λ provides a more linear

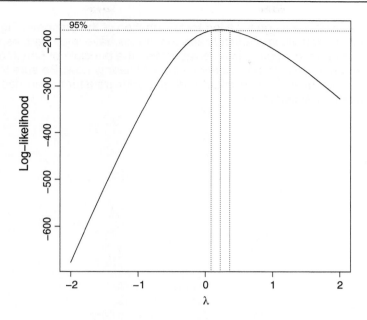

Figure 10.16   (Log)-likelihood as a function of lambda.

relationship with the covariates. The value of lambda can be positive or negative, when a λ of zero is suggested, then this implies a log transformation, while a λ of 1 implies that a transformation isn't necessary. The function boxcox () in the package MASS (Venables and Ripley, 2002) automates this procedure. This function yields a plot from which we can deduce the 'best' value of λ to use. This is a **likelihood** function, and we would like to find the value of λ that *maximises* the likelihood.

Box 10.9: Box-Cox and maximising the likelihood

The graph produced by boxcox () is the likelihood when the covariates are fitted to a model with $(y^\lambda - 1)/\lambda$ as the outcome. Whatever our preferred value for λ, this implies that fitting a model with y^λ is suggested: once λ is fixed, then we can rearrange the implied equation so that the outcome is y^λ instead of $(y^\lambda - 1)/\lambda$.

Applying boxcox () to our ozone pollution data produces the plot in Figure 10.16.

```
library (MASS)
boxcox (ozone ~ rad + temp + wind)
```

The plot suggests that a power transformation may be suitable. It's difficult to see exactly what value of λ that the maximum of the (log)-likelihood suggests, but this does not matter: a value in the right vicinity is all we need (and it's probably better to choose something that is easy to describe). Here, the maximum seems to happen around the 0.25 mark, suggesting that $y^{1/4}$ might be the way to go, but equally we could consider $\lambda = 0$ which suggests $\log(y)$ as this is also in the vicinity and might be easier to interpret and/or to explain to users of your model.

For ease of interpretation, let us go for a log transformation of the outcome. Figure 10.17 shows the resulting scatterplots, and we immediately see that things have improved, especially for `temp`. Though still not quite perfect, but taking into consideration the principle of parsimony, it is probably sensible to stop here: there isn't strong evidence against linearity now. Be sure to check the other model checking plots, however, as you could find that your transformation has had unintended consequences on the other assumptions.

```
ozone_mod9 <- lm (log (ozone) ~ wind + rad + temp)
summary (ozone_mod9)

Call:
lm(formula = log(ozone) ~ wind + rad + temp)

Residuals:
     Min       1Q    Median       3Q       Max
-2.06212 -0.29968 -0.00223  0.30767   1.23572

Coefficients:
              Estimate Std. Error t value Pr(>|t|)
(Intercept) -0.2611739  0.5534102  -0.472 0.637934
wind        -0.0615925  0.0157037  -3.922 0.000155 ***
rad          0.0025147  0.0005567   4.518 1.62e-05 ***
temp         0.0491630  0.0060863   8.078 1.07e-12 ***
---
Signif. codes:  0 '***' 0.001 '**' 0.01 '*' 0.05 '.' 0.1 ' ' 1

Residual standard error: 0.5085 on 107 degrees of freedom
Multiple R-squared:  0.6645,    Adjusted R-squared:  0.6551
F-statistic: 70.65 on 3 and 107 DF,  p-value: < 2.2e-16

ozone9_stdres <- rstandard (ozone_mod9)
plot (rad, ozone9_stdres, pch = 20, col = hue_pal () (3) [1],
    ylab = "Standardised residuals", xlab = "Solar radiation", ylim = c (-2, 4.5))
abline (a = 0, b = 0, lty = 3)
plot (temp, ozone9_stdres, pch = 20,  col = hue_pal () (3) [1],
    ylab = "Standardised residuals", xlab = "Air temperature", ylim = c (-2, 4.5))
abline (a = 0, b = 0, lty = 3)
plot (wind, ozone9_stdres, pch=20, col = hue_pal () (3) [1],
    ylab = "Standardised residuals", xlab = "Wind speed", ylim = c (-2, 4.5))
abline (a = 0, b = 0, lty = 3)
detach (ozone_pollution)
```

Finally, *not all ailments with linearity can be fixed by transforming the covariates and/or outcome*. Other approaches such as non-linear models may be necessary. See Chapters 12 and 14 for details.

Weighted least squares

The default is for all the values of the response to have equal weights (all equal to 1). This might not be what we want: we could, for example have more faith in some of the observations than others and may want to reflect this in the *weighting* that the observations are given in an analysis.

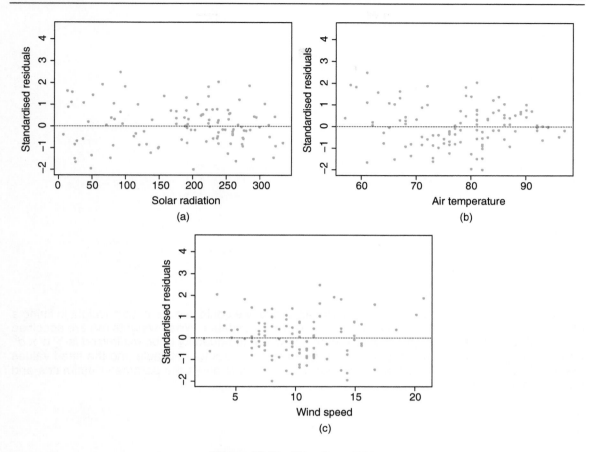

Figure 10.17 Transformations.

Where data points are to be weighted unequally, the classical approach is to weight each value by the inverse of the variance of the distribution from which that point is drawn. This downplays the influence of highly variable data and can result in a better fitting model. This strategy relies on us having a suitable variable which we can use to weight the observations, which is very unusual in practice.

Let us consider another dataset, where the response is seed production (Fruit) with a continuous explanatory variable (Root, Root diameter), and a two-level factor (Grazing, with levels Grazed and Ungrazed). Let us take a look at the data initially:

```
ipomopsis <- read.table ("ipomopsis.txt", header = T)
names (ipomopsis)

[1] "Root"    "Fruit"    "Grazing"

ipomopsis_mod1 <- lm (Fruit ~ Grazing + Root, data = ipomopsis)
summary (ipomopsis_mod1)
```

```
Call:
lm(formula = Fruit ~ Grazing + Root, data = ipomopsis)

Residuals:
     Min        1Q    Median        3Q       Max
-17.1920   -2.8224    0.3223    3.9144   17.3290

Coefficients:
                 Estimate Std. Error t value Pr(>|t|)
(Intercept)      -127.829      9.664  -13.23 1.35e-15 ***
GrazingUngrazed    36.103      3.357   10.75 6.11e-13 ***
Root               23.560      1.149   20.51  < 2e-16 ***
---
Signif. codes:  0 '***' 0.001 '**' 0.01 '*' 0.05 '.' 0.1 ' ' 1

Residual standard error: 6.747 on 37 degrees of freedom
Multiple R-squared:  0.9291,Adjusted R-squared:  0.9252
F-statistic: 242.3 on 2 and 37 DF,  p-value: < 2.2e-16
```

Instead of using initial root size as a covariate (as above) we could use `Root` as a weight in fitting a model with `Grazing` as the sole categorical explanatory variable. When weights (w) are specified the model is fitted using weighted least squares, in which the quantity to be minimized is $\sum w \times d^2$ (rather than $\sum d^2$), where d is the difference between the response variable and the fitted values predicted by the model. Needless to say, the use of weights alters the parameter estimates and their standard errors:

```
ipomopsis_mod2 <- lm (Fruit ~ Grazing, data = ipomopsis, weights = Root)
summary (ipomopsis_mod2)


Call:
lm(formula = Fruit ~ Grazing, data = ipomopsis, weights = Root)

Weighted Residuals:
     Min        1Q    Median        3Q       Max
-137.822   -53.551     0.381    30.259   145.132

Coefficients:
                Estimate Std. Error t value Pr(>|t|)
(Intercept)       70.725      4.849   14.59   <2e-16 ***
GrazingUngrazed  -16.953      7.469   -2.27    0.029 *
---
Signif. codes:  0 '***' 0.001 '**' 0.01 '*' 0.05 '.' 0.1 ' ' 1

Residual standard error: 62.51 on 38 degrees of freedom
Multiple R-squared:  0.1194,Adjusted R-squared:  0.0962
F-statistic: 5.151 on 1 and 38 DF,  p-value: 0.02899
```

Fitting root size as a statistical weight is scientifically wrong in this case: why should values from larger plants be given greater influence? Also, this analysis gives entirely the wrong interpretation

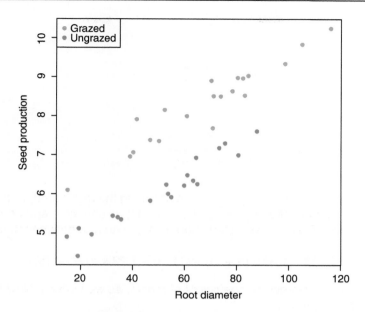

Figure 10.18 Plot of seed production by root diameter, coloured by grazing type.

of the data (ungrazed plants come out as being *less* fecund than the grazed plants). The original analysis in `ipomopsis_mod1` reverses this interpretation, showing that for a given root size, the grazed plants produced 36.013 *fewer* fruits than the ungrazed plants; the problem was that the big plants were almost all in the grazed treatment. We can see this clearly in Figure 10.18.

10.6 Using the model

10.6.1 Interpretation of model

There is little point in building a model unless we can interpret the results. This means not only understanding the output as described in Section 10.3 but also interpreting the regression coefficients: after all, if you have gone to the trouble of building a model to describe *how* a set of covariates impact the outcome, then it is reasonable to want to explain the role of each covariate in turn. The trick to doing this is to isolate the regression coefficient of interest. Understanding how this works in the case of the simple linear regression model is instructive, so we start by revisiting the caterpillar data from Section 10.1 for which the output is given again here for convenience.

```
summary (caterpillar_model)


Call:
lm(formula = growth ~ tannin, data = caterpillardata)

Residuals:
    Min       1Q   Median       3Q      Max
-2.4556  -0.8889  -0.2389   0.9778   2.8944
```

```
Coefficients:
            Estimate Std. Error t value Pr(>|t|)
(Intercept)  11.7556     1.0408  11.295 9.54e-06 ***
tannin       -1.2167     0.2186  -5.565 0.000846 ***
---
Signif. codes:  0 '***' 0.001 '**' 0.01 '*' 0.05 '.' 0.1 ' ' 1

Residual standard error: 1.693 on 7 degrees of freedom
Multiple R-squared:  0.8157,Adjusted R-squared:  0.7893
F-statistic: 30.97 on 1 and 7 DF,  p-value: 0.0008461
```

To *isolate* the intercept, we simply set `tannin = 0`. Isolating the (estimated) regression coefficient of tannin is also easy enough: take any value of tannin - let us say $a\%$ – and compare it to having $(a + 1)\%$ tannin in the diet. Then the expected change in growth rate between these two conditions of tannin is

$$(11.76 - 1.22 \times (a + 1)) - (11.76 - 1.22 \times a) = -1.22 \tag{10.6}$$

This leaves us with just the regression coefficient of tannin, as we wanted. Now let us think about how this converts into interpretation:

- the intercept tells us that when there is *no tannin* in the diet, the *expected* growth rate will be 11.76.

- the regression coefficient of tannin tells us that with a *one unit (one percent) increase* in tannin in the diet, the *expected* growth rate *decreases* by 1.22.

The italicised text above may seem pedantic, but without these caveats the interpretation wouldn't make sense. Notice also that the intercept here has a real-world interpretation, but this isn't always the case. If it doesn't make sense to set the covariate equal to zero, then by all means interpret the intercept but don't expect it to be meaningful. This *doesn't* mean that you don't need an intercept.

When we move to models with more than one covariate, the same ideas prevail. Take our experiment from Section 10.2.4 with weight as the response variable, and genotype, sex, and age as covariates. The first model we built was a multiple linear regression model without interactions (interactions make interpretation a little more tricky as we'll see shortly).

```
summary (gain_mod1)

Call:
lm(formula = Weight ~ Sex + Age + Genotype)

Residuals:
     Min       1Q    Median       3Q       Max
-0.40005 -0.15120 -0.01668  0.16953   0.49227

Coefficients:
            Estimate Std. Error t value Pr(>|t|)
(Intercept)  7.93701    0.10066  78.851  < 2e-16 ***
Sexmale     -0.83161    0.05937 -14.008  < 2e-16 ***
Age          0.29958    0.02099  14.273  < 2e-16 ***
```

```
GenotypeCloneB   0.96778      0.10282    9.412 8.07e-13 ***
GenotypeCloneC  -1.04361      0.10282  -10.149 6.21e-14 ***
GenotypeCloneD   0.82396      0.10282    8.013 1.21e-10 ***
GenotypeCloneE  -0.87540      0.10282   -8.514 1.98e-11 ***
GenotypeCloneF   1.53460      0.10282   14.925  < 2e-16 ***
---
Signif. codes:  0 '***' 0.001 '**' 0.01 '*' 0.05 '.' 0.1 ' ' 1

Residual standard error: 0.2299 on 52 degrees of freedom
Multiple R-squared:  0.9651, Adjusted R-squared:  0.9604
F-statistic: 205.7 on 7 and 52 DF,  p-value: < 2.2e-16
```

The intercept tells us that when all covariates are set to zero – so Age = 0, Sex = 0 which implies female, and all genotype dummy variables are zero implying Genotype Clone A (the reference category)- the *expected* weight will be 7.94.

The slope of Age tells us that with a *one unit (one year) increase* in age, the *expected* weight *increases* by 0.3, *holding all other covariates constant*. The last part tells us that we have to keep all other covariates the same if we want to isolate the slope of Age in order to interpret it (try something similar to equation (10.6) to see this is the case).

The remaining covariates are categorical. We could continue the same method of interpretation, but as we'll see, this has particular meaning in this case. Starting with sex, remember that a male has Sexmale = 1 while a female – the reference category – has Sexmale = 0. In this case, it doesn't always make sense to 'increase Sexmale by one unit' (what if Sexmale = 1 already?) so our comparison is always to the reference category (in other words, the 'increase by one unit' is represented by going from female to male here). The regression coefficient of Sexmale tells us therefore that the weight of males is 0.83 *lower* than that for females on average, if Genotype and Age remain unchanged.

Finally, the same interpretation applies for all the Genotype dummy variables, but this time we need to compare each one to the reference category. For example, the regression coefficient of GenotypeCloneD tells us therefore that the weight of those with Genotype Clone D is 0.82 *higher* than for those with Genotype Clone A on average, if Sex and Age don't change.

Box 10.10: Interpretation of regression coefficients

Putting all this together, the regression coefficients in multiple linear regression models *without* interaction terms can be interpreted as follows:

- the intercept tells us that for a female with Genotype Clone A and age zero, their *expected* weight is 7.94;

- the regression coefficient of age tells us that with a *one unit (one year) increase* in age, the *expected* weight *increases* by 0.3, if Genotype and Sex don't change;

- the regression coefficient of Sexmale tells us that the weight of males is *expected* to be 0.83 *lower* than that for females, if Genotype and Age remain don't change.

- the regression coefficient of GenotypeCloneD tells us that the weight of those with Genotype Clone D is 0.82 *higher* than that for those with Genotype Clone A on average, if Sex and Age don't change.

When we add in interactions, things get a little trickier. Take the model `gain_mod2`, for example in which we had an interaction between sex and age. According to this model, how do sex, age, and genotype now impact weight?

```
summary (gain_mod2)


Call:
lm(formula = Weight ~ Sex * Age + Genotype)

Residuals:
     Min       1Q    Median       3Q       Max
-0.37202 -0.15893 -0.00302  0.15263   0.45188

Coefficients:
               Estimate Std. Error t value Pr(>|t|)
(Intercept)     7.99759    0.11882  67.310  < 2e-16 ***
Sexmale        -0.95277    0.13933  -6.838 9.80e-09 ***
Age             0.27939    0.02970   9.406 9.98e-13 ***
GenotypeCloneB  0.96778    0.10290   9.405 1.00e-12 ***
GenotypeCloneC -1.04361    0.10290 -10.142 7.96e-14 ***
GenotypeCloneD  0.82396    0.10290   8.008 1.41e-10 ***
GenotypeCloneE -0.87540    0.10290  -8.507 2.36e-11 ***
GenotypeCloneF  1.53460    0.10290  14.914  < 2e-16 ***
Sexmale:Age     0.04039    0.04201   0.961    0.341
---
Signif. codes:  0 '***' 0.001 '**' 0.01 '*' 0.05 '.' 0.1 ' ' 1

Residual standard error: 0.2301 on 51 degrees of freedom
Multiple R-squared:  0.9658,   Adjusted R-squared:  0.9604
F-statistic: 179.8 on 8 and 51 DF,  p-value: < 2.2e-16
```

Let us start with the easy one: genotype isn't involved with any interaction term, so our interpretation of the estimated regression coefficients for each dummy variable for genotype is interpreted as before.

For sex, however, notice that it appears twice in the model: once as a main effect, and again as part of an interaction effect. If we want to understand what the main effect of sex is telling us, the only way to do this is to set age = 0, so that the interaction term effectively disappears. Then we proceed as per normal: using model `gain_mod2`, the regression coefficient of sex tells us that the expected weight of males is 0.95 *lower* than it is for females, when age = 0 and genotype remains the same.

For age, the same thought process is necessary: using model `gain_mod2`, the regression coefficient of age tells us that for a female (i.e. setting Sexmale = 0), the *expected* weight *increases* by 0.28 with a *one unit (one year) increase* in age, if Genotype doesn't change.

Finally, what about the interaction term itself? This one is even more cumbersome. Again, it might be easier to think about it as attempting to isolate this term from the model. The only way we can do this to compare:

- the expected change in weight for a one-year change in age for males, if genotype doesn't change;

- the expected change in weight for a one-year change in age for females, if genotype doesn't change.

The first comparison is estimated to be 0.28+0.04, while the second is estimated to be 0.28. Looking at the difference between the two gives the interaction effect.

Box 10.11: Interpretation of regression coefficients (including interactions)

Putting all this together, the regression coefficients in multiple linear regression models *with* interaction terms can be interpreted as follows:

- the intercept tells us that for a female with Genotype Clone A and age zero, their *expected* weight is 8;

- the regression coefficient of age tells us that for a female (i.e. setting `Sexmale = 0`), the *expected* weight *increases* by 0.28 with a *one unit (one year) increase* in age, if Genotype doesn't change;

- the regression coefficient of sex tells us that the expected weight of males is 0.95 lower than it is for females, when `age = 0` and genotype remains the same;

- the regression coefficient of `GenotypeCloneD` tells us that the weight of those with Genotype Clone D is 0.82 *higher* than that for those with Genotype Clone A on average, if Sex and Age remain unchanged;

- the regression coefficient of `Sexmale:Age` tells us that 0.04 is the expected difference between:

  - the expected change in weight for a one-year change in age for males, if genotype doesn't change;

  - the expected change in weight for a one-year change in age for females, if genotype doesn't change.

10.6.2 Making predictions

Using our model to make predictions about future observations is of interest in many situations. Using your model to make a point estimate of a future outcome, based on a set of covariates, is easy enough: you can think of it as plugging in the values of your covariates into the linear form of the model, along with the estimated regression coefficients. This is the *predicted mean* (or expected, or average) outcome based on your covariate values.

Before we make any predictions, you should be confident that the model fits the data well (otherwise, any prediction is unreliable at best) and that the values of the 'new' covariate(s) are in-line with what was used to build the model (otherwise, you are extrapolating outside the range of the data, for which you have no information).

R can, of course, automate the prediction using the `predict ()` function. Let us use `ozone_mod1` to predict the outcome when:

- `rad = 110, temp = 60` and `wind = 15.3`;

- `rad = 110, temp = 80` and `wind = 9.5`.

Both sets of values are reasonable given the range of the values within the dataset, but the first set is unusual in its *combination* of the three covariate values.

```
attach (ozone_pollution)
predict (ozone_mod1, data.frame (rad = c (110, 110), temp = c (60, 80),
wind = c (15.3, 9.5)))

          1         2
-9.647168 42.735054
```

While the second set of 'new' covariates gives a broadly sensible estimate of pollution level, the first is negative which is clearly nonsense. We need to be careful, therefore, that not only are the covariate values sensible but that their combination is in-line with the data used to build the model. In this case, it was obvious something had gone wrong, but it may not be the case in other examples.

As with any prediction, it is not enough simply to give a point estimate: we need to qualify it with some estimate of variability. This could be in the form of a standard error or a confidence interval. It's likely that a confidence interval is more appealing, and this can be requested when using the predict () function.

There's one complication before we can go further: *what type of prediction are you making*? Which of the following does your case fall in to?

1. Predicting the outcome for a *population*, given a specified set of covariate values;

2. Predicting the outcome for a *single observation*, given a specified set of covariate values.

The point estimate of these quantities will be the same, but their confidence intervals will differ: there is less variability in the (unknown) population (mean) outcome than there will be in the individual's outcome and so the confidence interval for the first case will be narrower than that of the second.

Box 10.12: Population vs individual prediction

This distinction is probably easier to visualise if we take a simple example. Imagine that you've built a model for the height of children, using age as a covariate. Suppose that you want to predict the height of a particular seven-year-old child, and also estimate the (mean) height of a population of seven-year-old children. There's a lot of variability in the heights of individual seven-year-olds, but when we think about the *population mean* height of seven-year-olds, there's a lot less uncertainty. The confidence interval we choose for our prediction must therefore reflect what we're trying to estimate.

Once you've decided what your prediction represents, you can specify this in the predict function as either:

1. interval = confidence when we want the confidence interval for the population (mean) outcome;

2. interval = prediction when we want the confidence interval for a specific observation.

```
predict (ozone_mod1, data.frame (rad = 110, temp = 80, wind = 9.5),
        interval = "confidence", level = 0.95)

      fit      lwr      upr
1 42.73505 37.20529 48.26482

predict (ozone_mod1, data.frame (rad = 110, temp = 80, wind = 9.5),
        interval = "prediction", level = 0.95)

      fit       lwr      upr
1 42.73505 0.4008949 85.06921

detach (ozone_pollution)
```

In the first, we request a 95% confidence interval for the population mean ozone concentration for the given covariate values, while in the second we assume that we want a confidence interval for a one-off observation. Notice how the latter is wider than the former, but the point estimate is the same for both.

10.7 Further types of regression modelling

We'll be extending the normal linear regression model over the next few chapters, and you will notice similarities in how we approach the modelling in *R*. Table 10.1 gives an overview of what's to come, including the relevant *R* function to fit the models.

For most of these models, a range of generic functions can be used to obtain information about the model, as we have in this chapter. The most important and most frequently used are listed in Table 10.2.

Table 10.1 Functions for various regression models.

lm ()	Fits a linear model with normal errors and constant variance; generally this is used for regression analysis using continuous explanatory variables.
glm ()	See Chapter 11. Fits generalised linear models to data using categorical or continuous explanatory variables, by specifying one of a family of **error structures** (e.g. Poisson for count data or binomial for proportion data) and a particular **link function**.
gam ()	See Chapter 12. Fits generalized additive models to data with one of a family of error structures (e.g. Poisson for count data or binomial for proportion data) in which the continuous explanatory variables can (optionally) be fitted as arbitrary smoothed functions using non-parametric smoothers rather than specific parametric functions.
lme (); lmer ()	See Chapter 13. Fit linear mixed-effects models with specified mixtures of fixed effects and random effects and allow for the specification of correlation structure among the explanatory variables and autocorrelation of the response variable (e.g. time series effects with repeated measures). lmer () allows for non-normal errors and non-constant variance with the same error families as a GLM.
nls ()	See Chapter 14. Fits a non-linear regression model via least squares, estimating the parameters of a specified non-linear function.

(continued)

Table 10.1   (Continued)

nlme ()	See Chapter 14. Fits a specified non-linear function in a mixed-effects model where the parameters of the non-linear function are assumed to be random effects; it allows for the specification of correlation structure among the explanatory variables and autocorrelation of the response variable (e.g. time series effects with repeated measures).
loess ()	See Chapter 12. Fits a local regression model with one or more continuous explanatory variables using non-parametric techniques to produce a smoothed model surface.
tree (); rpart()	See Chapter 20. Fits a regression tree model using binary recursive partitioning whereby the data are successively split along coordinate axes of the explanatory variables so that at any node the split is chosen that maximally distinguishes the response variable in the left and right branches. With a categorical response variable, the tree is called a classification tree, and the model used for classification assumes that the response variable follows a Multinomial distribution.

Table 10.2   Frequently used functions to extract information about regression models.

summary ()	produces parameter estimates and standard errors from lm ().
plot ()	produces diagnostic plots for model checking, including residuals against fitted values, normality checks, influence tests, etc.
anova ()	is a wonderfully useful function for comparing different models and producing ANOVA tables.
update ()	is used to modify the last model fit; it saves both typing effort and computing time.
coef ()	gives the coefficients (estimated parameters) from the model.
fitted ()	gives the fitted values, predicted by the model for the values of the explanatory variables included.
resid ()	gives the residuals (the differences between measured and predicted values of y).
predict ()	uses information from the fitted model to produce smooth functions for plotting a line through the scatterplot of your data. Make sure you provide a list or a dataframe containing all of the necessary information on each of the explanatory variables in your model to enable the prediction to be made.

References

Fox, J., & Weisberg, S. (2019). *An R companion to applied regression* (Third). Sage. https://socialsciences. mcmaster.ca/jfox/Books/Companion/.

Hebbali, A. (2020). *Olsrr: Tools for building OLS regression models* [R package version 0.5.3]. https://CRAN. R-project.org/package=olsrr.

Venables, W. N., & Ripley, B. D. (2002). *Modern applied statistics with S* (Fourth) [ISBN 0-387-95457-0]. Springer. https://www.stats.ox.ac.uk/pub/MASS4/.

Zeileis, A., & Hothorn, T. (2002). Diagnostic checking in regression relationships. *R News*, 2(3), 7–10. https:// CRAN.R-project.org/doc/Rnews/.

11

Generalised Linear Models

We saw in Section 10.5.8 that linear model assumptions may not be satisfied for our dataset, even after transformations. Fortunately, riding to our assistance are **Generalised Linear Models** or **GLMs** which are far more flexible and will also work with a much wider range of outcomes than linear models. Some examples of such outcomes are the following:

- Count data, such as the number of road accidents, where negative counts are not permitted;
- Binary data, such as dead or alive;
- Time to event (such as arrival of a train) data.

11.1 How GLMs work

This section offers a summary of the key features of GLMs: for more mathematical background and examples see, for instance, Dobson and Barnett, 2018. These features highlight the differences from and similarities to linear models.

11.1.1 Error structure

We saw in Chapter 10 that linear models have error terms that are assumed to have a Normal distribution. In practice, this may not be realistic, for instance we may have

- errors that are strongly skewed;
- errors that are strictly bounded (as in proportions);
- errors that cannot lead to negative fitted values (as in counts).

GLMs deal with this issue by assuming that the distribution of the outcome variable (Y_is), given the covariates (x_{ij}s), and thus the error distribution, comes from the **exponential family** (not to be

The R Book, Third Edition. Elinor Jones, Simon Harden and Michael J. Crawley.
© 2023 John Wiley & Sons Ltd. Published 2023 by John Wiley & Sons Ltd.
Companion website: www.wiley.com/go/jones/therbook3e

confused with the exponential distribution). The Normal distribution is part of this family, and so linear models are just examples of GLMs. Other examples are the following:

- Poisson errors, useful with count data;
- Binomial errors, useful with proportion data;
- Gamma errors, useful with data showing a constant coefficient of variation;
- Exponential errors, useful with data on time to an event.

In many of these cases, the relationship between the mean and variance is not constant, as assumed in linear models. Figure 11.1 illustrates this.

11.1.2 Linear predictor

The good news is that we don't have to forget everything we learnt about linear models. We still create a linear combination of the covariates (including interactions, etc.), but now that does not equal Y_i but

$$\eta_i = \beta_0 + \beta_1 x_{i1} + \dots \beta_p x_{ip}$$

the **linear predictor**, and the error term is taken care of elsewhere.

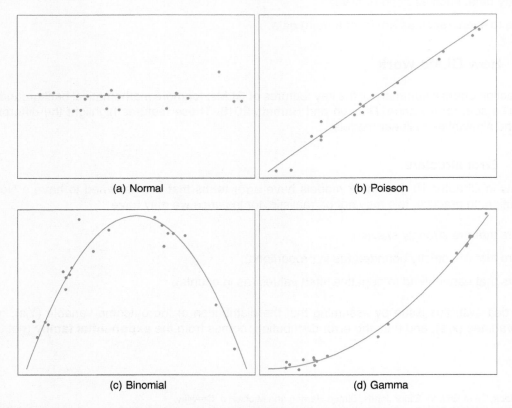

(a) Normal   (b) Poisson

(c) Binomial   (d) Gamma

Figure 11.1 Relationship between mean (x-axis) and variance (y-axis) for a range of error types.

11.1.3 Link function

The linear predictor and error distribution are brought together with the **link function**. So if the mean of any outcome variable, given the covariates is μ_i, i.e.

$$\mu_i = E(Y_i|X_i = x_i),$$

then the link function, $g()$, is defined so that:

$$\eta_i = g(\mu_i)$$

which is simple, but needs thinking about. The linear predictor emerges from the linear model as a sum of the terms for each of the p parameters. For instance, if our error terms come from a Normal distribution, the link function is usually the identity function:

$$\eta_i = \mu_i$$

and the mean of the linear predictor is also the mean of Y_i. Usually, however the mean of Y_i is obtained by applying the inverse link function to η_i, the linear combination of the covariates.

A more complex example arises with Poisson errors where the usual link function is

$$\eta_i = \ln(\mu_i)$$

One of the reasons for choosing this, and many other, link functions is to ensure that the fitted values stay within reasonable bounds. Here, for example, counts are all greater than or equal to 0 (negative count data would be nonsense), and so we need $g^{-1}(\eta_i) = e^{\eta_i}$ also to be non-negative, which is the case. Similarly, if the response variable was the proportion of individuals that died, then the fitted values would have to lie between 0 and 1 (fitted values greater than 1 or less than 0 would be meaningless). So the inverse of the **logit** link (Table 11.1) ensures that the linear predictor is transformed to a value between 0 and 1.

We can decide which link function we want to go with each error distribution. However, there are defaults used by R, known as **canonical link functions**, the most common being given in Table 11.1.

In the third line, we can see that the logit link, is actually the log of the odds of the event happening against it not happening: this is known as the **log odds ratio**. Note that, rather confusingly, R uses the argument `family` in order to select the error distribution. **Dispersion** allows, in some cases, flexibility between the variance of the linear predictor and that of the error distribution. See Section 11.2.2 for more details.

Once the GLM has been set up, the parameters of the model, the βs, and those from the error distribution are estimated from the data by a form of maximum likelihood.

Table 11.1 Common members of the exponential family

Error distribution name in R	Parameters	Canonical link	$g(\mu)$	Dispersion parameter
gaussian	μ, σ^2	identity	μ	σ^2
poisson	μ	log	$\ln(\mu)$	1
binomial	n, p	logit	$\ln\left(\frac{\mu}{1-\mu}\right)$	$\frac{1}{n}$
Gamma	α, λ	reciprocal	$\frac{1}{\mu}$	$\frac{1}{\alpha}$

Choosing between using a link function (e.g. log link) and transforming the response variable (i.e. having $log(Y_i)$ as the response variable rather than Y_i) takes a certain amount of experience. The decision is usually based on whether the variance is constant on the original scale of measurement. If the variance was constant, we might prefer use a link function. If the variance increased with the mean, we might be more likely to log-transform the response.

11.1.4 Model checking

To illustrate some of these ideas, we will return to the `ozone pollution` dataset discussed in the linear models chapter. We start by reproducing the model created using `lm ()`, but using the `glm ()` function: the argument `family = gaussian ()` is used to specify normally distributed errors. The full model is

$$E(Y_i | X_i = x_i) = \beta_0 + \beta_1 x_{i1} + \dots + \beta_p x_{ip} \ .$$

as the link function is just the identity function. This is equivalent to equation (10.3) in Section 10.2.1.

```
ozonepollution <- read.table ("ozone_pollution.txt", header = T)
lm_ozone <- glm (ozone ~ rad + temp + wind, family = gaussian (),
                    data = ozonepollution)
summary (lm_ozone)


Call:
glm(formula = ozone ~ rad + temp + wind, family = gaussian(),
    data = ozonepollution)

Deviance Residuals:
    Min       1Q    Median        3Q       Max
-40.485   -14.210   -3.556    10.124    95.600

Coefficients:
             Estimate Std. Error t value Pr(>|t|)
(Intercept) -64.23208   23.04204  -2.788  0.00628 **
rad           0.05980    0.02318   2.580  0.01124 *
temp          1.65121    0.25341   6.516 2.43e-09 ***
wind         -3.33760    0.65384  -5.105 1.45e-06 ***
---
Signif. codes:  0 '***' 0.001 '**' 0.01 '*' 0.05 '.' 0.1 ' ' 1

(Dispersion parameter for Gaussian family taken to be 448.2628)

    Null deviance: 121802  on 110  degrees of freedom
Residual deviance:  47964  on 107  degrees of freedom
AIC: 998.63

Number of Fisher Scoring iterations: 2
```

The summary of the GLM model looks a little different from that of a linear model. Some of the key features are the following:

- Near the top is a summary of **deviance residuals** rather than the residuals we are used to. The raw residuals are not generally appropriate for GLMs due to the relationship between the mean and the variance. Two types of residuals are usually created and this is the first;

- The middle section describing the coefficients is identical to that for linear models: be careful about its interpretation if the link function is not the identity;

- The **residual deviance** near the bottom is analogous to the RSS for linear models, i.e. we would like it to be as small as possible. The ratio of the residual deviance (4.7964118×10^4) to the number of degrees of freedom (107) should, in theory, be close to the `dispersion parameter`, whose theoretical Value is given in Table 11.1. Whether that is the case, is one of the factors in judging whether the model we have is a good one. We will come back to this in Section 11.2.2 when we examine **overdispersion** in count models;

- The AIC will be given wherever possible. This can be used for comparing models: the smaller the better.

We can create standardised residuals (the second type for GLMs) in a similar fashion to the way we did for linear models and Figure 11.2 compares them with fitted values from the model.

```
stdres_lm <- rstandard (lm_ozone)
plot (lm_ozone$fitted.values, stdres_lm, col = hue_pal ()(2)[1], pch = 20,
ylab = "standardised residuals", xlab = "fitted values")
```

As with linear models, we are looking for a random spread of dots. Although there are not too many residuals with absolute values greater than two, one of them is very large. In addition, the variance does appear to grow with the fitted values. Transformations were examined in Section 10.5.8, so

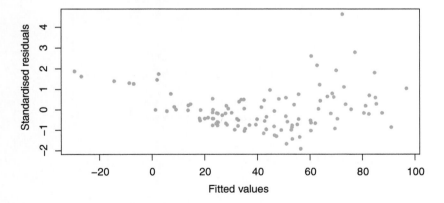

Figure 11.2 Linear model residuals from `ozonepollution`.

we will look at a different structure for the residuals. As the residuals appear to decrease and then increase, we will use a Gamma error distribution. This would give a model equation:

$$(E(Y_i|X_i = x_i))^{-1} = \beta_0 + \beta_1 x_{i1} + \ldots + \beta_p x_{ip} .$$

In order to account for the possible heteroscedasticity, we will also see whether a log-link function improves things and that model equation would be

$$\ln(E(Y_i|X_i = x_i)) = \beta_0 + \beta_1 x_{i1} + \ldots + \beta_p x_{ip} .$$

We won't write out any further model equations in full, but it's just a case of putting together the appropriate link function with the usual linear model equation:

```
glm_ozone_g <- glm (ozone ~ rad + temp + wind, family = Gamma (),
            data = ozonepollution)
glm_ozone_gl <- glm (ozone ~ rad + temp + wind, family = Gamma (link = "log"),
            data = ozonepollution)
summary (glm_ozone_g)


Call:
glm(formula = ozone ~ rad + temp + wind, family = Gamma(), data = ozonepollution)

Deviance Residuals:
    Min        1Q    Median        3Q       Max
-1.91389  -0.44403  -0.09569   0.29349   1.25129

Coefficients:
              Estimate Std. Error t value Pr(>|t|)
(Intercept)  1.061e-01  1.528e-02   6.940 3.13e-10 ***
rad         -6.821e-05  1.778e-05  -3.836 0.000212 ***
temp        -9.626e-04  1.567e-04  -6.144 1.40e-08 ***
wind         1.443e-03  3.465e-04   4.165 6.32e-05 ***
---
Signif. codes:  0 '***' 0.001 '**' 0.01 '*' 0.05 '.' 0.1 ' ' 1

(Dispersion parameter for Gamma family taken to be 0.2608118)

    Null deviance: 71.95  on 110  degrees of freedom
Residual deviance: 29.16  on 107  degrees of freedom
AIC: 939.81

Number of Fisher Scoring iterations: 6

summary (glm_ozone_gl)

Call:
glm(formula = ozone ~ rad + temp + wind, family = Gamma(link = "log"),
    data = ozonepollution)
```

```
Deviance Residuals:
    Min         1Q      Median        3Q        Max
-1.70970   -0.40806   -0.09134    0.24151    1.17971

Coefficients:
              Estimate Std. Error  t value  Pr(>|t|)
(Intercept)  0.4520877  0.5315684    0.850   0.39696
rad          0.0021026  0.0005347    3.933   0.00015 ***
temp         0.0430223  0.0058461    7.359 3.98e-11 ***
wind        -0.0659143  0.0150839   -4.370 2.89e-05 ***
---
Signif. codes:  0 '***' 0.001 '**' 0.01 '*' 0.05 '.' 0.1 ' ' 1

(Dispersion parameter for Gamma family taken to be 0.2385663)

    Null deviance: 71.950  on 110  degrees of freedom
Residual deviance: 25.853  on 107  degrees of freedom
AIC: 925.9

Number of Fisher Scoring iterations: 7
```

The log-link model has the smaller AIC (also smaller than that for the linear model), so let us run with that. Figure 11.3 shows the residuals.

```
stdres_glm <- rstandard (glm_ozone_gl)
plot (glm_ozone_gl$fitted.values, stdres_glm, col = hue_pal ()(2)[2], pch = 20,
ylab = "standardised residuals", xlab = "fitted values")
```

There are fewer points with absolute values greater than two, and they are less extreme, than in the linear model. On the face of it does look as if we have a larger variance for smaller fitted values; however, that may just be a consequence of there being more points for smaller values. Incidentally,

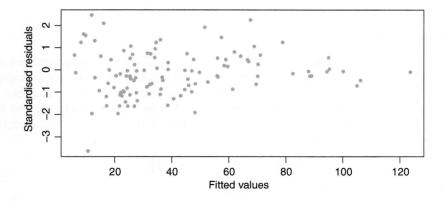

Figure 11.3 GLM with Gamma errors and log-link residuals from `ozonepollution`.

in Section 10.5.8, we wondered whether a transformation taking $y^{0.25}$ might be a good idea. With GLMs, we can use such a link function as follows:

```
glm_ozone_p <- glm (ozone ~ rad + temp + wind, family = Gamma (link =
                    power (0.25)),data = ozonepollution)
summary (glm_ozone_p)

Call:
glm(formula = ozone ~ rad + temp + wind, family = Gamma(link = power(0.25)),
    data = ozonepollution)

Deviance Residuals:
    Min        1Q      Median        3Q        Max
-1.70755   -0.45419   -0.06948    0.24978    1.17973

Coefficients:
              Estimate Std. Error t value Pr(>|t|)
(Intercept)  0.6798371  0.3104981   2.190 0.030732 *
rad          0.0010801  0.0003091   3.494 0.000693 ***
temp         0.0246121  0.0035039   7.024 2.08e-10 ***
wind        -0.0345243  0.0087976  -3.924 0.000154 ***
---
Signif. codes:  0 '***' 0.001 '**' 0.01 '*' 0.05 '.' 0.1 ' ' 1

(Dispersion parameter for Gamma family taken to be 0.2532739)

    Null deviance: 71.950  on 110  degrees of freedom
Residual deviance: 27.997  on 107  degrees of freedom
AIC: 935.1

Number of Fisher Scoring iterations: 11
```

but the AIC does not appear to be an improvement and the residuals plot (not shown) is very similar to that from the log link.

11.1.5 Interpretation and prediction

Having arrived at a model that we are happy with (`glm_ozone_gl`), how should we interpret it? The complicating factor is our log-link function. Since we take logs to arrive at the linear predictor, we need to go through the inverse of that function to understand how the linear predictor affects the outcome variable. We might want to know what the effect of an increase of 2 degrees in temperature might be on ozone estimates. Perhaps we discovered our thermometer was inaccurate or are interested in the effect of climate change:

1. Select the coefficient of wind in the model, $\beta_2 = 0.0430223$;

2. Multiply by the 2 degrees of interest to give, 0.0860447;

3. Take the exponential of the result, $e^{2\beta_2} = 1.089855$;

4. The effect on any ozone value can then be calculated by multiplying that value by the result from point 3.

Making predictions requires a similar approach, but we can use the `predict` () function in *R*, as we did for linear models. It is a little more complicated to derive the confidence interval, but here goes. Let us assume that we want to calculate 99% CIs for ozone levels for two sets of values of the covariates: (250,64, 10.3) and (200,62, 15.7).

```
covs <- data.frame (rad = c (250, 200), temp = c (64, 62), wind = c (10.3, 15.7))
z <- qnorm (0.995)
preds <- predict (glm_ozone_gl, newdata = covs, type = "response", se.fit = T)
point_est <- preds$fit
ci_lower <- preds$fit - z * preds$se.fit
ci_upper <- preds$fit + z * preds$se.fit
```

Fortunately, *R* handles the exponential transformation with the argument `type = "response"`. The CI for the first set of covariates, for instance, is then (`ci_lower[1]`, `ci_upper[1]`) or (15.45, 26.87). It is worth mentioning that it is dangerous to make predictions outside the area bounded by the covariate data that we have.

11.2   Count data and GLMs

Up to this point, most of our response variables have been continuous measurements such as weights, heights, lengths, temperatures, and growth rates. A great deal of the data collected by scientists, medical statisticians, and economists, however, is in the form of counts (whole numbers or integers). The number of individuals who died, the number of firms going bankrupt, the number of days of frost, the number of red blood cells on a microscope slide, and the number of craters in a sector of lunar landscape are all potentially interesting variables for study. With count data, the number 0 often appears as a value of the response variable (consider, for example what a 0 would mean in the context of the examples just listed). In this section, we deal with data on frequencies, where we count how many times something happened, although we have no way of knowing how often it did not happen (e.g. lightning strikes, bankruptcies, deaths, and births). This is in contrast to count data on proportions, where we know not only the number doing a particular thing but also the number not doing that thing (e.g. the proportion dying, sex ratios at birth, and proportions of different groups responding to a questionnaire).

Straightforward linear regression methods (assuming constant variance, Normal errors) are not appropriate for count data for four main reasons:

- the linear model might lead to the prediction of negative counts;

- the variance of the response variable is likely to increase with the mean;

- errors are unlikely be normally distributed;

- zeroes can be tricky to handle in transformations.

In *R*, count data are handled very elegantly in a generalised linear model by specifying `family = poisson` which sets errors to have a Poisson distribution and the default `link = log`. The log link ensures that all the fitted values are positive, while Poisson errors take account of the fact that the data are integers: the latter assume that their variances are equal to their means, and we shall revisit this assumption in Section 11.2.2.

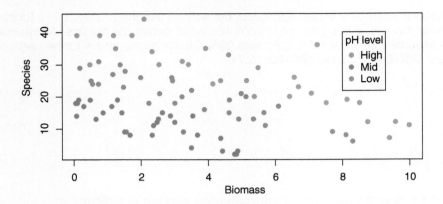

Figure 11.4 Dataset `species`.

11.2.1 A straightforward example

In this first example, the response is a count of the number of plant species on plots that have different biomass (a continuous explanatory variable) and different soil pH (a categorical variable with three levels: high, mid, and low), as pictured in Figure 11.4:

```
species <- read.table ("species.txt", header = T, colClasses = list (pH = "factor"))
head (species)

     pH    Biomass Species
1 high 0.4692972      30
2 high 1.7308704      39
3 high 2.0897785      44
4 high 3.9257871      35
5 high 4.3667927      25
6 high 5.4819747      29
cols = data.frame (pH = levels (species$pH), col = hue_pal () (3))
plot (species[,2:3], col = cols[match (species$pH, cols$pH),2],
      pch = 19)
legend (8, 40, legend = c ("high", "mid", "low"), pch = rep (19, 3),
        col = hue_pal () (3), title = "pH level")
```

We have created a dataframe, `cols`, matching each level of pH to a colour and then applying that to each point. It is clear that species declines with biomass, and that soil pH has a big effect on species, but does the slope of the relationship between species and biomass depend on pH? This is a question about interaction effects, and here, interaction effects are about differences between slopes. This is what we shall explore with our GLM, beginning with a model with no interaction.

```
species_mod1 <- glm (Species ~ Biomass + pH, poisson, data = species)
summary (species_mod1)

Call:
glm(formula = Species ~ Biomass + pH, family = poisson, data = species)
```

```
Deviance Residuals:
    Min      1Q   Median       3Q      Max
-2.5959  -0.6989  -0.0737   0.6647   3.5604


Coefficients:
            Estimate Std. Error z value Pr(>|z|)
(Intercept)  3.84894    0.05281  72.885  < 2e-16 ***
Biomass     -0.12756    0.01014 -12.579  < 2e-16 ***
pHlow       -1.13639    0.06720 -16.910  < 2e-16 ***
pHmid       -0.44516    0.05486  -8.114 4.88e-16 ***
---
Signif. codes:  0 '***' 0.001 '**' 0.01 '*' 0.05 '.' 0.1 ' ' 1


(Dispersion parameter for Poisson family taken to be 1)

    Null deviance: 452.346  on 89  degrees of freedom
Residual deviance:  99.242  on 86  degrees of freedom
AIC: 526.43

Number of Fisher Scoring iterations: 4
```

All the covariates appear to be important, so let us introduce an interaction and compare the two models:

```
species_mod2 <- glm (Species ~ Biomass * pH, poisson, data = species)
summary (species_mod2)

Call:
glm(formula = Species ~ Biomass * pH, family = poisson, data = species)

Deviance Residuals:
    Min      1Q   Median       3Q      Max
-2.4978  -0.7485  -0.0402   0.5575   3.2297

Coefficients:
               Estimate Std. Error z value Pr(>|z|)
(Intercept)     3.76812    0.06153  61.240  < 2e-16 ***
Biomass        -0.10713    0.01249  -8.577  < 2e-16 ***
pHlow          -0.81557    0.10284  -7.931 2.18e-15 ***
pHmid          -0.33146    0.09217  -3.596 0.000323 ***
Biomass:pHlow  -0.15503    0.04003  -3.873 0.000108 ***
Biomass:pHmid  -0.03189    0.02308  -1.382 0.166954
---
Signif. codes:  0 '***' 0.001 '**' 0.01 '*' 0.05 '.' 0.1 ' ' 1


(Dispersion parameter for Poisson family taken to be 1)

    Null deviance: 452.346  on 89  degrees of freedom
Residual deviance:  83.201  on 84  degrees of freedom
AIC: 514.39
```

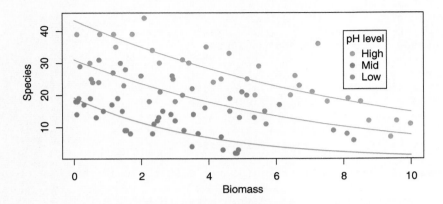

Figure 11.5 Dataset `species` with means of the fitted GLM.

```
Number of Fisher Scoring iterations: 4

anova (species_mod1, species_mod2, test = "Chi")

Analysis of Deviance Table

Model 1: Species ~ Biomass + pH
Model 2: Species ~ Biomass * pH
  Resid. Df Resid. Dev Df Deviance  Pr(>Chi)
1        86     99.242
2        84     83.201  2    16.04 0.0003288 ***
---
Signif. codes:  0 '***' 0.001 '**' 0.01 '*' 0.05 '.' 0.1 ' ' 1
```

Clearly, the small *p*-value suggests there is a difference between the models.

Poisson family models assume that the dispersion is 1 and so a good model would have the residual deviance and number of degrees of freedom close to each other (see Section 11.2.2 for more details). That is the case in our interaction model, whose AIC is also lower than the original simpler model.

The interaction between biomass and pH has an important effect on the number of species. We can plot the means of the fitted model to give Figure 11.5:

```
plot (species[,2:3], col = cols[match (species$pH, cols$pH),2])
legend (8, 40, legend = c ("high", "mid", "low"), pch = rep (19, 3),
        col = hue_pal ()(3), title = "pH level")
x <- seq (0, 10, 0.1)
for (levs in levels (species$pH)) {
  lines (x, exp (predict (species_mod2,
                          list (Biomass = x, pH = rep (levs, length (x))))),
        col = cols[match (levs, cols$pH),2])
}
```

11.2.2 Dispersion

In Table 11.1, we saw that attached to each error distribution is a dispersion parameter. Intuitively, this represents the ratio of the response variable to that of the linear predictor. Mathematically, we write it as follows:

$$\frac{Var(Y_i)}{Var(\mu_i)} = \frac{Var(Y_i)}{Var(g^{-1}(\beta_0 + \beta_1 x_{i1} + \ldots \beta_p x_{ip}))}.$$

In those distributions where the dispersion parameter is represented by a parameter of the distribution (e.g. Gamma with $\frac{1}{\alpha}$), the value of that latter parameter can be estimated based upon the dispersion of the data. However, for the Poisson and Binomial distributions, the dispersion parameter is fixed (1 and $\frac{1}{n}$, respectively), and so there is no way of rectifying any differences in the variances. Typically, $Var(Y_i)$ is larger than the denominator, and we have **overdispersion**, i.e. the data we observe are more widely spread (dispersed) than the explanatory variables.

The simplest way to deal with this is to find some more covariates that reduce the dispersion. If that is not possible, then GLMs do have a work around: the `quasi-Poisson` family can be used for count data and the following example illustrates that. However, it is worth stressing that this technique introduces another level of uncertainty into the analysis. Overdispersion happens for real, scientifically important reasons, and these reasons may throw doubt upon our ability to interpret the experiment in an unbiased way.

The response variable we will be examining is a count of infected blood cells per square millimetre on microscope slides prepared from randomly selected individuals. The explanatory variables are smoker (logical: yes or no), age (three levels: under 20, 21–59, 60, and over), sex (male or female), and body mass score (three levels: normal, overweight, and obese).

```
cellcounts <- read.table ("cells.txt", header = T,
                    colClasses = c ("numeric", rep ("factor", 4)))
names (cellcounts)

[1] "cells"   "smoker" "age"     "sex"     "weight"

head (cellcounts)

  cells smoker   age  sex weight
1    1       T young male normal
2    0       T young male normal
3    1       T young male normal
4    1       T young male normal
5    0       T young male normal
6    2       T young male normal
```

It is always a good idea with count data to get a feel for the overall frequency distribution of counts:

```
table (cellcounts$cells)

  0   1   2   3   4   5   6   7
314  75  50  32  18  13   7   2
```

Most subjects (314 of them) showed no damaged cells, and the maximum of 7 was observed in just two patients. We begin data inspection by tabulating the main effect means:

```
tapply (cellcounts$cells, cellcounts$smoker, mean)


        F         T
0.5478723 1.9111111

tapply (cellcounts$cells, cellcounts$weight,mean)


   normal      obese       over
0.5833333 1.2814371 0.9357143

tapply (cellcounts$cells, cellcounts$sex, mean)


   female       male
0.6584507 1.2202643

tapply (cellcounts$cells, cellcounts$age, mean)


      mid        old       young
0.8676471 0.7835821 1.2710280
```

It looks as if smokers had a substantially higher mean count than non-smokers, overweight and obese subjects had higher counts than those of normal weight, males had a higher count than females, and young subjects had a higher mean count than middle-aged or older people. We need to test whether any of these differences are important and to assess whether there are interactions between the explanatory variables.

We might start our model building with the very straightforward:

```
cells_mod1 <- glm (cells ~ smoker + sex + age + weight, poisson, data = cellcounts)
summary (cells_mod1)

Call:
glm(formula = cells ~ smoker + sex + age + weight, family = poisson,
    data = cellcounts)

Deviance Residuals:
    Min       1Q    Median       3Q       Max
-2.4787   -1.2493   -0.7866    0.5244    3.6826

Coefficients:
            Estimate Std. Error z value Pr(>|z|)
(Intercept) -1.228699   0.141585   -8.678  < 2e-16 ***
smokerT      1.305209   0.111522   11.704  < 2e-16 ***
sexmale      0.124044   0.109401    1.134    0.257
ageold       0.055447   0.125359    0.442    0.658
ageyoung    -0.003507   0.130616   -0.027    0.979
weightobese  0.925295   0.117704    7.861 3.80e-15 ***
```

```
weightover    0.531883    0.130218    4.085 4.42e-05 ***
---
Signif. codes:   0 '***' 0.001 '**' 0.01 '*' 0.05 '.' 0.1 ' ' 1

(Dispersion parameter for Poisson family taken to be 1)

    Null deviance: 1052.95  on 510   degrees of freedom
Residual deviance:  803.72  on 504   degrees of freedom
AIC: 1331.4

Number of Fisher Scoring iterations: 6
```

Aside from noting that weight and smoking appear to be critical factors in determining cell count, while age and gender do not, we can see that the ratio of residual deviance to degrees of freedom is 803.72/504 = 1.59 showing considerable overdispersion. If we cannot uncover further covariates that might explain this, then we could adapt our model:

```
cells_mod2 <- glm (cells ~ smoker + sex + age + weight, quasi-Poisson,
                   data = cellcounts)
summary (cells_mod2)


Call:
glm(formula = cells ~ smoker + sex + age + weight, family = quasi-Poisson,
    data = cellcounts)

Deviance Residuals:
    Min       1Q   Median       3Q      Max
-2.4787  -1.2493  -0.7866   0.5244   3.6826

Coefficients:
             Estimate Std. Error t value Pr(>|t|)
(Intercept) -1.228699   0.196355  -6.258 8.36e-10 ***
smokerT      1.305209   0.154662   8.439 3.41e-16 ***
sexmale      0.124044   0.151721   0.818  0.41399
ageold       0.055447   0.173852   0.319  0.74991
ageyoung    -0.003507   0.181143  -0.019  0.98456
weightobese  0.925295   0.163236   5.668 2.43e-08 ***
weightover   0.531883   0.180590   2.945  0.00338 **
---
Signif. codes:   0 '***' 0.001 '**' 0.01 '*' 0.05 '.' 0.1 ' ' 1

(Dispersion parameter for quasi-Poisson family taken to be 1.923312)

    Null deviance: 1052.95  on 510   degrees of freedom
Residual deviance:  803.72  on 504   degrees of freedom
AIC: NA

Number of Fisher Scoring iterations: 6
```

where the only change is to change `Poisson` to `Quasi-Poisson` (the default link function has not changed). It is worth comparing the outputs from the two models:

- the parameter estimates have not changed;

- however, the standard errors and, thus, the *p*-values have changed;

- this is as a result of the new parameter in our model, the dispersion, which is no longer 1 but is now estimated from the data;

- the AIC, to be used in model comparison, no longer has a value. This is because the quasi-Poisson is not a genuine probability distribution. So we cannot compare the two models we have produced so far in the usual ways (the `anova` function will not work as the models are not nested). However, we would probably decide that as our second model deals with the overdispersion, we will stick with that.

However, our model analysis is not complete as we have not examined interactions. The `anova ()` function can be used to compare quasi-Poisson models in the usual way, but it can also be used on individual models to examine the effect of adding in terms to the model. So for the maximal model:

```
cells_mod3 <- glm (cells ~ smoker * sex * age * weight, quasi-poisson,
                   data = cellcounts)
anova (cells_mod3, test = "F")

Analysis of Deviance Table

Model: Quasi-Poisson, link: log

Response: cells

Terms added sequentially (first to last)
```

	Df	Deviance	Resid. Df	Resid. Dev	F	Pr(>F)	
NULL			510	1052.95			
smoker	1	175.838	509	877.11	94.8007	< 2.2e-16	***
sex	1	3.250	508	873.86	1.7521	0.18624	
age	2	4.991	506	868.87	1.3455	0.26140	
weight	2	65.148	504	803.72	17.5620	4.372e-08	***
smoker:sex	1	6.441	503	797.28	3.4727	0.06300	.
smoker:age	2	4.055	501	793.22	1.0930	0.33604	
sex:age	2	6.670	499	786.56	1.7979	0.16677	
smoker:weight	2	11.714	497	774.84	3.1577	0.04341	*
sex:weight	2	2.584	495	772.26	0.6966	0.49877	
age:weight	4	4.939	491	767.32	0.6657	0.61608	
smoker:sex:age	2	6.570	489	760.75	1.7712	0.17125	
smoker:sex:weight	2	5.774	487	754.97	1.5566	0.21192	
smoker:age:weight	4	9.665	483	745.31	1.3027	0.26802	

```
sex:age:weight            4      7.442        479     737.87  1.0030   0.40551
smoker:sex:age:weight     2      1.538        477     736.33  0.4147   0.66080
---
Signif. codes:  0 '***' 0.001 '**' 0.01 '*' 0.05 '.' 0.1 ' ' 1
```

Note that we need to specify the F-test due to the presence of the dispersion parameter. We won't go through the gory details of picking our preferred model, but we might end up with something like:

```
cells_mod4 <- glm (cells ~ smoker * weight, quasi-Poisson, data = cellcounts)
summary (cells_mod4)

Call:
glm(formula = cells ~ smoker * weight, family = Quasi-Poisson,
    data = cellcounts)

Deviance Residuals:
    Min      1Q   Median      3Q      Max
-2.6511  -1.1742  -0.9148  0.5533   3.6436

Coefficients:
                    Estimate Std. Error t value Pr(>|t|)
(Intercept)          -0.8712     0.1760  -4.950 1.01e-06 ***
smokerT               0.8224     0.2479   3.318 0.000973 ***
weightobese           0.4993     0.2260   2.209 0.027598 *
weightover            0.2618     0.2522   1.038 0.299723
smokerT:weightobese   0.8063     0.3105   2.597 0.009675 **
smokerT:weightover    0.4935     0.3442   1.434 0.152226
---
Signif. codes:  0 '***' 0.001 '**' 0.01 '*' 0.05 '.' 0.1 ' ' 1

(Dispersion parameter for quasi-Poisson family taken to be 1.827927)

    Null deviance: 1052.95  on 510  degrees of freedom
Residual deviance:  792.85  on 505  degrees of freedom
AIC: NA

Number of Fisher Scoring iterations: 6
```

The intercept includes normal weight, and there does not appear to be a distinguishable difference between that and overweight (unlike between normal and obese), so we might choose to merge the normal and overweight levels. We can summarise the effect of the interaction:

```
tapply (cellcounts$cells, list (cellcounts$smoker, cellcounts$weight), mean)

      normal      obese       over
F  0.4184397  0.6893939  0.5436893
T  0.9523810  3.5142857  2.0270270
```

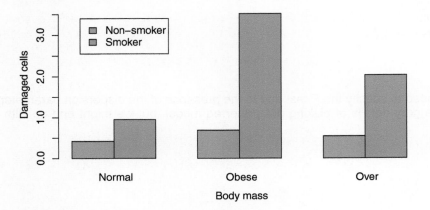

Figure 11.6 The effect of smoking and obesity in `cellcounts`.

The interaction arises because the response to smoking depends on body weight: smoking adds a mean of about 0.5 damaged cells for individuals with normal body weight, but adds 2.8 damaged cells for obese people. It is straightforward to turn the summary table into a barplot as in Figure 11.6:

```
barplot (tapply (cellcounts$cells, list (cellcounts$smoker, cellcounts$weight),
        mean),
        col = hue_pal () (2), beside = T,
        ylab = "damaged cells", xlab = "body mass")
legend (1.2,3.4, c("non-smoker", "smoker"), fill = hue_pal () (2))
```

There is also a `quasi-Binomial` error distribution that operates in a similar fashion and a more general `quasi` option. For the latter, we can specify a link function and a variance function, but no other distributional assumptions are made: it may be helpful to work with a statistician to understand exactly what is going on here.

11.2.3 An alternative to Poisson counts

The data analysed in this section refer to children from Walgett, New South Wales, Australia, who were classified by sex (with two levels: male (M) and female (F)), culture (also with two levels: Aboriginal (A) and not (N)), age group (with four levels: F0 (primary), F1, F2, and F3) and learner status (with two levels: average (AL) and slow (SL)). The response variable is a count of the number of days absent from school in a particular school year (Days). We pick up the data from one of the core *R* packages, MASS (Venables and Ripley, 2002):

```
library (MASS)
data (quine)
head (quine)
```

Before we proceed any further, it is worth looking at the number of data points in each combination of covariates:

```
ftable (table (quine$Eth, quine$Sex, quine$Age, quine$Lrn))
          AL SL

A F F0    4  1
    F1    5 10
    F2    1  8
    F3    9  0
  M F0    5  3
    F1    2  3
    F2    7  4
    F3    7  0
N F F0    4  1
    F1    6 11
    F2    1  9
    F3   10  0
  M F0    6  3
    F1    2  7
    F2    7  3
F3    7  0
```

There are zeroes, apparently because slow learners in the dataset never make it to F3. From a modelling point of view, this means that a maximal model (`Days ~ Eth * Age * Sex * Lrn`) will have lines where no analysis is possible.

We might begin with a minimal model:

```
quine_mod1 <- glm (Days ~ Eth + Age + Sex + Lrn, data = quine, family = poisson)
summary (quine_mod1)

Call:
glm(formula = Days ~ Eth + Age + Sex + Lrn, family = poisson,
    data = quine)

Deviance Residuals:
   Min      1Q   Median      3Q      Max
-6.808  -3.065   -1.119   1.818    9.909

Coefficients:
            Estimate Std. Error z value Pr(>|z|)
(Intercept)  2.71538    0.06468  41.980  < 2e-16 ***
EthN        -0.53360    0.04188 -12.740  < 2e-16 ***
AgeF1       -0.33390    0.07009  -4.764 1.90e-06 ***
AgeF2        0.25783    0.06242   4.131 3.62e-05 ***
AgeF3        0.42769    0.06769   6.319 2.64e-10 ***
```

```
SexM              0.16160       0.04253    3.799 0.000145 ***
LrnSL             0.34894       0.05204    6.705 2.02e-11 ***
---
Signif. codes:   0 '***' 0.001 '**' 0.01 '*' 0.05 '.' 0.1 ' ' 1

(Dispersion parameter for Poisson family taken to be 1)

    Null deviance: 2073.5  on 145  degrees of freedom
Residual deviance: 1696.7  on 139  degrees of freedom
AIC: 2299.2

Number of Fisher Scoring iterations: 5
```

Although all the elements of the model seem worth retaining, the ratio of residual deviance to degrees of freedom is shocking, so we should examine a quasi-Poisson model:

```
quine_mod2 <- glm (Days ~ Eth + Age + Sex + Lrn, data = quine,
family = quasi-Poisson)summary (quine_mod2)

Call:
glm(formula = Days ~ Eth + Age + Sex + Lrn, family = quasi-Poisson,
    data = quine)

Deviance Residuals:
   Min      1Q  Median      3Q      Max
-6.808  -3.065  -1.119   1.818    9.909

Coefficients:
            Estimate Std. Error t value Pr(>|t|)
(Intercept)   2.7154     0.2347  11.569  < 2e-16 ***
EthN         -0.5336     0.1520  -3.511 0.000602 ***
AgeF1        -0.3339     0.2543  -1.313 0.191413
AgeF2         0.2578     0.2265   1.138 0.256938
AgeF3         0.4277     0.2456   1.741 0.083831.
SexM          0.1616     0.1543   1.047 0.296914
LrnSL         0.3489     0.1888   1.848 0.066760.
---
Signif. codes:   0 '***' 0.001 '**' 0.01 '*' 0.05 '.' 0.1 ' ' 1

(Dispersion parameter for quasi-Poisson family taken to be 13.16691)

    Null deviance: 2073.5  on 145  degrees of freedom
Residual deviance: 1696.7  on 139  degrees of freedom
AIC: NA

Number of Fisher Scoring iterations: 5
```

The dispersion parameter seems to have taken care of the overdispersion, but ethnicity appears now to be the only key covariate. Once we start examining interactions using `anova (...,  test = "F")` for model comparison, the picture changes. Our preferred model, details omitted, might be

```
quine_mod3 <- glm (Days ~ Eth * Age + Sex * Age + Eth * Sex * Lrn,
                   data = quine, family = quasi-Poisson)
summary (quine_mod3)

Call:
glm(formula = Days ~ Eth * Age + Sex * Age + Eth * Sex * Lrn,
    family = quasi-Poisson, data = quine)

Deviance Residuals:
    Min        1Q    Median        3Q       Max
 -7.1369   -2.6852   -0.5919    1.6040    7.1049

Coefficients:
                Estimate Std. Error t value Pr(>|t|)
(Intercept)      2.83161    0.30489   9.287 4.98e-16 ***
EthN             0.09821    0.38631   0.254  0.79973
AgeF1           -0.20878    0.35933  -0.581  0.56224
AgeF2            0.16223    0.37481   0.433  0.66586
AgeF3           -0.25584    0.37855  -0.676  0.50036
SexM            -0.56268    0.38877  -1.447  0.15023
LrnSL            0.50311    0.30798   1.634  0.10479
EthN:AgeF1      -0.68742    0.46823  -1.468  0.14450
EthN:AgeF2      -1.07361    0.42449  -2.529  0.01264 *
EthN:AgeF3       0.01879    0.42914   0.044  0.96513
AgeF1:SexM      -0.26358    0.50673  -0.520  0.60385
AgeF2:SexM       0.94531    0.43530   2.172  0.03171 *
AgeF3:SexM       1.35285    0.42933   3.151  0.00202 **
EthN:SexM       -0.24554    0.37347  -0.657  0.51206
EthN:LrnSL      -0.65154    0.45857  -1.421  0.15778
SexM:LrnSL      -0.29570    0.41144  -0.719  0.47363
EthN:SexM:LrnSL  1.60463    0.57113   2.810  0.00573 **
---
Signif. codes:  0 '***' 0.001 '**' 0.01 '*' 0.05 '.' 0.1 ' ' 1

(Dispersion parameter for quasi-Poisson family taken to be 9.833478)

    Null deviance: 2073.5 on 145  degrees of freedom
Residual deviance: 1301.1 on 129  degrees of freedom
AIC: NA

Number of Fisher Scoring iterations: 5
```

Although none of the covariates would appear to warrant inclusion in the model on their own, they all appear in at least one of the interactions, and so they should all be retained.

We have seen that one of the disadvantages of the quasi approach to GLMs is the lack of an automatic AIC calculation. An alternative approach to overdispersed Poisson models which does provide this is to use the Negative Binomial distribution instead of the Poisson (see Section 9.3.2 for an example of a test which formally compares the two). The function for handling this, glm.nb (), also appears in the MASS library, so let us have a look at it for our minimal model:

```
quine_mod4 <- glm.nb (Days ~ Eth + Sex + Age + Lrn, data = quine)
summary (quine_mod4)

Call:
glm.nb(formula = Days ~ Eth + Sex + Age + Lrn, data = quine,
    init.theta = 1.274892646, link = log)

Deviance Residuals:
    Min        1Q    Median        3Q       Max
-2.7918   -0.8892   -0.2778    0.3797    2.1949

Coefficients:
            Estimate Std. Error z value Pr(>|z|)
(Intercept)  2.89458    0.22842  12.672  < 2e-16 ***
EthN        -0.56937    0.15333  -3.713 0.000205 ***
SexM         0.08232    0.15992   0.515 0.606710
AgeF1       -0.44843    0.23975  -1.870 0.061425 .
AgeF2        0.08808    0.23619   0.373 0.709211
AgeF3        0.35690    0.24832   1.437 0.150651
LrnSL        0.29211    0.18647   1.566 0.117236
---
Signif. codes:  0 '***' 0.001 '**' 0.01 '*' 0.05 '.' 0.1 ' ' 1

(Dispersion parameter for Negative Binomial (1.2749) family taken to be 1)

    Null deviance: 195.29 on 145  degrees of freedom
Residual deviance: 167.95 on 139  degrees of freedom
AIC: 1109.2

Number of Fisher Scoring iterations: 1

          Theta:  1.275
      Std. Err.:  0.161

2 x log-likelihood:  -1093.151
```

The output is slightly different than for a conventional GLM: we see the estimated second Negative Binomial parameter (here called Theta, but described in the *R* distributions functions as size) and its approximate standard error, together with the log-likelihood. Note that the residual deviance is far closer to the number of degrees of freedom than in the Poisson case above. There is also an AIC, which we can use, together with anova, to compare models. Having done that, details omitted to preserve sanity and paper, our preferred set of covariates and interactions appears to be the same as under the quasi-Poisson approach (that is not always the case):

```
quine_mod5 <- glm.nb (Days ~ Eth * Age + Sex * Age + Eth * Sex * Lrn,
                 data = quine)
summary (quine_mod5)

Call:
glm.nb(formula = Days ~ Eth * Age + Sex * Age + Eth * Sex * Lrn,
    data = quine, init.theta = 1.678619828, link = log)

Deviance Residuals:
    Min       1Q    Median       3Q       Max
-3.0246   -0.9449   -0.2228    0.4847    1.9002

Coefficients:
                 Estimate Std. Error z-value Pr(>|z|)
(Intercept)       2.91755    0.32626    8.942  < 2e-16 ***
EthN              0.05666    0.39515    0.143  0.88598
AgeF1            -0.32379    0.38373   -0.844  0.39878
AgeF2            -0.06383    0.42046   -0.152  0.87933
AgeF3            -0.34854    0.39128   -0.891  0.37305
SexM             -0.55047    0.39014   -1.411  0.15825
LrnSL             0.57697    0.33382    1.728  0.08392 .
EthN:AgeF1       -0.56613    0.43162   -1.312  0.18965
EthN:AgeF2       -0.89577    0.42950   -2.086  0.03702 *
EthN:AgeF3        0.08467    0.44010    0.192  0.84744
AgeF1:SexM       -0.08459    0.45324   -0.187  0.85195
AgeF2:SexM        1.13752    0.45192    2.517  0.01183 *
AgeF3:SexM        1.43124    0.44365    3.226  0.00126 **
EthN:SexM        -0.41608    0.37491   -1.110  0.26708
EthN:LrnSL       -0.78724    0.43058   -1.828  0.06750 .
SexM:LrnSL       -0.47437    0.45908   -1.033  0.30147
EthN:SexM:LrnSL   1.75289    0.58341    3.005  0.00266 **
---
Signif. codes:  0 '***' 0.001 '**' 0.01 '*' 0.05 '.' 0.1 ' ' 1

(Dispersion parameter for Negative Binomial (1.6786) family taken to be 1)

    Null deviance: 243.98 on 145 degrees of freedom
Residual deviance: 168.03 on 129 degrees of freedom
AIC: 1093.2

Number of Fisher Scoring iterations: 1


        Theta:  1.679
     Std. Err.:  0.227

2 x log-likelihood:  -1057.219
```

Not unexpectedly, the estimated parameters and their corresponding *p*-values are different from the equivalent quasi-Poisson model, but the model is probably easier to describe. We can plot our favourite residuals analyses in the usual way (`plot ()` uses the deviance residuals by default for

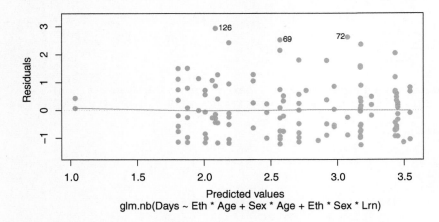

Figure 11.7   Deviance residuals vs fitted values for a Negative Binomial model for `quine`.

GLMs) to give Figure 11.7:

```
plot (quine_mod5, which = 1, col = hue_pal ()(1))
```

11.3   Count table data and GLMs

The analysis of count data with categorical explanatory variables comes under the heading of contingency tables, which we introduced in Section 9.3.3, in the context of testing. In this section, we will explore how we might visualise such data, in tables or plots, as we model them. Along the way, we will dig a little deeper into how we might compare models.

11.3.1   Log-linear models

A number of models that had been used for a long time were subsumed into the GLM family with its more general approach. The names of some of these models persist: we have already seen with the `ozone` dataset in Section 11.1.4 that the linear model is one of these. A **log-linear** model is just a linear model with a log-link function. There is a very useful way of displaying the residuals from such a model with categorical covariates, a mosaic plot. We can illustrate this using the `HairEyeColor` dataset in *R*:

```
mosaicplot (HairEyeColor, shade = T, type = "deviance")
```

Figure 11.8 shows the results for the deviance residuals. In this case (not always true), there is no difference in the analysis between these and the Pearson residuals.

11.3.2   All covariates might be useful

We saw in Section 10.4.5, the danger of building as many variables as possible into a model. However, there is also a danger, if we build models without thinking, of omitting some important

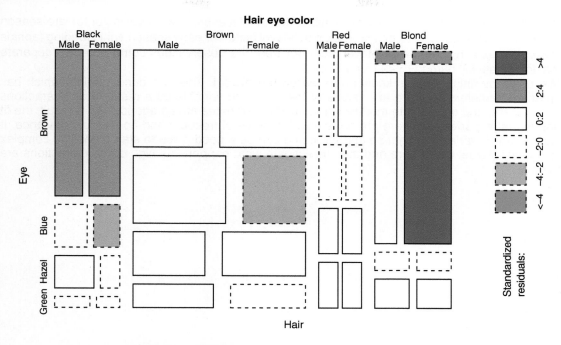

Figure 11.8   Visualisation of residuals from `HairEyeColor`.

explanatory variables. Subject matter expertise is critical here, but a thoughtful statistical analysis will also help. If we don't have the data, then that's life, and given that we make every effort to note the important factors, there is little we can do about it. The problem comes when we ignore factors that have an important influence on the response variable. This difficulty can be particularly acute if we aggregate data over important explanatory variables.

Suppose we are carrying out a study of induced defences in trees. A preliminary trial has suggested that early feeding on a leaf by aphids may cause chemical changes in the leaf which reduces the probability of that leaf being attacked later in the season by hole-making insects. To this end, we mark a large cohort of leaves, then score whether they were infested by aphids early in the season and whether they were holed by insects later in the year. The work was carried out on two different trees, and the results were as follows:

```
induced <- read.table ("induced.txt", header = T,
                   colClasses = c (rep ("factor", 3), "numeric"))
induced

  Tree   Aphid Caterpillar Count
1 Tree1  absent       holed    35
2 Tree1  absent         not  1750
3 Tree1 present       holed    23
4 Tree1 present         not  1146
5 Tree2  absent       holed   146
6 Tree2  absent         not  1642
7 Tree2 present       holed    30
8 Tree2 present         not   333
```

There are four variables: the response variable, `count` of leaves, a two-level factor for late-season feeding by caterpillars (`holed` or `intact`), a two-level factor for early season aphid feeding (aphids `present` or `absent`), and a two-level factor for tree (the observations come from two separate trees, imaginatively named `tree1` and `tree2`).

We begin by fitting what is known as a **saturated model**. This is a curious thing, which has as many parameters as there are values of the response variable as a result of all interactions being present, and occurs with models where all the covariates are categorical. As a result, the fit of the model is perfect, so there are no residual degrees of freedom and no residual deviance. It suggests which variables might be important and can be a good place to start modelling complex contingency tables: begin here and then investigate what happens as high-order interactions are dropped.

```
induced_mod1 <- glm (Count ~ Tree * Aphid * Caterpillar, family = poisson,
                  data = induced)
summary (induced_mod1)

Call:
glm(formula = Count ~ Tree * Aphid * Caterpillar, family = poisson,
    data = induced)

Deviance Residuals:
[1]  0  0  0  0  0  0  0  0  0

Coefficients:
                                   Estimate Std. Error z value Pr(>|z|)
(Intercept)                        3.555348   0.169031  21.034  < 2e-16 ***
TreeTree2                          1.428259   0.188204   7.589 3.23e-14 ***
Aphidpresent                      -0.419854   0.268421  -1.564  0.11778
Caterpillarnot                     3.912023   0.170713  22.916  < 2e-16 ***
TreeTree2:Aphidpresent            -1.162555   0.335011  -3.470  0.00052 ***
TreeTree2:Caterpillarnot          -1.491959   0.191314  -7.798 6.27e-15 ***
Aphidpresent:Caterpillarnot       -0.003484   0.271097  -0.013  0.98975
TreeTree2:Aphidpresent:Caterpillarnot -0.009634 0.342474 -0.028  0.97756
---
Signif. codes:  0 '***' 0.001 '**' 0.01 '*' 0.05 '.' 0.1 ' ' 1

(Dispersion parameter for Poisson family taken to be 1)

    Null deviance:  6.5734e+03 on 7  degrees of freedom
Residual deviance: -2.5580e-13 on 0  degrees of freedom
AIC: 73.521

Number of Fisher Scoring iterations: 3
```

The asterisk notation ensures that the saturated model is fitted, because all of the main effects and two-way interactions are fitted, along with the three-way Tree by Aphid by Caterpillar interaction. The model fit involves the estimation of $2 \times 2 \times 2 = 8$ parameters and exactly matches the eight values of the response variable, `Count`.

   The first real step in the modelling is to use `update ()` to remove the three-way interaction from the saturated model and then to use `anova ()` to test whether the three-way interaction is significant or not:

```
induced_mod2 <- update (induced_mod1, ~ . - Tree:Aphid:Caterpillar)
anova (induced_mod1, induced_mod2, test= "Chi")

Analysis of Deviance Table

Model 1: Count ~ Tree * Aphid * Caterpillar
Model 2: Count ~ Tree + Aphid + Caterpillar + Tree:Aphid + Tree:Caterpillar +
    Aphid:Caterpillar
  Resid. Df Resid. Dev Df    Deviance Pr(>Chi)
1         0 0.00000000
2         1 0.00079137 -1 -0.00079137   0.9776
```

The punctuation in the first line is very important (it is 'comma, tilde, dot, minus'), and note the use of colons rather than asterisks to denote interaction terms rather than main effects plus interaction terms. The test shows very clearly that the interaction between caterpillar attack and leaf holing does not differ from tree to tree (the p-value is large). Note that if this interaction had been significant, then we would have stopped the modelling at this stage. But it was not, so we leave it out and continue.

   What about the main question? Is there an interaction between aphid attack and leaf holing? The p-value is large in both our first two models, but let us test this by deleting the Caterpillar by Aphid interaction from the model:

```
induced_mod3 <- update (induced_mod2, ~ . - Aphid:Caterpillar)
anova (induced_mod2, induced_mod3, test= "Chi")

Analysis of Deviance Table

Model 1: Count ~ Tree + Aphid + Caterpillar + Tree:Aphid + Tree:Caterpillar +
    Aphid:Caterpillar
Model 2: Count ~ Tree + Aphid + Caterpillar + Tree:Aphid + Tree:Caterpillar
  Resid. Df Resid. Dev Df  Deviance Pr(>Chi)
1         1 0.0007914
2         2 0.0040853 -1 -0.003294   0.9542
```

There is absolutely no hint of an interaction (note also the decreasing AICs as our modelling has progressed). The interpretation is clear: this work provides no evidence at all for induced defences caused by early season caterpillar feeding.

   But look what happens when we do the modelling without thinking. Suppose we went straight for the interaction of interest, Aphid by Caterpillar. We might proceed like this:

```
induced_mod1a <- glm (Count~ Aphid * Caterpillar, family = poisson,
                  data = induced)
induced_mod2a <- update (induced_mod1a, ~ . - Aphid:Caterpillar)
```

```
anova (induced_mod1a, induced_mod2a, test = "Chi")

Analysis of Deviance Table

Model 1: Count ~ Aphid * Caterpillar
Model 2: Count ~ Aphid + Caterpillar
  Resid. Df Resid. Dev Df Deviance Pr(>Chi)
1         4     550.19
2         5     556.85 -1  -6.6594 0.009864 **
---
Signif. codes:  0 '***' 0.001 '**' 0.01 '*' 0.05 '.' 0.1 ' ' 1
```

The Aphid by Caterpillar interaction is highly significant, providing strong evidence for induced defences. This is wrong. By failing to include Tree in the model, we have omitted an important explanatory variable. As it turns out, and as we should really have determined by more thorough preliminary analysis, the trees differ enormously in their average levels of leaf holing:

```
as.table (by (induced$Count, INDICES = list (induced$Tree, induced$Caterpillar),
              FUN = sum))
      holed  not
Tree1    58 2896
Tree2   176 1975
```

Tree 2 has more than four times the proportion of its leaves holed by caterpillars than tree 1 does. If we had been paying more attention when we did the modelling the wrong way, we should have noticed that the model containing only Aphid and Caterpillar had massive overdispersion, and this should have alerted us that all was not well.

The moral is clear: always examine our data before we start modelling. With covariates that are all categorical, beginning with a saturated model and then gradually eliminating unimportant interactions is a sensible way to proceed. However, as discussed in Section 10.4.5, it is not guaranteed that we will arrive at our preferred model: it might also be worth starting with a linear model consisting of all covariates with no interactions and then adding in the latter gradually.

At this point, it is worth highlighting the reasons why we might prefer one model to another. We have seen a number of possibilities:

- using the `anova` () function to compare deviances. This only works with nested models;

- using AIC to compare log-likelihoods. This will work with all models where the data involved are the same;

- looking for overdispersion in count (and Binomial) models;

- examining residuals;

- one model makes more sense in the context being examined.

These criteria might not always point to one model being preferred: in fact, there may not be a preferred model. This is where subject matter expertise comes to the fore.

As an example, we might be interested in whether lizards show any niche separation across various ecological factors and, in particular, whether there are any interactions – for example, whether they show different habitat separation at different times of the day:

```
lizards <- read.table ("lizards.txt",header = T,
                        colClasses = c ("numeric", rep ("factor", 5)))
head (lizards)

   n   sun height  perch    time  species
1 20 Shade   High  Broad Morning opalinus
2 13 Shade    Low  Broad Morning opalinus
3  8 Shade   High Narrow Morning opalinus
4  6 Shade    Low Narrow Morning opalinus
5 34   Sun   High  Broad Morning opalinus
6 31   Sun    Low  Broad Morning opalinus

ftable (tapply (lizards$n, list (lizards$species,
                                 lizards$sun,
                                 lizards$height,
                                 lizards$perch,
                                 lizards$time),
sum))
```

				Afternoon	Mid-day	Morning
grahamii	Shade	High	Broad	4	1	2
			Narrow	3	1	3
		Low	Broad	0	0	0
			Narrow	1	0	0
	Sun	High	Broad	10	20	11
			Narrow	8	32	15
		Low	Broad	3	4	5
			Narrow	4	5	1
opalinus	Shade	High	Broad	4	8	20
			Narrow	5	4	8
		Low	Broad	12	8	13
			Narrow	1	0	6
	Sun	High	Broad	18	69	34
			Narrow	8	60	17
		Low	Broad	13	55	31
			Narrow	4	21	12

The response variable is n, the count for each contingency. The explanatory variables are all categorical: sun is a two-level factor (Sun and Shade within the bush), height is a two-level factor (High and Low within the bush), perch is a two-level factor (Broad and Narrow twigs), time is a three-level factor (Afternoon, Mid-day, and Morning), and there are two lizard species both belonging to the genus Anolis (A. grahamii and A. opalinus). It is important in creating our summary table to list our key variable, species, first. With categorical explanatory variables it can be difficult to see which are important by looking at tables or plots particularly, as here, when some of the combinations of variables have very few data instances.

As usual, we begin by fitting a saturated model, fitting all the interactions and main effects:

```
lizards_mod1 <- glm (n ~ sun * height * perch * time * species, poisson,
                      data = lizards)
lizards_mod1$aic
[1] 259.2488
```

Without painfully listing here a complex model, we can see that very few covariates have small *p*-values. At this point, it might be better to try a minimal model with no interactions, to see whether we can eliminate any of them.

```
lizards_mod2 <- glm (n ~ sun + height + perch + time + species, poisson,
                      data = lizards)
lizards_mod2$aic

[1] 329.8624
```

No. However, as the interaction between `species` and the other explanatory variables is what our subject matter expertise tells us is important, let us introduce those interactions.

```
lizards_mod3 <- glm (n ~ (sun + height + perch + time) * species, poisson,
                      data = lizards)
lizards_mod3$aic

[1] 281.642
```

This gives an AIC that is an improvement on our minimal model but not as good as the saturated one. Comparing the two by an alternative route suggests that we can improve upon `lizards_mod3`:

```
anova (lizards_mod3, lizards_mod1, test = "Chi")

Analysis of Deviance Table

Model 1: n ~ (sun + height + perch + time) * species
Model 2: n ~ sun * height * perch * time * species
  Resid. Df Resid. Dev Df Deviance  Pr(>Chi)
1        36     94.393
2         0      0.000 36   94.393 3.934e-07 ***
---
Signif. codes:  0 '***' 0.001 '**' 0.01 '*' 0.05 '.' 0.1 ' ' 1
```

And this is where things get tricky: we have 22 interaction terms that we could add in which leaves over a million models that we could try. It is unlikely that there is any *best* model across all the criteria listed above. One way to start may be to say that we can't really explain five-factor or four-factor interactions, so let us investigate what happens if we drop them:

```
lizards_mod4 <- update (lizards_mod1, ~ . - sun:height:perch:time:species -
                          height:perch:time:species -
                          sun:perch:time:species -
```

```
                           sun:height:time:species -
                           sun:height:perch:species -
                           sun:height:perch:time)
anova (lizards_mod4, lizards_mod1, test = "Chi")

Analysis of Deviance Table

Model 1: n ~ sun + height + perch + time + species + sun:height + sun:perch +
    height:perch + sun:time + height:time + perch:time + sun:species +
    height:species + perch:species + time:species + sun:height:perch +
    sun:height:time + sun:perch:time + height:perch:time + sun:height:species +
    sun:perch:species + height:perch:species + sun:time:species +
    height:time:species + perch:time:species
Model 2: n ~ sun * height * perch * time * species
  Resid. Df Resid. Dev Df Deviance Pr(>Chi)
1        11     13.231
2         0      0.000 11   13.231   0.2785

lizards_mod4$aic

[1]  250.4801
```

That looks better by both our formal criteria, `anova ()` and AIC, although we have skipped over the option of just leaving some of them out.

Returning to our bottom up modelling, we could take our interactions a step further by adding in three-factor interactions, but only if they involve `species`.

```
lizards_mod5 <- glm (n ~ (sun * height + perch * time + sun * perch +
                          sun * time + height * perch + height * time) * species,
                 poisson, data = lizards)
anova (lizards_mod5, lizards_mod4, test = "Chi")

Analysis of Deviance Table

Model 1: n ~ (sun * height + perch * time + sun * perch + sun * time +
    height * perch + height * time) * species
Model 2: n ~ sun + height + perch + time + species + sun:height + sun:perch +
    height:perch + sun:time + height:time + perch:time + sun:species +
    height:species + perch:species + time:species + sun:height:perch +
    sun:height:time + sun:perch:time + height:perch:time + sun:height:species +
    sun:perch:species + height:perch:species + sun:time:species +
    height:time:species + perch:time:species
  Resid. Df Resid. Dev Df Deviance Pr(>Chi)
1        18     19.963
2        11     13.231  7   6.7313   0.4574

anova (lizards_mod3, lizards_mod5, test = "Chi")

Analysis of Deviance Table
```

```
Model 1: n ~ (sun + height + perch + time) * species
Model 2: n ~ (sun * height + perch * time + sun * perch + sun * time +
    height * perch + height * time) * species
  Resid. Df Resid. Dev Df Deviance  Pr(>Chi)
1       36     94.393
2       18     19.963 18   74.431 7.929e-09 ***
---
Signif. codes:  0 '***' 0.001 '**' 0.01 '*' 0.05 '.' 0.1 ' ' 1

lizards_mod5$aic

[1] 243.2114
```

There seems to be no justification for the extra interactions in `lizards_mod4`, but these three-factor interactions do seem to be worth having. It is tempting to stop here, but we could see whether all these three-factor interactions are necessary. We could laboriously check dropping each of them term by term (which is probably what we ought to do), but let us take a short cut and use `step ()`, noting the problems with this function described in Section 10.4.5. We will do this by specifying that we want a model *between* `lizards_mod3` and `lizards_mod5`.

```
lizards_mod6 <- step (lizards_mod5, lower = lizards_mod3, upper = lizards_mod5,
                  trace = 0)
anova (lizards_mod6, lizards_mod5, test = "Chi")

Analysis of Deviance Table

Model 1: n ~ sun + height + perch + time + species + sun:height + perch:time +
    sun:time + height:perch + sun:species + height:species +
    perch:species + time:species + sun:height:species
Model 2: n ~ (sun * height + perch * time + sun * perch + sun * time +
    height * perch + height * time) * species
  Resid. Df Resid. Dev Df Deviance Pr(>Chi)
1       29     26.103
2       18     19.963 11   6.1408   0.8638

anova (lizards_mod3, lizards_mod6, test = "Chi")

Analysis of Deviance Table

Model 1: n ~ (sun + height + perch + time) * species
Model 2: n ~ sun + height + perch + time + species + sun:height + perch:time +
    sun:time + height:perch + sun:species + height:species +
    perch:species + time:species + sun:height:species
  Resid. Df Resid. Dev Df Deviance  Pr(>Chi)
1       36     94.393
2       29     26.103  7    68.29 3.272e-12 ***
---
Signif. codes:  0 '***' 0.001 '**' 0.01 '*' 0.05 '.' 0.1 ' ' 1
```

We have avoided all the detailed output using `trace = 0`. All the elements from `lower` must appear in any model, while `upper` describes the set of interactions that we would like to investigate. This model, `lizards_mod6`, appears to be the best we have seen so far using `anova ()`, subject matter expertise and AIC:

```
summary (lizards_mod6)

Call:
glm(formula = n ~ sun + height + perch + time + species + sun:height +
    perch:time + sun:time + height:perch + sun:species + height:species +
    perch:species + time:species + sun:height:species, family = poisson,
    data = lizards)

Deviance Residuals:
    Min       1Q    Median        3Q       Max
-2.2416   -0.4477   -0.1028    0.3693    1.4269

Coefficients:
                                  Estimate Std. Error z value Pr(>|z|)
(Intercept)                        1.06039    0.34470   3.076 0.002096 **
sunSun                             1.28872    0.33200   3.882 0.000104 ***
heightLow                         -2.34553    1.03851  -2.259 0.023911 *
perchNarrow                        0.05118    0.25367   0.202 0.840093
timeMid.day                       -1.21882    0.38436  -3.171 0.001519 **
timeMorning                       -0.09322    0.35844  -0.260 0.794808
speciesopalinus                    1.09914    0.35772   3.073 0.002122 **
sunSun:heightLow                   1.18783    1.06165   1.119 0.263205
perchNarrow:timeMid.day            0.46361    0.25099   1.847 0.064732.
perchNarrow:timeMorning            0.13262    0.27146   0.489 0.625154
sunSun:timeMid.day                 1.78928    0.31769   5.632 1.78e-08 ***
sunSun:timeMorning                 0.17181    0.28014   0.613 0.539670
heightLow:perchNarrow             -0.62891    0.19501  -3.225 0.001259 **
sunSun:speciesopalinus            -0.64637    0.33881  -1.908 0.056425.
heightLow:speciesopalinus          2.33058    1.05740   2.204 0.027520 *
perchNarrow:speciesopalinus       -0.77098    0.20934  -3.683 0.000231 ***
timeMid.day:speciesopalinus        0.88058    0.27353   3.219 0.001285 **
timeMorning:speciesopalinus        0.71650    0.29258   2.449 0.014330 *
sunSun:heightLow:speciesopalinus  -1.38050    1.08838  -1.268 0.204657
---
Signif. codes:  0 '***' 0.001 '**' 0.01 '*' 0.05 '.' 0.1 ' ' 1

(Dispersion parameter for Poisson family taken to be 1)

    Null deviance: 737.555  on 47  degrees of freedom
Residual deviance:  26.103  on 29  degrees of freedom
AIC: 227.35

Number of Fisher Scoring iterations: 5
```

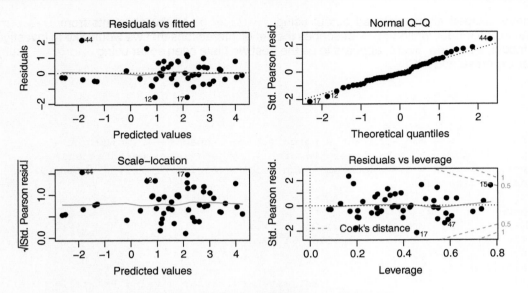

Figure 11.9   Residual plots for `lizards` model 6.

And it does not appear to be overdispersed. Finally, let us have a look at the standard residuals plots in Figure 11.9. They are the usual plots we should be familiar with from linear models (Section 10.5), where we are looking for:

- Residuals vs Fitted: non-linear patterns;
- Normal Q-Q: a pattern of points that deviates from the straight diagonal line;
- Scale-Location: a change in the spread of points, indicating heteroscedasticity;
- Residuals vs Leverage: points outside the dotted lines that might have undue influence.

```
par (mfrow = c (2, 2))
plot (lizards_mod6)
```

```
par (mfrow = c (1, 1))
```

There doesn't appear to be anything too concerning. We have certainly not explored all the possible models but have ended up with one that appears to be satisfactory from a statistical point of view, and also which is reasonably comprehensible from the point of view of somebody trying to interpret the data.

There is one final simplification that might reduce the complexity of the model. The `time` variable has three levels: `Morning`, `Mid.day`, and `Afternoon`. `Afternoon` is the default value in the intercept of our models, and it appears from the output of `lizards_mod6` that there is very little difference between that and the `Morning` (large *p*-values in all cases): something about the middle of the day is different from the rest of the time. So let us combine `Morning` and `Afternoon` for our final model.

```
levels (lizards$time)

[1] "Afternoon" "Mid.day"   "Morning"

levels (lizards$time)[c (1, 3)] <- "Not.mid.day"
lizards_mod5a <- glm (n ~ (sun * height + perch * time + sun * perch +
                           sun * time + height * perch + height * time) * species,
                 poisson, data = lizards)
lizards_mod6a <- step (lizards_mod5, lower = lizards_mod3, upper = lizards_mod5,
                       trace = 0)
summary (lizards_mod6a)

Call:
glm(formula = n ~ sun + height + perch + time + species + sun:height +
    perch:time + sun:perch + sun:time + height:perch + height:time +
    sun:species + height:species + perch:species + time:species +
    sun:height:species + sun:perch:species + sun:time:species +
    height:perch:species + height:time:species, family = poisson,
    data = lizards)

Deviance Residuals:
    Min       1Q    Median       3Q       Max
-2.8617  -0.5586  -0.1196   0.6015    1.8812

Coefficients:
                                      Estimate Std. Error z value Pr(>|z|)
(Intercept)                           1.046307   0.397387   2.633 0.008464 **
sunSun                                1.293375   0.438127   2.952 0.003157 **
heightLow                            -2.425150   1.058721  -2.291 0.021984 *
perchNarrow                           0.115169   0.520185   0.221 0.824780
timeMid.day                          -1.317651   0.769383  -1.713 0.086785 .
speciesopalinus                       1.497113   0.434556   3.445 0.000571 ***
sunSun:heightLow                      1.367695   1.076195   1.271 0.203778
perchNarrow:timeMid.day               0.299511   0.186869   1.603 0.108983
sunSun:perchNarrow                   -0.005545   0.558791  -0.010 0.992082
sunSun:timeMid.day                    2.012323   0.786212   2.560 0.010482 *
heightLow:perchNarrow                -0.314426   0.463790  -0.678 0.497804
heightLow:timeMid.day                -0.530622   0.477581  -1.111 0.266543
sunSun:speciesopalinus               -0.650635   0.482837  -1.348 0.177811
heightLow:speciesopalinus             2.447222   1.082506   2.261 0.023778 *
perchNarrow:speciesopalinus          -0.908819   0.579194  -1.569 0.116623
timeMid.day:speciesopalinus           0.786771   0.808520   0.973 0.330504
sunSun:heightLow:speciesopalinus     -1.440738   1.105941  -1.303 0.192668
sunSun:perchNarrow:speciesopalinus    0.275271   0.615174   0.447 0.654537
sunSun:timeMid.day:speciesopalinus   -0.395379   0.833931  -0.474 0.635418
heightLow:perchNarrow:speciesopalinus -0.353296   0.511734  -0.690 0.489948
heightLow:timeMid.day:speciesopalinus  0.297291   0.520378   0.571 0.567798
---
Signif. codes:  0 '***' 0.001 '**' 0.01 '*' 0.05 '.' 0.1 ' ' 1

(Dispersion parameter for Poisson family taken to be 1)
```

```
    Null deviance: 737.555  on 47  degrees of freedom
Residual deviance: 51.699  on 27  degrees of freedom
AIC: 256.95

Number of Fisher Scoring iterations: 5
```

We cannot compare `lizards_mod6` and `lizards_mod6a` formally as they do not share the same dataset (we have altered the `time` variable). However, this latest model appears to be overdispersed with many large p-values for the model terms. Also, the residuals plots (not shown) do not look as satisfactory as those for `lizards_mod6` so we will stick with that model.

We will have a final look at this dataset in Section 11.4.7, where we will treat the response variable as a proportion of species.

11.3.3 Spine plot

We will examine some interesting ways of plotting tables. Let us have a look at a **spine plot**: sometimes called a mosaic plot and introduced in Section 5.5.2. Suppose we have three treatments (placebo, drug A, and drug B) and the response variable is a five-level categorical variable (much worse, worse, no change, better, and much better). The data, one row per patient, consist of their current condition, and the treatment they were given:

```
spino <- read.table ("spino.txt", header = T, colClasses = rep ("factor", 2))
head (spino)

    condition treatment
1   no.change    placebo
2 much.better     drug.B
3   no.change     drug.B
4   no.change     drug.A
5   no.change     drug.B
6       worse     drug.A
```

The plot will be easier to interpret if we specify the order of the factor levels (they will be in alphabetic order by default):

```
spino$condition <- factor(spino$condition, c ("much.worse", "worse", "no.change",
                                               "better", "much.better"))
spino$treatment <- factor(spino$treatment, c ("placebo", "drug.A", "drug.B"))
```

Now, we can use `spineplot ()` like this to give Figure 11.10:

```
spineplot (condition ~ treatment, data = spino, col = hue_pal ()(5))
```

There are two things to notice about the spine plot, which is a bit like a more sophisticated bar plot. The partitions within the bars are the proportions of a given treatment in each of the five conditions,

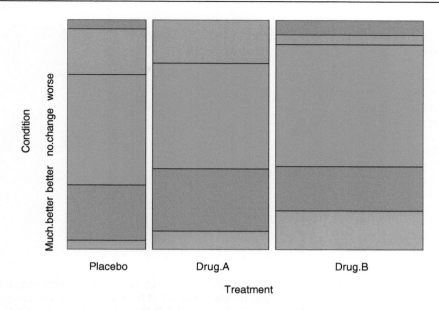

Figure 11.10   Spine plot for `spino`.

i.e. the conditional relative frequencies of *y*, `condition`, in every *x*, `treatment`, group (these are labelled on the left axis and quantified on the right axis). Where a category is empty (as in the `much worse level` with `drug.A`), the labels on the left can be confusing. The widths of the bars reflect the total sample sizes (there were more patients getting either drug than the placebo). It looks like `drug.B` is more effective than `placebo`, but the efficacy of `drug.A` is less clear. Here are the counts:

```
table (spino$condition, spino$treatment)

               placebo drug.A drug.B
  much.worse         1      0      3
  worse              5      7      2
  no.change         12     17     25
  better             6     10      9
  much.better        1      3      8
```

With so few patients showing changes in condition, we are going to struggle to find significant effects in this dataset. To do the stats, we need to create a dataframe of these counts with matching columns, one to show the level of treatment and one to show the level of condition. The tool for this is `as.data.frame.table ()`:

```
spino_df <- as.data.frame.table (table (spino$condition, spino$treatment))
colnames (spino_df) <- c ("condition", "treatment", "count")
spino_df
```

```
      condition treatment count
1   much.worse   placebo     1
2        worse   placebo     5
3    no.change   placebo    12
4       better   placebo     6
5  much.better   placebo     1
6   much.worse    drug.A     0
7        worse    drug.A     7
8    no.change    drug.A    17
9       better    drug.A    10
10 much.better    drug.A     3
11  much.worse    drug.B     3
12       worse    drug.B     2
13   no.change    drug.B    25
14      better    drug.B     9
15 much.better    drug.B     8
```

There is a line for each of the $5 \times 3 = 15$ combinations of condition and treatment. It is tempting to use aggregate () to do this, where the function we want to apply would be length () (for instance, to count how many patients receiving the placebo got much worse; we can see from the previous R output that the answer is 3 in this case).

```
spino_agg <- aggregate (spino, spino, length)
nrow (spino_agg)

[1] 14
```

As we can see, the problem is that aggregate () leaves out rows from the dataframe when there were zero cases (i.e. no patients receiving drug A got much worse), so there are only 14 rows in the dataframe, not the 15 we want for doing the statistics.

Despite the sparse data, let us attempt some model building by looking at models with and without interactions, and comparing them:

```
spino_mod1 <- glm (count ~ condition * treatment, poisson, data = spino_df)
spino_mod2 <- glm (count ~ condition + treatment, poisson, data = spino_df)
anova(spino_mod1, spino_mod2, test = "Chi")

Analysis of Deviance Table

Model 1: count ~ condition * treatment
Model 2: count ~ condition + treatment
  Resid. Df Resid. Dev Df Deviance Pr(>Chi)
1         0       0.00
2         8      12.85 -8   -12.85   0.1171
```

As we suspected, given the low replication, there is not enough data to spot an interaction between treatment and condition.

11.4 Proportion data and GLMs

An important class of problems involves count data on proportions such as:

- studies on death rates;
- infection rates of diseases;
- answers to questionnaires;
- proportion responding to clinical treatment;
- proportion admitting to particular voting intentions;
- sex ratios;
- data on proportional response to an experimental treatment.

What all these have in common is that we know how many of the experimental objects are in one category (dead, insolvent, male, or infected), and we also know how many are in another (alive, solvent, female, or uninfected). This contrasts with Poisson count data, where we, usually, knew how many times an event occurred, but not how many times it did not occur. We model processes involving proportional response variables in *R* by specifying a generalised linear model with `family = binomial`. The only complication is that whereas with Poisson errors we could simply specify `family = poisson`, with binomial errors, we must give the number of failures as well as the numbers of successes in a two-vector response variable. To do this, we bind together two vectors using `cbind ()` into a single object, *y*, comprising the numbers of successes and the number of failures. The binomial denominator, *n*, is the total sample size, and, for instance

```
number_of_failures <- n - number_of_successes
y <- cbind (number_of_successes, number_of_failures)
```

The old fashioned way of modelling this sort of data was to use a linear model and the mortality proportion as the response variable. There are four problems with this:

- the errors are not normally distributed;
- the variance is not constant;
- the response is bounded (by 1 above and by 0 below);
- by calculating the percentage, we lose information on the size of the sample, *n*, from which the proportion was estimated.

There are some kinds of proportion data, such as percentage cover, which are best analysed using conventional linear models (assuming Normal errors and constant variance) following arcsine transformation. The response variable, *y*, measured in radians, is

$$\sin^{-1}(0.01 \times p)$$

where *p* is percentage cover.

If, however, the response variable takes the form of a percentage change in some continuous measurement (such as the percentage change in weight on receiving a particular diet), then rather than arcsine-transforming the data, it is usually better treated by either

- using final weight as the response variable and initial weight as a covariate; or

- by specifying the response variable as a relative growth rate, measured as log (final weight/initial weight),

both of which can be analysed as linear models with Normal errors without further transformation.

11.4.1 Theoretical background

The traditional transformations of proportion data were arcsine (see Section 2.1.2) and probit ($\Phi^{-1}(p)$, where Φ is the CDF for the standard Normal distribution). The arcsine transformation took care of the error distribution, while the probit transformation was used to linearize the relationship between percentage mortality and log dose in a bioassay. There is nothing wrong with these transformations, and they are available within R, but a simpler approach is often preferable and is likely to produce a model that is easier to interpret. The major difficulty with modelling proportion data is that the responses are strictly bounded. There is no way that the percentage dying can be greater than 100% or less than 0%. But if we use simple techniques such as regression or analysis of covariance, then the fitted model could quite easily predict negative values or values greater than 100%, especially if the variance was high, and many of the data were close to 0% or to 100%.

The logistic curve (see Figure 2.7 for a selection) is commonly used to describe data on proportions, because unlike the straight-line model, it asymptotes at 0 and 1 so that negative proportions and responses of more than 100% cannot be predicted. Throughout this discussion, we shall use p to describe the proportion of individuals observed to respond in a given way. Because much of their jargon was derived from the theory of gambling, statisticians call these **successes**, although to a demographer measuring death rates, this may seem somewhat macabre. The proportion of individuals that respond in other ways (the statistician's failures) is therefore $1 - p$, and we shall call this proportion q. The third variable is the size of the sample, n, from which p was estimated (this is the binomial denominator, and the statistician's number of attempts).

An important point about the binomial distribution is that the variance is not constant. In fact, the variance of a binomial distribution with mean np is

$$npq,$$

so that the variance changes with the mean as in Figure 11.11.

The variance is low when p is very high or very low, and the variance is greatest when $p = q = 0.5$. As p gets smaller, so the binomial distribution gets closer and closer to the Poisson distribution. We can see why this is so by considering the formula for the variance of the Binomial (above). Remember that for the Poisson, the variance is equal to the mean, np. Now, as p gets smaller, so q gets closer and closer to 1, so the variance of the Binomial converges to the mean:

$$npq \to np \qquad (q \to 1).$$

Using a GLM to model a proportional response is sometimes known as **logistic regression**. For the sake of simplicity, if we assume a simple linear predictor $a + bx$, then the **logistic function** for p as a function of x is given by

$$p = \frac{e^{a+bx}}{1 + e^{a+bx}},$$

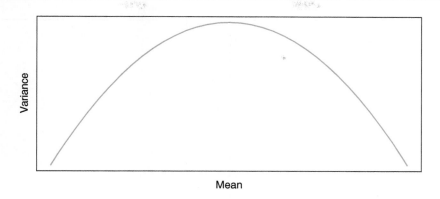

Figure 11.11 Mean vs variance for a Binomial distribution.

and there are no prizes for realizing that the model is not linear. But if $x = -\infty$, then $p = 0$, and if $x = +\infty$, then $p = 1$, so the model is strictly bounded. If $x = 0$, then $p = e^a/(1 + e^a)$. The trick of linearising the logistic model actually involves a very simple transformation. Bookmakers specify probabilities by quoting the odds, for instance against a particular horse winning a race (they might give odds of 2 to 1 on a reasonably good horse or 25 to 1 on an outsider). This is a rather different way of presenting information on probabilities than scientists are used to dealing with. Thus, where the scientist might state a proportion as 0.333 (one chance of winning in three), the bookmaker would give odds of 2 to 1 (based on the counts of outcomes: one success against two failures). In symbols, this is the difference between the scientist stating the probability p, and the bookmaker stating the odds p/q. Now, if we take the odds p/q and substitute this into the formula for the logistic, we get

$$\frac{p}{q} = \frac{e^{a+bx}}{1 + e^{a+bx}}\left(1 - \frac{e^{a+bx}}{1 + e^{a+bx}}\right)^{-1} = e^{a+bx}$$

Taking natural logs and recalling that $\ln(e^x) = x$ will simplify matters even further, so that

$$\ln(p/q) = a + bx.$$

This gives a linear predictor, $a + bx$, not for p but for the **logit** transformation of p, namely $ln(p/q)$. In the jargon of GLMs, the logit is the link function relating the linear predictor to the value of p. Figure 11.12 p as a function of x (left panel) and $logit(p)$ as a function of x (right panel) for the logistic model with $a = 1$ and $b = 0.1$.

```
x <- seq (-60, 60, 0.1)
a <- 1
b <- 0.1
p <- exp (a + b * x) / (1 + exp (a + b * x))
plot (x, p, xlab = "x", ylab = "p", type = "l", col = hue_pal () (2) [1])
plot (x, log (p / (1 - p)), xlab = "x", ylab = "logit = log (p / q)",
      type = "l", col = hue_pal () (2) [2])
```

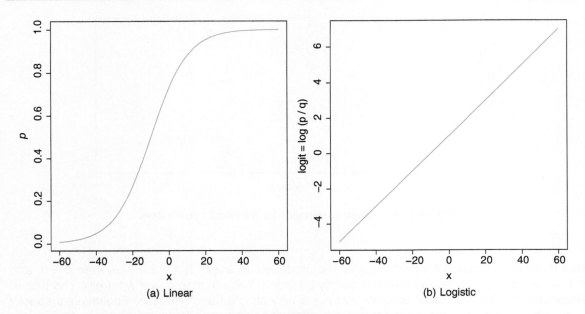

Figure 11.12 Relationships between *x* and functions of *p*.

We might ask at this stage: 'why not simply do a linear regression of $ln(p/q)$ against the explanatory *x*-variable?'. GLM with binomial errors has three great advantages here:

1. it allows for the non-constant binomial variance;

2. it deals with the fact that logits for *p*s near 0 or 1 are infinite;

3. it allows for differences between the sample sizes by weighted regression.

That the errors are binomially distributed is an assumption, not a fact. When we have overdispersion, this assumption is wrong, and we need to deal with it: we describe how to do this in our final theoretical excursion.

All the different statistical procedures that we have met in earlier chapters can also be used with data on proportions. Factorial analysis of variance, multiple regression, and a variety of models in which different regression lines are fitted in each of several levels of one or more factors, can be carried out. The only difference is that we assess the significance of terms compared with the χ^2 distribution – using the increase in scaled deviance that results from removal of the term from the current model.

The important point to bear in mind is that hypothesis testing with Binomial errors is less clear-cut than with Normal errors. While the chi-squared approximation for changes in scaled deviance is reasonable for large samples (i.e. larger than about 30), it is poorer with small samples. Most worrying is the fact that the degree to which the approximation is satisfactory is itself unknown. This means that considerable care must be exercised in the interpretation of tests of hypotheses on parameters, especially when the parameters are marginally significant or when they explain a very small fraction of the total deviance. With Binomial or Poisson errors, we cannot hope to provide exact *p*-values for our tests using the `anova ()` function in *R*. When we have obtained the minimal adequate model, the residual scaled deviance should be roughly equal to the residual degrees of freedom.

Overdispersion occurs when the residual deviance is considerably larger than the residual degrees of freedom. There are two possibilities: either the model is mis-specified, or the probability of success, p, is not constant within a given treatment level. The effect of randomly varying p is to increase the binomial variance from npq to $npq + n(n-1)\sigma^2$, leading to a large residual deviance. This occurs even for models that would fit well if the random variation were correctly specified.

One simple solution is to assume that the variance is not npq but $npq\phi$, where ϕ is an unknown scale parameter, greater than 1. We obtain an estimate of the scale parameter from the data and then compare that to the residual deviance divided by the degrees of freedom. To accomplish this, we use `family = quasi-Binomial` rather than `family = binomial` when there is overdispersion.

To summarise, the most important points to emphasise in modelling with binomial errors are as follows:

- create a two-column object for the response, using `cbind` to join together the two vectors containing the counts of success and failure;

- fit a model or models, perhaps beginning with the maximal model and removing interaction terms and main effects as necessary;

- check for overdispersion (residual deviance greater than the residual degrees of freedom) and correct for it by using `family = quasi-Binomial` rather than `family = binomial` if necessary;

- remember that we do not obtain exact p-values with binomial errors: the χ^2 approximations are sound for large samples, but small samples may present a problem;

- the fitted values are two sets of counts, like the response variable;

- the linear predictor is in logits (the log of the odds $= ln(p/q)$);

- we can back-transform from logits (z) to proportions (p) by $p = 1/[1 + e^{-z}]$

- use `plot ()` to examine residuals.

11.4.2 Logistic regression with binomial errors

This example concerns sex ratios in insects (the proportion of all individuals that are males). In the species in question, it has been observed that the sex ratio is highly variable, and an experiment was set up to see whether population density was involved in determining the fraction of males.

```
sexratio <- read.table ("sexratio.txt", header = T)
head (sexratio)

  density females males
1       1       1     0
2       4       3     1
3      10       7     3
4      22      18     4
5      55      22    33
6     121      41    80
```

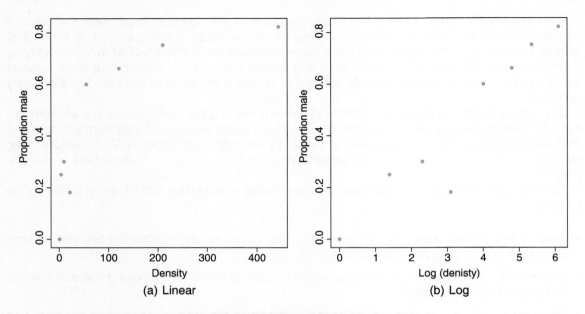

Figure 11.13   Proportions of males in `sexratio`.

From Figure 11.13 it certainly looks as if there are proportionally more males at high density, but we should plot the data as proportions to see this more clearly:

```
p <- sexratio$males / (sexratio$males + sexratio$females)
plot (sexratio$density, p, ylab = "proportion male", xlab = "density",
      col = hue_pal () (2) [1])
plot (log (sexratio$density), p, ylab = "proportion male",
      xlab = "log (denisty)", col = hue_pal () (2) [2])
```

Evidently, a logarithmic transformation of the explanatory variable is likely to improve the model fit. We shall see in a moment.

The question is whether increasing population density leads to a significant increase in the proportion of males in the population – or, more briefly, whether the sex ratio is density-dependent. It certainly looks from the plot as if it is.

The response variable is a matched pair of counts that we wish to analyse as proportion data using a GLM with binomial errors. First, we use `cbind` to bind together the vectors of male and female counts into a single object that will be the response in our analysis. This means that *y* will be interpreted in the model as the proportion of all individuals that were male. We then specify the model:

```
y <- cbind (sexratio$males, sexratio$females)
sex_mod1 <- glm (y ~ density, binomial, data = sexratio)
summary (sex_mod1)

Call:
glm(formula = y ~ density, family = binomial, data = sexratio)
```

```
Deviance Residuals:
    Min       1Q    Median      3Q      Max
-3.4619   -1.2760  -0.9911   0.5742   1.8795

Coefficients:
             Estimate Std. Error z value Pr(>|z|)
(Intercept) 0.0807368  0.1550376   0.521    0.603
density     0.0035101  0.0005116   6.862 6.81e-12 ***
---
Signif. codes:  0 '***' 0.001 '**' 0.01 '*' 0.05 '.' 0.1 ' ' 1

(Dispersion parameter for Binomial family taken to be 1)

    Null deviance: 71.159  on 7  degrees of freedom
Residual deviance: 22.091  on 6  degrees of freedom
AIC: 54.618

Number of Fisher Scoring iterations: 4
```

This says that the object called `sex_mod1` is a generalised linear model in which *y* (the sex ratio) is modelled as a function of a single continuous explanatory variable (called *density*), using an error distribution from the Binomial family.

The model table looks just as it would for a straightforward regression. The first parameter in the coefficients table is the intercept, and the second is the slope of the graph of sex ratio against population density. The *p*-value corresponding to the slope is effectively 0 and as the slope is greater than 0, there appears to be proportionately more males at higher population density, but there is substantial overdispersion (residual deviance = 22.09 is much greater than the degrees of freedom, 6). We can see if log transformation of the explanatory variable improves this:

```
sex_mod2 <- glm (y ~ log (density), binomial, data = sexratio)
summary (sex_mod2)

Call:
glm(formula = y ~ log(density), family = binomial, data = sexratio)

Deviance Residuals:
    Min       1Q    Median      3Q      Max
-1.9697   -0.3411   0.1499   0.4019   1.0372

Coefficients:
             Estimate Std. Error z value Pr(>|z|)
(Intercept)  -2.65927    0.48758  -5.454 4.92e-08 ***
log(density)  0.69410    0.09056   7.665 1.80e-14 ***
---
Signif. codes:  0 '***' 0.001 '**' 0.01 '*' 0.05 '.' 0.1 ' ' 1

(Dispersion parameter for Binomial family taken to be 1)
```

```
    Null deviance: 71.1593  on 7  degrees of freedom
Residual deviance:  5.6739  on 6  degrees of freedom
AIC: 38.201

Number of Fisher Scoring iterations: 4
```

This is a big improvement, so we shall adopt it. In the model with `log (density)`, there is no evidence of overdispersion (residual deviance = 5.67 on 6 degrees of freedom), whereas the lack of fit introduced by the curvature in our first model caused substantial overdispersion. Note also the reduction in AIC.

Model checking involves the use of `plot (sex_mod2)` (not shown). As we will see, there is no pattern in the residuals against the fitted values, and the QQ plot is reasonably linear. Point no. 4 is highly influential (it has a large Cook's distance), but the model is still an improvement with this point omitted. One shouldn't draw too strong a conclusion from residual plots with such a small number of points, but there is nothing too worrying there.

We conclude that the proportion of animals that are males increases significantly with increasing density, and that the logistic model is linearised by logarithmic transformation of the explanatory variable (population density). We finish by drawing the fitted mean line through the scatter plot to produce Figure 11.14. Note the use of `type = "response"` to back-transform from the logit scale to the S-shaped proportion scale.

```
xv <- seq (0, 6, 0.01)
ev <- data.frame (density = exp (xv))
yv <- predict (sex_mod2, newdata = ev,
              type = "response")
plot (log (sexratio$density), p, ylab = "Proportion male",
     xlab = "log (density)", col = hue_pal () (2) [2])
lines (xv, yv, col = hue_pal () (2) [2])
```

11.4.3 Predicting *x* from *y*

The next dataset consist of numbers dead and initial batch size for five doses of pesticide application, and we wish to know what dose kills 50% of the individuals (or 90% or 95%, as required). The

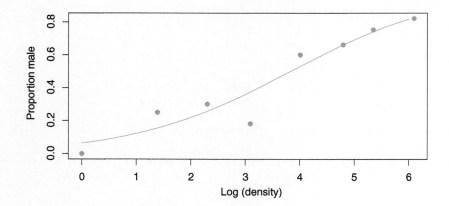

Figure 11.14 Fitted line in `sexratio` logistic model.

tricky statistical issue is that one is using a value of *y* (50% dead), the outcome, to predict a value of *x* (the relevant dose), the explanatory variable, and to work out a standard error on the x-axis.

```
bioassay <- read.table ("bioassay.txt", header = T)
head (bioassay)

  dose dead batch
1    1    2   100
2    3   10    90
3   10   40    98
4   30   96   100
5  100   98   100
```

The logistic regression is carried out in the usual way after we have created a response of the dead and not-dead:

```
y <- cbind (bioassay$dead, bioassay$batch - bioassay$dead)
bioassay_mod <- glm (y ~ log(bioassay$dose), binomial)
```

Then the function `dose.p ()` from the MASS library is run with the model object, specifying the proportions killed for which we want the predicted log (doses) (0.5 is the default):

```
dose.p (bioassay_mod, p = c (0.5,0.9,0.95))

             Dose         SE
p = 0.50: 2.306981 0.07772065
p = 0.90: 3.425506 0.12362080
p = 0.95: 3.805885 0.15150043
```

As our model took logs of the doses we will need to reverse that to give the predicted dose. So for 50%, we need to calculate $e^{2.307} = 10.04$.

11.4.4 Proportion data with categorical explanatory variables

This next example concerns the germination of seeds of two genotypes of the parasitic plant Orobanche and two extracts from host plants (bean and cucumber) that were used to stimulate germination. It is a two-way factorial analysis of deviance:

```
germination <- read.table ("germination.txt", header = T,
                     colClasses = c (rep ("numeric", 2),
                                     rep ("factor", 2)))
head (germination)

  count sample Orobanche   extract
1    10     39       a75      bean
2    23     62       a75      bean
3    23     81       a75      bean
4    26     51       a75      bean
5    17     39       a75      bean
6     5      6       a75  cucumber
```

The count is the number of seeds that germinated out of a batch of size = sample. So the number that did not germinate is sample − count, and we construct the response vector like this:

```
y <- cbind (germination$count, germination$sample - germination$count)
```

Each of the categorical explanatory variables has two levels:

```
levels (germination$Orobanche)

[1] "a73" "a75"

levels (germination$extract)

[1] "bean"      "cucumber"
```

We want to test the hypothesis that there is no interaction between Orobanche genotype (a73 or a75) and plant extract (bean or cucumber) on the germination rate of the seeds. This requires a factorial analysis using the asterisk * operator like this:

```
germ_mod1 <- glm (y ~ Orobanche * extract, binomial, data = germination)
summary (germ_mod1)

Call:
glm(formula = y ~ Orobanche * extract, family = binomial, data = germination)

Deviance Residuals:
    Min        1Q     Median        3Q        Max
-2.01617  -1.24398   0.05995   0.84695   2.12123

Coefficients:
                             Estimate Std. Error z value Pr(>|z|)
(Intercept)                   -0.4122     0.1842  -2.238   0.0252 *
Orobanchea75                  -0.1459     0.2232  -0.654   0.5132
extractcucumber                0.5401     0.2498   2.162   0.0306 *
Orobanchea75:extractcucumber   0.7781     0.3064   2.539   0.0111 *
---
Signif. codes:  0 '***' 0.001 '**' 0.01 '*' 0.05 '.' 0.1 ' ' 1

(Dispersion parameter for Binomial family taken to be 1)

    Null deviance: 98.719  on 20  degrees of freedom
Residual deviance: 33.278  on 17  degrees of freedom
AIC: 117.87

Number of Fisher Scoring iterations: 4
```

At first glance, it looks as if there is a highly significant interaction term, but we need to check that the model is sound. The first thing is to check for is overdispersion. The residual deviance divided by the residual degrees of freedom is 1.96, so the model is quite badly overdispersed: the overdispersion factor is almost 2. The simplest way to take this into account is to use what is called an 'empirical scale parameter' to reflect the fact that the errors are not binomial as we assumed, but were larger than this (i.e. overdispersed) by a factor of almost 2. We refit the model using quasi-Binomial errors to account for the overdispersion, checking whether the interaction term is still important:

```
germ_mod2 <- glm (y ~ Orobanche * extract, quasi-Binomial, data = germination)
germ_mod3 <- update (germ_mod2, ~ . - Orobanche:extract)
anova (germ_mod3, germ_mod2, test = "F")

Analysis of Deviance Table

Model 1: y ~ Orobanche + extract
Model 2: y ~ Orobanche * extract
  Resid. Df Resid. Dev Df Deviance      F  Pr(>F)
1        18     39.686
2        17     33.278  1   6.4081 3.4418 0.08099.
---
Signif. codes:  0 '***' 0.001 '**' 0.01 '*' 0.05 '.' 0.1 ' ' 1
```

Remember that we use an F-test instead of a χ^2 test to compare the original and simplified models because now we have estimated two parameters from the model (the mean plus the empirical scale parameter). Now, we see that adding the interaction does not appear to improve the model. There is no compelling evidence that different genotypes of Orobanche respond differently to the two plant extracts.

The next step is to see if any further model simplification is possible by using the anova () function on just the latest model:

```
anova (germ_mod3, test = "F")

Analysis of Deviance Table

Model: Quasi-Binomial, link: logit

Response: y

Terms added sequentially (first to last)


          Df Deviance Resid. Df Resid. Dev       F    Pr(>F)
NULL                        20     98.719
Orobanche  1    2.544        19     96.175  1.1954    0.2887
extract    1   56.489        18     39.686 26.5412 6.692e-05 ***
---
Signif. codes:  0 '***' 0.001 '**' 0.01 '*' 0.05 '.' 0.1 ' ' 1
```

The *p*-value for extract is very small, but it is not obvious that we need to keep Orobanche genotype in the model. We try removing it:

```
germ_mod4 <- update (germ_mod3, ~ . - Orobanche)
anova (germ_mod4, germ_mod3, test = "F")

Analysis of Deviance Table

Model 1: y ~ extract
Model 2: y ~ Orobanche + extract
  Resid. Df Resid. Dev Df Deviance       F Pr(>F)
1        19     42.751
2        18     39.686  1    3.065 1.4401 0.2457
```

There is no justification for retaining Orobanche in the model. So the minimal adequate model contains just two parameters:

```
coef (germ_mod4)

    (Intercept) extractcucumber
-0.5121761          1.0574031
```

However, what exactly do these two numbers mean? Remember that the coefficients are from the linear predictor. They are on the transformed scale, so because we are using quasi-binomial errors, they are in logits: $(\ln(p/(1-p)))$. To turn them into the germination rates for the two plant extracts, we require a little calculation. To go from a *logit*(x) to a proportion *p*, we need to calculate:

$$p = \frac{1}{1 + e^{-x}}$$

So our first *x* value is -0.512, and we calculate

```
1 / ( 1 + exp(0.512))

[1] 0.3747248
```

This says that the mean germination rate of the seeds with the first plant extract (bean) was 37%. What about the parameter for extract (1.057)? Remember that with categorical explanatory variables, the parameter values are differences between means. So to get the second germination rate, we add 1.057 to the intercept before back-transforming:

```
1 / (1 + exp(0.5122-1.0574))

[1] 0.6330212
```

This says that the germination rate was nearly twice as great (63%) with the second plant extract (cucumber). Obviously, we want to generalise this process and also to speed up the calculations of the estimated mean proportions. We can use `predict` to help here, because `type="response"` makes predictions on the back-transformed scale automatically:

```
tapply (predict (germ_mod4, type="response"), germination$extract, mean)

    bean  cucumber
0.3746835 0.6330275
```

It is interesting to compare these figures with the averages of the raw proportions. First, we need to calculate the proportion germinating, p, in each sample:

```
p <- germination$count / germination$sample
```

Then we can find the average germination rates for each extract:

```
tapply (p, germination$extract, mean)

    bean  cucumber
0.3487189 0.6031824
```

We see that this gives different answers. Not too different in this case, but different nonetheless. The correct way to average proportion data is to add up the total counts for the different levels of abstract, and only then to turn them into proportions:

```
tapply (germination$count, germination$extract, sum)

    bean cucumber
148      276
```

This means that 148 seeds germinated with bean extract and 276 with cucumber. But how many seeds were involved in each case?

```
tapply (germination$sample, germination$extract, sum)

    bean cucumber
395      436
```

This means that 395 seeds were treated with bean extract and 436 seeds were treated with cucumber. So the answers we want are 148/395 and 276/436 (i.e. the correct mean proportions). We can automate the calculation like this:

```
as.vector (tapply (germination$count, germination$extract, sum)) /
as.vector (tapply (germination$sample, germination$extract, sum))

[1] 0.3746835 0.6330275
```

These are the correct mean proportions that were produced by the GLM. The moral here is that we calculate the average of proportions by using total counts and total samples and not by averaging the raw proportions.

Just to clarify, here is another example showing what not to do. We have four proportions:

$$0.2, 0.17, 0.2, 0.53.$$

So surely to find the overall proportion, we just add them up and divide by 4. This gives $1.1/4 = 0.275$. Wrong! And not by just a little bit. We need to look at the counts on which the proportions were based. These turn out to be

$$1/5, 1/6, 2/10, 53/100.$$

The correct way to average proportions is to add up the total count of successes ($1 + 1 + 2 + 53 = 57$) and divide this by the total number of samples ($5 + 6 + 10 + 100 = 121$). The correct mean proportion is $57/121 = 0.4711$. This is nearly double our incorrect answer (0.275).

11.4.5   Binomial GLM with ordered categorical covariates

We now look at the dataset `esoph` where the outcome is whether subjects have cancer, based on covariates which are categorical but ordered. The dataset comes with *R*:

```
head (esoph)

   agegp      alcgp       tobgp ncases ncontrols
1  25-34 0-39g/day  0-9g/day        0        40
2  25-34 0-39g/day     10-19        0        10
3  25-34 0-39g/day     20-29        0         6
4  25-34 0-39g/day       30+        0         5
5  25-34     40-79  0-9g/day        0        27
6  25-34     40-79     10-19        0         7
```

More details can be found at `help (esoph)`, but in summary the covariates are age group (`agegp`, with six ordered levels each spanning 10 years), alcohol consumption (`alcgp`, with four ordered levels), and tobacco consumption (`tobgp`, with four ordered levels). There are too few cases to fit a full factorial of `agegp * tobgpacco * alcgp`, so we start with a maximal model that has a main effect for age and an interaction between tobacco and alcohol (which doesn't seem a stupid area to explore):

```
esoph_mod1 <- glm (cbind (ncases, ncontrols) ~ agegp + alcgp * tobgp, binomial,
                   data = esoph)
summary (esoph_mod1)

Call:
glm(formula = cbind(ncases, ncontrols) ~ agegp + alcgp * tobgp,
    family = binomial, data = esoph)

Deviance Residuals:
    Min       1Q   Median       3Q      Max
-1.9069  -0.6470  -0.2356   0.5557   2.4011
```

```
Coefficients:
                Estimate Std. Error z value Pr(>|z|)
(Intercept)     -1.16933    0.20767  -5.631 1.79e-08 ***
agegp.L          3.97135    0.69286   5.732 9.94e-09 ***
agegp.Q         -1.58715    0.61943  -2.562   0.0104 *
agegp.C          0.09866    0.47331   0.208   0.8349
agegp^4          0.09950    0.32816   0.303   0.7617
agegp^5         -0.27067    0.21516  -1.258   0.2084
alcgp.L          2.42627    0.28829   8.416  < 2e-16 ***
alcgp.Q          0.12999    0.25418   0.511   0.6091
alcgp.C          0.36600    0.22252   1.645   0.1000
tobgp.L          1.10809    0.27042   4.098 4.17e-05 ***
tobgp.Q          0.26586    0.25419   1.046   0.2956
tobgp.C          0.29394    0.24026   1.223   0.2212
alcgp.L:tobgp.L -0.42942    0.58589  -0.733   0.4636
alcgp.Q:tobgp.L  0.04169    0.53027   0.079   0.9373
alcgp.C:tobgp.L -0.25088    0.47211  -0.531   0.5951
alcgp.L:tobgp.Q  0.33676    0.56764   0.593   0.5530
alcgp.Q:tobgp.Q -0.62384    0.50922  -1.225   0.2205
alcgp.C:tobgp.Q  0.02303    0.44197   0.052   0.9584
alcgp.L:tobgp.C -0.15742    0.54313  -0.290   0.7719
alcgp.Q:tobgp.C -0.06700    0.48120  -0.139   0.8893
alcgp.C:tobgp.C -0.17340    0.40908  -0.424   0.6717
---
Signif. codes:  0 '***' 0.001 '**' 0.01 '*' 0.05 '.' 0.1 ' ' 1

(Dispersion parameter for Binomial family taken to be 1)

    Null deviance: 367.953  on 87  degrees of freedom
Residual deviance:  76.886  on 67  degrees of freedom
AIC: 233.94

Number of Fisher Scoring iterations: 6
```

The residual deviance is close to the number of degrees of freedom, which is promising. We have not seen before how ordered factor levels (see later in this Section for how to order/unorder levels) are displayed in the `summary.glm` table:

- L means 'linear', testing whether there is evidence for a straight-line relationship with the response variable (look at the sign to see if it is increasing or decreasing);

- Q means 'quadratic', testing whether there is evidence for curvature in the response (look at the sign to see if the curvature is U-shaped or upside-down U-shaped);

- C means 'cubic', testing whether there is evidence for more than one point of inflection in the relationship;

- numbers like 4, 5, etc., test for higher-order polynomial effects, like local maxima and local minima in the relationship.

We shall not attempt to interpret the output until we have finished with model simplification. There is no indication of an interaction between smoking and drinking, so we remove this and compare with the first model:

```
esoph_mod2 <- glm (cbind (ncases, ncontrols) ~ agegp + alcgp + tobgp, binomial,
                data = esoph)
anova (esoph_mod1, esoph_mod2, test = "Chisq")

Analysis of Deviance Table

Model 1: cbind(ncases, ncontrols) ~ agegp + alcgp * tobgp
Model 2: cbind(ncases, ncontrols) ~ agegp + alcgp + tobgp
  Resid. Df Resid. Dev Df Deviance Pr(>Chi)
1        67     76.886
2        76     82.337 -9  -5.4506   0.7934
```

Where our outcome variable is Binomial or Poisson, we need to specify a χ^2 test; otherwise, we can stick to the default F-test. The null hypothesis is that we could omit the deleted variables from the model with minimal consequences, and there is no evidence against that, so we will retain the new model (which also has a lower AIC):

```
summary (esoph_mod2)

Call:
glm(formula = cbind(ncases, ncontrols) ~ agegp + alcgp + tobgp,
    family = binomial, data = esoph)

Deviance Residuals:
    Min       1Q   Median       3Q      Max
-1.9507  -0.7376  -0.2438   0.6130   2.4127

Coefficients:
            Estimate Std. Error z value Pr(>|z|)
(Intercept) -1.19039    0.20737  -5.740 9.44e-09 ***
agegp.L      3.99663    0.69389   5.760 8.42e-09 ***
agegp.Q     -1.65741    0.62115  -2.668  0.00762 **
agegp.C      0.11094    0.46815   0.237  0.81267
agegp^4      0.07892    0.32463   0.243  0.80792
agegp^5     -0.26219    0.21337  -1.229  0.21915
alcgp.L      2.53899    0.26385   9.623  < 2e-16 ***
alcgp.Q      0.09376    0.22419   0.418  0.67578
alcgp.C      0.43930    0.18347   2.394  0.01665 *
tobgp.L      1.11749    0.24014   4.653 3.26e-06 ***
tobgp.Q      0.34516    0.22414   1.540  0.12358
tobgp.C      0.31692    0.21091   1.503  0.13294
---
Signif. codes:  0 '***' 0.001 '**' 0.01 '*' 0.05 '.' 0.1 ' ' 1

(Dispersion parameter for Binomial family taken to be 1)
```

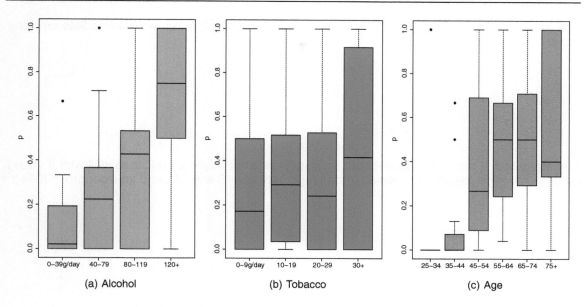

Figure 11.15 Prevalence of cancer by covariate in `esoph`.

```
    Null deviance: 367.953   on 87   degrees of freedom
Residual deviance:  82.337   on 76   degrees of freedom
AIC: 221.39

Number of Fisher Scoring iterations: 6
```

There is strong evidence for linear effects of all three covariates, with a quadratic (decelerating) effect of age on cancer risk. We shall now consider factor-level reduction, particularly for higher-order elements. Let us look at the outcome data as proportions of the number of cases (p) and plot the covariates, as in Figure 11.15, each time displaying the results as the other covariates vary:

```
p <- esoph$ncases / (esoph$ncases + esoph$ncontrols)
plot (p ~ alcgp, col = hue_pal ()(3)[1], data = esoph, xlab = "",
    cex.lab = 1.5, cex.axis = 1.5)
plot (p ~ tobgp, col = hue_pal ()(3)[2], data = esoph, xlab = "",
    cex.lab = 1.5, cex.axis = 1.5)
plot (p ~ agegp, col = hue_pal ()(3)[3], data = esoph, xlab = "",
    cex.lab = 1.5, cex.axis = 1.5)
```

The plots suggest some model simplifications: let us reduce each covariate to just three groups. For the alcohol response, we could combine the middle two groups:

```
esoph$alcgp2 <- esoph$alcgp
levels (esoph$alcgp2)[2:3] <- "40-119"
levels (esoph$alcgp2)

[1] "0-39g/day" "40-119"    "120+"
```

The tobacco response could probably be simplified by combining the two intermediate smoking rates:

```
esoph$tobgp2 <- esoph$tobgp
levels (esoph$tobgp2)[2:3] <- "10-30"
levels (esoph$tobgp2)


[1] "0-9g/day" "10-30"    "30+"
```

The age effect is most complicated, but a three-level factor might work just as well with a young group (under age 45), an intermediate group (age between 45 and 54), and an older group (55+):

```
esoph$agegp2 <- esoph$agegp
levels (esoph$agegp2)[4:6] <- "55+"
levels (esoph$agegp2)[1:2] <- "under45"
levels (esoph$agegp2)


[1] "under45" "45-54"    "55+"
```

Updating our model, `esoph_mod2` for that, reduces the number of terms (as there are fewer levels of the covariates):

```
esoph_mod3 <- glm (cbind (ncases, ncontrols) ~ agegp2 + alcgp2 + tobgp2, binomial,
            data = esoph)
summary (esoph_mod3)

Call:
glm(formula = cbind(ncases, ncontrols) ~ agegp2 + alcgp2 + tobgp2,
    family = binomial, data = esoph)

Deviance Residuals:
    Min       1Q   Median       3Q      Max
-1.8944  -0.7976  -0.3094   0.8586   2.0751

Coefficients:
            Estimate Std. Error z value Pr(>|z|)
(Intercept)  -1.1913     0.1632  -7.299 2.89e-13 ***
agegp2.L      2.1472     0.2602   8.252  < 2e-16 ***
agegp2.Q     -0.5952     0.2112  -2.819  0.00482 **
alcgp2.L      2.4664     0.2674   9.223  < 2e-16 ***
alcgp2.Q      0.1420     0.1782   0.797  0.42565
tobgp2.L      1.0549     0.2357   4.476 7.62e-06 ***
tobgp2.Q      0.2307     0.1766   1.307  0.19131
---
Signif. codes:  0 '***' 0.001 '**' 0.01 '*' 0.05 '.' 0.1 ' ' 1

(Dispersion parameter for Binomial family taken to be 1)
```

```
    Null deviance: 367.953  on 87  degrees of freedom
Residual deviance:  97.619  on 81  degrees of freedom
AIC: 226.67

Number of Fisher Scoring iterations: 5
```

We can't use AIC to compare `esoph_mod2` and `esoph_mod3`, as we have played around with the data by combining factors, and we can't use the `anova ()` function as the models are not nested. However, simpler is better, so let us stick with the newer model.

Having established that our ordered factors should all stay in the model, it might be interesting to examine what happens if we take away the ordering:

```
esoph$alcgp3 <- factor (esoph$alcgp, ordered = FALSE)
esoph$agegp3 <- factor (esoph$agegp2, ordered = FALSE)
esoph$tobgp3 <- factor (esoph$tobgp2, ordered = FALSE)
esoph_mod4 <- glm (cbind (ncases, ncontrols) ~ agegp3 + alcgp3 + tobgp3, binomial,
                data = esoph)
summary (esoph_mod4)

Call:
glm(formula = cbind(ncases, ncontrols) ~ agegp3 + alcgp3 + tobgp3,
    family = binomial, data = esoph)

Deviance Residuals:
    Min       1Q   Median       3Q      Max
-1.8967  -0.8038  -0.3366   0.7228   2.4536

Coefficients:
             Estimate Std. Error z value Pr(>|z|)
(Intercept)   -5.2314     0.4202 -12.449  < 2e-16 ***
agegp345-54    2.1941     0.3924   5.591 2.25e-08 ***
agegp355+      2.9868     0.3692   8.089 6.02e-16 ***
alcgp340-79    1.3906     0.2458   5.658 1.53e-08 ***
alcgp380-119   1.9254     0.2785   6.913 4.76e-12 ***
alcgp3120+     3.4805     0.3770   9.231  < 2e-16 ***
tobgp310-30    0.4409     0.1989   2.216   0.0267 *
tobgp330+      1.4747     0.3350   4.402 1.07e-05 ***
---
Signif. codes:  0 '***' 0.001 '**' 0.01 '*' 0.05 '.' 0.1 ' ' 1

(Dispersion parameter for Binomial family taken to be 1)

    Null deviance: 367.953  on 87  degrees of freedom
Residual deviance:  92.602  on 80  degrees of freedom
AIC: 223.66

Number of Fisher Scoring iterations: 5
```

We can see that even without the ordering, all the different levels in our factors seem to belong in the model. As with all such models, we could continue permuting factor levels and interactions, but we should be careful about doing that until we reach a result that we might have imagined beforehand.

11.4.6 Binomial GLM with categorical and continuous covariates

We now turn to an example concerning flowering in five varieties of perennial plant. Replicated individuals in a fully randomized design were sprayed with one of six doses of a controlled mixture of growth promoters. After six weeks, plants were scored as flowering or not flowering. The count of flowering individuals forms the response variable. We have both continuous (dose) and categorical (variety) explanatory variables. We use logistic regression because the response variable is a count (flowered) that can be expressed as a proportion (flowered/total):

```
flowering <- read.table ("flowering.txt", header = T,
                         colClasses = list (variety = "factor"))
head (flowering)
  flowered number dose variety
1        0     12    1       A
2        0     17    4       A
3        4     10    8       A
4        9     11   16       A
5       10     10   32       A
6        0     17    1       B
```

We can plot the data in Figure 11.16:

```
y <- cbind (flowering$flowered, flowering$number - flowering$flowered)
pf <- flowering$flowered / flowering$number
plot (flowering$dose, jitter (pf), xlab = "dose", ylab = "proportion flowered",
      col = hue_pal () (5) [as.vector (as.numeric (factor (flowering$variety)))])
legend (1, 0.9, legend = levels (flowering$variety),
        pch = rep (19, 5), title = "variety",
        col = hue_pal () (5))
```

We use a sneaky trick to colour the points by variety: we can convert levels of a factor to numbers by using as.numeric () (we then need to convert the result of that into a vector!). Using jitter () stops common values hiding one another.

There is clearly a substantial difference between the plant varieties in their response to the flowering stimulant. The modelling proceeds in the usual way. We begin by fitting the maximal model with different slopes and intercepts for each variety (estimating 10 parameters in all):

```
flow_mod1 <- glm (y ~ dose * variety, binomial, data = flowering)
summary (flow_mod1)

Call:
glm(formula = y ~ dose * variety, family = binomial, data = flowering)

Deviance Residuals:
    Min       1Q   Median       3Q      Max
-2.6648  -1.1200  -0.3769   0.5735   3.3299
```

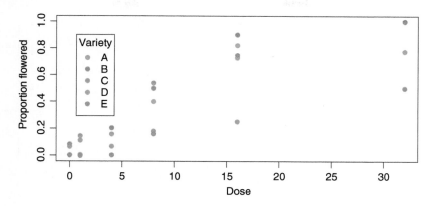

Figure 11.16 `flowering` by variety and dose.

```
Coefficients:
             Estimate Std. Error z value Pr(>|z|)
(Intercept)  -4.59165    1.03215  -4.449 8.64e-06 ***
dose          0.41262    0.10033   4.113 3.91e-05 ***
varietyB      3.06197    1.09317   2.801 0.005094 **
varietyC      1.23248    1.18812   1.037 0.299576
varietyD      3.17506    1.07516   2.953 0.003146 **
varietyE     -0.71466    1.54849  -0.462 0.644426
dose:varietyB -0.34282   0.10239  -3.348 0.000813 ***
dose:varietyC -0.23039   0.10698  -2.154 0.031274 *
dose:varietyD -0.30481   0.10257  -2.972 0.002961 **
dose:varietyE -0.00649   0.13292  -0.049 0.961057
---
Signif. codes:  0 '***' 0.001 '**' 0.01 '*' 0.05 '.' 0.1 ' ' 1

(Dispersion parameter for Binomial family taken to be 1)

    Null deviance: 303.350  on 29  degrees of freedom
Residual deviance:  51.083  on 20  degrees of freedom
AIC: 123.55

Number of Fisher Scoring iterations: 5
```

The model exhibits substantial overdispersion, but this could be due to poor model selection rather than extra, unmeasured variability. Let us investigate this by plotting the fitted curves through the scatter plot to give Figure 11.17.

```
y <- cbind (flowering$flowered, flowering$number - flowering$flowered)
pf <- flowering$flowered / flowering$number
plot (flowering$dose, jitter (pf), xlab = "dose", ylab = "proportion flowered",
      col = hue_pal ()(5)[as.vector (as.numeric (factor (flowering$variety)))])
legend (1, 0.9, legend = levels (flowering$variety),
        pch = rep (19, 5), title = "variety",
```

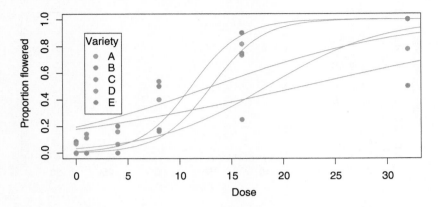

Figure 11.17 `flowering` by variety and dose with fitted logistic lines.

```
        col = hue_pal () (5))
xv <- seq (0,35,0.1)
for (i in 1:5) {
  vn <- rep (levels (flowering$variety) [i], length (xv))
  yv <- predict (flow_mod1, list (variety = factor(vn), dose = xv),
    type = "response")
  lines (xv, yv, col = hue_pal () (5)[i])
}
```

As we can see, the model is reasonable for two of the genotypes (A and E), moderate for one genotype (C) but very poor for two of them, (B and D). For both of the latter, the model greatly overestimates the proportion flowering at zero dose, and for genotype B, there seems to be some inhibition of flowering at the highest dose because the graph falls from 90% flowering at dose 16 to just 50% at dose 32. Variety D appears to be asymptoting at less than 100% flowering.

```
tapply (pf, list (flowering$dose, flowering$variety), mean)

           A           B           C           D           E
0  0.0000000 0.08333333 0.00000000 0.06666667 0.0000000
1  0.0000000 0.00000000 0.14285714 0.11111111 0.0000000
4  0.0000000 0.20000000 0.06666667 0.15789474 0.0000000
8  0.4000000 0.50000000 0.17647059 0.53571429 0.1578947
16 0.8181818 0.90000000 0.25000000 0.73076923 0.7500000
32 1.0000000 0.50000000 1.00000000 0.77777778 1.0000000
```

These failures of the model should focus attention for future work. The moral is that the fact that we have proportion data does not mean that the data will necessarily be well described by the logistic model. For instance, in order to describe the response of genotype B, the model would need to have a hump, rather than to asymptote at $p = 1$ for large doses. It is essential to look closely at the data, both with plots and with tables, before accepting the model output. *Model choice is a very big deal*. The logistic was a poor choice for two of the five varieties in this case.

   We did rather gloss over whether accounting for overdispersion would improve matters. As we discussed in Section 11.2.2, the parameter estimates, and thus the predictions, will not change if we use `family = quasi-Binomial` so Figure 11.17 would look exactly the same. However, if we put confidence intervals around these lines (they are mean estimates), then things would be different. This does not change the conclusion that the model we have requires improvement: more data would help as well.

11.4.7 Revisiting lizards

In Section 11.3.2, we examined the `lizards` dataset, treating the response as a count of lizards from one of two species. We can work with the proportion of all lizards that are text Anolis grahamii as the response variable, instead of analysing the counts of the numbers of text *A. grahamii* and *A. opalinus* separately. This requires us to reformat the dataset.

First, we need to make absolutely sure that all the explanatory variables are in exactly the same order for both species of lizards. The reason for this is that we are going to `cbind ()` the counts for one of the lizard species onto the half dataframe containing the other species counts and all of the explanatory variables. Any mistakes here would be disastrous because the count would be lined up with the wrong combination of explanatory variables, and the analysis would be wrong and utterly meaningless.

```
lizards_sort <- lizards[order (lizards$species,
                               lizards$sun,
                               lizards$height,
                               lizards$perch,
                               lizards$time),]
```

If we examine the new dataset, we will see that the first half is all the `grahamii` entries, and the second is those for `opalinus`, with the order of the other variables the same in each half. Next, we need to extract the top half of this dataframe (i.e. rows 1–24):

```
lizards_sort_top <- lizards_sort[1:24,]
names (lizards_sort_top)[1] <- "Ag"
lizards_sort_top <- lizards_sort_top[,-6]
head (lizards_sort_top)

   Ag  sun height  perch       time
25  2 Shade   High  Broad Not.mid.day
41  4 Shade   High  Broad Not.mid.day
33  1 Shade   High  Broad     Mid.day
27  3 Shade   High Narrow Not.mid.day
43  3 Shade   High Narrow Not.mid.day
35  1 Shade   High Narrow     Mid.day
```

We have also renamed the count column, `n`, as it is now just a count of text A. grahamii, and deleted the final column as all the entries, `grahamii`, are the same. We can now add the counts for text A. opalinus into a new column:

```
lizards_new <- data.frame(lizards_sort$n[25:48], lizards_sort_top)
names (lizards_new)[1] <- "Ao"
head (lizards_new)
```

```
    Ao Ag    sun height   perch        time
25 20  2 Shade   High   Broad Not.mid.day
41  4  4 Shade   High   Broad Not.mid.day
33  8  1 Shade   High   Broad     Mid.day
27  8  3 Shade   High  Narrow Not.mid.day
43  5  3 Shade   High  Narrow Not.mid.day
35  4  1 Shade   High  Narrow     Mid.day
```

We can now analyse these data in a similar fashion to other datasets in this section. We have probably seen enough of modelling lizards in Section 11.3.2, so will not repeat the exercise. However, it would be interesting to consider whether we might end up with a similar model to that we built earlier.

11.5 Binary Response Variables and GLMs

Many statistical problems involve binary response variables. For example, we often classify individuals as

- dead or alive;

- occupied or empty;

- healthy or diseased;

- male or female;

- literate or illiterate;

- mature or immature;

- solvent or insolvent;

- employed or unemployed; or

- good or bad at statistics.

It is interesting to understand the factors that are associated with an individual being in one class or the other. Binary analysis will be a useful option when at least one of our explanatory variables is continuous (rather than categorical). In a study of company insolvency, for instance, the data would consist of a list of measurements made on the insolvent companies (their age, size, turnover, location, management experience, workforce training, and so on,) and a similar list for the solvent companies. The question then becomes which, if any, of the explanatory variables increase the probability of an individual company being insolvent.

The response variable contains only 0s and 1s; for example, 0 to represent dead individuals and 1 to represent live ones. Thus, there is only a single column of numbers for the response, in contrast to proportion data where two vectors (successes and failures) were bound together to form the response (see Section 11.4). The way that R treats binary data is to assume that the 0s and 1s come from a binomial trial with sample size 1. If the probability that an individual is dead is p, then the probability of obtaining y (where y is either dead or alive, 0 or 1) is given by an abbreviated form of the Binomial distribution with $n = 1$, known as the Bernoulli distribution:

$$P(y) = p^y \times (1 - p)^{1-y}.$$

The random variable y has a mean of p and a variance of $p(1 - p)$, and the objective is to determine how the explanatory variables influence the value of p. The trick to using binary response variables effectively is to know when it is worth using them, and when it is better to lump the successes and failures together and analyse the total counts of dead individuals, occupied patches, insolvent firms, or whatever. The question we need to ask is: do we have unique values of one or more explanatory variables for each and every individual case?

If the answer is 'yes', then analysis with a binary response variable is likely to be fruitful. If the answer is 'no', then there is nothing to be gained, and we should reduce our data by aggregating the counts to the resolution at which each count does have a unique set of explanatory variables. For example, suppose that all our explanatory variables were categorical – sex (male or female), employment (employed or unemployed), and region (urban or rural). In this case, there is nothing to be gained from analysis using a binary response variable because none of the individuals in the study have unique values of any of the explanatory variables. It might be worthwhile if we had each individual's body weight, for example, then we could ask whether, when we control for sex and region, heavier people are more likely to be unemployed than lighter people: the, usually, unique values from the continuous variable make the analysis possible. In the absence of unique values for any explanatory variables, there are two useful options:

1. Analyse the data as a contingency table using Poisson errors, with the count of the total number of individuals in each of the eight contingencies ($2 \times 2 \times 2$) as the response variable (see Section 11.3) in a dataframe with just eight rows; or

2. decide which of our explanatory variables is the key (perhaps we are interested in gender differences), then express the data as proportions (the number of males and the number of females) and recode the binary response as a count of a two-level factor. The analysis is now of proportion data (the proportion of all individuals that are female, for instance) using Binomial errors (see Section 11.4).

If we do have unique measurements of one or more explanatory variables for each individual, these are likely to be continuous variables such as body weight, income, medical history, distance to the nuclear reprocessing plant, geographic isolation, and so on. This being the case, successful analyses of binary response data tend to be multiple regression analyses or complex analyses of covariance.

In order to carry out modelling on a binary response variable, we take the following steps:

• create a single vector containing 0s and 1s as the response variable;

• use a GLM with `family = binomial`;

• consider changing the link function from the default logit to complementary log-log;

• fit the model in the usual way;

• test the importance of model terms by deletion of terms from the maximal model (or adding in to the minimal one), and compare the change in deviance with a χ^2 test.

Note that there is no such thing as overdispersion with a binary response variable, and hence, no need to change to using the quasi-Binomial when the residual deviance is large. The choice of link function is generally made by trying both links and selecting the link that gives the lowest deviance. The logit link that we used earlier is symmetric in p and q, but the **complementary log-log** link is asymmetric. We may also improve the fit by transforming one or more of the explanatory variables. Bear in mind that we can fit non-parametric smoothers to binary response variables using Generalised Additive Models (as described in Chapter 12) instead of carrying out parametric logistic regression.

11.5.1   A straightforward example

In this example, the response variable is called `incidence`: a value of 1 means that an island was occupied by a particular species of bird, and 0 means that the bird did not breed there. The explanatory variables are the `area` of the island (km^{2}2) and the `isolation` of the island (distance from the mainland, km).

```
isolation <- read.table ("isolation.txt", header = T)
head (isolation)

  incidence area isolation
1         1 7.928     3.317
2         0 1.925     7.554
3         1 2.045     5.883
4         0 4.781     5.932
5         0 1.536     5.308
6         1 7.369     4.934
```

There are two continuous explanatory variables, so the appropriate analysis is multiple regression. The response is binary, so we shall do logistic regression with binomial errors. We begin by fitting a complex model involving an interaction between isolation and area:

```
iso_mod1 <- glm( incidence ~ area * isolation, binomial, data = isolation)
```

Then we fit a simpler model with only main effects for isolation and area:

```
iso_mod2 <- glm( incidence ~ area + isolation, binomial, data = isolation)
```

We now compare the two models:

```
anova (iso_mod2, iso_mod1, test = "Chi")

Analysis of Deviance Table

Model 1: incidence ~ area + isolation
Model 2: incidence ~ area * isolation
  Resid. Df Resid. Dev Df Deviance Pr(>Chi)
1        47     28.402
2        46     28.252  1  0.15043   0.6981
```

The simpler model does not appear to be worse, so we accept this for the time being, and inspect the parameter estimates and standard errors:

```
summary (iso_mod2)

Call:
glm(formula = incidence ~ area + isolation, family = binomial,
    data = isolation)

Deviance Residuals:
    Min        1Q    Median        3Q       Max
-1.8189   -0.3089    0.0490    0.3635    2.1192

Coefficients:
             Estimate Std. Error z value Pr(>|z|)
(Intercept)    6.6417     2.9218   2.273  0.02302 *
area           0.5807     0.2478   2.344  0.01909 *
isolation     -1.3719     0.4769  -2.877  0.00401 **
---
Signif. codes:  0 '***' 0.001 '**' 0.01 '*' 0.05 '.' 0.1 ' ' 1

(Dispersion parameter for Binomial family taken to be 1)

    Null deviance: 68.029  on 49  degrees of freedom
Residual deviance: 28.402  on 47  degrees of freedom
AIC: 34.402

Number of Fisher Scoring iterations: 6
```

The estimates and their standard errors are in logits. We see that `area` has a positive effect (islands are more likely to be occupied), but `isolation` has a very strong negative effect (isolated islands are much less likely to be occupied). This is the minimal adequate model. We should plot the fitted model through the scatterplot of the data. We can see the effect of each covariate separately in Figure 11.18.

```
iso_moda <- glm (incidence ~ area, binomial, data = isolation)
iso_modi <- glm (incidence ~ isolation, binomial, data = isolation)
xva <- seq (0, 9, 0.01)
yva <- predict (iso_moda, list (area = xva), type = "response")
plot (isolation$area, isolation$incidence, xlab = "area", ylab = "incidence")
lines (xva, yva, col = hue_pal () (2) [1])
xvi <- seq (0, 10, 0.01)
yvi <- predict (iso_modi, list (isolation = xvi), type = "response")
plot (isolation$isolation, isolation$incidence, xlab = "isolation",
ylab = "incidence")
lines (xvi, yvi, col = hue_pal () (2) [2])
```

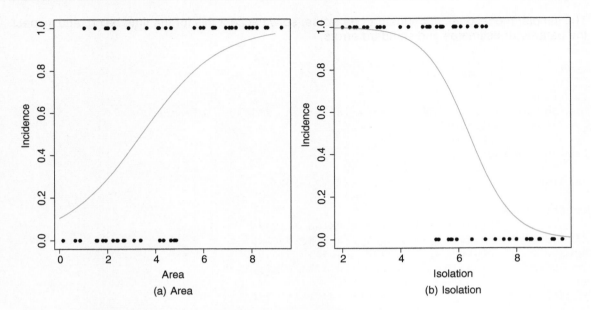

Figure 11.18   Covariates shown individually for fitted models in `isolation`.

This shape of plot is typical of that for logistic regression. It is the middle section, where it begins and ends, that is the interesting part of the curve. Obviously, the values for incidence can only be 0 or 1 so are not very compelling on their own.

11.5.2   Graphical tests of the fit of the logistic curve to data

The logistic plots above are all well and good, but it is very difficult to know how good the fit of the model is when the data are shown only as 0s or 1s. Some people have argued for putting histograms instead of rugs on the top and bottom axes, but there are issues here about the arbitrary location of the bins. Rugs are a one-dimensional addition to the bottom (or top) of the plot showing the locations of the data points along the x-axis. The idea is to indicate the extent to which the values are clustered at certain values of the explanatory variable, rather than evenly spaced out along it. If there are many values at the same value of *x*, it will be useful to use the jitter function to spread them out (by randomly selected small distances).

A different tack is to cut the data into a number of sectors and plot empirical probabilities (ideally with their standard errors) as a guide to the fit of the logistic curve, but this, too, can be criticized on the arbitrariness of the boundaries to do the cutting, coupled with the fact that there are often too few data points to give acceptable precision to the empirical probabilities and standard errors in any given group. For what it is worth, here is an example of this approach. The response is `occupation` of territories (0 or 1) and the explanatory variable is `resources` available in each territory:

```
occupation <- read.table ("occupation.txt", header = T)
head (occupation)

  resources occupied
1  14.18154        0
```

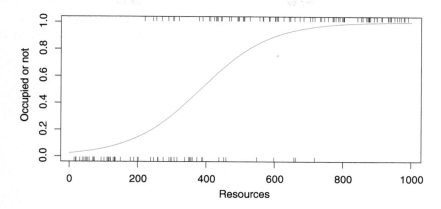

Figure 11.19 Rug plot for `isolation`.

2	18.68306	0
3	20.22156	0
4	30.75129	0
5	38.16026	0
6	43.15511	0

Figure 11.19 is a rug plot with a fitted logistic curve:

```
plot (occupation$resources, occupation$occupied, type = "n",
      xlab = "resources", ylab = "occupied or not")
rug (occupation$resources[occupation$occupied == 0])
rug (occupation$resources[occupation$occupied == 1], side = 3)
occ_mod <- glm (occupied ~ resources, binomial, data = occupation)
xv <- 0:1000
yv <- predict (occ_mod, list(resources = xv), type = "response")
lines (xv, yv, col = hue_pal ()(2)[1])
```

There is no need to add jitter as `resources` is continuous and so exact overlap is unlikely.

The idea is to cut up the ranked values on the x-axis (`resources`) into five categories and then work out the mean and the standard error of the proportions of `occupied` in each group. We shall, slightly arbitrarily, pick five groups:

```
occ_cut <- cut (occupation$resources, 5)
tapply (occupation$occupied, occ_cut, sum)

(13.2,209]   (209,405]   (405,600]   (600,795]   (795,992]
         0          10          25          26          31
```

The `cut ()` function is impressive. It has taken the continuous variable called `resources`, and cut it up into five bins creating a factor called `occ_cut`. The margins of the bins are defined within curved and square brackets which are read as follows: (13.2, 209] means 'from, but not including, 13.2 to, and including, 209'. So the figure next to the round bracket is excluded from this bin and is included in the adjacent bin (to the left in this case). This option is called `right = TRUE` and is the default for `cut ()`. We use the table function to count the number of cases in each bin:

```
table (occ_cut)
occ_cut
(13.2,209]    (209,405]    (405,600]    (600,795]    (795,992]
        31           29           30           29           31
```

So the empirical probabilities are given by

```
occ_probs <- tapply(occupation$occupied, occ_cut, sum) / table (occ_cut)
occ_probs

(13.2,209]    (209,405]    (405,600]    (600,795]    (795,992]
0.0000000    0.3448276    0.8333333    0.8965517    1.0000000
```

We can plot these probabilities against the mean value of `resources` in each bin, in the logistic regression plot, and add a standard error (we will estimate this using a Binomial distribution on the empirical probabilities for each bin: $\sqrt{p(1-p)/n}$) to express uncertainty, to give Figure 11.20.

```
occ_probs <- as.vector (occ_probs)
resmeans <- as.vector (tapply (occupation$resources, occ_cut, mean))
se <- as.vector (sqrt (occ_probs * (1 - occ_probs) / table (occ_cut)))
up <- occ_probs + se
down <- occ_probs - se
points (resmeans, occ_probs, cex=2, col = hue_pal ()(2)[2])
for (i in 1:5) {
  lines (rep (resmeans[i], 2), c (up[i], down[i]), col = hue_pal ()(2)[2])
}
```

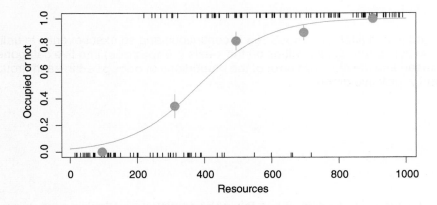

Figure 11.20   Rug plot for `isolation`.

Evidently, the logistic regression is a good fit to the data above resources of 800 (not surprising, though, given that there were no unoccupied patches in this region), but it is rather a poor fit for resources between 400 and 800, as well as below 200, despite the fact that there were no occupied patches in the latter region (empirical probability is zero).

11.5.3   Mixed covariate types with a binary response

In our next example, the binary response variable is `infected` (abset or present) and the explanatory variables are `weight` and `age` (continuous) and `sex` (categorical).

```
infection <- read.table ("infection.txt", header = T,
                    colClasses = c ("factor", rep ("numeric", 2), "fac-
tor"))
head (infection)

  infected age weight    sex
1   absent   2      1 female
2   absent   9     13 female
3  present  15      2 female
4   absent  15     16 female
5   absent  18      2 female
6   absent  20      9 female
```

Figure 11.21 displays some of the data.

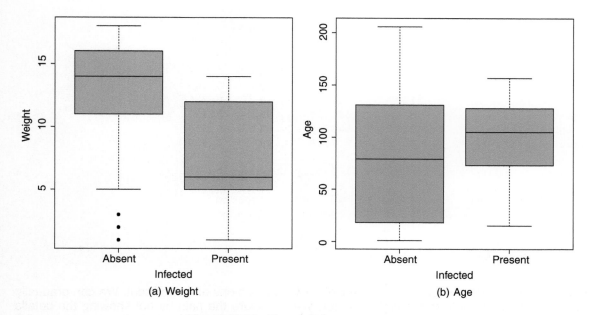

(a) Weight   (b) Age

Figure 11.21   Box plots for `infection`.

```
boxplot (weight ~ infected, data = infection, col = hue_pal ()(2)[1])
boxplot (age ~ infected, data = infection, col = hue_pal ()(2)[2])
table (infection$sex, infection$infected)
```

```
          absent present
  female      17      11
  male        47       6
```

Infected individuals are substantially lighter than uninfected individuals and occur in a much narrower range of ages. The infection is also much more prevalent in females (11/28) than in males (6/53).

We now proceed, as usual, to fit a maximal model with different slopes for each level of the categorical variable:

```
inf_mod1 <- glm (infected ~ age * weight * sex, family = binomial,
                 data = infection)
summary (inf_mod1)

Call:
glm(formula = infected ~ age * weight * sex, family = binomial,
    data = infection)

Deviance Residuals:
    Min       1Q   Median       3Q      Max
-2.1767  -0.5359  -0.2494  -0.1691   2.3149

Coefficients:
                      Estimate Std. Error z value Pr(>|z|)
(Intercept)          -0.109124   1.375388  -0.079    0.937
age                   0.024128   0.020874   1.156    0.248
weight               -0.074156   0.147678  -0.502    0.616
sexmale              -5.969109   4.278066  -1.395    0.163
age:weight           -0.001977   0.002006  -0.985    0.325
age:sexmale           0.038086   0.041325   0.922    0.357
weight:sexmale        0.213830   0.343265   0.623    0.533
age:weight:sexmale   -0.001651   0.003419  -0.483    0.629


(Dispersion parameter for Binomial family taken to be 1)

    Null deviance: 83.234  on 80  degrees of freedom
Residual deviance: 55.706  on 73  degrees of freedom
AIC: 71.706

Number of Fisher Scoring iterations: 6
```

It certainly does not look as if any of the high-order interactions are significant. We can gradually remove them starting from the highest order. We will spare the pain by not showing the details (using either AIC or anova () for comparison purposes), but the upshot is that we would not wish to retain any of them. So we now might examine the model which just has main effects:

```
inf_mod2 <- glm (infected ~ age + weight + sex, family = binomial,
                 data = infection)
summary (inf_mod2)

Call:
glm(formula = infected ~ age + weight + sex, family = binomial,
    data = infection)

Deviance Residuals:
    Min       1Q    Median       3Q      Max
-1.9481  -0.5284  -0.3120  -0.1437   2.2525

Coefficients:
            Estimate Std. Error z value Pr(>|z|)
(Intercept)  0.609369   0.803288   0.759 0.448096
age          0.012653   0.006772   1.868 0.061701 .
weight      -0.227912   0.068599  -3.322 0.000893 ***
sexmale     -1.543444   0.685681  -2.251 0.024388 *
---
Signif. codes:  0 '***' 0.001 '**' 0.01 '*' 0.05 '.' 0.1 ' ' 1

(Dispersion parameter for Binomial family taken to be 1)

    Null deviance: 83.234  on 80  degrees of freedom
Residual deviance: 59.859  on 77  degrees of freedom
AIC: 67.859

Number of Fisher Scoring iterations: 5
```

Weight is clearly worth retaining, sex is quite significant (not just for the survival of the human race), and age is marginally interesting. All of these conclusions chime with our preliminary data analysis. It is worth establishing whether there is any evidence of non-linearity in the response of infection to weight or age. We might begin by fitting quadratic terms for the two continuous explanatory variables:

```
inf_mod3 <- glm (infected ~ age + weight + sex + I (weight^2) + I (age^2),
                 family = binomial, data = infection)
summary (inf_mod3)

Call:
glm(formula = infected ~ age + weight + sex + I(weight^2) + I(age^2),
    family = binomial, data = infection)

Deviance Residuals:
    Min       1Q    Median       3Q      Max
-1.70226  -0.44412  -0.19584  -0.02505   2.36653

Coefficients:
            Estimate Std. Error z value Pr(>|z|)
(Intercept) -3.4475839  1.7978359  -1.918   0.0552 .
```

```
age            0.0829364  0.0360205    2.302    0.0213 *
weight         0.4466284  0.3372352    1.324    0.1854
sexmale       -1.2203683  0.7683288   -1.588    0.1122
I(weight^2)   -0.0415128  0.0209677   -1.980    0.0477 *
I(age^2)      -0.0004009  0.0002004   -2.000    0.0455 *
---
Signif. codes:  0 '***' 0.001 '**' 0.01 '*' 0.05 '.' 0.1 ' ' 1


(Dispersion parameter for Binomial family taken to be 1)

    Null deviance: 83.234  on 80  degrees of freedom
Residual deviance: 48.620  on 75  degrees of freedom
AIC: 60.62

Number of Fisher Scoring iterations: 6
```

Evidently, both relationships appear to be curvilinear. It is worth looking at these non-linearities in more detail, to see if we can do better with other kinds of models (e.g. non-parametric smoothers, piecewise linear models or step functions). A Generalised Additive Model (GAM) is often a good way to start when we have continuous covariates. We shall leave the example on a cliffhanger at this point and return to it in Section 12.2.

11.5.4 Spine plot and logistic regression

In a spinogram (see Section 11.3.3), the response is categorical, but the explanatory variable is continuous. The following data show parasitism (a binary response, `parasitised` or `not`) as a function of host population density:

```
wasps <- read.table ("wasps.txt", header = T, colClasses = list (fate = "fac-
tor"))
head (wasps)

  density fate
1       1  not
2       2  not
3       2  not
4       4  not
5       4  not
6       4  not

table (wasps$density, wasps$fate)

     not paratised
  1    1         0
  2    2         0
  4    3         1
  8    6         2
 16   11         5
 32   12        20
 64   12        52
```

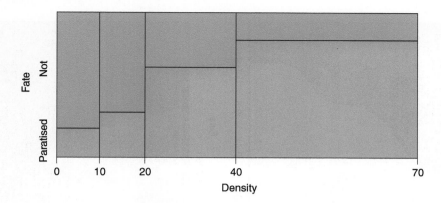

Figure 11.22   Spine plot for `wasps`.

Apparently, the proportion of hosts parasitised increases as host density is increased, as we can see in Figure 11.22:

```
spineplot (fate ~ density, data = wasps, col = hue_pal ()(2))
```

The trend of increasing parasitism with density is very clear. In these plots, the width of the sector indicates how many of the data fell in this range of population densities; there were equal numbers of hosts in the first two bins, but twice as many in the highest density category than in the category below, with a peak of just over 80% parasitised. Alternatively, if we want a smooth curve, we can use the conditional density plot `cdplot ()` like this to give Figure 11.23a:

```
cdplot (fate ~ density, data = wasps, col = hue_pal ()(2))
cdplot (fate ~ log (density), data = wasps, col = hue_pal ()(2))
```

The trend is quantified using logistic regression:

```
wasps_mod1 <- glm (fate ~ density, binomial, data = wasps)
wasps_mod2 <- glm (fate ~ log (density), binomial, data = wasps)
summary (wasps_mod2)

Call:
glm(formula = fate ~ log(density), family = binomial, data = wasps)

Deviance Residuals:
    Min      1Q   Median      3Q      Max
-1.8044  -1.0124   0.6612   0.6612   2.1522

Coefficients:
             Estimate Std. Error z value Pr(>|z|)
(Intercept)   -4.0230     1.0585  -3.801 0.000144 ***
log(density)   1.3062     0.2942   4.440 8.99e-06 ***
---
Signif. codes:  0 '***' 0.001 '**' 0.01 '*' 0.05 '.' 0.1 ' ' 1
```

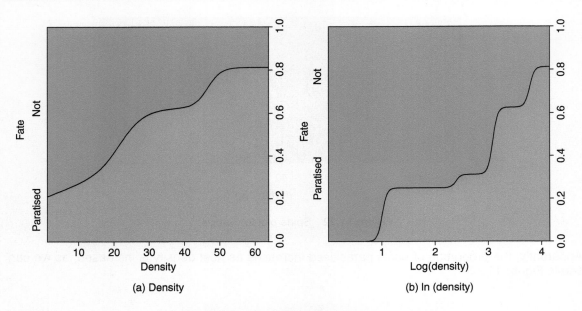

Figure 11.23 Smoothed spine plot for `wasps`.

```
(Dispersion parameter for Binomial family taken to be 1)

    Null deviance: 167.39  on 126  degrees of freedom
Residual deviance: 139.08  on 125  degrees of freedom
AIC: 143.08

Number of Fisher Scoring iterations: 4
```

It's a little tricky to see from Figure 11.23a, but the relationship between `density` and proportion `parasitised` does not appear to be linear (see Figure 11.23b), which is why we have looked at both models with the second one having a lower AIC, so we will stick with that.

We can plot the data and regression line. We will do that using the model coefficients. However, first, we need to convert the outcome into numbers as `fate` is a factor. We have seen before that levels can be converted into numbers using `as.numeric ()`, but those numbers start at one, so we need to deduct one from each value. This gives us Figure 11.24:

```
plot (jitter (log (wasps$density)), as.numeric (wasps$fate) - 1, col = hue_pal
     ()(3)[1],       xlim = c (0, 5), xlab = "jittered ln (density)",
     ylab = "proportion parasitised")
xv <- seq (0, 5, 0.01)
yv <- 1 / (1 + 1 / exp (coef (wasps_mod2)[1] + coef (wasps_mod2)[2] * xv))
lines (xv, yv, col = hue_pal ()(3)[2])
```

The logistic plot might be improved by overlaying the empirical frequencies, as well as showing the raw data as 0s and 1s. We might choose four bins in an example like this, averaging the four

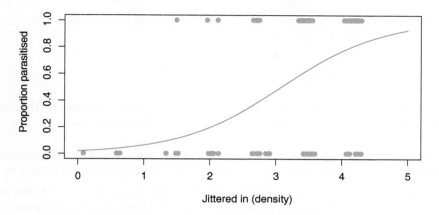

Figure 11.24 Data and regression line for `wasps` model 2.

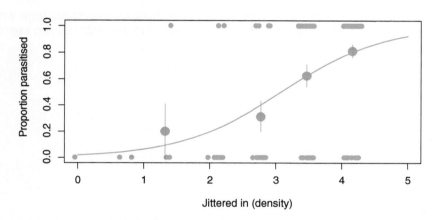

Figure 11.25 Data and regression line for `wasps` model 2.

lowest density classes, and using the counts data from the three highest classes (16, 32, and 64). To add error bars, `eb`, to show plus and minus one standard error of the estimated proportion, we use:

$$SE_p = \sqrt{\frac{p(1-p)}{n}}$$

This gives us Figure 11.25:

```
den <- c (3.75, 16, 32, 64)
pd <- c(3/15, 5/16, 20/32, 52/64)
points (log (den), pd, cex = 2,, col = hue_pal ()(4)[3])
eb <- sqrt (pd * (1 - pd) / den)
for (i in 1:4) {
  lines (rep (log (den[i]), 2), c (pd[i] - eb[i], pd[i] + eb[i]),
        col = hue_pal ()(4)[4])
}
```

This has the virtue of illustrating the excellent fit of the model at high densities, but the rather less good although not terrible fit at lower densities.

11.6 Bootstrapping a GLM

We introduced the bootstrap in Section 9.4, but it has much wider applicability than just for tests and CIs. There are two contrasting ways of bootstrapping statistical models:

1. fit the model lots of times by selecting cases for inclusion at random with replacement, so that some data points are excluded and others appear more than once in any particular model fit;

2. fit the model once and calculate the residuals and the fitted values, then shuffle the residuals lots of times and add them to the fitted values in different permutations, fitting the model to the many different data sets.

In both cases, we will obtain a distribution of parameter values for the model from which we can derive confidence intervals. Here we use the `timber` dataset to illustrate the two approaches:

```
timber <- read.table ("timber.txt", header = T)
head (timber)

  volume  girth height
1 0.7458 0.6623   21.0
2 0.7458 0.6862   19.5
3 0.7386 0.7022   18.9
4 1.1875 0.8379   21.6
5 1.3613 0.8538   24.3
6 1.4265 0.8618   24.9
```

Modelling attempts to derive the `volume` in cubic metres from the `girth` and `height`, both in metres. There is a similar dataset in the achingly modern imperial measurements named `trees` in *R*, but the data are different. We shall use what is, in fact, a linear model, but it illustrates the point in a straightforward way:

```
timber_model <- glm (log (volume) ~ log (girth) + log (height), data = timber)
summary (timber_model)

Call:
glm(formula = log(volume) ~ log(girth) + log(height), data = timber)

Deviance Residuals:
      Min         1Q     Median         3Q        Max
-0.168619  -0.048504   0.002509   0.063703   0.129248

Coefficients:
            Estimate Std. Error t value Pr(>|t|)
(Intercept) -2.89938    0.63767  -4.547 9.56e-05 ***
```

```
log(girth)    1.98267     0.07503   26.426   < 2e-16 ***
log(height)   1.11714     0.20448    5.463 7.83e-06 ***
---
Signif. codes:  0 '***' 0.001 '**' 0.01 '*' 0.05 '.' 0.1 ' ' 1

(Dispersion parameter for Gaussian family taken to be 0.006626731)

    Null deviance: 8.30893  on 30  degrees of freedom
Residual deviance: 0.18555  on 28  degrees of freedom
AIC: -62.697

Number of Fisher Scoring iterations: 2
```

We will use the `boot` library (Canty and Ripley, 2021) and, as we saw in Section 9.4, the hard part of using this is writing the sampling function correctly. It has at least two arguments: the first must be the data on which the resampling is to be carried out (in this case, the whole dataframe called timber), and the second must be the index (the randomized subscripts showing which data values are to be used in a given realization; some cases will be repeated, others will be omitted).

For the first approach, we create a new dataframe inside the function based on the randomly selected indices, then fit the model to this new data set. Finally, the function should return the coefficients of the model. Here is the 'statistic' function in full:

```
library (boot)
model.boot1 <- function (data, indices){
  sub_data <- data[indices,]
  model <- glm (log(volume) ~ log (girth) + log (height), data = sub_data)
  coef (model)
}
```

We can run this function 2000 times using the `boot ()` function:

```
timber_boot <- boot (timber, model.boot1, R = 2000)
timber_boot

ORDINARY NONPARAMETRIC BOOTSTRAP

Call:
boot(data = timber, statistic = model.boot1, R = 2000)


Bootstrap Statistics:
     original         bias    std. error
t1* -2.899379 -0.025232199  0.65937400
t2*  1.982665 -0.000664192  0.06164977
t3*  1.117138  0.008103604  0.21297723
```

There is very little bias in any of the three parameter estimates, and the bootstrapped standard errors are close to their parametric equivalents.

For the second approach, we fit the GLM and extract the fitted values ($\hat{y}$ or *yhat*), which will be the same each time, and the residuals, which will be independently shuffled each time:

```
yhat <- fitted (timber_model)
resids <- resid (timber_model)
```

Then we make a dataframe that will be fed into the bootstrap, containing the residuals to be shuffled, along with the two covariates:

```
res_data <- data.frame (resids, timber$girth, timber$height)
```

We write the 'statistic' function to do the work within boot. The first argument is always the dataframe and the second is always the index i, which controls the shuffling:

```
model.boot2 <- function (res_data, i) {
  y <- yhat + res_data[i,1]
  nd <- data.frame (y, timber$girth, timber$height)
  model <- glm (y ~ log (timber$girth) + log (timber$height), data = nd)
  coef(model)
}
```

Inside the function, we create a particular vector of *y* values by adding the shuffled residuals (res_data[i,1]) to the fitted values, then put this vector along with the covariates into a new dataframe, nd, that will be different each time the GLM is fitted. The function returns the three coefficients from the particular fitted model, which are the 'statistics' of the bootstrap, hence, the name of the function. Finally, because we want to shuffle the residuals rather than sample them with replacement, we specify sim = "permutation" in the call to the boot function:

```
perms <- boot (res_data, model.boot2, R = 2000, sim = "permutation")
perms

DATA PERMUTATION


Call:
boot(data = res_data, statistic = model.boot2, R = 2000, sim = "permutation")


Bootstrap Statistics:
     original         bias     std. error
t1* -2.899379  0.0133097979   0.60946493
t2*  1.982665  0.0009428575   0.07218387
t3*  1.117138 -0.0042702801   0.19549132
```

with similarly effective results to the first method.

Finally, we can create 99% CIs for each of the parameter estimates, selecting the usually preferred BCa method (using the adjusted bootstrap percentage method):

```
boot.ci (perms, index = 1, conf = 0.99)$bca[c (1, 4, 5)]
[1]   0.990000 -4.596246 -1.532413
boot.ci (perms, index = 2, conf = 0.99)$bca[c (1, 4, 5)]
[1] 0.990000 1.767156 2.142671
boot.ci (perms, index = 3, conf = 0.99)$bca[c (1, 4, 5)]
[1] 0.990000 0.678363 1.658917
```

Remember that these intervals are for the intercept, and the coefficients of `log (girth)` and `log (height)`, respectively.

References

Canty, A., & Ripley, B. D. (2021). *Boot: Bootstrap R (S-plus) functions* [R package version 1.3-28].

Dobson, A. J., & Barnett, A. J. (2018). *An introduction to generalized linear models* (Fourth). CRC Press.

Venables, W. N., & Ripley, B. D. (2002). *Modern applied statistics with S* (Fourth) [ISBN 0-387-95457-0]. Springer. https://www.stats.ox.ac.uk/pub/MASS4/.

12

Generalised Additive Models

Up to this point, we have introduced covariates into linear models or into the linear predictors of GLMs (see Section 11.1.2), by taking the covariate data directly or possibly using some function of those data. It may well be that the covariate data do not have a neat linear (or function of linear such as *ln*) relationship with the outcome variable (even when the link function is taken into account), and we need some non-parametric representation of the covariate to be introduced into the linear predictor. These representations are known as **smoothers**: they attempt to represent the covariate data by a smooth line. For instance, if we had some count data with a single covariate, then with a GLM we might use a log-link function so that

$$\ln(\mu_i) = \eta_i = \beta_0 + \beta_1 x_i$$

where μ_i is the mean of the Poisson distribution for Y_i. With **Generalised additive models** or **GAMs** we have

$$\ln(\mu_i) = \eta_i = \beta_0 + s(x_i)$$

where the function s (.), a smoother, attempts to create a smooth line to represent the x_is, which don't have a shape that can be represented by a regular parametric function.

Generalised additive models (implemented in *R* by the gam () function) extend the range of application of generalised linear models by allowing non-parametric smoothers in addition to parametric forms, and these can be associated with a range of link functions. All of the error families allowed with GLMs are available with GAMs (binomial, poisson, Gamma, etc.). Indeed, gam () has many of the attributes of both glm () and lm (), and the output can be modified using update (). We can use all of the familiar methods such as summary (), anova (), predict () and fitted () after a GAM has been fitted to data. The gam () function used in this book is in the mgcv package contributed by Simon Wood who has also written a book (Wood, 2017, where many of the arguments to gam (), which we have not covered, are discussed):

```
library (mgcv, quietly = T)

This is mgcv 1.8-36. For overview type 'help("mgcv-package")'.
```

The R Book, Third Edition. Elinor Jones, Simon Harden and Michael J. Crawley.
© 2023 John Wiley & Sons Ltd. Published 2023 by John Wiley & Sons Ltd.
Companion website: www.wiley.com/go/jones/therbook3e

Before we look at building models, we will look at an example of smoothing. Then we will review some straightfoward examples before returning to how the smoothers work and some more complex models.

12.1   Smoothing example

One of the simplest model-fitting functions is `loess ()` (which replaces its predecessor called `lowess ()`). This, and other functions such as `splines ()`, can be used where we are interested in exploring the simple relationship between two variables without the complexity of a GLM. The following example shows the log of population change from year to year, $Delta(t) = \ln(N(t + 1)/N(t))$, as a function of population density ($N(t)$) in an investigation of density dependence in a sheep population. The data are shown in Figure 12.1:

```
soay <- read.table ("soaysheep.txt", header = T)
head (soay)

  Year Population      Delta
1 1955        710  0.08759806
2 1956        775  0.22546344
3 1957        971  0.12382949
4 1958       1099  0.20124957
5 1959       1344 -0.78994656
6 1960        610  0.39998564

attach (soay)
plot (Population, Delta, col = hue_pal ()(2)[1])
```

```
detach (soay)
```

We are not examining trends over time but trying to understand whether we can predict the log change, given the current year's population. Broadly speaking, population change is positive at low densities ($Delta > 0$) and negative at high densities ($Delta < 0$), but there is a great deal of scatter,

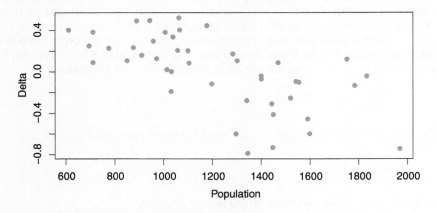

Figure 12.1   Log of population change from year to year.

and it is not at all obvious what shape of smooth function would best describe the data. Here is the default `loess` at work:

```
soay_mod1 <- loess (Delta ~ Population, data = soay)
summary (soay_mod1)

Call:
loess(formula = Delta ~ Population, data = soay)

Number of Observations: 44
Equivalent Number of Parameters: 4.66
Residual Standard Error: 0.2616
Trace of smoother matrix: 5.11   (exact)

Control settings:
    span    :   0.75
    degree  :   2
    family  :   gaussian
    surface:   interpolate         cell = 0.2
  normalize:   TRUE
 parametric:   FALSE
drop.square:   FALSE
```

While the summary output is not particularly illuminating, it does tell us that the equivalent of 4.66 parameters was used in building the model. Remember a straight line has two parameters, a quadratic (e.g. a parabola) three, etc. The 0.66 is a little confusing, but it does give some sense of the complexity of the line representing the smooth fit. Now, we can draw the smoothed line using `predict ()` in the usual way to extract the predicted values from the model and plot them in Figure 12.2:

```
xv <- seq (600, 2000, 1)
yv <- predict (soay_mod1, data.frame (Population = xv))
lines (xv, yv, col = hue_pal ()(3)[2])
```

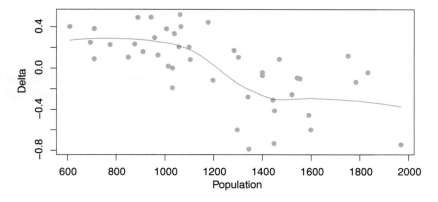

Figure 12.2 Log of population change with smoothed line.

The smooth curve looks rather like a step function. We can compare this smooth function with a step function, using a tree model (see Section 20.2 and Ripley, 2019) as an objective way of determining the threshold for splitting the data into low- and high-density parts:

```
library (tree)
thresh <- tree (Delta ~ Population, data = soay)
print (thresh)

node), split, n, deviance, yval
      * denotes terminal node

 1) root 44 5.2870  0.006208
   2) Population < 1289.5 25 0.8596  0.226500
     4) Population < 1009.5 13 0.2364  0.277600 *
     5) Population > 1009.5 12 0.5525  0.171200
      10) Population < 1059.5 5 0.1631  0.072120 *
      11) Population > 1059.5 7 0.3053  0.241900 *
   3) Population > 1289.5 19 1.6180 -0.283700
     6) Population < 1459 9 0.7917 -0.349500 *
     7) Population > 1459 10 0.7519 -0.224400 *
```

The threshold for the first split of the tree model is at Population = 1289.5, so we define this as the threshold density:

```
th <- 1289.5
```

Then we can use this threshold to create a two-level factor for fitting two constant rates of population change using aov ():

```
soay_mod2 <- aov (Delta ~ (Population > th), data = soay)
summary (soay_mod2)

                Df Sum Sq Mean Sq F value    Pr(>F)
Population > th  1  2.810   2.810   47.63 2.01e-08 ***
Residuals       42  2.477   0.059
---
Signif. codes:  0 '***' 0.001 '**' 0.01 '*' 0.05 '.' 0.1 ' ' 1
1 observation deleted due to missingness
```

showing a residual error variance of 0.059. This compares with the residual of $0.2616^2 = 0.068$ from the loess () model above. To draw the step function, we need the average low-density population increase and the average high-density population decline:

```
tapply (soay$Delta[-45], (soay$Population[-45] > th), mean)

     FALSE        TRUE
0.2265084 -0.2836616
```

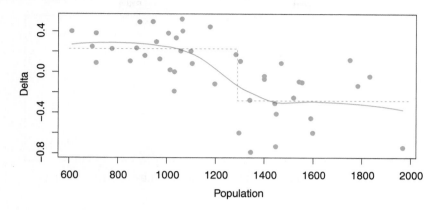

Figure 12.3   Log of population change with smoothed line and step function.

Note the use of negative subscripts to drop the NA from the last value of Delta. Then use these figures to draw the step function, shown in Figure 12.3:

```
lines (x = c (600, th, th, 2000), y = c (0.2265, 0.2265, -0.2837, -0.2837),
       lty = 2, col = hue_pal () (3) [3])
```

It is a moot point which of these two models is the most realistic scientifically, but the step function involved three estimated parameters (two averages and a threshold), while the loess is based on 4.66 degrees of freedom, so parsimony favours the step function (it also has a slightly lower residual sum of squares). It is also worth noting that there are very few points to the right-hand side of the plot and so any fitted model above 1600 would have a very large standard error.

12.2   Straightforward examples of GAMs

Sometimes we can see that the relationship between *y* and *x* is non-linear, but we do not have any theory or any mechanistic model to suggest a particular functional form (mathematical equation) to describe the relationship. In such circumstances, GAMs are particularly useful because they fit non-parametric smoothers to the data without requiring us to specify any particular mathematical model to describe the non-linearity. Here is a toy example, using the dataset hump, plotted in Figure 12.4:

```
hump <- read.table ("hump.txt", header = T)
head (hump)

      y     x
1 3.741 0.907
2 2.295 0.761
3 1.498 1.108
4 2.881 1.016
5 0.760 1.189
6 3.120 1.001
```

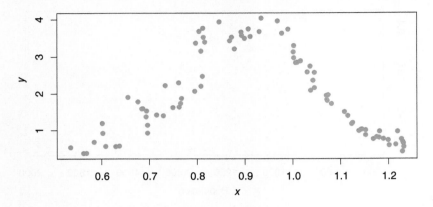

Figure 12.4 Scatter plot of hump.

```
attach (hump)
plot (x, y, col = hue_pal ()(2)[1])
```

```
detach (hump)
```

There is no obvious formula which could relate the *x* and *y* values. The model is specified very simply by showing which explanatory variables (in this case just *x*) are to be fitted as smoothed functions: it is set up exactly as a GLM, except that we use s (x) to say that we wish to smooth the *x* data:

```
hump_mod <- gam (y ~ s (x), data = hump)
summary (hump_mod)


Family: gaussian
Link function: identity

Formula:
y ~ s(x)


Parametric coefficients:
            Estimate Std. Error t value Pr(>|t|)
(Intercept)  1.95737    0.03446    56.8   <2e-16 ***
---
Signif. codes:  0 '***' 0.001 '**' 0.01 '*' 0.05 '.' 0.1 ' ' 1

Approximate significance of smooth terms:
      edf Ref.df     F p-value
s(x) 7.452  8.403 116.7  <2e-16 ***
---
Signif. codes:  0 '***' 0.001 '**' 0.01 '*' 0.05 '.' 0.1 ' ' 1

R-sq.(adj) =  0.919   Deviance explained = 92.6%
GCV = 0.1156  Scale est. = 0.1045     n = 88
```

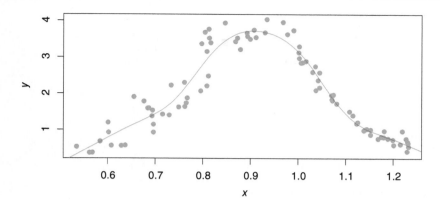

Figure 12.5 Scatter plot of `hump` with fitted model.

The output looks reasonably familiar, but there are a couple of things worth pointing out:

- the smoothed term has been taken out of the `Parametric coefficients` section of the output and is shown instead under the `Approximate significance of smoothed terms` heading. The estimated degrees of freedom column (**edf**: 7.452) gives some measure of the complexity of the curve that has been created;

- the **Deviance explained** estimates how much of the uncertainty in *y* is explained by the model.

We can use the `predict` function to show the fitted model over the range of *x* values by adding the following to give Figure 12.5:

```
xv <- seq (0.5, 1.3, 0.01)
yv <- predict (hump_mod,list (x = xv))
lines (xv, yv, col = hue_pal () (2) [2])
```

Our second straightforward example takes us back to Section 11.5.3 and the `infection` data set. We had got as far as determining that the linear predictor seemed to behave more acceptably with squared terms for age and weight. We will create a new GAM model with smoothers for these variables:

```
inf_mod4 <- gam (infected ~ sex + s (age) + s (weight), family = binomial,
                 data = infection)
summary (inf_mod4)


Family: binomial
Link function: logit

Formula:
infected ~ sex + s(age) + s(weight)
```

```
Parametric coefficients:
            Estimate Std. Error z value Pr(>|z|)
(Intercept)  -1.4763      0.5716  -2.583   0.0098 **
sexmale      -1.3099      0.7279  -1.800   0.0719.
---
Signif. codes:  0 '***' 0.001 '**' 0.01 '*' 0.05 '.' 0.1 ' ' 1

Approximate significance of smooth terms:
            edf Ref.df Chi.sq p-value
s(age)    2.150  2.715  6.191 0.07667.
s(weight) 1.957  2.446 10.954 0.00722 **
---
Signif. codes:  0 '***' 0.001 '**' 0.01 '*' 0.05 '.' 0.1 ' ' 1

R-sq.(adj) =  0.359   Deviance explained = 40.3%
UBRE = -0.23574  Scale est. = 1          n = 81
```

This does not appear to help very much with age, but the *p*-value associated with weight is small. If we revert the age term back to `age + I (age`^{2}`)`, we find that sex does not have a substantial influence, and so our final GAM model would be, with the smoothed fitted line for weight, as in Figure 12.6:

```
inf_mod5 <- gam (infected ~ I (age^2) + s (weight), family = binomial,
                 data = infection)
summary (inf_mod5)


Family: binomial
Link function: logit

Formula:
infected ~ I(age^2) + s(weight)

Parametric coefficients:
             Estimate Std. Error z value Pr(>|z|)
(Intercept) -2.218e+00  5.877e-01  -3.773 0.000161 ***
I(age^2)     2.779e-05  3.162e-05   0.879 0.379407
---
Signif. codes:  0 '***' 0.001 '**' 0.01 '*' 0.05 '.' 0.1 ' ' 1

Approximate significance of smooth terms:
            edf Ref.df Chi.sq p-value
s(weight) 2.198  2.742  13.39 0.00335 **
---
Signif. codes:  0 '***' 0.001 '**' 0.01 '*' 0.05 '.' 0.1 ' ' 1

R-sq.(adj) =  0.228   Deviance explained = 26.6%
UBRE = -0.14183  Scale est. = 1          n = 81

plot (inf_mod5, col = hue_pal ()(2)[1], shade = T, shade.col = hue_pal ()(2)[2])
```

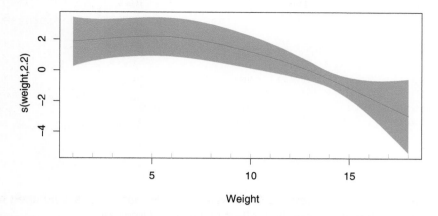

Figure 12.6 Plot of `infection` fitted model 5 showing the smoothed weight function.

Unlike for GLMs and linear models, the `plot ()` function for GAMs will plot each of the fitted smoothed variables (we will examine residuals for GAMs in Section 12.4.1). We can see that the weight smoothed function seems to have a threshold, where it drops steeply at somewhere between 8 and 12. We could leave the model as it is now. However, if we wanted a final model that was a GLM, we could incorporate that threshold point as follows.

We could try a piecewise linear fit for weight, estimating the threshold weight at a range of values (say 8–14) and selecting the threshold that gives the lowest residual deviance; this turns out to be a threshold of 12. The piecewise regression is specified by the term:

```
I((weight - 12) * (weight > 12))
```

The `I` ('as is') is necessary to stop the * being evaluated as an interaction term in the model formula. What this expression says is 'regress infection on the value of weight - 12, but only do this when weight > 12 is true'. Otherwise, assume that infection is independent of weight. So our final model is

```
inf_mod6 <- glm (infected ~ age + I (age^2) + I((weight - 12) * (weight > 12)),
            family = binomial, data = infection)
summary (inf_mod6)


Call:
glm(formula = infected ~ age + I(age^2) + I((weight - 12) * (weight >
    12)), family = binomial, data = infection)

Deviance Residuals:
    Min        1Q      Median        3Q        Max
-1.42301   -0.50141   -0.13277   -0.01416    2.11658

Coefficients:
                          Estimate  Std. Error  z value  Pr(>|z|)
(Intercept)             -3.1207552   1.2665593   -2.464    0.0137 *
age                      0.0765784   0.0323376    2.368    0.0179 *
I(age^2)                -0.0003843   0.0001846   -2.081    0.0374 *
```

```
I((weight - 12) * (weight > 12)) -1.3511706  0.5134681  -2.631   0.0085 **
---
Signif. codes:  0 '***' 0.001 '**' 0.01 '*' 0.05 '.' 0.1 ' ' 1

(Dispersion parameter for binomial family taken to be 1)

    Null deviance: 83.234  on 80  degrees of freedom
Residual deviance: 51.953  on 77  degrees of freedom
AIC: 59.953

Number of Fisher Scoring iterations: 7
```

which has a lower AIC than our previous GLM. We conclude that there is a humped relationship between infection and age and a threshold effect of weight on infection.

12.3   Background to using GAMs

GAMs are an extension of GLMs and the gam () function inherits many of the features of glm (), such as the model formula, family, and link function. The extra feature is the smoothing of certain covariates. The theory and implementation of this feature is very complex. However, in this section, we will first attempt to explain what smoothing is doing and then cover how this might be applied in practice, particularly where there are multiple smoothed covariates. The gam () function can be run without understanding any of the technical background, as it has various default arguments built in.

12.3.1   Smoothing

We saw in Section 12.1 an example of trying to fit a smooth curve to a series of points. The basic idea is to take lots of short sections along the x-axis, fit a curve (known as a **spline**) to each of them and then make sure that each of these splines join up smoothly (i.e. they meet at a point or **knot** with the same gradient and, possibly more features in common described by further derivatives of the splines). The most obvious curve would just link up all the covariate values precisely. However, as our data will only be a sample from a population, we will have **overfitted** the curve to that sample: a different sample would then be likely to fit that curve badly. So the fitting process **penalises** the use of too many knots or too much **wiggliness**. To complicate this even further, the penalty has a coefficient, known as a **smoothing parameter**, which determines how strict the penalisation is. There are a range of methods for estimating this parameter from the data and details can be found in help (gam).

In practice, we are interested in the fitted curve, and Figure 12.7 shows the results of various types of fit. Bad fits might arise from the wrong number of knots or an incorrect smoothing parameter, etc.: we don't need to worry about those as gam () takes care of that for us.

12.3.2   Suggestions for using gam ()

There are many ways of specifying the model in a GAM: all of the continuous explanatory variables *x*, *w*, and *z* can enter the model as non-parametrically smoothed functions like this:

```
y ~ s (x) + s (w) + s (z).
```

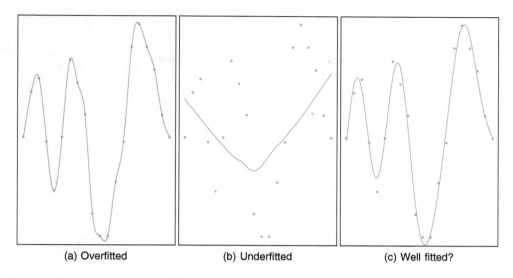

| (a) Overfitted | (b) Underfitted | (c) Well fitted? |

Figure 12.7 Various types of fitted splines.

Alternatively, the model can contain a mix of parametrically estimated parameters (*x* and *z*) and smoothed variable *w*:

```
y ~ x + s (w) + z.
```

Formulae can involve nested (two-dimensional) terms in which the smoothing *s*() terms have more than one argument, implying a multi-dimensional smooth:

```
y ~ s (x) + s (z) + s (x, z).
```

This does not represent an interaction between *x* and *z*. The appropriate formula for that is

```
y ~ z + s (x, by = z),
```

where the `by` argument ensures that the smooth function gets multiplied by covariate *z*. However, GAM smooths are centred (average value zero), so the parametric term for *z* is needed as well. If we wanted a relationship

$$E(y) = f(x)z,$$

then the appropriate formula would be

```
y ~ z + s (x, by = z) - 1.
```

Finally, the smoothers can have overlapping terms such as

```
y ~ s (x, z) + s (z, w).
```

12.4 More complex GAM examples

The use of GAMs can be extended to any situation where we might use a GLM, but where one or more of our covariates does not have an obvious functional relationship with the outcome variable. In this section, we will examine a few such examples.

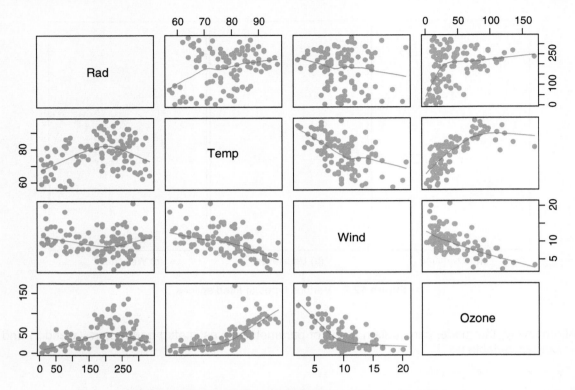

Figure 12.8 Pairwise scatter plots for `ozonepollution`.

12.4.1 Back to `Ozone`

We have explored the dataset which looks at levels of ozone in relation to wind temperature and solar radiation in the chapters on both linear regression (Section 10.2) and GLMs (Section 11.1.4). Here we will return to it in the context of GAMs. For data inspection, we use pairs with a non-parametric smoother, `lowess` to give Figure 12.8:

```
ozonepollution <- read.table ("ozone_pollution.txt", header = T)
pairs (ozonepollution, panel = function (x,y) {
  points (x, y, col = hue_pal () (2) [1])
  lines (lowess (x, y), col = hue_pal () (2) [2])
}
)
```

Now, let us fit all three explanatory variables using a GAM:

```
ozone_gam1 <- gam (ozone ~ s (rad) + s (temp) + s (wind), data = ozonepollution)
summary (ozone_gam1)


Family: gaussian
```

```
Link function: identity

Formula:
ozone ~ s(rad) + s(temp) + s(wind)

Parametric coefficients:
            Estimate Std. Error t value Pr(>|t|)
(Intercept)    42.10       1.66   25.36  <2e-16 ***
---
Signif. codes:  0 '***' 0.001 '**' 0.01 '*' 0.05 '.' 0.1 ' ' 1

Approximate significance of smooth terms:
          edf Ref.df       F p-value
s(rad)  2.763  3.451   3.964 0.00859 **
s(temp) 3.841  4.762  11.612 < 2e-16 ***
s(wind) 2.918  3.666  13.770 < 2e-16 ***
---
Signif. codes:  0 '***' 0.001 '**' 0.01 '*' 0.05 '.' 0.1 ' ' 1

R-sq.(adj) =  0.724   Deviance explained = 74.8%
GCV =      338   Scale est. = 305.96    n = 111
```

Note that the intercept is estimated as a parametric coefficient and the three explanatory variables are fitted as smooth terms. All three have small p-values, but radiation's is the largest. For illustration purposes, we can compare a GAM with and without a term for radiation using ANOVA in the usual way (there doesn't seem to be a good reason for excluding radiation in practice):

```
ozone_gam2 <- gam (ozone ~ s (temp) + s (wind), data = ozonepollution)
anova (ozone_gam2, ozone_gam1, test = "F")

Analysis of Deviance Table

Model 1: ozone ~ s(temp) + s(wind)
Model 2: ozone ~ s(rad) + s(temp) + s(wind)
  Resid. Df Resid. Dev    Df Deviance      F Pr(>F)
1    101.10      34885
2     98.12      30742 2.9757   4142.2 4.5496 0.0051 **
---
Signif. codes:  0 '***' 0.001 '**' 0.01 '*' 0.05 '.' 0.1 ' ' 1
```

Clearly, it would be silly to exclude radiation. However, we need to recognise that the F-test for GAMs, unlike that for GLMs, is only approximate and the resulting p-values should not be interpreted too precisely (a good lesson in all circumstances). Figure 12.8 suggests that there might be an interaction between wind and temperature, as there appears to be a clear trend in the scatter plot, so let us investigate that

```
ozone_gam3 <- gam (ozone ~ s (temp) + s (wind) + s (rad) + s (wind, by = temp),
                   data = ozonepollution)
summary (ozone_gam3)


Family: gaussian
Link function: identity
```

```
Formula:
ozone ~ s(temp) + s(wind) + s(rad) + s(wind, by = temp)

Parametric coefficients:
            Estimate Std. Error t value Pr(>|t|)
(Intercept)   0.7802     1.5017    0.52    0.605

Approximate significance of smooth terms:
              edf Ref.df       F  p-value
s(temp)     3.826  4.769   6.479 5.18e-05 ***
s(wind)     3.310  4.181   4.764  0.00127 **
s(rad)      2.834  3.537   3.861  0.00946 **
s(wind):temp 2.000 2.000 176.395  < 2e-16 ***
---
Signif. codes:  0 '***' 0.001 '**' 0.01 '*' 0.05 '.' 0.1 ' ' 1

Rank: 37/38
R-sq.(adj) =  0.726   Deviance explained = 75.3%
GCV = 339.97  Scale est. = 303.26    n = 111
```

That seems to improve things: note the increased Deviance explained figure. It is worth investigating the order in which the interaction term is presented (`s (wind, by = temp)` vs `s (temp, by = wind)` as the answers may well be different, due to the approximate nature of smoothing). We can examine the residuals from this model as given in Figure 12.9:

```
par (mfrow = c (2,2))
plot (ozone_gam3, residuals = T)

par (mfrow = c (1, 1))
```

There are three plots comparing smoothed curve with points representing the residuals for each covariate, together with one for the interaction. The residuals are displayed alongside the fitted lines. The plot at the bottom right represents the interaction term. The residuals do seem to be fairly randomly spread about the fitted line, which is what we are looking for in a well-fitted model.

12.4.2   An example with strongly humped data

The `SemiPar` package (Wand, 2018) contains a number of useful data sets where parametric modelling, such as in GLMs, is not entirely satisfactory. We will use the `ethanol` dataframe which contains 88 sets of measurements for variables from an experiment in which ethanol was burned in a single cylinder automobile test engine. The response variable, NOx, is the concentration of nitric oxide (NO) and nitrogen dioxide (NO2) in engine exhaust, normalised by the work done by the engine, and the two continuous explanatory variables are C (the compression ratio of the engine), and E (the equivalence ratio at which the engine was run, which is a measure of the richness of the air-ethanol mix). Pairwise scatter plots are shown in Figure 12.10.

```
library (SemiPar)
data (ethanol)
head (ethanol)
```

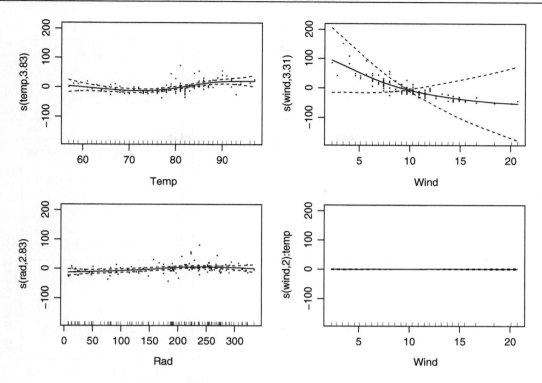

Figure 12.9 Residual plots for `ozonepollution` model 3.

```
    NOx  C     E
1 3.741 12 0.907
2 2.295 12 0.761
3 1.498 12 1.108
4 2.881 12 1.016
5 0.760 12 1.189
6 3.120  9 1.001

pairs (ethanol, col = hue_pal () (6))
```

Because NOx is such a strongly humped function of the equivalence ratio, E, we start with a model that fits E as a smoothed term and estimates a parametric term for the compression ratio:

```
ethanol_mod1 <- gam (NOx ~ s (E) + C, data = ethanol)
summary (ethanol_mod1)


Family: gaussian
Link function: identity

Formula:
NOx ~ s(E) + C
```

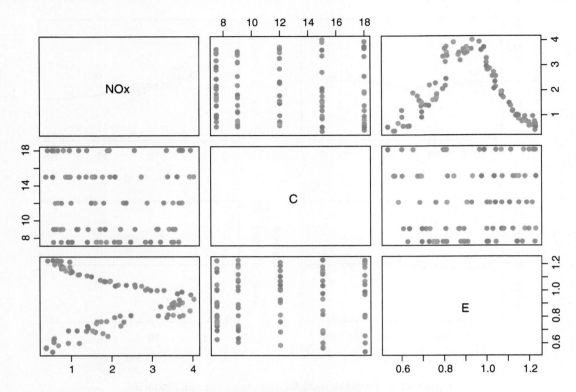

Figure 12.10   Pairwise scatter plots for `ethanol`.

```
Parametric coefficients:
            Estimate Std. Error t value Pr(>|t|)
(Intercept) 1.291342   0.088898  14.526  < 2e-16 ***
C           0.055345   0.007062   7.837 1.88e-11 ***
---
Signif. codes:  0 '***' 0.001 '**' 0.01 '*' 0.05 '.' 0.1 ' ' 1

Approximate significance of smooth terms:
      edf Ref.df      F p-value
s(E) 7.553  8.469 208.8  <2e-16 ***
---
Signif. codes:  0 '***' 0.001 '**' 0.01 '*' 0.05 '.' 0.1 ' ' 1

R-sq.(adj) =  0.953   Deviance explained = 95.8%
GCV = 0.067206  Scale est. = 0.05991   n = 88
```

This looks to be a useful model, but we have not really thought about C. The `coplot ()` function is helpful in showing where the effect of C on NOx was most marked, as given in Figure 12.11:

```
coplot (NOx ~ C | E, panel = panel.smooth, data = ethanol, col = hue_pal ()(10))
```

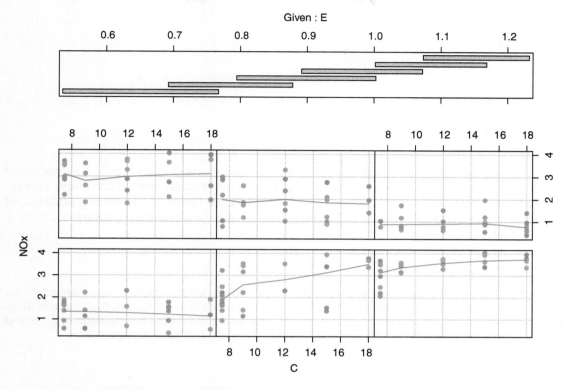

Figure 12.11   Coplot for explaining the effect of C on NOx in ethanol.

This set of plots divides the variable we are not interested in, E, into six overlapping sets of values (se top plot) and then, for each of them, starting at the bottom left, plots the five levels of C against NOx, together with a smoothed line of best fit. There is a pronounced positive effect of C on NOx only in panel 2 (ethanol, $0.7 < E < 0.9$ from the bars or **shingles** in the upper panel), but only slight effects elsewhere (most of the smoothed lines are roughly horizontal). So we can introduce an interaction effect into our model:

```
ethanol_mod2 <- gam (NOx ~ s (E) + s (E, by = C), data = ethanol)
summary (ethanol_mod2)


Family: gaussian
Link function: identity

Formula:
NOx ~ s(E) + s(E, by = C)

Parametric coefficients:
            Estimate Std. Error t value Pr(>|t|)
(Intercept)  1.28594    0.06537   19.67   <2e-16 ***
---
Signif. codes:  0 '***' 0.001 '**' 0.01 '*' 0.05 '.' 0.1 ' ' 1
```

```
Approximate significance of smooth terms:
        edf Ref.df      F p-value
s(E)   6.328  7.236 38.62  <2e-16 ***
s(E):C 4.710  5.407 36.54  <2e-16 ***
---
Signif. codes:  0 '***' 0.001 '**' 0.01 '*' 0.05 '.' 0.1 ' ' 1

R-sq.(adj) =  0.976   Deviance explained = 97.9%
GCV = 0.036159  Scale est. = 0.031213  n = 88
```

Note that if we had introduced the interaction the other way round (s (C, by = E)), we would have received an error message, essentially because E is continuous, and we don't have enough data points for the number of actual values of E. C only has five levels so that is not a problem. All elements of this new model have (nearly) zero p-values, and the deviance explained is 97.9%: a cracking result.

12.4.3 GAMs with binary data

GAMs are particularly valuable with binary response variables (for background, see Section 11.5). To illustrate the use of gam () for modelling binary response data, we return to the example analysed by logistic regression in Section 11.5.1. We want to understand how the isolation of an island and its area influence the probability that the island is occupied by our study species.

```
isolation <- read.table ("isolation.txt", header = T)
head (isolation)

  incidence  area isolation
1         1 7.928     3.317
2         0 1.925     7.554
3         1 2.045     5.883
4         0 4.781     5.932
5         0 1.536     5.308
6         1 7.369     4.934
```

In the logistic regression analysis, isolation had a negative effect on the probability that an island will be occupied by our species, and area (island size) had a positive effect on the likelihood of occupancy. But we have no a priori reason to believe that the logit of the probability should be linearly related to either of the explanatory variables. We can try using a GAM to fit smoothed functions to the incidence data:

```
iso_gam1 <- gam (incidence ~ s (area) + s (isolation), binomial, data = isola-
tion)
summary (iso_gam1)


Family: binomial
Link function: logit

Formula:
incidence ~ s(area) + s(isolation)
```

```
Parametric coefficients:
            Estimate Std. Error z value Pr(>|z|)
(Intercept)   1.6371     0.9898   1.654    0.0981 .
---
Signif. codes:  0 '***' 0.001 '**' 0.01 '*' 0.05 '.' 0.1 ' ' 1

Approximate significance of smooth terms:
              edf Ref.df Chi.sq p-value
s(area)     2.429  3.066  3.455 0.32945
s(isolation) 1.000  1.000  7.480 0.00624 **
---
Signif. codes:  0 '***' 0.001 '**' 0.01 '*' 0.05 '.' 0.1 ' ' 1

R-sq.(adj) =   0.63   Deviance explained = 63.1%
UBRE = -0.32096  Scale est. = 1          n = 50
```

This suggests that `area` might be worth dropping from the model. Let us have a look at the residuals to see what is going on (Figure 12.12):

```
par (mfrow = c (1, 2))
plot (iso_gam1, residuals = T)

par (mfrow = c (1, 1))
```

This suggests a strong effect of `area`, with very little scatter, but only above a threshold of about `area` = 5. As there are relatively few points in that range, it might explain why the *p*-value in the model is large, despite there appearing to be something going on. We assess the significance of area by deletion:

```
iso_gam2 <- gam (incidence ~ s (isolation), binomial, data = isolation)
anova (iso_gam2, iso_gam1, test = "Chisq")
```

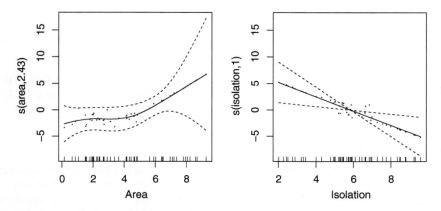

Figure 12.12 Fitted plots with residuals for a GAM for `isolation`.

```
Analysis of Deviance Table

Model 1: incidence ~ s(isolation)
Model 2: incidence ~ s(area) + s(isolation)
  Resid. Df Resid. Dev      Df Deviance Pr(>Chi)
1    45.191    29.127
2    44.934    25.094 0.25709    4.033 0.007425 **
---
Signif. codes:  0 '***' 0.001 '**' 0.01 '*' 0.05 '.' 0.1 ' ' 1
```

and clearly should not delete `area`. This shows the value of exploring a model and not just deleting terms because of a large *p*-value.

From Figure 12.12, it looks as if the relationship between `isolation` and `indicence` might be roughly linear. Look what happens if we don't smooth `isolation`:

```
iso_gam3 <- gam (incidence ~ s (area) + isolation, binomial, data = isolation)
summary (iso_gam3)


Family: binomial
Link function: logit

Formula:
incidence ~ s(area) + isolation

Parametric coefficients:
            Estimate Std. Error z value Pr(>|z|)
(Intercept)   9.5755     3.1859   3.006  0.00265 **
isolation    -1.3555     0.4956  -2.735  0.00624 **
---
Signif. codes:  0 '***' 0.001 '**' 0.01 '*' 0.05 '.' 0.1 ' ' 1

Approximate significance of smooth terms:
         edf Ref.df Chi.sq p-value
s(area) 2.429  3.066  3.455   0.329

R-sq.(adj) =   0.63  Deviance explained = 63.1%
UBRE = -0.32096  Scale est. = 1          n = 50
```

There is no difference in the deviance explained between this and the first model. We might have anticipated this by looking at the `edf` value for `isolation` in that model: it is exactly 1, suggesting a straight-line relationship which will also appear in our final model.

12.4.4 Three-dimensional graphic output from `gam`

Here is an example by Simon Wood (the author of `mgcv`) which shows the kind of three-dimensional graphics that can be obtained from `mgcv` using `vis.gam ()`, when there are two or more continuous explanatory variables. Note that in this example, the smoother works on both variables together, $y \sim s(x, z)$, to give Figure 12.13 showing the fitted model over a wide range of covariate values:

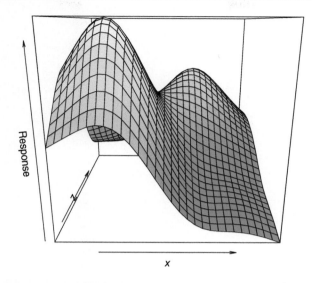

Figure 12.13   Fitted plots with residuals for a GAM for `isolation`.

```
some_function <- function (x, z, sx = 0.3, sz = 0.4) {
  (pi^sx * sz) * (1.2 * exp (-(x - 0.2)^2 / sx^2 - (z - 0.3)^2 / sz^2) +
                  0.8 * exp (- (x - 0.7)^2 / sx^2 - (z - 0.8)^2 / sz^2))
}
n <- 500
x <- runif(n)
z <- runif(n)
y <- some_function (x, z) + rnorm (n) * 0.1
some_model <- gam (y ~ s (x, z))
vis.gam (some_model, type = "response")
```

The details of the function which generates the data don't matter – it's just complex with some added noise (`rnorm (n) * 0.1`). We can choose whether to plot the linear predictor or the response. In this case, they are the same as there is no link function.

References

Ripley, B. (2019). *Tree: classification and regression trees* [R package version 1.0-40]. https://CRAN.R-project .org/package=tree.

Wand, M. (2018). *SemiPar: semiparametic regression* [R package version 1.0-4.2]. https://CRAN.R-project .org/package=SemiPar.

Wood, S. N. (2017). *Generalized additive models: an introduction with R* (2nd ed.). Chapman; Hall.

13

Mixed-Effect Models

13.1 Regression with categorical covariates

Up to this point, we have treated all categorical explanatory variables in regression models by defining dummy variables to represent the levels of the variable. Effectively, this partitions the data into groups with observations within a group in some sense more similar than those from different groups. This has worked well so far for our examples, allowing us to take account of such explanatory variables with little fuss.

Let us delve into this idea a bit further because, as we'll see, this isn't the only way of incorporating information about categorical explanatory variables. Indeed, in some instances, this method would be downright silly as we'll now show.

Let us first consider a simple example where we have a regression model with a categorical covariate, sex, which has two levels: male and female. For any individual that we find, the knowledge that it is, say, female conveys a great deal of information about the individual, and this information draws on experience gleaned from many other individuals that were female. A female will have a whole set of attributes (associated with her being female) no matter what population that individual was drawn from.

Now, take a different example where we are looking at the effect of adding fertiliser (F, a binary variable) on crop yield (Y), where the experiment was conducted on plots located in many different fields so that there are potentially many observations from the same field. We could model this as in equation (13.1), with f_i denoting the presence of fertiliser for the ith observation.

$$Y_i = \beta_0 + \beta_1 f_i + \epsilon_i, \tag{13.1}$$

where $\epsilon_i \sim N(0, \sigma^2)$. This model seems perfectly sensible: we probably *want* to understand the effect of fertiliser on yield, and an estimate of the regression coefficient (and associated information) from a regression output would be desirable.

One criticism of this model is that it ignores the possibility that the field in which the plot was located may have an effect on crop yield. In other words, plots within the same field are likely to be in some way similar, or alternatively, the yields from plots within the same field are likely to be correlated with one another. We need to take account of this as it violates a basic assumption of a normal linear regression model: loosely speaking, that the observations are independent of one another once we account for the predictors. Our go-to method would be to create dummy variables

The R Book, Third Edition. Elinor Jones, Simon Harden and Michael J. Crawley.
© 2023 John Wiley & Sons Ltd. Published 2023 by John Wiley & Sons Ltd.
Companion website: www.wiley.com/go/jones/therbook3e

to represent the various fields (let us say M of them) involved in the study like this:

$$Y_i = \beta_0 + \beta_1 f_i + \beta_2 g_{i2} + \cdots + \beta_{iM} g_{iM} + \epsilon_i .$$ (13.2)

This is rather messy with all the dummy variables introduced, but it's worth thinking about what they are actually doing. These dummy variables are adjusting the intercept for each field.

Let us write this in an alternative way where now Y_{ij} represents the i'th observation from the jth field (and similarly, f_{ij} and ϵ_{ij} represent the fertiliser and error term for the i'th observation from the jth field):

$$Y_{ij} = \beta_{0j} + \beta_1 f_{ij} + \epsilon_{ij}.$$ (13.3)

Notice the intercept term: this changes for each field as we go from $j = 1$ through to $j = M$. The expression in (13.3) is a lot tidier than that in (13.2).

However, though this looks tidier, all those dummy variables are still there despite our new notation. This formulation, where we have one dummy variable for each field, leads to at least two inconveniences.

First, the experiment may have been conducted using a large number of fields which would translate into a large number of dummy variables in our model in equation (13.2) or equivalently in equation (13.3). Do we really want to use up valuable degrees of freedom in including these dummy variables in the model?

Second, what if we want to generalise the results beyond the fields that were used in the study? If we were to use dummy variables to account for field-to-field differences, then our model is tied to those particular fields (compare this with the dummy variable for fertiliser, where we have already agreed that it is useful to compare yield with and without fertiliser, and there is no reason why our findings on the effect of fertiliser on yield can't be generalised). We don't really want to do this, and indeed, we probably aren't all that interested in these *particular* fields anyway. So what do we do? We could ignore the field effect as in our simpler model in equation (13.1), but then we're not accounting for potential dependence in yield between observations that came from the same field and the subsequent structure inherent in our data. Or we could use an alternative approach: account for the field effect using **random effects**.

13.2   An alternative method: random effects

So far the regression coefficients in equations (13.1)–(13.2) contain only so-called **fixed** effects. They are *fixed* in the sense that we estimate each of them, though this term can be rather confusing: take, for example, equation (13.2) where the intercept varies by field.

Random effects have factor levels that are drawn from a large (potentially very large) population in which the units of observation differ in many ways, but we do not know exactly how or why they differ (and, frankly, we may not care as in our plots within fields example). Whether we class a categorical variable as a random or fixed effect is really our choice and will depend, at least in part, on what we are interested in investigating.

How do these random effects make their way into our model? Let us go back to our hypothetical example. Rather than incorporate information about field using dummy variables (and so we have regression coefficients to estimate), let us instead think of the effect that field has on crop as a random variable. We need to assume a distribution for this random variable, and a common choice is to assume that the distribution is Normal. We follow the same apparent structure as in equation (13.3), that is:

$$Y_{ij} = \beta_{0j} + \beta_1 f_{ij} + \epsilon_{ij},$$ (13.4)

but now we assume that $\beta_{0j} \sim N(\beta_0, \tau^2)$ for $j = 1, \ldots, M$ as well as $\epsilon_{ij} \sim N(0, \sigma^2)$ for all i and j. This assumption on β_{0j} is different to what we assumed in equation (13.3).

Note that we don't intend to estimate each of the β_{0j}, but we are interested in estimating the *parameters* of its assumed distribution, β_0 and τ, in the same way we're interested in estimating σ from the distribution of the error term. These models are known as **random intercept** models (or more generally **random effect models**) because the intercept is treated as a random effect (or more generally because there are random effects in the model). As we are interested in estimating the regression coefficient of fertiliser directly, we call this a **fixed** effect. Models with both fixed- and random effects are often referred to as **mixed effects models**.

Before moving on, let us compare the random effect model in equation (13.4) to the so-called **fixed effect** model in equation (13.2) or (13.3) (the term 'fixed' just means that we assume there is an underlying (fixed) value to the parameter and we try to estimate it).

- In our fixed effects model, we estimate the value of β_{0j} for each value of j. This means a total of $M + 2$ parameters to estimate (the intercept, the $(M - 1)$ regression coefficients attached to each field, the regression coefficient of F, and σ);

- In our random effects model, we treat β_{0j} as a random variable from a $N(\beta_0, \tau^2)$ distribution. We don't estimate each individual β_{0j}, but we are interested in estimating β_0 and τ^2. This means a total of 4 parameters to estimate ($\beta_0, \tau^2, \beta_1, \sigma$).

Now we're in a situation where we are accounting for the differences between fields but without constraining ourselves to the pitfalls of doing this with dummy variables. But what if, for example, we also thought that there might be some interaction between the field and whether fertiliser was applied. Now what?

The idea of random effects comes in handy here too. Let us go back to using dummy variables as in equation (13.2). An interaction means that we are now allowing the slope to vary by group as well as the intercept (the latter is just due to having a categorical covariate). When we've dealt with interactions in the past, we've estimated each and every one of these slopes, but we don't need to do this unless this information is of interest in its own right. We can, instead, treat these varying slopes as random variables. In our example, this would amount to

$$Y_{ij} = \beta_{0j} + \beta_{1j} f_{ij} + \epsilon_{ij}, \tag{13.5}$$

where now we assume that $\beta_{0j} \sim N(\beta_0, \tau_0^2)$, along with $\beta_{1j} \sim N(\beta_1, \tau_1^2)$, in addition to $\epsilon_{ij} \sim N(0, \sigma^2)$ for all i and j. Again, when we treat this as a random slope what we're really interested is in estimating the parameters of the distribution, so now we're estimating $\beta_0, \tau_0, \beta_1, \tau_1$ as well as the usual σ. This makes a total of five things to estimate. Had we have gone for the fixed effects model with interaction this would have meant a total of $(3M + 1)$ parameters to estimate.

13.3 Common data structures where random effects are useful

It's vitally important to think about the structure of our data before applying random effects. The modelling which we'll come to shortly relies on us specifying the correct structure of the data. This ensures that we're applying random effects in the correct way, but relies on us to get it right in the first place. Here are some common data structures.

13.3.1 Nested (hierarchical) structures

We saw a simple example of a nested structure earlier, with plots nested within fields. This is often referred to as a two-level model: level 2 corresponds to the overarching fields, whereas level 1 is the plots (and, of course, these are nested within the level 2 units). It is helpful to visualise the data structure as in Figure 13.1, noting that we don't need the same number of plots per field.

In our example, where we applied fertiliser (or not) to plots, we say that the variable fertiliser is at level 1.

We're not restricted to two levels. Three- and four-level nested models are not uncommon though as the number of levels grows, so does the complexity of fitting the model. Let us modify our example, supposing that the fields are nested within farms. We're not interested in specifically modelling farms, but we can add it as a random effect so that we are taking into account that fields are nested within farms (and so may have some commonalities), and then plots are nested within fields. Figure 13.2 shows a common visualisation for this type of data structure.

At level 1 we have the plots, at level 2 we have the fields, and at level 3 we have the farms themselves. As before, fertiliser enters the model at level 1 (plots), though we will probably want to treat fertiliser as a fixed effect.

13.3.2 Non-nested structures

Let us take another example, where the structure isn't nested. Three experienced dentists measure the remaining dentin thickness between a cavity in a tooth and the pulp in a number of children's teeth using radiographs (an image). For each tooth and subsequent radiograph, two dentists measure the remaining dentin thickness. We'd like to model remaining dentin thickness, but we should account for two things: that the two measurements taken on the same radiograph are likely to be highly correlated, and that measurements taken by a particular dentist are likely to be somehow connected (they're taken by the same person after all!). The specific tooth and particular dentist doesn't really matter here, so it makes sense to introduce these structures into the data using random effects, along with any other information (let us suppose they're all fixed effects) that we have access to.

We could argue that there are two measurements per tooth (radiograph) and, therefore, we have a two-level model. But what about the dentists? Are the teeth nested within dentists? Neither approach works, of course. These are non-nested data.

Non-nested data are trickier to analyse. We don't consider this in much detail, but see, for example Faraway, 2016.

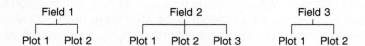

Figure 13.1 Two-level data structure.

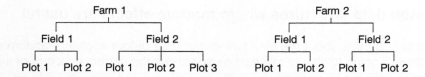

Figure 13.2 Three-level data structure.

13.3.3 Longitudinal structures

Longitudinal structures are very common. This is when we take multiple measurements of the unit of interest over time. We might for example look at the growth of children from age five to nine, measuring their height every 6 months. Modelling the growth of any particular child might not be of interest (immediately we think of random effects), but we obviously need to take account of the fact that there are multiple measurements from each child as these are going to be highly correlated.

In this case, we could simply state that the measurements are nested within child, which would be true. What this ignores is time: these are *ordered* observations. We will need to be careful to incorporate time into our model so that we can model the growth of children over the 5-year period.

13.4 *R* packages to deal with mixed effects models

There are several *R* packages that fit models with random effects. Two popular packages are `nlme` (Pinheiro et al., 2021) and `lme4` (Bates et al., 2015). Both have functions to fit linear mixed models using the functions `lme ()` and `lmer ()`, respectively. Most examples in this book will fit linear mixed models using the `nlme` package, though we will also look at an example using `lme4`.

At the end of this chapter, we'll consider generalised linear mixed models, which is akin to extending (normal) linear models to generalised linear models. For this, the `lme4` package is well suited as it has a dedicated function for such models, `glmer ()`.

13.4.1 The `nlme` package

The `nlme` package fits linear mixed effects models (those with normally distributed errors), along with non-linear mixed effects models (again with normally distributed errors). See Bates et al., 2015, for an excellent introduction to the `nlme` package.

We'll concentrate on linear mixed effect models in this chapter, for which the relevant package function is `lme ()`. The format of this function separates the fixed and random parts of the model, and we specify each separately as follows (in its most basic format):

```
lme (fixed, random, data)
```

The fixed effect (a compulsory part of the `lme ()` structure) is just the overall mean value of the response variable, for example `y ~ 1` or `y ~ x + z`.

The random effects show the identities of the random variables and their relative locations in the hierarchy and is *not* optional. Let us suppose that we have three random effects a, b, and c, with c nested within b which in turn is nested within a. In most mixed-effects models, we assume that the random effects have a mean of zero and that we are interested in quantifying variation in the intercept caused by differences between the factor levels of the random effects. After the intercept comes the vertical bar | which is read as 'given the following spatial arrangement of the random variables'. We would specify this using `random = 1 | a/b/c`. (Now, we see the importance of thinking about the *structure* of data!) An important detail to notice is that the name of the response variable (y here) is not repeated in the random-effects formula.

Putting this together we have, for example:

```
lme (fixed = y ~ 1, random = ~ 1 | a / b / c, data)
```

If we also had a fixed effect, x, and just one random effect a, but we want to specify a random slope as well as a random intercept for x, we would write

```
lme(fixed = y ~ x, random = ~ x | a, data)
```

13.4.2 The `lme4` package

The `lme4` package not only fits linear mixed models (like the `nlme` package) using the `lmer ()` function but also fits *generalised* linear mixed models using the `glmer ()` function. We'll see an example at the end of this chapter where the outcome of interest is binary, not continuous, and so we need to use a *logistic* mixed model instead of a (normal) mixed model. We'll concentrate on linear mixed models using `lmer ()` for now.

There is just one formula in `lmer ()`, not separate formulae for the fixed and random effects. In its most basic format we have, for example

```
lmer (formula, data)
```

where the formula structure requires the fixed effects to be specified first, followed by a plus sign, then one or more random terms enclosed in parentheses. In the following example, we use the same model as we did previously where we have a random intercept specified in layers with c nested within b which in turn is nested within a:

```
lmer (y ~ 1 + (1 | a / b / c), data)
```

If we also had a fixed effect, x, and just one random effect a, but we want to specify a random slope as well as a random intercept for x, we would write:

```
lmer (y ~ x + (x | a), data)
```

13.4.3 Methods for fitting mixed models

When we were dealing with normal linear models, in which we only had fixed effects, least squares was a simple approach to estimating the model's parameters. However, if we tried it for models with random effects, we have the downside of, for example, potentially negative variance for random effects. See Faraway, 2016 for an in-depth discussion. We need to find another method.

So what alternatives do we have? Maximum likelihood (ML) – see Section 2.5.2 – has good properties but requires assuming a distribution for the random effects (usually we assume normality). That would be fine for our (normal) linear mixed models, but ML estimates can be biased.

Another approach, restricted maximum likelihood (REML), tries to correct this. In general, REML is preferred because of its attempt to correct this bias. However, REML has its downsides too: because of the underlying mathematics, if we want to compare models (i.e. test one model against another), then we can only compare REML-fitted models if they have the same fixed effect structure (i.e. any difference is in the random effects only). If we want to compare two models where the fixed-effect structure differs, then we can't use REML to fit the models initially. In this case, it is common for researchers to fit the models using ML instead, where there is no such restriction in comparing models.

13.5 Examples of implementing random effect models

13.5.1 Multilevel data (two levels)

This example involves a regression of plant size against local point measurements of soil nitrogen *N* at five places within each of 24 farms. It is expected that plant size and soil nitrogen will be positively correlated. There is only one measurement of plant size and soil nitrogen at any given point. We have here an example of *two-level* data: the five places (level 1) are *nested within* a farm (level 2). We also have a covariate, soil nitrogen, which is measured at level 1.

Our first port of call is to plot the data.

```
farms <- read.table ("farms.txt" , header = T)
attach (farms)
head (farms)

         N        size farm
1 18.18014 96.48147    1
2 20.47343 98.64003    1
3 21.34757 99.36465    1
4 18.41299 93.19268    1
5 19.75629 98.39972    1
6 29.02022 99.53934    2

plotcol <- hue_pal ()(24)
plot (N, size, col = plotcol[farm], pch = 16,
      ylab = "Plant size", xlab = "Soil nitrogen level")
```

With 24 farms to consider, the plot in Figure 13.3 is tricky to read. The most obvious pattern, however, is that there is substantial variation in mean values of both soil nitrogen and plant size across the farms: the minimum-yielding fields have a mean *y* value of less than 80, while the maximum fields have a mean *y* value above 110.

The key distinction to understand is between:

1. fitting lots of linear regression models (one for each farm);

2. fitting one linear regression model using dummy variables to represent farms;

3. fitting one mixed-effects model, taking account of the differences between farms in terms of their contribution to the variance in response.

The first strategy is simple to implement but doesn't make the most of the data by borrowing strength across the whole dataset, and we end up with 24 linear regression models for specific farms that we can't generalise. The second strategy is again simple to implement, but the resulting model will be cumbersome owing to a large number of dummy variables to account for farm effect. Though we are making good use of our data here by pooling information across farms, we are still limited to a model that is specific to the 24 farms which formed the study. The third strategy, though perhaps slightly more complicated to implement, makes good use of the data *and* allows us to learn about the variation in size across farms while controlling for nitrogen.

Let us start with a simple random effects model which takes into account the structure (size readings are nested within farms), but ignores the information on soil nitrogen.

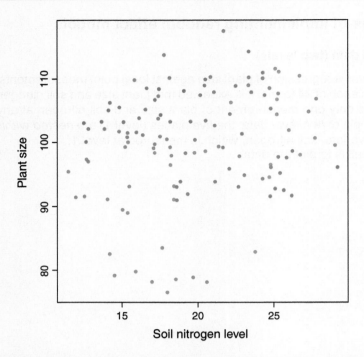

Figure 13.3   A plot of plant size against nitrogen level, coloured by farm.

```
library(nlme)
farms_mod1 <- lme (size ~ 1, random = ~ 1 | farm, data = farms)
summary (farms_mod1)

Linear mixed-effects model fit by REML
  Data: farms
       AIC      BIC    logLik
  655.1033 663.4406 -324.5516

Random effects:
 Formula: ~1 | farm
        (Intercept) Residual
StdDev:    8.361411 2.443197

Fixed effects:  size ~ 1
               Value Std.Error DF  t-value p-value
(Intercept) 99.65783  1.721277 96 57.89763       0

Standardized Within-Group Residuals:
        Min         Q1         Med         Q3         Max
-2.43265571 -0.58669857 -0.00948166  0.63447518  2.44336463

Number of Observations: 120
Number of Groups: 24
```

Let us take a closer look at the `Random effects` and `Fixed effects` parts of the output. The fixed effects section tells us that the average size is around 100. Meanwhile, the random effects output reveals considerable variation in size. This has been estimated at the farm level (i.e. how much of the variation in size is due to farm), and residual (unexplained) variation. The total variance is about $8.361^2 + 2.443^2 \approx 75.88$ with $8.361^2/75.88 \approx 0.92$ or 92% of the total variation in size due to differences between farms.

We would ideally make use of the soil nitrogen readings, so let us add that into our model. This next model has an intercept for each farm, but the slope (of soil nitrogen) is assumed to be the same for each farm.

```
farms_mod2 <- lme (size ~ N, random = ~ 1 | farm, data = farms)
summary (farms_mod2)

Linear mixed-effects model fit by REML
  Data: farms
      AIC       BIC     logLik
  614.3687 625.4515 -303.1844

Random effects:
 Formula: ~1 | farm
        (Intercept) Residual
StdDev:    8.506147 1.929859

Fixed effects:  size ~ N
              Value Std.Error DF  t-value p-value
(Intercept) 85.56750 2.5406539 95 33.67932       0
N            0.70875 0.0928735 95  7.63133       0
 Correlation:
  (Intr)
N -0.727

Standardized Within-Group Residuals:
       Min          Q1         Med          Q3         Max
-2.79070207 -0.62807448  0.02781053  0.70358230  2.18211935

Number of Observations: 120
Number of Groups: 24
```

Now, we can see that nitrogen and size appear to be positively correlated, as expected. On adding information on soil nitrogen, the total variance (of the random effects) is roughly $8.506^2 + 1.930^2 \approx 76.079$ with $8.506^2/76.079 \approx 95\%$ of this estimated to be due to differences in sizes between farms.

Finally, what if we thought that the effect of soil nitrogen might change from farm to farm? That is, is there an interaction between farm and soil nitrogen in their effect on size of plants? This is equivalent to asking for a random slope (in addition to the random intercept). Here's how we can incorporate this:

```
farms_mod3 <- lme (size ~ N, random = ~ N | farm, data = farms)

Error in lme.formula(size ~ N, random = ~N | farm, data = farms): nlminb
problem,
convergence error code = 1 message = iteration limit reached without
convergence (10)
```

In this case, the model won't run, and we get an error message stating that the model hasn't converged. There are various choices of algorithm underpinning mixed models, all of which depend on a fancy version of trial-and-error until repeated updates no longer improve the estimates. Here, the algorithm hasn't found a point after which the estimates stabilise under the default REML method, but we can try another algorithm instead (and increase the number of iterations from the default of 50–100). This time we try optimising using optim (see ?optim for more information about this algorithm), but ask *R* to print out information about the algorithm using msVerbose = TRUE (the additional information is printed after running the model).

```
farms_mod4 <- lme (size ~ N, random = ~ N | farm, data = farms,
          control = list (msMaxIter = 100 , opt = "optim" , msVerbose = TRUE))
initial  value 417.290973
final  value 417.024640
converged

summary (farms_mod4)
Linear mixed-effects model fit by REML
  Data: farms
      AIC      BIC    logLik
  617.978 634.6021 -302.989

Random effects:
 Formula: ~N | farm
 Structure: General positive-definite, Log-Cholesky parametrization
            StdDev      Corr
(Intercept) 7.29765460 (Intr)
N           0.09435962 0.583
Residual    1.91987488

Fixed effects:  size ~ N
              Value Std.Error DF  t-value p-value
(Intercept) 85.82944 2.3595804 95 36.37488       0
N            0.69860 0.0940528 95  7.42779       0
 Correlation:
  (Intr)
N -0.68

Standardized Within-Group Residuals:
       Min          Q1         Med          Q3         Max
-2.76289733 -0.68265159  0.05158404  0.69169645  2.18451345

Number of Observations: 120
Number of Groups: 24
```

This now works, and we see that the total variance (of the random effects) is about $7.298^2 + 0.094^2 + 1.920^2 \approx 56.95$ with $7.298^2/56.95 \approx 93.5\%$ of this estimated to be due to differences in intercepts and a mere 0.00016% due to differences in slopes. The remaining (residual) variance in size is unexplained. We are also informed that the correlation between the random intercept and random slope is about 0.583. We probably don't need the random slope here, but we could test whether this was the case using the anova () function:

```
anova (farms_mod4, farms_mod2)

           Model df      AIC      BIC    logLik   Test   L.Ratio p-value
farms_mod4     1  6 617.9780 634.6021 -302.9890
farms_mod2     2  4 614.3687 625.4515 -303.1844 1 vs 2 0.3907332  0.8225
```

With a large *p*-value, it seems that our addition of a random slope doesn't really do much and so on balance we would probably prefer the simpler model.

Before we finish up here, we should check that the model fits the data reasonably well. The model checking process is similar in spirit to that for linear models in Section 10.5. We'll look at a plot of standardised residuals vs. fitted values (we would ideally see a cloud-like pattern), the observed vs. fitted values, and QQ-plots to check for normality (the latter for the random intercept *and* for the usual residuals). A nice package for this is `predictmeans` (Luo et al., 2021), which can be used across the mixed models packages.

```
library (predictmeans)
residplot (farms_mod2)
detach (farms)
```

The plots in Figure 13.4 look reasonable here, and we have no strong evidence to suggest that the model is unsuitable.

13.5.2 Multilevel data (three levels)

The following classic example comes from Snedecor, 1989. Three experimental treatments were administered to rats, and the glycogen content of the rats' livers was analysed as the response variable. There were two rats per treatment, so the total sample was $n = 3 \times 2 = 6$. The tricky bit was that after each rat was killed, its liver was cut up into three pieces: a left-hand bit, a central bit, and a right-hand bit. So now there are six rats, each producing three bits of liver, so a total of $6 \times 3 = 18$ bits of liver to analyse. Finally, two separate preparations were made from each macerated bit of liver to assess the measurement error associated with the analytical machinery. There are therefore $2 \times 18 = 36$ observations in the dataframe.

```
rats <- read.table ("rats.txt" , header = T)
attach (rats)
names (rats)

[1] "Glycogen"  "Treatment" "Rat"       "Liver"

head (rats)

  Glycogen Treatment Rat Liver
1      131         1   1     1
2      130         1   1     1
3      131         1   1     2
4      125         1   1     2
5      136         1   1     3
6      142         1   1     3
```

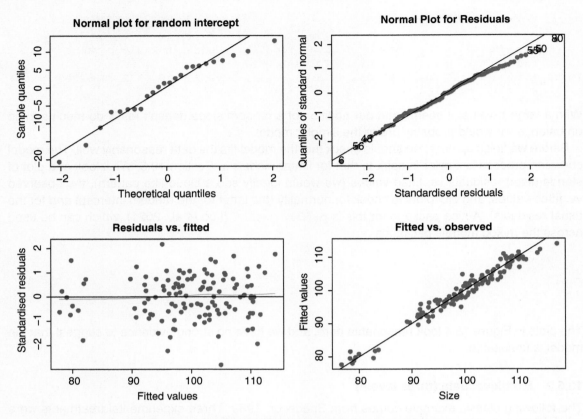

Figure 13.4   Model checking for our chosen two-level model.

The factor levels are numbers, so we need to declare the explanatory variables to be categorical before we begin. Our first problem is that the data are presented with rat coded as either '1' or '2' within each treatment. We need to explicitly tell *R* that we have six *different* rats here rather than two different rats who were each subjected to each treatment.

```
rats$Rat <- factor (Rat)
rats$Liver <- factor (Liver)
rats$Treatment <- factor (Treatment)
rats$rat_num <- cumsum (!duplicated (rats[2:3]))
head (rats, 8)

  Glycogen Treatment Rat Liver rat_num
1      131         1   1     1       1
2      130         1   1     1       1
3      131         1   1     2       1
4      125         1   1     2       1
5      136         1   1     3       1
6      142         1   1     3       1
7      150         1   2     1       2
8      148         1   2     1       2
```

Let us take a closer look at the difference between `Rat` and `rat_num` by producing a table of each of these variables:

```
table (rats$Rat)

 1  2
18 18

table (rats$rat_num)

1 2 3 4 5 6
6 6 6 6 6 6
```

It makes sense to treat 'Treatment' as a fixed effect, but we will probably want to consider 'Rat' and 'Liver' as random effects. Notice here that the samples are nested within 'Liver' which in turn is nested within 'Rat'. We need to take account of this nested structure of the data. We need not only a random effect at the level of the rat but also at the level of liver (which is nested within rat).

Now, we can build our model with treatment as a fixed effect and random effects to account for the structure of observations within liver, nested within rat. Let us use the function `lmer ()` this time from the `lme4` package.

```
library (lme4)
rats_mod1 <- lmer (Glycogen ~ Treatment + (1 | rat_num / Liver), data = rats)
summary (rats_mod1)

Linear mixed model fit by REML ['lmerMod']
Formula: Glycogen ~ Treatment + (1 | rat_num/Liver)
   Data: rats

REML criterion at convergence: 219.6

Scaled residuals:
    Min       1Q    Median       3Q       Max
-1.48212 -0.47263   0.03062  0.42934   1.82935

Random effects:
 Groups         Name         Variance Std.Dev.
 Liver:rat_num  (Intercept)  14.17    3.764
 rat_num        (Intercept)  36.06    6.005
 Residual                    21.17    4.601
Number of obs: 36, groups:  Liver:rat_num, 18; rat_num, 6

Fixed effects:
            Estimate Std. Error t value
(Intercept)  140.500      4.707  29.848
Treatment2    10.500      6.657   1.577
Treatment3    -5.333      6.657  -0.801
```

```
Correlation of Fixed Effects:
           (Intr) Trtmn2
Treatment2 -0.707
Treatment3 -0.707  0.500
```

The output doesn't include *p*-values, but we can see from the rather small t-values that treatment 2 doesn't appear to be significantly different from treatment 1, and neither is treatment 3. This may be due to the size of the dataset, however.

From the output, we can compute the contribution of the various components to the variability in glycogen. We see that the total variance is about $14.17 + 36.06 + 21.17 = 71.40$ and so about 50% of the variation is between rats within treatments, 19.8% is between liver bits within rats and 29.6% is between readings within liver bits within rats.

Once again, we should check that our model is suitable using the `residplot ()` function from `predictmeans`. We can do so as follows, and this time we should specify the level at which we want to do this: level 1 and level 2. The resulting plots are not shown.

```
library (predictmeans)
residplot (rats_mod1, level = 1)
residplot (rats_mod1, level = 2)
detach (rats)
```

13.5.3   Designed experiment: split-plot

The first example is a classic designed experiment set-up, known as a split-plot experiment. We want to model crop yield from the application of three different treatments: irrigation (with two levels, irrigated or not), sowing density (with three levels: low, medium, and high), and fertiliser application (with three levels: low, medium, and high). See Section 16.2.1 for another analysis using these data.

The largest plots were the four whole fields (or **block**), each of which was split in half, and irrigation was allocated at random to one half of the field. Each irrigation plot was split into three, and one of three different seed-sowing densities (low, medium, or high) was allocated at random (independently for each level of irrigation and each block). Finally, each density plot was divided into three, and one of three fertiliser nutrient treatments, N, P, or N and P together, was allocated at random. Each field, therefore, has a yield observation for each combination of the treatments applied.

```
yields <- read.table ("splityield.txt" , header = T)
attach (yields)
head (yields)

  yield block irrigation density fertilizer
1    90    A     control    low        N
2    95    A     control    low        P
3   107    A     control    low       NP
4    92    A     control  medium       N
5    89    A     control  medium       P
6    92    A     control  medium      NP
```

Now, let us think about how we'll analyse these data. The three fertilisers are likely to be of direct interest so it makes sense to incorporate this information as fixed effects. On the other hand, one complicating factor is that we need to account for the effect of a particular field ('block' variable in the data): observations taken from the same field are more likely to be similar to each other than observations from different fields. Unless we take this structure into account we risk losing vital information about the variability in yield between fields. These particular fields are unlikely to be of direct interest in themselves, so we account for this structure using random effects. This is equivalent to having a random intercept for the model.

The fixed-effect part of the model is specified in just the same way as in a straightforward factorial experiment, as below. The random-effect part of the model says that we want the random variation to enter via effects on the intercept, denoted by `1` as per normal. Finally, we define the spatial structure of the random effects after the vertical line (which we read as 'given that density is nested within irrigation, which is nested within block' in this example) reflecting the progressively smaller plot sizes. There is no need to specify the smallest spatial scale (fertiliser plots). Here we extract only the table of estimated coefficients and *p*-values instead of the whole output: with so many covariates the output becomes very cumbersome.

```
library (nlme)
yields_mod1 <- lme (yield ~ irrigation * density * fertilizer,
                    random = ~ 1 | block / irrigation / density)
summary (yields_mod1)$tTable[, c (1, 5)]


                                                     Value        p-value
(Intercept)                                          80.50  8.249709e-16
irrigationirrigated                                  31.75  3.180453e-02
densitylow                                            5.50  5.159119e-01
densitymedium                                        14.75  9.782620e-02
fertilizerNP                                          5.50  4.081089e-01
fertilizerP                                           4.50  4.978391e-01
irrigationirrigated:densitylow                      -39.00  5.712055e-03
irrigationirrigated:densitymedium                   -22.25  7.964592e-02
irrigationirrigated:fertilizerNP                     13.00  1.703904e-01
irrigationirrigated:fertilizerP                       5.50  5.576461e-01
densitylow:fertilizerNP                               3.25  7.285769e-01
densitymedium:fertilizerNP                           -6.75  4.723096e-01
densitylow:fertilizerP                               -5.25  5.756095e-01
densitymedium:fertilizerP                            -5.50  5.576461e-01
irrigationirrigated:densitylow:fertilizerNP           7.75  5.590671e-01
irrigationirrigated:densitymedium:fertilizerNP        3.75  7.770156e-01
irrigationirrigated:densitylow:fertilizerP           20.00  1.367861e-01
irrigationirrigated:densitymedium:fertilizerP         4.00  7.626005e-01
```

We could consider testing whether the three-way interaction was actually important in predicting yield. We can do so with `anova ()`, but this will only work if we compare the models when they have both been fitted with ML rather than REML. This is because the two models have different fixed effects, which REML can't cope with (see Section 13.4.3).

To fit the models with ML rather than REML, we use `method = "ML"` in `lme ()` or `REML = FALSE` in `lmer ()`. Let us re-run the model above, this time fitting with ML rather than REML, then build a simpler model that omits the three-way interaction but keeps the two-way interactions.

```
yields_mod1 <- lme (yield ~ irrigation * density * fertilizer,
                random = ~ 1 | block / irrigation / density, method = "ML")
yields_mod2 <- lme (yield ~ (irrigation + density + fertilizer) ^ 2 ,
                random = ~ 1 | block / irrigation / density, method = "ML")
anova (yields_mod1, yields_mod2)


            Model df      AIC      BIC   logLik   Test  L.Ratio p-value
yields_mod1     1 22 573.5108 623.5974 -264.7554
yields_mod2     2 18 569.0046 609.9845 -266.5023 1 vs 2 3.493788  0.4788
```

With a large *p*-value from the ANOVA, it seems that having the three-way interaction isn't really helping to explain the variability in yield, therefore, it is sensible to omit it.

We can continue this process to simplify the model as necessary. Finally, we may settle on a much simplified model with irrigation, density, and fertiliser as fixed effects, together with irrigation–density and irrigation–fertiliser interactions, which seems almost as good as the second model we considered:

```
yields_mod3 <- lme (yield ~ irrigation * density + irrigation * fertilizer,
                random = ~ 1 | block / irrigation / density, method = "ML")
anova (yields_mod1, yields_mod3)


            Model df      AIC      BIC   logLik   Test  L.Ratio p-value
yields_mod1     1 22 573.5108 623.5974 -264.7554
yields_mod3     2 14 565.1933 597.0667 -268.5967 1 vs 2 7.682562  0.4651

summary (yields_mod3)

Linear mixed-effects model fit by maximum likelihood
  Data: NULL
      AIC      BIC   logLik
 565.1933 597.0667 -268.5967


Random effects:
 Formula: ~1 | block
         (Intercept)
StdDev: 0.0005335774


 Formula: ~1 | irrigation %in% block
         (Intercept)
StdDev:    1.716893


 Formula: ~1 | density %in% irrigation %in% block
         (Intercept) Residual
StdDev:    5.722412 8.718327

Fixed effects: yield ~ irrigation * density + irrigation * fertilizer
                            Value Std.Error DF  t-value p-value
(Intercept)              82.08333  4.756285 44 17.257868  0.0000
irrigationirrigated      27.80556  6.726402  3  4.133793  0.0257
densitylow                4.83333  5.807346 12  0.832279  0.4215
```

```
densitymedium                                   10.66667  5.807346 12  1.836754  0.0911
fertilizerNP                                     4.33333  3.835553 44  1.129781  0.2647
fertilizerP                                      0.91667  3.835553 44  0.238992  0.8122
irrigationirrigated:densitylow                 -29.75000  8.212827 12 -3.622382  0.0035
irrigationirrigated:densitymedium              -19.66667  8.212827 12 -2.394628  0.0338
irrigationirrigated:fertilizerNP                16.83333  5.424290 44  3.103325  0.0033
irrigationirrigated:fertilizerP                 13.50000  5.424290 44  2.488805  0.0167
 Correlation:
                                   (Intr) irrgtn dnstyl dnstym frtlNP frtlzP
irrigationirrigated                -0.707
densitylow                         -0.610  0.432
densitymedium                      -0.610  0.432  0.500
fertilizerNP                       -0.403  0.285  0.000  0.000
fertilizerP                        -0.403  0.285  0.000  0.000  0.500
irrigationirrigated:densitylow      0.432 -0.610 -0.707 -0.354  0.000  0.000
irrigationirrigated:densitymedium   0.432 -0.610 -0.354 -0.707  0.000  0.000
irrigationirrigated:fertilizerNP    0.285 -0.403  0.000  0.000 -0.707 -0.354
irrigationirrigated:fertilizerP     0.285 -0.403  0.000  0.000 -0.354 -0.707
                                   irrgtnrrgtd:dnstyl irrgtnrrgtd:dnstym irr:NP
irrigationirrigated
densitylow
densitymedium
fertilizerNP
fertilizerP
irrigationirrigated:densitylow
irrigationirrigated:densitymedium   0.500
irrigationirrigated:fertilizerNP                       0.000
irrigationirrigated:fertilizerP                        0.000                    0.500

Standardized Within-Group Residuals:
      Min          Q1         Med          Q3          Max
-2.58166957 -0.51480864  0.07893418  0.60157089  2.19570827


Number of Observations: 72
Number of Groups:
                                 block               irrigation %in% block
                                   4                            8
density %in% irrigation %in% block
24

detach (yields)
```

We should also consider whether our chosen model fits the data well and we can do so in the same manner as the previous two examples.

13.5.4 Longitudinal data

A common cause of non-independence between observations is when each individual is measured several times as it grows during the course of an experiment. The next example is as simple as possible: we have a single fixed effect (a two-level categorical variable, with fertiliser added or not) and six replicate plants in each treatment, with each plant measured on five occasions (after 2, 4, 6, 8, and 10 weeks of growth). The response variable is root length, measured non-destructively through a glass panel, which is opened to the light only when the root length measurements are being taken.

```
fert_results <- read.table ("fertilizer.txt" , header = T)
attach (fert_results)
head (fert_results)

  root week plant fertilizer
1  1.3    2   ID1      added
2  3.5    4   ID1      added
3  7.0    6   ID1      added
4  8.1    8   ID1      added
5 10.0   10   ID1      added
6  2.0    2   ID2      added
```

We begin with data inspection. For the kind of data involved in mixed-effects models, there are some excellent built-in plotting functions (variously called panel plots, trellis plots, or lattice plots). To use trellis plotting, we begin by turning our dataframe called `fert_results` into a `grouped-Data ()` object. To do this, we specify the nesting structure of the random effects and indicate the fixed effect by defining `fertilizer` as `outer` to this nesting. Because `fert_results` is now a `groupedData` object, the plotting is fantastically simple:

```
library (nlme)
library (lattice)
fert_results <- groupedData (root ~ week | plant,
                             outer = ~ fertilizer, fert_results)
plot (fert_results)
```

Now, in Figure 13.5, we get separate a plot of growth for each of the individual plants (created, in this case, by joining the dots, which is the default option), with plant identities ranked from bottom left (ID5) to top right (ID7) on the basis of mean root length.

It is often informative to group together the six replicates within each treatment and to have one panel for each of the treatment levels (i.e. one for the fertilised plants and one for the controls in this case). This is very straightforward, using `outer` to indicate the grouping:

```
plot (fert_results, outer = T)
```

It is clear from Figure 13.6 that by week 10, there is virtually no overlap between the two treatment groups. The largest control plant has about the same root length as the smallest fertilised plant (about 9 cm).

Now for the statistical modelling, it makes sense to have fertiliser as a fixed effect, and we ought to account for time in this way too. In the first instance, let us allow a random intercept by plant, and also allow the slope of the growth over the 10-week period to vary by plant. This is probably unnecessary: look at Figure 13.5 or 13.6 and notice that the slopes don't really vary by plant all that much.

In any case, notice the way we now specify the random effects: we use `week | plant`, rather than `1 | plant`, as the latter would give us just a random intercept. Notice also that we once again switch to a different algorithm, `optim`, and increase the number of iterations here to 200 in order for the model to converge.

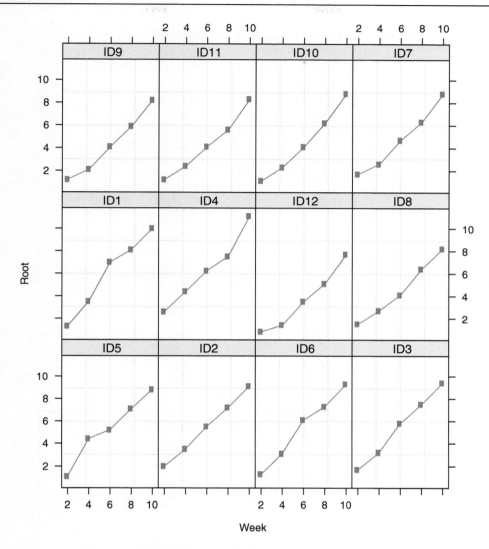

Figure 13.5 Growth over 10 weeks by plant.

Our model is now:

```
fert_mod1 <- lme (root ~ fertilizer + week, random = ~ week | plant,
                  control = list (msMaxIter = 200 , opt = "optim" ))
summary (fert_mod1)
Linear mixed-effects model fit by REML
  Data: NULL
      AIC       BIC      logLik
  117.9317 132.2331 -51.96587

Random effects:
 Formula: ~week | plant
```

```
 Structure: General positive-definite, Log-Cholesky parametrization
            StdDev        Corr
(Intercept) 0.12799038  (Intr)
week        0.03879304  0.755
Residual    0.47643219

Fixed effects:  root ~ fertilizer + week
                    Value    Std.Error DF  t-value   p-value
(Intercept)       -0.0289046 0.18354447 47 -0.15748  0.8755
fertilizercontrol -1.1445241 0.21462754 10 -5.33261  0.0003
week               0.9375000 0.02446016 47 38.32764  0.0000
 Correlation:
                  (Intr) frtlzr
fertilizercontrol -0.585
week              -0.562  0.000

Standardized Within-Group Residuals:
       Min         Q1         Med         Q3         Max
-1.5850053 -0.6309136 -0.1337281  0.5333399  2.2062078

Number of Observations: 60
Number of Groups: 12
```

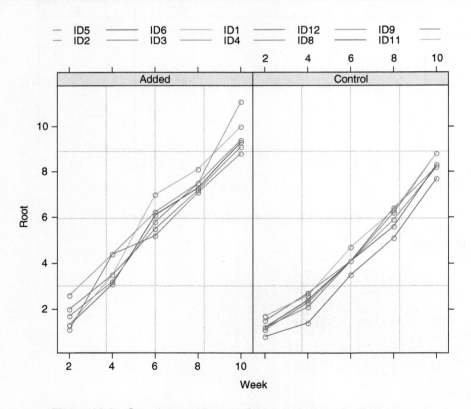

Figure 13.6   Growth over 10 weeks for each plant, by fertiliser status.

The mean reduction in root size associated with the unfertilised controls, in the same week, is estimated to be around 1.14 and this has a standard error of 0.21. Do we really need the random slope, though? Let us build a model without this and use anova () to investigate. Notice here that since we are only changing the random effects structure, we can continue to use REML and still use anova () (see Section 13.4.3 for more information).

```
fert_mod2 <- lme (root ~ fertilizer + week, random = ~ 1 | plant,
                  control = list (msMaxIter = 200 , opt = "optim" ))
anova (fert_mod1, fert_mod2)

          Model df       AIC       BIC     logLik   Test  L.Ratio p-value
fert_mod1     1  7 117.9317 132.2331 -51.96587
fert_mod2     2  5 115.3551 125.5704 -52.67756 1 vs 2 1.423382  0.4908
```

With a *p*-value of around 0.49, there doesn't seem to be much evidence for keeping the random slope, and this tallies with what we saw in Figures 13.5 and 13.6. Let us go with our simpler model, therefore:

```
summary (fert_mod2)

Linear mixed-effects model fit by REML
  Data: NULL
       AIC       BIC     logLik
  115.3551 125.5704 -52.67756

Random effects:
 Formula: ~1 | plant
         (Intercept)  Residual
StdDev:    0.3269795 0.4911157

Fixed effects:  root ~ fertilizer + week
                     Value   Std.Error DF  t-value p-value
(Intercept)       0.0526667 0.20963942 47  0.25123  0.8027
fertilizercontrol -1.3076667 0.22741630 10 -5.75010  0.0002
week               0.9375000 0.02241626 47 41.82231  0.0000
 Correlation:
                  (Intr) frtlzr
fertilizercontrol -0.542
week              -0.642  0.000

Standardized Within-Group Residuals:
       Min         Q1        Med         Q3        Max
-1.7022503 -0.6297164 -0.1275204  0.4571003  2.4393620

Number of Observations: 60
Number of Groups: 12

detach (fert_results)
```

Notice that there is quite a bit of unexplained variation in root size. The total variance is about $0.33^2 + 0.49^2 \approx 0.35$ with $0.49^2/0.35 \approx 69\%$ of this unexplained.

Model checking follows the same procedure as for other examples in this chapter.

13.6   Generalised linear mixed models

We are not restricted to *normal* hierarchical models. Just as we were able to extend the idea of (normal) linear models to generalised linear models, we can extend the idea of (normal) mixed effect models to generalised linear mixed effects models using `lmer ()` with a specified error family.

The default method for fitting generalised linear model is now the Laplace method. The `lmer ()` function can deal with the same error structures as a generalised linear model, namely Poisson (for count data), binomial (for binary data or proportion data), or gamma (for continuous data, where the variance increases with the square of the mean). The model call is just like a mixed-effects model but with the addition of the name of the error family. Some examples of the formulation are the following:

```
glmer (y ~ fixed + (time | random), family = binomial)
glmer (y ~ fixed + (1 | random), family = poisson)
```

Note that the model formula has the same structure as for `lmer ()`, but we're also specifying a family.

13.6.1   Logistic mixed model

In the `bacteria` dataframe, which is part of the `MASS` library (Venables and Ripley, 2002), we have repeated assessment of bacterial infection (yes or no, coded as `y` or `n`) in a series of patients allocated at random to one of three treatments: `placebo`, `drug` and drug plus supplement (`drug+`). The trial lasted for 11 weeks and different patients were assessed on different numbers of occasions. The question is whether the two treatments significantly reduced bacterial infection.

```
library (MASS)
attach (bacteria)
head (bacteria)

  y ap hilo week  ID     trt
1 y  p   hi     0 X01 placebo
2 y  p   hi     2 X01 placebo
3 y  p   hi     4 X01 placebo
4 y  p   hi    11 X01 placebo
5 y  a   hi     0 X02   drug+
6 y  a   hi     2 X02   drug+
```

The data are binary, so we need to use `family = binomial`. There are repeated measures on the same patients so we cannot use `glm ()`. The ideal solution is to use a generalised mixed models function, for which we need `glmer ()`. Like `glm ()`, the `glmer ()` function can take text (e.g. a two-level factor like `y`) as the response variable. We start by looking at the data:

```
table (y, trt)

   trt
y   placebo drug drug+
  n       12   18    13
  y       84   44    49

table (y, week)

   week
y    0  2  4  6 11
  n  5  4 11 11 12
  y 45 40 31 29 32
```

Preliminary data inspection suggests that the drug might be effective because only 12 out of 96 patient visits were bacteria-free in the placebos, compared with 31 out of 124 for the treated individuals. There is also some evidence that week might prove to be important in modelling the outcome too.

The modelling goes like this. It makes sense to have both treatment and week as fixed effects, but let us account for the repeated assessment of patients by introducing a random intercept and allow the slope of week to vary by patient:

```
library (lme4)
bacteria_mod1 <- glmer (y ~ trt + week + (week | ID), family = binomial)
summary (bacteria_mod1)

Generalized linear mixed model fit by maximum likelihood (Laplace
  Approximation) [glmerMod]
 Family: binomial  ( logit )
Formula: y ~ trt + week + (week | ID)

    AIC       BIC   logLik deviance df.resid
  210.6     234.4    -98.3    196.6      213

Scaled residuals:
    Min      1Q  Median      3Q     Max
-4.1130  0.2191  0.2839  0.3840  1.3666

Random effects:
 Groups Name        Variance Std.Dev. Corr
 ID     (Intercept) 0.40495  0.6364
        week        0.01876  0.1369   1.00
Number of obs: 220, groups:  ID, 50

Fixed effects:
            Estimate Std. Error z value Pr(>|z|)
(Intercept)  2.84912    0.63533   4.484 7.31e-06 ***
trtdrug     -1.30207    0.66459  -1.959   0.0501.
trtdrug+    -0.65443    0.70285  -0.931   0.3518
week        -0.08225    0.09085  -0.905   0.3653
```

```
---
Signif. codes:  0 '***' 0.001 '**' 0.01 '*' 0.05 '.' 0.1 ' ' 1

Correlation of Fixed Effects:
         (Intr) trtdrg trtdr+
trtdrug  -0.652
trtdrug+ -0.641  0.512
week     -0.558  0.147  0.223
optimizer (Nelder_Mead) convergence code: 0 (OK)
boundary (singular) fit: see ?isSingular
```

Variation in intercepts across the patients (variance of around 0.41) explained a lot more than that for variation in slopes (variance of around 0.02). In the first instance, let us test whether we really need the random slope.

```
bacteria_mod2 <- glmer (y ~ trt + week + (1 | ID), family = binomial)
anova (bacteria_mod1, bacteria_mod2)

Data: NULL
Models:
bacteria_mod2: y ~ trt + week + (1 | ID)
bacteria_mod1: y ~ trt + week + (week | ID)
              npar    AIC    BIC  logLik deviance  Chisq Df Pr(>Chisq)
bacteria_mod2    5 207.77 224.74 -98.885   197.77
bacteria_mod1    7 210.62 234.37 -98.308   196.62 1.1553  2     0.5612
```

The simpler `bacteria_mod2` is not much worse than the more complex `bacteria_mod1` ($p = 0.56$), so we adopt the simpler model.

```
summary (bacteria_mod2)

Generalized linear mixed model fit by maximum likelihood (Laplace
  Approximation) [glmerMod]
 Family: binomial  ( logit )
Formula: y ~ trt + week + (1 | ID)

    AIC      BIC   logLik deviance df.resid
  207.8    224.7    -98.9    197.8      215

Scaled residuals:
    Min      1Q  Median      3Q     Max
-3.8175  0.1755  0.2958  0.4171  1.2930

Random effects:
 Groups Name        Variance Std.Dev.
 ID     (Intercept) 1.314    1.146
Number of obs: 220, groups:  ID, 50

Fixed effects:
           Estimate Std. Error z value Pr(>|z|)
```

```
(Intercept)  3.14392    0.62249   5.051 4.41e-07 ***
trtdrug     -1.32014    0.64240  -2.055  0.03988 *
trtdrug+    -0.79544    0.65198  -1.220  0.22245
week        -0.14369    0.05099  -2.818  0.00484 **
---
Signif. codes:  0 '***' 0.001 '**' 0.01 '*' 0.05 '.' 0.1 ' ' 1

Correlation of Fixed Effects:
         (Intr) trtdrg trtdr+
trtdrug  -0.618
trtdrug+ -0.580  0.492
week     -0.591  0.118  0.085

detach (bacteria)
```

The interpretation is straightforward: holding week constant, there is evidence in this experiment that the treatment significantly reduces bacterial infection, though curiously there is no evidence that the drug plus supplement regime is any different from the placebo. This might be because the trial is too small to demonstrate the significance of its efficacy.

13.7   Alternatives to mixed models

Random effects aren't the only way to deal with data for which observations aren't independent. Another class of models, **Generalised Estimating Equations** (also known as GEEs), extend the ideas underpinning generalised linear models of Chapter 11.

In mixed models, we explicitly model the random effects: we interpret the output as **subject specific**. That is, we interpret the regression coefficients in terms of the individual units of observation. For GEEs, however, we average over these random effects and so the interpretation of regression coefficients is now **population averaged**. In other words, if we consider the outcome of interest conditional on the covariates in the model, we interpret the GEE output as being averaged over the population.

The advantage of the GEE is that it doesn't suffer the same potential issues with convergence as a mixed model might. The choice of mixed or GEE model should, however, depend on the modelling interest: are we interested in modelling on an individual or population-averaged basis?

An excellent introduction to GEEs can be found in Hardin, 2012 and also in Ziegler, 2011.

References

Bates, D., Mächler, M., Bolker, B., & Walker, S. (2015). Fitting linear mixed-effects models using lme4. *Journal of Statistical Software, Articles, 67*(1), 1–48. https://doi.org/10.18637/jss.v067.i01.

Faraway, J. J. (2016). *Extending the linear model with R: generalized linear, mixed effects and nonparametric regression models / Julian J. Faraway* (Second). CRC Press.

Hardin, J. W. (2012). *Generalized estimating equations / James W. Hardin, Joseph M. Hilbe* (Second). Chapman and Hall/CRC.

Luo, D., Ganesh, S., & Koolaard, J. (2021). *Predictmeans: calculate predicted means for linear models* [R package version 1.0.6]. https://CRAN.R-project.org/package=predictmeans.

Pinheiro, J., Bates, D., DebRoy, S., Sarkar, D., & R Core Team. (2021). *nlme: Linear and nonlinear mixed effects models* [R package version 3.1-152]. https://CRAN.R-project.org/package=nlme.

Snedecor, G. W. (1989). *Statistical methods* (Eighth / George W. Snedecor, William G. Cochran). Blackwell.

Venables, W. N., & Ripley, B. D. (2002). *Modern applied statistics with S* (Fourth) [ISBN 0-387-95457-0]. Springer. https://www.stats.ox.ac.uk/pub/MASS4/.

Ziegler, A. (2011). *Generalized estimating equations / Andreas Ziegler*. Springer.

14

Non-linear Regression

When it comes to building a model, sometimes a *linear* model just won't do, and we resort to using a *non-linear* model instead. These terms might, at first glance, be confusing.

Consider a regression model where we have a covariate x and a response Y, and we choose to transform the covariate (let us say to x^2 to achieve the best *linear* fit between the covariate and response). The model equation looks something like

$$Y = a + bx^2,$$

and if we were to plot the (x, y) relationship, it wouldn't be linear.

Is this still a linear model? It might seem strange, but this is still a linear model because it is *linear in its parameters*, that is, it is linear in a and b. It might help to consider re-labelling x^2 to, say, z. Now, if we were to plot the (z, Y) relationship, we'd see a *linear* relationship. The model is still classed as a linear model.

The same idea goes for the generalised linear models (GLMs) of Chapter 11. These are still *linear* models, as the name suggests, even though the relationship between an outcome (or a function thereof) and the covariates may not appear linear. The format of a GLM, assuming just one covariate here, is

$$g(\mu) = a + bx,$$

where $g()$ is a link function and μ is the expected response given the covariate. This is a *linear* model since $g(\mu)$ is a linear function of the parameters a and b.

It is not always possible to build an adequate model for some relationships through linear models. That is, the sort of relationship required cannot be *linearized* like the example above. This leads to the idea of non-linear models.

Our first problem is that when we move away from linear models, we have an unlimited choice of structure or format for our non-linear model. Unlike linear models, we must explicitly specify the form (or shape) of our non-linear model and then we can consider estimating the parameters therein. Table 14.1 lists some common forms, some of which are also discussed in Section 2.1.6.

Our second problem is that we need to specify an initial guess for each of the parameters in our model, though some common non-linear models have 'self-starting' versions which bypass this step. We consider these later in Section 14.3.

Once we have the format of our model sorted (and starting values, if necessary), then we can use `nls ()` instead of `lm ()` to build our model. Then, instead of say `y ~ x`, we write out the functional form of the model, e.g. `y ~ a - b * exp(-c * x)` to spell out the precise non-linear model we want to fit to the data.

The R Book, Third Edition. Elinor Jones, Simon Harden and Michael J. Crawley.
© 2023 John Wiley & Sons Ltd. Published 2023 by John Wiley & Sons Ltd.
Companion website: www.wiley.com/go/jones/therbook3e

Table 14.1 Useful non-linear functions

Type	Equation
Asymptotic functions	
Michaelis–Menten	$y = \frac{ax}{1+bx}$
two-parameter asymptotic exponential	$y = a(1 - e^{-bx})$
three-parameter asymptotic exponential	$y = a - be^{-cx}$
S-shaped functions	
two-parameter logistic	$y = \frac{e^{a+bx}}{1+e^{a+bx}}$
three-parameter logistic	$y = \frac{a}{1+be^{-cx}}$
four-parameter logistic	$y = a + \frac{b-a}{1+e^{(c-x)/d}}$
Weibull	$y = a - be^{-(cx^d)}$
Gompertz	$y = ae^{-be^{-cx}}$
Humped curves	
Ricker curve	$y = axe^{-bx}$
first-order compartment	$y = k\exp(-\exp(a)x) - \exp(-\exp(b)x)$
bell-shaped	$y = a\exp(-(bx)^2)$
biexponential	$y = ae^{bx} - ce^{-dx}$

A good reference for principles of non-linear models can be found in Seber, 2004, while Ritz, 2008 is an excellent source for non-linear modelling specifically in *R*.

14.1   Example: modelling deer jaw bone length

Our first example requires us to model jaw bone length as a function of age in deer. Our first port of call is to plot the data to see what we're dealing with which is shown in Figure 14.1.

```
jaws <- read.table ("jaws.txt", header = T)
attach (jaws)
names (jaws)
```

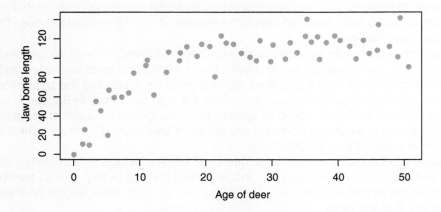

Figure 14.1   A plot of jaw bone length against age of deer

```
[1] "age"   "bone"

plot (age, bone, col = hue_pal () (3) [1],
      ylab = "Jaw bone length" , xlab = "Age of deer")
```

We'll look at two different modelling strategies: initially assuming an exponential relationship (as theory indicates this would be a suitable model), then using the Michaelis–Menten model.

14.1.1   An exponential model for the deer data

Theory indicates that the relationship between age (here denoted x) and jaw bone length (denoted y) is an asymptotic exponential with three parameters (a, b, c):

$$y = a - b \exp(-cx).$$

Our plot in Figure 14.1 provides useful information to work out sensible starting values. It always helps in cases like this to work out the equation's 'behaviour at the limits'–that is to say, to find the values of y when $x = 0$ and when $x = \infty$. For $x = 0$, we have $\exp(-0)$ which is 1, and $1 \times b = b$, so $y = a - b$. For $x = \infty$, we have $\exp(-\infty)$ which is 0, and $0 \times b = 0$, so $y = a$. That is to say, the asymptotic value of y is a, and the intercept is $a - b$.

Inspection suggests that a reasonable estimate of the asymptote is $a \approx 120$ and intercept ≈ 10, so $b = 120 - 10 = 110$. Our guess at the value of c is slightly harder. Where the curve is rising most steeply, jaw length is about 40, where age is 5. Rearranging the equation gives

$$c = -\frac{\log((a - y)/b)}{x} = -\frac{\log(120 - 40)/110)}{5} \approx 0.064.$$

We can check the adequacy of our initial values using the `nlstools` package (Baty et al., 2015), which plots the data together with the curve defined by our initial guesses of parameters. The plot is generated using the `preview ()` function and is shown in Figure 14.2: it looks pretty good. Notice that the function also gives us the residual sum of squares (RSS) for this particular model (the sum of the squared differences between observed and predicted jaw bone length, based on the initial model given).

```
library(nlstools)
preview (bone ~ a - b * exp (-c * age), data = jaws,
         list (a = 120, b = 110, c = 0.064))
```

```
RSS:   15900
```

We go ahead and fit our non-linear model using `nls ()`.

```
jaws_mod1 <- nls (bone ~ a - b * exp (-c * age),
           start = list (a = 120, b = 110, c = 0.064))
summary (jaws_mod1)
```

```
Formula: bone ~ a - b * exp(-c * age)
```

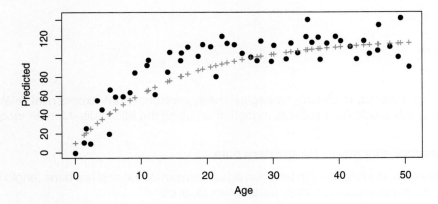

Figure 14.2 A plot of jaw bone length against age of deer, with the model corresponding to the initial values of the parameters superimposed

```
Parameters:
   Estimate Std. Error t value Pr(>|t|)
a 115.2528      2.9139    39.55  < 2e-16 ***
b 118.6875      7.8925    15.04  < 2e-16 ***
c   0.1235      0.0171     7.22 2.44e-09 ***
---
Signif. codes:  0 '***' 0.001 '**' 0.01 '*' 0.05 '.' 0.1 ' ' 1

Residual standard error: 13.21 on 51 degrees of freedom

Number of iterations to convergence: 5
Achieved convergence tolerance: 2.383e-06
```

All parameters appear to be significantly different from zero. Beware, however. This does not necessarily mean that all the parameters need to be retained in the model. In this case, $a = 115.2528$ with standard error 2.9139 doesn't appear all that different from $b = 118.6875$ with standard error 7.8925. So we should try fitting the simpler two-parameter model instead:

$$y = a(1 - e^{-cx}).$$

```
jaws_mod2 <- nls (bone ~ a * (1 - exp (-c * age)),
              start = list (a = 120, c = 0.064), data = jaws)
anova (jaws_mod1, jaws_mod2)

Analysis of Variance Table

Model 1: bone ~ a - b * exp(-c * age)
Model 2: bone ~ a * (1 - exp(-c * age))
  Res.Df Res.Sum Sq Df  Sum Sq F value Pr(>F)
1     51     8897.3
2     52     8929.1 -1 -31.843  0.1825  0.671
```

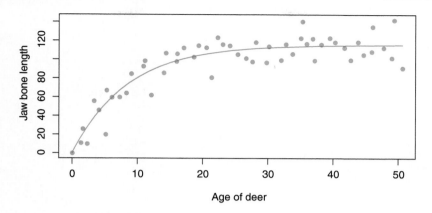

Figure 14.3 The final fitted non-linear model for the deer jawbone data

Model simplification seems justified ($p = 0.671$), so we accept the two-parameter version, jaws_mod2, as our minimal adequate model. We finish by plotting the curve through the scatterplot. A useful function from the `nlstools` package is the `plotfit ()` function which allows us to informally inspect the fit of our model. Note that the data set needs to be specified in the `nls ()` call in order for `plotfit ()` to work. The argument `smooth` instructs that a continuous curve should be plotted as opposed to a sequence of dots. It looks pretty good in Figure 14.3.

```
plotfit (jaws_mod2, smooth = TRUE, ylab = "Jaw bone length" , xlab = "Age of deer",
         col.obs = hue_pal () (3) [1], col.fit = hue_pal () (3) [2], pch.obs = 16)
```

We can use the usual `summary ()` function, or `overview ()` from `nlstools` to get parameter estimates and other information. The latter contains everything that is produced by the former, but with a little more detail (most helpfully, confidence intervals for the parameter estimates).

```
overview (jaws_mod2)

------
Formula: bone ~ a * (1 - exp(-c * age))

Parameters:
   Estimate Std. Error t value Pr(>|t|)
a 115.58056    2.84365  40.645  < 2e-16 ***
c   0.11882    0.01233   9.635 3.69e-13 ***
---
Signif. codes:  0 '***' 0.001 '**' 0.01 '*' 0.05 '.' 0.1 ' ' 1

Residual standard error: 13.1 on 52 degrees of freedom

Number of iterations to convergence: 5
Achieved convergence tolerance: 1.369e-06

------
```

```
Residual sum of squares: 8930

------
t-based confidence interval:
          2.5%        97.5%
a 109.87435953 121.2867506
c   0.09407099   0.1435604


------
Correlation matrix:
           a           c
a  1.0000000 -0.6795024
c -0.6795024  1.0000000
```

Our final fitted model is of the form

$$Y_i = 115.58(1 - \exp(-0.12x_i)) + \epsilon_i,$$

where, approximately, $\epsilon \sim N(0, 13.1^2)$.

14.1.2   A Michaelis–Menten model for the deer data

Model choice is always an important issue in curve fitting. We shall compare the fit of the asymptotic exponential of Section 14.1.1 with a Michaelis–Menten model which is of the form:

$$y = \frac{ax}{1 + bx} .$$

As to starting values for the parameters, it is clear that a reasonable estimate for the asymptote would be 100 (this is a/b). The curve passes close to the point (5, 40), so we can guess a value of a of $40/5 = 8$, and hence, $b = 8/100 = 0.08$. We can check how sensible our starting values are. They don't seem too bad, and roughly the right area, as shown in Figure 14.4.

```
preview (bone ~ a * age / (1 + b * age), data = jaws, list (a = 8, b = 0.08))
```

```
RSS:   82600
```

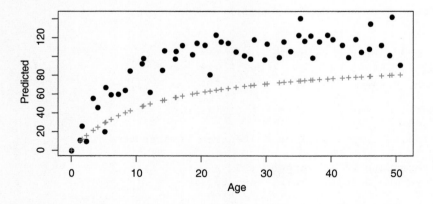

Figure 14.4   Checking the adequacy of the initial values of parameters

Now, use `nls ()` to estimate the parameters:

```
jaws_mod3 <- nls (bone ~ a * age / (1 + b * age), data = jaws, list (a = 8, b = 0.08))
summary (jaws_mod3)

Formula: bone ~ a * age/(1 + b * age)

Parameters:
  Estimate Std. Error t value Pr(>|t|)
a 18.72539    2.52587   7.413 1.09e-09 ***
b  0.13596    0.02339   5.814 3.79e-07 ***
---
Signif. codes:  0 '***' 0.001 '**' 0.01 '*' 0.05 '.' 0.1 ' ' 1

Residual standard error: 13.77 on 52 degrees of freedom

Number of iterations to convergence: 7
Achieved convergence tolerance: 1.553e-06
```

We can check the fit of the model, and the plots don't look too ominous in Figure 14.5, with the possibility that we have a little heteroscedasticity of the variance of the error term, like with the previous model. We'll look at model checking in a little more detail in Section 14.4.1, including using the package `nlstools` to generate these plots directly.

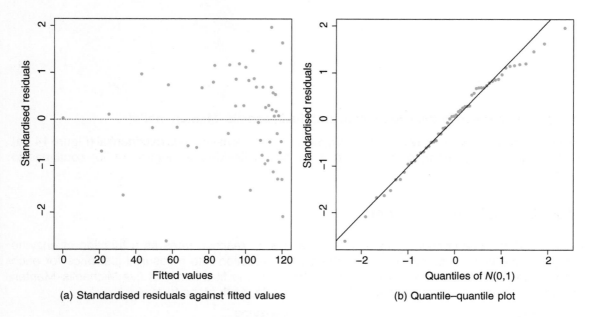

(a) Standardised residuals against fitted values

(b) Quantile–quantile plot

Figure 14.5 Checking the fit of the Michaelis–Menten model for the deer jawbone data

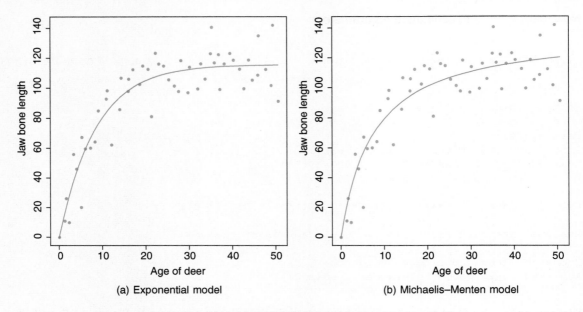

Figure 14.6   Two models for the deer jawbone length data

```
jaws_mod3_resids <- nlsResiduals (jaws_mod3)
plot (nlsResiduals (jaws_mod3)[[2]][,1], nlsResiduals (jaws_mod3)[[2]][,2],
      col = hue_pal ()(3)[1], pch = 16,
      ylab = "Standardized residuals", xlab = "Fitted values")
abline(a=0, b=0, lty=3)
qqnorm (nlsResiduals (jaws_mod3)[[2]][,2], col = hue_pal ()(3)[1], main="", pch = 16,
        ylab = "Standardized Residuals", xlab = "Quantiles of N(0,1)")
qqline (nlsResiduals (jaws_mod3)[[2]][,2])
```

14.1.3   Comparison of the exponential and the Michaelis–Menten model

Finally, we can compare the two models. We can see that the asymptotic exponential (Figure 14.6a) tends to get to its asymptote first, and that the Michaelis–Menten (Figure 14.6b) continues to increase.

14.2   Example: grouped data

Here is a dataframe containing experimental results on reaction rates as a function of enzyme concentration for five different bacterial strains, with reaction rate measured just once for each strain at each of 10 enzyme concentrations. The idea is to fit a family of five Michaelis–Menten functions with parameter values depending on the strain, each of the form:

$$\text{rate} = c + \frac{a \times \text{enzyme}}{1 + b \times \text{enzyme}}.$$

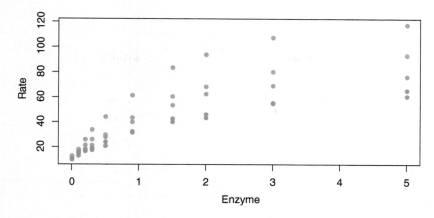

Figure 14.7   Plot of rate by enzyme concentration, for five bacterial strains

Our first port of call is to plot the data. It is clear from Figure 14.7 that the different strains will require different parameter values, but there is a reasonable hope that the same functional form will describe the response of the reaction rate of each strain to enzyme concentration.

```
reaction <- read.table ("reaction.txt", header=T)
attach (reaction)
names (reaction)


[1] "strain" "enzyme" "rate"


plotcol <- hue_pal () (5)
plot (enzyme, rate, pch=16, col = plotcol[strain])
```

We could also plot the data separately by strain, which we can see in Figure 14.8, that we achieve by using the `groupedData ()` function from the `nlme` package (Pinheiro et al., 2021).

```
library (nlme)
reaction <- groupedData (rate ~ enzyme | strain, data = reaction)
plot (reaction, pch=16, col = hue_pal () (1) [1])
```

We'll use the `nlme` package to fit such a model which allows us to fit a model for each of the five strains in the dataset. Note here that this is just a fixed effects model (no random effects as yet): we are just fitting an `nls ()` to each group. The function we need is `nlsList ()`, which fits the same functional form to a group of subjects (as indicated by the horizontal 'given' operator). Figure 14.8 is helpful for choosing starting values. For example, c is the rate when we have no enzyme, and a starting value of $c = 10$ seems reasonable. We could use the `preview ()` function from `nlstools` to experiment with values of a and b. We settle on $a = 20$ and $b = 0.25$.

```
react_mod1 <- nlsList (rate ~ c + a * enzyme / (1 + b * enzyme) | strain,
                       data = reaction, start = c (a = 20, b = 0.25, c = 10))
summary (react_mod1)
```

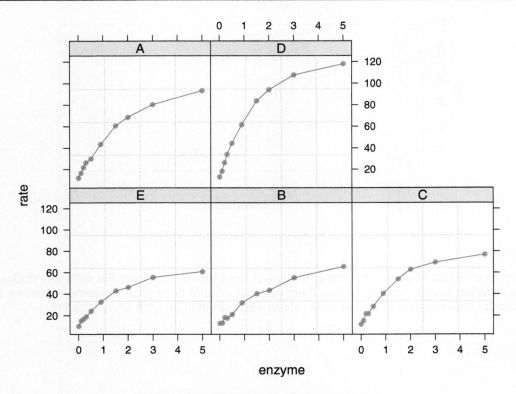

Figure 14.8   Plot of rate, enzyme and strain.

```
Call:
  Model: rate ~ c + a * enzyme/(1 + b * enzyme) | strain
   Data: reaction

Coefficients:
  a
 Estimate  Std. Error    t-value         Pr(>|t|)
E 37.50984    4.840749   7.748768   6.462816e-06
B 26.05893    3.063474   8.506335   2.800345e-05
C 51.86774    5.086678  10.196781   7.842354e-05
A 51.79746    4.093791  12.652687   1.943004e-06
D 94.46245    5.813975  16.247482   2.973297e-06
   b
  Estimate  Std. Error    t value         Pr(>|t|)
E 0.5253479  0.09354863   5.615774   5.412404e-05
B 0.2802433  0.05761532   4.864041   9.173723e-04
C 0.5584897  0.07412453   7.534479   5.150212e-04
A 0.4238572  0.04971637   8.525506   2.728564e-05
D 0.6560539  0.05207361  12.598587   1.634553e-05
   c
  Estimate  Std. Error    t value         Pr(>|t|)
E 10.30139    1.240664   8.303123   4.059886e-06
```

```
B 11.73312    1.120451 10.471780 7.049414e-06
C 10.53219    1.254928  8.392664 2.671650e-04
A 11.46498    1.194155  9.600916 1.244487e-05
D 10.40964    1.294447  8.041767 2.909373e-04

Residual standard error: 1.81625 on 35 degrees of freedom
```

This procedure fitted a non-linear model to each group, but an alternative approach is to build a non-linear model that includes random effects to account for the group structure (see Chapter 13 for further details). It seems that the coefficients *b* and *c* may suffice as fixed effects as the output of `react_mod1` indicated that the coefficient *a* varies quite a bit between strains, but *b* and *c* don't vary all that much. That's what we'll do next.

```
react_mod2 <- nlme (rate ~ c + a * enzyme / (1 + b * enzyme), fixed
           = a + b + c ~ 1, random = a ~ 1 | strain, data = reaction,
           start = c (a = 20, b = 0.25, c = 10))
summary (react_mod2)

Nonlinear mixed-effects model fit by maximum likelihood
  Model: rate ~ c + a * enzyme/(1 + b * enzyme)
  Data: reaction
      AIC    BIC  logLik
  259.5399 269.1 -124.77

Random effects:
 Formula: a ~ 1 | strain
                a Residual
StdDev: 17.15369 2.196028

Fixed effects:  a + b + c ~ 1
     Value Std.Error DF   t-value p-value
a 54.18450  8.314779 43  6.516649       0
b  0.54019  0.034627 43 15.600302       0
c 10.48476  0.672268 43 15.596111       0
 Correlation:
  a       b
b  0.295
c -0.237 -0.622

Standardized Within-Group Residuals:
      Min          Q1         Med         Q3         Max
-2.6753956 -0.5190895  0.1192612  0.6285120  1.8587493

Number of Observations: 50
Number of Groups: 5
```

The fixed effects in this model are the means of the parameter values over the five strains. To see the separate parameter estimates of *a* for each strain, use `coef ()`:

```
coef (react_mod2)

          a         b         c
E 37.96432 0.5401869 10.48476
B 37.79126 0.5401869 10.48476
C 50.93771 0.5401869 10.48476
A 60.25090 0.5401869 10.48476
D 83.97829 0.5401869 10.48476


detach (reaction)
```

The parameter estimates are close to, but not equal to, the values estimated by `nlsList ()`. The efficiency of the random effects model in terms of degrees of freedom is illustrated by contrasting the numbers of parameters estimated by `nlsList ()`, for which we have 15 (three values for each of the parameters) and by `nlme ()`, for which we have five (made up of three parameters plus two variances). This gives residual degrees of freedom of 35 and 45, respectively, for the two models we considered.

14.3 Self-starting functions

One of the most likely things to go wrong in non-linear model is that the model fails because our initial guesses for the starting parameter values were too far off. The simplest solution is to use one of *R*'s 'self-starting' models, which work out the starting values automatically. Table 14.2 lists the most frequently used self-starting functions.

We'll look at examples of using self-starting functions next.

14.3.1 Self-starting Michaelis–Menten model

In our next example, reaction rate is a function of enzyme concentration: reaction rate increases quickly with concentration at first but asymptotes once the reaction rate is no longer enzyme-limited. *R* has a self-starting version called `SSmicmen ()`, parameterised as

$$y = \frac{ax}{b+x},$$

where the two parameters are *a* (the asymptotic value of *y*) and *b* (which is the *x* value at which half of the maximum response, *a*/2, is attained). In the field of enzyme kinetics, *b* is called the Michaelis parameter (in the *R* help file, the two parameters are called `Vm` and `K`, respectively).

Let us load the data and plot it as in Figure 14.9. There's a good case to be made for a non-linear model here, and the shape seems to be in-line with a Michaelis–Menten shaped model.

```
mm <- read.table("mm.txt", header = T)
names (mm)


[1] "conc" "rate"


plot (mm$rate ~ mm$conc, col = hue_pal ()(1)[1],
      xlab = "Concentration", ylab = "Reaction rate")
```

To fit the non-linear model, just put the name of the response variable (`rate`) on the left of the tilde, ~, then put `SSmicmen (conc, a, b))` on the right of the tilde, with the name of the explanatory

Table 14.2 Useful non-linear self-starting functions

Function	Purpose
SSasymp ()	asymptotic regression model
SSasympOff ()	asymptotic regression model with an offset
SSasympOrig ()	asymptotic regression model through the origin
SSbiexp ()	biexponential model
SSfol ()	first-order compartment model
SSfpl ()	four-parameter logistic model
SSgompertz ()	Gompertz growth model
SSlogis ()	logistic model
SSmicmen ()	Michaelis–Menten model
SSweibull ()	Weibull growth curve model

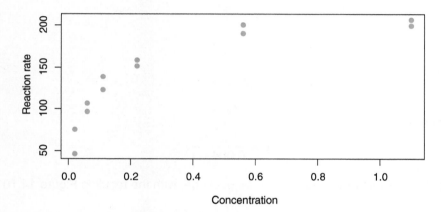

Figure 14.9 Plot of reaction rate by enzyme concentration

variable first in the list of arguments (conc in this case), then the names for the two parameters (*a* and *b*, as defined above):

```
mm_mod1 <- nls (rate ~ SSmicmen (conc, a, b), data = mm)
summary (mm_mod1)


Formula: rate ~ SSmicmen(conc, a, b)

Parameters:
   Estimate Std. Error t value Pr(>|t|)
a 2.127e+02  6.947e+00  30.615 3.24e-11 ***
b 6.412e-02  8.281e-03   7.743 1.57e-05 ***
---
Signif. codes:  0 '***' 0.001 '**' 0.01 '*' 0.05 '.' 0.1 ' ' 1

Residual standard error: 10.93 on 10 degrees of freedom
```

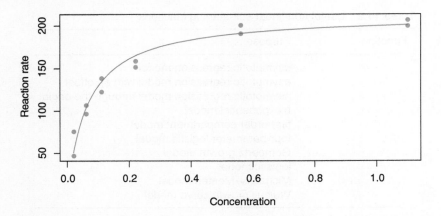

Figure 14.10 Plot of reaction rate by enzyme concentration, with superimposed model

```
Number of iterations to convergence: 0
Achieved convergence tolerance: 1.937e-06
```

So the equation is

$$y = \frac{212.7x}{0.064 + x},$$

and we can plot it like this using the `nlstools` package, with the result in Figure 14.10.

```
plotfit (mm_mod1, smooth = TRUE, ylab = "Reaction rate" , xlab = "Concentration",
         col.obs = hue_pal ()(3)[1], col.fit = hue_pal ()(3)[2], pch.obs = 16)
```

14.3.2 Self-starting asymptotic exponential model

The three-parameter asymptotic exponential is usually written like this:

$$y = a - be^{-cx}.$$

In *R*'s self-starting version, `SSasymp ()`, the parameters are as follows:

- *a* is the horizontal asymptote on the right-hand side (called `Asym` in the *R* help file);
- $b = a - R0$, where *R*0 is the intercept (the response when *x* is zero);
- *c* is the rate constant (the log of `lrc` in the *R* help file).

Here is `SSasymp` applied to the jaws data:

```
jaws <- read.table ("jaws.txt", header = T)
attach (jaws)
names (jaws)


[1] "age"  "bone"


jaws_ss_mod1 <- nls (bone ~ SSasymp (age, a, b, c))
summary (jaws_ss_mod1)


Formula: bone ~ SSasymp(age, a, b, c)

Parameters:
  Estimate Std. Error t value Pr(>|t|)
a 115.2527     2.9139  39.553   <2e-16 ***
b  -3.4348     8.1961  -0.419    0.677
c  -2.0915     0.1385 -15.101   <2e-16 ***
---
Signif. codes:  0 '***' 0.001 '**' 0.01 '*' 0.05 '.' 0.1 ' ' 1

Residual standard error: 13.21 on 51 degrees of freedom

Number of iterations to convergence: 0
Achieved convergence tolerance: 2.45e-07
```

The plot of this fit was shown in Section 14.1.1 along with the simplified model without the parameter *b* which looks unnecessary.

Alternatively, one can use the two-parameter form that passes through the origin, `SSasympOrig` (), which fits the function $y = a(1 - e^{-bx})$. The final form of the asymptotic exponential allows one to specify the function with an offset, *d*, on the *x* values, using `SSasympOff` (), which fits the function $y = a - be^{-c(x-d)}$. For example:

```
jaws_ss_mod2 <- nls (bone ~ SSasympOrig (age, a, b))
summary (jaws_ss_mod2)


Formula: bone ~ SSasympOrig(age, a, b)

Parameters:
  Estimate Std. Error t value Pr(>|t|)
a 115.5805     2.8436   40.65   <2e-16 ***
b  -2.1302     0.1038  -20.52   <2e-16 ***
---
Signif. codes:  0 '***' 0.001 '**' 0.01 '*' 0.05 '.' 0.1 ' ' 1

Residual standard error: 13.1 on 52 degrees of freedom

Number of iterations to convergence: 0
Achieved convergence tolerance: 6.915e-07


detach (jaws)
```

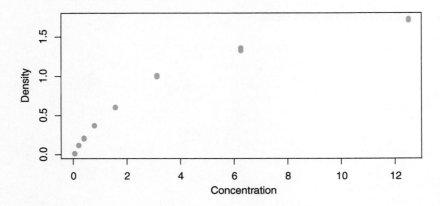

Figure 14.11   Plot of density by concentration

14.3.3 Self-starting logistic

This is one of the most commonly used three-parameter growth models, producing a classic
S-shaped curve. The form of the function is

$$y = \frac{a}{1 + be^{-cx}}.$$

Let us apply this form to a set of data which record the density for differing concentration levels,
which we plot in Figure 14.11.

```
sslogistic <- read.table ("sslogistic.txt", header = T)
attach (sslogistic)
names (sslogistic)


[1] "density"        "concentration"


plot (density ~ concentration, col = hue_pal ()(1)[1],
      xlab = "Concentration", ylab = "Density")
```

We estimate the three parameters (*a*, *b*, *c*) using the self-starting function `SSlogis ()`:

```
sslogis_mod1 <- nls (density ~ SSlogis (log (concentration), a, b, c),
            data = sslogistic)
summary (sslogis_mod1)


Formula: density ~ SSlogis(log(concentration), a, b, c)


Parameters:
  Estimate Std. Error t value Pr(>|t|)
a  2.34518    0.07815    30.01 2.17e-13 ***
b  1.48309    0.08135    18.23 1.22e-10 ***
c  1.04146    0.03227    32.27 8.51e-14 ***
```

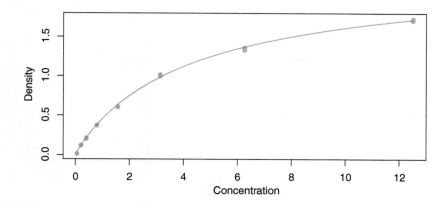

Figure 14.12 Plot of density by concentration, with superimposed model

```
---
Signif. codes:   0 '***' 0.001 '**' 0.01 '*' 0.05 '.' 0.1 ' ' 1

Residual standard error: 0.01919 on 13 degrees of freedom

Number of iterations to convergence: 0
Achieved convergence tolerance: 8.283e-06
```

Here *a* is the asymptotic value, *b* is the mid-value of *x* when *y* is *a*/2, and *c* is the scale.

Now draw the fitted line using `plotfit ()` from the package `nlstools`. We see in Figure 14.12 that the fit is rather good.

```
plotfit (sslogis_mod1, smooth = TRUE, xlab = "Concentration", ylab = "Density",
         col.obs = hue_pal () (3) [1], col.fit = hue_pal () (3) [2], pch.obs = 16)
```

```
detach (sslogistic)
```

14.3.4 Self-starting four-parameter logistic

This model allows a lower asymptote (the fourth parameter) as well as an upper. The four-parameter logistic is given by

$$y = a + \frac{b-a}{1 + \exp\left(\frac{d-x}{c}\right)}.$$

The parameters are *a*, the horizontal asymptote (for low values of *x*); *b*, the horizontal asymptote (for large values of *x*); *d* the value of *x* at the point of inflection of the curve; and *c* is a numeric scale parameter on the x-axis.

The chicks data set contains information on chick weight at varying time points. Applying a four-parameter logistic model to the chicks data we get the following, including the plot in Figure 14.13.

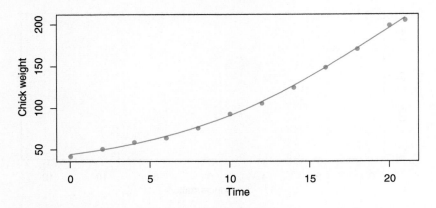

Figure 14.13   Plot of chick weight by time, with superimposed model

```
chicks <- read.table ("chicks.txt" , header = T)
attach (chicks)
names (chicks)


[1] "weight" "Time"


chicks_mod1 <- nls (weight ~ SSfpl (Time, a, b, c, d), data = chicks)
summary (chicks_mod1)


Formula: weight ~ SSfpl(Time, a, b, c, d)

Parameters:
  Estimate Std. Error t value Pr(>|t|)
a   27.453      6.601   4.159 0.003169 **
b  348.971     57.899   6.027 0.000314 ***
c   19.391      2.194   8.836 2.12e-05 ***
d    6.673      1.002   6.662 0.000159 ***
---
Signif. codes:  0 '***' 0.001 '**' 0.01 '*' 0.05 '.' 0.1 ' ' 1

Residual standard error: 2.351 on 8 degrees of freedom

Number of iterations to convergence: 0
Achieved convergence tolerance: 2.476e-07


plotfit (chicks_mod1, smooth = TRUE, ylab = "Chick weight" , xlab = "Time",
         col.obs = hue_pal ()(3)[1], col.fit = hue_pal ()(3)[2],
         pch.obs = 16)


detach (chicks)
```

The parameterised model would be written like this:

$$y = 27.453 + \frac{348.971 - 27.453}{1 + \exp((19.391 - x)/6.673)}.$$

14.4 Further considerations

There are a whole host of other considerations, for example model evaluation, confidence intervals for parameters, and predictions to name but a few. The package `nlstools`, which was useful in checking the form and initial values for a non-linear regression, also contains functionality that is very useful in using and assessing non-linear models.

14.4.1 Model checking

It's prudent to check how well the model actually fits the data which we do by plotting the residuals in various ways. We can use the `nlsResiduals ()` function from `nlstools` to do this, and then plot in the usual way.

There are a range of possible plots, but we only look at those which are useful in this context. Which plots are produced is controlled by the `which` argument. A standardised residuals vs. fitted values plot is generated when `which = 2`, which is useful for checking for evidence of heteroscedasticity of the variance of the error term. A quantile–quantile plot (QQ-plot) is generated when `which = 6`.

Let us apply this to the deer jawbone data from Section 14.1, where we settled on the an exponential model of the form

$$y = a(1 - \exp(-c \times age)).$$

The resulting model was plotted in Figure 14.3 and was referred to as `jaws_mod2` which we'll continue with here for convenience.

We'll start with a standardised residual vs. fitted values plot (checking for evidence of heteroscedasticity), and a QQ-plot (checking for evidence of departure from the assumption of normally distributed errors).

```
library (nlstools)
jaws_mod2 <- nls (bone ~ a * (1 - exp (-c * age)),
                  start = list (a = 120, c = 0.064), data = jaws)
jaws_mod2_resids <- nlsResiduals (jaws_mod2)
plot (jaws_mod2_resids, which = 2)
plot (jaws_mod2_resids, which = 6)
```

The plots in Figure 14.14 aren't too bad, and the model seems to fit reasonably well.

Another question of interest is whether we have any highly influential observations in our data set. Again, we can use `nlstools` to help us here using the `nlsJack` functionality.

```
jaws_mod2_jack <- nlsJack (jaws_mod2)
summary (jaws_mod2_jack)


------
Jackknife statistics
```

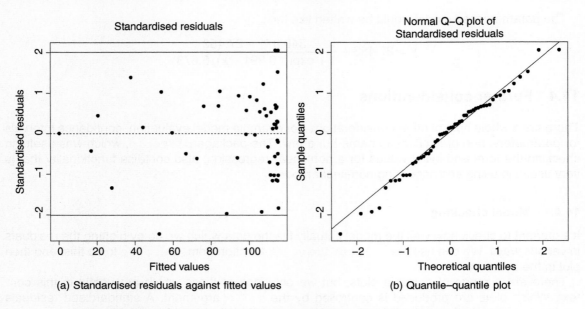

Figure 14.14 Checking the fit of the exponential model for the deer jawbone data

```
    Estimates          Bias
a 115.435903 0.144651976
c   0.117775 0.001040679


------
Jackknife confidence intervals
            Low            Up
a 109.56824584 121.3035604
c   0.09051351   0.1450365


------
Influential values
* Observation 4 is influential on a
* Observation 50 is influential on a
* Observation 53 is influential on a
* Observation 54 is influential on a
* Observation 2 is influential on c
* Observation 16 is influential on c
```

The jackknife procedure flags some possible influential observations and helpfully tells us how they are influential. We shouldn't be too surprised about this here: the data set is small so it's quite natural for there to be some influential observations (Figure 14.14).

This procedure also produces confidence intervals for regression coefficients, but bootstrap (see Section 14.4.2) may be more reliable (Baty et al., 2015).

14.4.2   Confidence intervals

There are many ways of estimating confidence intervals for, e.g. parameter estimates, and we have already seen one possibility in Section 14.4.1. Other methods include **profile confidence intervals** (which attempts to remove the assumption of normality of regression coefficients) and **bootstrapped confidence intervals**. The former can be a little cumbersome. Once again, nlstools provides an easy method for generating the latter. Let us stick to our deer jawbone data again to see it in action.

```
library (nlstools)
jaws_mod2 <- nls (bone ~ a * (1 - exp (-c * age)),
                start = list (a = 120, c = 0.064), data = jaws)
summary (jaws_mod2)


Formula: bone ~ a * (1 - exp(-c * age))

Parameters:
    Estimate Std. Error t value Pr(>|t|)
a 115.58056    2.84365   40.645  < 2e-16 ***
c   0.11882    0.01233    9.635 3.69e-13 ***
---
Signif. codes:  0 '***' 0.001 '**' 0.01 '*' 0.05 '.' 0.1 ' ' 1

Residual standard error: 13.1 on 52 degrees of freedom

Number of iterations to convergence: 5
Achieved convergence tolerance: 1.369e-06

jaws_mod2_boot <- nlsBoot (jaws_mod2)
summary (jaws_mod2_boot)


------
Bootstrap statistics
      Estimate Std. error
a 115.7844936 2.80065156
c   0.1191837 0.01249085


------
Median of bootstrap estimates and percentile confidence intervals
      Median         2.5%         97.5%
a 115.841325 110.2276768 121.3381662
c   0.118575   0.0969314   0.1449641
```

The least squares estimates and bootstrapped estimates of the regression coefficient are very similar, as one would expect.

References

Baty, F., Ritz, C., Charles, S., Brutsche, M., Flandrois, J.-P., & Delignette-Muller, M.-L. (2015). A toolbox for nonlinear regression in R: the package nlstools. *Journal of Statistical Software, Articles*, *66*(5), 1–21. https://doi.org/10.18637/jss.v066.i05.

Pinheiro, J., Bates, D., DebRoy, S., Sarkar, D., & R Core Team. (2021). *nlme: Linear and nonlinear mixed effects models* [R package version 3.1-152]. https://CRAN.R-project.org/package=nlme.

Ritz, C. (2008). *Nonlinear regression with R / Christian Ritz, Jens Carl Streibig*. Springer.

Seber, G. A. F. (2004). *Nonlinear regression / G.A.F. Seber and C.J. Wild*. Wiley.

15

Survival Analysis

A great many studies in statistics deal with deaths or with failures of components: they involve the numbers of deaths, the timing of death, or the risks of death to which different classes of individuals are exposed. The analysis of survival data is a major focus of the statistics business (see Kalbfleisch and Prentice, 2002; Miller et al., 1998; Fleming and Harrington, 2011), for which *R* supports a wide range of tools. The main theme of this chapter is the analysis of data that take the form of measurements of the **time to death**, or the **time to failure** of a component. Up to now, we have dealt with mortality data by considering the proportion of individuals that were dead *at a given time*. In this chapter, each individual is followed until it dies, then the time of death is recorded (this will be the response variable). Individuals that survive to the end of the experiment will die at an unknown time in the future; they are said to be **censored** (as explained below).

15.1 Handling survival data

Since everything dies eventually, it is often not interesting to analyse the results of survival experiments in terms of the proportion that were killed; in due course, they *all* die. We'll use the package `survival` (Therneau and Grambsch, 2000) to handle survival analyses in this chapter which offers a range of functions for graphical representations, hypothesis testing, and model building.

15.1.1 Structure of a survival dataset

Let us start with an example which looks at the changing probability of survival over time. The data come from a study of cancer patients undergoing one of four-drug treatment programmes (drugs A, B, and C and a placebo).

The R Book, Third Edition. Elinor Jones, Simon Harden and Michael J. Crawley.
© 2023 John Wiley & Sons Ltd. Published 2023 by John Wiley & Sons Ltd.
Companion website: www.wiley.com/go/jones/therbook3e

```
library (survival)
cancer <- read.table ("cancer.txt", header = T)
attach (cancer)
head (cancer)

  death treatment status
1     4     DrugA      1
2    26     DrugA      1
3     2     DrugA      1
4    25     DrugA      1
5     7     DrugA      1
6     6     DrugA      0
```

This data set has three variables: `death` indicates time of death, or survival time (some of these death times aren't necessarily deaths, however); `treatment` indicates which treatment the patient had been allocated; `status` indicates any censoring of the death times listed (whether the death time is an actual death, or the last time the patient was seen). The 'event' of interest here is death, as morbid as that may be, and our goal might be to model the time to event for example.

Let us first look at the variable `death`, the time of death, or survival time. Its distribution is skewed, as we can see from the histogram in Figure 15.1a, and the times themselves are of course always positive. Any analysis we use needs to be able to handle these key features of the data. We could also view this information using a so-called **Kaplan–Meier plot**, which is given in Figure 15.1b. This represents the proportion still alive at particular times. Notice that the function decreases each time a death is observed, creating a stepped pattern. The Kaplan–Meier plot is discussed in more detail in Section 15.2.1.

More interesting, perhaps, is to split death times according to `treatment`. This would allow us to assess whether treatment had any effect on survival time. A nice way of viewing this information is via a Kaplan–Meier plot, which is given in Figure 15.2a, but this time we have one Kaplan–Meier function for each drug.

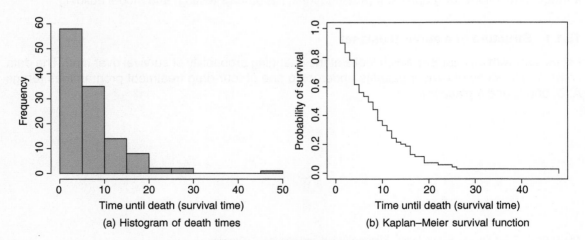

(a) Histogram of death times

(b) Kaplan–Meier survival function

Figure 15.1   Plots of time until death, or survival time

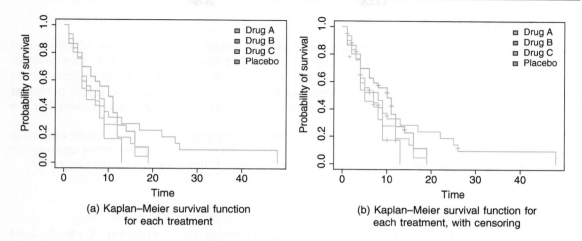

(a) Kaplan–Meier survival function
for each treatment

(b) Kaplan–Meier survival function for
each treatment, with censoring

Figure 15.2 Survival of different groups of patients over time

It is clear that the treatments caused different patterns of mortality, but all four start out with 100% survival, and if we continued the study indefinitely, all four would end up with zero. We could pick some arbitrary point in the middle of the distribution at which to compare the percentage survival, but this may be difficult in practice because the treatments might have few observations at the same location. Also, the choice of when to measure the difference is entirely subjective and hence open to bias. It is much better to use R's powerful facilities for the analysis of survival data than it is to pick an arbitrary time at which to compare two proportions.

A complicating feature of survival data is that the time to event for every observation may not be known. This is known as **censoring**. This comes about principally because some individuals outlive the experiment, while others leave the experiment before they die. Another reason for censoring occurs when individuals are lost from the study: they may be killed in accidents, they may emigrate, or they may lose their identity tags. We know when we last saw them alive, but we have no way of knowing their age at death. In general, then, our survival data may be a mixture of times at death and times after which we have no more information on the individual. We deal with this by setting up an extra variable called the **censoring indicator** to distinguish between the two kinds of numbers. If a time really is a time to death, then the censoring indicator takes the value 1. If a time is just the last time we saw an individual alive, then the censoring indicator is set to 0.

The column `status` in our cancer data tells us whether an observation is the death time of an individual (as is the case for the first five), or whether the observation was censored (as it is for the sixth individual). Censorship in this case may have happened because the individual dropped out of the study but is actually still alive, or they may have died, but this was not recorded.

We can update the plot in Figure 15.2a to include information about censoring: such times are marked by a cross in Figure 15.2b. A cross denotes the last time we saw an individual, but we do not know what happened to them afterwards. These individuals contribute *something* to our knowledge of survival, so we do not remove these observations from our data set, but we do need to ensure that they are appropriately handled.

Often, in a survival analysis, our aim is to understand the role of covariates in influencing the time until an event. In our cancer example, our only covariate is the treatment type. We're not limited to just one covariate, nor are we limited to only categorical covariates. In Section 15.3, we'll consider how to build a (regression) model for time to event data using any number of covariates.

15.1.2 Survival data in *R*

The survival package in *R* contains a suite of tools to model survival data with which we can create graphics as in Figure 15.2. It also allows us to estimate important quantities in survival analysis (Section 15.2) and build models for our time-to-event data (Section 15.3). But before we do any of this, we need to ensure that *R* knows that we are dealing with survival data, and in particular which variable contains information on survival time and which holds information on whether the observation was censored.

This is achieved using the Surv () command from the package survival, which creates a survival object in *R*. Its arguments are the time until an event (time), and whether the observation is censored (event). For our cancer data, the following gives *R* the necessary information:

```
Surv (time = death, event = status)
```

It makes sense that the object that results – information on time to death/censoring – is usually used as the *outcome* variable in a survival analysis, and we'll frequently use Surv () inside other survival functions.

15.2 The survival and hazard functions

There are two important quantities that are of interest in the analysis of survival data: the **survival function** and the **hazard function**. Both describe the distribution of time until an event, but in different ways. These will form the basis of an analysis. Initial analysis (including graphical representations and basic hypothesis testing) generally involves the survival function, whereas any modelling of survival data usually boils down to modelling the hazard function:

- The survival function at time *t*, $S(t)$, is the probability that an individual will survive beyond time *t*.

- The hazard function at time *t*, $h(t)$, is the instantaneous risk of an event at time *t*, given that the individual has survived up until time *t*. This is not a probability, but it is a measure of risk: the greater the hazard, the greater the risk.

The survival and hazard functions are, of course, closely related. For those familiar with the idea of derivatives, the relationship is described by

$$h(t) = -\frac{\partial}{\partial t} \log S(t),$$

but we needn't worry about this detail as *R* does all the hard work for us.

The usual starting point for a survival analysis is to estimate and plot the survival function. Figure 15.2 shows the (empirical) survival function per treatment for our cancer data, one for each treatment group. Notice how the survival function – the probability of surviving beyond a particular time – is decreasing with time but at different rates for the various drug groups, and we can immediately see that patients taking drug A are more likely to survive beyond 20 units of time. With this much information available at-a-glance from a plot of the (estimated) survival function, it is no wonder that they are a popular tool in the analysis of time-to-event data and often the first port of call.

We may want to plot the survival function for all observations, or we may want to compare between groups as we did for our cancer data. Either way, there are two broad options in estimating the survival function: we can choose not to make distributional assumptions about it (so-called *non-parametric* estimation), or alternatively, make assumptions about its form (so-called *parametric* estimation). The former is far more common, especially as an initial analysis.

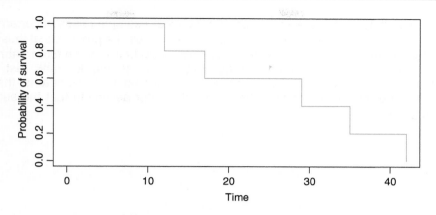

Figure 15.3   Survival function for the toy data set

15.2.1   Non-parametric estimation of the survival function

The most common non-parametric estimation technique for the survival function is that given by Kaplan–Meier. This gives a stepped survival function that accrues information as each death occurs. Indeed, we have already seen such an example in Figure 15.2a (without displaying censoring) and Figure 15.2b (displaying censoring).

It is, perhaps, easier to understand how the Kaplan–Meier survival function is generated by considering a toy example. Suppose we had $n = 5$ individuals and that the times at death were 12, 17, 29, 35, and 42 weeks after the beginning of a trial. The probability of survival remains at 1 until the first death at time 12. The curve then steps down to 0.8 because 80% of the initial cohort is now alive. It continues at 0.8 until time 17 when the curve steps down to 0.6 (40% of the individuals are now dead), and so on, until all of the individuals are dead at time 42. This stepped survival function is shown in Figure 15.3.

In general, therefore, we have two variables at any one time: the number of deaths and the number at risk (i.e. those that have not yet died: the survivors). The Kaplan–Meier survivor function then produces a step at every time at which one or more deaths occurs.

Censoring complicates matters a little, but it is easy enough for *R* to denote censored observations on the plot by inserting a cross as we saw in Figure 15.2b. However, these aren't *events* per se, so we need to adjust the number at risk. This makes sense: if an observation is censored, then it is not at risk so we reduce this accordingly. Therefore, the number at risk changes not only when we observe a death but also when we consider a censored observation.

All these calculations are automated in *R* with the `survfit ()` function. The plots in Figure 15.2 were produced by creating an object `cancer_surv` (notice the use of `Surv ()` here) before plotting. The statement `mark.time` requests that censored observations be marked on the plot (using a cross), which then gives us Figure 15.2b.

```
cancer_surv <- survfit (Surv (death, status) ~ treatment, type = "kaplan-meier")
plot (cancer_surv, ylab = "Probability of survival", xlab = "Time",
      mark.time = TRUE, col = hue_pal () (4) [1:4])
legend ("topright", legend = c ("Drug A", "Drug B", "Drug C", "Placebo"),
        fill = hue_pal () (4) [1:4], bty = "n")
```

Comparing survival functions between groups in our cancer example raises important questions. Did patients on drug A live longer than those on the placebo? Are the prospects of those on drug B different to those on drug C? Is there any difference in survival between the four treatments?

The most common statistical procedure applicable here is the log-rank test. This is a non-parametric test and can cope with censored observations. It compares the observed and expected number of deaths for each treatment, the latter assuming that the survival is the same for each group.

```
compare_treat <- survdiff (Surv (death, status) ~ treatment)
compare_treat

Call:
survdiff(formula = Surv(death, status) ~ treatment)

                    N Observed Expected (O-E)^2/E (O-E)^2/V
treatment=DrugA    30       25     30.4     0.960     1.838
treatment=DrugB    30       25     27.5     0.226     0.373
treatment=DrugC    30       25     20.2     1.131     1.658
treatment=placebo  30       21     17.9     0.543     0.802

Chisq = 3.6 on 3 degrees of freedom, p = 0.3

detach (cancer)
```

Here, with a *p*-value of 0.3, there is no evidence that the survival functions differ between the four groups. This may come as a surprise, given the plot in Figure 15.2b. If we look closely, however, only 5 of the 30 individuals on drug A survived beyond time 20. This makes the survival curve for drug A look better, but is based on a small number of observations.

15.2.2 Parametric estimation of the survival function

If we are confident that the survival function will behave in a predictable way, parametric estimation may be suitable. Common distributions include the Exponential, Weibull, Gompertz, log-Logistic, among many others. Each has its own set of characteristics, which should be carefully considered if contemplating parametric estimation of the survival function. The format of these survival functions are given in Table 15.1, and examples are given in Figure 15.4.

Given that there is a close relationship between the survival and hazard functions, if we model the survival function using a particular distribution (as we have done in Figure 15.4), then this also tells us what the associated hazard function looks like (Figure 15.5). The simplest of these distributions – the Exponential – gives a *constant* hazard over time, while the other hazard functions

Table 15.1 Common parametric forms of the survival and hazard functions

Distribution	Survival function	Hazard function
Exponential	$\exp(-at)$	a
Weibull	$\exp(-(at)^b)$	$ab(at)^{b-1}$
Gompertz	$\exp(-(a/b)(\exp(bt)-1))$	$a\exp(bt)$
log-Logistic	$1/(1+at^b)$	$(abt^{b-1})/(1+at^b)$

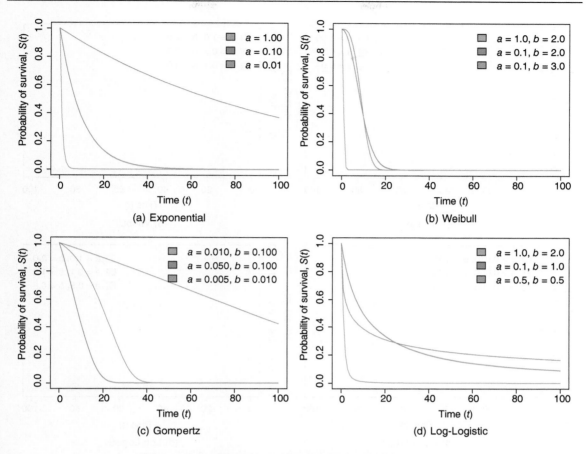

Figure 15.4   Examples of (parametric) survival functions

change over time. Plotting parametric survival or hazard functions requires first building a (parametric) model, which we'll do in Section 15.3.

15.3   Modelling survival data

Modelling survival data generally means modelling failure times using *regression models*. This allows us to model the effect of covariates on the failure time. The most common models for survival data are proportional hazard (PH) models in medical applications, while accelerated failure time (AFT) models are more common in other applications (e.g. in engineering).

Proportional hazard models model the hazard function and take the form

$$h(t|\mathbf{x_i}) = h_0(t) \exp(\beta_0 + \beta_1 x_{i1} + \cdots + \beta_p x_{ip}) = h_0(t) \exp(\mathbf{x_i^T} \beta). \tag{15.1}$$

The function $h_0(t)$ describes the baseline hazard of failure for all individuals and in particular is not dependent on the covariates (think of this as setting all covariates equal to zero). Our specific choice of model will dictate the form of $h_0(t)$. The remaining term may or may not have an intercept,

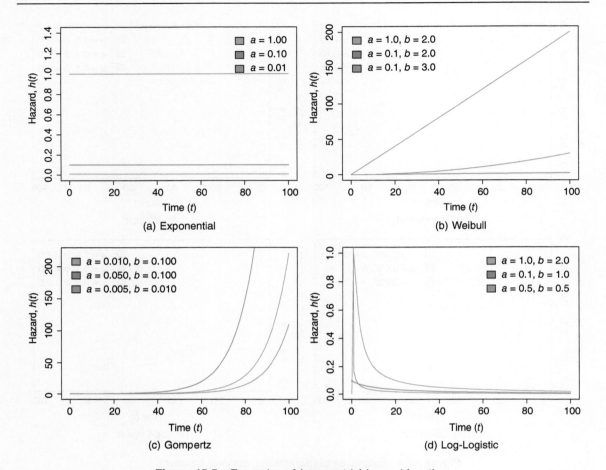

Figure 15.5 Examples of (parametric) hazard functions

again depending on our choice of model. Notice that the covariates (and indeed the regression coefficients) are fixed and do not vary with time in this set-up.

The term 'proportional hazard' comes from the idea that changing the covariates $\mathbf{x}_1$ to $\mathbf{x}_2$ results in a new hazard function $h(t|\mathbf{x}_2)$ that is *proportional* to the original hazard function $h(t|\mathbf{x}_1)$. That is, the ratio of these two hazards is constant over t, see Box 15.1 for details. This is shown graphically by the blue line in Figure 15.6.

Box 15.1: Proportional hazards

We can see that under the model in equation (15.1), the ratio of two hazard functions using the sets of covariates $\mathbf{x}_1$ and $\mathbf{x}_2$ is

$$\frac{h(t|\mathbf{x}_2)}{h(t|\mathbf{x}_1)} = \frac{h_0(t)\exp(\mathbf{x}_2^{\mathsf{T}}\beta)}{h_0(t)\exp(\mathbf{x}_2^{\mathsf{T}}\beta)} = \frac{\exp(\mathbf{x}_2^{\mathsf{T}}\beta)}{\exp(\mathbf{x}_1^{\mathsf{T}}\beta)}.$$

That is, a constant, thereby the hazards are said to be proportional.

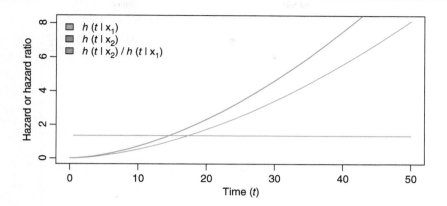

Figure 15.6 Hazard functions (or ratios) over time

Accelerated failure time models consider the time to event, T, and are usually written in the form

$$\log T_i = \alpha_0 + \alpha_1 x_{i1} + \cdots + \alpha_p x_{ip} + \sigma \epsilon_i , \qquad (15.2)$$

for which we choose a particular distribution for ϵ_i, where for some distributions, a scalar σ is required. It is perhaps easier to see the similarities and differences between the PH and AFT models if we re-write equation (15.2) in terms of the hazard function. This gives

$$h(t|\mathbf{x}_i) = h_0(t \exp(-\mathbf{x}_i^\mathsf{T} \alpha)) \exp(-\mathbf{x}_i^\mathsf{T} \alpha). \qquad (15.3)$$

These model classes are not mutually exclusive. Some models are both PH *and* AFT models.

We'll start by looking at the most common PH model, the **Cox proportional hazard model** in Section 15.3.2, which is the most common model in medicine. AFT models are then discussed in Section 15.3.3. But before doing this, let us take a look at another survival data set which we'll use for building models. This time we have two possible covariates to consider, unlike our cancer data set which had only one.

15.3.1 The data

We'll apply these techniques on the `roaches` data set. This contains three groups of insects (labelled A, B, and C), their weight, and time until death. Our aim is to understand the impact of insect group and weight on the insects' survival time.

```
roaches <- read.table ("roaches.txt", header = TRUE)
attach (roaches)
summary (roaches)

     death            status            weight         group
Min.   : 1.00    Min.    :0.0000    Min.   : 0.055    A:50
1st Qu.: 1.00    1st Qu.:1.0000    1st Qu.: 2.459    B:50
Median : 7.00    Median :1.0000    Median : 6.316    C:50
Mean   :15.17    Mean    :0.8667    Mean    : 9.390
3rd Qu.:21.00    3rd Qu.:1.0000    3rd Qu.:11.955
Max.   :50.00    Max.    :1.0000    Max.    :42.090
```

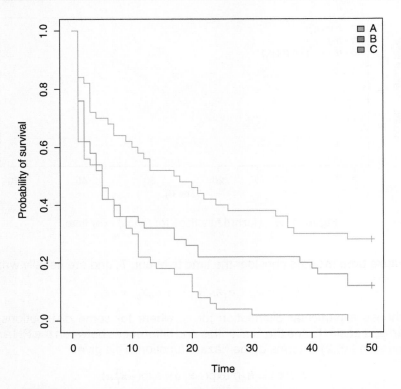

Figure 15.7 Kaplan–Meier survival for the three groups of insects

First, we plot the Kaplan–Meier curves of the three groups, which is displayed in Figure 15.7. There are clearly big differences between the death rates in the three groups. The crosses + at the end of the survivorship curves for groups A and B indicate that there was censoring in these groups (not all of the individuals were dead at the end of the experiment). We've not considered the covariate `weight` yet, which we'll do in the following sections, first using a Cox proportional hazard model in Section 15.3.2 and then using an accelerated failure time model in Section 15.3.3.

15.3.2 The Cox proportional hazard model

This is the most widely used regression model for survival data, which has the same basic form as that in equation (15.1). The Cox proportional hazard model doesn't assume a specific form for the baseline hazard, $h_0(t)$. These models are therefore known as **semi-parametric models** (we still make parametric assumptions on how the covariates act upon failure times, but not on the baseline hazard, hence *semi*-parametric). Usually, our main interest is in understanding how the covariates impact failure times, and not on the baseline hazard, which may explain the popularity of this class of models.

We can use the function `coxph ()` to fit a Cox proportional hazard model to our roaches data.

```
roach_model_ph1 <- coxph (Surv (death, status) ~ weight + group)
summary (roach_model_ph1)


Call:
coxph(formula = Surv(death, status) ~ weight + group)

  n= 150, number of events= 130

           coef exp(coef)  se(coef)      z Pr(>|z|)
weight 0.007425  1.007453  0.009953  0.746   0.4557
groupB 0.507645  1.661374  0.237918  2.134   0.0329 *
groupC 0.967882  2.632362  0.233350  4.148 3.36e-05 ***
---
Signif. codes:  0 '***' 0.001 '**' 0.01 '*' 0.05 '.' 0.1 ' ' 1

       exp(coef) exp(-coef) lower.95 upper.95
weight     1.007     0.9926    0.988    1.027
groupB     1.661     0.6019    1.042    2.648
groupC     2.632     0.3799    1.666    4.159


Concordance= 0.608  (se = 0.03)
Likelihood ratio test= 21.09  on 3 df,   p=1e-04
Wald test             = 20.54  on 3 df,   p=1e-04
Score (logrank) test = 21.69  on 3 df,   p=8e-05
```

The output gives us both the estimated regression coefficients, `coef`, the exponentiated coefficients, `exp(coef)`, together with other information relating to the coefficients (hypothesis tests and the upper and lower bound of the 95% confidence interval). The final part of the output gives a popular measure of goodness-of-fit of the model (`Concordance`), together with three hypothesis tests for the model overall (the likelihood ratio, Wald, and Score (logrank) tests). The concordance gives the proportion of all pairs of observations for which the predicted survival times of a pair are in the same order as was observed. That is if the pair in question is observations 1 and 2, and the death time of observation 1 is larger than for observation 2, then the pair is concordant if the predicted survival time of observation 1 is also larger than that for observation 2. The following three hypothesis tests compare the model with removing all covariates: it asks whether a model with no predictors is (almost) as good as our model. If we get a large p-value here, we are in trouble: it tells us that the covariates aren't really doing anything to explain survival time. All three tests listed here are *asymptotically* equivalent, meaning as the sample size grows, the p-values they produce will coincide.

Note that `weight` doesn't appear to be particularly influential, so we remove this covariate. The resulting model is

```
roach_model_ph2 <- coxph (Surv (death, status) ~ group)
summary (roach_model_ph2)


Call:
coxph(formula = Surv(death, status) ~ group)

  n= 150, number of events= 130

        coef exp(coef)  se(coef)      z Pr(>|z|)
```

```
groupB 0.5607     1.7520     0.2257 2.485     0.013 *
groupC 1.0084     2.7412     0.2263 4.456 8.33e-06 ***
---
Signif. codes:  0 '***' 0.001 '**' 0.01 '*' 0.05 '.' 0.1 ' ' 1

       exp(coef) exp(-coef) lower.95 upper.95
groupB     1.752     0.5708     1.126     2.727
groupC     2.741     0.3648     1.759     4.271

Concordance= 0.607  (se = 0.027)
Likelihood ratio test= 20.55  on 2 df,     p=3e-05
Wald test             = 19.86  on 2 df,     p=5e-05
Score (logrank) test = 20.98  on 2 df,     p=3e-05
```

Notice here that no information is given about the baseline hazard. This is treated almost like a nuisance parameter, and only information relating to the covariates is presented. To this end, our estimated hazard is of the form

$$h(t|\mathbf{x_i}) = h_0(t)\exp(0.56 \times \text{groupB}_i + 1.01 \times \text{groupC}_i)$$

Evidently, insects in group A lived longer than those in either group B or C (positive regression coefficients): the hazard of death for those from groups B or C is higher than that for A.

Although we've fitted a proportional hazards model, and not made assumptions about the form of the baseline hazard, we should check whether proportional hazards are a reasonable assumption. The function cox.zph () allows us to do this and obtain both formal hypothesis tests and graphical displays for this purpose.

```
roach_ph <- cox.zph (roach_model_ph2)
print (roach_ph)

       chisq df  p
group   1.82  2 0.4
GLOBAL  1.82  2 0.4

plot (roach_ph)
```

The *p*-values we see check the covariates individually, as well as a global check of the PH assumption. As the null hypothesis is that the hazards are proportional, the *p*-values here give us no cause for concern. The plots in Figure 15.8 look at a particular type of *residual* (specifically the *Schoenfeld* residuals) against time. Given that we are assuming proportional hazards, the regression coefficients should be constant over time, and so the solid black line should be (close to) horizontal. When this is not the case, proportional hazards is a dubious assumption to make. Here, it doesn't seem too bad an assumption. Of course, no such plot with real data will ever give us totally horizontal lines so this is a judgement call (the *p*-values help here!).

15.3.3 Accelerated failure time models

Unlike the (semi-parametric) Cox proportional hazard model, AFT models are *parametric*: they make assumptions about the form of the baseline hazard and how the covariates impact the survival

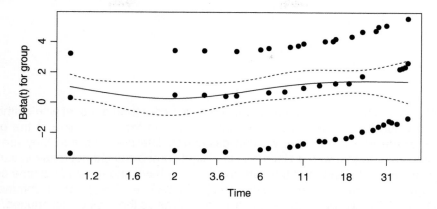

Figure 15.8 Graphic check of PH assumption

time. Just as we had to ensure that the proportional hazard assumption was reasonable in Section 15.3.2, here it is likely that we'll need to try a range of distributions to see which fits the data best.

That AFT models in equation (15.2) can be fit using the `survreg ()` command for which we need to specify the distribution to be used. Distributional options include Exponential, Weibull, Gaussian, Logistic, log-Normal, and log-Logistic. We'll consider the Exponential and Weibull options for our roaches data.

The exponential model, which assumes that T has an Exponential distribution, is actually one of the simplest AFT models. Here, $\sigma = 1$ in equation (15.2), and recall that under this assumption, the (baseline) hazard is constant (see Table 15.1) which we can write as, say, $\exp(-\alpha_0)$ so that the notation is consistent with that in equation (15.2). Rewriting the exponential AFT model in terms of the hazard function, as we did in equation (15.3):

$$h(t|\mathbf{x_i}) = \exp(-\alpha_0 - \alpha_1 x_{i1} - \cdots - \alpha_p x_{ip}) \,.$$

Notice that this model automatically satisfies the PH assumption and could be called an 'exponential proportional hazards model'. So that it is of the same form as in equation (15.1), we take $\beta_j = -\alpha_j$: this proportional hazards model is a re-parameterisation of the AFT model.

Fitting the exponential AFT model in R, we get the following:

```
roach_model_exp1 <- survreg (Surv (death, status) ~ weight + group,
                     dist = "exponential")
summary (roach_model_exp1)

Call:
survreg(formula = Surv(death, status) ~ weight + group, dist = "exponential")
            Value Std. Error      z       p
(Intercept)  3.51541    0.17340 20.27  < 2e-16
weight      -0.01002    0.00993 -1.01     0.31
groupB      -0.60456    0.23564 -2.57     0.01
groupC      -1.32170    0.22889 -5.77 7.7e-09

Scale fixed at 1
```

```
Exponential distribution
Loglik(model)= -481.5   Loglik(intercept only)= -502.1
Chisq= 41.35 on 3 degrees of freedom, p= 5.5e-09
Number of Newton-Raphson Iterations: 5
n= 150
```

The output tells us that the model with both covariates is better than a model with neither covariate included (the p-value for this likelihood ratio test is given in the `Chisq` line of the output). The estimates are for the AFT model, but we can easily translate these so that they are for the PH model as above. We see that with an increase in weight comes a slight decrease in survival (small negative regression coefficient), and that Groups B and C have shorter survival time compared to the reference group A (again, negative coefficients). The `Scale fixed at 1` comment refers to $\sigma = 1$ in equation (15.2). Allowing σ to deviate from one gives us the Weibull distribution, so it makes sense to try that next.

Like the exponential model, the Weibull AFT model also satisfies the PH assumption, but these are the only two distributions to have this property. The connection between the estimates that `survreg ()` give and the proportional hazards parameterisation of the model is a little more involved this time; we won't go into detail here.

```
roach_model_weil <- survreg (Surv (death, status) ~ weight + group)
summary (roach_model_weil)

Call:
survreg(formula = Surv(death, status) ~ weight + group)
               Value Std. Error     z        p
(Intercept)   3.5149      0.2370 14.83  < 2e-16
weight       -0.0115      0.0135 -0.85    0.395
groupB       -0.7401      0.3248 -2.28    0.023
groupC       -1.4701      0.3129 -4.70 2.6e-06
Log(scale)    0.3119      0.0704  4.43 9.4e-06

Scale= 1.37

Weibull distribution
Loglik(model)= -470.1   Loglik(intercept only)= -483.3
Chisq= 26.34 on 3 degrees of freedom, p= 8.1e-06
Number of Newton-Raphson Iterations: 5
n= 150
```

The fact that the scale parameter is greater than 1 indicates that the risk of death increases with time in this case (which makes sense given the context). Is the scale parameter significantly different from one? This would imply that the Weibull is superior to the exponential model which fixes $\sigma = 1$. The output indicates that it is: a hypothesis test for the logarithm of the scale being zero is given – equivalent to testing whether the $\sigma = 1$ – gives a very small p-value. We conclude that the Weibull `roach_model_weil` is superior to the exponential so we continue with it.

Furthermore, there is no evidence that the regression coefficient of `weight` is not zero; therefore, we remove this covariate. The resulting model is

```
roach_model_wei2 <- survreg (Surv (death, status) ~ group)
summary (roach_model_wei2)

Call:
survreg(formula = Surv(death, status) ~ group)
              Value Std. Error     z       p
(Intercept)  3.4593     0.2283 15.15  < 2e-16
groupB      -0.8222     0.3097 -2.65  0.0079
groupC      -1.5403     0.3016 -5.11 3.3e-07
Log(scale)   0.3145     0.0705  4.46 8.1e-06

Scale= 1.37

Weibull distribution
Loglik(model)= -470.5    Loglik(intercept only)= -483.3
Chisq= 25.63 on 2 degrees of freedom, p= 2.7e-06
Number of Newton-Raphson Iterations: 5
n= 150
```

It is clear that groups B and C are significantly different to group A in terms of their survival. Using the model, the predicted mean ages at death are given, along with the mean ages of insects that actually died and the ages when insects were last seen (dead or alive):

```
#Prediction of mean age at death, roach_model_wei2, for each group
tapply (predict (roach_model_wei2), group, mean)

        A         B         C
31.796137 13.972647  6.814384

#Mean age at death for each group, using only death (non-censored) times
tapply (death [status == 1], group [status == 1], mean)

        A         B         C
12.611111  9.568182  8.020000

#Mean age at death/censoring for each group
tapply (death, group, mean)

    A     B     C
23.08 14.42  8.02
```

The predicted ages at death are substantially greater than the observed ages at last sighting. This is not surprising: an observation that is censored at time *t*, say, is still alive and so the model incorporates a prediction for how long the individual will remain alive *after* being censored. This means that when we have lots of censoring, predictions of time to death will potentially be

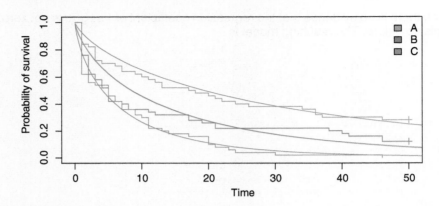

Figure 15.9 Parametric survival functions superimposed on the Kaplan–Meier estimate for the three groups of insects

significantly larger than the sample mean time to death suggests. We can plot the parametric survival functions using the Weibull AFT for the roaches data using the following code, the result of which is in Figure 15.9.

```
plot (roach_group, ylab = "Probability of survival", xlab = "Time", mark.time = TRUE,
     col=hue_pal () (3) [1:3])
legend ("topright", legend=c("A", "B", "C"), fill = hue_pal () (3) [1:3], bty = "n")
lines (predict (roach_model_wei2, newdata = list (group = "A"), type="quantile",
               p = seq (0.01, 0.99, by = 0.01)), seq (0.99, 0.01, by = -0.01),
     col = hue_pal () (3) [1])
lines (predict (roach_model_wei2, newdata = list (group = "B"), type = "quantile",
               p = seq (0.01, 0.99, by = 0.01)), seq (0.99, 0.01, by = -0.01),
     col = hue_pal () (3) [2])
lines (predict (roach_model_wei2, newdata = list (group = "C"), type = "quantile",
               p = seq (0.01, 0.99, by = 0.01)), seq (0.99, 0.01, by = -0.01),
     col = hue_pal () (3) [3])
```

```
detach (roaches)
```

While fitting a parametric model is very easy, we might consider which distribution to choose. Choosing between an Exponential and a Weibull is easy as we saw above, but what if we also want to consider other distributions? In some fields, there are specific distributions that are known to describe events well, while in others, it is a case of trial-and-error to find a distribution. One straightforward way of doing this is by plotting the survival function from the model on top of a (non-parametric) Kaplan–Meier curve. If these match pretty well then it is not unreasonable to think that the model is doing a pretty good job at describing the data. The parametric survival functions using the Weibull AFT for the roaches data, given in Figure 15.9, shows a pretty good fit with the Kaplan–Meier estimate.

This approach only works with categorical covariates, of course; that is, when the covariates separate the survival data into groups. Other approaches include looking at the AIC for the model, which can be accessed using the `extractAIC ()` function.

15.3.4 Cox proportional hazard or a parametric model?

In cases where we have censoring, or where we want to use a more complex error structure, we need to choose between a parametric model, fitted using `survreg ()`, and a non-parametric model, fitted using `coxph ()`. If we want to use the model for prediction, then there is no choice: we must use the parametric `survreg ()` because `coxph ()` does not extrapolate beyond the last observation. Traditionally, medical studies use a Cox model, while engineering studies use AFT models, but both disciplines could fruitfully use either technique depending on the nature of the data and the precise question being asked. Here is a typical question addressed with a Cox model: 'How much does the risk of dying decrease if a new drug treatment is given to a patient?' In contrast, parametric techniques are typically used for questions like this: 'What proportion of patients will die in 2 years based on data from an experiment that ran for just 4 months?'

References

Fleming, T. R., & Harrington, D. P. (2011). *Counting processes and survival analysis*. John Wiley & Sons.

Kalbfleisch, J. D., & Prentice, R. L. (2002). *The statistical analysis of failure time data* (Second). John Wiley & Sons.

Miller, R. G., Gong, G., & Alvaro, M. (1998). *Survival analysis*. John Wiley & Sons.

Therneau, T. M., & Grambsch, P. M. (2000). *Modeling survival data: extending the Cox model*. Springer.

16

Designed Experiments

There are a number of analyses using *R* that commonly arise when we design our own study or experiment and those that are not covered in the other modelling chapters are included here. They can be used for observational studies, etc., but, typically, they work most effectively where we have control over the process that is being analysed. A good introduction to and discussion of the design and analysis of experiments can be found in Cox and Reid, 2000. In this chapter, we will assume that we have the data and want to draw every last ounce/gram/grain of information from them.

16.1 Factorial experiments

A **factorial experiment** is a designed experiment where all the covariates are categorical, usually each having a small number of levels, and the outcome is usually continuous. The experiment is usually carried out for each combination of factor levels. If each combination is repeated, then we have **replicates**. For instance, we might be interested in the volume of a loaf of bread where we have low and high levels of both `yeast` and `flour` together with a proving `time`, where the mixture rests and expands, of 20 and 40 minutes. Although the final explanatory variable is numerical, it takes only two values and so we shall consider it as categorical. There are eight combinations of the three factors and as each has two levels this is known as a 2^3 experiment. There are also eight terms in a saturated model (i.e. with all the interactions), and in order to add an understanding of variation in our model estimates, replicates are necessary. We would want to test each of the eight combinations and if we did that three times for each combination we would have 3 replicates and 24 experimental runs.

Our example comes from a farm-scale trial of animal diets. There are two factors: `diet` and `supplement`. Diet is a factor with three levels: `barley`, `oats`, and `wheat`. Supplement is a factor with four levels: `control`, `agrimore`, `supergain`, and `supersupp`. The response variable is weight `gain` after six weeks, and there are four replicates so $3 \times 4 \times 4 = 48$ runs in total.

The R Book, Third Edition. Elinor Jones, Simon Harden and Michael J. Crawley.
© 2023 John Wiley & Sons Ltd. Published 2023 by John Wiley & Sons Ltd.
Companion website: www.wiley.com/go/jones/therbook3e

```
growth <- read.table ("growth.txt", header = T,
                      colClasses = list (diet = "factor", supplement = "factor"))
head (growth)


  supplement  diet      gain
1  supergain wheat  17.37125
2  supergain wheat  16.81489
3  supergain wheat  18.08184
4  supergain wheat  15.78175
5    control wheat  17.70656
6    control wheat  18.22717
```

Data inspection is carried out using `barplot (.., beside = T, ...)` to get the bars in adjacent clusters rather than vertical stacks, and this gives Figure 16.1:

```
attach (growth)
barplot (tapply (gain, list (diet, supplement), mean),
         beside = T, col = hue_pal ()(3), ylim = c (0, 30))
legend (6.2, 30, legend = c ("barley", "oats", "wheat"), fill = hue_pal ()(3))


detach (growth)
```

Note that the second factor in the list (`supplement`) appears as groups of bars from left to right in alphabetical order by factor level, from `agrimore` to `supersupp`. The first factor (`diet`) appears as three levels within each group of bars, again in alphabetical order by factor level. We need a key to explain the levels of diet, and we have increased the default scale on the *y*-axis to make enough room for the legend box. It is worth remembering that to find the numerical value on the *x*-axis for plotting a `barplot ()` legend, we can run the plot without any output:

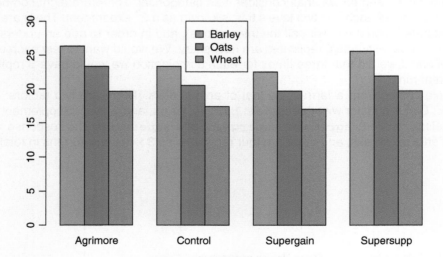

Figure 16.1 Initial factor analysis for `growth`

```
attach (growth)
barplot (tapply (gain, list (diet, supplement), mean),
         beside = T, plot = F)

      [,1]  [,2]  [,3]  [,4]
[1,]   1.5   5.5   9.5  13.5
[2,]   2.5   6.5  10.5  14.5
[3,]   3.5   7.5  11.5  15.5

detach (growth)
```

The values given are the location of the start of the bars on the *x*-axis, and we have chosen to position the legend just after the third bar in the control set.

There certainly appears to be a difference in gain due to diet, but the effects due to supplement and any interactions are less clear. We can inspect the mean values that have been plotted:

```
attach (growth)
tapply (gain, list (diet, supplement), mean)

       agrimore   control  supergain  supersupp
barley 26.34848  23.29665   22.46612   25.57530
oats   23.29838  20.49366   19.66300   21.86023
wheat  19.63907  17.40552   17.01243   19.66834

detach (growth)
```

Then we use aov () or lm () to fit a factorial analysis of variance (the choice affects only whether we get an ANOVA table or a list of parameters estimates as the default output from summary), as we would with any model. We can create a linear model and then summarise it in either form:

```
growth_mod1 <- lm (gain ~ diet * supplement, data = growth)
summary (aov (growth_mod1))

                Df  Sum Sq  Mean Sq  F value    Pr(>F)
diet             2  287.17   143.59    83.52  3.00e-14 ***
supplement       3   91.88    30.63    17.82  2.95e-07 ***
diet:supplement  6    3.41     0.57     0.33     0.917
Residuals       36   61.89     1.72
---
Signif. codes:  0 '***' 0.001 '**' 0.01 '*' 0.05 '.' 0.1 ' ' 1

summary (growth_mod1)

Call:
lm(formula = gain ~ diet * supplement, data = growth)

Residuals:
```

```
     Min        1Q    Median       3Q       Max
-2.48756 -1.00368 -0.07452  1.03496   2.68069


Coefficients:
                                Estimate Std. Error t value Pr(>|t|)
(Intercept)                      26.3485     0.6556  40.191  < 2e-16 ***
dietoats                         -3.0501     0.9271  -3.290 0.002248 **
dietwheat                        -6.7094     0.9271  -7.237 1.61e-08 ***
supplementcontrol                -3.0518     0.9271  -3.292 0.002237 **
supplementsupergain              -3.8824     0.9271  -4.187 0.000174 ***
supplementsupersupp              -0.7732     0.9271  -0.834 0.409816
dietoats:supplementcontrol        0.2471     1.3112   0.188 0.851571
dietwheat:supplementcontrol       0.8183     1.3112   0.624 0.536512
dietoats:supplementsupergain      0.2470     1.3112   0.188 0.851652
dietwheat:supplementsupergain     1.2557     1.3112   0.958 0.344601
dietoats:supplementsupersupp     -0.6650     1.3112  -0.507 0.615135
dietwheat:supplementsupersupp     0.8024     1.3112   0.612 0.544381
---
Signif. codes:  0 '***' 0.001 '**' 0.01 '*' 0.05 '.' 0.1 ' ' 1

Residual standard error: 1.311 on 36 degrees of freedom
Multiple R-squared:  0.8607,Adjusted R-squared:  0.8182
F-statistic: 20.22 on 11 and 36 DF,  p-value: 3.295e-12
```

This is a rather complex model, because there are 12 estimated parameters (the number of rows in the linear model table): the intercept, five main effects and six interactions. The parameter labelled Intercept is the overall mean with both factor levels set to their first in the alphabet (diet = barley and supplement = agrimore). The remaining lines are the differences between the parameters in those lines and those in the intercept. The aov () output is shorter and suggests that, overall, the interaction does not appear to be important. The lm () output has large *p*-values for all interaction combinations and, in fact, suggests that there is little difference between agrimore and supersupp, which the barplot seems to bear out. Also, if we look carefully at the table of means, we can see that the effect sizes of two of the supplements, control and supergain are not very different from one another in any of the three rows, but this has not been highlighted in the output as neither is in the intercept, which just compares their differences with agrimore. This means that we cannot just count up the number of rows with stars in order to determine the number of factor levels that show differences.

Next, we might simplify the model by leaving out the interaction term:

```
growth_mod2 <- lm (gain ~ diet + supplement, data = growth)
summary (growth_mod2)


Call:
lm(formula = gain ~ diet + supplement, data = growth)

Residuals:
    Min       1Q    Median       3Q       Max
-2.30792 -0.85929 -0.07713  0.92052   2.90615
```

```
Coefficients:
                    Estimate Std. Error t value Pr(>|t|)
(Intercept)          26.1230     0.4408  59.258  < 2e-16 ***
dietoats             -3.0928     0.4408  -7.016 1.38e-08 ***
dietwheat            -5.9903     0.4408 -13.589  < 2e-16 ***
supplementcontrol    -2.6967     0.5090  -5.298 4.03e-06 ***
supplementsupergain  -3.3815     0.5090  -6.643 4.72e-08 ***
supplementsupersupp  -0.7274     0.5090  -1.429     0.16
---
Signif. codes:  0 '***' 0.001 '**' 0.01 '*' 0.05 '.' 0.1 ' ' 1

Residual standard error: 1.247 on 42 degrees of freedom
Multiple R-squared:  0.8531,Adjusted R-squared:  0.8356
F-statistic: 48.76 on 5 and 42 DF,  p-value: < 2.2e-16
```

It is clear that we need to retain all three levels of `diet`, but it is not clear that we need four levels of `supplement`: `supersupp` is not obviously different from `agrimore` (from the *p*-value and barplot). We have already discussed that `supergain` is not obviously different from the `control` group. We shall try a new two-level factor to replace the four-level supplement, and see if this reduces the model's explanatory power: `agrimore` and `supersupp` are recoded as `best` and `control` and `supergain` as `worst`, using their numerical position in the default alphabetical order:

```
supp_new <- growth$supplement
levels (supp_new)


[1] "agrimore"  "control"   "supergain" "supersupp"


levels (supp_new)[c(1,4)] <- "best"
levels (supp_new)[c(2,3)] <- "worst"
levels (supp_new)


[1] "best"  "worst"


growth <- cbind (growth, supp_new)
```

And now we can compare the models:

```
growth_mod3 <- lm (gain ~ diet + supp_new, data = growth)
anova (growth_mod3, growth_mod2)


Analysis of Variance Table

Model 1: gain ~ diet + supp_new
Model 2: gain ~ diet + supplement
  Res.Df    RSS Df Sum of Sq      F Pr(>F)
1     44 71.284
2     42 65.296  2    5.9876 1.9257 0.1584
```

The new model has saved 2 degrees of freedom, and there is no justification for the more complex original model. Our final model is thus:

```
summary (growth_mod3)


Call:
lm(formula = gain ~ diet + supp_new, data = growth)

Residuals:
    Min      1Q  Median      3Q     Max
-2.6716 -0.9432 -0.1918  0.9293  3.2698

Coefficients:
               Estimate Std. Error t value Pr(>|t|)
(Intercept)     25.7593     0.3674  70.106  < 2e-16 ***
dietoats        -3.0928     0.4500  -6.873 1.76e-08 ***
dietwheat       -5.9903     0.4500 -13.311  < 2e-16 ***
supp_newworst   -2.6754     0.3674  -7.281 4.43e-09 ***
---
Signif. codes:  0 '***' 0.001 '**' 0.01 '*' 0.05 '.' 0.1 ' ' 1

Residual standard error: 1.273 on 44 degrees of freedom
Multiple R-squared:  0.8396,Adjusted R-squared:  0.8286
F-statistic: 76.76 on 3 and 44 DF, p-value: < 2.2e-16
```

16.1.1 Expanding data

There is a useful function for generating all the different combinations of factor levels. Suppose we have three variables: `height` with five levels between 60 and 80 in steps of 5, `weight` with five levels between 100 and 300 in steps of 50, and two genderss. Then we have $5 \times 5 \times 2 = 50$ observations:

```
expanded_factors <- expand.grid (height = seq (60, 80, 5),
                                 weight = seq (100, 300, 50),
                                 sex = c ("Male", "Female"))
head (expanded_factors)


  height weight  sex
1     60    100 Male
2     65    100 Male
3     70    100 Male
4     75    100 Male
5     80    100 Male
6     60    150 Male


tail (expanded_factors)
```

```
   height weight      sex
45     80    250  Female
46     60    300  Female
47     65    300  Female
48     70    300  Female
49     75    300  Female
50     80    300  Female
```

16.2   Pseudo-replication

Pseudo-replication is where the sample size (and thus the number of degrees of freedom available for testing) is incorrectly stated as being too high. It typically arises in

- nested sampling, when repeated measurements are taken from the same individual, or observational studies are conducted at several different spatial scales (mostly random effects); or

- split-plot analysis, when designed experiments have different treatments applied to plots of different sizes (mostly fixed effects).

We will look at an example of the latter. A discussion of fixed and random effects can be found in Section 13.2.

16.2.1   Split-plot effects

In a split-plot experiment, different treatments are applied to plots of different sizes. Each different plot size is associated with its own error variance, so instead of having one error variance (as in all the ANOVA tables up to this point), we have as many error terms as there are different plot sizes. The analysis is presented as a series of component ANOVA tables, one for each plot size, in a hierarchy from the largest plot size with the lowest replication at the top, down to the smallest plot size with the greatest replication at the bottom. The following example refers to a designed field experiment on crop `yield` with three treatments: `irrigation` (with two levels, irrigated or not), sowing `density` (with three levels, low, medium, and high), and `fertiliser` application (with three levels).

```
splityield <- read.table ("splityield.txt", header = T)
head (splityield)

  yield block irrigation density fertiliser
1    90     A    control     low          N
2    95     A    control     low          P
3   107     A    control     low         NP
4    92     A    control  medium          N
5    89     A    control  medium          P
6    92     A    control  medium         NP
```

The largest plots were the four whole fields (`block`), each of which was split in half, and irrigation was allocated at random to one half of the field. Each irrigation plot was split into three, and one of three different seed-sowing densities was allocated at random (independently for each level of irrigation and each block). Finally, each density plot was divided into three, and one of three fertiliser nutrient treatments (N, P, or N and P together) was allocated at random.

The problem here is pseudo-replication. There are four blocks, each split in half, with one half irrigated and the other as a control. The dataframe for an analysis of this experiment should therefore contain just 8 rows (not 72 rows as in the present case). There should be seven degrees of freedom in total, three for blocks, one for irrigation and just $7 - 3 - 1 = 3$ d.f. for error. The danger is that the model could be run as if it had 72 independent trials representing massive pseudo-replication.

The model is specified as a factorial experiment, using the asterisk notation. The error structure is defined in the `Error ()` term, with the plot sizes listed from left to right, from largest to smallest, with each variable separated by the slash operator. Note that the smallest plot size, `fertiliser`, does not need to appear in the Error term:

```
splityield_mod1 <- aov (yield ~ irrigation * density * fertilizer +
                        Error (block/irrigation/density), data = splityield)
summary (splityield_mod1)


Error: block
          Df Sum Sq Mean Sq F value Pr(>F)
Residuals  3  194.4   64.81


Error: block:irrigation
            Df Sum Sq Mean Sq F value Pr(>F)
irrigation   1   8278    8278   17.59 0.0247 *
Residuals    3   1412     471
---
Signif. codes:  0 '***' 0.001 '**' 0.01 '*' 0.05 '.' 0.1 ' ' 1


Error: block:irrigation:density
                  Df Sum Sq Mean Sq F value Pr(>F)
density            2   1758   879.2   3.784 0.0532.
irrigation:density 2   2747  1373.5   5.912 0.0163 *
Residuals         12   2788   232.3
---
Signif. codes:  0 '***' 0.001 '**' 0.01 '*' 0.05 '.' 0.1 ' ' 1


Error: Within
                            Df Sum Sq Mean Sq F value   Pr(>F)
fertiliser                   2 1977.4   988.7  11.449 0.000142 ***
irrigation:fertiliser        2  953.4   476.7   5.520 0.008108 **
density:fertiliser           4  304.9    76.2   0.883 0.484053
irrigation:density:fertiliser 4  234.7    58.7   0.680 0.610667
Residuals                   36 3108.8    86.4
---
Signif. codes:  0 '***' 0.001 '**' 0.01 '*' 0.05 '.' 0.1 ' ' 1
```

Here we see the four ANOVA tables, one for each plot size: `blocks` are the biggest plots, half blocks get the `irrigation` treatment, one-third of each half block gets a sowing `density` treatment, and one-third of a sowing density treatment gets each `fertiliser` treatment. Note that although main effect for `density` has a large *p*-value, it appears in an interaction with `irrigation` that we

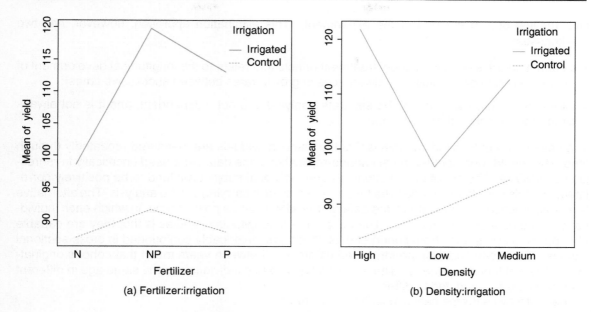

Figure 16.2   Interactions plots for `splityield`

would like to keep and so we will retain it. The best way to understand the two interesting interaction terms is to plot them using `interaction.plot ()` like this, as shown in Figure 16.2:

```
attach (splityield)
interaction.plot (fertilizer, irrigation, yield, col = hue_pal ()(4)[1:2])
interaction.plot (density, irrigation, yield, col = hue_pal ()(4)[3:4])
detach (splityield)
```

Irrigation increases yield proportionately more on the N-fertilised plots than on the P-fertilised plots. On the irrigated plots, yield is lowest on the low-density plots, but on control plots yield is lowest on the high-density plots.

When there are one or more missing values (NA), then factors have effects in more than one stratum and the same main effect turns up in more than one ANOVA table. In such a case, use `lme ()` or `lmer ()` rather than `aov ()`. The output of `aov ()` is not to be trusted under these circumstances.

16.2.2   Removing pseudo-replication

This section includes reference to fixed and random effects which are defined in Section 13.2.

If we are principally interested in fixed effects in a model, then the best response to pseudo-replication in a data set is simply to eliminate it. Spatial pseudo-replication can be averaged away. We will always get the correct effect size and *p*-value from the reduced, non-pseudo-replicated dataframe. Note also that we should not use `anova` to compare different models for the fixed effects when using `lme` or `lmer` with REML (see Section 13.4.3). Temporal pseudo-replication can be dealt with by carrying out carrying out separate ANOVAs, one at each time (or just one at the end of the experiment). This elimination approach, however, has two weaknesses:

- it cannot address questions about treatment effects that relate to the longitudinal development of the mean response profiles (e.g. differences in growth rates between successive times);

- inferences made with each of the separate analyses are not independent, and it is not always clear how they should be combined.

The key feature of longitudinal data is that the same individuals are measured repeatedly through time. This would represent temporal pseudo-replication if the data were used uncritically in regression or ANOVA. The set of observations on one individual subject will tend to be positively correlated, and this correlation needs to be taken into account in carrying out the analysis. The alternative is a cross-sectional study, with all the data gathered at a single point in time, in which each individual contributes a single data point. The advantage of longitudinal studies is that they are capable of separating age effects from cohort effects; these are inextricably confounded in cross-sectional studies. This is particularly important when differences between years mean that cohorts originating at different times experience different conditions so that individuals of the same age in different cohorts would be expected to differ.

There are two extreme cases in longitudinal studies:

- a few measurements on a large number of individuals;

- a large number of measurements on a few individuals.

In the first case, it is difficult to fit an accurate model for change within individuals, but treatment effects are likely to be tested effectively. In the second case, it is possible to get an accurate model of the way that individuals change though time, but there is less power for testing the significance of treatment effects, especially if variation from individual to individual is large. In the first case, less attention will be paid to estimating the correlation structure, while in the second case, the covariance model will be the principal focus of attention. The aims are the following:

- to estimate the average time course of a process;

- to characterise the degree of heterogeneity from individual to individual in the rate of the process;

- to identify the factors associated with both of these, including possible cohort effects.

The response is not the individual measurement, but the sequence of measurements on an individual subject. This enables us to distinguish between age effects and year effects; see Diggle et al., 1994 for details.

16.2.3 Derived variable analysis

An alternative approach is to get rid of the pseudo-replication by reducing the repeated measures into a set of summary statistics (slopes, intercepts, or means), then analyse these summary statistics using standard parametric techniques such as ANOVA or regression. This technique is weak when the values of the explanatory variables change through time. Derived variable analysis makes most sense when it is based on the parameters of scientifically interpretable non-linear models from each time sequence. However, the best model from a theoretical perspective may not be the best model from the statistical point of view.

There are three qualitatively different sources of random variation that might be taken into account:

- random effects, where experimental units differ (e.g. genotype, history, size, and physiological condition) so that there are intrinsically high responders and other low responders;

- serial correlation, where there may be time-varying stochastic variation within a unit (e.g. market forces, physiology, ecological succession, and immunity) so that correlation depends on the time separation of pairs of measurements on the same individual, with correlation weakening with the passage of time;

- measurement error, where, for instance, the assay technique may introduce an element of correlation (e.g. shared bioassay of closely spaced samples; different assay of later specimens).

16.3 Contrasts

Contrasts are used to compare outcome means or groups of means based on specific values for categorical covariates, in what are known as single-degree-of-freedom comparisons. There are two sorts of contrasts we might be interested in

- contrasts we had planned to examine at the experimental design stage (these are referred to as **a priori contrasts**);

- contrasts that look interesting after we have seen the results (these are referred to as **a posteriori contrasts**).

Some people are very snooty about a posteriori contrasts, on the grounds that they were unplanned: we are not supposed to decide what comparisons to make after we have seen the analysis. There is some sense to this, but scientists do it all the time. The key point is that we should only do contrasts after the ANOVA has established that there really are significant differences to be investigated, and then take account of the fact that you are carrying out multiple tests (see Section 9.5). It is not good practice to carry out tests to compare the largest mean with the smallest mean, if the ANOVA has failed to reject the null hypothesis (tempting though this may be).

If we have k levels of a factor, we should remember:

- there is a huge number of possible contrasts, even for relatively small k; and

- there are only $k - 1$ mutually orthogonal contrasts.

Two contrasts are said to be **orthogonal** to one another if the comparisons are statistically independent. Technically, two contrasts are orthogonal if the products of their contrast coefficients sum to zero (we shall see what this means in a moment).

Let us take a simple example. Suppose we have one factor with five levels, and the factor levels are called a, b, c, d, e. Let us start writing down the possible contrasts. Obviously, we could compare each mean singly with every other:

$$a \times b; a \times c; a \times d; a \times e; b \times c; b \times d; b \times e; c \times d; c \times e; d \times e.$$

But we could also compare pairs of means:

$$[a,b] \times [c,d]; [a,b] \times [c,e]; [a,b] \times [cd,e]; [a,c] \times [b,d]; [a,c] \times [d,e], \ldots$$

or triplets of means:

$$[a,b,c] \times d; [a,b,c] \times e; [a,b,d] \times c; [a,b,d] \times e; [a,b,e] \times c; \ldots$$

or groups of four means:

$$[a,b,c,d] \times e; [a,b,c,e] \times d; [a,b,d,e] \times c; [a,c,d,e] \times b, [b,c,d,e] \times a,$$

and so on. There are absolutely masses of possible contrasts. In practice, however, we should only compare things once, either directly or implicitly. So the two contrasts $a \times b$ and $a \times c$ implicitly contrast $b \times c$. This means that if we have carried out the first two contrasts then the third contrast is not an orthogonal contrast because we have already carried it out, implicitly. Which particular contrasts are orthogonal depends very much on our choice of the first contrast to make. Suppose there were good reasons for comparing $[a,b,c,e] \times d$. For example, d might be the placebo and the other four might be different kinds of drug treatment, so we make this our first contrast. Because $k - 1 = 4$ we only have three possible contrasts that are orthogonal to this. There may be a priori reasons to group $[a,b]$ and $[c,e]$, so we make this our second orthogonal contrast. This means that we have no degrees of freedom in choosing the last two orthogonal contrasts: they have to be $a \times b$ and $c \times e$. Just remember that with orthogonal contrasts we only compare things once.

16.3.1 Contrast coefficients

Contrast coefficients are a numerical way of embodying the hypothesis we want to test. The rules for constructing contrast coefficients are straightforward, each level of the covariate in question getting a number:

- factor levels to be lumped together get the same sign (plus or minus);
- levels to be contrasted get the opposite sign;
- levels to be excluded get a contrast coefficient of 0;
- the contrast coefficients must add up to 0.

Suppose that with our five-level factor, $\{a,b,c,d,e\}$, we want to begin by comparing the four levels $[a,b,c,e]$ with the single level d. All levels enter the contrast, so none of the coefficients is 0. The four terms a,b,c,e are grouped together, so they all get the same sign (minus, for example, although it makes no difference which sign is chosen). They are to be compared to d, so it gets the opposite sign (plus, in this case). The choice of what numeric values to give the contrast coefficients is not constrained. Most people use whole numbers rather than fractions, but it really does not matter. All that matters is that the coefficients sum to 0. The positive and negative coefficients have to add up to the same value. In our example, comparing four means with one mean, a natural choice of coefficients would be -1 for each of a,b,c,e, and $+4$ for d. Alternatively, we could select $+0.25$ for each of a,b,c,e, and -1 for d.

Factor level:	a	b	c	d	e
contrast 1 coefficients:	−1	−1	−1	4	−1

Similarly, suppose the second contrast is to compare $[a, b]$ with $[c, e]$. Because this contrast excludes d, we set its contrast coefficient to 0. a, b get the same sign (say, plus) and c, e get the opposite sign. Because the number of levels on each side of the contrast is equal (2 in both cases), we can use the name numeric value for all the coefficients. The value 1 is the most obvious choice (but we could use π, if we wanted to be perverse):

Factor level:	a	b	c	d	e
Contrast 2 coefficients:	1	1	−1	0	−1

There are only two possibilities for the remaining orthogonal contrasts, $a \times b$ and $c \times e$:

Factor level:	a	b	c	d	e
Contrast 3 coefficients:	1	−1	0	0	0
Contrast 4 coefficients:	0	0	1	0	−1

The variation in the outcome variable attributable to a particular contrast is called the **contrast sum of squares**. The importance of a contrast is judged by an F-test, dividing the contrast sum of squares by the error variance.

16.3.2   An example of contrasts using R

The following example comes from the a competition experiment, in which the biomass of control plants is compared to the biomass of plants grown in conditions (clipping), where competition was reduced in one of four different ways. There are two treatments in which the roots of neighbouring plants were cut (to 5 or 10 cm depth) and two treatments in which the shoots of neighbouring plants were clipped (25% or 50% of the neighbours were cut back to ground level).

```
comp <- read.table ("competition.txt", header = T,
                    colClasses = list (clipping = "factor"))
head (comp)

  biomass clipping
1    551      n25
2    457      n25
3    450      n25
4    731      n25
5    499      n25
6    632      n25

attach (comp)
comp_means <- tapply (biomass, clipping, mean)
detach (comp)
comp_means

 control       n25       n50       r10        r5
465.1667  553.3333  569.3333  610.6667  610.5000
```

We start with the one-way analysis of variance:

```
comp_mod1 <- aov (biomass ~ clipping, data = comp)
summary (comp_mod1)


            Df Sum Sq Mean Sq F value  Pr(>F)
clipping     4  85356   21339   4.302 0.00875 **
Residuals   25 124020    4961
---
Signif. codes:  0 '***' 0.001 '**' 0.01 '*' 0.05 '.' 0.1 ' ' 1
```

Clipping treatment has a clear effect on biomass. But have we fully understood the result of this experiment? Probably not. For example, which factor levels had the biggest effect on biomass, and were all of the competition treatments significantly different from the controls? To answer these questions, we need to use the `lm ()` analysis. In fact, unless we specifically need to look at the values of sums of squares, this output is always more useful:

```
comp_mod1 <- lm (biomass ~ clipping, data = comp)
summary (comp_mod1)

Call:
lm(formula = biomass ~ clipping, data = comp)

Residuals:
     Min       1Q   Median       3Q      Max
-103.333  -49.667    3.417   43.375  177.667

Coefficients:
            Estimate Std. Error t value Pr(>|t|)
(Intercept)   465.17      28.75  16.177  9.4e-15 ***
clippingn25    88.17      40.66   2.168  0.03987 *
clippingn50   104.17      40.66   2.562  0.01683 *
clippingr10   145.50      40.66   3.578  0.00145 **
clippingr5    145.33      40.66   3.574  0.00147 **
---
Signif. codes:  0 '***' 0.001 '**' 0.01 '*' 0.05 '.' 0.1 ' ' 1

Residual standard error: 70.43 on 25 degrees of freedom
Multiple R-squared:  0.4077,Adjusted R-squared:  0.3129
F-statistic: 4.302 on 4 and 25 DF,  p-value: 0.008752
```

The *F*-statistic and consequent *p*-value from `aov ()` are both present here. It looks as if all levels of the factor are important to the model, because all five rows of the summary table have small *p*-values. In fact, this is not the case. This example highlights the major shortcoming of treatment contrasts: they do not show how many significant factor levels we need to retain in the minimal adequate model because all of the rows are being compared with the intercept (with the controls in this case, simply because the factor level name for `control` comes first in the alphabetic list of levels).

In this experiment, there are several planned comparisons we should like to make. The obvious place to start is by comparing the `control` plants, exposed to the full rigours of competition, with all of the other treatments. That is to say, we want to contrast the first level of clipping with the other four levels. The contrast coefficients, therefore, would be 4, −1, −1, −1, −1. The next planned comparison might contrast the shoot-pruned treatments (`n25` and `n50`) with the root-pruned treatments (`r10` and `r5`). Suitable contrast coefficients for this would be 0, 1, 1, −1, −1 (because we are ignoring the `control` in this contrast). A third contrast might compare the two depths of root pruning; 0, 0, 0, 1, −1. The last orthogonal contrast would, therefore, have to compare the two intensities of shoot pruning: 0, 1, −1, 0, 0 (in order to preserve orthogonality: see below). Because the factor called `clipping` has five levels there are only $5 - 1 = 4$ orthogonal contrasts. *R* is outstandingly good at dealing with contrasts, and we can associate these five user-specified a priori contrasts with the categorical variable called `clipping` like this:

```
contrasts (comp$clipping) <-
  cbind (c (4, -1, -1, -1, -1),
         c (0, 1, 1, -1, -1),
         c (0, 0, 0, 1, -1),
         c (0, 1, -1, 0, 0))
```

We can check that this has done what we wanted by typing:

```
comp$clipping[[2]]
```

```
[1] n25
attr(,"contrasts")
        [,1] [,2] [,3] [,4]
control    4    0    0    0
n25       -1    1    0    1
n50       -1    1    0   -1
r10       -1   -1    1    0
r5        -1   -1   -1    0
Levels: control n25 n50 r10 r5
```

This produces the matrix of contrast coefficients that we specified. One contrast is contained in each column. Note that all the columns add to zero (i.e. each set of contrast coefficients is correctly specified). Note also that the products of any two of the columns sum to zero (this shows that all the contrasts are orthogonal, as intended): for example, comparing contrasts 1 and 2 gives products $(4 \times 0) + (-1 \times 1) + (-1 \times 1) + (-1 \times -1) + (-1 \times -1) = 0$. Now, we can refit the model and inspect the results of our specified contrasts, rather than using the default treatment contrasts:

```
comp_mod2 <- lm (biomass ~ clipping, data = comp)
summary (comp_mod2)

Call:
lm(formula = biomass ~ clipping, data = comp)

Residuals:
     Min       1Q   Median       3Q      Max
 -103.333  -49.667    3.417   43.375  177.667
```

```
Coefficients:
            Estimate Std. Error t value Pr(>|t|)
(Intercept) 561.80000   12.85926  43.688  < 2e-16 ***
clipping1   -24.15833    6.42963  -3.757 0.000921 ***
clipping2   -24.62500   14.37708  -1.713 0.099128.
clipping3     0.08333   20.33227   0.004 0.996762
clipping4    -8.00000   20.33227  -0.393 0.697313
---
Signif. codes:  0 '***' 0.001 '**' 0.01 '*' 0.05 '.' 0.1 ' ' 1

Residual standard error: 70.43 on 25 degrees of freedom
Multiple R-squared:  0.4077,Adjusted R-squared:  0.3129
F-statistic: 4.302 on 4 and 25 DF,  p-value: 0.008752
```

Notice that `comp_mod2` appears to be identical to `comp_mod1`. However, as we have reorganised `clipping` with a different set of contrasts, the output from the two models will be different. This analysis suggests that the only contrast we are interested in is that between the `control` and the four competition treatments. All the other comparisons have relatively large *p*-values. When we specify the contrasts, the intercept is the overall (grand) mean:

```
mean (comp$biomass)
```

```
[1] 561.8
```

The second row, labelled `clipping1`, estimates, like all contrasts, the difference between two means. But which two means, exactly? We have already seen the means for all the different factor levels. Thus, this first contrast compares the `control` mean with the mean of the other four treatments. The simplest way to get this other mean is to create a new factor, `c1` that has value 1 for the controls and 2 for the rest:

```
c1 <- factor (1 + (comp$clipping != "control"))
tapply (comp$biomass, c1, mean)
```

```
       1        2
465.1667 585.9583
```

The estimate reflecting the first contrast is the difference between the overall mean and the mean of the four non-control treatments:

```
mean (comp$biomass) - tapply (comp$biomass,c1,mean)[2]
```

```
        2
-24.15833
```

and we see the estimate in row 2 of `summary (comp_mod2)` is -24.15833. What about the second contrast? This compares the root-pruned and shoot-pruned treatments, and `c2` is a factor that lumps together the required treatments:

```
c2 <- factor (2 * (comp$clipping == "n25") + 2 * (comp$clipping == "n50") +
            (comp$clipping == "r10") + (comp$clipping == "r5"))
(tapply (comp$biomass, c2, mean) [3] - tapply (comp$biomass, c2, mean) [2]) / 2


      2
-24.625
```

So the second contrast is half the difference between the root- and shoot-pruned treatments. What about the third contrast? This is between the two root-pruned treatments. We know their values already from above:

```
(comp_means [4] - comp_means [5]) / 2


       r10
0.08333333
```

The third contrast is half the difference between the two means. The final contrast compares the two shoot-pruning treatments, and the contrast is half the difference between these two means:

```
(comp_means [2] - comp_means [3]) / 2

n25
 -8
```

To recap:

- the first contrast compares the overall mean with the mean of the four non-control treatments;
- the second contrast is half the difference between the root and shoot-pruned treatment means;
- the third contrast is half the difference between the two root-pruned treatments; and
- the fourth contrast is half the difference between the two shoot-pruned treatments.

It is important to note that the first four standard errors in the summary.lm table are all different from one another. As we have just seen, the estimate in the first row of the table is a mean, while all the other rows contain estimates that are differences between means. For instance, the overall mean on the top row is based on 30 numbers so the standard error of the mean is $\sqrt{\frac{4961}{30}}$, where the 4961 comes from summary (comp_mod1):

```
sqrt (4961 / 30)

[1] 12.8595
```

The next row compares two means so we need the standard error of the difference between two means. The complexity comes from the fact that the two means are each based on different numbers of numbers. The overall mean is based on all five factor levels, while the non-control mean with which it is compared is based on four means. Each factor level has $n = 6$ replicates, so the denominator in the standard error formula is $5 \times 4 \times 6 = 120$. Thus, the standard error of the difference between these two means is

```
sqrt (4961 / 120)
```

```
[1] 6.429749
```

The complexity of these calculations is a good reason for preferring treatment contrasts rather than user-specified contrasts as the default. The advantage of orthogonal contrasts, however, is that the summary.lm table gives us a much better idea of the number of parameters required in the minimal adequate model (two in this case).

Overall, what we have seen suggests that each of the clipping procedures is an improvement on the control but that there appears to be very little difference between them.

16.3.3 Model simplification for contrasts

The analysis we carried out in Section 16.3.2 would probably have been decided upon before we carried out the experiment, i.e. it was a priori. In this section, we will look at an interactive approach to the data that we might carry out once we have collected them, i.e. a posteriori. To demonstrate this, we revert to treatment contrasts. First, we switch off our user-defined contrasts:

```
comp$clipping[[2]]
```

```
[1] n25
attr(,"contrasts")
        [,1] [,2] [,3] [,4]
control    4    0    0    0
n25       -1    1    0    1
n50       -1    1    0   -1
r10       -1   -1    1    0
r5        -1   -1   -1    0
Levels: control n25 n50 r10 r5

contrasts (comp$clipping) <- NULL
comp$clipping[[2]]
```

```
[1] n25
Levels: control n25 n50 r10 r5
```

If we refer back to the table of means at the start of the previous section, we see that the levels that are most similar are the effects of root pruning to 10 and 5 cm (610.7 vs. 610.5). We shall begin by simplifying these to a single root-pruning treatment called root. We start by copying the original factor name:

```
clipping2 <- comp$clipping
levels (clipping2)[4:5] <- "root"
levels (clipping2)


[1] "control" "n25"      "n50"      "root"


comp <- data.frame (comp, clipping2)
```

The levels we want to merge are the fourth and fifth in alphabetical order. Now, we can fit the new model and compare it to our initial one:

```
comp_mod3 <- lm (biomass ~ clipping2, data = comp)
anova (comp_mod3, comp_mod1)


Analysis of Variance Table

Model 1: biomass ~ clipping2
Model 2: biomass ~ clipping
  Res.Df    RSS Df Sum of Sq  F Pr(>F)
1     26 124020
2     25 124020  1  0.083333  0 0.9968
```

As expected, this model simplification was completely justified. The next step is to investigate the remaining effects:

```
summary (comp_mod3)


Call:
lm(formula = biomass ~ clipping2, data = comp)


Residuals:
     Min      1Q  Median      3Q      Max
-103.333  -49.667   3.417  43.417  177.667


Coefficients:
              Estimate Std. Error t value Pr(>|t|)
(Intercept)     465.17      28.20  16.498 2.72e-15 ***
clipping2n25     88.17      39.87   2.211 0.036029 *
clipping2n50    104.17      39.87   2.612 0.014744 *
clipping2root   145.42      34.53   4.211 0.000269 ***
---
Signif. codes:  0 '***' 0.001 '**' 0.01 '*' 0.05 '.' 0.1 ' ' 1

Residual standard error: 69.07 on 26 degrees of freedom
Multiple R-squared:  0.4077,Adjusted R-squared:  0.3393
F-statistic: 5.965 on 3 and 26 DF,  p-value: 0.003099
```

It looks as if the two shoot-clipping treatments are not significantly different from one another (they differ by just 16.0 with a standard error of 23.904). We can lump these together into a single shoot-pruning treatment as follows:

```
clipping3 <- comp$clipping2
levels (clipping3)[2:3] <- "shoot"
levels (clipping3)

[1] "control" "shoot"    "root"

comp <- data.frame (comp, clipping3)
```

We can build another model and compare, again concluding that the simpler model is worth retaining:

```
comp_mod4 <- lm (biomass ~ clipping3, data = comp)
anova (comp_mod4, comp_mod3)

Analysis of Variance Table

Model 1: biomass ~ clipping3
Model 2: biomass ~ clipping2
  Res.Df    RSS Df Sum of Sq      F Pr(>F)
1     27 124788
2     26 124020  1       768 0.161 0.6915

summary (comp_mod4)

Call:
lm(formula = biomass ~ clipping3, data = comp)

Residuals:
     Min       1Q   Median      3Q      Max
-111.333  -48.021    3.417  43.417  169.667

Coefficients:
               Estimate Std. Error t value Pr(>|t|)
(Intercept)      465.17      27.75  16.760 8.52e-16 ***
clipping3shoot    96.17      33.99   2.829 0.008697 **
clipping3root    145.42      33.99   4.278 0.000211 ***
---
Signif. codes:  0 '***' 0.001 '**' 0.01 '*' 0.05 '.' 0.1 ' ' 1

Residual standard error: 67.98 on 27 degrees of freedom
Multiple R-squared:  0.404,Adjusted R-squared:  0.3599
F-statistic: 9.151 on 2 and 27 DF, p-value: 0.0009243
```

It is definitely worth checking whether a final simplification that merges all the treatments is better:

```
clipping4 <- comp$clipping3
levels (clipping4)[2:3] <- "pruned"
levels (clipping4)


[1] "control" "pruned"

comp <- data.frame (comp, clipping4)
comp_mod5 <- lm (biomass ~ clipping4, data = comp)
anova (comp_mod5, comp_mod4)


Analysis of Variance Table

Model 1: biomass ~ clipping4
Model 2: biomass ~ clipping3
  Res.Df    RSS Df Sum of Sq      F  Pr(>F)
1     28 139342
2     27 124788  1     14553 3.1489 0.08726 .
---
Signif. codes:  0 '***' 0.001 '**' 0.01 '*' 0.05 '.' 0.1 ' ' 1


summary (comp_mod5)


Call:
lm(formula = biomass ~ clipping4, data = comp)

Residuals:
     Min      1Q   Median      3Q      Max
-135.958  -49.667   -4.458   50.635  145.042

Coefficients:
                Estimate Std. Error t value Pr(>|t|)
(Intercept)        465.2       28.8  16.152 1.01e-15 ***
clipping4pruned    120.8       32.2   3.751 0.000815 ***
---
Signif. codes:  0 '***' 0.001 '**' 0.01 '*' 0.05 '.' 0.1 ' ' 1

Residual standard error: 70.54 on 28 degrees of freedom
Multiple R-squared:  0.3345,Adjusted R-squared:  0.3107
F-statistic: 14.07 on 1 and 28 DF,  p-value: 0.0008149
```

Definitely. The model has just two parameters: the mean for the controls (465.2) and the difference between the control mean and the four treatment means (120.8):

```
tapply (comp$biomass, comp$clipping4, mean)


 control    pruned
465.1667 585.9583
```

If we were to compare our final model with that containing just an intercept then the *p*-value for the *F*-test comparison is given in two places in the model summary. We have come to a similar conclusion to our analysis in Section 16.3.2, namely that treatment matters but which one isn't really important.

16.3.4 Helmert contrasts

So far we have seen the default **treatment** contrasts and our hand crafted alternatives. *R* does have other built-in contrasts, and the first of them we shall look at is the **Helmert contrast**:

```
contrasts (comp$clipping)


        n25 n50 r10 r5
control   0   0   0  0
n25       1   0   0  0
n50       0   1   0  0
r10       0   0   1  0
r5        0   0   0  1


options (contrasts = c ("contr.helmert", "contr.poly"))
contrasts (comp$clipping)


        [,1] [,2] [,3] [,4]
control  -1   -1   -1   -1
n25       1   -1   -1   -1
n50       0    2   -1   -1
r10       0    0    3   -1
r5        0    0    0    4
```

We have set two types of contrast: the second, `"contr.poly"`, is for ordered covariates and we will examine it in Section 16.3.6. The first contrast compares the `control` with n25, the second [control, n25] with n50, etc. Let us build a model which incorporates these contrasts:

```
comp_mod6 <- lm (biomass ~ clipping, data = comp)
summary (comp_mod6)


Call:
lm(formula = biomass ~ clipping, data = comp)
```

```
Residuals:
     Min       1Q    Median       3Q       Max
-103.333   -49.667     3.417   43.375   177.667

Coefficients:
             Estimate Std. Error t value Pr(>|t|)
(Intercept)   561.800     12.859  43.688   <2e-16 ***
clipping1      44.083     20.332   2.168   0.0399 *
clipping2      20.028     11.739   1.706   0.1004
clipping3      20.347      8.301   2.451   0.0216 *
clipping4      12.175      6.430   1.894   0.0699 .
---
Signif. codes:  0 '***' 0.001 '**' 0.01 '*' 0.05 '.' 0.1 ' ' 1

Residual standard error: 70.43 on 25 degrees of freedom
Multiple R-squared:  0.4077,Adjusted R-squared:  0.3129
F-statistic: 4.302 on 4 and 25 DF,  p-value: 0.008752
```

The *R* code is exactly the same as for our first model, but we have changed the universal `options` and so the output is different. With Helmert contrasts, the intercept, as usual, is the overall mean (561.8). The first contrast (labelled `clipping1`) compares the first mean in alphabetical sequence with the average of the first and second factor levels in alphabetical sequence (`control` plus `n25`): its parameter estimate is the mean of the first two factor levels, minus the mean of the first factor level:

```
mean (comp_means[1:2]) - comp_means[1]

 control
44.08333
```

The other estimates can be calculated in similar ways. This approach is less intuitive than that for treatment contrasts but does provide an alternative method for gradually building a minimal model. Superficially, it does seem from the above output that we might keep `n25` and `r10` in our model as they appear to make a difference when they are added in. However, it is important to remember what `clipping3` represents. It represents the comparison between `r10` and `control`, `n25`, `n50` and is not something we have studied before. We will need to consider whether for this example, it is a sensible comparison to make.

16.3.5 Sum contrasts

A further option in *R* is sum contrasts:

```
options (contrasts = c ("contr.sum", "contr.poly"))
contrasts (comp$clipping)


        [,1] [,2] [,3] [,4]
control    1    0    0    0
n25        0    1    0    0
n50        0    0    1    0
```

```
r10              0     0     0     1
r5              -1    -1    -1    -1
```

The four contrasts are the differences between the grand mean and the first four factor means (control, n25, n50 and r10). We can see this by building our usual model:

```
comp_mod7 <- lm (biomass ~ clipping, data = comp)
summary (comp_mod7)


Call:
lm(formula = biomass ~ clipping, data = comp)

Residuals:
      Min        1Q    Median        3Q       Max
 -103.333   -49.667     3.417    43.375   177.667

Coefficients:
              Estimate Std. Error t value Pr(>|t|)
(Intercept)    561.800     12.859  43.688  < 2e-16 ***
clipping1      -96.633     25.719  -3.757 0.000921 ***
clipping2       -8.467     25.719  -0.329 0.744743
clipping3        7.533     25.719   0.293 0.772005
clipping4       48.867     25.719   1.900 0.069019 .
---
Signif. codes:  0 '***' 0.001 '**' 0.01 '*' 0.05 '.' 0.1 ' ' 1

Residual standard error: 70.43 on 25 degrees of freedom
Multiple R-squared:  0.4077, Adjusted R-squared:  0.3129
F-statistic: 4.302 on 4 and 25 DF,  p-value: 0.008752
```

The estimates are easily calculated:

```
comp_means[1:4] - mean (comp_means)


   control         n25         n50         r10
-96.633333   -8.466667    7.533333   48.866667
```

There definitely appears to be a difference between control and the overall mean (which includes control). Again, it is a subject matter decision as to whether that is interesting or useful to know. However, it might be more useful to compare the overall mean with each of the four possible treatments. In order to do that, we need to change the order of the levels so that contrast appears last, and then build our model:

```
comp$clipping <- factor (comp$clipping, levels = c ("n25", "n50", "r5", "r10",
                                                    "control"))
comp_mod8 <- lm (biomass ~ clipping, data = comp)
summary (comp_mod8)
```

```
Call:
lm(formula = biomass ~ clipping, data = comp)

Residuals:
     Min       1Q   Median       3Q      Max
-103.333  -49.667    3.417   43.375  177.667

Coefficients:
            Estimate Std. Error t value Pr(>|t|)
(Intercept)  561.800     12.859  43.688   <2e-16 ***
clipping1     -8.467     25.719  -0.329   0.7447
clipping2      7.533     25.719   0.293   0.7720
clipping3     48.700     25.719   1.894   0.0699 .
clipping4     48.867     25.719   1.900   0.0690 .
---
Signif. codes:  0 '***' 0.001 '**' 0.01 '*' 0.05 '.' 0.1 ' ' 1

Residual standard error: 70.43 on 25 degrees of freedom
Multiple R-squared:  0.4077, Adjusted R-squared:  0.3129
F-statistic: 4.302 on 4 and 25 DF,  p-value: 0.008752
```

It does not seem as if any of the treatments is an improvement on the mixture of everything, not something we have seen before (where, for instance, we compared individual treatments with just the `control`).

16.3.6   Polynomial contrasts

There is a further setting for contrasts in *R*: **polynomial contrasts** where we attempt to fit a polynomial to the response data, based on different values of our categorical covariate. Clearly, this will only have a valid interpretation if the covariate is ordered and the different levels represent roughly equal widths. For instance, in the following data set, we are measuring the `response` to four different levels of dietary supplement, the `treatment`: very low, low, medium, and high. They might represent the ranges (in mg / day) of 0–5, 5.1–10, 10.1–15, 15.1–20 and, in that case, fitting a curve to the four levels makes some sense: the four intervals have roughly the same width. One might then predict the response for specific values of the supplement. However, if the lowest category was 0 and the remaining three levels were 0.1–5, 5.1–10, 10.1–15, then fitting a curve would make no sense as the intervals have different widths. Anyway, here are the data, plotted in Figure 16.3:

```
poly <- read.table ("poly.txt", header = T, colClasses = list
(treatment = "factor"))
head (poly)

  treatment response
1   verylow         3
2       low         6
3    medium         7
4      high         5
5   verylow         2
6       low         6
```

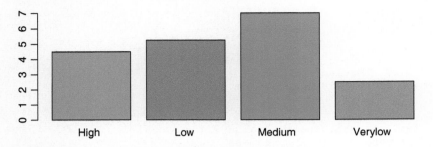

Figure 16.3 `response` for different unordered levels of `treatment` in `poly`

```
attach (poly)
poly_means <- tapply (response, treatment, mean)
poly_means

   high     low  medium verylow
   4.50    5.25    7.00    2.50


barplot (poly_means, names = levels (treatment), col = hue_pal ()(5))


detach (poly)
```

The problem is that *R*'s default is to take the factor levels in alphabetical order leading to a plot that is difficult to interpret, and the default model likewise:

```
summary (lm (response ~ treatment, data = poly))

Call:
lm(formula = response ~ treatment, data = poly)

Residuals:
   Min     1Q Median     3Q    Max
 -1.25  -0.50   0.00   0.50   1.00

Coefficients:
            Estimate Std. Error t value Pr(>|t|)
(Intercept)   4.8125     0.1875  25.667 7.45e-12 ***
treatment1   -0.3125     0.3248  -0.962    0.355
treatment2    0.4375     0.3248   1.347    0.203
treatment3    2.1875     0.3248   6.736 2.09e-05 ***
---
Signif. codes:  0 '***' 0.001 '**' 0.01 '*' 0.05 '.' 0.1 ' ' 1

Residual standard error: 0.75 on 12 degrees of freedom
Multiple R-squared:  0.8606, Adjusted R-squared:  0.8258
F-statistic:  24.7 on 3 and 12 DF,  p-value: 2.015e-05
```

At the end of Section 16.3.5, we saw how to change the order of factor levels. However, here we need to go one step further and tell *R* that the levels are ordered:

```
poly$treatment <- ordered (poly$treatment,
                           levels = c ("verylow", "low", "medium", "high"))
levels (poly$treatment)

[1] "verylow" "low"     "medium"  "high"

poly_means <- tapply (poly$response, poly$treatment, mean)
```

We have recreated `poly_means` after the reordering so that we can use it directly in a new bar plot. Now, we can build a model which may look a little strange at first:

```
poly_mod1 <- lm (response ~ treatment, data = poly)
summary (poly_mod1)

Call:
lm(formula = response ~ treatment, data = poly)

Residuals:
   Min     1Q Median     3Q    Max
 -1.25  -0.50   0.00   0.50   1.00

Coefficients:
            Estimate Std. Error t value Pr(>|t|)
(Intercept)   4.8125     0.1875  25.667 7.45e-12 ***
treatment.L   1.7330     0.3750   4.621 0.000589 ***
treatment.Q  -2.6250     0.3750  -7.000 1.43e-05 ***
treatment.C  -0.7267     0.3750  -1.938 0.076520 .
---
Signif. codes:  0 '***' 0.001 '**' 0.01 '*' 0.05 '.' 0.1 ' ' 1

Residual standard error: 0.75 on 12 degrees of freedom
Multiple R-squared:  0.8606,Adjusted R-squared:  0.8258
F-statistic:  24.7 on 3 and 12 DF,  p-value: 2.015e-05
```

The default in *R* for ordered factor levels is to build a model where the contrasts are polynomial terms (`treatment.L` is linear, `treatment.Q` is quadratic, `treatment.C` is cubic, etc.), all mutually orthogonal. We saw in Section 16.3.4 when we changed to Helmert contrasts that we actually typed `options (contrasts = c ("contr.helmert", "contr.poly"))`: we had to specify contrasts for both unordered and ordered data.

The model suggests that a linear and quadratic term would be useful in fitting a curve. The details of the contrasts *R* has created are given by

```
contrasts (poly$treatment)

            .L      .Q         .C
[1,]  -0.6708204   0.5  -0.2236068
[2,]  -0.2236068  -0.5   0.6708204
[3,]   0.2236068  -0.5  -0.6708204
[4,]   0.6708204   0.5   0.2236068
```

The rows represent the four levels, and we can recover their means by multiplying each row of the contrast matrix by the appropriate model coefficients and adding in the intercept:

```
pm_coefs <- coef (poly_mod1)
contrasts (poly$treatment) %*% pm_coefs[2:4] + pm_coefs[1]


      [,1]
[1,] 2.50
[2,] 5.25
[3,] 7.00
[4,] 4.50
```

We can now add the fitted quadratic curve to the bar plot. We need to create a new model as we want to fit *x*-values (one to four) to the means of the four categories. However, we have to go through the process of finding the *x*-coordinates for the mid-point of each bar and adjusting the *x*-coordinates for our fitted curve, resulting in Figure 16.4:

```
x <- 1:4
barplot (poly_means ~ x, names = names (poly_means),
         col = hue_pal ()(5)[1:4])
xv <- seq (1, 4, 0.01)
poly_mod2 <- lm (poly_means ~ poly (x, 3))
yv <- predict (poly_mod2, list (x = xv))
bar_x <- barplot (poly_means, plot = F)
xv_map <- lm (bar_x ~ I(1:4))
xs <- coef (xv_map)[1] + coef (xv_map)[2] * xv
lines (xs, yv, col = hue_pal ()(5)[5], lwd = 2)
```

16.3.7 Contrasts with multiple covariates

Finally, we will examine a data set where there is more than one covariate. We will keep it relatively simple by making the second covariate continuous, but extending contrasts to more than one categorical variable is relatively straightforward with a clear head. Our dataset looks at the dependence of `weight` on `sex` and `age` in Costa Rican stoats, as illustrated in Figure 16.5:

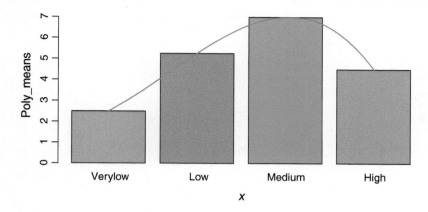

Figure 16.4   `response` for different ordered levels of `treatment` in `poly`

```
stoats <- read.table ("stoats.txt", header = T)
head (stoats)


    weight   sex age
1   5.311580 male   1
2   7.340586 male   2
3   6.561460 male   3
4 10.151011 male   4
5   9.976946 male   5
6 12.076808 male   6


stoats_male <- stoats[stoats$sex == "male",]
stoats_female <- stoats[stoats$sex == "female",]
plot (stoats_male$age, stoats_male$weight, type = "b",
      main = "", xlab = "age", ylab = "weight (kgs)",
      ylim = range (stoats$weight), col = hue_pal ()(2)[1])
lines (stoats_female$age, stoats_female$weight, type = "b",
      col = hue_pal ()(2)[2])
legend (2, 18, legend = c ("male", "female"), , col = hue_pal ()(2),
        lwd = rep (2, 2))
```

The two sets of data appear relatively linear so we might attempt to fit two lines. However, there are several different ways of expressing the values of the four parameters involved:

- two slopes, and two intercepts;

- one slope and one difference between slopes, and one intercept and one difference between intercepts;

- the overall mean slope and the overall mean intercept, and one difference between slopes and one difference between intercepts.

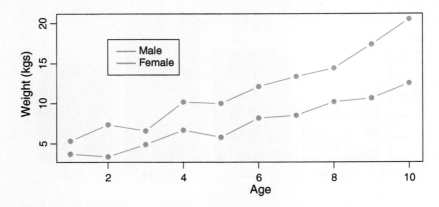

Figure 16.5 Weights of Costa Rican stoats in `weight`

We can look at a variety of regression models where we just regress on `age`:

```
lm (weight ~ age, data = stoats)

Call:
lm(formula = weight ~ age, data = stoats)

Coefficients:
(Intercept)           age
     2.541         1.279

lm (weight ~ age, data = stoats_male)

Call:
lm(formula = weight ~ age, data = stoats_male)

Coefficients:
(Intercept)           age
     3.115         1.561

lm (weight ~ age, data = stoats_female)

Call:
lm(formula = weight ~ age, data = stoats_female)

Coefficients:
(Intercept)           age
    1.9663        0.9962
```

These show a wide range of intercept and slope values.

Now, let us look at the full model with interaction for a range of contrasts. First, the default treatment contrast:

```
stoats_mod1 <- lm (weight ~ age * sex, data = stoats)
summary (stoats_mod1)


Call:
lm(formula = weight ~ age * sex, data = stoats)

Residuals:
      Min       1Q   Median       3Q      Max
-1.23614 -0.60421  0.05658  0.65660  1.77263

Coefficients:
            Estimate Std. Error t value Pr(>|t|)
(Intercept)  2.54073    0.44319   5.733 3.08e-05 ***
age          1.27851    0.07143  17.899 5.26e-12 ***
sex1        -0.57445    0.44319  -1.296  0.21331
age:sex1    -0.28230    0.07143  -3.952  0.00114 **
---
Signif. codes:  0 '***' 0.001 '**' 0.01 '*' 0.05 '.' 0.1 ' ' 1

Residual standard error: 0.9175 on 16 degrees of freedom
Multiple R-squared:  0.9652, Adjusted R-squared:  0.9587
F-statistic: 147.8 on 3 and 16 DF,  p-value: 7.101e-12
```

All the parameter estimates can be extracted from the above models. The `intercept` is just that for females (first alphabetically), `age` is the female slope, `sexmale` is the difference between the two gender intercepts and `age:sexmale` the difference between the two gender slopes. From a model point of view, we would retain all the terms, even though the difference in intercepts has a large p-value, as the interaction is clearly important.

Moving to Helmert contrasts:

```
options (contrasts = c ("contr.helmert", "contr.poly"))
stoats_mod2 <- lm (weight ~ age * sex, data = stoats)
summary (stoats_mod2)


Call:
lm(formula = weight ~ age * sex, data = stoats)

Residuals:
      Min       1Q   Median       3Q      Max
-1.23614 -0.60421  0.05658  0.65660  1.77263

Coefficients:
            Estimate Std. Error t value Pr(>|t|)
(Intercept)  2.54073    0.44319   5.733 3.08e-05 ***
age          1.27851    0.07143  17.899 5.26e-12 ***
sex1         0.57445    0.44319   1.296  0.21331
age:sex1     0.28230    0.07143   3.952  0.00114 **
```

```
---
Signif. codes:  0 '***' 0.001 '**' 0.01 '*' 0.05 '.' 0.1 ' ' 1

Residual standard error: 0.9175 on 16 degrees of freedom
Multiple R-squared:  0.9652,Adjusted R-squared:  0.9587
F-statistic: 147.8 on 3 and 16 DF,  p-value: 7.101e-12
```

The `intercept` is the overall intercept, `age` is the overall slope, `sex1` represents what needs to be added to (for males) or taken away from (for females) the overall intercept to arrive at the gender intercepts and `age:sex1` similarly to get the two gender slopes. Once we understand where the numbers come from, the interpretation would remain the same as in the treatment contrast model.

Finally, we look at sum contrasts:

```
options (contrasts = c ("contr.sum", "contr.poly"))
stoats_mod3 <- lm (weight ~ age * sex, data = stoats)
summary (stoats_mod3)

Call:
lm(formula = weight ~ age * sex, data = stoats)

Residuals:
     Min       1Q   Median       3Q      Max
-1.23614 -0.60421  0.05658  0.65660  1.77263

Coefficients:
            Estimate Std. Error t value Pr(>|t|)
(Intercept)  2.54073    0.44319   5.733 3.08e-05 ***
age          1.27851    0.07143  17.899 5.26e-12 ***
sex1        -0.57445    0.44319  -1.296  0.21331
age:sex1    -0.28230    0.07143  -3.952  0.00114 **
---
Signif. codes:  0 '***' 0.001 '**' 0.01 '*' 0.05 '.' 0.1 ' ' 1

Residual standard error: 0.9175 on 16 degrees of freedom
Multiple R-squared:  0.9652,Adjusted R-squared:  0.9587
F-statistic: 147.8 on 3 and 16 DF,  p-value: 7.101e-12
```

This is very similar to the Helmert contrasts in this case, with the signs of the final two estimates reversed. Note that in all three models the R^2 and F-test values remain the same.

References

Cox, D. R., & Reid, N. (2000). *The theory of design of experiments*. Chapman & Hall.
Diggle, P. J., Liang, K. Y., & Zeger, S. L. (1994). *Analysis of longitudinal data*. Clarendon Press.

## 17

Meta-Analysis

There is a compelling case to be made that analysts should look at the whole body of evidence rather than trying to understand individual studies in isolation. The **systematic review** of a body of evidence is known as **meta-analysis**. The idea is to draw together all of the appropriate studies that have addressed the same question and attempted to estimate the same effect, and calculate an overall effect and an overall measure of uncertainly for it.

In an ideal world, we should be able to extract from every published study the exact question addressed, the estimated effect size, the variance of that effect, the sample size, and enough detail on the methods used to be confident that the study was comparable with the others that we have already included. This allows us to calculate a suitable overall effect size and that would be it. It sounds simple enough, but there are many pitfalls to watch out for.

We'll merely scratch the surface in this chapter, but an excellent source of information is the Cochrane Training webpage, https://training.cochrane.org/, which houses the Cochrane Handbook (Higgins et al., 2021).

17.1   Elements of a meta-analysis

There is a lot to think about when embarking on a meta-analysis. Broadly speaking we need to decide:

1. which studies to include in the analysis;

2. what effect is of interest and whether this is calculable from the information we have;

3. how to weight the evidence from each study;

4. what model to use for the meta-analysis.

These are briefly addressed below in turn.

The R Book, Third Edition. Elinor Jones, Simon Harden and Michael J. Crawley.
© 2023 John Wiley & Sons Ltd. Published 2023 by John Wiley & Sons Ltd.
Companion website: www.wiley.com/go/jones/therbook3e

17.1.1   Choosing studies for a meta-analysis

You cannot do a meta-analysis without collating a set of suitable studies which have attempted to address the same question. Gathering these studies is often the most time-consuming and difficult aspect of a meta-analysis.

It is important to think very carefully about the following:

- What do we mean by 'the same question'?
- What is an appropriate study?
- What makes a study inappropriate?
- How different can a study be and still be worth including in the meta-analysis?
- What are the publication biases in the various studies?

In reality, it would be rare to find a set of studies that have been conducted in *exactly* the same way. Subject knowledge will be needed to decide which studies are similar enough and which are not. Now, come up with clear rules for the selection (and omission) of studies.

Be aware that **publication bias** is a real problem for meta-analysis. We can never know how many experiments were carried out but not published, and it is highly likely that proportionately more studies go unpublished if they failed to find a significant effect. If they don't make it to publication, we have no hope of accounting for the information they contained in our meta-analysis. This will, unfortunately, bias our results. We can attempt to investigate publication bias via **funnel plots** (which we'll see in Section 17.3) though the method won't work well if there are only a small number of studies in the meta-analysis.

17.1.2   Effects and effect size

Meta-analysis can work with a variety of effect types. The list below isn't exhaustive, but it gives some sense of the broad scope of meta-analysis.

- Measures from continuous variable(s):
  - Means;
  - Mean differences and standardised mean differences between two independent groups;
  - Mean differences and standardised mean differences, paired observations;
  - Ratio of means (response ratio);
  - Correlation coefficients.
- Measures from categorical variable(s):
  - Proportions;
  - Rates;
  - Risk difference;
  - Odds ratios;
  - Risk ratios (relative risk).

For some studies in a meta-analysis, the measure of interest might already be computed in the relevant paper or other publication. In other cases, that won't be the case. For example, interest might be in estimating a particular odds ratio. While some studies might include their estimated odds ratio in their publication, others may publish a 2×2 contingency table of results from which the odds ratio will need to be computed.

It is important to note that the effect type from each study needs to be the same. That is, if one study reports an odds ratio and another study reports a risk difference, the results can't be combined into a single meta-analysis unless the data are available from which a single effect type for all studies can be computed.

17.1.3 Weights

It would be a poor quality meta-analysis if we were just to combine the study results without thinking about the quality of the evidence provided by individual studies. More precise studies should be given heavier weights in comparison to less precise studies, rather than simply taking the arithmetic mean of the effect size of interest across studies.

But what do we mean by 'precision' and how should we measure it? There are a number of options. Sample size weighting is one such option, with larger studies allocated higher weight. In some ways, this makes sense and is appealing due to its simplicity. A large sample size doesn't always guarantee that the estimate itself is particularly precise, however: there could be considerable uncertainty around the estimate despite a large sample size, whereas a smaller study might have less uncertainty. Here, of course, we're referring to the standard error (or equivalently the variance) of the effect size as a measure of uncertainty.

It therefore makes sense to consider using the standard error of the effect size as a tool for weighting studies, and that is exactly what is used in many meta-analyses. This gives more weight to studies with smaller standard error (less uncertainty around the estimated effect size) than those with larger standard error. A common way of doing this is by using **inverse variance weighting**, where 'variance' refers to the squared standard error.

How does this compare to the sample size weighting? Typically, studies with larger sample size have smaller standard error/variance, which leads to a heavier weighting in the meta-analysis. This isn't always the case, but often is in practice.

We'll use inverse variance weighting from now on. In this case, if we have effect sizes $\hat{\mu}_1, \dots, \hat{\mu}_N$ from N studies, and corresponding estimated standard errors $\hat{v}_1, \dots, \hat{v}_N$ for these effects, then a *basic* inverse-variance meta-analysis of these effect size would give an overall effect size of

$$\frac{\sum_{i=1}^{N} \hat{\mu}_i / \hat{v}_i^2}{\sum_{i=1}^{N} 1/\hat{v}_i^2}. \tag{17.1}$$

The numerator weights the individual study effects and the denominator then scales this back to the original scale. As straightforward as (17.1) is, this method might not adequately reflect the overall effect estimate as we'll see next.

17.1.4 Fixed vs. random effect models

There will naturally be variation in the effect sizes from different studies. In some instances, it might be possible to justify that there is a *single true effect size* (for instance, if many studies are trying to estimate the same physical constant), and that any differences between studies is purely down to sampling error. In this case, supposing that the true effect is denoted μ, then the k'th study's estimate of it, $\hat{\mu}_k$, can be represented by

$$\hat{\mu}_k = \mu + \epsilon_k$$

where ϵ_k is study k's sampling error and typically we assume that $\epsilon_k \sim N(0, v_k^2)$.

The aim of a meta-analysis under these assumptions is to estimate μ in the best way. This is known as a fixed-effect model, and the resulting analysis a **fixed effects meta-analysis**. Equation (17.1) would be an appropriate method to estimate the inverse-variance weighted overall effect size.

It is much more likely in practice, however, that the effect being estimated varies with the context (e.g. with location, genetics, or environmental conditions). That is, the k'th study's estimate of the effect size, $\hat{\mu}_k$, has some underlying true value μ_k, and this varies from study to study. These true study effects $\mu_1, \dots, \mu_N$ will centre around μ, say, and study k's true effect size will deviate from this by some amount δ_k. Therefore, study k's estimate, $\hat{\mu}_k$, can be written as follows:

$$\hat{\mu}_k = \mu_k + \epsilon_k$$
$$= \mu + \delta_k + \epsilon_k \qquad (17.2)$$

where $\epsilon_k \sim N(0, v_k^2)$ and $\delta_k \sim N(0, \tau^2)$.

Our aim is still to estimate μ via a meta-analysis, but now we have two sources of 'error' to contend with:

- error arising because of the difference between study k's true effect size and study k's estimated effect (denoted by ϵ_k), known as sampling error or error *within* studies;

- error arising due to the difference between study k's true effect size and the overall effect size (denoted by δ_k) known as the heterogeneity *between* studies.

With a model as defined in (17.2), the resulting meta-analysis is referred to as a **random effects meta-analysis** as the δ_k act as random effects.

The weighting method in (17.1) is no longer suitable under (17.2) because the weights would only take into account the sampling error within study rather than the heterogeneity between studies. The appropriate weighting of study effects is now:

$$\frac{\sum_{i=1}^{N} \hat{\mu}_i / (\hat{v}_i^2 + \tau^2)}{\sum_{i=1}^{N} 1 / (\hat{v}_i^2 + \tau^2)} . \qquad (17.3)$$

We can approximate the v_i^2's easily as before, but what about τ^2? There are a number of ways of doing this, the most common being an approach by DerSimonian and Laird, 1986 which also happens to be one of the simplest methods. This is what we'll use in the examples of Section 17.3.

A natural question would be whether the added complexity of a random effects meta-analysis is worth it, especially if we have only a small number of studies. Do we really need to take into account heterogeneity between studies, or can we get away with a fixed effects meta-analysis? It might be that there is external knowledge about the effect size of interest which dictates one way or another whether a fixed- or random effects meta-analysis is suitable. Otherwise, we could use the data in hand to investigate further.

Common ways to check whether there is heterogeneity between studies includes Cochran's Q, the I^2 statistic, or the H^2 statistic. The first two are usually printed as part of the output for meta-analysis studies whatever package is used, along with H^2 and other statistics to boot. These are by no means perfect ways of measuring the extent of heterogeneity between studies, but they are easily accessible and provide a rough guide.

Cochran's Q provides a test of heterogeneity, with the null hypothesis stating no heterogeneity (that is, there is no variation in the underlying studies' true effect size and so a fixed effects analysis will suffice) and the alternative hypothesis stating the opposite. A small p-value here indicates that the evidence is against the null hypothesis, and so a random effect meta-analysis is likely necessary.

The I^2 statistic depends on Q and provides a value between 0 and 1. It is a rough measure of the proportion of variability in the effect sizes that is due to differences between studies. The larger this value, the more evidence we have that we need a random effects meta-analysis.

The H^2 statistic also depends on Q and estimates the ratio of the total variability between effect sizes (whether between or within studies) to the variability within studies. As the total variability will be at least as large as the variability in effect size within studies, H^2 will be at least 1. The further away H^2 is from 1, the more likely it is that we need a random effects meta-analysis.

An excellent source of accessible further reading on the nuances of random effects meta-analysis can be found in Harrer et al., 2021.

17.2 Meta-analysis in *R*

There are many packages to do the number crunching for a meta-analysis. Two commonly used packages, both with a wide range of functionality and documentation, are `meta` (Balduzzi et al., 2019) and `metafor` (Viechtbauer, 2010). The `metafor` package has more advanced capabilities than `meta`. Though the examples in this chapter could easily be done using either package, we'll demonstrate these with `metafor` as you may need to use its more advanced functions for your future analyses.

The main workhorse functions included in the `metafor` package are `escalc ()`, and the `rma ()` function or its equivalent, `rma.uni ()`. While `escalc ()` computes (if necessary) the effect of interest from each study plus the relevant standard error, `rma ()` conducts the meta-analysis itself.

17.2.1 Formatting information from studies

Before we start using `metafor`, we need to import the information from our included studies into *R*. It is necessary to compile all information into a single data set with one row per study. The information to be extracted from each study will vary depending on the type of effect of interest, but this will become second nature with a bit of practice. We'll see examples in Section 17.3.

Typically, for effects based on continuous measures, information on the estimated effect and some measure of variability from each study should be included. When interest is an effect based on categorical data, such as an odds ratio, either the computed effect size and its variance is needed or in some cases it might be possible to specify the 'raw' data from each study (e.g. for an odds ratio, the underlying entries of the relevant 2×2 contingency table).

17.2.2 Computing the inputs of a meta-analysis

The `metafor` package provides a very useful tool in its `escalc ()` function. Its purpose is to compute the relevant effect size and appropriate variance for each study. It may sound strange that there is a function to compute the effect sizes and their variances, but remember that the information from studies might not be in the format required. For example:

- interest is in the mean difference of a response between a treatment and control group (or between different time points), but each study reports the results for the treatment and control groups separately (or results at the time points separately);

- an odds ratio is needed but each study reports a 2×2 contingency table instead;

- the information about the uncertainty in an effect estimate might not be in the right format, or in the case of our 2×2 table example above, needs to be computed from the table itself. Watch out for the type of uncertainty estimate reported: 'standard deviation' and 'standard error' sound very similar, but are distinct measures.

The arguments of `escalc ()` change depending on the effect of interest, but example set-ups are given below for some common effect types. The output of this function is saved as an object, which then becomes the input for the meta-analysis. It is important to *think* before using `escalc ()`: are the data already in the correct format? If so, using `escalc ()` is pointless.

More examples can be found in Viechtbauer, 2010, which also explains further capabilities of the `escalc ()` function.

Single mean

Each study estimates a single mean. The measure in this case is coded as `"MN"`. The dataframe containing the study information, here called `study_data`, needs to be specified along with the names of the columns of the dataframe relating to the:

- sample size, `n1i`;
- mean, `m1i`;
- standard deviation, `sd1i`.

For example, if the sample size was in `study_data` in a column called `study_size`, the mean in a column called `study_mean`, and the standard deviation in a column called `study_stdev`, then we'd use:

```
dat_mean <- escalc (measure = "MN",
                    n1i = study_size, m1i = study_mean, sd1i = study_stdev,
                    data = study_data)
```

Mean difference

Here, each study will have looked at two groups (we'll call them group 1 and group 2) and estimated the mean response for each. We're interested in looking at the mean difference between these groups, which we'll assume hasn't been computed. The measure in this case is coded as `"MD"`.

The dataframe containing the study information, here called `study_data`, needs to be specified along with the column of the dataframe relating to the:

- group 1 sample size, `n1i`;
- group 2 sample size, `n2i`;
- group 1 mean, `m1i`;
- group 2 mean, `m2i`;
- group 1 standard deviation, `sd1i`;
- group 2 standard deviation, `sd2i`.

The function can then be written as follows, substituting in the relevant column names as necessary:

```
dat_meandiff <- escalc (measure = "MD",
                        n1i, n2i, m1i, m2i, sd1i, sd2i,
                        data = study_data)
```

Standardised mean difference

Each study will have looked at two groups (we'll call them group 1 and group 2) and estimated the mean response for each. This time we want the standardised mean difference. This is useful when studies target the same outcome but may have measured it in different ways. The measure in this case is coded as `"SMD"`. The dataframe containing the study information, here called `study_data`, needs to be specified along with the column of the dataframe relating to the:

- group 1 sample size, `n1i`;
- group 2 sample size, `n2i`;
- group 1 mean, `m1i`;
- group 2 mean, `m2i`;
- group 1 standard deviation, `sd1i`;
- group 2 standard deviation, `sd2i`.

The function can then be written as follows, substituting in the relevant column names as necessary:

```
dat_meandiff <- escalc (measure = "SMD",
                        n1i, n2i, m1i, m2i, sd1i, sd2i,
                        data = study_data)
```

Correlation

Each study measures a correlation coefficient (same type in each study, e.g. all Pearson correlation coefficients). The measure in this case is coded as `"COR"`. The dataframe containing the study information, here called `study_data`, needs to be specified along with the column of the dataframe relating to the:

- raw correlation coefficients, `ri`;

- sample size, `ni`.

The function can then be written as follows, substituting in the relevant column names as necessary:

```
dat_corr <- escalc (measure = "COR",
                    ri, ni,
                    data = study_data)
```

Odds ratios, risk ratios and risk differences

Supposing that each study provides a 2×2 contingency table and that interest is in estimating either the odds ratio, risk ratio, or risk difference. The measures in this case are coded as `"OR"`, `"RR"` and `"RD"`, respectively. The dataframe containing the study information, here called `study_data`, needs to be specified along with the column of the dataframe relating to the:

- upper left cell from 2×2 contingency table, `ai`;

- lower left cell from 2×2 contingency table, `ci`;

- EITHER: upper right cell from 2×2 contingency table, `bi`, and lower right cell, `di`;

- OR upper row total, `n1i`, and lower row total, `n2i`.

Note that the tables need to be set up in the same way to do this (that is, the columns and rows must be in the same order for all contingency tables under consideration).

The function can then be written as follows (depending on information given), substituting `"OR"` for either of the other two measures as necessary, and using the relevant column names:

```
dat_corr <- escalc (measure = "OR",
                    ai, bi, ci, di,
                    data = study_data)
dat_corr <- escalc (measure = "OR",
                    ai, ci, n1i, n2i,
                    data = study_data)
```

17.2.3 Conducting the meta-analysis

Once we've computed everything we need, which may or may not have required the use of `escalc ()`, we can run the meta-analysis. This is very easy using `rma ()`. The effect estimate from each study, known as `yi`, together with its variance, known as `vi`, needs to be supplied. The method, fixed- or random- effects meta-analysis will need to be specified and if the latter, the method used to compute the heterogeneity between studies, τ^2.

At this point, it is instructive to see some examples of meta-analyses using the `metafor` package.

17.3 Examples

17.3.1 Meta-analysis Of scaled differences

This example comes from Borenstein et al., 2021 and concerns six studies each with a treatment and a control group, with sample size varying from 40 to 200 for each group in each study:

```
metadata <- read.table ("metadata.txt", header = T)
head (metadata)

  study meanT sdT  nT meanC sdC  nC
1     A    94  22  60    92  20  60
2     B    98  21  65    92  22  65
3     C    98  28  40    88  26  40
4     D    94  19 200    82  17 200
5     E    98  21  50    88  22  45
6     F    96  21  85    92  22  85
```

The effect size for each study in this case is going to be the scaled difference between the treatment and control means. We'll use `metafor` to do the heavy lifting for us, from calculating the effect size from each study to conducting the meta-analysis.

Let us first use `escalc ()` to define a new dataset, `dat_boren`, that includes the effects and variances.

```
library (metafor)
dat_boren <- escalc (measure = "SMD", m1i = meanT, m2i = meanC,
                     sd1i = sdT, sd2i = sdC, n1i = nT, n2i = nC,
                     data = metadata)
head (dat_boren)

  study meanT sdT  nT meanC sdC  nC     yi     vi
1     A    94  22  60    92  20  60 0.0945 0.0334
2     B    98  21  65    92  22  65 0.2774 0.0311
3     C    98  28  40    88  26  40 0.3665 0.0508
4     D    94  19 200    82  17 200 0.6644 0.0106
5     E    98  21  50    88  22  45 0.4618 0.0433
6     F    96  21  85    92  22  85 0.1852 0.0236
```

The `escalc ()` function has computed the effect size (shown in the column labelled `yi`) and the associated variance (shown as `vi`). This is much easier and less error prone than doing the calculations by hand.

Now we're ready to run the meta-analysis using `rma ()`. We need to decide at this point whether we want a fixed effects meta-analysis or a random effects meta-analysis. Let us run both to see the difference, starting with the fixed-effects version.

```
fixed_boren <- rma (yi = yi, vi = vi, data = dat_boren, method = "FE")
fixed_boren

Fixed-Effects Model (k = 6)

I^2 (total heterogeneity/total variability):   58.03%
H^2 (total variability/sampling variability):  2.38

Test for Heterogeneity:
Q(df = 5) = 11.9138, p-val = 0.0360

Model Results:

estimate      se     zval     pval    ci.lb    ci.ub
  0.4150  0.0643   6.4557   <.0001   0.2890   0.5410   ***

---
Signif. codes:  0 '***' 0.001 '**' 0.01 '*' 0.05 '.' 0.1 ' ' 1
```

The output gives us the estimate of the overall effect size, which is 0.415. The output also includes the 95% confidence interval for our overall estimate, which is (0.289, 0.541).

Of interest, perhaps, is the output relating to the summaries for heterogeneity between studies. The output for Q, I^2, and H^2 all point to there being evidence of some heterogeneity between studies. These are only indicators, however, so if it makes scientific sense to run only a fixed effects meta-analysis here, then do only that.

Let us take a look at the random effects version of this meta-analysis. The rma () function just needs a small tweak to the method argument. We have a choice of methods in how we run a random effects meta-analysis, which boils down to options in computing the between-study variance, τ^2. The most common is DerSimonian and Laird's method, but others are listed in the documentation for the metafor package. We'll stick to DerSimonian and Laird's method by specifying method = "DL".

```
random_boren <- rma (yi = yi, vi = vi, data = dat_boren, method = "DL")
random_boren

Random-Effects Model (k = 6; tau^2 estimator: DL)

tau^2 (estimated amount of total heterogeneity): 0.0372 (SE = 0.0421)
tau (square root of estimated tau^2 value):        0.1930
I^2 (total heterogeneity/total variability):       58.03%
H^2 (total variability/sampling variability):      2.38

Test for Heterogeneity:
Q(df = 5) = 11.9138, p-val = 0.0360

Model Results:

estimate      se     zval     pval    ci.lb    ci.ub
  0.3585  0.1055   3.3996   0.0007   0.1518   0.5652   ***

---
Signif. codes:  0 '***' 0.001 '**' 0.01 '*' 0.05 '.' 0.1 ' ' 1
```

The output gives us the estimate of the overall effect size, which is 0.358. We see that the 95% confidence interval for our overall estimate is $(0.152, 0.565)$. Note the difference in estimates between the fixed- and random-effect versions, and this time we also get an estimate of the between-study variance, τ^2.

A forest plot is an excellent way of displaying the individual study effects together with the estimated overall effect. Let us use our random effects meta-analysis as an example. We tell the function `forest ()` which meta-analysis object to use, request that headers be included for the study label and standardised mean difference columns, and that we use the study names as taken from the data set.

```
forest (random_boren, header = TRUE, slab = paste (dat_boren$study))
```

The study effect size is graphically represented by a solid black box in Figure 17.1. The bigger the box, the more weight was assigned to the study. This tallies with the size of the variance in the data set generated by `escalc ()`: the larger this variance, the smaller the weight and the resulting box. The whiskers from the box represent the 95% confidence interval for each estimate. These estimates are also written on the right-hand side of the plot. The overall effect size is represented by a diamond at the bottom of the plot, the width of which indicates the 95% confidence interval around this estimate. Helpfully, the plot also includes a reminder that a random effects model (RE Model) was used.

We can see in Figure 17.1 that the confidence interval for four of the six study estimates cross zero. A zero indicates no difference between the groups, and this is indicated on the plot by a

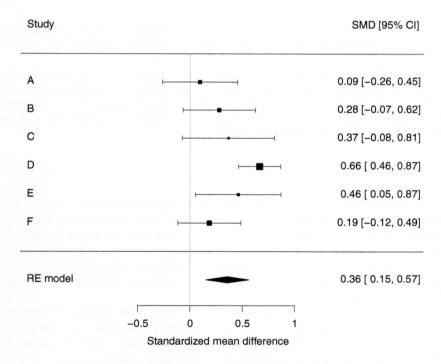

Figure 17.1 Forest plot for the random effects meta-analysis.

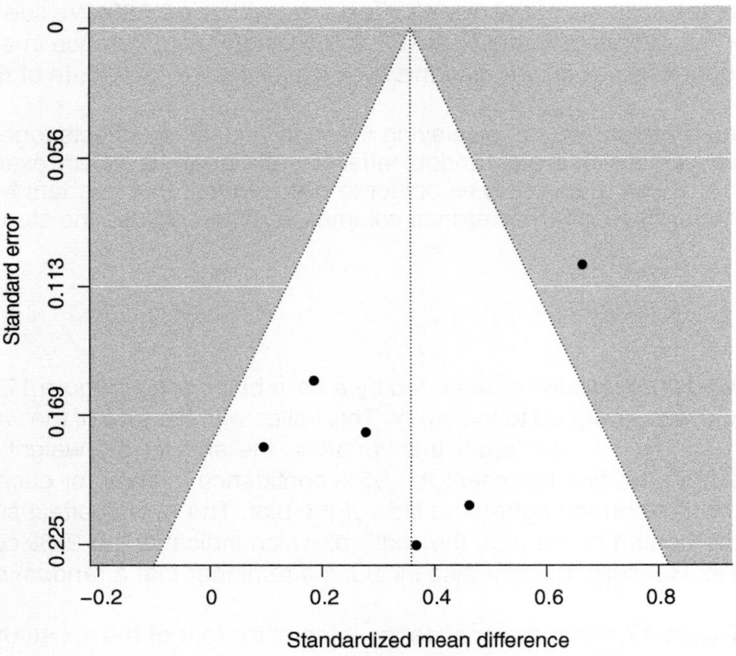

Figure 17.2 Funnel plot for the studies included in our meta-analysis.

vertical dashed line. However, we can see that the largest weight was assigned to study D – which happened to have the largest sample size too – and in this study, we can see a clear difference between the two groups.

Finally, though the sample size (number of studies) is relatively small, we could consider a funnel plot to check for any evidence of publication bias. These types of graphics plot the effect size on the *x*-axis, and the associated variance on the *y*-axis. We would expect to see a triangular pattern (or upside-down funnel shape) as indicated in Figure 17.2, though Higgins et al., 2021 recommend a minimum of 10 studies for this to be meaningful.

```
funnel (random_boren, xlab = "Standardized Mean Difference")
```

Each study is plotted in Figure 17.2. The location of the apex of the white triangle coincides with the overall effect estimate, while the triangle itself represents the area we would expect all studies to lie. The smaller the standard error (square root of the variance of the effect estimate), the more information the study contains (which is related to its weight in the meta-analysis) and in turn we'd expect such studies to produce similar effect estimates (at the top of the white triangle). Meanwhile, for studies with larger standard errors, we'd expect the effect sizes to vary more from study to study (bottom of the white triangle).

We start to worry when there are systematic gaps in the funnel, but this is hard to judge when we have only a handful of studies as we have here. For example, if we see that gaps in the area indicating 'no difference' – effect size of zero in our example – this points to studies that may not have been published due to not finding 'statistically significant' results.

The picture in Figure 17.2 is unclear, but we have only six studies so we shouldn't read too much into this plot.

17.4   Meta-analysis of categorical data

Next, we demonstrate a random effects meta-analysis on six studies, each with two treatments (control, C, and treated, T), looking at the number of deaths for each treatment. Rather morbidly, deaths are counted as 'successes' in the data set. The data come from Borenstein et al., 2021.

```
metadata2 <- read.table ("metadata2.txt", header = T)
metadata2

  study successT failureT  nT successC failureC  nC
1     A       12       53  65       16       49  65
2     B        8       32  40       10       30  40
3     C       14       66  80       19       61  80
4     D       25      375 400       80      320 400
5     E        8       32  40       11       29  40
6     F       16       49  65       18       47  65
```

The effect of interest is the *log*-odds ratio rather than the odds ratio. This is because it makes the mathematics easier. Roughly speaking, the odds ratio takes values in $[0, \infty)$ with an odds ratio of 1 indicating no difference between treatment and control. Resulting confidence intervals, for example, will not be symmetric around the estimated odds ratio, making the maths cumbersome. By taking the log of the odds ratio, the value can be anything in $(-\infty, \infty)$ with a log odds ratio of 0 indicating no difference between treatment and control. Our confidence intervals will now be symmetric around the estimate, and the maths is far easier to handle. We can, of course, reverse engineer our results so that we see the odds ratios rather than the log odds ratios.

The data tell us that for study A, for example, we have 65 individuals allocated to the treatment (of which 12 died), and another 65 individuals were allocated to the control group (with 16 deaths observed). The information on each study in the data set could be written as a contingency table, which for study A is given in Table 17.1.

For this particular study, the odds ratio is $(12 \times 49)/(53 \times 16) = 0.693$, so that the log-odds is -0.366, but we can use `escalc ()` to do all calculations for us including the appropriate variance. We input the number of deaths and number who survived for each treatment, taking care that `ai` and `bi` relate to one group and `ci` and `di` relates to the other.

```
library (metafor)
dat_categ <- escalc (measure = "OR", ai = successT, bi = failureT,
                     ci = successC, di = failureC,
                     data = metadata2)
head (dat_categ)
```

Table 17.1   Data from Study A.

	Deaths	Survived	TOTAL
Treatment	12	53	65
Control	16	49	65
TOTAL	28	102	130

	study	successT	failureT	nT	successC	failureC	nC	yi	vi
1	A	12	53	65	16	49	65	-0.3662	0.1851
2	B	8	32	40	10	30	40	-0.2877	0.2896
3	C	14	66	80	19	61	80	-0.3842	0.1556
4	D	25	375	400	80	320	400	-1.3218	0.0583
5	E	8	32	40	11	29	40	-0.4169	0.2816
6	F	16	49	65	18	47	65	-0.1595	0.1597

The function `escalc ()` has computed everything we need, with each study's estimated log odds ratio in the column `yi` and the estimated variance in the column `vi`. Let us get on with the meta-analysis, for which we'll assume a random effects set-up using the DerSimonian and Laird method once again.

```
random_categ <- rma (yi = yi, vi = vi, data = dat_categ, method = "DL")
random_categ

Random-Effects Model (k = 6; tau^2 estimator: DL)

tau^2 (estimated amount of total heterogeneity): 0.1729 (SE = 0.2148)
tau (square root of estimated tau^2 value):        0.4158
I^2 (total heterogeneity/total variability):      52.61%
H^2 (total variability/sampling variability):      2.11

Test for Heterogeneity:
Q(df = 5) = 10.5512, p-val = 0.0610

Model Results:

estimate      se     zval     pval    ci.lb    ci.ub
 -0.5663  0.2388  -2.3711   0.0177  -1.0344  -0.0982   *


---
Signif. codes:  0 '***' 0.001 '**' 0.01 '*' 0.05 '.' 0.1 ' ' 1
```

The overall estimate of the log odds ratio is below zero (all studies indicated this, see the estimates from `escalc ()`), and the 95% confidence interval lies entirely below zero too indicating that there is a difference between the treatment and control groups in terms of number of deaths.

Let us take a look at the associated forest plot:

```
forest (random_categ, header = TRUE, slab = paste (dat_categ$study))
```

In Figure 17.3, we see that the study with the most weight (and also the largest sample size, as would be expected) – Study D – is the only one with a confidence interval that *doesn't* cross zero. Remember that a zero on the log odds ratio scale indicates no difference in proportion of deaths between treatment and control group.

We may want to display the forest plot in terms of odds ratios rather than log odds ratios. We can transform the results in Figure 17.3 by specifying `atransf = exp` in the `forest ()` function. This takes the exponential of the log odds ratios, which puts us back on the odds ratio scale. Notice the asymmetry in the confidence intervals on the right-hand side of the plot in Figure 17.4, though the *x*-axis is on a natural log scale so they appear symmetric in the plot.

```
forest (random_categ, header = TRUE, slab = paste (dat_categ$study), atransf = exp)
```

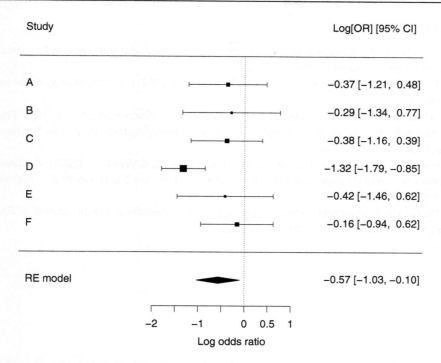

Figure 17.3 Forest plot for the random effects meta-analysis of log odds ratios.

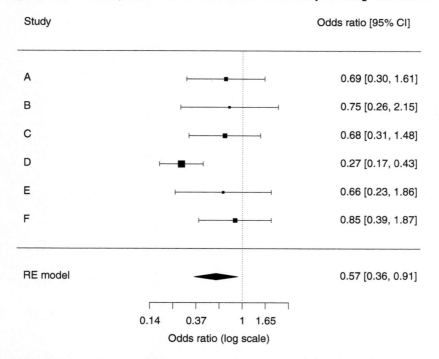

Figure 17.4 Forest plot for the random effects meta-analysis of odds ratios (with a log scale on the *x*-axis).

References

Balduzzi, S., Rücker, G., & Schwarzer, G. (2019). How to perform a meta-analysis with R: a practical tutorial. *Evidence-Based Mental Health*, *22*(4), 153–160.

Borenstein, M., Hedges, L. V., Higgins, J. P. T., & Rothstein, H. (2021). *Introduction to meta-analysis*. John Wiley & Sons, Inc.

DerSimonian, R., & Laird, N. (1986). Meta-analysis in clinical trials. *Controlled Clinical Trials*, *7*(3), 177–188.

Harrer, M., Cuijpers, P., Furukawa, T. A., & Ebert, D. D. (2021). *Doing meta-analysis with R: a hands-on guide* (First). Chapman & Hall/CRC Press.

Higgins, J., Thomas, J., Chandler, J., Cumpston, M., Li, T., Page, M., & Welch, V. (2021). Cochrane handbook for systematic reviews of interventions version 6.2 (updated february 2021). *Cochrane*. http://www.training.cochrane.org/handbook.

Viechtbauer, W. (2010). Conducting meta-analyses in R with the metafor package. *Journal of Statistical Software*, *36*(3), 1–48. https://doi.org/10.18637/jss.v036.i03.

18

Time Series

Time series data are vectors of numbers, typically regularly spaced in time. Yearly counts of animals, daily prices of shares, monthly means of temperature, and minute-by-minute details of blood pressure are all examples of time series, but they are measured on different time scales. Sometimes the interest is in the time series itself (e.g. whether or not it is cyclic, or how well the data fit a particular theoretical model), and sometimes the time series is incidental to a designed experiment (e.g. repeated measures). We cover each of these cases in turn.

Three key concepts in time series analysis are

- trend;

- serial dependence; and

- stationarity.

Many time series analyses assume that the data are **untrended**. If they do show a consistent upward or downward trend, then they can be detrended before analysis (e.g. by differencing). Serial dependence arises because the values of adjacent members of a time series may well be connected, as one might expect in all the examples listed above. Stationarity is a technical concept, but it can be thought of simply as meaning that the time series has the same properties wherever we start looking at it and is an assumption made in many models (after the trend has been removed). We will have a look at some examples that cover many common themes of time series before returning to the theory in a little more detail with an example. Finally, we look at simulating time series. A longer introduction to using R with time series can be found, for instance, at Cowpertwait and Metcalfe, 2009.

18.1 Moving average

A good way of seeing patterns in time series data is to plot the moving average. For instance, a three-point moving average:

$$y_t = \frac{y_{t-1} + y_t + y_{t+1}}{3}$$

The R Book, Third Edition. Elinor Jones, Simon Harden and Michael J. Crawley.
© 2023 John Wiley & Sons Ltd. Published 2023 by John Wiley & Sons Ltd.
Companion website: www.wiley.com/go/jones/therbook3e

We could write a simple function in *R* to calculate the moving average of length *n* of a series of numbers of length *l*:

```
ma <- function (y, n) {
  l <- length (y)
  y_new <- numeric (l - n + 1)
  for (i in 1:length (y_new)) {
    y_new[i] <- mean (y[i:(i + n - 1)])
  }
  y_new
}
```

A time series of 13 years of mean monthly temperatures will illustrate the use of the moving average, resulting in Figure 18.1:

```
temp <- read.table ("temp.txt", header = T)
attach (temp)
plot (temps, col = hue_pal ()(4)[1])
lines (temps, col = hue_pal ()(4)[2])
plot (temps, col = hue_pal ()(4)[1])
lines (x = 2:155, y = ma (temps, 3), col = hue_pal ()(4)[3])
plot (temps, col = hue_pal ()(4)[1])
lines (x = seq (6.5, 150.5, 1), y = ma (temps, 12), col = hue_pal ()(4)[4])
detach (temp)
```

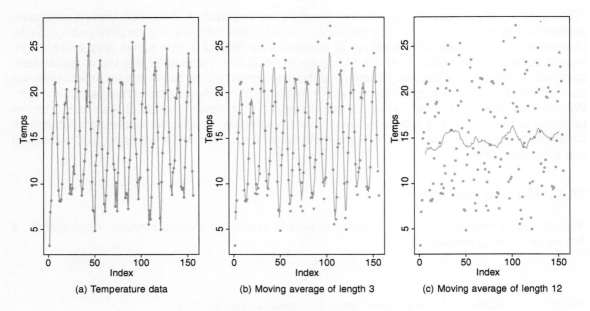

(a) Temperature data   (b) Moving average of length 3   (c) Moving average of length 12

Figure 18.1 Time series plots for `temp`.

In the first plot, we have just joined the plotted dots with a line (i.e. a moving average of length one: an alternative would just be to use `plot (temps, type = "b")`, although this looks a little ungainly). We just need to be careful to plot the moving average at the right points on the x-axis: the first point is at $(n + 1)/2$ and the last at $l - (n - 1)/2$. R uses the term `Index` to denote the x values of data, where y values exist. We can see that the three-point moving average smooths out the extreme values, while the twelve-point version compensates for the annual seasonal effect.

18.2 Blowflies

The Australian ecologist, A.J. Nicholson, reared blowfly larvae on pieces of liver in laboratory cultures that his technicians kept running continuously for almost 7 years (361 weeks, to be exact). The data are just the count for each week:

```
blowfly <- read.table ("blowfly.txt" , header = T)
head.matrix(blowfly)

     flies
1    948
2    942
3    911
4    858
5    801
6    676
```

R has a particular format for storing time series, and we can convert the data into that and then plot them to give Figure 18.2:

```
flies <- ts (blowfly$flies)
plot (flies, col = hue_pal ()(1))
```

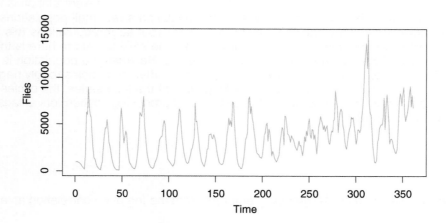

Figure 18.2 Time series plot for `blowfly`.

The plot () function recognises that we have a time series and plots accordingly (in fact using plot.ts ()). This classic time series has two clear features:

- For the first 200 weeks, the system exhibits beautifully regular cycles;
- After week 200, things change (perhaps a genetic mutation had arisen); the cycles become much less clear-cut, and the population begins a pronounced upward trend.

Two important ideas to understand in time series analysis are autocorrelation and partial autocorrelation. **Autocorrelation** describes how this week's population is related to last week's population. This is the autocorrelation at (time) lag 1: it can also be measured for any lag. **Partial autocorrelation** describes the relationship between this week's population and the population at lag t once we have controlled for the correlations between all of the intervening weeks between this week and week t. The definition should become clear if we draw the scatterplots from which, for instance, the first four autocorrelation terms are calculated (lags 1–4).

There is a snag, however. The vector of flies at lag 1 is shorter (by one) than the original vector because the first element of the lagged vector is the second element of flies. The coordinates of the first data point to be drawn on the scatterplot are (flies[1],flies[2]) and the coordinates of the last plot that can be drawn are (flies[360], flies[361]) because the original vector is 361 element long:

```
length (flies)
```

```
[1] 361
```

Thus, the lengths of the vectors that can be plotted go down by one for every increase in the lag of one. We can produce the four plots for lags 1–4 in a function like this, which produces Figure 18.3:

```
sapply (1:4, function (x) plot (flies[-(361: (361 - x + 1))], flies[-(1:x)],
                                xlab = "", ylab = "", col = hue_pal () (8) [x]) )
```

So, for instance, at lag 3 (i.e. x = 3), we are plotting flies[-(361:359)] which equals flies[1:358] against flies[-(1:3)] which is flies[4:361]. The correlation is very strong at lag 1, but notice how the variance increases with population size: small populations this week are invariably correlated with small populations next week, but large populations this week may be associated with large or small populations next week. The striking pattern here is the way that the correlation fades away as the size of the lag increases. Because the population is cyclic, the correlation goes to zero, then becomes weakly negative and then becomes strongly negative. This occurs at lags that are half the cycle length. Looking back at the time series, the cycles look to be about 20 weeks in length. So let us repeat the exercise by producing scatterplots at lags of 7, 8, 9, and 10 weeks in Figure 18.4:

```
sapply (7:10, function (x) plot (flies[-(361: (361 - x + 1))], flies[-(1:x)],
                                 xlab = "", ylab = "", col = hue_pal () (8) [x - 2]) )
```

The negative correlation at lag 10 gradually emerges from the fog of no correlation at lag 7.

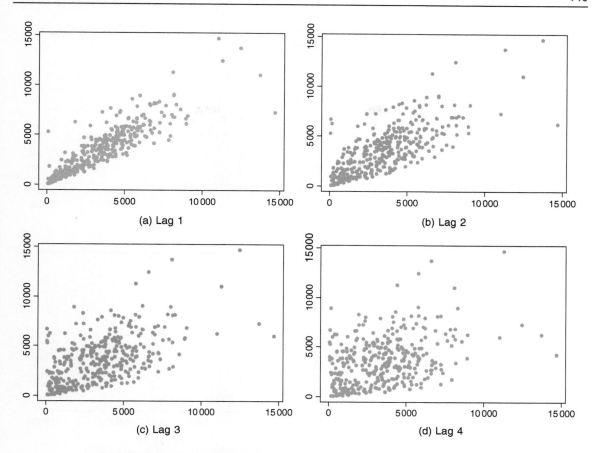

Figure 18.3 Scatter plots comparing `blowfly` numbers at different lags.

We can investigate the **autocorrelation** and **partial autocorrelation** using R's `acf ()` function, which calculates the two types of correlation for increasing lags, to produce Figure 18.5:

```
acf (flies, col = hue_pal () (2) [1], main = "")
acf (flies, type = "p", col = hue_pal () (2) [2], main = "")
```

The autocorrelation plot (Figure 18.5a) shows a gradually decreasing positive association between the value at a time point and that 6 weeks later, followed by a negative relationship for a lag of 7–12 weeks, and then a positive link peaking at about week 19. This is consistent with the time series plot in Figure 18.2, even taking into account the changes from week 200 or thereabouts. The dotted blue lines attempt to show where the size of the autocorrelation might be deemed to be significant. These should be taken with a very large pinch of salt, as with all claims about statistical significance, and subject matter expertise is a much better judge of important levels of association.

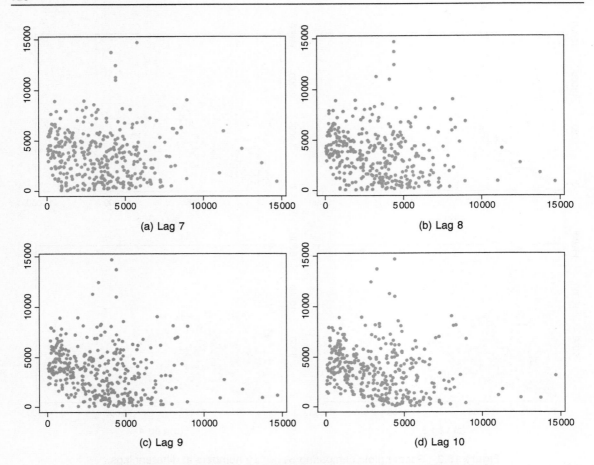

Figure 18.4 Scatter plots comparing `blowfly` numbers at different lags.

What kinds of time lags are involved in the generation of these cycles? We use partial autocorrelation (`type = "p"`) to find this out as shown in Figure 18.5b. The density-dependent effects are most manifest at lags of two and three weeks, with other negative effects at lags of four and five weeks. These lags reflect the duration of the larval and pupal period (one and two periods, respectively). The cycles are clearly caused by overcompensating density dependence, resulting from intra-specific competition between the larvae for food (what Nicholson christened 'scramble competition'). There is a curious positive feedback at a lag of 12 weeks (12–16 weeks, in fact). What might be the cause for this?

We might have decided that the behaviour of the time series is consistent (**stationary**, approximately) over the first 200 weeks, but then changes after that. We could investigate the behaviour of the second half of the time series in the hope that that might also be stationary, albeit in a different way form the first half. Let us examine the data from week 201 onwards:

```
flies_2 <- flies[201:361]
```

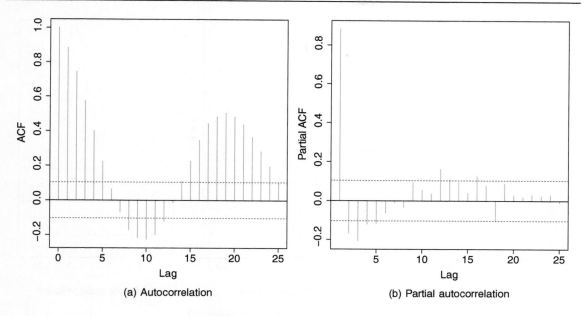

(a) Autocorrelation   (b) Partial autocorrelation

Figure 18.5   Correlation plots for `blowfly`.

We can test for a linear **trend** in mean fly numbers against day number, from 1 to `length`
(`flies_2`):

```
blowfly_mod <- lm (flies_2 ~ I (1:length (flies_2)))
summary (blowfly_mod)


Call:
lm(formula = flies_2 ~ I(1:length(flies_2)))

Residuals:
    Min      1Q  Median      3Q     Max
-4584.8 -1205.5  -138.0   968.6  9375.7

Coefficients:
                      Estimate Std. Error t value Pr(>|t|)
(Intercept)           2827.531    336.661   8.399 2.37e-14 ***
I(1:length(flies_2))    21.945      3.605   6.087 8.29e-09 ***
---
Signif. codes:  0 '***' 0.001 '**' 0.01 '*' 0.05 '.' 0.1 ' ' 1

Residual standard error: 2126 on 159 degrees of freedom
Multiple R-squared:  0.189,Adjusted R-squared:  0.1839
F-statistic: 37.05 on 1 and 159 DF,  p-value: 8.289e-09
```

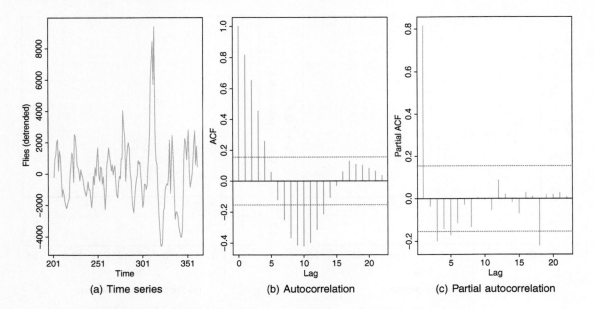

Figure 18.6 Time series plots for `blowfly`, weeks 201–361, detrended.

Note the use of I in the model formula (for 'as is') to tell *R* that the colon we have used is to generate a sequence of *x* values for the regression (and not an interaction term as it would otherwise have assumed).

   This shows that there is a definite upward trend of about 22 extra flies on average each week in the second half of the time series. We can detrend the data by subtracting the fitted values from the linear regression of second on day number:

```
flies_detrended <- flies_2 - predict (lm (flies_2 ~ I (1:length (flies_2))))
```

Now let us have another look at our time series plots but based around the detrended data. Figure 18.6 shows all three plots.

```
plot.ts (flies_detrended, col = hue_pal ()(3)[1],
          ylab = "flies (detrended)", xaxt = "n")
axis (1, at = seq (0, 150, 50), labels = seq (201, 361, 50))
acf (flies_detrended, col = hue_pal ()(3)[2], main = "")
acf (flies_detrended, type = "p", col = hue_pal ()(3)[3], main = "")
```

We have amended the *x*-axis to show the original week numbers. These new plots seem to show a cycle but which seems more damped than in the first 20 weeks and which seems to peak a couple of weeks earlier, presumably caused by the increasing population. There is also a curious large negative partial autocorrelation. For comparison purposes, autocorrelation plots for weeks 1–200 are shown in Figure 18.7, where there is also some evidence of the 18 week lag weirdness.

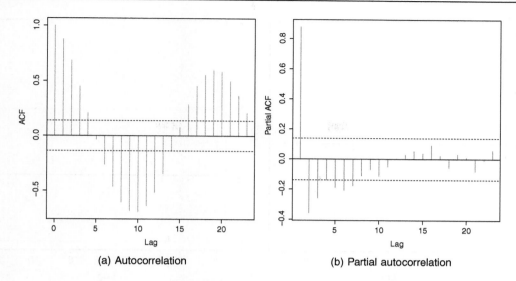

(a) Autocorrelation (b) Partial autocorrelation

Figure 18.7 Autocorrelation plots for `blowfly`, weeks 1–200.

```
flies_1 <- flies[1:200]
acf (flies_1, col = hue_pal ()(2)[1], main = "")
acf (flies_1, type = "p", col = hue_pal ()(2)[2], main = "")
```

18.3 Seasonal data

We saw a straightforward example of some temperature data in Section 18.1. Here are daily maximum and minimum temperatures (together with rainfall) from Silwood Park in south-east England over a 19-year period, beginning in 1987:

```
silwood <- read.table ("silwoodweather.txt", header = T)
head (silwood)
```

```
  upper lower rain month   yr
1  10.8   6.5 12.2     1 1987
2  10.5   4.5  1.3     1 1987
3   7.5  -1.0  0.1     1 1987
4   6.5  -3.3  1.1     1 1987
5  10.0   5.0  3.5     1 1987
6   8.0   3.0  0.1     1 1987
```

To simplify matters and make each year the same length, we will delete the leap day data. This won't have a great effect on temperature trends but, obviously, wouldn't be appropriate if we were examining cumulative rainfall:

```
silwood <- silwood[-seq (365 + 31 + 29, nrow (silwood), 365 * 4 + 1),]
```

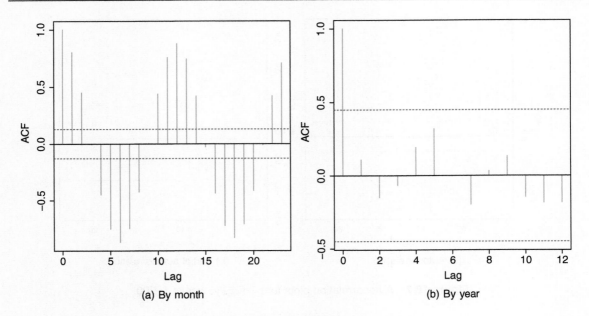

Figure 18.8   Autocorrelation plots for `silwood`.

18.3.1   Point of view

As we have seen, one way of spotting trends or seasonal effects is to review the autocorrelation plot. We will do that here by month and then by year in Figure 18.8:

```
month_ts <- ts (as.vector (tapply (silwood$upper, list (silwood$month, silwood
                                    $yr), mean)))
acf (month_ts, main = "", col = hue_pal () (2) [1])
year_ts <- ts (as.vector (tapply (silwood$upper, list (silwood$yr), mean)))
acf (year_ts, main = "", col = hue_pal () (2) [2])
```

There is a perfect monthly cycle with period 12 (as expected). What about patterns across years? Nothing! The pattern we may (or may not) see depends upon the scale at which we look for it. There is a strong pattern between days within months (tomorrow will be like today). There is very strong pattern from month to month within years (January is cold, July is warm). But there may be no pattern at all from year to year (there may be progressive global warming, but it is not apparent within this recent time series, and there is absolutely no evidence for un-trended serial correlation).

18.3.2   Built in `ts ()` functions

Our analysis of `blowfly` was a little informal and did not make the most of the tools available to us in *R*. Our analysis is more straighforward to carry out, and the graphics are better labelled, if we convert the temperature data into a regular time series object using `ts ()`, as we saw in the previous section. We need to specify the first date (January 1987) as `start = c (1987, 1)`, and the number of data points per year as `frequency = 365` (this is much simpler since we standardised the year length):

```
upper_ts <- ts (silwood$upper, start = c (1987, 1), frequency = 365)
```

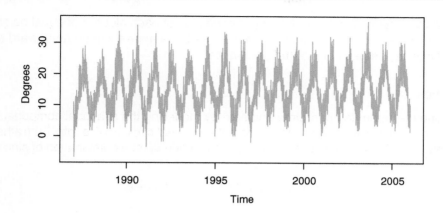

Figure 18.9   Correctly labelled time series plot for `silwood`.

Now, we can use `plot ()` to see a plot of the time series, correctly labelled by years in Figure 18.9:
.

```
plot (upper_ts, ylab = "degrees", col = hue_pal ()(1))
```

Having done that, there is a function, `stl ()`, that might help us decompose the time series into seasonal, trend, and irregular components using `loess ()` (see Section 12.1 for a discussion of the function). This gives us Figure 18.10

```
upper_decomp <- stl (upper_ts, "periodic")
plot (upper_decomp, col = hue_pal ()(2)[1], col.range = hue_pal ()(2)[2])
```

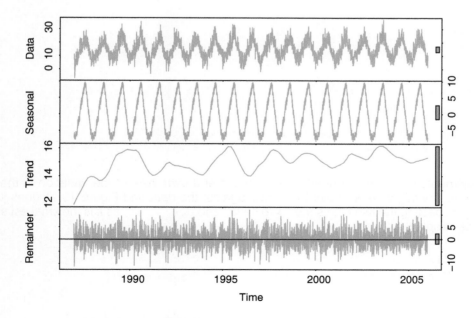

Figure 18.10   Decomposition of `silwood` using `loess ()`.

There is an annual cycle. The bars at the right-hand side of each plot are of equal heights (as can be seen by looking at the y-axes), so that we can see there appears to be an upward trend, but it is relatively small in comparison with the data range.

18.3.3 Cycles

Let us examine maximum temperatures and start by modelling the seasonal component. The simplest models for cycles are scaled so that a complete annual cycle is of length 1.0 (rather than 365 days). The equation for the seasonal (or any) cycle is made up of a combination of sine and cosine curves:

$$y_t = \alpha + \beta sin(2\pi t) + \gamma cos(2\pi t) + \epsilon_t$$

This is a linear model, so we can estimate its three parameters very simply:

```
time = (1:nrow (silwood) / 365)
silwood_mod1 <- lm (upper ~ sin (time * 2 * pi) + cos (time * 2 * pi),
                    data = silwood)
summary (silwood_mod1)


Call:
lm(formula = upper ~ sin(time * 2 * pi) + cos(time * 2 * pi),
    data = silwood)

Residuals:
     Min       1Q    Median       3Q       Max
-14.1386  -2.4136   -0.1275   2.2212   14.6645

Coefficients:
                    Estimate Std. Error t value Pr(>|t|)
(Intercept)         14.96134    0.04091  365.74   <2e-16 ***
sin(time * 2 * pi)  -2.52503    0.05785  -43.65   <2e-16 ***
cos(time * 2 * pi)  -7.24301    0.05785 -125.20   <2e-16 ***
---
Signif. codes:  0 '***' 0.001 '**' 0.01 '*' 0.05 '.' 0.1 ' ' 1

Residual standard error: 3.407 on 6932 degrees of freedom
Multiple R-squared:  0.7172, Adjusted R-squared:  0.7171
F-statistic:  8790 on 2 and 6932 DF, p-value: < 2.2e-16
```

All three elements of the model need to be retained and over 70% of the variation in the data is taken care of. We might want to plot the model against the data and Figure 18.11 does just that. We start by inspecting the two time series. We have used `pch = "."` as it is the smallest standard point we can display.

```
plot (silwood$upper, ylab = "upper", pch = ".", col = hue_pal ()(2)[1])
lines (1:(nrow (silwood)), predict (silwood_mod1), col = hue_pal ()(2)[2])
```

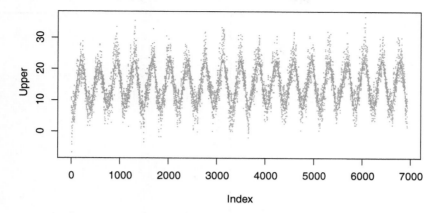

Figure 18.11 Data and predictions for `silwood` model 1.

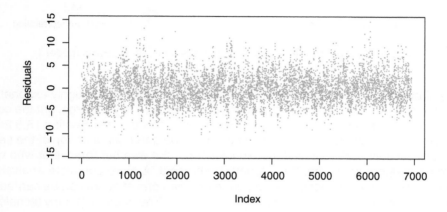

Figure 18.12 Residuals for `silwood` model 1.

We can investigate the residuals to look for patterns (e.g. trends in the mean, or autocorrelation structure). Remember that the residuals are stored as part of the model object, and they are given in Figure 18.12:

```
plot (silwood_mod1$resid, ylab = "residuals", pch = ".", col = hue_pal ()(1))
```

There looks to be some periodicity in the residuals, roughly matching the yearly patterns, but there are too many data points to pick out trends. To look for serial correlation in the residuals, we use the `acf ()` function like this to give Figure 18.13:

```
acf (silwood_mod1$resid, main = "", col = hue_pal ()(2)[1])
acf (silwood_mod1$resid, type = "p", main = "", col = hue_pal ()(2)[2])
```

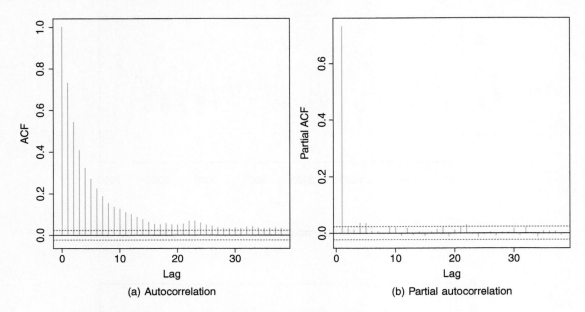

Figure 18.13   Autocorrelation analysis for residuals of `silwood` model 1.

There is very strong serial correlation in the residuals, and this drops off roughly exponentially with increasing lag (Figure 18.13a). The partial autocorrelation at lag 1 is very large, but the correlations at higher lags are much smaller. This suggests that an AR (1) model (see Section 18.5.2: basically, the previous year has an effect on the current year) might be appropriate on top of the seasonality. This is the statistical justification behind the old joke about the weather forecaster who was asked what tomorrow's weather would be. "Like today's", she said. A more complete analysis of cyclic data using sines and cosines (most cycles require more than one of each) can be carried out using **spectral decomposition**, using the function `spectrum ()`. The analysis is fairly technical and will not be considered here.

18.3.4   Testing for a time series trend

We saw from the decomposition in Figure 18.10 that there may be a trend in the Silwood maximum daily temperature data, and in Section 18.3.3 the possibility of an AR (1) model in the residuals suggested the same thing. There are many ways we could investigate this, but one option would be to take the `trend + remainder` elements from the decomposition and build a simple linear model:

```
trend_rem <- upper_decomp$time.series[,"trend"] +
  upper_decomp$time.series[,"remainder"]
silwood_mod2 <- lm (trend_rem ~ I (1: length (trend_rem)))
summary (silwood_mod2)
```

```
Call:
lm(formula = trend_rem ~ I(1:length(trend_rem)))

Residuals:
    Min      1Q   Median      3Q      Max
-13.4156  -2.2655  -0.1474   2.1437  12.5823

Coefficients:
                           Estimate Std. Error t value Pr(>|t|)
(Intercept)               1.431e+01  7.807e-02 183.251  <2e-16 ***
I(1:length(trend_rem))    1.888e-04  1.950e-05   9.685  <2e-16 ***
---
Signif. codes:  0 '***' 0.001 '**' 0.01 '*' 0.05 '.' 0.1 ' ' 1

Residual standard error: 3.25 on 6933 degrees of freedom
Multiple R-squared:  0.01335,Adjusted R-squared:  0.01321
F-statistic: 93.81 on 1 and 6933 DF,  p-value: < 2.2e-16
```

We have just regressed the data without the cycle on a simple index of days. There certainly appears to be a trend of 1.9×10^{-4} degrees per day or 0.07 degrees per year, although the small value for R^2 suggests there is a lot more going on besides that. Residual plots, which we can generate in the usual way, show nothing unusual.

18.4   Multiple time series

When we have two or more time series measured over the same period, the question naturally arises as to whether or not the ups and downs, or indeed any other pattern or trend of the different series are correlated. It may be that we suspect that change in one of the variables causes changes in the other (e.g. changes in the number of predators may cause changes in the number of prey, because more predators means more prey eaten). We need to be careful, of course, because it will not always be obvious which way round the causal relationship might work (e.g. predator numbers may go up because prey numbers are higher; ecologists call this a numerical response). Suppose we have the following sets of counts:

```
twoseries <- read.table ("twoseries.txt", header = T)
head (twoseries)

    x   y
1 101 121
2 210 111
3 314 234
4 221 512
5  13 226
6 222 137

twoseries <- ts (twoseries)
```

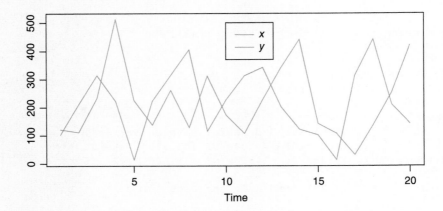

Figure 18.14 Time series plots of `twoseries`.

The two series are informatively titled *x* and *y*. We start by inspecting the two time series in Figure 18.14:

```
ts.plot (twoseries, col = hue_pal ()(2))
legend (10, 500, legend = c ("x", "y"), lwd = 1, col = hue_pal ()(2))
```

In a change to our usual function, we have used `ts.plot ()` rather than `plot ()` (which defaults to `plot.ts ()` for time series) as it puts the two sequences in the same plot and offers more flexibility for multiple time series. There is some evidence of periodicity (at least in *x*) and it looks as if *y* lags behind *x* by roughly two periods (sometimes 1). Now, let us carry out straightforward partial autocorrelation analyses on each time series separately and the cross-correlation between the two series, as in Figure 18.15. The stand-alone plots for *x* and *y* are the first and last plots. The top right-hand plot is the partial autocorrelation between the two going forward in time and that in the bottom left going backwards.

```
acf (twoseries, type = "p", col = hue_pal ()(10))
```

As we suspected, the evidence for periodicity is stronger in *x* than in *y*: the partial autocorrelation is large and negative at lag 2 for *x*, but not for *y*. The interesting point is the cross-correlation between *x* and *y* which is significant at lags 1 and 2 (top right). Positive changes in *x* are associated with negative changes in *y* and vice versa.

18.5 Some theoretical background

So far, we have examined time series data but not built models, except for the trend, that might help us analyse the data or even make predictions. In this section, we will look at some standard models, which will cover all stationary time series, and more. All of them assume that the error terms (similar but not the same as those used in linear models) are independent from each other. There are models, known as **GARCH models**, where that is not the case, which we will not cover here. Let us begin with something that we have already seen, namely the autocorrelation.

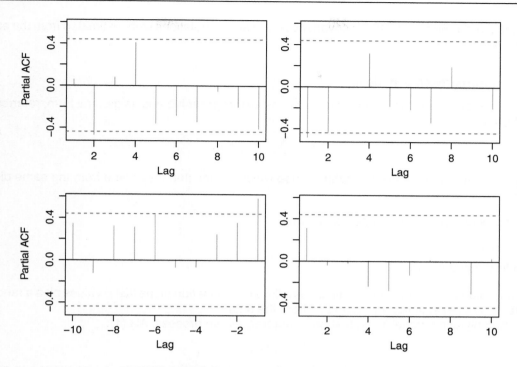

Figure 18.15 Time series plots of `twoseries`.

18.5.1 Autocorrelation

We have seen plots of autocorrelation and so will have a general idea of what the value represents. Here we will formalise the idea. Let us assume that we have a time series represented by $\{Y_t : t = 0, 1, \ldots\}$ where, for instance, Y_1 represents the value at time 1. Then we define the **autocovariance** function, γ_k, (in an analogous fashion to covariance) at lag k as follows:

$$\gamma_k = cov(Y_{t-k}, Y_t).$$

So this looks at the relationship between the two elements of the right-hand side at lag k over all values of t. The **autocorrelation**, ρ_k, (again in an analogous fashion to correlation) is then

$$\rho_k = \frac{\gamma_k}{\gamma_0}.$$

Clearly, γ_0 is just the variance of Y_t. The most important properties of the autocorrelation coefficient are as follows:

- they are symmetric backwards and forwards, so $\rho_k = \rho_{-k}$;
- the limits are $-1 \le \rho_k \le 1$, similar to correlation;
- when Y_t and Y_{t-k} are independent, then $\rho_k = 0$;
- the converse of the previous point is not true, so that $\rho_k = 0$ does not imply that Y_t and Y_{t-k} are independent (look at the scatterplot for $k = 7$ in Figure 18.4).

For the plots in Section 18.2, the covariances and autocorrelations were estimated from the sample data that we have.

18.5.2 Autoregressive models

The first type of model we will look at is known as **autoregressive** and its general form, referred to as **AR (p)**, is

$$Y_t = \sum_{i=1}^{p} \alpha_i Y_{t-i} + \epsilon_t.$$

The ϵ_t (error) terms are known as **white noise** which means that they come from the same distribution;

- independently of all other white noise terms;
- with mean 0;
- with finite variance σ^2.

So, the value of our time series at time t, is a linear combination of the last p values plus a random error term. We (R) estimate the α_i and σ^2 from the data.

A commonly used model is the first-order autoregressive process, AR (1):

$$Y_t = \alpha Y_{t-1} + \epsilon_t.$$

which is simple to interpret. In that case, if $-1 < \alpha < 1$, then the process is stationary and going back to autocorrelation:

$$\rho_k = \alpha^k, \qquad k = 0, 1, 2, \ldots .$$

If we decide that we are going to use an AR (p) model, perhaps by looking at the autocorrelation plot, then how do we pick p, the **order**? One method is to use the partial autocorrelation function.

18.5.3 Partial autocorrelation

Partial autocorrelation is the relationship between the current value of Y_t and that at lag t when we have controlled for the correlations between all of the successive weeks between this week and week t. That is to say, the partial autocorrelation is the correlation between Y_t and Y_{t+k} after regression of Y_t on $Y_{t+1}, Y_{t+2}, \ldots, Y_{t+k-1}$. The technical details are more complex than those for autocorrelation, but, in practice, we obtain it by solving a set of equations based on the data in our time series.

We have already seen that the partial autocorrelation function may be useful in interpreting our data. We can also use it to estimate p, the order of an AR (p) process. When we look at a partial autocorrelation plot, we would expect to see the partial autocorrelation to be roughly zero from lag $p + 1$ onwards. See Section 18.7 for an example. An alternative is to use AIC for model comparison.

18.5.4 Moving average models

These **moving average** models of order q, **MA (q)**, are the other type of independent error model: we shouldn't confuse them with the more general term, moving average. We define the model by

$$Y_t = \mu + \epsilon_t + \sum_{i=1}^{q} \beta_i \epsilon_{t-i}$$

where the ϵ_i are white noise as in AR (p) models. So the value of the time series at any point is some mean (frequently omitted by subtracting the mean from all values) plus an error term plus the moving average of a limited number of previous error terms. These models are always stationary. Again, we (or R) estimate the parameters, β_i and σ^2, from the data, albeit in a less straightforward way than for AR (p) models. The key decisions here are: when do we use an MA (q) model, and what should we use as q. The autocorrelation plot may guide us here in a similar way to the partial autocorrelation plot for AR () models: we might pick $q + 1$ to be the first small value in the plot. See Section 18.7 for an example. Again, AIC can also be used.

18.5.5 More general models: ARMA and ARIMA

We can combine types of independent error model with both autoregressive and moving average elements. An **ARMA (p, q)** model is

$$Y_t = \sum_{i=1}^{p} \alpha_i Y_{t-i} + \epsilon_t + \mu + \sum_{i=1}^{q} \beta_i \epsilon_{t-i}.$$

Once again, R will do all the work, once we have chosen p and q. AN ARMA model will be able to represent any stationary time series.

Finally (phew), the most general model is known as **ARIMA (p, d, q)** (the I stands for **integrated**). We might find that we have a time series that is definitely not stationary, for instance there may be a trend or seasonality. We could not then use the models described above, which only hold for stationary series. However, there is a technique, known as **differencing** whereby we replace the time series with one which is just the differences between consecutive terms. So the new series might be $\{Z_t\}$, where

$$z_t = y_t - y_{t-1}$$

If we carry out this process one or more (d) times, then we may end up with a series that appears to be stationary, and we can use an ARMA model. We can select our value of d by carrying out differencing and then looking at the time series plot for stationarity. If there is just a single repeated cycle then, usually $d = 1$. What we have ended up with is an **ARIMA (p, d, q)** model. R does all the dirty work for us using `arima ()`. In Section 18.6, we will have a look at an example.

18.6 ARIMA example

Records of the number of skins of predators (lynx) and prey (snowshoe hares) returned by trappers were collected over many years by the Hudson's Bay Company. The data set `lynx` has the lynx numbers:

```
lynx <- read.table ("lynx.txt", header = T)
head (lynx)

   Lynx
1   269
2   321
3   585
4   871
5  1475
6  2821
```

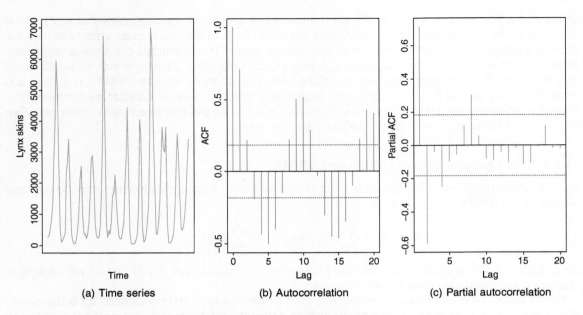

Figure 18.16 Time series plots for `lynx`.

Figure 18.16 shows the usual time series plots

```
plot.ts (lynx$Lynx, col = hue_pal ()(3)[1], ylab = "lynx skins", xaxt = "n")
acf (lynx$Lynx, col = hue_pal ()(3)[2], main = "")
acf (lynx$Lynx, type = "p", col = hue_pal ()(3)[3], main = "")
```

It looks as if there is a seasonal cycle, so we might think that $d = 1$. Figure 18.16c has large values up to $p = 2$ suggesting that we might incorporate AR (2) into our model. Picking a value for q is a bit tricky because of the differencing, so let us run an AIC analysis on a range of values for q, say 0 to 5:

```
lynx_aics <- numeric (6)
names (lynx_aics) <- 0:5
for (q in 0:5) {
  lynx_aics[q + 1] <- arima (lynx$Lynx, order = c (2, 1, q))$aic
}
lynx_aics


        0         1         2         3         4         5
1895.150  1865.770  1867.537  1864.522  1852.578  1877.075
```

This suggests we use $q = 4$. So, let us have a look at the model output:

```
lynx_mod <- arima (lynx$Lynx, order = c (2, 1, 4))
lynx_mod
```

```
Call:
arima(x = lynx$Lynx, order = c(2, 1, 4))

Coefficients:
          ar1       ar2       ma1      ma2      ma3       ma4
       1.5877   -0.9990   -1.8541   0.7477   0.8136   -0.7070
s.e.   0.0057    0.0022    0.1036   0.1779   0.1431    0.0969

sigma^2 estimated as 613727:   log likelihood = -919.29,   aic = 1852.58
```

In our terminology, α_1 is represented by `ar1` and β_2 by `ma2`, etc. The estimate of the variance of the white noise, σ^2 is huge: the standard error is larger than any of the data values (the 'noise' is larger than the 'signal') which suggests that this might not be a great model for the data (perhaps the error terms are not independent). Anyway, this gives us a good idea of how to create ARIMA models. Predictions can be made in the usual way using `predict ()`.

18.7   Simulation of time series

Once we have built our time series model and are happy with it, we can simulate from it, perhaps to investigate what happens beyond the period for which we have data. **This is dangerous**, as it assumes that the same model assumptions about errors, p, d, and q hold beyond the period for which we have data. However, it may be useful to explore multiple simulations in order to understand the possible range of future outcomes. As the models we have built are mostly stationary, one option with a non-stationary dataset would be to take out non-stationary elements, simulate from the stationary remainder and then add back the non-stationary features.

Simulations also serve to illustrate how we might expect the time series and autocorrelation plots for different models to look and that is what we will investigate in this section. Fortunately, *R* has a function that will do all the work for us, `arima.sim ()`. Let us start by having a look at some white noise, in Figure 18.17:

```
set.seed (271828)
white_noise <- arima.sim (list (order = c (0, 0, 0)), n = 1000)
plot (white_noise, ylab = "", col = hue_pal ()(15)[1])
acf (white_noise, main = "", col = hue_pal ()(15)[2])
acf (white_noise, type = "p", main = "", col = hue_pal ()(15)[3])
```

We have not specified an error term variance (it can be set using `sd =`) so the default is 1, and the parameters of our ARIMA (p, d, q) model are entered using `list (order = c (0, 0, 0))`. As we just want white noise in this case, all three are zero and the white noise itself will be picked up in the AR (0) part of the model. We have fixed the seeds (`set.seed (271828)`) for all the simulations in this section so that we can comment on the specific outputs.

The plots are what we might expect: the occasional large value in all three arising by chance but no overall pattern. In particular both of the autocorrelation plots show occasional lines (here at lags 4 and 21) that exceed the dotted lines. This is an inevitable consequence of random sampling, and it can be dangerous to read too much into such readings should they occur in a real dataset. The dotted lines should be treated as guidance, not as an absolute measure of importance.

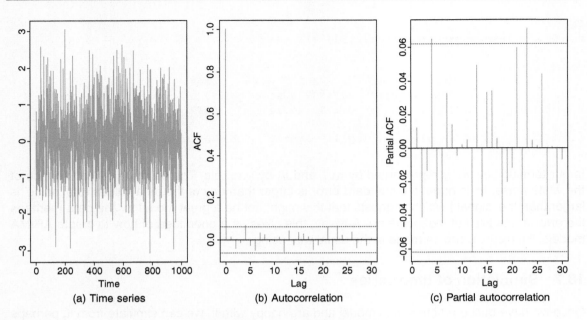

Figure 18.17 White noise simulation.

Next, Figure 18.18 shows an AR (2) model with $\alpha_1 = 1$ and $\alpha_2 = -0.7$:

```
set.seed (182845)
ar2 <- arima.sim (list (order = c (2, 0, 0), ar = c (1, -0.7)), n = 1000)
plot (ar2, ylab = "", col = hue_pal ()(15)[4])
acf (ar2, main = "", col = hue_pal ()(15)[5])
acf (ar2, type = "p", main = "", col = hue_pal ()(15)[6])
```

There is far greater variation in the time series plot, and it is very clear from the partial autocorrelation plot that $p = 2$ is appropriate.

Figure 18.19 shows an MA (3) model with no mean, $\beta_1 = 2$, $\beta_2 = -1$ and $\beta_3 = 1.3$:

```
set.seed (904523)
ma3 <- arima.sim (list (order = c (0, 0, 3), ma = c (2, -1, 1.3)), n = 1000)
plot (ma3, ylab = "", col = hue_pal ()(15)[7])
acf (ma3, main = "", col = hue_pal ()(15)[8])
acf (ma3, type = "p", main = "", col = hue_pal ()(15)[9])
```

The effect of the three weighted white noise terms is to produce a much wider range of values for the series than just the white noise alone. The autocorrelation plot with large terms to lag 3 certainly suggests that $q = 3$ fits the data well.

In both the preceding simulations, if we had decided that they were AR () or MA (), then finding the order is relatively straightforward: if we hadn't settled on the type of model, perhaps from understanding the subject matter background of the data set, then things would not have been so clear.

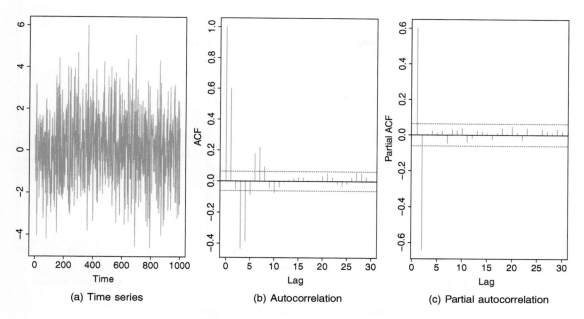

Figure 18.18   AR (2) simulation.

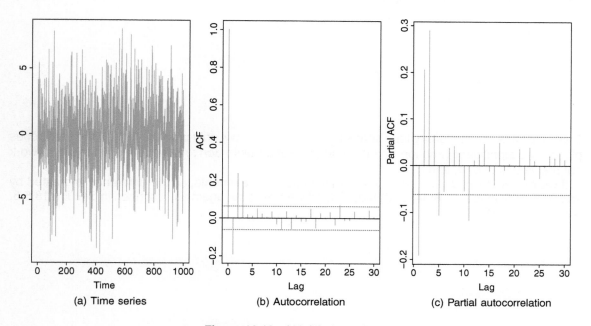

Figure 18.19   MA (3) simulation.

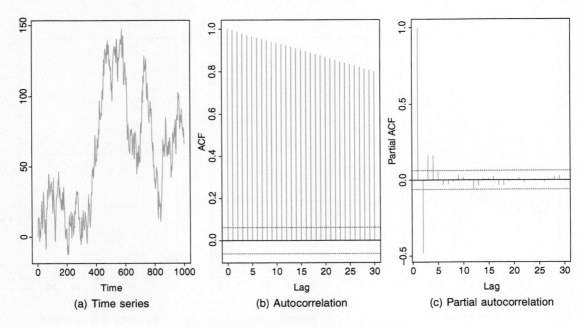

Figure 18.20   ARIMA (2, 1, 3) simulation.

Finally, just to complicate things further, we will add a differencing term of order 1 on top of both models seen already, to give Figure 18.20:

```
set.seed (536028)
ar2d1ma3 <- arima.sim (list (order = c (2, 1, 3), ar = c (1, -0.7),
                       ma = c (2, -1, 1.3)), n = 1000)
plot (ar2d1ma3, ylab = "", col = hue_pal ()(15)[10])
acf (ar2d1ma3, main = "", col = hue_pal ()(15)[11])
acf (ar2d1ma3, type = "p", main = "", col = hue_pal ()(15)[12])
```

Given that this is a stationary time series (`arima.sim ()` will only produce those), the time series plot shows significant variation and the autocorrelation plots don't really help us in trying to work out the values of p, d, and q.

If we examine `ar2d1ma3`, we will see that it has 1001 elements, as the difference is created by adding it back in to an ARMA (2, 3) model. So if we take it out again as described in Section 18.5.5, we get Figure 18.21:

```
set.seed (747135)
ar2ma3 <- arima.sim (list (order = c (2, 0, 3), ar = c (1, -0.7),
                     ma = c (2, -1, 1.3)), n = 1000)
plot (ar2ma3, ylab = "", col = hue_pal ()(15)[13])
acf (ar2ma3, main = "", col = hue_pal ()(15)[14])
acf (ar2ma3, type = "p", main = "", col = hue_pal ()(15)[15])
```

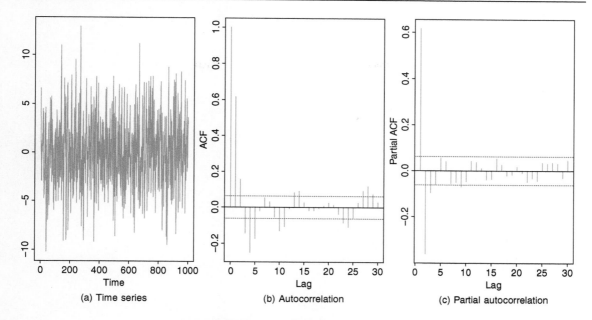

Figure 18.21 ARMA (2, 3) simulation.

The autocorrelation plots suggest that we might select $p = 3$ and $q = 5$. We could compare AIC for that combination with the orders that actually generated the data:

```
sim_mod1 <- arima (ar2d1ma3, order = c (3, 0, 5))
sim_mod1$aic

[1] 4711.538

sim_mod2 <- arima (ar2d1ma3, order = c (2, 0, 3))
sim_mod2$aic

[1] 4743.492
```

The AIC deduced from the plots is smaller than that from the model that the generated data: fitting time series models is a very inexact science!

Reference

Cowpertwait, P. S. P., & Metcalfe, A. V. (2009). *Introductory time series with R* (First). Springer.

19

Multivariate Statistics

This class of statistical methods is fundamentally different from many others in the book because there may not be a response variable. Instead of trying to understand variation in a response variable in terms of explanatory variables, in multivariate statistics we look for *structure in the data*. The problem is that structure is rather easy to find, and all too often it is a feature of that particular data set alone. The real challenge is to find *general* structure that will apply to other data sets as well. Unfortunately, there is no guaranteed means of detecting pattern, and a great deal of ingenuity has been shown by statisticians in devising means of pattern recognition in multivariate data sets. The main division is between methods that assume a given structure and seek to divide the cases into groups, and methods that seek to discover structure from inspection of the data. The really important point is that we need to know exactly what the question is that we are trying to answer. Do not mistake the opaque for the profound.

R incorporates a wide range of multivariate techniques, many of them in extra packages. A good summary can be found at https://cran.r-project.org/web/views/Multivariate.html. The subjects covered in this chapter together are the following:

- visualising data;

- multivariate analysis of variance;

- principal component analysis: analyses the main sources of variation in the data;

- factor analysis: picks out hidden variables that explain correlation in the data;

- cluster analysis: splits the data into groups based upon similarity;

- discriminant analysis: explains how data contributes to classification into known groups;

- neural networks: finds pattern in data using a black box.

These techniques are *not* recommended unless we know exactly what we are doing, and exactly *why* we are doing it. Beginners are sometimes attracted to multivariate techniques because of the complexity of the outputs they produce. These techniques (with the exception of discriminant analysis and neural networks) are also described as **unsupervised learning**, i.e. they attempt to find patterns in data without any guidance as to what these patterns might be.

The R Book, Third Edition. Elinor Jones, Simon Harden and Michael J. Crawley.
© 2023 John Wiley & Sons Ltd. Published 2023 by John Wiley & Sons Ltd.
Companion website: www.wiley.com/go/jones/therbook3e

19.1 Visualising data

As usual, before carrying out fancy statistical analyses it is always worth spending time understanding a dataset. Multivariate data often exists in high dimensions (e.g. a record of my physical characteristics might contain hundreds of pieces of information such as height, left big toe length), and so it can be difficult to produce helpful summary statistics and plots. A couple of such plots are illustrated here but many more are available with *R*.

A good starting point is appropriate univariate plots for each variable (barchart, histogram, or boxplot for instance) and bivariate scatter plots between pairs. Fortunately, we can combine the two using the function `chart.Correlation ()` which can be found in the `PerformanceAnalytics` package (Peterson and Carl, 2020). We illustrate this using the `taxonomy` data set that we will examine in more detail in Section 19.5.1. For now, we just need to know that there are 120 observations of 7 plant characteristics, and they are displayed in Figure 19.1:

```
library (PerformanceAnalytics)
taxa <- read.table ("taxonomy.txt", header = T, colClasses = list
                  (Taxon = "factor"))
chart.Correlation (taxa[, 2:8], histogram = TRUE, pch = 20)
```

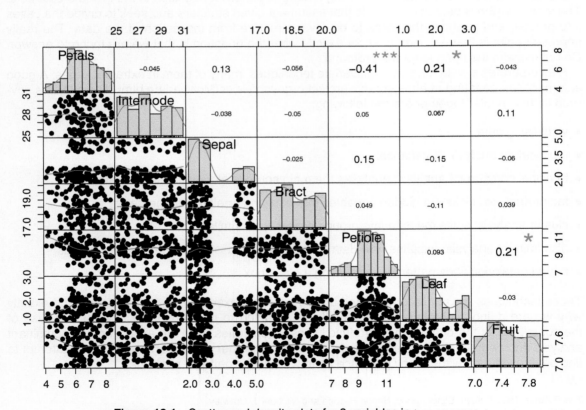

Figure 19.1 Scatter and density plots for 8 variables in `taxonomy`.

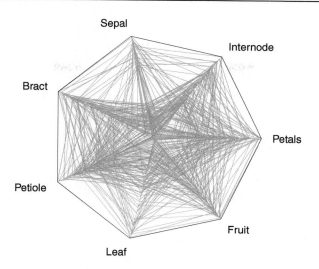

Figure 19.2   Radar plot for `taxonomy`.

Histograms of individual variables appear down the diagonal while scatter plots between all pairs of variables are in the lower left hand triangle. The numbers in the upper right-hand triangle are correlation coefficients and lines of best fit have been added to the histograms and scatter plots. There is very little flexibility in altering colours, etc. It seems clear that there are no strong relationships between any of the pairs of variables, and that most of the individual variables are a long way from being normally distributed. Note the `sepal` data are split into two parts.

An alternative approach is to focus on the observations rather than the variables. We could create a **radar or cobweb plot** as in Figure 19.2:

```
stars (taxa[,2:8], locations = c (0, 0), key.loc = c (0, 0), radius = F,
      col.lines = hue_pal ()(120))
```

We can track individual observations around the seven variables by following individual lines. The 120 lines have different colours, gradually changing through the colour spectrum. The plot would look quite different if the order of the variables were to be changed. There do appear to be different characteristics between the observations at the blue and red ends of the spectrum, the reason for which will become clear in Section 19.6.

Clearly, both of the plots displayed here are only useful for relatively small numbers of observations and variables but then big data inhabits a separate universe.

19.2   Multivariate analysis of variance

Two or more response variables are sometimes measured in the same experiment. Of course, we can analyse each response variable separately, and that is the typical way to proceed. But there are occasions where we want to treat the group of response variables as one multivariate response. The function for this is `manova ()`, the multivariate analysis of variance. The data set `manova` investigates the effect of two categorical covariates, `rate` and `additive`, on three outcomes describing plastic packaging material: `tear`, `gloss`, and `opacity`.

```
plastic <- read.table ("manova.txt", header = T)
head (plastic)


  tear gloss opacity rate additive
1  6.5   9.5     4.4  Low      Low
2  6.2   9.9     6.4  Low      Low
3  5.8   9.6     3.0  Low      Low
4  6.5   9.6     4.1  Low      Low
5  6.5   9.2     0.8  Low      Low
6  6.9   9.1     5.7  Low     High
```

We then bind the three outcomes together and fit a model:

```
plastic_out <- cbind (plastic$tear, plastic$gloss, plastic$opacity)
colnames (plastic_out) <- colnames (plastic)[1:3]
plastic_mod1 <- manova (plastic_out ~ plastic$rate * plastic$additive)
summary (plastic_mod1)

                            Df  Pillai approx F num Df den Df   Pr(>F)
plastic$rate                 1 0.61814   7.5543      3     14 0.003034 **
plastic$additive             1 0.47697   4.2556      3     14 0.024745 *
plastic$rate:plastic$additive 1 0.22289  1.3385      3     14 0.301782
Residuals                   16
---
Signif. codes:  0 '***' 0.001 '**' 0.01 '*' 0.05 '.' 0.1 ' ' 1
```

This shows that both rate and additive are important, but the interaction appears not to be. Note that the F-tests are based on 3 (outcomes) and 14 (data - minus variables - intercept) degrees of freedom (not 1 and 16). However, it would be useful also to see the effect on responses separately, and we might as well eliminate the interaction term:

```
plastic_mod2 <- manova (plastic_out ~ plastic$rate + plastic$additive)
summary.aov (plastic_mod2)


 Response tear:
                 Df Sum Sq Mean Sq F value    Pr(>F)
plastic$rate      1 1.7405 1.74050  16.769 0.0007549 ***
plastic$additive  1 0.7605 0.76050   7.327 0.0149597 *
Residuals        17 1.7645 0.10379
---
Signif. codes:  0 '***' 0.001 '**' 0.01 '*' 0.05 '.' 0.1 ' ' 1

 Response gloss:
                 Df Sum Sq Mean Sq F value  Pr(>F)
plastic$rate      1 1.3005 1.30050  6.9688 0.01720 *
plastic$additive  1 0.6125 0.61250  3.2821 0.08774.
Residuals        17 3.1725 0.18662
---
Signif. codes:  0 '***' 0.001 '**' 0.01 '*' 0.05 '.' 0.1 ' ' 1
```

```
Response opacity:
                 Df Sum Sq Mean Sq F value Pr(>F)
plastic$rate      1  0.421  0.4205  0.1038 0.7513
plastic$additive  1  4.901  4.9005  1.2094 0.2868
Residuals        17 68.884  4.0520
```

We are now carrying out multiple tests so need to be careful about the *p*-values we are considering (see Section 9.5). As there are three models, a rule of thumb might be to multiply the *p*-values by three. In that case, `rate` seems to have a strong impact on `tear` and a not very strong effect on `gloss`, and `rate` also has a marginal effect on `gloss`. How we interpret the model overall will depend upon subject matter knowledge, and whether we genuinely want to consider the three responses as one.

19.3 Principal component analysis

The idea of principal component analysis (**PCA**) is to find a small number of orthogonal (i.e. at right angles or independent from each other) *linear combinations* of the variables which capture most of the variation in the data as a whole. With a large number of variables, it may be easier to consider a small number of combinations of the original data rather than the entire data set.

Suppose, for example that 54 plants species are grown in 89 plots for 10 years and the average annual yield (in grams of dry weight) for each species is collected:

```
pgdata <- read.table ("pgfull.txt", header = T)
names (pgdata)

 [1] "AC"      "AE"      "AM"      "AO"      "AP"     "AR"
 [7] "AS"      "AU"      "BH"      "BM"      "CC"     "CF"
[13] "CM"      "CN"      "CX"      "CY"      "DC"     "DG"
[19] "ER"      "FM"      "FP"      "FR"      "GV"     "HI"
[25] "HL"      "HP"      "HS"      "HR"      "KA"     "LA"
[31] "LC"      "LH"      "LM"      "LO"      "LP"     "OR"
[37] "PL"      "PP"      "PS"      "PT"      "QR"     "RA"
[43] "RB"      "RC"      "SG"      "SM"      "SO"     "TF"
[49] "TG"      "TO"      "TP"      "TR"      "VC"     "VK"
[55] "plot"    "lime"    "richness" "hay"    "pH"
```

The data set contains the yield for 89 observations of 54 variables (species: `AC` to `VK`) together with experimental treatments (plot and lime) and covariates (species richness, hay biomass and soil pH). More details can be found in Crawley et al., 2005. The questions we might be interested in are: what are the principal species that explain the variation in outputs and what environmental factors are associated with them?

We shall use PCA for the first question. The general idea is, rather than trying to order 54 species or linear combinations of 54 species to explain the variability, to pick, say, the top three linear combinations or, perhaps, the top *n* combinations that explain 90% of the variability. Each of these combinations is independent of all others. Calculating principal components is easy. Interpreting what the components mean in scientific terms is hard and open to multiple viewpoints. We need to be more than usually circumspect when evaluating multivariate statistical analyses.

There are two main functions for carrying out PCA in *R*. For greater numerical accuracy, it is better to use `prcomp ()` rather than `princomp ()`. We have used `scale. = T`, as one usually should, because there are considerable differences in the species' yield, and this argument scales the variables to have a common unit variance. We have also just extracted the first 10 components, for brevity of display. For more details of the values that `prcomp ()` outputs, see `?prcomp`.

Here, we extract the 54 variables that refer to the species' abundances, create a PCA for those data and then display the first component (PC1) in terms of a linear combination (known as the **loading**) of the species:

```
pgfull <- pgdata[,1:54]
pg_pca10 <- prcomp (pgfull, scale. = T, rank. = 10)
pg_pca10$rotation[,1]
```

```
           AC             AE             AM             AO             AP             AR
-0.094847022   0.248199360  -0.128231348  -0.008367024   0.233093832  -0.030684541
           AS             AU             BH             BM             CC             CF
 0.203834353  -0.041862654   0.117061802  -0.217853150  -0.119046926  -0.018751538
           CM             CN             CX             CY             DC             DG
 0.013378707  -0.152355483  -0.140626502  -0.163562365  -0.032789664   0.180978637
           ER             FM             FP             FR             GV             HI
 0.028176293  -0.038214150  -0.010737382  -0.109946159  -0.029589100  -0.111970784
           HL             HP             HS             HR             KA             LA
 0.057332986  -0.177241015   0.243955132  -0.077531394  -0.176949315  -0.034599396
           LC             LH             LM             LO             LP             OR
-0.235911073  -0.245943408   0.017753865  -0.227519292   0.100217825  -0.034801791
           PL             PP             PS             PT             QR             RA
-0.004037382   0.194184981  -0.232368593   0.211780957   0.001242644   0.080241568
           RB             RC             SG             SM             SO             TF
-0.183676488   0.159629849   0.004071989  -0.156285598  -0.091038026  -0.084247592
           TG             TO             TP             TR             VC             VK
 0.065843619   0.179495609   0.073639589  -0.075703493  -0.065371782   0.027504448
```

The output shows the loading assigned to each `species` in the first principal component. The species `AP`, `AE`, and `HS` have strong positive loadings on PC1 and `LC`, `PS`, `BM`, and `LO` have strong negative loadings. The first principal component would thus begin:

$$-0.095x_{AC} + 0.248x_{AE} - 0.128x_{AM} \cdots .$$

We can compare the loadings across the first two components (PC1 and PC2) in the **biplot** of Figure 19.3:

```
biplot (pg_pca10)
```

The numbers represent the rows in the original dataframe, and the directions of the arrows show the relative loadings of the species on the first and second principal components. For instance, the species `AP` which, as we saw, has a strong positive loading in PC1, has a very slightly negative loading on PC2: it can be seen on the right-hand side of Figure 19.3.

We can summarise and plot the variances accounted for by the 10 components in Figure 19.4a (sometimes known as a **scree plot**):

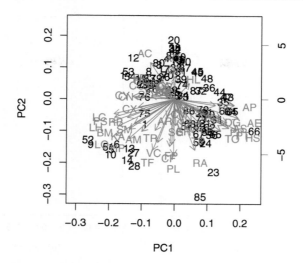

Figure 19.3 Biplot for components 1 and 2 for `pgfull`.

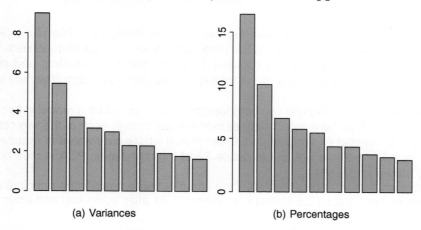

(a) Variances   (b) Percentages

Figure 19.4 Scree plots from PCA for data set `pgfull`.

```
summary (pg_pca10)

Importance of first k=10 (out of 54) components:
                          PC1     PC2     PC3      PC4      PC5      PC6      PC7
Standard deviation      3.0048  2.3358  1.9317  1.78562  1.73303  1.51187  1.50878
Proportion of Variance  0.1672  0.1010  0.0691  0.05904  0.05562  0.04233  0.04216
Cumulative Proportion   0.1672  0.2682  0.3373  0.39639  0.45201  0.49434  0.53649
                          PC8     PC9     PC10
Standard deviation      1.37586 1.32441 1.27318
Proportion of Variance  0.03506 0.03248 0.03002
Cumulative Proportion   0.57155 0.60403 0.63405

barplot (pg_pca10$sdev[1:10]^2, main = "", col = hue_pal ()(2)[1], cex.axis = 2,
        ylab = "")
```

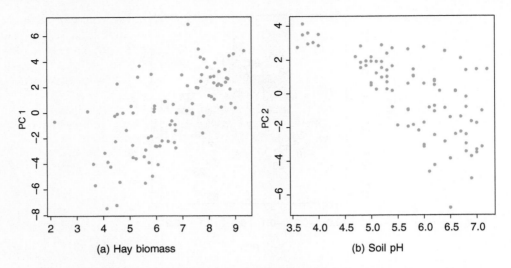

Figure 19.5 Comparison of components with covariates for `pgfull`.

We have calculated the variances by squaring the standard deviations. The plot in Figure 19.4b shows percentages of the total variance of the data rather than their absolute values. We can see that the first principal component (PC1) explains 16.7% of the total variation, and only the next four (PC2–PC5) explain more than 5% of the total remaining variation each (they are presented in decreasing order of size).

If we built a model from just the first two components, then it would be a model in two dimensions rather than 54. It would thus be a much simpler model even though each of the two components is a combination of our original 54 species. In a linear model where we wanted to reduce the number of dimensions from 54 to 2, we would just delete 52 of the covariates. PCA is thus not only more subtle but also harder to interpret.

If there are explanatory variables available, we can plot these against the principal components to look for patterns and Figure 19.5 shows key relationships after some trial and error:

```
yv <- predict (pg_pca10) [,1]
yv2 <- predict (pg_pca10) [,2]
plot (pgdata$hay, yv, xlab = "", ylab = "PC 1", col= hue_pal () (2) [1], cex.lab = 2)
plot (pgdata$pH, yv2, xlab = "", ylab = "PC 2", col= hue_pal () (2) [2], cex.lab = 2)
```

For Figure 19.5a, we build a model just using the first component, predict total yields for each plot, and then compare those with the hay biomass covariate. We can see the first principal component is associated with increasing biomass (and hence increasing competition for light) and, using a similar approach, that the second principal component is associated with declining soil pH (increasing acidity). Now the real work would start, because we are interested in the mechanisms that underlie these patterns.

19.4 Factor analysis

With PCA we were interested in the sources of variation in the data and explored this by looking at variances of individual components. In **factor analysis**, we are trying to understand whether there are underlying factors that explain the correlations or covariances between pairs of variables. This approach is popular in the social sciences where the aim is to provide usable numerical values for quantities such as intelligence or social status (**latent variables** that are not directly measurable). In terms of Figure 19.1, PCA could be thought of as an analysis of the variation in the univariate plots down the diagonal while factor analysis examines the variation in the off diagonal bivariate plots.

Compared with PCA, the variables themselves are of relatively little interest in factor analysis; it is gaining an understanding of the hypothesised underlying factors that is the main aim. The idea is that the correlations amongst the variables are explained by the common factors. The function `factanal ()` performs maximum likelihood factor analysis on a covariance matrix or data matrix. We will make use again of the `pgfull` data set that we introduced in Section 19.3 and will just look at the first eight factors:

```
pg_fact8 <- factanal (pgfull, 8)
loadings (pg_fact8)
```

```
Loadings:
    Factor1 Factor2 Factor3 Factor4 Factor5 Factor6 Factor7 Factor8
AC -0.512 -0.268                           0.121
AE  0.925 -0.107          -0.146          -0.118
AM -0.206  0.413  0.213           0.163   0.115   0.153   0.186
AO -0.312 -0.196 -0.151 -0.105          -0.148  -0.102
AP  0.827 -0.173 -0.195 -0.167          -0.123
AR         0.150           0.111                  0.127
AS  0.778
AU                                                         0.996
BH  0.380
BM -0.116  0.292          0.695                   0.380
CC -0.152                 0.159           0.943
CF         0.539                  0.342
CM                 0.434 -0.110
CN -0.276  0.143                          0.541   0.147
CX                        0.628           0.169   0.146
CY -0.211        -0.162   0.340                   0.270
DC        -0.125                           0.372
DG  0.738                -0.127            0.145
ER                                0.960
FM -0.108                                 0.133
FP  0.245  0.226          0.478   0.493           -0.176
FR -0.386        -0.144
GV -0.134
HI -0.202 -0.129 -0.163   0.182                   0.216
HL        -0.157         -0.127          -0.139
HP -0.155  0.832                                  0.240
HS  0.746 -0.102  0.257 -0.152
HR -0.155 -0.107 -0.122   0.101                   0.150
KA -0.167  0.774 -0.169   0.139
LA                                        0.829
LC -0.306  0.378 -0.125   0.529                            0.328
LH -0.256  0.556 -0.132   0.421           0.223   0.195
```

	Factor1	Factor2	Factor3	Factor4	Factor5	Factor6	Factor7	Factor8
LM				0.112	0.221			
LO	-0.129	0.432		0.781		0.251		
LP	0.115		0.745					
OR							0.996	
PL		0.369	0.675		0.337			
PP	0.527		0.226	-0.167		-0.175		
PS	-0.212	0.301	-0.130	0.681		0.150	0.158	
PT	0.741			-0.100	0.150	-0.105		
QR	-0.194	-0.135						
RA	0.195	0.227	0.578		0.205	-0.166	-0.107	
RB	-0.122	0.158		0.272		0.934		
RC	0.361			-0.198		-0.176	-0.152	
SG					0.806			
SM		0.388				0.787		
SO		-0.100	0.386					
TF	0.702	0.260						
TG	0.141		0.583	-0.110		0.367	0.107	
TO	0.418		0.567	-0.158				
TP			0.818					
TR		0.141	0.306	0.238		0.458		
VC		0.403	0.246	0.309	-0.169			
VK					0.909			

	Factor1	Factor2	Factor3	Factor4	Factor5	Factor6	Factor7	Factor8
SS loadings	5.840	3.991	3.577	3.540	3.028	2.644	2.427	2.198
Proportion Var	0.108	0.074	0.066	0.066	0.056	0.049	0.045	0.041
Cumulative Var	0.108	0.182	0.248	0.314	0.370	0.419	0.464	0.505

The main loadings table shows, for each factor, its correlation with each variable (values in $(-0.1, 0.1)$ are not shown). We are interested in strong positive or negative correlations. The bottom table explains, as in PCA, the proportion of variability explained by the factor (Box 19.1).

Box 19.1: Warning

Factors in factor analysis are *not* the same as the categorical explanatory variables we have been calling factors throughout the rest of this book

---

We need a good understanding of the data to be able to interpret them. On factor 1 we see strong positive correlations with AE, AP, and AS and negative correlations with AC, AO, and FR: this has a natural interpretation as a gradient from tall neutral grassland (positive correlations) to short, acidic grasslands (negative correlations). On factor 2, low-growing species associated with moderate-to-high soil pH (AM, CF, HP, KA) have large positive values and low-growing acid-loving species (AC, AO) have negative values. Factor 3 picks out the key nitrogen-fixing (legume) species LP and TP with high positive values, and so on. It is not a coincidence that PCA and factor analysis result in similar components and factors (see, for instance those with large positive values in PC1 and factor 1) – that is frequently the case.

Factor analysis could be seen as an exploratory precursor to structural equation modelling which involves building testable models for latent variables. The subject is outside the scope of this book, but the packages `sem` and `lavaan` are good places to start.

19.5 Cluster analysis

Cluster analysis is a set of techniques that look for groups (clusters) in the data. Objects belonging to the same group resemble each other. Objects belonging to different groups are dissimilar. Sounds simple, doesn't it? The problem is that there are a multitude of ways of determining what sorts of clusters are required and what determines how similar data items are. We will review two of the most popular methods, both of which have a number of flavours:

- k-means: partitioning into a number of clusters (k) specified by the user;
- hierarchical: not a single clustering but a set of cluster groupings ranging from each data item belonging to its own cluster to a single cluster. These are displayed to look like an upside down tree.

19.5.1 *k*-means

We try to find clusters of data that are close to each other so that the total variation within clusters is minimised. Mathematically speaking, assume that our dataset has m numerical variables so that each data item can be thought of as a point in m-dimensional space, with coordinates the values of the m variables. The **k-means** algorithm determines k cluster centres (**centroids**) in m-dimensional space and then each data item belongs to the cluster whose centroid is closest (using the standard Euclidean distance function). The centroids are chosen to minimise the sum of the variances of the distances to the items within each cluster.

As a toy example, we have some (x, y) data (i.e. $m = 2$) that we know belong to six groups, by some unknown criteria, as in Figure 19.6a:

```
kmd <- read.table ("kmeansdata.txt", header = T)
head (kmd)
attach (kmd)
plot (x, y, col = hue_pal ()(6)[group])
```

```
          x          y group
1   2.918896  8.587122     2
2  10.724510  8.194907     1
3   5.588091 10.382890     2
4   6.619314  5.399704     5
5   8.725792  4.253471     5
6   9.923255  3.216071     4
```

We then use `kmeans ()` to estimate the clusters for $k = 4, 5, 6$ in the remaining plots of Figure 19.6.

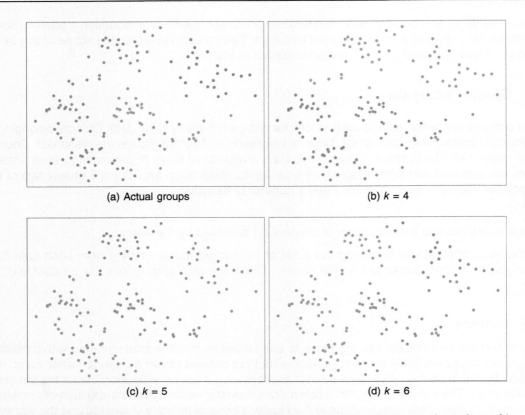

Figure 19.6 Data set `kmeansdata` with *k*-means clustering based upon varying values of *k*.

```
model4 <- kmeans (kmd[, 1:2], 4)
plot (x, y, col = hue_pal ()(4)[model4[[1]]], xlab = "", ylab = "")
model5 <- kmeans (kmd[, 1:2], 5)
plot (x, y, col = hue_pal ()(5)[model5[[1]]], xlab = "", ylab = "")
model6 <- kmeans (kmd[, 1:2], 6)
plot (x, y, col = hue_pal ()(6)[model6[[1]]], xlab = "", ylab = "")
detach (kmd)
```

Even when we know how many clusters there should be, there are some points that have been assigned to the wrong groups (as Euclidean distance is not exactly the measure by which the original cluster allocation was made). However, the real weakness of the approach is revealed when we use the wrong number of clusters – allocations vary considerably. For instance, if we want to allocate people to personality clusters based on their performance in a range of assessments, what is *k*? The best approach may be to try a range of values for *k* and then compare the resulting clusters in considerable detail.

A further issue with k-means clustering is that it is fairly crude. For instance, the data set `taxonomy`, which we reviewed briefly in Section 19.1 has measurements of seven variables ($m = 7$) on 120 individual plants. The data actually come from plants on four separate islands (the `Taxon` column with values I–IV), and the question is whether the *k*-means approach will spot that.

```
head (taxa)

  Taxon    Petals Internode    Sepal    Bract  Petiole     Leaf     Fruit
1     I 5.621498  29.48060 2.462107 18.20341 11.27910 1.128033 7.876151
2     I 4.994617  28.36025 2.429321 17.65205 11.04084 1.197617 7.025416
3     I 4.767505  27.25432 2.570497 19.40838 10.49072 1.003808 7.817479
4     I 6.299446  25.92424 2.066051 18.37915 11.80182 1.614052 7.672492
5     I 6.489375  25.21131 2.901583 17.31305 10.12159 1.813333 7.758443
6     I 5.785868  25.52433 2.655643 17.07216 10.55816 1.955524 7.880880
```

The variables are plotted in Figure 19.1, where we can see that there appears to be excellent data separation on sepal length, and reasonable separation on petiole length and leaf width, but nothing obvious for the other variables.

In this case, we *know* that there are four groups. In reality, of course, we would not know this, and finding out the number of groups would be one of the central aims of the study. Let us see how kmeans () allocates individuals to four groups:

```
taxa_kn <- kmeans (taxa[, 2:8], 4)
taxa_kn$centers

    Petals Internode    Sepal    Bract  Petiole     Leaf    Fruit
1 5.496332  27.47250 2.561201 18.80867 10.840511 1.608050 7.526214
2 6.566806  29.91864 3.002083 18.31510  9.802510 1.945407 7.529972
3 6.996461  26.56658 4.614698 18.32699 10.059406 1.653439 7.425915
4 6.998258  26.55506 2.468164 18.37792  9.076467 1.852448 7.440706


taxa_kn$cluster

  [1] 2 1 1 1 4 4 1 1 1 1 1 1 1 1 1 1 1 1 1 1 1 2 1 1 2 2 2 1 1 2 2 4 4 2 2 4 4
 [38] 4 4 4 2 2 4 4 4 2 4 4 1 4 4 4 4 2 4 2 2 2 4 2 4 4 4 2 2 4 4 4 4 2 2 1 2 4
 [75] 4 4 4 2 2 2 4 1 4 4 2 2 2 4 1 2 3 2 3 2 3 3 2 1 3 3 2 3 3 3 3 2 3 3 3 3 3
[112] 2 2 3 3 3 2 3 2 2
```

The kmeans object that we have created contains a lot of information, but we have pulled out two items:

- centers: The seven-dimensional centroids discussed above;

- cluster: How each data point is allocated to a cluster (if we study the original data in detail we will see that the correct clusters are four sets of 30 data points each grouped together).

We can also compare how the data are grouped correctly (I–IV) and using kmeans (1–4):

```
table (taxa$Taxon, taxa_kn$cluster)

       1   2   3   4
  I   21   7   0   2
  II   1   9   0  20
  III  3  13   0  14
  IV   1  10  19   0
```

Not very impressive at all – we can see how the two sets of four groups match up (e.g. II with 4) but only just over half of the data points have been correctly clustered. Of course, the computer was doing its classification blind. See the end of Section 19.6 for a discussion.

19.6 Hierarchical cluster analysis

The idea behind hierarchical cluster analysis is to show which of a (potentially large) set of samples are most similar to one another, and to group these similar samples in the same limb of a tree. Groups of samples that are distinctly different are placed in other limbs (see Figure 19.7 for an example). The trick is in defining what we mean by 'most similar'. Each of the samples can be thought of as a sitting in an *m*-dimensional space (similar to *k*-means clusters in Section 19.5.1), defined by the *m* variables (columns) in the dataframe. We define similarity on the basis of the *distance* between two samples in this *m*-dimensional space. Several different distance measures could be used, but the default is Euclidean distance (for the other options, see `?dist`), and this is used to work out the distance from every sample to every other sample. Initially, each sample is assigned to its own cluster, and then the `hclust ()` algorithm proceeds iteratively, at each stage joining the two most similar clusters, continuing until there is just a single cluster.

We return to our `pgfull` data, introduced in Section 19.3, which shows the distribution of 54 plant species over 89 plots receiving different experimental treatments. The aim is to see which plots are most similar in their botanical composition, and whether there are reasonably homogeneous groups of plots that might represent distinct plant communities. We label each plot with its number and lime composition:

```
labels <- paste (pgdata$plot, letters[pgdata$lime], sep = "")
```

The first step is to turn the matrix of measurements on individual plots into a dissimilarity matrix, i.e. we need to calculate the 'distances' between each row in the dataframe (plot) and every other using

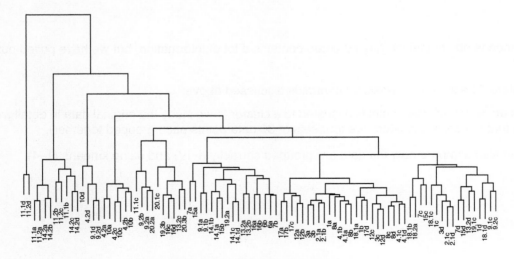

Figure 19.7   Hierarchical clustering for `pgfull`.

`dist ()`. These distances are then used to carry out hierarchical cluster analysis using `hclust ()`:

```
pgdist <- dist (pgdata[,1:54])
hpg <- hclust (pgdist)
```

We can plot the resulting object called `hpg`, and we specify that the leaves of the hierarchy are labelled by their plot/lime labels to give Figure 19.7:

```
plot (hpg, labels = labels, main = "", xlab = "", ylab = "", axes = F, sub = "",
      cex = 0.6)
```

If we view this object in full-screen mode within *R*, we will be able to read all the plot labels and to work out the groupings. It turns out that the groupings have very natural scientific interpretations. The highest break, for instance, separates the two plots dominated by Holcus lanatus (`11.1d` and `11.2d`) from the other 87 plots. The second break distinguishes the high nitrogen plots also receiving phosphorus (plots `11` and `14`). The third break takes out the acidified plots (numbers `9`, `10`, and `4.2`). The plots on the right-hand side all have soils that exhibit phosphorus deficiency. The leftmost groups are all from plots receiving high rates of nitrogen and phosphorus input, and so on. The `hclust ()` function has done an excellent job of recognising real-plant communities over the top seven splits.

Let us try hierarchical clustering on the taxonomic data, described in Section 19.5.1, and leading to Figure 19.8:

```
plot (hclust (dist (taxa)), main = "", xlab = "", ylab = "", axes = F, sub = "",
      cex = 0.6)
```

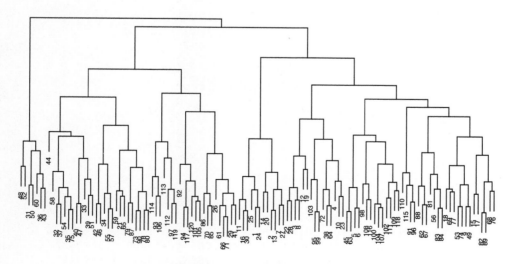

Figure 19.8 Hierarchical clustering for `taxonomy`.

Because in this example we know that the first 30 rows in the dataframe come from group 1, rows 31–60 from group 2, rows 61–90 from group 3, and rows 91–120 from group 4, we can see that the grouping produced by `hclust ()` is pretty woeful. Most of the rows in the leftmost major split are from group 2, but the rightmost split contains members from groups 1, 4, and 3. Neither `kmeans ()` nor `hclust` is up to the job in this case. When we *know* the group identities, then it is easy to use tree models to devise the optimal means of distinguishing and classifying individual cases (see Section 20.3.2).

So there we have it, when we *know* the identity of the species, then clustering models are wonderfully efficient at constructing keys to distinguish between the individuals, and at allocating them to the relevant categories. When we do *not* know the identities of the individuals, then the statistical task is much more severe, and inevitably ends up being much more error-prone. Even knowing the number of clusters used to generate the data is not particularly helpful. Multivariate clustering without a response variable is fundamentally difficult and uncertain.

19.7   Discriminant analysis

In **discriminant analysis**, we know the identity of each individual (unlike cluster analysis) and want to know how the explanatory variables contribute to the correct classification of individuals. It is thus quite similar to regression with outcome variable, group membership: there is a form of regression that deals with more than two categorical outcomes (**multinomial regression**), but interpretation can be difficult. Discriminant analysis works by uncovering relationships among the groups' covariance matrices to discriminate between groups. With k groups, we will have $k - 1$ discriminators. However, note that an assumption that needs to be checked is that all explanatory variables are normally distributed for each outcome value (see Section 9.2.5). The R functions we will need for discriminant analysis are available in the MASS library (Venables and Ripley, 2002a), part of the base installation.

Returning to the `taxonomy` data set (see Section 19.5.1: we know that there are four groups), we illustrate the use of `lda ()` to carry out a linear discriminant analysis (other types such as quadratic discriminant analysis, using `qda ()`, are available), assuming that the appropriate normality checks have been carried out:

```
library (MASS)
lda_model <- lda (Taxon ~ ., data = taxa)
lda_model


Call:
lda(Taxon ~., data = taxa)

Prior probabilities of groups:
   I   II  III   IV
0.25 0.25 0.25 0.25

Group means:
      Petals Internode    Sepal    Bract  Petiole     Leaf    Fruit
I   5.476128  27.91886 2.537955 18.60268 10.864184 1.508029 7.574642
II  7.035078  27.69834 2.490336 18.47557  8.541085 1.450260 7.418702
III 6.849666  27.99308 2.446003 18.26330  9.866983 2.588555 7.482349
IV  6.768464  27.78503 4.532560 18.42953 10.128838 1.645945 7.467917
```

```
Coefficients of linear discriminants:
                LD1            LD2            LD3
Petals     -0.01891137    0.034749952    0.559080267
Internode   0.03374178    0.009670875    0.008808043
Sepal       3.45605170   -0.500418135    0.401274694
Bract       0.07557480    0.068774714   -0.024930728
Petiole     0.25041949   -0.343892260   -1.249519047
Leaf       -1.13036429   -3.008335468    0.647932763
Fruit       0.18285691   -0.208370808   -0.269924935

Proportion of trace:
   LD1    LD2    LD3
0.7268 0.1419 0.1313
```

We can isolate the critical elements of each discriminant by finding the largest absolute coefficients. We would thus base our model on sepal first (3.46), then leaf (−3.008), and then petiole (−1.25). Compare this with the key uncovered by the tree model in Section 20.3.2, or the histograms in Figure 19.1, where those three variables are most clearly bimodal. Plots showing how pairs of discriminants distinguish between groups are given in Figure 19.9.

```
plot (lda_model, col = rep (hue_pal ()(4), each = 30))
```

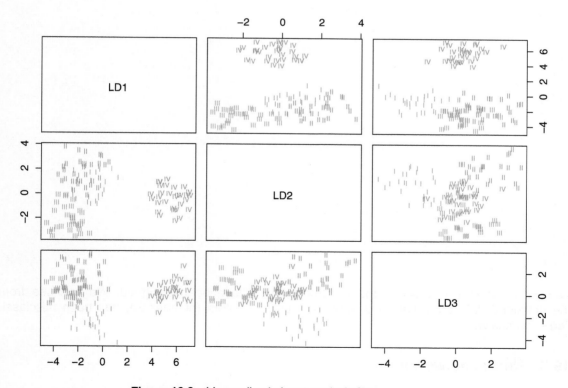

Figure 19.9 Linear discriminant analysis for `taxonomy`.

Without going into the technical detail, we can see that the linear discriminants LD1 and LD2 clearly separate taxon IV (i.e. cases from island IV) without error and make a reasonable stab at taxon III, but the former is easy because there is no overlap in sepal length between this taxon, and the others. LD2 and LD3 are quite good at finding taxons I and II, and LD1 and LD3 are quite good at getting taxon I.

In common with other supervised learning techniques (see Chapter 20), the model is often trained on data where we know the outcome (here, taxon/island) and then used on cases where we don't. So let us use a random subset of half the cases for training:

```
train <- sort (sample (1:120, 60))
table (taxa$Taxon[train])


   I   II  III   IV
  13   16   17   14
```

We can see that our sample is fairly representative of the population (remember, if we try this, we will get a different sample). Now, use this for training to create a second model with which we can predict the outcome of the unused (non-training) data:

```
lda_model2 <- lda (Taxon ~., data = taxa, subset = train)
untrained <- taxa[-train,]
not_train <- predict (lda_model2, untrained)
not_train$class

 [1] I   I   I   I   I   I   I   I   I   I   I   I   I   I   I   I   I   II  II
[20] I   II  II  II  II  II  II  II  II  II  II  II  III III III III III III III
[39] III III III III III III IV  IV  IV  IV  IV  IV  IV  IV  IV  IV  IV  IV  IV
[58] IV  IV  IV
Levels: I II III IV


lda_cm <- table (taxa$Taxon[-train], not_train$class)
lda_cm


       I  II  III  IV
  I   17   0    0   0
  II   1  13    0   0
  III  0   0   13   0
  IV   0   0    0  16
```

The `class` output lists where the untrained plants have been assigned. We can see from the untrained data predictions and table that only one item (number 20) has been misclassified – impressive!

19.8 Neural networks

These are computationally intensive methods for finding pattern in data sets that are so large, and contain so many explanatory variables, that standard methods such as multiple regression are

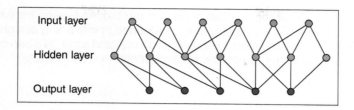

Figure 19.10 A simplified neural network where information travels along lines and is processed at nodes.

impractical (they would simply take too long to plough through). A simplified representation of a neural network is given in Figure 19.10.

Data arrives in the input layer and leaves from the output layer. The key feature of **neural network** models is that they contain at least one *hidden layer*: each node in the hidden layer receives information from each of many inputs, carries out some mathematical operations (giving rise to a large number of variants), and then produces many outputs. A neural network can operate like multiple regression when the outputs are continuous variables, or like classification when the outputs are categorical. The concept arose by trying to mimic the human brain – not quite there yet though.

As with discriminant analysis in Section 19.7, there is some training. We shall use the same data set, `taxonomy`, and the same training set. The *R* package is called `nnet` (Venables and Ripley, 2002b) and comes as part of the base *R* installation. It is fairly straightforward to use:

```
library (nnet)
nn_model <- nnet (Taxon ~., data = taxa, subset = train, size = 4, decay = 1.0e-5,
                  maxit = 200)

# weights:   52
initial  value 106.567639
iter  10 value 82.843632
iter  20 value 82.843468
iter  30 value 80.592149
iter  40 value 43.336877
iter  50 value 36.031598
iter  60 value 32.098723
iter  70 value 31.613884
iter  80 value 31.223533
iter  90 value 21.820788
iter 100 value 15.581749
iter 110 value 14.309256
iter 120 value 12.472875
iter 130 value 10.643250
iter 140 value 8.486192
iter 150 value 7.918626
iter 160 value 6.879530
iter 170 value 5.986390
iter 180 value 5.047090
iter 190 value 4.803050
iter 200 value 4.698925
final  value 4.698925
stopped after 200 iterations
```

We have specified `size = 4` for the number of units in our hidden layer. This came about through trial and error: fewer or more units resulted in all the untrained plants being assigned to III. Similarly, the decay is a technical parameter, given a value through trial and error. We can compare the actual classification (rows) with that using the neural network (columns) as follows:

```
nn_cm <- table (taxa$Taxon[-train], predict (nn_model, untrained, type="class"))
nn_cm


      I II III IV
  I   4  4   8  1
  II  2 12   0  0
  III 2  1   9  1
  IV  0  0   0 16
```

The result (19 cases misclassified) is not as good as linear discriminant analysis (just 1) and that was after quite a bit of tweaking – only possible because we knew the outcome. Note that `nnet ()` involves a random process and so will give a slightly different outcome each time it is run.

So only use neural networks when small sample techniques can't be used (e.g. for extremely large data sets) and talk to an expert before using them.

References

Crawley, M. J., Johnston, A. E., Silvertown, J., Dodd, M., de Mazancourt, C., Heard, M., Henman, D. F., & Edwards, G. R. (2005). Determinants of species richness in the park grass experiment. *American Naturalist*, *165*, 348–362.

Peterson, B. G., & Carl, P. (2020). *Performanceanalytics: econometric tools for performance and risk analysis* [R package version 2.0.4]. https://CRAN.R-project.org/package=PerformanceAnalytics.

Venables, W. N., & Ripley, B. D. (2002a). *Modern applied statistics with S* (Fourth) [ISBN 0-387-95457-0]. Springer. https://www.stats.ox.ac.uk/pub/MASS4/.

Venables, W. N., & Ripley, B. D. (2002b). *Modern applied statistics with S* (Fourth) [ISBN 0-387-95457-0]. Springer. https://www.stats.ox.ac.uk/pub/MASS4/.

## 20

Classification and Regression Trees

Classification and regression tree models (**CARTs**) are computationally intensive methods that are used in situations where there are many explanatory variables and we would like guidance about, possibly, including them in the model: **classification trees** are where the outcome is discrete and **regression trees** where the outcome is continuous. Often, there are so many explanatory variables that we simply could not investigate them all, even if we wanted to invest the huge amount of time that would be necessary to complete such a complicated multiple regression exercise. The great virtues of tree models are as follows:

- they are very simple to implement, understand, and interpret;

- they are excellent for initial data inspection;

- they give a very clear picture of the structure of the data;

- they provide a highly intuitive insight into the kinds of interactions between variables.

Let us begin by looking at a tree model in action, before thinking about how it works. Here is an air pollution example that we might want to analyse as a multiple regression: the outcome is continuous (Pollution) and the covariates are self-explanatory, although the units used are a little opaque in places. We will begin by using the package tree, then illustrate the more modern package rpart (Ripley, 2019), which stands for **recursive partitioning**, which is what is going on here. The regression tree is displayed in Figure 20.1:

```
library (tree)
pollute <- read.table ("pollute.txt", header = T)
head (pollute)

  Pollution Temp Industry Population Wind  Rain Wet.days
1        24 61.5      368        497  9.1 48.34      115
2        30 55.6      291        593  8.3 43.11      123
3        56 55.9      775        622  9.5 35.89      105
4        28 51.0      137        176  8.7 15.17       89
```

The R Book, Third Edition. Elinor Jones, Simon Harden and Michael J. Crawley.
© 2023 John Wiley & Sons Ltd. Published 2023 by John Wiley & Sons Ltd.
Companion website: www.wiley.com/go/jones/therbook3e

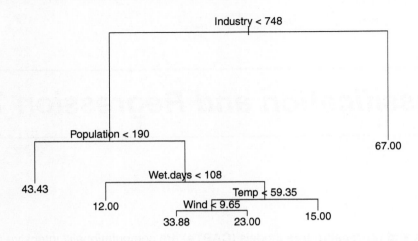

Figure 20.1   Regression tree for `pollute`.

```
5          14 68.4       136      529  8.8 54.47      116
6          46 47.6        44      116  8.8 33.36      135


pollute_mod1 <- tree (pollute)
plot (pollute_mod1)
text (pollute_mod1)
```

It shows, for ranges of values of the covariates, what the mean `Pollution` level might be, e.g. for `Industry` with values < 748 and `Population` with values < 190, the mean `Pollution` level is predicted to be 43.43. Our first question might be: why is `Industry` at the top (other questions will be considered later)? Well, if we build a simple linear model that might give us a clue:

```
pollute_mod2 <- lm (Pollution ~ Temp + Industry + Wind + Rain + Wet.days,
                    data = pollute)
summary (pollute_mod2)

Call:
lm(formula = Pollution ~ Temp + Industry + Wind + Rain + Wet.days,
    data = pollute)

Residuals:
    Min      1Q  Median      3Q     Max
-20.483  -8.785  -3.149   7.120  58.013

Coefficients:
             Estimate Std. Error t value Pr(>|t|)
(Intercept) 135.825337  49.993685   2.717  0.01017 *
Temp         -1.771656   0.635532  -2.788  0.00852 **
Industry      0.025606   0.004597   5.571 2.84e-06 ***
Wind         -3.750067   1.948589  -1.925  0.06245 .
Rain          0.622758   0.387777   1.606  0.11727
```

```
Wet.days      -0.055288    0.174421   -0.317  0.75314
---
Signif. codes:  0 '***' 0.001 '**' 0.01 '*' 0.05 '.' 0.1 ' ' 1

Residual standard error: 15.77 on 35 degrees of freedom
Multiple R-squared:  0.6052,Adjusted R-squared:  0.5488
F-statistic: 10.73 on 5 and 35 DF,  p-value: 2.621e-06
```

`Industry` has the smallest *p*-value suggesting that, by some measure, its influence on `Pollution` might be the most important. As well as helping us understand the relationship between outcomes and explanatory variables, CART models are important tools in making decisions: given particular covariate values, which outcome should we select? We will now examine how these trees work in a little more detail.

20.1 How CARTs work

A CART model is fitted using **binary recursive partitioning**, whereby the data are successively split along co-ordinate axes of each of the explanatory variables so that, at any node, the split which maximally distinguishes the response variable in the left and the right branches is selected. Splitting continues until nodes are pure or the data are too sparse (fewer than six cases, by default). The decisions about which variable to work with next and where it should be split are made based on which point most clearly distinguishes between the items on either side of the split. There are many different algorithms to do this, and the details shouldn't bother us unduly: the key thing is that this is not a black box process, but one that can be understood. For instance, looking at the first split for `pollute`, as selected by our model, in Figure 20.2:

```
attach (pollute)
low_ind <- (Industry < 748)
ind_means <- tapply (Pollution, low_ind, mean)
ind_means

    FALSE       TRUE
67.00000 24.91667

plot (Industry, Pollution, col = hue_pal ()(3)[1])
abline (v = 748, lty = 2, col = hue_pal ()(3)[2])
```

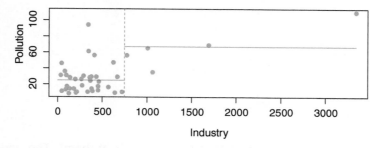

Figure 20.2 Splitting `pollute` by `Industry` at 748.

```
lines (c (0, 748), rep (ind_means[2], 2), col = hue_pal ()(3)[3])
lines (c (748, max (Industry)), rep (ind_means[1], 2), col = hue_pal ()(3)[3])
```

```
detach (pollute)
```

Splitting `Industry` at 748 (vertical line) in Figure 20.1 produces the greatest difference between `Pollution` means (horizontal lines) for any covariate and point: it explains the greatest amount of variation or deviance.

The process then continues with all the variables apart from those used already, in this case `Industry`. In defiance of gravity, the first split is at the **root**, and the lowest points are **leaves** or **classes** for discrete outcomes.

20.2 Regression trees

Regression trees have continuous outcomes, and in this section, we will continue with the `pollution` data set, but compare the `tree` package with `rpart` and with linear regression.

20.2.1 The `tree` package

When we created `pollute_mod1` we just specified the dataset, `pollute`. By default, `tree ()` takes the first column as the outcome and the remainder as covariates. We could have been more specific and arrived at the same model by specifying:

```
pollute_mod1 <- tree (Pollution ~ ., data = pollute)
```

`Pollution ~.` means explore `Pollution` as a function of the rest of the data columns. As well as a visual output, `tree` also has a standard textual one:

```
print (pollute_mod1)

node), split, n, deviance, yval
      * denotes terminal node

 1) root 41 22040 30.05
   2) Industry < 748 36 11260 24.92
     4) Population < 190 7   4096 43.43 *
     5) Population > 190 29  4187 20.45
    10) Wet.days < 108 11     96 12.00 *
    11) Wet.days > 108 18   2826 25.61
      22) Temp < 59.35 13   1895 29.69
        44) Wind < 9.65 8   1213 33.88 *
        45) Wind > 9.65 5    318 23.00 *
      23) Temp > 59.35 5    152 15.00 *
 3) Industry > 748 5   3002 67.00 *
```

The terminal nodes or leaves are denoted by * (there are six of them). The node number is on the left, labelled by the variable on which the split at that node was made. Next comes the **split**

criterion which shows the threshold value of the variable that was used to create the split. The number of cases going into the split (or into the terminal node) comes next. The penultimate figure is the deviance at that node. Notice how the deviance goes down as non-terminal nodes are split. The last figure on the right is the mean value of the response variable within that node or at that that leaf.

In the root, based on all $n = 41$ data points, the deviance is the sum of squares and the value is the overall mean for `Pollution`. The highest mean pollution (67.00) was in node 3 and the lowest (12.00) was in node 10. Note how the nodes are nested: within node 2, for example node 4 is terminal, but node 5 is not; within node 5, node 10 is terminal, but node 11 is not; within node 11, node 23 is terminal but node 22 is not, and so on. Frankly, it is probably simpler to begin with the graphic of the tree and only then progressing to review the text.

Tree models lend themselves to circumspect and critical analysis of complex dataframes. In the present example, the aim is to understand the causes of variation in air pollution levels from case to case. The interpretation of the regression tree would precede something like this:

- the five most extreme cases of `Industry` stand out (mean = 67.00) and need to be considered separately;

- for the rest, `Population` is the most important variable but, interestingly, it is low populations that are associated with the highest levels of pollution (mean = 43.43). Why might that be?

- for high levels of `Population` (greater than 190), the number of `Wet.days` is a key determinant of pollution; the places with the fewest wet days (less than 108 per year) have the lowest pollution levels of anywhere in the dataframe (mean = 12.00);

- for those places with more than 108 wet days, it is `Temperature` that is most important in explaining variation in pollution levels; the warmest places have the lowest air pollution levels (mean = 15.00);

- for the cooler places with lots of wet days, it is `Wind` speed that matters: the windier places are less polluted than the still places.

This kind of complex and contingent explanation is much easier to see, and to understand, in tree models than in the output of a multiple regression.

20.2.2 The `rpart` package

There is a newer package, `rpart` (Therneau and Atkinson, 2019), which differs from `tree` in the way it decides on which variables to split, and where, but which has many shared features. There is a good technical introduction with example (**vignette**), `longintro`, which can be found once the package has been installed by typing `help (rpart)`. The name of the package and the function we will use stands for 'recursive partitioning'. We can compare the outputs of `rpart ()` (left) and `tree ()` (right) for the pollution data in Figure 20.3:

```
library (rpart)
pollute_mod3 <- rpart (Pollution ~ ., data = pollute)
plot (pollute_mod3)
text (pollute_mod3)
pollute_mod1 <- tree (Pollution ~ ., data = pollute)
plot (pollute_mod1)
text (pollute_mod1)
```

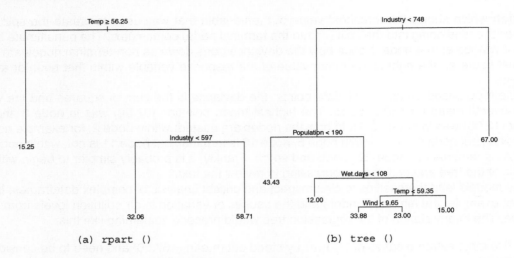

Figure 20.3 Tree diagrams for `pollute`.

The trees are different due to the criteria for which variables are to be selected for splitting and where they are split. The function `rpart ()` is much better at anticipating the results of model simplification, because it considers interactions. We have thus ended up with just three leaves, but their mean values are very distinct. Analysing `Temp` and `Industry` using the values from the tree and a simple linear regression:

```
temp_big <- factor (pollute$Temp >= 56.25)
ind_small <- factor (pollute$Industry < 597)
pollute_mod4 <- lm (pollute$Pollution ~ temp_big * ind_small)
summary (pollute_mod4)

Call:
lm(formula = pollute$Pollution ~ temp_big * ind_small)

Residuals:
    Min      1Q  Median      3Q     Max
-29.714  -8.071  -3.071   6.286  61.944

Coefficients:
                    Estimate Std. Error t value Pr(>|t|)
(Intercept)           29.085      4.053   7.176 1.66e-08 ***
temp_big1             16.300      4.053   4.021 0.000274 ***
ind_small1             5.022      4.053   1.239 0.223165
temp_big1:ind_small1   8.308      4.053   2.050 0.047544 *
---
Signif. codes:  0 '***' 0.001 '**' 0.01 '*' 0.05 '.' 0.1 ' ' 1

Residual standard error: 18.48 on 37 degrees of freedom
Multiple R-squared:  0.4267,Adjusted R-squared:  0.3802
F-statistic:  9.18 on 3 and 37 DF,  p-value: 0.0001132
```

This displays an important interaction (analogous to the split on the right branch of the tree diagram). The `rpart ()` model does not allow the inclusion of any other covariates. For instance, if we added `Population` to the linear model (the second most important variable according to `tree`), the original interaction between `Temp` and `Industry` as well as the `Industry` split becomes less critical:

```
pollute_mod5 <- lm (pollute$Pollution ~ temp_big * ind_small +
                    pollute$Population)
summary (pollute_mod5)

Call:
lm(formula = pollute$Pollution ~ temp_big * ind_small + pollute$Population)

Residuals:
    Min      1Q  Median      3Q     Max
-25.169  -8.664  -3.351   8.142  64.778

Coefficients:
                      Estimate Std. Error t value Pr(>|t|)
(Intercept)          17.801554   6.615974   2.691 0.010744 *
temp_big1            15.204906   3.912219   3.887 0.000419 ***
ind_small1           -0.594108   4.706707  -0.126 0.900256
pollute$Population    0.013817   0.006564   2.105 0.042341 *
temp_big1:ind_small1  6.851516   3.938714   1.740 0.090486 .
---
Signif. codes:  0 '***' 0.001 '**' 0.01 '*' 0.05 '.' 0.1 ' ' 1

Residual standard error: 17.68 on 36 degrees of freedom
Multiple R-squared:  0.4895,    Adjusted R-squared:  0.4328
F-statistic: 8.631 on 4 and 36 DF,  p-value: 5.432e-05
```

In summary, the `tree ()` function seems to be stronger for data inspection, because it shows more detail about the potential interaction structure in the dataframe. On the other hand, `rpart ()` is much better at anticipating the results of model simplification. It is probably best to use them both and get the benefit of two perspectives on the data set before embarking on the time-consuming business of carrying out a comprehensive multiple regression exercise.

20.2.3 Comparison with linear regression

To see how a tree model works when there is a single, continuous response variable, it is instructive to compare the output with a simple linear regression model. Take the relationship between `Mileage` and `Weight` in the `car.test.frame` data set (part of the `rpart` package) with the tree diagram and scatter plot shown in Figure 20.4:

```
data ("car.test.frame")
car_mod1 <- tree (Mileage ~ Weight, data = car.test.frame)
plot (car_mod1)
text (car_mod1)
plot (car.test.frame$Weight, car.test.frame$Mileage, xlab = "Weight",
      ylab = "Mileage", col = hue_pal ()(3)[1])
```

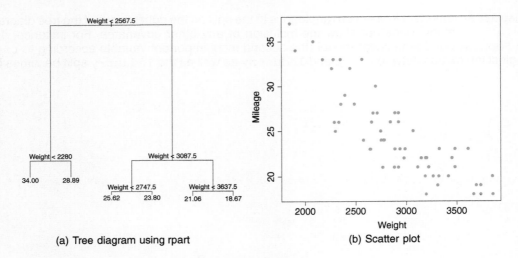

(a) Tree diagram using rpart   (b) Scatter plot

Figure 20.4   Exploratory plots for `car.test.frame`.

As there is only one covariate considered, `rpart (Mileage ~ Weight, data = car.test.` `frame)` produces exactly the same tree as `tree (Mileage ~ Weight, data = car.test.` `frame)`.

We can see that the heavier cars do fewer miles per gallon, but there is a lot of scatter. The tree model starts by finding the `Weight` that splits the mileage data in a way that explains the maximum deviance or variation in `Mileage`. This weight turns out to be 2567.5. We can add the effect of this to the scatter plot to give Figure 20.5:

```
weight_low <- mean (car.test.frame$Mileage[car.test.frame$Weight < 2567.5])
weight_high <- mean (car.test.frame$Mileage[car.test.frame$Weight >= 2567.5])
abline (v = 2567.5, lty = 2, col = hue_pal ()(3)[2])
lines (c (1500, 2567.5), rep (weight_low, 2), col = hue_pal ()(3)[3])
lines (c (2567.5, 4000), rep (weight_high, 2), col = hue_pal ()(3)[3])
```

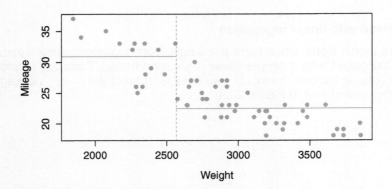

Figure 20.5   Splitting `car.test.frame` by `Weight` at 2567.58.

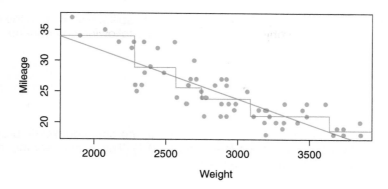

Figure 20.6 Splitting `car.test.frame` by `Weight` for the whole tree with linear regression line.

The vertical line denotes the split and the horizontal lines the mean value of `Mileage` at any `weight` after the split. The next thing the tree model does is to work out the threshold weight that would best split the mileage data for the lighter cars: this turns out to be 2280. It then works out the threshold split for the heavier cars: this turns out to be 3087.5, and so the process goes on, until there are too few cars in each split to justify continuation. To see the full regression tree in a plot, we can use the `predict ()` function which joins up our vertical and horizontal lines (they represent different things) to give Figure 20.6:

```
plot (car.test.frame$Weight, car.test.frame$Mileage, xlab = "Weight",
     ylab = "Mileage", col = hue_pal () (3) [1])
wt <- seq (1500,4000)
ml <- predict (car_mod1, list (Weight = wt))
lines (wt, ml, col = hue_pal () (3) [3])
car_lm <- lm (Mileage ~ Weight, data = car.test.frame)
abline (a = coef (car_lm) [1], b = coef (car_lm) [2], col = hue_pal () (3) [2])
```

We have also added the straightforward linear regression line for comparison. We would not normally do all this, of course (and we could not do it with more than two explanatory variables), but it is a good way of showing how tree models work with a continuous response variable. In linear regression (or GLMs), all the data contribute to the fitted model (here, the straight line). In a regression tree, just those points in the same leaf contribute to the mean value at that leaf.

20.2.4 Model simplification

Model simplification in regression trees is based on a cost-complexity measure, as opposed to AIC or `anova ()`. This reflects the trade-off between fit and explanatory power (a model with a perfect fit would have as many parameters as there were data points (it would be overfitted)), and would consequently have no explanatory power at all). We return to the `pollution` example analysed earlier, where we fitted the tree model object called `pollute_mod1`.

Regression trees can be over-elaborate and can respond to random features of the data, particularly if we decide to build the model based on a subset (**training set**) of the data. To deal with this, *R* contains a set of procedures to prune trees on the basis of a cost-complexity measure (details are not particularly interesting). The function `prune.tree ()` (there is an equivalent `prune.rpart ()` for the `rpart` package) determines a nested sequence of sub-trees of the supplied tree by recursively 'snipping' off the least important splits, based upon the cost-complexity measure. The function returns an object which contains the following components:

```
prune.tree (pollute_mod1)$size
```

```
[1] 6 5 4 3 2 1
```

This shows the number of terminal nodes in each tree in the cost-complexity pruning sequence: the original model had six terminal nodes (see Figure 20.1). This is not very interesting, but fairly standard (`car_mod1` gives the same sequence).

```
prune.tree (pollute_mod1)$dev
```

```
[1]    8876.589   9240.484 10019.992 11284.887 14262.750 22037.902
```

This is the total deviance of each tree in the cost-complexity pruning sequence.

```
prune.tree (pollute_mod1)$k
```

```
[1]       -Inf   363.8942   779.5085 1264.8946 2977.8633 7775.1524
```

This shows the value of the cost-complexity pruning parameter of each tree in the sequence. If determined algorithmically (as here, k is not specified as an input), its first value defaults to $-\infty$. We can compare `size` with `deviance` to give Figure 20.7 (the `plot.tree.sequence ()` function which actually does the plotting appears to have an issue with the colouring of the outline box!):

```
plot (prune.tree (pollute_mod1), col = hue_pal ()(1)[1])
```

This shows the way that deviance declines as complexity is increased. The total deviance is 22,037.902 (`size = 1`), and this is reduced as the complexity of the tree increases up to six nodes. An alternative is to specify the number of nodes to which we want the tree to be pruned;

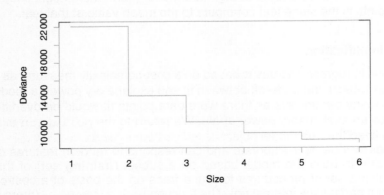

Figure 20.7   Effect of pruning `pollute` on deviance.

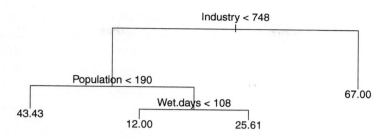

Figure 20.8 Tree for `pollute` with four leaves.

this uses the `best =` option. Figure 20.8 shows the tree with four nodes or leaves. We can see that the bottom two splits have just been deleted from Figure 20.1.

```
pollute_mod6 <- prune.tree (pollute_mod1, best = 4)
plot (pollute_mod6)
text (pollute_mod6)
```

20.3   Classification trees

Classification trees, for discrete outcomes, are derived using the same *R* functions as for regression trees. Some of the technical goings on under the bonnet may be different, but the interpretation remains broadly the same.

20.3.1   Classification trees with categorical explanatory variables

Tree models are a superb tool for helping to write efficient and effective taxonomic keys. Suppose that all of our explanatory variables are categorical, and that we want to use tree models to write a dichotomous key (i.e. we want to find a combination of covariates which uniquely identifies each species). There is only one entry for each species, so we want the twigs of the tree to be the individual rows of the dataframe (i.e. we want to fit a tree perfectly to the data).

The following example relates to the nine lowland British species in the genus Epilobium (Onagraceae). We have eight categorical explanatory variables, and we want to find the optimal dichotomous key. The dataframe looks like this:

```
epilobium <- read.table ("epilobium.txt", header = T, colClasses = rep
                         ("factor", 9))
epilobium
```

	species	stigma	stem.hairs	glandular.hairs	seeds	pappilose	stolons
1	hirsutum	lobed	spreading	absent	none	uniform	absent
2	parviflorum	lobed	spreading	absent	none	uniform	absent
3	montanum	lobed	spreading	present	none	uniform	absent
4	lanceolatum	lobed	spreading	present	none	uniform	absent
5	tetragonum	clavate	appressed	present	none	uniform	absent
6	obscurum	clavate	appressed	present	none	uniform	stolons

```
7      roseum clavate  spreading        present        none  uniform absent
8    palustre clavate  spreading        present   appendage  uniform absent
9    ciliatum clavate  spreading        present   appendage   ridged absent
   petals     base
1   >9mm  rounded
2  <10mm  rounded
3  <10mm  rounded
4  <10mm  cuneate
5  <10mm  rounded
6  <10mm  rounded
7  <10mm  cuneate
8  <10mm  rounded
9  <10mm  rounded
```

In our tree model, we need to specify two extra arguments to ensure that the splitting process goes as far as it can:

- `minsize = 2`. This sets the smallest level at which we will continue to create splits. Selecting 2 ensures that we will continue to carry on splitting, even if we have just two items in a set.

- `mindev = 0`. This is the maximum deviance remaining that we will tolerate. In practice, it is better to specify a very small value for the minimum deviance (say, 10^{-6}) rather than zero.

Figure 20.9 shows the resulting model.

```
epi_mod1 <- tree (species ~ ., mindev = 10e-6, minsize = 2, data = epilobium)
plot (epi_mod1)
text (epi_mod1, cex = 0.7)
```

Each species is uniquely identified by the explanatory variables. The computer has produced a working key to a difficult group of plants. The result stands as testimony to the power and usefulness of tree models. The same principle underlies good key-writing as is used in tree models: find

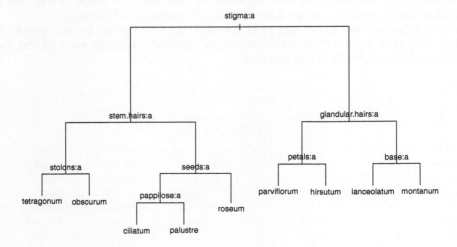

Figure 20.9 Tree for `epilobium` with maximum number of leaves.

the characters that explain most of the variation, and use these to split the cases into roughly equal-sized groups at each dichotomy.

20.3.2 Classification trees for replicated data

In this next example from plant taxonomy, the response variable is a four-level categorical variable called `Taxon` (it is a label expressed as Roman numerals I–IV). The aim is to use the measurements from the seven morphological explanatory variables to construct the best key to separate these four taxa (the **best key** is the one with the lowest error rate – the key that misclassifies the smallest possible number of cases). We also considered this data set in Chapter 19 when reviewing multi-variate statistical techniques.

```
taxonomy <- read.table ("taxonomy.txt", header = T,
                        colClasses = list (Taxon = "factor"))
head (taxonomy)

   Taxon   Petals Internode    Sepal    Bract  Petiole     Leaf     Fruit
1      I 5.621498  29.48060 2.462107 18.20341 11.27910 1.128033 7.876151
2      I 4.994617  28.36025 2.429321 17.65205 11.04084 1.197617 7.025416
3      I 4.767505  27.25432 2.570497 19.40838 10.49072 1.003808 7.817479
4      I 6.299446  25.92424 2.066051 18.37915 11.80182 1.614052 7.672492
5      I 6.489375  25.21131 2.901583 17.31305 10.12159 1.813333 7.758443
6      I 5.785868  25.52433 2.655643 17.07216 10.55816 1.955524 7.880880
```

The tree, illustrated in Figure 20.10 is surprisingly simple.

```
tax_mod1 <- tree (Taxon ~ ., data = taxonomy)
plot (tax_mod1)
text (tax_mod1)
```

With only a small degree of rounding on the suggested break points, the tree model suggests a simple (and for these 120 plants, completely error-free) key for distinguishing the four taxa:

1. Sepal length > 3.5   *Taxon IV*
1. Sepal length ≤ 3.5   2.
2. Leaf width > 2.0   *Taxon III*
2. Leaf width ≤ 2.0   3.
3. Petiole length < 9.9   *Taxon II*
3. Petiole length ≥ 9.9   *Taxon I*

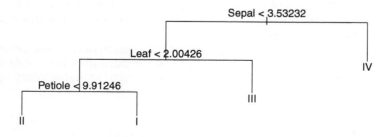

Figure 20.10   Default tree for `taxonomy`.

We have not yet considered the `summary ()` function for a tree, which is always worth a stab, so here goes:

```
summary (tax_mod1)


Classification tree:
tree(formula = Taxon ~., data = taxonomy)
Variables actually used in tree construction:
[1] "Sepal"   "Leaf"    "Petiole"
Number of terminal nodes:  4
Residual mean deviance:  0 = 0 / 116
Misclassification error rate: 0 = 0 / 120
```

Three of the seven variables were chosen for use (`Sepal`, `Leaf` and `Petiole`); four variables were assessed and rejected (`Petals`, `Internode`, `Bract`, and `Fruit`). The key has four nodes, and hence, three dichotomies. As we can see, the misclassification error rate was an impressive 0 out of 120. It is noteworthy that this classification tree does much better than the multivariate classification methods described in Chapter 19.

For classification trees, the print method produces a great deal of information:

```
print (tax_mod1)

node), split, n, deviance, yval, (yprob)
      * denotes terminal node

1) root 120 332.70 I ( 0.2500 0.2500 0.2500 0.2500 )
  2) Sepal < 3.53232 90 197.80 I ( 0.3333 0.3333 0.3333 0.0000 )
    4) Leaf < 2.00426 60  83.18 I ( 0.5000 0.5000 0.0000 0.0000 )
       8) Petiole < 9.91246 30   0.00 II ( 0.0000 1.0000 0.0000 0.0000 ) *
       9) Petiole > 9.91246 30   0.00 I ( 1.0000 0.0000 0.0000 0.0000 ) *
    5) Leaf > 2.00426 30   0.00 III ( 0.0000 0.0000 1.0000 0.0000 ) *
3) Sepal > 3.53232 30   0.00 IV ( 0.0000 0.0000 0.0000 1.0000 ) *
```

The node number is followed by the split criterion (e.g. `Sepal` < 3.53 at node 2). Then comes the number of cases passed through that node (90 in this case, versus 30 going into node 3, which is the terminal node for taxon IV). The remaining deviance within this node is 197.8 (compared with zero in node 3, where all the individuals are alike; they are all taxon IV). Next is the name of the factor level(s) left in the split (I, II, and III in this case, with the convention that the first in the alphabet is listed), then a list of the empirical probabilities (the fractions of all the cases at that node that are associated with each of the levels of the response variable – in this case, the 90 cases are equally split between taxa I, II, and III, and there are no individuals of taxon IV at this node, giving 0.33, 0.33, 0.33, and 0 as the four probabilities).

Incidentally, there is quite a useful plotting function for classification trees called `partition. tree ()`, but it can only be used when the model has no more than two explanatory variables. Its use is illustrated in Figure 20.11 by taking the two most important explanatory variables, `Sepal` and `Leaf`:

```
tax_mod2 <- tree (Taxon ~ Sepal + Leaf, data = taxonomy);
partition.tree (tax_mod2)
```

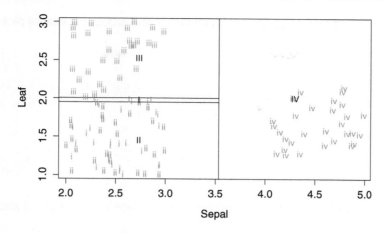

Figure 20.11   Partition tree for `taxonomy` with just `Sepal` and `Leaf`.

```
tax_label <- ifelse (taxonomy$Taxon == "I", "i",
                ifelse (taxonomy$Taxon == "II","ii",
                    ifelse(taxonomy$Taxon == "III","iii","iv")))
text (taxonomy$Sepal, taxonomy$Leaf, label = tax_label,
      col = hue_pal () (4) [as.numeric (factor (tax_label))])
```

The `partition.tree ()` shows how the phase space defined by sepal length and leaf width has been divided up between the four taxa (using capital roman numerals), but it does not show where the data fall. We have added them using lower-case roman numerals. We can see that taxa III and IV are beautifully separated on the basis of sepal length and leaf width, but taxa I and II are all jumbled up (recall that they are separated from one another on the basis of petiole length).

20.4   Looking for patterns

Tree diagrams can help us look for patterns in the data. As a fairly extreme example, let us revisit the `ethanol` database, part of the `lattice` package (Sarkar, 2008), that we looked at in Section 12.4.2. We are interested in the dependence of NOx on E:

```
library (lattice)
data (ethanol)
head (ethanol)

    NOx   C      E
1 3.741 12 0.907
2 2.295 12 0.761
3 1.498 12 1.108
4 2.881 12 1.016
5 0.760 12 1.189
6 3.120  9 1.001
```

We can create a function that will accept the two variables and produce a scatter plot with the default tree fit:

```
plot_tree <- function (x, y) {
  plot (x, y,  col = hue_pal ()(2)[1], xlab = deparse (substitute (x)),
        ylab = deparse (substitute (y)))
  tree_mod <- tree (y ~ x)
  x_grid <- seq (min (x) * 0.9, max (x) * 1.1, length.out = 1000)
  y_tree <- predict (tree_mod, list (x = x_grid))
  lines (x_grid, y_tree, col = hue_pal ()(2)[2])
}
```

Note the impenetrable but functional code to extract the axis labels. Figure 20.12 shows three plots:

(a) all the data;

(b) all the data with an E value < 1.007;

(c) all the data with an E value < 1.006.

Even though all three plots show the data dropping at the right-hand side, the `tree ()` function, which fits a line to the data, requires a minimum number of points (which can be reset as in Section 20.3.1), in this case $E < 1.007$, to show that drop in the tree diagram: beware of arbitrarily cutting off the data.

```
attach (ethanol)
plot_tree (E, NOx)
plot_tree (E[E < 1.007], NOx[E < 1.007])
plot_tree (E[E < 1.006], NOx[E < 1.006])
detach (ethanol)
```

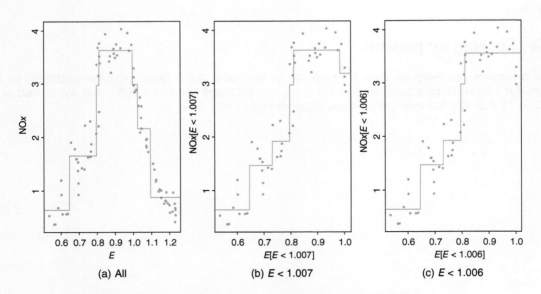

Figure 20.12   Tree plots for `ethanol` for varying subsets of the data.

References

Ripley, B. (2019). *Tree: classification and regression trees* [R package version 1.0-40]. https://CRAN.R-project
.org/package=tree.

Sarkar, D. (2008). *Lattice: multivariate data visualization with R* [ISBN 978-0-387-75968-5]. Springer. http://
lmdvr.r-forge.r-project.org.

Therneau, T., & Atkinson, B. (2019). *Rpart: Recursive partitioning and regression trees* [R package version
4.1-15]. https://CRAN.R-project.org/package=rpart.

21

Spatial Statistics

Spatial statistics enables us to build models for data that are set in more than one dimension; for instance, the spread of mould on the surface of a piece of cheese in two dimensions or the locations of galaxies in three dimensions. The critical issue is that what goes on at one location might affect what happens nearby. There are two kinds of data sets that we will explore here:

- data which occur at specific points, e.g. trees in a forest or crimes on a map, and are known as **spatial point patterns**;
- data that take values across the whole of the space, e.g. pollution levels in a city, and are known as **geospatial statistics**, from their origin in mining.

We are interested in modelling the location and, possibly, the value of the data at specific points or over an area. We will just give a flavour of the possible analyses.

Modelling using spatial statistics usually requires extra *R* packages and a list of these is given at https://cran.r-project.org/web/views/Spatial.html. This should give some idea of the range of functionality and techniques encompassed by spatial statistics. There are also some links to data sources.

21.1 Spatial point processes

If our data form a spatial point pattern, then we model them using **spatial point processes**. For most of this section, we will use the `spatstat` package (Baddeley et al., 2015a) to examine the data and build those processes: the package is extremely comprehensive and Baddeley et al., 2015b is an equally comprehensive guide to its use and to the general principles of spatial point processes.

```
library (spatstat)
```

Before we can analyse our data, we need to represent them in a point pattern in a format that `spatstat` can recognise (technically an object of type `ppp`): if we are working in two dimensions, then we need to specify the *x* and *y* coordinates of each point together with the **window** within

The R Book, Third Edition. Elinor Jones, Simon Harden and Michael J. Crawley.
© 2023 John Wiley & Sons Ltd. Published 2023 by John Wiley & Sons Ltd.
Companion website: www.wiley.com/go/jones/therbook3e

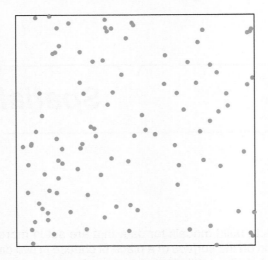

Figure 21.1 100 randomly generated points.

which those points lie. For instance, we can create a point pattern, summarise it and then plot it in Figure 21.1 using:

```
xcoord <- runif (100)
ycoord <- runif (100)
ran_pts <- ppp (x = xcoord, y = ycoord, window = square (r = 1))
summary (ran_pts)

Planar point pattern:  100 points
Average intensity 100 points per square unit

Coordinates are given to eight decimal places

Window: rectangle = [0, 1] x [0, 1] units
Window area = 1 square unit

plot (ran_pts, cols = hue_pal ()(3)[1], main = "", pch = 20)
```

We have changed the representation of a point using the argument `pch = 20`. There are many ways to describe a window, but here we have specified a square with sides of length one, and so our randomly drawn *x* and *y* coordinates fit within that. Data can also be imported from spreadsheets or standard formats used by Geographic Information Systems. This may require the use of other *R* packages such as `maptools` or `shapefiles`.

Box 21.1: Plot functions

The plot function used for Figure 21.1 is actually `plot.ppp ()`, as *R* recognises the object to be plotted is of type ppp and selects the appropriate `plot.()` function

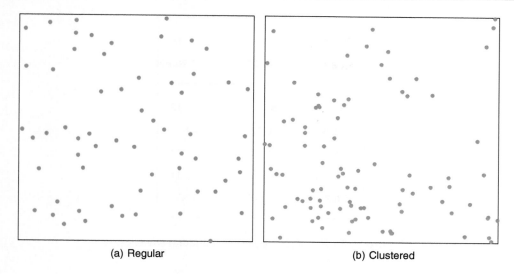

(a) Regular   (b) Clustered

Figure 21.2   Types of point pattern.

The first question we consider is whether there is any evidence to allow rejection of the null hypothesis of **complete spatial randomness** (CSR), sometimes described as a **Poisson Process**. In a **random** pattern (Figure 21.1), the distribution of each individual point is completely independent of the distribution of every other. Individuals neither inhibit nor promote one another. In a **regular** pattern (Figure 21.2a), individuals are more spaced out than in a random one, presumably because of some mechanism (such as competition) that eliminates individuals that are too close together. In a **clustered** pattern (Figure 21.2b), individuals are more clumped than in a random one, presumably because of some process such as reproduction with limited dispersal, or because of underlying spatial heterogeneity (e.g. good patches and bad patches).

21.1.1   How can we check for randomness?

As we can see from Figures 21.1 and 21.2, it may be quite difficult to discriminate between randomness and other patterns in part or all of a window just by inspection. A number of more formal approaches have thus been developed to check for randomness and also to understand where regularity or clustering may occur. None of them is perfect so it is a good idea to use more than one of them on any data. To explore these techniques, we will use the `ponderosa` data set from `spatstat` which describes tree locations (see `?ponderosa` for details):

```
summary (ponderosa)


Planar point pattern:  108 points
Average intensity 0.0075 points per square metre


Coordinates are given to 3 decimal places
i.e. rounded to the nearest multiple of 0.001 metres


Window: rectangle = [0, 120] x [0, 120] metres
Window area = 14400 square metres
Unit of length: 1 metre
```

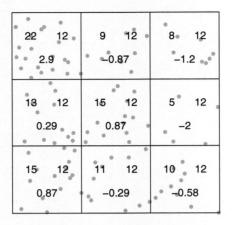

Figure 21.3   Ponderosa points and quadrat statistics.

The first approach uses a **quadrat test** wherein the window is divided into quadrats. The number of points in each quadrat is compared to the number we would expect from randomness (i.e. total number of points in the window divided by the number of quadrats) using a χ^2 goodness of fit test (see Section 9.3.2). The relevant statistics are overlaid on the data in Figure 21.3 which shows an area 120 m on each side:

```
pond_quad <- quadrat.test (ponderosa, nx = 3, ny = 3)
plot (ponderosa, main = "", cols = hue_pal ()(1), pch = 20)
plot (pond_quad, add = T)
```

In each quadrat, the first number is the count of points, the second the expected number given randomness and the third the Pearson residuals (see Section 10.5.1). There are a couple of large residuals figures and the formal test gives

```
pond_quad


Chi-squared test of CSR using quadrat counts

data:  ponderosa
X2 = 16.5, df = 8, p-value = 0.07152
alternative hypothesis: two.sided

Quadrats: 3 by 3 grid of tiles
```

The output is fairly self-explanatory. By inspection, there do appear to be more points the further left one moves. So far, there appears to be some evidence against randomness, but it is not overwhelming. The number of quadrats to use will be determined by how many data points we have: we need a reasonable number in each quadrat for the test to work, but want to be able to have as many quadrats as possible to detect where any non-randomness occurs. R's default is 5×5 but the area under study may not be square. In this case, we have chosen 3×3 as there is not a huge amount of data. If we had chosen 5×5, then the expected number of points in each quadrat would have been fewer than five and the χ^2 test would have not been valid (see Section 9.3.2).

The second approach to exploring randomness is to select a (mathematical) function that takes values at every point in the window (perhaps a covariate such as direction or slope) and then compare its empirical cumulative distribution function (CDF) acting on the data with the CDF that would have arisen from CSR, using a Kolmogorov–Smirnov test (Section 9.2.4): for instance we might compare the percentage of points that have slope less than 30 degrees between our actual data and CSR. In this example, as there appears to be a trend along the x-axis (more points for smaller x), we shall test for that:

```
cdf.test (ponderosa, covariate = "x", test = "ks")



Spatial Kolmogorov--Smirnov test of CSR in two dimensions

data:  covariate 'x' evaluated at points of 'ponderosa'
    and transformed to uniform distribution under CSR
D = 0.15035, p-value = 0.01515
alternative hypothesis: two-sided
```

There appears to be good evidence against no trend in that direction. Incidentally, there is no strong evidence of a trend along the y-axis:

```
cdf.test (ponderosa, covariate = "y", test = "ks")



Spatial Kolmogorov--Smirnov test of CSR in two dimensions

data:  covariate 'y' evaluated at points of 'ponderosa'
    and transformed to uniform distribution under CSR
D = 0.061672, p-value = 0.8059
alternative hypothesis: two-sided
```

Although we have used the Kolmogorov–Smirnov test, other tests are available, so we may choose our favourite.

The third approach to randomness is a little more complicated but, in many cases, more informative. Again, we pick a function, but this time it takes values at distances from zero up to the longest distance in the window. And again, we compare the empirical CDF of that function (i.e. the proportions of points with associated distances less than or equal to any distance) with CSR. The functions most commonly used are (there are many more):

F The distance from anywhere in the window to the nearest point. In practice, a very fine grid is used rather than anywhere;

G The distance from any point to its nearest neighbouring point;

K The number of points within a certain distance of any point. A more stable version of this is the **L** function.

Before we perform any calculations, we need to consider an issue that may cause problems. All our distance functions work well in the middle of the window and for small distances. However, as we

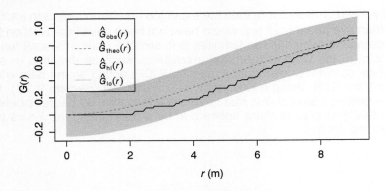

Figure 21.4 Ponderosa G statistic.

move towards the edges, the distance may well extend outside the window: our data are often just a sample from a larger area and so any calculations will omit that larger area. This explains why we need to specify a window for any point pattern and, fortunately, spatstat deals with this **edge effect** for us.

Plotting the output for our data using the G function gives Figure 21.4:

```
plot (envelope (ponderosa, Gest, nsim = 19, verbose = F, global = T), main = "")
```

As this is an important type of plot that comes up frequently in spatial point processes it is worth exploring in detail:

- The black line ($\hat{G}_{obs}(r)$) is the empirical CDF. For instance, about 40% of the points have a nearest neighbour less than or equal to 6 m away;

- The red line ($G_{theo}(r)$) is the theoretical equivalent to the black line, i.e. if there were 108 trees (as there are) and the distances between them came as precisely as possible from a Poisson Process (i.e. they were exponentially distributed: a feature of Poisson Processes), then this would be the CDF;

- The grey-shaded region (or **envelope**) represents the outer limits of a random sample of size 19 drawn from the distribution described in the previous point. So if we run the envelope command again, we will get a slightly different envelope;

- We are interested in whether our data are random. This plot represents a hypothesis test with null hypothesis that the data are random. The sample size of 19 generates an envelope, based on that randomness assumption, which is equivalent to checking whether the p-value is less than 0.05 (the equivalent to a p-value of 0.01 would be a sample size of 99). If the black line moves outside the envelope, then there is evidence against the null hypothesis at the 5% level and at the distance r where the edge of the envelope is broken;

- The conclusion from this test is that between 4 and 6 m there is some evidence against randomness. As the line is close to the edge of the envelope than elsewhere, at those distances, there are not enough neighbouring points, giving some evidence of regularity. We have not just carried out a test, but we have also some indication of the distance at which we need to probe further into non-randomness.

None of the three types of tests we have described completely captures the extent to which our data are randomly distributed. They should be used as indicators in building a model rather than conclusive in themselves (as should all statistical tests!). There appears to be evidence of both a trend along the x-axis, and some regularity for distances between 4 and 6 m.

21.1.2 Models

Our goal in building spatial point process models is usually to explain why the points are where they are (there are more complex aims, such as investigating values at points, but we will leave those for now). We can get some sense of the underlying **intensity** of points across a window just by looking at the points as in Figure 21.3. An alternative approach is to look at a heat map which gives a rough idea of the intensity of points across the whole window. This is shown, psychedelically, in Figure 21.5 for the `ponderosa` data:

```
plot (density (ponderosa), main = "")
```

The values represent the number of trees per square metre, and the overall pattern backs up the indication that there are more trees the further to the left that we go.

The outcome that we will model is this intensity (denoted by λ). In fact, for technical reasons, we model the log intensity so that if we want to build a model with the x direction as a covariate we would use either of the two following equivalent equations:

$$\log(\lambda) = \beta_0 + \beta_1 x$$
$$\lambda = e^{\beta_0 + \beta_1 x}$$

and then generate the model as follows:

```
ponderosa_model1 <- ppm (ponderosa, ~x)
ponderosa_model1
```

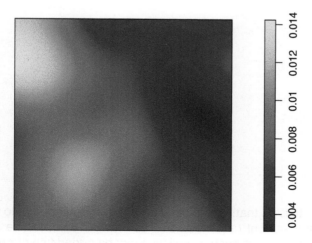

Figure 21.5 Ponderosa heat map.

```
Non-stationary Poisson process

Log intensity:  ~x

Fitted trend coefficients:
 (Intercept)               x
-4.475504135  -0.007515171

                  Estimate        S.E.       CI95.lo       CI95.hi  Ztest       Zval
(Intercept)   -4.475504135  0.173949717  -4.81643932  -4.134568954  ***  -25.728723
x             -0.007515171  0.002834888  -0.01307145  -0.001958893   **   -2.650959
```

where the `ppm ()` function performs a similar role to that which `lm ()` does for linear models. The interpretation is akin to that of a generalised linear model with a log-link function (Section 11.1.3) and the parameter estimators have been calculated using a maximum likelihood approach. The fitted intensity function (rounded to four decimal places) is

$$\lambda(x) = e^{-4.4755 - 0.0075x}$$

Box 21.2: Warning

There is not just one heat map for any spatial point pattern. There are an infinite number which can be produced by varying the bandwidth (see `?density` for more details). This is analogous to varying the appearance of a histogram by changing the widths of the cells

---

The mean value of the intensity at the left-hand side of the window (i.e. when $x = 0$) is $e^{-4.4755} = 0.0114$ and every time we move one metre to the right that mean is multiplied by $e^{-0.0075} = 0.9925$. The `Ztest` column suggests that the x covariate is significant, but we can compare it more specifically with a Poisson Process without a covariate (the intensity is just the number of trees):

```
ponderosa_model0 <- ppm (ponderosa)
anova (ponderosa_model0, ponderosa_model1, test = "Chisq")


Analysis of Deviance Table

Model 1: ~1  Poisson
Model 2: ~x  Poisson
  Npar Df Deviance Pr(>Chi)
1    1
2    2  1     7.17 0.007413 **
---
Signif. codes:  0 '***' 0.001 '**' 0.01 '*' 0.05 '.' 0.1 ' ' 1
```

The `test = "Chisq"` tells us that we are carrying out a loglikelihood ratio test, and the covariate model is clearly an improvement (a *p*-value of 0.0074). AIC can also be used for comparisons between models. Other covariates such as soil type can be added into our models using the `data` argument in `ppm ()`.

Incidentally, if we felt that the data showed, for instance, a quadratic relationship with *x*, then we could model that and then compare it with `ponderosa_model1` as follows:

```
ponderosa_model2 <- ppm (ponderosa, ~polynom (x, 2))
anova (ponderosa_model1, ponderosa_model2, test = "Chisq")

Analysis of Deviance Table

Model 1: ~x   Poisson
Model 2: ~x + I(x^2)   Poisson
  Npar Df Deviance Pr(>Chi)
1   2
2   3  1    0.345    0.557
```

but this does not appear to be an improvement.

As usual, once we have created a model, we should check how well the model fits the data. The first approach to doing this is to run the randomness tests described above but with `ponderosa_model1` rather than just the data:

```
cdf.test (ponderosa_model1, covariate = "x", test = "ks")

Spatial Kolmogorov--Smirnov test of inhomogeneous Poisson process in two
dimensions

data:  covariate 'x' evaluated at points of 'ponderosa'
     and transformed to uniform distribution under 'ponderosa_model1'
D = 0.047307, p-value = 0.969
alternative hypothesis: two-sided
```

and the *p*-value is now clearly not significant, whereas with just the data it was far smaller (0.02).

Alternatively, or additionally, we could examine residuals in an analogous fashion to linear models. Both the residuals and the resulting plots are more complex than those we have met before due to the multi-dimensional nature of our data. The four default plots are shown in Figure 21.6 for `ponderosa_model1`:

```
diagnose.ppm (ponderosa_model1, main = "")
```

Detailed descriptions of the plots can be found in `?diagnose.ppm`. In brief, the top-right and bottom-left plots show cumulative residuals with 5% significance lines. The residuals sneak outside the outer lines at about *x* = 8 m and *y* = 115 m, but if we run the plots for `ponderosa_model0`, we will see that what we have now is a vast improvement.

Box 21.3: Interactions

The interactions discussed here are completely different from the model term interactions we have met in linear models (Section 10.2.4). The former describe how the location of one point affects the locations of those nearby, while the latter examine whether covariates interact with each other in a way that significantly affects the model outcome

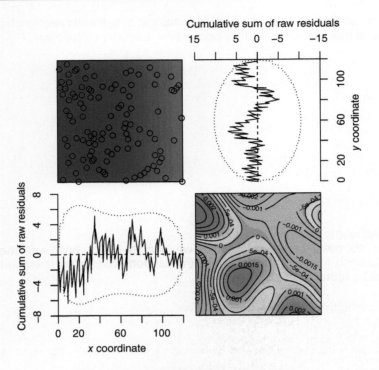

Figure 21.6   Ponderosa model1 residuals.

We have dealt with the *x* trend, but not the regularity. We can incorporate clustering or regularity into our models by adding features (known as **Gibbs or interaction processes**) that include either of these types of interaction between points.

There is an ever-growing list of available Gibbs processes in spatstat (see `?ppm`), and they can be used to fit clustering or regularity at different distances between pairs or larger groups of points.

In the `Ponderosa` data set, there appears to be regularity up to about 6 m. The Strauss model is a fairly straightforward model for dealing with interactions between pairs of points. To use it, we need to specify the distance (*r*) up to which we believe the interactions are taking place. We will set *r* = 6, but we could play around with this value to see what results in the most satisfactory set of residuals. More complicated models may require more than one such distance (described in `spatstat` as **irregular** parameters), and there are not completely satisfactory automated techniques for estimating them (see `?ppm`).

We introduce the Strauss model as follows:

```
ponderosa_model3 <- ppm (ponderosa, ~x, interaction = Strauss (r = 6))
ponderosa_model3


Nonstationary Strauss process

Log trend:  ~x

Fitted trend coefficients:
```

```
(Intercept)                   x
-3.63131827  -0.01403956

Interaction distance: 6
Fitted interaction parameter gamma:        0.5990555

Relevant coefficients:
Interaction
 -0.5124009

For standard errors, type coef(summary(x))
```

We can see that, compared to `ponderosa_model1`, both the intercept and the coefficient of the *x* covariate have changed slightly, but they can still be interpreted in the same way. We also have an estimate of the interaction parameter: $\gamma = 0.599$. What on earth does that mean? The actual value is not critical, but $\gamma < 1$ implies that we have fitted a model with regularity up to 6 m. $\gamma > 1$ would suggest clustering and $\gamma \sim 1$ neither (i.e. the residuals appear to come from a Poisson Process). Model fitting (including estimation of these parameters) is carried out using a **pseudolikelihood** (an approximation to the likelihood).

To see how good the fit for `ponderosa_model3` is, we can examine the residuals for distance functions. We would expect these to cluster around zero at all distances but with greater uncertainty for larger distances. A plot of these for the G function is displayed in Figure 21.7a:

```
plot (Gres (ponderosa_model3), main = "", legend = F)
```

The black and red lines represent the residuals from the model after adjusting for the edge effect in two different ways. The outer bands are simulated from the model and represent a sort of envelope: they suggest where we might look for further model refinement. In this case, the residuals fall well

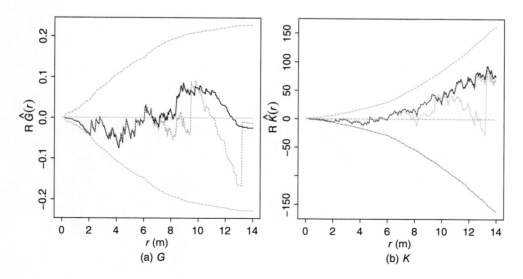

Figure 21.7   Ponderosa model3 residuals plots.

within the outer bands and it appears that no further refinement of the model is necessary. However, it is always worth examining residuals for more than one function:

```
plot (Kres (ponderosa_model3), xlim = c (0, 14), main = "", legend = F)
```

The plot for K residuals is shown in Figure 21.7b (we have kept the same *x* range as the G plot): it appears to confirm our diagnosis.

Data may exhibit different clustering or regularity at different distances and multiple interaction processes can be introduced into **hybrid** models using `interactions = Hybrid (S = Strauss (r = 5), ...)` (Baddeley et al., 2013). Gibbs processes are good at representing regularity but are not always ideal for clustering. For the latter, an alternative approach is to use Cox or cluster processes. However, these cannot currently be combined with other processes into hybrid models.

21.1.3 Marks

In many spatial point processes there may be data, known as **marks**, attached to each point. For instance, in the ragwort data set, four different types of ragwort are recorded, and they are shown in Figure 21.8.

```
ragwort_data <- read.table ("ragwortmap2.txt", header = T,
                            colClasses = c (type = "factor"))
ragwort <- ppp (x = ragwort_data$x, y = ragwort_data$y, xrange = c (0, 3000),
                yrange = c (0, 1500), marks = ragwort_data$type)
summary (ragwort)


Marked planar point pattern:  3359 points
Average intensity 0.0007464444 points per square unit

Coordinates are integers,
i.e. rounded to the nearest unit

Multitype:
          frequency proportion    intensity
regrowth        135 0.04019053 3.000000e-05
```

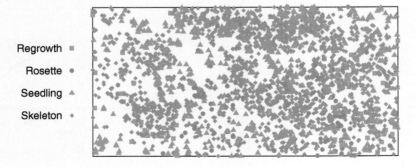

Regrowth ▪
Rosette •
Seedling ▲
Skeleton ◦

Figure 21.8   Ragwort.

```
rosette          146 0.04346532 3.244444e-05
seedling        1100 0.32747840 2.444444e-04
skeleton        1978 0.58886570 4.395556e-04

Window: rectangle = [0, 3000] x [0, 1500] units
Window area = 4500000 square units

plot (ragwort, main = "", cols = hue_pal () (4), pch = 15:18)
```

The mark is the species of ragwort, given in column `type` which must be a factor, and the window is specified using the ranges of *x* and *y* coordinates. In this case, the types are categorical: there are four different species as summarised above. Marks can also be continuous. For instance, in the ragwort data set, we can see that some entries have a diameter. As there are fewer options for building models with continuous marks, it is often simplest to divide them into a small number of multi-type categories (e.g. diameters < 4, 5–8 etc) using the `cut ()` function.

It is important with marked data to be sure that a spatial point process model is still appropriate, i.e. that the locations of the points result from some random pattern that we are interested in investigating. So if we wanted to study the overall prevalence of the four species of ragwort but were not bothered about location then a spatial point process model would not be suitable (we could treat the location as a covariate). However, if we were studying the effect of species on the locations of other species, then it would. It is important to be clear up front about the research question that is being investigated.

Many of the techniques described for unmarked point patterns can be applied to marked patterns but, inevitably, the marks introduce another layer of complexity. We will just touch on some of the possibilities in the remainder of this section. For instance, heat plots for each of the species can be easily produced (plots not shown):

```
plot (density (split (ragwort)))
```

However, they do not give any sense of the relative frequency of each of the four species. This can be shown in Figure 21.9 using the `relrisk ()` function:

```
plot (relrisk (ragwort), zlim = c(0, 1), main = "")
```

The `zlim` argument standardises the plots so that a shade in any of the plots represents the same frequency of plant relative to the total. As we had already seen, there are very few regrowth and rosette plants compared with seedlings and skeletons.

One way of exploring how the different species interact is to plot the distance functions (e.g. G) described in Section 21.1.1 for pairs of species. We can create Figure 21.10 as follows:

```
plot (alltypes (ragwort, "G"), title = "")
```

Each plot shows the extent to which one species is clustered or regular compared to another species and can be interpreted in a similar way to the lines in Figure 21.4. For instance, as one might expect, the diagonal plots show that all species tend to cluster together: the red, green, and black lines, representing different sorts of edge correction, are well above the blue randomness line. The

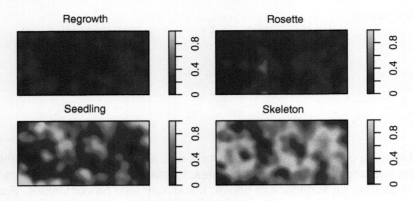

Figure 21.9 Relative heat maps for the ragwort data.

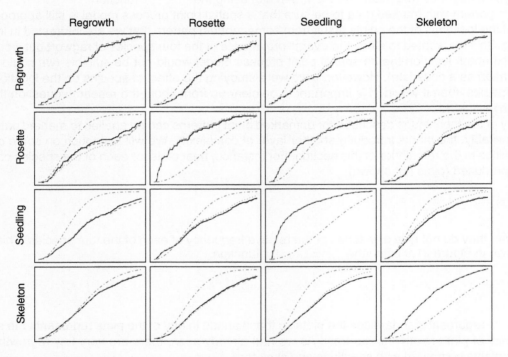

Figure 21.10 G functions for pairs of species. Blue lines represent randomness: the rest, different types of edge correction.

plot in row two, column three is interesting as it suggests that at short distances seedlings cluster around rosettes but that thereafter they tend to keep their distance. Envelopes can be added in the `alltypes ()` function for randomness tests. We might expect the matrix of plots to be symmetrical, but if, for instance, seedlings cluster around rosettes there is no expectation that rosettes will cluster around seedlings: there may be a variety of patterns that might account for the initial clustering.

Point process models can be built which take the marks into account:

```
ppm (ragwort, ~ marks)

Stationary multi-type Poisson process

Possible marks: 'regrowth', 'rosette', 'seedling' and 'skeleton'

Log intensity:  ~marks

Intensities:
beta_regrowth  beta_rosette beta_seedling beta_skeleton
 3.000000e-05  3.244444e-05  2.444444e-04  4.395556e-04


              Estimate       S.E.      CI95.lo      CI95.hi Ztest       Zval
(Intercept) -9.1991409 0.03129634  -9.2604806  -9.1378012   ***  -293.93663
marks1      -1.2151723 0.06843365  -1.3492998  -1.0810448   ***   -17.75694
marks2      -1.1368405 0.06636353  -1.2669106  -1.0067703   ***   -17.13050
marks3       0.8826184 0.03786828   0.8083979   0.9568388   ***    23.30759
```

In this case, the first mark alphabetically, regrowth, is built into the intercept, and then differences of intensity compared with other the other marks are displayed as covariates. Unsurprisingly, seedlings and skeletons show a significantly different intensity from regrowth, whereas rosettes do not. Covariates such as soil type or distance in the x direction can be added in the usual way.

Finally, we can add in Gibbs processes to our model to take account of regularity. For instance, the multi-type Strauss process allows us to specify, for each pair of species, different distances up to which regularity interactions are taking place (see ?MultiStrauss for more details). At present, spatstat in common with other packages does not have processes that deal with multi-type clustering in an analogous way.

21.2 Geospatial statistics

There are many R packages for exploring data which take values at all locations in two or three dimensions. We will use geoR (Ribeiro Jr. et al., 2020), a useful, and not too technical, introduction to this area.

```
library (geoR)
```

The following example is a geographic-scale trial to compare the yields of 56 different varieties of wheat. What makes the analysis more challenging is that the farms carrying out the trial were spread out over a wide range of latitudes and longitudes. We shall ignore the specific varieties of wheat for now.

```
wheat <- read.table ("wheat.txt", header = T)
head (wheat)

  Block  variety yield latitude longitude
1     1   LANCER 29.25      4.3      19.2
```

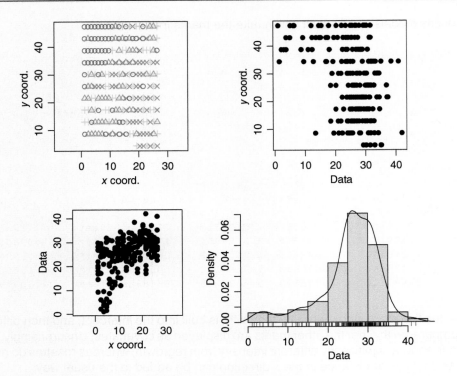

Figure 21.11 Exploratory plots for wheat.

2	1	BRULE	31.55	4.3	20.4
3	1	REDLAND	35.05	4.3	21.6
4	1	CODY	30.10	4.3	22.8
5	1	ARAPAHOE	33.05	4.3	24.0
6	1	NE83404	30.25	4.3	25.2

We transform our data into the format (class) recognised by geoR (possible covariates could also be added in here) and then the plot () function is actually plot.geodata () from the package: this results in Figure 21.11

```
wheat_geo <- as.geodata (wheat, coords.col = 5:4, data.col = 3)
plot (wheat_geo)
```

The values of the yield (referred to as 'data' in the plots) are represented by colour in the first plot (blue being low and red high). It seems to show a trend from the NW (low) to the SE (high) which is borne out by the following two plots. However, note that the trend does not look linear.

21.2.1 Models

There are many types of models that we could work with, but a common one, where s represents any point in the area we are considering and $Y(s)$ is the value (e.g. wheat yield) at that point, is

$$Y(s) = \mu(s) + S(s) + Z(s)$$

Examining each of the elements on the right-hand side in turn:

- $\mu(S)$: the **trend** or deterministic part of the yield consisting of covariates including location data. In our case that might be latitude or wheat variety;

- $S(s)$: a value which allows statistical variation over the area we are considering but which ensures that points near to each other have similar variation and are therefore correlated. Technically, this is a **Gaussian process**;

- $Z(s)$: a final statistical variation term which takes into account measurement errors or differences in techniques, wherever data have been gathered. This term is similar to the error term in linear models (see Section 10.1.1).

We will examine how we might explore the first two elements.

As usual with model building, having examined the data our first task is to create the deterministic elements or, in geostatistical terminology, **trend**. We can introduce a term to take account of the non-linear location pattern in the data as follows:

```
plot (wheat_geo, trend = '2nd', lowess = T)
```

The `trend = '2nd'` argument refers to a second-order trend in direction with terms including x^2, y^2, and xy. Figure 21.12 shows residuals rather than data, after the trend has been added. As usual,

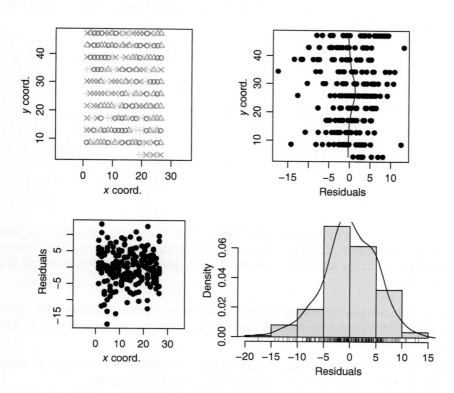

Figure 21.12 Exploratory plots for wheat with second-order trend.

we are looking for randomness: there is less of a clear pattern to the values in the first plot and the residuals mapped against the *x* and *y* coordinates display far more randomness than before, as can be seen from the fitted line.

The next task in our model building is to capture the correlation in values between points that are spatially close to each other. We will do this by building a **stationary model** which assumes that:

1. the values at each location have a constant mean throughout the area we are considering once the trend has been taken into account;

2. the variogram of any two points depends only upon the distance between them (not their location or relative direction).

The **variogram** is a plot of distance against variability between points at that distance apart. Unlike a linear model, for instance, we would not expect the residuals of two data points to be independent from each other: the spatial nature of the data will not permit that. For two points that are close together, one would expect little difference in the variability of their values and so the variogram is low. As the distance between the pair increases, the variogram will rise until there is no connection between the variability whereupon the variogram will meander randomly. The assumptions given above are rarely precisely true in practice, but they provide a surprisingly effective approach to describing spatial variability. Technically, the variogram is a function of the covariance between points at a particular distance.

We begin to model this spatial correlation using an empirical variogram plot (we have chosen `max.dist = 20` as there is no discernible pattern in the data at larger distances) which compares distance with variogram value:

```
wheat_var <- variog (wheat_geo, trend = "2nd", max.dist = 20)
plot (wheat_var, main = "",
xlab = "distance (h)", ylab = "variogram", col = "red", pch = 19)
```

```
variog: computing omnidirectional variogram
variofit: covariance model used is exponential
variofit: weights used: npairs
variofit: minimisation function used: optim
variofit: covariance model used is spherical
variofit: weights used: npairs
variofit: minimisation function used: optim
```

Figure 21.13a shows the empirical variogram for our data. It collects distances between pairs of points into groups (**bins**) and works out the average variogram value for each group. Various quaintly named features of the variogram plot, which give away its origin in geological prospecting, have then been added:

- **nugget:** the minimum value of the variogram for points very close together. The problem in this case is that none of the pairs of points are particularly close and so we end up with a large value for the nugget;

- **sill:** the value of the variogram where the points appear to flatten out or begin to show randomness. The **partial sill** is the difference between the sill and the nugget;

- **range:** the distance at which the sill occurs.

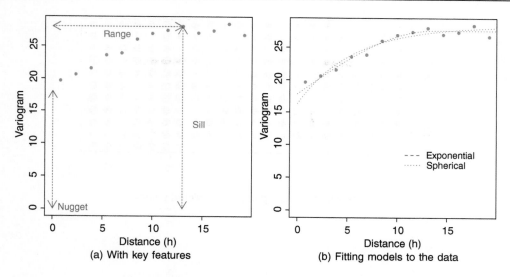

Figure 21.13   Empirical variograms for wheat.

We use these initial values to help fit a curve to the variogram plot. There are a number of standard curves we could use and the features help us estimate their parameters. Figure 21.13b shows a couple of these curves (exponential and spherical: there are many more options) after they have been fitted to the data using the function variofit ():

```
nug <- 18
sill <- 28
partial_sill <- sill - nug
range <- 13
plot (wheat_var, main = "", cex.lab = 1.5,
     xlab = "distance (h)", ylab = "variogram", col = "red", pch = 19)
exp_est <- variofit (wheat_var, cov.model = "exp",
                        ini.cov.pars = c (partial_sill, range), nugget = nug)
sph_est <- variofit (wheat_var, cov.model = "sph",
                        ini.cov.pars = c (partial_sill, range), nugget = nug)
lines (exp_est, col = "brown", lty = 3, lwd = 2)
lines (sph_est, col = "blue", lty = 3, lwd = 2)
legend (10, 10, legend = c ("exponential", "spherical"), lty = c (2, 3),
lwd = rep (2, 2), bty = "n", cex = 1.5, col = c ("blue", "brown"))
```

The exponential curve appears to fit best. If we investigate summary (exp_est), we will find that the final value for the partial sill is 5.53 and the range 12.09. This completes our model in that we now have details of the covariances between residuals to go with the trend.

Our final step might be to estimate values at any point in the area we are considering. For instance, Figure 21.14 shows a circle plot of the data together with the prediction for a number of points (in red):

```
plot (wheat$longitude, wheat$latitude, xlab = "", ylab = "", col = "blue",
     pch = 20, cex = wheat$yield / 10)
```

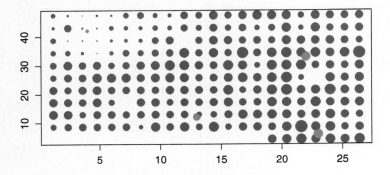

Figure 21.14 Circle plot with predicted values.

```
pred_pts <- matrix (c (4, 22, 13, 23, 42, 33, 12, 6), ncol = 2)
krige_pts <- krige.conv (wheat_geo, loc = pred_pts,
                         krige = krige.control (obj.m = exp_est))


krige.conv: model with mean given by a second-order polynomial on the
coordinates
krige.conv: Kriging performed using global neighbourhood


points (pred_pts, col = "red", pch = 20, cex = krige_pts$predict / 10)
```

This can be extended to give a heat map of predicted values for the whole area using `pred_grid ()` and `krige_surf ()`.

References

Baddeley, A., Rubak, E., & Turner, R. (2015a). *Spatial point patterns: methodology and applications with R*. Chapman & Hall/CRC Press. https://www.routledge.com/Spatial-Point-Patterns-Methodology-and-Applications-with-R/Baddeley-Rubak-Turner/9781482210200/.

Baddeley, A., Rubak, E., & Turner, R. (2015b). *Spatial point patterns: methodology and applications with R*. CRC Press. https://doi.org/10.1201/b19708.

Baddeley, A., Turner, R., Mateu, J., & Bevan, A. (2013). Hybrids of Gibbs point process models and their implementation. *Journal of Statistical Software*, *55*(11), 1–43. https://www.jstatsoft.org/v55/i11/.

Ribeiro Jr., P. J., Diggle, P. J., Schlather, M., Bivand, R., & Ripley, B. (2020). *geoR: Analysis of geostatistical data* [R package version 1.8-1]. https://CRAN.R-project.org/package=geoR.

## 22

Bayesian Statistics

Instead of asking 'what do my data show?', the Bayesian analyst asks 'how do my data alter our view of the world?'. It may not sound like much, but it is a fundamental change of outlook. The idea is that the results of the new study are assessed in the light of the existing knowledge to establish an updated assessment of parameter values and their uncertainties.

Imagine we have a model in mind for a data set. Whether we are Bayesian or not, there will be parameters, $\theta = (\theta_1, \ldots, \theta_m)$, in this model that we want to estimate (or learn about). The way that a Bayesian and frequentist view these parameters differs:

- A frequentist would view the parameters θ as *fixed* quantities whose true values are unknown to us.

  - The key here is that the parameters are thought of as fixed (i.e. a single number which is unknown to us).
  - The aim is to estimate these parameters.

- A Bayesian would view the parameters θ as *random variables*, represented by a probability distribution.

  - These are *not* thought of as fixed.
  - For a specified model with parameters θ, we combine our existing (pre-data) information about the parameters (in the form of a **prior** probability distribution on the parameters θ) with our data.
  - This gives us the **posterior** distribution of θ. We can view the process as updating our prior beliefs about θ using the data.
  - Once we have a good handle on the posterior probability distribution of θ, we can use it to compute all sorts of summary statistics of interest, e.g. means and variances of the parameters.

This fundamental difference in the way we think about parameters has further nice consequences which we'll discuss in Section 22.1.6. For now, let us explore the elements of a Bayesian analysis.

The R Book, Third Edition. Elinor Jones, Simon Harden and Michael J. Crawley.
© 2023 John Wiley & Sons Ltd. Published 2023 by John Wiley & Sons Ltd.
Companion website: www.wiley.com/go/jones/therbook3e

22.1   Components of a Bayesian Analysis

If we were to grossly simplify the process of fitting a frequentist model, we could describe it as follows:

- Choose a suitable (class of) models, e.g. normal linear regression model, which will have a fixed set of assumptions;
- Estimate the parameters of the model using a pre-defined algorithm;
- Check, as far as possible, that the underlying assumptions of the model are not violated.

A Bayesian analysis feels quite different:

- Construct a (bespoke) model from scratch, where *we* define every aspect of the structure and assumptions that will be made (though often the structure is borrowed directly from 'standard' frequentist models);
- Gather existing knowledge about the parameters in the model and channel this information into probability distributions (the **prior** information we have about the model parameters);
- Estimate the **posterior** distribution of the parameters, which combines information from the likelihood (the model we constructed plus the data) and the prior information;
- Use the posterior distribution to estimate any quantities of interest about the parameters.

This gives the Bayesian analyst ultimate flexibility: whereas frequentists tend to be restricted to off-the-shelf models with prescribed formats and assumptions, a Bayesian can create a bespoke model with no restrictions. While this sounds great, it comes with a lot of responsibility and requires excellent understanding of what we're doing. A good source of background, examples, and computational methods on each of these steps is given in Gelman et al., 2004.

22.1.1   The likelihood (the model and data)

Model choice is a very important part of Bayesian data analysis. We'll create a model from scratch each time we want to run a Bayesian analysis. This may sound like a lot of work, but this gives the researcher ultimate flexibility. It is probably easiest to get your head around this using an example.

Suppose that we want to build a simple linear regression model of the form:

$$y_i = a + bx_i + \epsilon_i \tag{22.1}$$

where we have data on a covariate $\mathbf{x} = (x_1, \ldots, x_n)$ and an outcome $\mathbf{y} = (y_1, \ldots, y_n)$. Other than the format given in (22.1), we would also need to specify the distribution of our error term, ϵ. Usually, if we were to run this model as a frequentist, we would assume that $\epsilon_i \sim N(0, \sigma^2)$ and that these terms are independent. That is not necessary here: we can build the model however we want.

For now let us say that we're willing to assume that the errors are independent and come from a *t*-distribution with unknown degrees of freedom, v. That is, $\epsilon_i \sim t_v$. Our model is defined by

$$y_i = a + bx_i + \epsilon_i$$

$$\epsilon_i \sim t_v$$

This model structure combined with the data will give us our **likelihood**. We won't go into the exact format of the likelihood here: it isn't particularly instructive if we are just looking to competently run a Bayesian analysis. This is taken care of by the software we'll be using to run our models.

22.1.2 Priors

Continuing with the example in Section 22.1.1, the (unknown) parameters are a, b, v. Remember that in a Bayesian framework these are considered random variables so that they have some underlying probability distribution.

For each of these parameters, we need to specify our prior information in the form of a probability distribution (that is, we need to encode our prior beliefs in this format). This prior information will eventually be combined with the likelihood to produce a *posterior* distribution for each of a, b, v: this gives the *updated* information about the parameters having seen the data.

There is no such thing as a 'correct' prior, and you and I may well have different opinions on what prior is suitable. I may make the assumption that the prior information on the parameter a is encapsulated by a prior of the form $N(3, 5^2)$, but it is highly likely that you will choose something different. This is one of the often-quoted downsides of a Bayesian: the prior information is at least somewhat subjective. The potential problem with this is, since the prior information is combined with the data, the posterior distribution is at least partially dependent on the prior chosen.

The good news is that a change in prior information doesn't always change the end result of our analysis too drastically as long as there is enough information in the data. When this is the case, the information in the data essentially dominates the information in the prior. This isn't always the case, however, so be warned. We should, at the very least, be able to robustly defend our choice of prior. This could be based on expert knowledge, as we describe below.

But how do we go about trying to condense our current knowledge of the parameters into suitable (prior) distributions? Let us suppose that in the example in (22.1) the outcome represents the height in centimetres of girls, and the covariate represents their age in months ranging from 24 to 60 months.

The intercept, a, denotes the mean height (or length) of a newborn, for which information is readily available. The mean is around 49 cm, and we might for example use a normal prior for a with mean 49 cm and standard deviation of 1 cm to be on the safe side though this is probably overkill. A normal prior is common, but there is an obvious disadvantage in this case: it is not limited to positive numbers. This shouldn't be too much of an issue here as we have a small standard deviation and our analysis is limited to children of at least 24 months old (that is, though the intercept is necessary, it's not of interest in its own right).

The slope, b, denotes the average rate of change of height between 24 and 60 months. Again, we can find information on this: a girl in this age range would be expected to grow on average 0.5 cm per month. We could opt for a normal prior with mean 0.5 and a standard deviation of, say, 0.1 cm.

Finally, we need to think about the degrees of freedom for our t-distribution which captures information about the error term, ϵ. It has been suggested that a reasonable prior to use for the degrees of freedom is a Gamma distribution with parameters 2 and 0.1 (Juárez and Steel, 2010) (this may sound a little strange, but degrees of freedom don't have to be whole numbers). This Gamma distribution places most of its weight on values below 50 – so the estimated degrees of freedom for the t-distribution is likely to be less than 50 unless the data dictates otherwise – which in turn implies that the resulting t-distribution is rather different to the (standard) Normal distribution.

In this example, we were able to select reasonable prior information, and each prior is justifiable in this sense. In others, we may have very little information to go on. In these cases, we often resort to using rather *vague* priors. That is, priors with large variance that cover a wide range of possibilities. We will frequently find vague priors being referred to as 'uninformative priors', but this isn't technically true: all priors give some information even if that information isn't particularly strong.

22.1.3 The Posterior

A Bayesian analysis combines our likelihood (function of our model and data) with the prior information on the unknown parameters of the model. This produces our 'updated' probability distribution for these unknown parameters (which are random variables), known as the **posterior distribution**.

Let us take the parameter a from (22.1), which represents the intercept for our model. A Bayesian analysis will combine the likelihood and the prior information and provide us with a posterior distribution for a. We can think of the data as having 'updated' the prior to give us the posterior.

But how do we elicit the posterior? The underlying idea is that we make use of Bayes's theorem (hence the name 'Bayesian'!). Bayes's theorem states that for any two events A and B with $P(B) \neq 0$ we have

$$P(A|B) = \frac{P(B|A)P(A)}{P(B)} \ .$$

See Section 2.4.2 for a more in-depth treatment. Another format of Bayes's theorem states, for our model parameters θ and data $\mathbf{z}$:

$$p(\theta|\mathbf{z}) = \frac{p(\mathbf{z}|\theta)p(\theta)}{p(\mathbf{z})}$$

where we have:

- the posterior distribution of the parameters, $p(\theta|\mathbf{z})$ (that is, the updated distribution of the parameters after we take into consideration the data);
- the prior distribution of the parameters, $p(\theta)$; and
- the information from our model and data, $p(\mathbf{z}|\theta)$.

The term $p(\mathbf{z})$ is just a constant (it doesn't depend on the unknown θ which is what we're trying to extract information about), and so it's easier to say that:

$$p(\theta|\mathbf{z}) \propto p(\mathbf{z}|\theta)p(\theta) \ . \tag{22.2}$$

This turns out to be very helpful believe it or not, as it tells us how to modify our existing beliefs, $p(\theta)$ in the light of our model and data, $p(\mathbf{z}|\theta)$, to give us our posterior distribution, $p(\theta|\mathbf{z})$.

In some cases, it is possible to derive the exact posterior distribution analytically, because the mathematics in (22.2) works out nicely. One such case is when the posterior belongs to the same class of distributions as the prior. When this is the case, we say that the prior is a **conjugate** prior. Conjugate priors are useful if we are aiming for an analytical solution, but not essential if we intend to investigate our posterior distribution numerically.

Estimating the posterior distribution numerically is necessary in the vast majority of cases, but this requires computing power (and a clever algorithm). Indeed, until the 1980s, the idea of a Bayesian analysis was novel but often impractical to conduct because the posterior distribution was just too complex to compute. Models and associated priors were restricted to those which had a posterior distribution that could be derived analytically. The rapid development of computing power meant that we could approximate the posterior by simulation instead of determining it analytically. This is where **Markov chain Monte Carlo** (or **MCMC** for short) comes into its own: it allows us to simulate from the posterior distribution which enables us to build up a picture of what the posterior 'looks' like. Bayesian analysis is now commonplace thanks to this innovative idea.

22.1.4 Markov chain Monte Carlo (MCMC)

The basic idea behind the MCMC algorithm is to generate a sequence of random values for our unknown model parameters such that the next value drawn depends only on the previous value, and that taken collectively the values generated represent draws from the posterior distribution.

Let us suppose we only have one unknown parameter, θ_1, though this idea extends to however many parameters we have in our model. We start with an **initial value** for θ_1, either chosen by the researcher or randomly sampled from a sensible distribution (e.g. if the parameter is a variance, we don't want the initial value to be negative!). Subsequent samples – generally called **iterations** – for θ_1 are drawn sequentially, with the distribution of the next draw depending only on the last sample drawn. This is the 'Markov chain' bit: the current 'value' is dependent only on the last value drawn. The Monte Carlo part of the name refers to random draws (the gambling part).

The clever bit of MCMC is that eventually (i.e. if we do this for long enough) these samples will be representative of samples drawn from the posterior distribution of θ_1 (Gelman et al., 2004). But why is this useful? If we can draw samples from the posterior distribution of θ_1, then we can learn a lot about this parameter:

- we can get a good feel for the *shape* of the posterior distribution (e.g. we could draw a histogram using these samples, or better still approximate with a kernel density plot);

- we can compute summary statistics for the posterior distribution (e.g. if we want to estimate the mean of the posterior, then compute the mean of the samples drawn).

Don't be fooled at this point into thinking that there is just one 'MCMC algorithm': that isn't the case. There are various algorithms that can be used, all with the same underlying idea of generating sequences of numbers that can eventually be used to learn about the posterior. The simplest is probably the Gibbs sampling algorithm, with the Metropolis and Metropolis–Hastings algorithms better for more complicated models. We needn't worry about which to use when using *R*: the default is often Gibbs sampling, but functions to run Bayesian analysis will often switch to another algorithm behind the scenes if it runs into trouble.

22.1.5 Considerations for MCMC

Using MCMC involves three important practical considerations:

- the burn-in period;
  - 'how long does it take until my MCMC algorithm is spitting out values that are representative of the posterior?'

- the number of iterations;
  - 'once my MCMC algorithm is producing values that are representative of the posterior, how long should we continue to run the algorithm?'

- the number of 'chains'.
  - 'can I run multiple MCMC algorithms simultaneously to see if they all come to the same conclusion about the posterior?'

It's important to note that the first few iterations of the MCMC algorithm won't produce samples from the posterior: we need to run the algorithm for a while before we can treat the samples generated as coming from it.

One option is to run the chain for a long time. That way, even if the first few (possibly thousands of!) samples aren't representative of the posterior, this will be a drop in the ocean compared to the total number of samples. These won't therefore make much difference when taken together with the rest of the samples.

A more popular option is to **burn** the first few samples generated. This is a fancy way of saying that we delete them, and the term **burn-in period** is often used to denote the iterations we ignore. How long should the burn-in period last? Once we're confident that the algorithm is drawing samples from the posterior distribution, how many iterations do we need? There are no clear-cut answers here. It is, however, clear that we need to make every effort to check that the algorithm has run long enough to *reach* the posterior – often referred to as reaching or converged to equilibrium – and once that has happened, that we generate a sufficient number of samples from the posterior to get a very good feel for the distribution.

Of course, there won't be a specific point at which we switch from 'not yet sampling from the posterior' to 'sampling from the posterior', no more than there'll be a point at which we switch from 'not enough samples from the posterior' to 'enough samples from the posterior'. If we have multiple parameters in our model, what might be a sufficient number of iterations of the algorithm for one may not be enough for the others. This makes it very tricky, but the long and the short of it is this: the more we are willing to 'burn' initially and the more samples we generate after the burn-in period, the better. There's no such thing as too many samples, though we generally have constraints on how long we're willing to wait.

There are various tools available to help determine if we've run our chain for long enough, and whether we've discarded a sufficient number of initial samples. A really useful method is to use trace plots. These plot the iteration number on the *x*-axis and the sampled value on the *y*-axis, with one of these plots per parameter of interest. What we would like to see is a thick solid horizontal band: this shows that the algorithm has settled down and is churning out values that are, on average, not changing.

For example, consider a model with two parameters, `parameter.1` and `parameter.2`. We run the model for 5000 iterations. The trace plot in Figure 22.1a looks just about acceptable: we can see that the samples for `parameter.1` are consistent and form a classic solid band indicative of

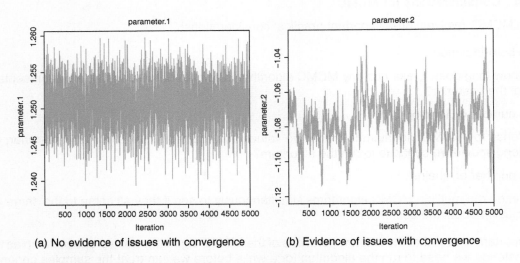

(a) No evidence of issues with convergence   (b) Evidence of issues with convergence

Figure 22.1   Trace plots for two parameters after a Bayesian analysis (5000 iterations).

the algorithm having converged. Ideally, we'd run it for a tad longer, just to make sure. Meanwhile, the trace plot in Figure 22.1b indicates that the MCMC sequence of samples are still wandering around and haven't yet settled: we need to run the model for a lot longer, despite `parameter.1` looking OK. The burn-in period should therefore be even larger than 5000 iterations in this case. We'll see further examples in Section 22.3 of how to generate these plots and what to look out for.

Finally, note that it's possible to set off more than one MCMC chain at a time. This is often a very sensible idea as long as we specify different starting values for each chain. To see why this is the case, imagine that the correct posterior is a multimodal distribution. We set off a single MCMC algorithm, and after a while, the chain seems to reach equilibrium. It seems very stable, and we think we've got a good handle on the posterior. Great! But what if the MCMC algorithm got 'stuck' in one of the 'humps' of the *true* posterior distribution, and didn't make it over to visit the other humps? Our inference would be very wrong indeed about this parameter.

There are two broad ways we can try to avoid this problem. The first is to note that if we run the MCMC algorithm for long enough, it will eventually visit all the nooks and crannies of the posterior distribution. But how long is 'long enough' (how long is a piece of string)? Our trace plots may look great, and *still* we haven't explored the whole posterior distribution. To try to avoid this problem, a common tactic is to run multiple chains each starting from a different initial value. If all the chains start from different places, and all the chains seem to be pointing to roughly the same posterior distribution by the time we stop the MCMC algorithm, then we should have more confidence that we have explored the whole of the posterior rather than getting stuck in one part of it.

The idea of **thinning** a chain is also common. Because the MCMC process is based on a Markov chain, successive values of the parameters show strong serial correlations, so successive values typically give little extra information about the shape of the posterior distribution. Thinning a chain involves taking every nth sample rather than using them all. This is often unnecessary, unless there is evidence that our chain isn't moving well around the posterior distribution (again, trace plots are helpful).

22.1.6 Inference

Once we run our Bayesian analysis and we're happy that the model has converged, we'll want to inspect the output and make inferences about the parameters of interest. One of the strengths of the Bayesian approach is the ease of interpretation of the output.

The MCMC algorithm will have produced samples from the posterior distribution of each parameter of interest. From there we can

- get a feel for the shape of the posterior by plotting the samples for each parameter;
  - a rudimentary way of doing this would be to create a histogram;
  - software to run Bayesian analyses generally plot kernal densities instead (see Figure 22.3 for a sneak preview).
- find summary statistics for each parameter of interest, say θ;
  - find the (estimated) mean of the posterior of a parameter, θ, by computing the mean of the samples for θ;
  - find an interval $[l, u]$ so that with probability 0.95 the value of θ lies within it (and with probability 0.025 the value is less than l, and with probability 0.025 the value is greater than u).

The last example is a **95% credible interval** for the parameter of interest. Notice how nice the interpretation is: the value of the parameter lies within these bounds with probability 0.95.

Compare this with a frequentist approach, and in particular, the idea of a confidence interval. A (frequentist) confidence interval for a parameter tells us that, if we re-ran our data-collecting exercise over and over again, computing a 95% confidence interval for the parameter each time, then 95% of these 95% confidence intervals would contain the true value of the parameter. That is a far more complicated interpretation, and possibly less useful, than a Bayesian credible interval.

22.1.7   The Pros and Cons of going Bayesian

The advantages of Bayesian analysis include the following:

- models can be as complex as necessary to describe the question in hand: we have complete control over the structure of the model and the assumptions we make;
- the assumptions we make are transparent because we have to specify them all in our model;
- we can incorporate prior information about the parameters, which can help strengthen the evidence we collect at the end of our analysis;
- we can combine information from multiple sources easily and in a coherent manner;
- interpretation of complex models is much more straightforward;
- we can carry out sequential analyses, where we continue to update our knowledge of parameters as new data are collected.

However, a Bayesian analysis has a number of disadvantages:

- we need to know much more maths and statistics to do it competently;
- we have complete control over the model and assumptions, so we need to know what we're doing;
- the choice of priors can be both controversial and consequential, especially with small sample sizes.

Does this mean that Bayesian analyses should not be trusted? Not at all. When we analyse our data, be it by selecting a frequentist model or going Bayesian, we're making decisions about the structure and assumptions to be made. That's an important point: often, we forget that all frequentist models make assumptions because many of them are implicit. We shouldn't be building a frequentist model if we don't believe the underlying assumptions it makes, no more than we should be building a Bayesian model if the assumptions we specify are clearly nonsense.

With the addition of prior information, we *do* need to be careful. With sufficient data, the influence of the priors won't be too dramatic, and the information will come mostly from the data. If we do find ourselves in the situation where a change of prior results in dramatic changes in the results, then this tells us that we don't have very much information in the data to start with. Back to the drawing board, in that case.

22.2   Bayesian analysis in *R*

There is a huge amount of information and a great many computing resources for Bayesian analysis available on the CRAN website. This is summarised in the Bayesian Inference Task View

(Park et al., 2021). The Task View subdivides the packages under five headings:

- Bayesian packages for general model fitting;
- Bayesian packages for specific models or methods;
- post-estimation tools;
- packages for learning Bayesian statistics;
- packages that link *R* to other sampling engines (like `R2jags`, `R2WinBUGS`, `R2OpenBUGS`).

Applied researchers interested in Bayesian statistics are increasingly attracted to *R* because of the ease with which one can code algorithms to sample from posterior distributions as well as the significant number of packages contributed to CRAN. In particular, there are several choices for MCMC sampling. For many years, the most popular of these was WinBUGS (Spiegelhalter et al., 2003), and this can still be run from *R* using the package `R2WinBUGS` (Sturtz et al., 2005). This is not used here because WinBUGS does not run on a Mac, and the software is no longer being developed. The final manifestation of WinBUGS, frozen at version 1.4.3, is still perfectly functional on some operating systems.

Two other options are OpenBUGS (this replaced WinBUGS) and JAGS. We'll illustrate this chapter using JAGS. It is fairly straightforward to learn to use another package once we know one of them.

22.2.1   Installing JAGS

JAGS stands for 'Just Another Gibbs Sampler' (Plummer, 2003). It is a program for analysis of Bayesian hierarchical models using MCMC simulation. It is very like BUGS in spirit and language.

First, install JAGS. Do this by visiting http://mcmc-jags.sourceforge.net/. Click on 'files page' under Downloads, then 'Download Latest Version', then click on Download JAGS. Then run the program and chose all the default options that are offered.

The next thing to do is install the `R2jags` package (Su and Yajima, 2020) that allows *R* to communicate with JAGS and vice versa. Inside *R*, while running *R* as administrator, install the package in the usual way. Now, we are ready to start Bayesian modelling.

22.2.2   Running JAGS in *R*

The first thing to appreciate is that most of the hard work is done *outside R*. We have to use the BUGS language to write down our model together with the priors. We don't need anything fancy here: a basic text editor will do and we'll be saving our models as `.txt` files. Only now can we go into *R* to start the modelling. This is the sequence of events:

- Write the model in a text editor, using BUGS language, and save it somewhere sensible.
- Use `read.table ()` to enter the data into a dataframe in the usual way.
- (Optional) `attach ()` the dataframe and make a list of the variable names that need to be passed into the BUGS code. If we don't do that, we will need to specify where the variables can be found using the dollar sign.
- Choose the initial values of each parameter and each chain (or leave JAGS to choose them later down the line).

- Load the `R2jags` package using `library (R2jags)`.

- Run the JAGS model using the `jags ()` function by specifying the name of the list of variables, the initial conditions (optional), the path and name of the file where the BUGS code is to be found, and the number of Markov chains to run (a popular choice is three).

With any luck the JAGS model will run, and its progress is indicated by a slowly moving horizontal bar. Once the model has finished, we can inspect the parameter estimates and their uncertainty measures, and create various plots.

22.2.3 Writing BUGS models

BUGS stands for 'Bayesian inference Using Gibbs Sampling' (Lunn et al., 2009). Information about the history of BUGS can be found at the OpenBUGS website https://www.mrc-bsu.cam.ac.uk/software/bugs/openbugs/.

The trick is to learn how to express a particular model in BUGS code. The code looks superficially like *R*, but it is fundamentally different. We write it in a text editor (notepad or similar will do the trick, or even directly in RStudio), and save it as a text file outside of *R*. The name of the file containing the BUGS model is provided as an argument to the `jags ()` function in *R*.

There are lots of clear examples of the way that different kinds of models are expressed in BUGS code on the website for WinBUGS (Spiegelhalter et al., 2003) at https://www.mrc-bsu.cam.ac.uk/software/bugs/the-bugs-project-the-bugs-book/bugs-book-examples/. It is worth spending time browsing through these examples to find the one closest to the problem you are trying to solve, then edit the code to tailor it to your specific requirements. Three examples are described in detail below (a simple regression, a longitudinal study, and an experiment involving proportion data with overdispersion).

Let us code up a couple of examples, starting with a simple model then using the slightly more complex running example from Section 22.1.

BUGS model for Bernoulli data

Let us suppose we have 100 observations from a Bernoulli distribution with unknown probability of success, `theta`. We want to learn about `theta` and set up a Bayesian model. We choose a `Beta(1,1)` prior for `theta` (this is equivalent to a Uniform distribution over the interval [0,1]). We can now write our BUGS model as follows.

```
model {
  for (i in 1:100) {
    x[i] ~ dbern(theta)
  }
  theta ~ dbeta(1,1)
}
```

We can think of the contents of `model { }` as describing the likelihood, while the remaining line of code corresponds to the single prior.

Note that:

- all model files start with `model{ ;`

- we have 100 observations, here indexed by `i`, and we want to loop around these which we do using `for (i in 1:100){ ;`

- each of our 100 observations, `x[1]` through `x[100]`, has the same distribution;
- the Bernoulli distribution is denoted `dbern` and similarly for the Beta distribution;
- we use a twiddles, ~, to denote distribution, e.g. `x[i] ~ dbern(theta)` denotes that the random variable `x[i]` has a Bernoulli distribution with some parameter `theta`;
- notice that that we close the `for (i in 1:100){` loop before we specify the prior on `theta`, since `theta` does not depend on `i`;
- remember that we opened the BUGS code with `model{` so we need to close this at the end with a `}`.

BUGS code for a simple linear regression model

In Section 22.1, we considered a linear regression model. Suppose that we have 500 observations of an outcome, $(y_1, \ldots, y_{500})$, the associated covariate of interest, $(x_1, \ldots, x_{500})$, and we wanted to code for a model of the following format where the unknown parameters are a, b and σ:

$$y_i = a + bx_i + \epsilon_i$$
$$\epsilon_i \sim N(0, \sigma^2)$$

For now, we are assuming normally distributed errors.

Another way of writing this, since a, b, x are considered constants, would be

$$y_i \sim N(a + bx_i, \sigma^2)$$

Or yet another way would be

$$y_i \sim N(\mu_i, \sigma^2)$$
$$\mu_i = a + bx_i$$

It is this latter format that's required in BUGS code, and it is written as follows:

```
model {
  for (i in 1:500) {
    y[i] ~ dnorm(mu[i], tau)
    mu[i] <- a + b*x[i]
  }
  a ~ dnorm(0, 0.01)
  b ~ dnorm(0, 0.01)
  tau ~ dunif(0.1, 100)
}
```

The model contains a mixture of deterministic and random elements. The deterministic components are indicated by '`<-`', for example

$$\text{mu[i] <- a + b*x[i]}.$$

The random components are indicated by a tilde (~), for example

$$\text{y[i] ~ dnorm(mu[i], tau)}$$

and similarly for the prior for the intercept

$$a \sim dnorm(0, \ 0.01).$$

Notice here that BUGS code uses **precision**, rather than variance (precision is just the inverse of the variance). So in our model above, `tau` is the precision, and we would need its reciprocal for the variance. We choose here to set the prior on `tau` directly, but this isn't mandatory. Many prefer to set a prior on the standard deviation, then convert that information into the precision.

In Section 22.1, we assumed a t-distribution for the error term. How do we write the BUGS code with this information? It's simple, as shown below, though now we have an unknown degrees of freedom parameter (in place of σ). We place a gamma prior on the degrees of freedom, and a uniform prior on the standard deviation which we then convert to a precision by inverting the square of the standard deviation, `pow(sigma, 2)`. The function `pow` raises the first argument to the *power* given in the second argument.

```
model {
   for (i in 1:500) {
      y[i] ~ dt(mu[i], tau, df)
      mu[i] <- a + b*x[i]
   }
   a ~ dnorm(0, 0.01)
   b ~ dnorm(0, 0.01)
   tau <- 1/pow(sigma, 2)
   sigma ~ dunif(0.1, 100)
   df ~ dgamma(2, 0.1)
}
```

22.3 Examples

22.3.1 MCMC for a simple linear regression

In this example (analysed in detail as a linear model in Section 10.1.2, the response variable is growth and the continuous explanatory variable is the concentration of tannin in the diet. We start by reading the data into *R*:

```
growth_data<- read.table ("regression.txt", header = T)
head (growth_data)

   growth tannin
1      12      0
2      10      1
3       8      2
4      11      3
5       6      4
6       7      5
```

Here is a reminder of the output of the simple linear regression for comparison with the JAGS output in due course:

```
summary (lm (growth ~ tannin, data = growth_data))

Call:
lm(formula = growth ~ tannin, data = growth_data)
```

```
Residuals:
    Min      1Q  Median      3Q     Max
-2.4556 -0.8889 -0.2389  0.9778  2.8944

Coefficients:
            Estimate Std. Error t value Pr(>|t|)
(Intercept)  11.7556     1.0408  11.295 9.54e-06 ***
tannin       -1.2167     0.2186  -5.565 0.000846 ***
---
Signif. codes:  0 '***' 0.001 '**' 0.01 '*' 0.05 '.' 0.1 ' ' 1

Residual standard error: 1.693 on 7 degrees of freedom
Multiple R-squared:  0.8157,Adjusted R-squared:  0.7893
F-statistic: 30.97 on 1 and 7 DF,  p-value: 0.0008461
```

We'll emulate the structure of this model this time, though note that this is not required: we can choose whatever structure we want for the model. Also note that a Bayesian analysis requires prior information on all parameters, which also differentiates this analysis from the frequentist version.

Outside *R*, write the BUGS model and save it as a text file. This is the part that is most difficult at first. The model contains the information on the structure of the model and the nature of the priors. We've opted for normal priors on the intercept and slope, centred at zero with a *precision* of 0.0001 (so a variance of 10 000). These priors are rather vague given the magnitude of the variance, but they are not entirely uninformative. In an ideal world, we'd have a bit more information on these parameters and could feed that into the priors.

We choose a Gamma distribution with parameters 0.001 and 0.001 for the precision of `growth`. We also define `sigma` to be the standard deviation: doing this means that we can request results on the standard deviation which might be easier to interpret than results on the precision. We could repeat this analysis with different priors to assess how sensitive it is to these assumptions.

The resulting BUGS code is similar in spirit to the second example in Section 22.2.3. The code is saved to a file called `regressionbugs.txt` in this example. This is what the model file looks like:

```
model {
  for (i in 1:9) {
    growth[i] ~ dnorm(mu[i], tau)
    mu[i] <- a + b * tannin[i]
  }
  a ~ dnorm(0.0, 1.0E-4)
  b ~ dnorm(0.0, 1.0E-4)
  tau ~ dgamma(1.0E-3, 1.0E-3)
  sigma <- 1/sqrt(tau)
}
```

Now go back into *R*. We need to open the library to connect our *R* session with the JAGS program:

```
library (R2jags)
```

We'll be using the `jags ()` function to run the analysis, and we'll need to pass on several important bits of information to it:

- where to find the data;
- initial values for the parameters (we can omit this, and let JAGS choose values);

- a list of the unknown parameters that we want output for (it is not always the case that we'll want output for *all* our parameters: some of these may be 'nuisance' parameters that are not really of interest);

- where to find the BUGS model code;

- the number of chains we want to simulate;

- the number of iterations per chain;

- the burn-in period (by default, the burn-in is half the number of iterations);

- any thinning required (by default, jags decides on the level of thinning by looking at the number of iterations specified and the burn-in).

Run the `jags ()` function to produce the model. Here we ask for three chains (with different starting points), with 10 000 iterations each, and burning (ignoring) the first 1000 iterations per chain (or 3000 iterations in total). We choose not to thin the chain here, by specifying the thinning to be 1:

```
growth_mod1 <- jags (data = growth_data,
                parameters.to.save = c ("a", "b", "tau"),
                n.iter = 10000, n.burnin = 3000, n.thin = 1, n.chains = 3,
                model.file = "regressionbugs.txt", progress.bar = "none")


Compiling model graph
    Resolving undeclared variables
    Allocating nodes
Graph information:
    Observed stochastic nodes: 9
    Unobserved stochastic nodes: 3
    Total graph size: 45

Initializing model
```

We've opted for `progress.bar = "none"` here, but we can omit this to view real-time information on the number of iterations completed.

Before inspecting the output, we should check that we're happy that the chains have converged and that our burn-in was sufficient. We can do that with the function `traceplot ()`. Note that the plots *don't* show the iterations relegated to the burn-in period, so all we're looking for here is that the trace plots don't provide evidence against the assumption that we're simulating from the posterior. Though this doesn't guarantee that all is OK, there's nothing in the trace plots of Figure 22.2 that suggests otherwise.

```
col_trace <- hue_pal()(3)
traceplot (growth_mod1, ask = FALSE, varname = c ("a", "b", "tau"),
        mfrow = c (2,2), col = col_trace)
```

Now, we can inspect the model output with a fair degree of confidence:

```
growth_mod1

Inference for Bugs model at "regressionbugs.txt", fit using jags,
 3 chains, each with 10000 iterations (first 3000 discarded)
```

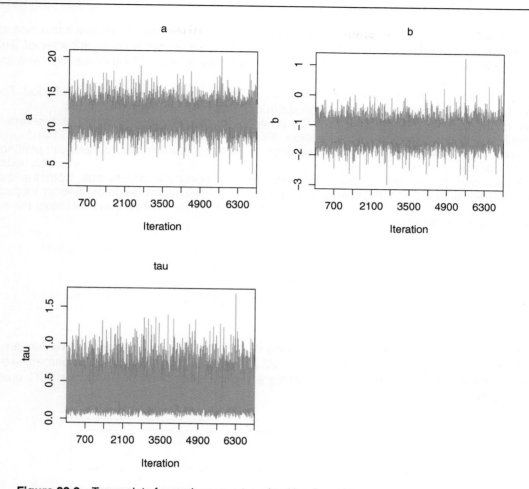

Figure 22.2 Trace plots for each parameter, checking for evidence of convergence issues.

```
n.sims = 21000 iterations saved
          mu.vect sd.vect    2.5%    25%    50%    75%  97.5%  Rhat n.eff
a          11.758   1.231   9.314 11.020 11.758 12.499 14.222 1.001 21000
b          -1.217   0.258  -1.728 -1.373 -1.217 -1.062 -0.709 1.001 21000
tau         0.347   0.183   0.086  0.212  0.317  0.448  0.780 1.001  8000
deviance   36.339   2.926  33.029 34.217 35.580 37.654 44.113 1.001 21000

For each parameter, n.eff is a crude measure of effective sample size,
and Rhat is the potential scale reduction factor (at convergence, Rhat=1).

DIC info (using the rule, pD = var(deviance)/2)
pD = 4.3 and DIC = 40.6
DIC is an estimate of expected predictive error (lower deviance is better).
```

The parameter estimates are very close to those obtained by the linear model. The output suggests for example that the posterior distribution for the intercept, a, has a mean of around 11.8 and the

95% credible interval for this parameter is roughly $(9.3, 14.2)$. Remember that this has a nice interpretation: there is a 0.95 probability that the true value of the intercept is within this interval. This is *not* the same as the interpretation of a (frequentist) confidence interval for the intercept, and so the two are not comparable.

There is also an additional parameter, `deviance`, which is computed from the likelihood. This is useful for model comparison, and is described in more detail in Gelman et al., 2004.

We might want to see the shape of the posterior distribution for our three parameters. We can estimate these using the `coda` package (Plummer et al., 2006) (need to load the `lattice` package). As we are selecting particular parameters to plot (i.e. we're not interested in plotting the posterior of the deviance), we use `growth_mod1$BUGSoutput$sims.matrix`. This extracts the BUGS output from the model, and then requests particular parameters from the matrix that holds all samples for all parameters in the model. We might be interested in inspecting `growth_mod1$BUGSoutput$sims.matrix` on its own, but be warned that it will have the same number of rows as iterations.

```
library (coda)
library (lattice)
growth_mod1_mcmc <- as.mcmc (growth_mod1$BUGSoutput$sims.matrix
                             [,c ("a", "b", "tau")])
densityplot (growth_mod1_mcmc)
```

Connecting these plots to the output, and taking the parameter `a` as an example, we can see that the mean of the posterior distribution in Figure 22.3 is around 11.7, while the 2.5th percentile of the posterior is about 9.3 and the 97.5th percentile is around 14.2. In other words, the 95% credible interval is $(9.3, 14.2)$.

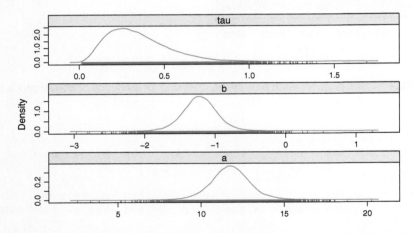

Figure 22.3   Estimated posterior distribution for each of the three parameters of interest.

22.3.2   MCMC for longitudinal data

The root growth of 12 plants was measured over five time periods which were two weeks apart. Six of these were allocated to receive fertiliser, while the other six didn't. In Section 13.5.3, we settled on a linear mixed-effect model for these data with time and fertiliser as fixed effects and a random intercept for each plant considered. Here are the data once again.

```
fertilizer_data <- read.table ("fertilizer.txt", header = T)
head (fertilizer_data)

  root week plant fertiliser
1  1.3    2   ID1      added
2  3.5    4   ID1      added
3  7.0    6   ID1      added
4  8.1    8   ID1      added
5 10.0   10   ID1      added
6  2.0    2   ID2      added
```

We'll develop a Bayesian version of the earlier (frequentist) hierarchical model, and the easiest way of writing the BUGS model would be as follows. Priors have also been specified below. We could probably do better here with a little thought, but for now we'll stick to unimaginative normally distributed priors for regression coefficients and gamma distributed priors for precisions.

```
model{
  for( i in 1: 12) {
    for( j in 1: 5) {
      root[i, j] ~ dnorm(mu[i, j], tau)
      mu[i, j] <- alpha[i] + beta[i] * week[j] + gamma[i] * fertilizer[i]
    }
    alpha[i] ~ dnorm(alpha.mu, alpha.tau)
    beta[i] ~ dnorm(beta.mu, beta.tau)
    gamma[i] ~ dnorm(gamma.mu, gamma.tau)
  }
  tau ~ dgamma(0.001, 0.001)
  alpha.mu ~ dnorm(0, 0.001)
  beta.mu ~ dnorm(0, 0.001)
  gamma.mu ~ dnorm(0, 0.001)
  alpha.tau ~ dgamma(0.001, 0.001)
  beta.tau ~ dgamma(0.001, 0.001)
  gamma.tau ~ dgamma(0.001, 0.001)
  sigma <- 1 / sqrt(tau)
}
```

Notice that the outcome (root) is indexed by `[i, j]`. Here, `i` notes the plant number, ranging from 1 to 12, while `j` tracks the timepoint, ranging from 1 to 5 (weeks 2 through 10). Helpfully, the data have already been ordered, first by plant ID then by week then by fertiliser status.

For each plant at each timepoint, the root length is described by a Normal distribution with a mean that depends on the plant and timepoint, and some common *precision* `tau`. This mean is a linear combination of time and fertiliser, with the coefficients (`alpha`, `beta`, `gamma`) depending on the plant.

Notice how we open two loops at the start (indexed by `i` and `j`), close the one relating to `j` before specifying the priors on the regression coefficients (which depend on `i` and so must be within this loop), then detailing the remaining priors which depend on neither `i` or `j`.

We save our model to a text file called `bayeslme.txt`. Here we choose to place priors on the precisions, and also create a new parameter, `sigma`, the standard deviation of the Normal distribution applied to the outcome. This means we can get output on the standard deviation, which might be easier to digest than information on the precision.

The issues in this example concern the *shape* of the data. Note from the BUGS code that the response (root length) needs to be a matrix with the plants as the rows, not a single vector as `root` is at present. Some minor restructuring is required, which leads to a matrix with rows corresponding to plants, and columns corresponding to weeks:

```
root <- fertilizer_data$root
dim (root) <- c (5, 12)
root <- t (root)
root

       [,1]  [,2]  [,3]  [,4]  [,5]
 [1,]   1.3   3.5  7.00   8.1  10.0
 [2,]   2.0   3.5  5.50   7.2   9.1
 [3,]   1.7   3.2  5.80   7.5   9.4
 [4,]   2.6   4.4  6.23   7.5  11.1
 [5,]   1.1   4.4  5.20   7.1   8.8
 [6,]   1.3   3.1  6.10   7.3   9.3
 [7,]   1.7   2.6  4.70   6.3   8.8
 [8,]   1.5   2.7  4.10   6.4   8.2
 [9,]   1.2   2.1  4.10   5.9   8.2
[10,]   1.1   2.3  4.10   6.2   8.8
[11,]   1.2   2.4  4.10   5.6   8.3
[12,]   0.8   1.4  3.50   5.1   7.7
```

The explanatory variables, `week` and `fertilizer`, need to be vectors of length 5 and 12, respectively (look at the code: `week` is indexed by j which runs from 1 to 5, and `fertiliser` is indexed by i which runs from 1 to 12). We can simply code the week from 1 to 5, whereas for `fertiliser`, the first six plants listed in the data set had fertiliser added and the rest did not. We can conveniently code this as a binary vector, with 1 indicating fertiliser added:

```
week <- c (1:5)
fertilizer <- c (rep (1, 6) , rep (0, 6))
```

We need to provide `jags ()` with the names of the variables containing the data so we define the following:

```
fertilizer_data_jags <- list ("root", "week", "fertilizer")
```

Finally, we can run `jags ()`, specifying three chains each with 100 000 iterations (this is probably overkill) and a burn-in for each chain of 10 000 iterations. Again, we choose not to thin the iterations, and notice that we only ask for *some* of the unknown parameters to be monitored. In this example, there would otherwise be a total of 44 parameters which would take up too many pages here.

```
fert_mod1 <- jags (data = fertilizer_data_jags,
                   parameters.to.save = c ("tau", "alpha.mu", "alpha.tau",
                                           "beta.mu", "beta.tau", "gamma.mu",
                                           "gamma.tau", "sigma"),
                   model.file = "bayeslme.txt", n.chains = 3, n.iter = 100000,
                   n.burnin = 10000, n.thin = 1, progress.bar = "none" )
```

```
Compiling model graph
   Resolving undeclared variables
   Allocating nodes
Graph information:
   Observed stochastic nodes: 60
   Unobserved stochastic nodes: 43
   Total graph size: 257

Initialising model
```

This may take a while to execute, but once done, we should consider whether there is any evidence of not having reached convergence. We could ask for the full set of trace plots (there would be a lot!), but we stick to just a few here.

```
col_trace <- hue_pal ()(3)
traceplot (fert_mod1, ask = FALSE,
          varname = c ("tau", "alpha.mu", "alpha.tau", "beta.mu",
                       "beta.tau", "gamma.mu", "gamma.tau"),
mfrow = c (4,2), col = col_trace)
```

All seems in order in Figure 22.4. Notice how the parameters `alpha.tau`, `beta.tau`, `gamma.tau` are bounded below by zero, creating a rather different looking trace plot to what can be seen for the other parameters. This is because these are precisions and can't be less than zero and a zero (or close to zero) precision appears to be consistent with the data, model, and prior combination. The same doesn't happen for the other precision, `tau`, because the data, model, and priors point to this parameter being quite different from zero. Now, we're ready to investigate the posterior estimates of the parameters:

```
fert_mod1

Inference for Bugs model at "bayeslme.txt", fit using jags,
 3 chains, each with 1e+05 iterations (first 10000 discarded)
 n.sims = 270000 iterations saved
          mu.vect sd.vect    2.5%     25%     50%     75%    97.5% Rhat n.eff
alpha.mu   -1.184   0.213  -1.585  -1.315  -1.186  -1.055   -0.785 1.004   830
alpha.tau 193.408 389.452   4.154  16.794  49.888 184.806 1301.504 1.001 11000
beta.mu     1.874   0.055   1.770   1.840   1.875   1.909    1.979 1.006  2200
beta.tau  266.705 379.122  28.714  78.169 140.824 287.292 1339.548 1.001  4000
gamma.mu    1.171   0.265   0.638   1.009   1.173   1.339    1.678 1.003  1100
gamma.tau 204.191 402.915   2.307  14.851  52.010 202.408 1363.242 1.001 82000
sigma       0.489   0.056   0.398   0.451   0.485   0.521    0.606 1.001 88000
tau         4.328   0.922   2.724   3.677   4.259   4.906    6.322 1.001 88000
deviance   83.734   7.145  72.119  78.866  83.121  87.911   98.497 1.001 28000

For each parameter, n.eff is a crude measure of effective sample size,
and Rhat is the potential scale reduction factor (at convergence, Rhat=1).

DIC info (using the rule, pD = var(deviance)/2)
pD = 25.5 and DIC = 109.3
DIC is an estimate of expected predictive error (lower deviance is better).
```

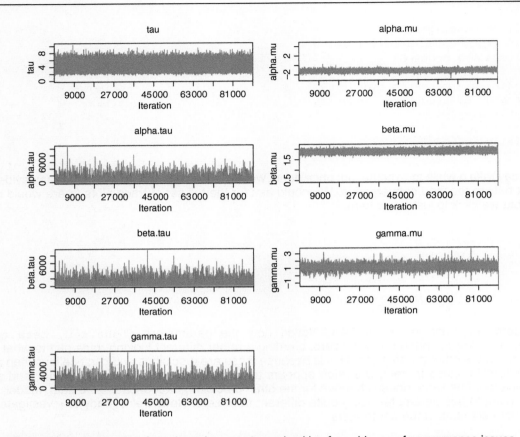

Figure 22.4 Trace plots for selected parameters, checking for evidence of convergence issues.

There seems to be some uncertainty in the values of the precision for `alpha`, `beta` and `gamma`, which was also evident in the range of values we saw for these parameters in the trace plots. This isn't surprising: we have a small data set, a relatively complex model due to the hierarchical nature of the data, and priors which contain little information. The consequence of this is that we haven't learnt a huge amount about the parameters of interest. We could attempt to remedy this by collecting more data (this is often implausible), or thinking carefully about the information we provide via the prior distributions in the hope that this would strengthen our inference, or alternative reconsider the structure of the model we use.

22.4 MCMC for a model with binomial errors

We analysed data for the percentage germination of seeds from a factorial experiment involving two genotypes of *Orobanche* and two extracts as a quasi-binomial model (i.e. including an overdispersion parameter) in Section 11.4.4. The response, `count`, is the number germinating out of an initial `sample` of seeds (i.e. 10 germinated out of 39 seeds in the first case):

```
germ_data <- read.table ("germination.txt", header = T)
attach (germ_data)
```

```
head (germ_data)

  count sample Orobanche   extract
1    10     39       a75      bean
2    23     62       a75      bean
3    23     81       a75      bean
4    26     51       a75      bean
5    17     39       a75      bean
6     5      6       a75  cucumber
```

Write the BUGS model and save it in a text file called `bayesglm.txt`:

```
model{
  for( i in 1: 21) {
    count[i] ~ dbin(p[i], sample[i])
    b[i] ~ dnorm(0, tau)
    logit(p[i]) <- alpha0 + alpha1 * Orobanche[i] + alpha2 * extract[i] +
                   alpha12 * Orobanche[i] * extract[i] + b[i]
  }
  alpha0 ~ dnorm(0, 1.0E-6)
  alpha1 ~ dnorm(0, 1.0E-6)
  alpha2 ~ dnorm(0, 1.0E-6)
  alpha12 ~ dnorm(0, 1.0E-6)
  tau ~ dgamma(0.001, 0.001)
  sigma <- 1 / sqrt(tau)
}
```

We define the number germinating, `count`, as binomially distributed with probability of success, `p`, and the number of trials equal to the number of observations in each case, `sample`. We model the logit of the proportion, `p`, as a linear combination of `Orobanche` and `extract` plus their interaction. For the overdispersion, we define `b[i]` ~ `dnorm(0,tau)`.

In terms of priors, we use vague normal priors for the intercept, the two main effects and the interaction term (`alpha0`, `alpha1`, `alpha2` and `alpha12`), with `tau` selected from a Gamma distribution. Such vague priors may be the result of genuine lack of information, or perhaps laziness. With these types of priors, we should hope that the information in the data is sufficient to yield useful inference.

The data we need to provide to the model are the following:

```
germ_data_jags <- list ("count", "sample", "Orobanche", "extract")
```

Now run the model:

```
germ_mod1 <- jags (data = germ_data_jags,
                   parameters.to.save = c ("alpha0", "alpha1", "alpha2",
                                           "alpha12","tau"),
                   model.file = "bayesglm.txt", n.chains = 3, n.iter = 10000,
                   n.burnin = 3000, n.thin = 1, progress.bar = "none" )

Compiling model graph
   Resolving undeclared variables
```

```
    Allocating nodes
Graph information:
   Observed stochastic nodes: 21
   Unobserved stochastic nodes: 26
   Total graph size: 166

Initialising model

col_trace <- hue_pal ()(3)
traceplot (germ_mod1, ask=FALSE,
          varname = c ("alpha0", "alpha1", "alpha2", "alpha12", "tau"),
          mfrow = c (3,2), col = col_trace)
```

All seems to be OK with the trace plots in Figure 22.5, though there considerable uncertainty in the precision of the overdispersion component (to be expected, since there we have a very small

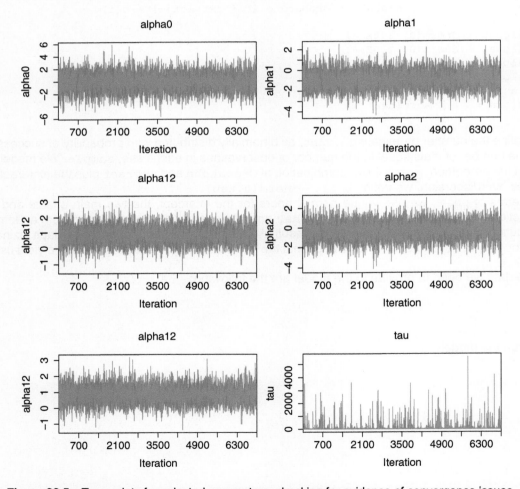

Figure 22.5   Trace plots for selected parameters, checking for evidence of convergence issues.

sample size). We can see this in the model estimates too. We could consider running the model for more iterations, or improving the prior information to try to remedy this. Once we're happy we can inspect our model and make our conclusions. The model summary as described in the trace plots in Figure 22.5 are given here.

```
germ_mod1

Inference for Bugs model at "bayesglm.txt", fit using jags,
 3 chains, each with 10000 iterations (first 3000 discarded)
 n.sims = 21000 iterations saved
          mu.vect sd.vect    2.5%     25%     50%     75%   97.5% Rhat n.eff
alpha0     -0.093   1.153  -2.409  -0.822  -0.081   0.645   2.173 1.001 21000
alpha1     -0.910   0.689  -2.278  -1.351  -0.915  -0.477   0.473 1.001  6600
alpha12     0.823   0.437  -0.035   0.547   0.816   1.094   1.711 1.001 21000
alpha2     -0.290   0.727  -1.749  -0.746  -0.285   0.178   1.143 1.001 21000
tau        52.326 178.330   2.918   7.239  13.013  28.974 399.775 1.008   420
deviance  101.969   6.858  90.161  96.878 101.414 106.658 116.043 1.005   570

For each parameter, n.eff is a crude measure of effective sample size,
and Rhat is the potential scale reduction factor (at convergence, Rhat=1).

DIC info (using the rule, pD = var(deviance)/2)
pD = 23.4 and DIC = 125.4
DIC is an estimate of expected predictive error (lower deviance is better).

detach (germ_data)
```

References

Gelman, A., Carlin, J. B., Stern, H. S., & Rubin, D. B. (2004). *Bayesian data analysis* (Second). Chapman & Hall/CRC.

Juárez, M. A., & Steel, M. F. J. (2010). Non-Gaussian dynamic Bayesian modelling for panel data. *Journal of Applied Econometrics*, 25(7), 1128–1154. https://doi.org/10.1002/jae.1113.

Lunn, D., Spiegelhalter, D., Thomas, A., & Best, N. (2009). The BUGS project: evolution, critique and future directions. *Statistics in Medicine*, 28(25), 3049–3067.

Park, J. H. P., Martin, A. D., & Quinn, K. M. (2021). CRAN task view: Bayesian inference [Version 2021-09-04]. http://cran.r-project.org/web/views/Bayesian.html.

Plummer, M. (2003). JAGS: A program for analysis of Bayesian graphical models using Gibbs sampling.

Plummer, M., Best, N., Cowles, K., & Vines, K. (2006). CODA: Convergence diagnosis and output analysis for MCMC. *R News*, 6(1), 7–11. https://journal.r-project.org/archive/.

Spiegelhalter, D., Thomas, A., Best, N., Lunn, D., & MRC Biostatistics Unit (2003). WinBUGS user manual (Version 1.4).

Sturtz, S., Ligges, U., & Gelman, A. (2005).R2WinBUGS: A package for running winBUGS from R. *Journal of Statistical Software*, 12(3), 1–16. http://www.jstatsoft.org.

Su, Y.-S., & Yajima, M. (2020). *R2jags: Using R to run 'JAGS'* [R package version 0.6-1]. https://CRAN.R-project.org/package=R2jags.

23
Simulation Models

Simulation modelling is an enormous topic, and all we will do here is to demonstrate a few very simple temporal and spatial simulation techniques that give the flavour of what is possible in *R*, which has very powerful simulation capabilities. Simulation models are typically used for investigating dynamics in time, in space, or in both space and time together.

23.1 Temporal dynamics

For temporal dynamics, we might be interested in:

- the transient dynamics (the behaviour after the start but before equilibrium is attained – if indeed equilibrium is ever attained);

- equilibrium behaviour (after the transients have damped away);

- chaos (random-looking, but actually deterministic temporal dynamics that are extremely sensitive to initial conditions).

23.1.1 Chaotic dynamics in population size

Biological populations typically increase exponentially when they are small, but individuals perform less well as population density rises, because of competition, predation, or disease. In aggregate, these effects on birth and death rates are called **density-dependent processes**, and it is the nature of the density-dependent processes that determine the temporal pattern of population dynamics. The simplest density-dependent model of population dynamics is known as the **quadratic map**. It is a first-order non-linear difference equation:

$$N(t + 1) = \lambda N(t)[1 - N(t)],$$

where $N(t)$ is the population size at time t and the single parameter, λ, is known as the **per-capita multiplication rate**. The population can only increase when the population is small if $\lambda > 1$, the so-called **invasion criterion**. But how does the system behave as λ increases above 1?

The R Book, Third Edition. Elinor Jones, Simon Harden and Michael J. Crawley.
© 2023 John Wiley & Sons Ltd. Published 2023 by John Wiley & Sons Ltd.
Companion website: www.wiley.com/go/jones/therbook3e

We begin by simulating time series of populations for different values of λ and plotting them to see what happens. We create a function that plots the output for times in $[1, n]$, with a starting value of $x1$ and any value of λ:

```
quad_fn <- function (x1, lambda, n) {
  x <- numeric (n)
  x[1] <- x1
  for (t in 2:n) {
    x[t] <- lambda * x[t - 1] * (1 - x[t - 1])
  }
  plot (1:n, x, type = "l", ylim = c (0, 1),
        xlab = "time", ylab = "population",
        main = substitute (paste (lambda, " = ", a), list (a = lambda)),
        cex.main = 2, col = hue_pal ()(100)[sample (1:100, 1)])
}
```

Note the use of `substitute (paste ())` to combine text, a Greek letter and the value of a variable in the heading. Figure 23.1 shows the output for $\lambda = 2, 3.3, 3.5, 4$:

```
par (mfrow = c (2, 2))
quad_fn (0.6, 2, 40)
quad_fn (0.6, 3.3, 40)
quad_fn (0.6, 3.5, 40)
quad_fn (0.6, 4, 40)

par (mfrow = c (1, 1))
```

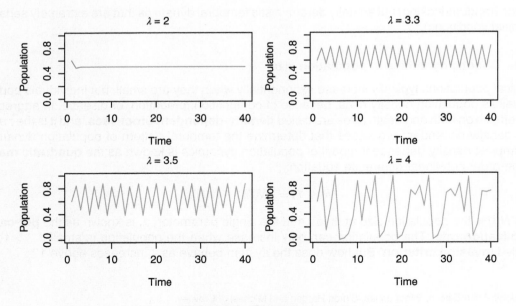

Figure 23.1 Quadratic maps.

For $\lambda = 2$, the population falls very quickly from its initial value (0.6) to equilibrium (0.5) and stays there; this system has a **stable point equilibrium**. For $\lambda = 3.3$, the dynamics show persistent two point cycles. For $\lambda = 3.5$, we have four point cycles. Finally, for $\lambda = 4$, this looks interesting. The dynamics do not repeat in any easily described pattern. They are said to be **chaotic** because the pattern shows extreme sensitivity to initial conditions: tiny changes in initial conditions can have huge consequences on numbers at a given time in the future.

23.1.2 Investigating the route to chaos

We have seen four snapshots of the relationship between λ and population dynamics. To investigate this more fully, we can write a function to describe the dynamics as a function of λ, and extract a set of (say, 20) sequential population densities, after any transients have died away, in the range $[n1, n2]$. Here is the function, which is an updated version of that seen in the previous section:

```
chaos_fn <- function (x1, lambda, n1, n2) {
  x <- numeric (n2)
  x[1] <- x1
  for (t in 2:n2) {
    x[t] <- lambda * x[t - 1] * (1 - x[t - 1])
  }
  x[n1:n2]
}
```

Although we need to calculate all values of the sequence up to index $n2$, we only output those in the specified interval. We will now run this function for a range of values between two and four, looking at outputs in [380,400] and plot the resulting values, as in Figure 23.2:

```
plot (c (2, 4), c (0, 1), type = "n", xlab = substitute (paste (lambda)),
      ylab = "population")
for (i in seq (2, 4, 0.01)) {
```

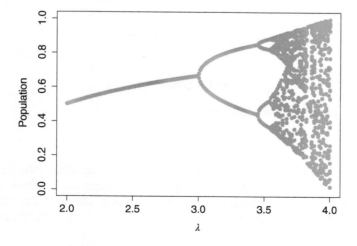

Figure 23.2 The quadratic map and chaos.

```
    outs <- chaos_fn (0.6, i, 380, 400)
    points (rep (i, length (outs)), outs, col = hue_pal ()(201)[i * 100 - 199])
}
```

What is interesting is the boundary of the apparently unpredictable area, the **edge of chaos**: what values for the settings determine whether we are in a relatively predictable situation or whether we cannot foresee what might occur. More details can be found, for instance, in May, 1976.

23.2   Spatial simulation models

For spatial dynamics, we might use simulation models to study:

- meta-population dynamics (where local extinction and re-colonisation of patches characterise the long-term behaviour, with constant turnover of occupied patches);
- neighbour relations (in spatially explicit systems where the performance of individuals is determined by the identity and attributes of their immediate neighbours);
- pattern generation (dynamic processes that lead to the generation of emergent, but more or less coherent patterns).

We will examine examples of all three.

23.2.1   Meta-population dynamics

The theory is very simple. The world is divided up into many patches, all of which are potentially habitable. Populations on inhabited patches go extinct with a density-independent probability, e. Occupied patches all contain the same population density and produce migrants (**propagules**) at a rate m per patch. Empty patches are colonised at a rate proportional to the total density of propagules and the availability of empty patches that are suitable for colonisation. The response variable is the proportion of patches that are occupied, p. The dynamics of p, therefore, are just gains minus losses, so

$$\frac{dp}{dt} = p(1 - p)m - ep.$$

At equilibrium, $\frac{dp}{dt} = 0$, and so

$$p(1 - p)m = ep,$$

giving the equilibrium proportion of occupied patches, p^*, as

$$p^* = 1 - \frac{e}{m}.$$

This draws attention to a critical result: there is a threshold migration rate ($m = e$) below which the meta-population cannot persist, and the proportion of occupied patches will drift inexorably to zero. Above this threshold, the meta-population persists in dynamic equilibrium with patches continually going extinct (the mean lifetime of a patch is $1/e$) and other patches becoming colonised by immigrant propagules. This model is due to Levins, 1969.

The simulation produces a moving cartoon of the occupied and empty patches. We begin by setting the parameter values which will ensure that the simulation keeps going:

```
m <- 0.15
e <- 0.1
```

We create a square universe of 10 000 patches in a 100 × 100 array, but this is not a spatially explicit model, and so the map-like aspects of the image should be ignored. The response variable is just the proportion of all patches that are occupied. Here are the initial conditions, placing 100 (or nearly) occupied patches at random in a sea of unoccupied patches:

```
s <- (1 - e)
N <- matrix (rep (0, 10000), nrow = 100)
xs <- sample (1:100, replace = T)
ys <- sample (1:100, replace = T)
for (i in 1:100){
  N[xs[i],ys[i]] <- 1
}
image (1:100, 1:100, N)
box (col = "black")
```

We have used the `image` () function, to give Figure 23.3, with its default colours, as it plots exactly what we require.

We want the simulation to run over 1000 generations. We have broken the loop into segments in order to understand the detail of what is going on:

```
for (t in 1:1000) {
```

First, we model the survival (or otherwise) of occupied patches. Each cell of the universe gets an independent random number from a uniform distribution (a real number between 0 and 1). If the random number is bigger than or equal to the survival rate s (= $1 - e$, above), then the patch

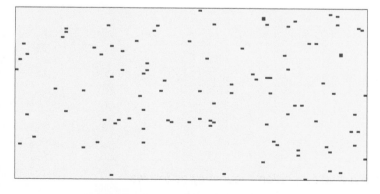

Figure 23.3　Initial meta-population plot.

survives for another generation. If the random number is greater than *s*, then the patch goes extinct and the corresponding value in the matrix *N* is set to zero:

```
S <- matrix (runif (10000), nrow = 100)
N <- N * (S < s)
```

Note that this one statement updates the whole matrix of 10 000 patches. Next, we work out the production of propagules, im, by the surviving patches (the rate per patch is *m*):

```
im <- floor (sum (N * m))
```

We assume that the settlement of the propagules is random, some falling in empty patches, but others being *wasted* by falling in already occupied patches:

```
placed <- matrix (sample (c (rep (1, im), rep (0, 10000 - im))), nrow = 100)
  N <- N + placed
N <- apply (N, 2, function(x) ifelse (x > 1, 1, x))
```

The last line is necessary to keep the values of *N* as just 0 (empty) or 1 (occupied) because our algorithm gives *N* = 2 when a propagule falls in an occupied patch. Now, we can draw the map of the occupied patches at each iteration (or just at the end by moving the image () and box () lines after }):

```
image (1:100, 1:100, N)
  box (col = "black")
}
```

Because the migration rate (*m* = 0.15) exceeds the extinction rate (*e* = 0.1), the meta-population is predicted to persist. The analytical solution for the long-term proportion of patches occupied is one-third of patches (1 − 0.1/0.15). If we run our simulation for 1000 iterations, showing the loop in one code chunk, then we arrive at Figure 23.4:

```
for (t in 1:1000) {
  S <- matrix (runif (10000), nrow = 100)
  N <- N * (S < s)
  im <- floor (sum (N * m))
  placed <- matrix (sample (c (rep (1, im), rep (0, 10000 - im))), nrow = 100)
  N <- N + placed
  N <- apply (N, 2, function(x) ifelse (x > 1, 1, x))
}
image (1:100, 1:100, N)
box (col = "black")
```

We can work out the actual proportion occupancy as follows:

```
sum (N) / length (N)
```

```
[1] 0.2934
```

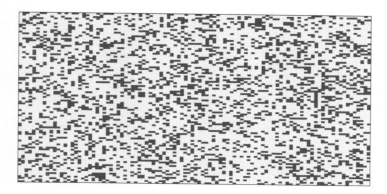

Figure 23.4 Meta-population plot after 1000 iterations.

There were 2934 occupied patches in this map by the time we stopped. Remember that a meta-population model is not spatially explicit, so we should not read anything into any of the apparent neighbour relations in this plot (the occupied patches should be distributed at random over the surface: randomness is not uniform).

23.2.2 Coexistence resulting from spatially explicit (local) density dependence

We have two species which would not coexist in a well-mixed environment because the fecundity of species A is greater than the fecundity of species B, and this would lead, sooner or later, to the competitive exclusion of species B and the persistence of a monoculture of species A. The idea is to see whether the introduction of local neighbourhood density dependence is sufficient to prevent competitive exclusion and allow long-term coexistence of the two species.

The kind of mechanism that might allow such an outcome is the build-up of specialist natural enemies such as insect herbivores or fungal pathogens in the vicinity of groups of adults of species A, that might prevent recruitment by species A when there were more than a threshold number, say T, of individuals of species A in a neighbourhood.

The problem with spatially explicit models is that we have to model what happens at the edges of the universe. All locations need to have the same numbers of neighbours in the model, but patches on the edge have fewer neighbours than those in the middle. The simplest solution is to model the universe as having *wrap-around margins* in which the left-hand edge is assumed to have the right-hand edge as its left-hand neighbour (and vice versa), while the top edge is assumed to have the bottom edge as its neighbour above (and vice versa). The four corners of the universe are assumed to be reciprocal diagonal neighbours: this results in a torus rather than the initial rectangle.

We need to define who is a neighbour of whom. The simplest method, adopted here, is to assume a square grid in which a central cell has eight neighbours – three above, three below, and one to either side, as in Figure 23.5:

```
plot (c (0, 1), c (0, 1),xaxt = "n", yaxt = "n",
      type = "n", xlab = "", ylab = "")
abline (v = c (1 / 3, 2 / 3))
abline (h = c (1 / 3, 2 / 3))
text (x = rep (c (1 / 6, 3 / 6, 5 / 6), 3)[-5],
```

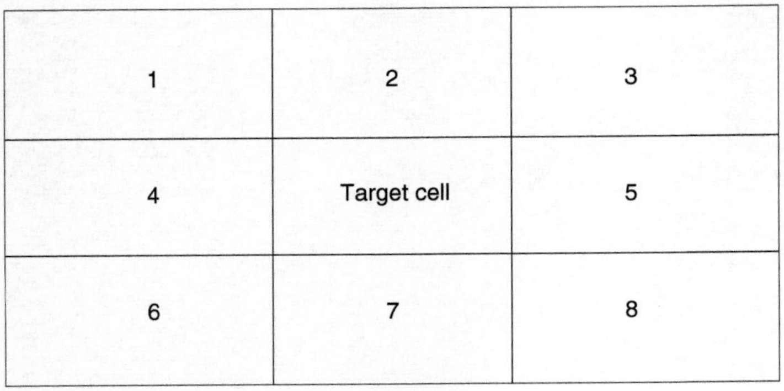

Figure 23.5 Target cell and immediate neighbours.

```
    y = rep (c (5 / 6, 3 / 6, 1 / 6), each = 3) [-5],
    labels = (1:9) [-9])
text (3 / 6, 3 / 6, "target cell")
```

Note how we create `text` that would put the numbers 1–9 in all cells, but then omit the middle item. This produces a plot showing a target cell in the centre of a matrix, and the numbers in the other cells indicate its **first-order neighbours**.

  We need to write a function to define the margins for cells on the top, bottom, and edge of our universe, *N*, and which determines all the neighbours of the four corner cells. Our universe is 100×100 cells and so the matrix containing all the neighbours will need to be 102×102. Note the use of subscripts:

```
margins <- function (N) {
  edges <- matrix (rep (0, 10404), nrow = 102)
  edges[2:101, 2:101] <- N
  edges[1, 2:101] <- N[100,]
  edges[102, 2:101] <- N[1,]
  edges[2:101, 1] <- N[,100]
  edges[2:101, 102] <- N[,1]
  edges[1, 1] <- N[100, 100]
  edges[102, 102] <- N[1, 1]
  edges[1, 102] <- N[100, 1]
  edges[102, 1] <- N[1, 100]
  edges
}
```

Next, we need to write a function to count the number of species A in the eight neighbouring cells, for any cell [*i,j*] in our matrix or universe *X*:

```
nhood <- function (X, i, j) {
  sum (X[(i - 1):(i + 1), (j - 1):(j + 1)] == 1)
}
```

Figure 23.6   Initial coexistence plot.

Now, we can set the parameter values: the reproductive rates of species A and B, the death (*d*) and survival (*s*) rates of adults (which determine the space freed up for recruitment) and the threshold number (*T*) of species A (out of the eight neighbours) above which recruitment cannot occur:

```
RA <- 3
RB <- 2.0
d <- 0.25
s <- (1 - d)
T <- 6
```

Our initial conditions fill one half of the universe with species A and the other half with species B, giving Figure 23.6:

```
N <- matrix (c (rep (1, 5000), rep(2, 5000)), nrow = 100)
image (1:100, 1:100, N)
box (col = "black")
```

We run the simulation for 1000 time steps, again breaking the loop down into comprehensible chunks:

```
for (t in 1:1000) {
```

First, we need to see if the occupant of a cell survives or dies. For this, we compare a uniformly distributed random number between 0 and 1 with the specified survival rates = $s = 1 - d$. If the random number is less than *s* the occupant survives, otherwise, it dies:

```
S <- 1 * (matrix (runif (10000), nrow = 100) < s)
```

The 1 * translates TRUEs and FALSEs into 1s and 0s. We kill the necessary number of cells to open up space for recruitment:

```
N <- N * S
space <- 10000 - sum (S)
```

We would expect `space` to be roughly equal to $d \times 10\,000$. Next, we need to compute the neighbourhood density of `A` for every cell (using the wrap-around margins), `tots`:

```
nt <- margins (N)
  tots <- matrix (rep (0, 10000), nrow = 100)
  for (a in 2:101) {
    for (b in 2:101) {
      tots[a - 1, b - 1] <- nhood (nt, a, b)
    }
}
}
```

The survivors produce seeds, in proportions *fA* and *fB*, as follows:

```
seedsA <- sum (N == 1) * RA
seedsB <- sum (N == 2) * RB
all_seeds <- seedsA + seedsB
fA <- seedsA / all_seeds
fB <- 1 - fA
```

Seeds settle over the universe at random:

```
setA <- ceiling (10000 * fA)
placed <- matrix (sample (c (rep (1, setA),
                             rep (2, 10000 - setA))),
                  nrow = 100)
```

Seeds only produce recruits in empty cells, i.e. if `N[i,j] == 0`. If the occupant of an empty cell (placed) is species B, then species B gets that cell. If species A is supposed to occupy a cell, then we need to check that it has fewer than *T* neighbours of species A. If so, species A gets the cell. If not, the cell is forfeited to species B.

```
for (i in 1:100) {
  for(j in 1:100) {
    if (N[i,j] == 0) {
      if (placed[i,j] == 2) {
        N[i,j] <- 2
      } else {
        if (tots[i,j] >= T) {
          N[i,j] <- 2
        } else {
          N[i,j] <- 1
        }
      }
    }
  }
}
}
```

Figure 23.7 Coexistence plot after 1000 iterations.

Finally, we can draw the map, showing species A in the darker colour:

```
  image (1:100, 1:100, N)
  box (col = "black")
}
```

We can watch as the initial half-and-half pattern breaks down, and species A increases in frequency at the expense of species B. Eventually, however, species A gets to the point where most of the cells have six or more neighbouring cells containing species A, and its recruitment begins to fail. At equilibrium, species B persists in isolated cells or in small lighter-coloured patches, where the neighbouring cells have six or more occupants that belong to species A. Figure 23.7 shows the result for the parameters listed above. If we set the threshold $T = 9$ (i.e. there is no limit to A's neighbours of its own species), species A drives species B to extinction. Here is the whole loop in one go:

```
for (t in 1:1000) {
  S <- 1 * (matrix (runif (10000), nrow = 100) < s)
  N <- N * S
  space <- 10000 - sum (S)
  nt <- margins (N)
  tots <- matrix (rep (0, 10000), nrow = 100)
  for (a in 2:101) {
    for (b in 2:101) {
      tots[a - 1, b - 1] <- nhood (nt, a, b)
    }
  }
  seedsA <- sum (N == 1) * RA
  seedsB <- sum (N == 2) * RB
  all_seeds <- seedsA + seedsB
  fA <- seedsA / all_seeds
  fB <- 1 - fA
  setA <- ceiling (10000 * fA)
  placed <- matrix (sample (c (rep (1, setA),
                                rep (2, 10000 - setA))),
```

```
                        nrow = 100)
  for (i in 1:100) {
    for(j in 1:100) {
      if (N[i,j] == 0) {
        if (placed[i,j] == 2) {
          N[i,j] <- 2
        } else {
          if (tots[i,j] >= T) {
            N[i,j] <- 2
          } else {
            N[i,j] <- 1
          }
        }
      }
    }
  }
}
image (1:100, 1:100, N)
box (col = "black")
```

23.2.3 Pattern generation resulting from dynamic interactions

In this section, we look at an example of an ecological interaction between a species and its parasite. The interaction is unstable in a non-spatial model, with increasing oscillations in numbers leading quickly to extinction of the host species and then, in the next generation, its parasite. The *non-spatial* dynamics look like this Figure 23.8. The parasite increases in generation number 1 and drives the host to extinction in generation 2, subsequently going extinct itself in generation 3. The challenge is to see if making the interaction *spatially* explicit can promote coexistence, and if so, through what pattern of spatial and temporal dynamics.

In a spatial model, we allow that hosts and parasites can move from the location in which they were born to any one of the eight first-order neighbouring cells (Figure 23.5). For the

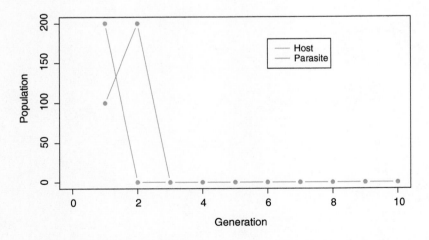

Figure 23.8 Non-spatial dynamics of a species and its parasite.

purposes of dispersal, the universe is assumed to have wrap-around margins for both species (see Section 23.2.2). The interaction is interesting because it is capable of producing beautiful spatial patterns that fluctuate with host and parasite abundance. We begin by setting the parameter values for the dynamics of the host (*r*) and the parasite (*a*) and the migration rates of the host (*Hmr*) and parasite (*Pmr*). In this case, the hosts are relatively sedentary, and the parasites are highly mobile:

```
r <- 0.4
a <- 0.1
Hmr <- 0.1
Pmr <- 0.9
```

Next, we set up the 100×100 matrices of host (N) and parasite (P) abundance. These will form what is termed a **coupled map lattice**:

```
N <- matrix (rep (0, 10000), nrow = 100)
P <- matrix (rep (0, 10000), nrow = 100)
```

The simulation is seeded by introducing 200 hosts and 100 parasites into a single cell at location [33, 33]:

```
N[33,33] <- 200
P[33,33] <- 100
```

We need to define a function called `host ()` to calculate the next host population as a function of current numbers of hosts (*N*) and parasites and (*P*), and a similar function called `parasite ()`: this gives us a **Nicholson–Bailey model**:

```
host <- function (N, P) {
  N * exp (r - a * P)
}
parasite <- function (N,P) {
  N * (1 - exp (- a * P))
}
```

We then need a function to define the wrap-around margins for defining the destinations of migrants from each cell and a function to count the number of neighbouring individuals, as discussed in Section 23.2.2:

```
margins <- function (N) {
  edges <- matrix (rep (0, 10404), nrow = 102)
  edges[2:101, 2:101] <- N
  edges[1, 2:101] <- N[100,]
  edges[102, 2:101] <- N[1,]
  edges[2:101, 1] <- N[,100]
  edges[2:101, 102] <- N[,1]
  edges[1, 1] <- N[100, 100]
  edges[102, 102] <- N[1, 1]
  edges[1, 102] <- N[100, 1]
```

```
   edges[102, 1] <- N[1, 100]
   edges
}
nhood <- function (X, i, j) {
  sum (X[(i - 1):(i + 1), (j - 1):(j + 1)])
}
```

We also need a function to count the number of migrants of either sort arriving in any cell:

```
migration <- function (edges) {
  migs <- matrix (rep (0, 10000), nrow = 100)
  for (a in 2:101) {
    for (b in 2:101) {
      migs[a - 1, b - 1] <- nhood (edges, a, b)
    }
  }
  migs
}
```

Finally, we run the simulation for 600 generations. We will only plot the final status, but by taking the `image ()` lines into the loop, we can watch the balance of host and parasite evolve: the initial introduction at [33, 33] spreads out and both host and parasite populations pulse in abundance. Eventually, the wave of migration reaches the margin and appears on the right-hand edge. The fun starts when the two waves meet one another. The result is shown in Figure 23.9.

```
for (t in 1:600) {
  he <- margins (N)
  pe <- margins (P)
  Hmigs <- migration (he)
  Pmigs <- migration (pe)
  N <- N - Hmr * N + Hmr * Hmigs / 9
  P <- P - Pmr * P + Pmr * Pmigs / 9
  Ni <- host (N,P)
```

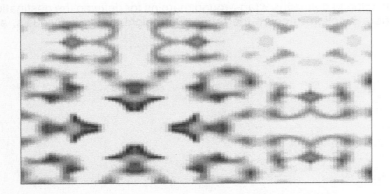

Figure 23.9   Non-spatial dynamics of a species and its parasite.

```
    P <- parasite (N,P)
    N <- Ni
}
image (1:100, 1:100, N)
box (col = "black")
```

23.3 Temporal and spatial dynamics: random walk

The spatial models that we saw in Section 23.2 also involved time, but the emphasis was primarily spatial. We will now demonstrate the classic probabilistic example of a random walk in two dimensions. The idea is to follow an individual as it staggers its way around a two-dimensional surface, starting at the point [50, 50] and leaving a trail of lines on a square island which scales from 0 to 100. First, we need to define what we mean by our random walk. Suppose that in the x direction the individual could move one step to the left in a given time period, stay exactly where it is for the whole time period, or move one step to the right. We need to specify the probabilities of these three outcomes. Likewise, in the y direction the individual could move one step up in a given time period, stay exactly where it is for the whole time period, or move one step down. Again, we need to specify probabilities. In R, the three movement options are `c (1, 0, -1)` for each of the types of motion (left, stay or right, and up, stay or down), and we might as well say that each of the three motions is equally likely. We need to select one of the three motions at random independently for the x and y directions at each time period. In R, we use the `sample ()` function for this:

```
sample (c (1, 0, -1), 1)
```

```
[1] 0
```

which selects one value (the last argument) with equal probability from the three listed options. Out of 99 repeats of this procedure, we should expect an average of 33 ups and 33 downs, 33 lefts and 33 rights. We simulate a walk of 10 000 steps (each time we run this it will differ) resulting in Figure 23.10

```
plot (0:100, 0:100, type = "n", xlab = "", ylab = "")
x <- integer (10001)
y <- integer (10001)
x[1] <- 50
y[1] <- 50
points (x[1], y[1], col = hue_pal ()(2)[1])
for (i in 1:10000) {
  x[i + 1] <- x[i] + sample (c (1, 0, -1), 1)
  y[i + 1] <- y[i] + sample (c (1, 0, -1), 1)
  if (x[i + 1] > 100 | x[i + 1] < 0 | y[i + 1] > 100 | y[i + 1] < 0) {
    x <- x[1:i]
    y <- y[1:i]
    break
  }
}
lines (x, y, col = hue_pal ()(2)[2])
```

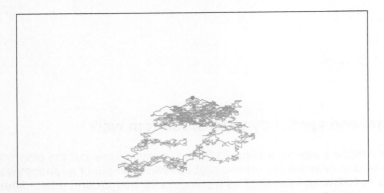

Figure 23.10   Random walk of up to 10 000 steps.

Our walker falls into the water and stops walking once he reaches the edge of the island. We could make the walk more sophisticated by providing wrap-around margins (see Section 23.2.2). On average, of course, the random walk should stay in the middle, where it started, but as we will see by running this model repeatedly, most random walkers do nothing of the sort. Instead, the average hides interesting activity: they usually wander off and drown.

References

Levins, R. (1969). Some demographic and genetic consequences of environmental heterogeneity for biological control. *Bulletin of the Entomological Society of America*, *15*, 237–240.

May, R. M. (1976). Simple mathematical models with very complicated dynamics. *Nature*, *261*, 459–467.

Index

Text in `typewriter` font denotes R functions or packages / libraries. The latter are all listed under the 'package' entry and where appropriate under specific functions or other entries. All datasets are listed under the heading 'datasets'. Page references in **bold** give the definition of a term or the first major usage of a function.

The R Book, Third Edition. Elinor Jones, Simon Harden and Michael J. Crawley.
© 2023 John Wiley & Sons Ltd. Published 2023 by John Wiley & Sons Ltd.
Companion website: www.wiley.com/go/jones/therbook3e